CASE STUDIES IN MARKETING MANAGEMENT

Edited by

Dr. S. Ramesh Kumar

Professor of Marketing

Indian Institute of Management Bangalore

India

Pearson

Published by Dorling Kindersley (India) Pvt. Ltd, Licensees of Pearson Education in South Asia.

ISBN 978-81-317-6139-7

First Impression
Current Impression, 2026

This edition is manufactured in India and is authorized for sale only in India, Bangladesh, Bhutan, Pakistan, Nepal, Sri Lanka and the Maldives. Circulation of this edition outside of these territories is UNAUTHORIZED.

Published by Pearson India Education Services Pvt. Ltd, CIN: U72200TN2005PTC057128.

Head Office: 1st Floor, Berger Tower, Plot No. C-001A/2, Sector 16B, Noida - 201 301, Uttar Pradesh, India.

Registered Office: 6th Floor, Tower A, Unit A and B, International Tech Park, CapitaLand Chennai, 200 Feet Radial Road,Zamin Pallavaram, Old Pallavaram Chennai – 600117, Tamil Nadu, India

Website: in.pearson.com; Email: companysecretary.india@pearson.com

Digitally printed in India by Trinity Academy for Corporate Training Ltd, New Delhi in the year of 2026.

CONTENTS

CASE INDEX

Chapters	Case Title
Chapter 1: Understanding Marketing	Shanghai Jahwa: Liushen Shower Cream (A)
Chapter 2: Marketing Strategies and Planning Them	HyundaiCard's Marketing Strategy
Chapter 3: Environmental Analysis	ITC in Rural India
Chapter 4: Importance of Marketing Research	Ontario Machinery Ring (A) - Problem Definition
Chapter 5: Creating and Nurturing Customer Value	Cineplex Entertainment: The Loyalty Program
Chapter 6: Consumer Behaviour	Super Shampoo Products and the Indian Mass Market
Chapter 7: Business to Business Markets	Tinplate Company of India: Need for a Conceptual Focus
Chapter 8: Market Segmentation and Targeting	Shoppers Stop: Targeting the Young
Chapter 9: Brand Equity Dimensions	Air Miles Canada: Rebranding the Air Miles Rewards Program
Chapter 10: Brand Positioning Strategy	Romantic Rides or Fiery Thrills: Positioning a Motorcycle Brand in the Indian Context
Chapter 11: Competitive Strategies	Kids Market Consulting
Chapter 12: Product-based Strategies	The Wii: Nintendo's Video Game Revolution
Chapter 13: Managing Services	SaskTel
Chapter 14: Pricing Strategies	Hanson Production: Pricing for Opening Day
Chapter 15: Marketing Channels	Synnex International: Transforming Distribution of High-tech Products
Chapter 16: Retailing and Wholesaling	Shiny Stores: Retailing Challenges in the Indian Context
Chapter 17: Integrated Marketing Communications	Brand in the Hand: Mobile Marketing at Adidas
Chapter 18: Advertising and Communications	Nike Inc.: Developing an Effective Public Relations Strategy
Chapter 19: Communications Other Than Mass Advertising	Spectrum Brands, Inc. - The Sales Force Dilemma
Chapter 20: New Market Offerings	Launch of the Ford Fiesta Diesel: The World's Most Efficient Car
Chapter 21: Globalization of Markets	Dabur India Ltd. - Globalization
Chapter 22: Organizational Aspects in Marketing	Sat & Co.: Market Orientation
Strategic Marketing Cases *(to be attempted by students at the end of the basic course in Marketing)*	Infosys: The Challenge of Global Branding
	Nano Tata-Logy: The People's Car
	Louis Vuitton in India

NOTE TO INSTRUCTORS/PROFESSORS

Instructors/Professors using this book will have access to teaching material that will enable them to teach the cases with the perspectives that have been captured by the author/s of the respective case.

PREFACE

Just as economies and markets are termed as "emerging", academic contexts too are "emerging" in this part of the world. The Indian emerging context is one of diversity in terms of its demographics, lifestyles, spending patterns and cultural aspects. Students of marketing depend on academics, practitioners and their own observation of the environment to appreciate the application of marketing knowledge that they derive from text books to the practical context. Cases supplement text books not only in terms of learning but also in terms of combining concepts with the realities of the environment.

The Indian marketing scenario is characterized by a unique set of challenges that are different from what companies face in developed economies. The co-existence of one time usage of shampoo packets with super-premium brands of shampoos, the presence of brands like Mont Blanc and Tag Heur with the unorganized sector that comprise of cheap assembled watches, the fragmented retail outlets (called *kirana* shops numbering about 15 million) competing with the glitz of modern retail outlets, the haggling consumer segments shopping in crowded bazaars while their upmarket counterparts indulging in hedonic shopping and the emergence of a strong rural market that contributes to the extent of fifty per cent of sales volume in several fast moving consumer goods are just some of the striking contrasts that challenge marketers in the Indian context as compared the western markets.

While the realities of the Indian context has changed radically in the past decade, students of marketing have not been able to experience the excitement of marketing concepts inside the classroom, due to the non-availability of appropriate marketing cases.

Several cases that have been written in the Indian context do not lend themselves amenable to teaching the concepts of marketing (they are not teaching cases though they may provide a descriptive commentary of marketing practices in the country). I felt that there was a distinctive need for a book of cases that would address the students in a structured and methodical manner while they go through the basic course on marketing basics. I felt it was not enough if students have a sporadic exposure to cases while going through the basic marketing course; students have to go through a set of cases that are closely tied to several chapters in a text book.

While there are a dearth of cases that reflect the Indian market realities, academics in this context also face the challenges posed by an emerging academic environment: non-availability of data, unreliable consumer responses in research, lukewarm response of several companies to part with data for case writing purposes and building up a strong team that can work continuously on developing teaching cases are just some of these challenges that an academic faces in this context.

Given the challenges faced by the students of marketing and the limitations imposed by the environment, I have selected a set of cases from the Ivey Business School case collection (well known for its case contributions) that addresses conceptual issues related to the text. The cases chosen are, to the extent possible, relevant to the marketing issues present in the prevailing Indian environment. I have incorporated cases matched with chapters that a student may find in most text books on marketing management. This would mean that this book on cases can be followed by an instructor regardless of the text book being prescribed for the basic marketing course.

I have ensured that the difficulty level of cases would be appropriate for business schools in Indian universities.

There are not too many Indian cases as the academic context in India is just "emerging". There was a need to strike a balance between cases that reflect the Indian context and the western context based cases chosen with a view to reflect the Indian context's issues I have made an attempt to strike this balance by including Indian cases applicable to a few chapters. I have also provided a set of strategic marketing cases (associated with the Indian context) that can be attempted by students after going through significant parts of the marketing management text book during the course.

I trust that this book of cases will be useful both to the students of marketing and the faculty members teaching the basic marketing course in Indian universities.

ACKNOWLEDGEMENTS

New ventures and attempts are a part of any environment and more specifically such endeavours are important for academics in an emerging academic environment like India. Every step taken towards academic experimentation, however incremental it may be, adds value, in my view, to the academic context. Prof. Paul Beamish's (Director, Engaging Emerging Markets Research Centre, Ivey Business School) suggestions on having a case book to suit the Indian context was indeed the basic motivational trigger that set me working on this project. His grasp of the Indian environment and the need for a conceptual book on marketing cases to address the environment opened up a dialogue between us on a host of important issues that were important to such a proposition in the Indian context. I thank him for triggering the project into action.

Gigi Wong (Regional Manager, Ivey Publishing), with all her involvement and commitment, ensured that I discussed several combinations of cases before choosing a set that we thought would be the best fit. She was also instrumental in handling several legal issues that had to be sorted out before the contract was signed. I thank her for all her efforts and focus that were critical to the endeavour.

J. Saravanan (former General Manager, Marketing) and Raza Khan of Pearson Education were highly excited about the project. They did everything they could to ensure that the various points of coordination were taken care of without any barriers to the completion of this project. I thank them for encouraging the project and being open to such "new to the environment's" proposition. I would also like to thank A. Maran for the timely coordination provided for this project.

I thank Dr Pankaj Chandra of Indian Institute of Management Bangalore, India, for the facilities that were provided to me during this project.

Finally, I thank my parents who have always had a word of encouragement to any endeavour of mine and my wife Amrith Ramesh and daughter Sahana for providing a conducive environment that enabled me to focus on the work. Last but not the least, I would like to recall with gratitude, my association with Dr B. Ilango, former Vice Chancellor of Bharathiar University, who had provided unflinching support to my initial academic endeavours.

S. Ramesh Kumar
Professor of Marketing
Indian Institute of Management Bangalore
rkumar@iimb.ernet.in

ABOUT THE EDITOR

S. Ramesh Kumar is Professor in the Marketing Area, Indian Institute of Management Bangalore, India. He has a mix of industrial and teaching experience of thirty years. S. Ramesh Kumar was awarded the ICFAI Best Teacher Award by Association for Indian Management Schools (AIMS).

S. Ramesh Kumar has published a number of articles and case studies in reputed journals (national and international), business magazines and business newspapers. His several international publications include papers in refereed journals of repute, which are known both for their academic rigor and practice orientation. His papers have appeared in the *Journal of Integrated Marketing Communication*, *Journal of Brand Management*, *Ivey Business Journal*, and his co-authored papers have been published in *Marketing Review*, *Journal of Customer Behaviour*, *Asia Pacific Journal on Economics and Business* and Richard Ivey Business School's case collection. Ramesh Kumar specializes in the application of marketing and consumer behaviour concepts to the Indian context and has written six books on the theme. *Marketing and Branding—The Indian Scenario* deals with Indian examples based on basic marketing concepts and the book has commendations from world class academics and marketing practitioners. Ramesh Kumar's book *Marketing Nuggets—Conceptual Dimensions in Marketing* won the first prize awarded by The Federation of Educational Publishers in India. His second book *Application Exercises in Marketing* deals with exercises concerning practical issues across product categories in the Indian context. This book provides exercises for conceptual applications in Marketing. His third book *Managing Indian Brands—Marketing Concepts and Strategies* deals with the application of marketing and consumer behaviour concepts to the Indian context. His fourth book on consumer behaviour, *Conceptual Issues in Consumer Behaviour—The Indian Context* provides the Indian interface for several concepts in consumer behaviour and supplements the text book on the subject. Ramesh Kumar's expanded book on consumer behaviour is *Consumer Behaviour and Branding—Concepts, Readings and Cases—The Indian Context*. He has co-authored a text book *Consumer Behaviour* with Leon Schiffman and Lezlie Kanuk in collaboration with Joseph Wisenblit.

Ramesh Kumar has also presented papers in international conferences and these include paper presentation in conferences conducted by the American Marketing Association at Vanderbilt University, the U.S.; Maastricht University; the Netherlands; University of Queensland; Australia; Academy of Marketing Conference at the U.K. and International Congress of Psychology conducted by the Swedish Psychological Association at Stockholm. He has been an invited speaker/visiting scholar in universities abroad for delivering specialized lectures on marketing in the Indian context.

Ramesh Kumar is on the editorial board of *Journal of Asian Business Studies* along with academics drawn from the best of business schools in the world.

Ramesh Kumar has conducted a number of training programs for corporate executives in Indian and multinational organizations.

S. Ramesh Kumar

1

Shanghai Jahwa

Liushen Shower Cream (A)

Peter Yuan prepared this case under the supervision of Professor Niraj Dawar solely to provide material for class discussion. The authors do not intend to illustrate either effective or ineffective handling of a managerial situation. The authors may have disguised certain names and other identifying information to protect confidentiality.

On the first Friday after the Spring Festival in 1993, Mr. Ge, general manager of Shanghai Jahwa Corporation, walked back to his office after the weekly competitive and market review meeting with the marketing department. During the meeting, Mr. Qing, the brand manager of Liushen, had handed him a proposal for launching a new product, a shower cream. This morning, the focus had been on Unilever's activities on the Lux brand. Unilever was one of the most active European multinationals in the Chinese personal care market, and a direct competitor of Jahwa in skin care and hair care products. In 1990, it had launched the first shower cream in China, and had been the only brand in the category for three years now. Adoption of the product seemed to be slow, but recent sales growth had convinced many in the industry that shower cream had potential. Rumors suggested that other multinationals were considering launching similar products. When Mr. Qing briefed the group on the proposal, there was muted discussion and some skepticism. Mr. Ge understood his colleagues' concerns: was the timing right? How could Jahwa compete against an entrenched multinational? Would the Liushen brand be the appropriate vehicle to carry the shower cream? He knew Jahwa had to make a decision soon. Mr. Qing believed the best time for the launch was just before the summer, in May.

PEOPLE'S REPUBLIC OF CHINA

Known for its large (1.2 billion) population, 5,000 year history and as the largest communist country, China has been one of the focal points in global business ever since it embarked on an ambitious modernization program in 1978, often referred to as "reform and opening to the outside world" (Exhibit 1). The government billed this program as "building a socialist market economy with Chinese characteristics." With real GDP growth at an impressive 10 per cent per annum over the previous five years and inflation at eight per cent, the growth program appeared to be performing well. Nevertheless, the country faced numerous challenges in revitalizing the state-owned industrial sector, upgrading its infrastructure, and rationalizing the allocation of resources. A key part of the program was to allow private ownership and to encourage foreign direct investment. While industry output and market demand increased substantially, rapid urbanization was taking a toll on farming land and mobilizing large parts of the rural population, which originally accounted for some 80 per cent of the entire country (Exhibits 2(a) and 2(b)). Much of this mobilized population migrated to the coastal regions in search of a better life. Regional income disparity was growing (Exhibit 3).

COSMETICS AND PERSONAL CARE INDUSTRY

As the market liberalized in the 1980s and early 1990s, the number of cosmetic and personal care producers mushroomed. Among the 1,500 companies that operated in the sector in 1993, 25 had annual sales between RMB 100 million and RMB 1.5 billion. Another 90 ranged from RMB 10 million to RMB 100 million. The rest were small, mostly entrepreneurial start-ups that operated in regional markets. The industry was concentrated in the richer regions. For example, Shanghai and Guangdong, two of the fastest growing coastal regions with a population of around 80 million, accounted for 30 per cent of the total output.

Foreign Invested Enterprises (FIEs) had been the fastest growing subgroup in the industry. Import tariffs on cosmetics and personal care products were still high (Exhibit 4), and foreign players wanting to operate in China preferred to set up manufacturing operations locally. Those attracted by the potential of the Chinese market had set up beachheads as early as the 1980s. The total value of FDI in the industry between 1979 and 1988 was approximately US$20 million. Investment had grown significantly in recent years. It was estimated that in the present year, over 100 FIEs would enter the sector, with some US$70 million of total investment. The most formidable of FIEs were multinationals such as P&G, Unilever, Johnson & Johnson (J&J), Henkel, Shiseido and Kao. Armed with international brands, superior products, marketing expertise and enviable financial resources, they were quickly taking over the leadership role in many product categories (Exhibit 5).

Industry observers agreed that FIEs, especially the multinationals, were driving the spectacular market growth. They had demonstrated to their local competitors the power of marketing.

Most domestic producers had limited resources for product development and marketing efforts. Few had brand-building expertise. Many of the lower-end companies competed on price, with low quality and often a short-lived presence on the market. At the other extreme, when international brands were launched in China, they were selling at up to 500 per cent premium over these local brands. The difference between the long-term, brand-oriented approach of the multinationals and the short-term focus of most local producers was stark. Although they were not competing for the same consumers, multinationals quickly established benchmarks for the industry and consumers. Television advertising was widely used by these new entrants. Often, they used advertisements developed for other Asian Chinese markets, which focused on building associations with a better lifestyle, beauty and glamor, personal success, and professional care. These messages played well with the affluent young urban Chinese market.

Retail sales of cosmetics and personal care products reached RMB 6 billion in 1992. Growth had averaged 35 per cent between 1985 and 1990. Some forecast that by 2000, the market would reach RMB 30 billion. However, the distribution of this growth was uneven (Exhibits 6 and 7). Urban consumption was five to 10 times higher than in the rural areas. A Jahwa manager felt that products that did sell in rural markets "tended to be low priced, colorful, oily and heavily fragranced." The selection in local village shops was very limited. Even among the urban population, there were sharp differences between regional cities and provincial capitals, and between inland provinces and coastal provinces. Living standards had always been higher in the capitals and along the coast. Disparities had only been exacerbated after reform. Coastal region populations tended to be better educated and had greater exposure to the outside world. Guangdong province households, for example, had access to Hong Kong television channels. Chinese versions of *Elle*, *Vogue* and other fashion magazines were available at news-stands in Shanghai and Beijing, but not in smaller cities or inland.

As a result, cosmetics and personal care multinationals had chosen 18-to-35-year-old urban, affluent to middle-income women as their key target segment. Some of these consumers would spend up to 20 per cent of their income on cosmetics, especially in the middle-income segment (earning RMB 500 to RMB 2,000 per month). This target segment tended to be "fashion oriented," open to new concepts, and willing to try new products. They were easily accessible through mass media, especially television and fashion magazines, and patronized downtown department stores.

SHANGHAI JAHWA

Shanghai Jahwa traced its history back to 1898, when Guangshen Company was established in Hong Kong as a cosmetics manufacturer. In the early 1930s, it set up a cosmetics manufacturing plant in Shanghai, which developed well-regarded brand names such as Shuangmei (Chinese eau de toilette). After the communist revolution in 1949, the company was nationalized and merged with three other personal care producers into a state-owned company named Shanghai Mingxing Household Products Factory. During the 1960s, Youyi and Yashuang from Mingxing became the best-selling brands of moisturizing cream in China. In 1967, Mingxing changed its name to Shanghai Household Chemical Factory (known as Jahwa). During the planned economy era (from 1949 to around 1980), the government set prices (retail, as well as wholesale) and allocated a production quota, both in terms of products and volume, to each factory. All output was "purchased" by a state monopoly distributor. Promotion was not deemed necessary, as the government "planned" for everything from raw material supply to final consumption. Starting in 1978, when China adopted reforms, the planning mechanism was gradually abolished.

During the 1980s, the company launched a number of successful products under a variety of brands. In the late 1980s and early 1990s, Jahwa launched three new national brands: Liushen, Mingxing and Chinf de Chinf. In 1990, Jahwa invested in a joint venture with S.C. Johnson & Son in Shanghai, the Ruby Johnson Cosmetics Co. Ltd. Some of Jahwa's brands, including Maxam and Ruby brands, were incorporated into the new joint venture. Sales independent of the joint venture reached RMB 260 million in 1992 (Exhibit 8).

Much of Jahwa's recent success was attributed to its general manager, Mr. Ge Wenyao. He was a firm believer in modern management techniques and an ardent advocate of a modernized Chinese industrial sector. He joined Jahwa in 1985 as general manager and quickly set out to restructure the company by streamlining production, setting up several specialized manufacturing plants in the vicinity of Shanghai, and emphasizing product quality and lower costs. Mr. Ge then promoted the concept of "high contribution" inside Jahwa:

> If one compares the average contribution in Jahwa with leading international companies or foreign invested joint ventures in China, they are somewhere between 40 per cent and 60 per cent, and we were around 12 per cent. Most of the state-owned enterprises are only measured on net profit. It gives management an incentive to cut expenses, especially for marketing and R&D. It seems that the company is making a profit, but that is at the expense of long-term growth. There is little money left for building brands or developing new products. Selling price is low but products are also low value-added. In the long run, the company loses its competitiveness.

Mr. Ge set a target contribution of 35 per cent, to be met by 1998. Accordingly, Jahwa rationalized its product line and set a higher minimum contribution bar for new products. Managers at Jahwa quickly realized that higher contributions could only be achieved by offering higher value-added products.

In the late 1980s, Mr. Ge implemented the brand manager system (Exhibit 9). He recruited college-educated managers and gave them responsibility for market research, new product launches, design and execution of marketing programs and the overall positioning of the brand. Apart from various in-house training programs, Jahwa also sent some managers to be trained abroad.

Brand managers worked closely with R&D, market research, and the sales departments. Mr. Ge was convinced that new product development and quality improvement were fundamental to Jahwa's ability to compete with multinationals. Jahwa invested aggressively both in people and equipment. The company offered competitive compensation packages, and no "glass ceiling," a phenomenon that locals usually complained about when working for multinationals. Jahwa had extensive co-operation agreements with local universities and institutes for basic research. In addition, it also selectively obtained technology from international companies through licensing agreements (Exhibit 10).

In 1988, Jahwa abandoned an outdated sole distributor relationship in favor of a sales network with 24 regional offices around the country. Regional offices were responsible for developing local distributors, supervising delivery to wholesalers and managing the "Jahwa counter" in some 1,000 department stores. As Mr. Ge said: "the sales department is responsible for total channel management." The new sales network proved to be a crucial element of Jahwa's success. It not only improved logistics, but more importantly, it brought Jahwa much closer to its customers and consumers. Consumer trends, recent market developments and competitive information were rapidly fed back to Jahwa's management in Shanghai.

SHOWER CREAM

Shower cream was developed in the United States in the 1980s as a moisturizing alternative to soap. Traditionally, an alkaline base gives soap its cleaning power, but can be harsh to the skin as the surface is left "unprotected." The result is a "dry skin" sensation after soap use. Shower cream uses surfactant instead of an alkaline base. It covers the skin with a fine membrane that controls water evaporation from the surface, providing moisturizing. It was quickly accepted in Europe and America, as consumers liked its "silky" feeling on the skin. Brands of shower cream proliferated with major players entering the market: Lux and Lifebuoy from Unilever, Safeguard from P&G, Biore from Kao and Baby from J&J competed in European, American and Japanese markets. Each had developed a unique positioning, and price differences were small. Most of these brands had also recently been introduced in other markets in Asia, including Thailand and Hong Kong.

SHOWER CREAM IN CHINA

Shower cream was introduced into China in 1990 by Unilever. The European edible-oils-to-cosmetics conglomerate was among the most aggressive players in the personal care market in China. It offered a wide range of products under its well-known brands, including Pond's moisturizing cream, Vaseline moisturizing lotion, Hazeline Snow moisturizing cream, and Lux soap and shower creams. Some of the products were produced in China by Unilever's joint ventures, others, including the shower cream, were imported from its manufacturing facilities in other parts of Asia. During 1992, there had been reports that Unilever may have been negotiating other joint ventures, including for the production of shower cream in the Shanghai region. This would reduce their costs dramatically, and could even lead to a decrease in prices.

Most of Unilever's products were sold at 100 per cent to 200 per cent premium over local products, some even higher. The premium gave these brands a high-quality image. The brands were very focused and consistently positioned: Pond's for basic skin care, Hazeline for purity, and Lux for beauty and glamor. In China, Unilever used extensive television advertisements to promote its brand images. Lux soap ran a series of advertisements that featured glamorous international and Asian stars such as Nastasja Kinski and Jialin Liu. The launch of Lux shower cream in China allowed Unilever to capitalize on the established brand image of Lux soap.

Like most of Unilever's products, Lux shower cream was first launched through downtown department stores in major cities such as Beijing, Shanghai and Guangzhou, spreading quickly into more regions and more stores as the market accepted the products. Two initial sizes launched were: the 350 millilitres (ml) size retailing at RMB 40, and the 700 ml size at RMB 70. Adoption of shower cream was slow. Sales grew at an average 40 per cent in the first three years, much lower than the 150 per cent to 300 per cent norm for new products in the personal care industry in China. In 1992, sales of Lux shower cream reached around RMB 33 million at retail. It was clearly a luxury item for most Chinese. Soap sold for around RMB 1 to RMB 5 a bar, while Rejoice shampoo from P&G was priced around RMB 15 for 200 ml.

Of greater concern was the impression that the product category, shower cream, did not seem to fit into the habits and lifestyles of Chinese consumers. Housing reform started in the late 1980s in some selected cities in China. Before then, the government built and owned most of the residential buildings and assigned apartments to people based on age and family size in return for a nominal rent of between RMB 10 and RMB 50 per month. The units varied from one bedroom to three bedrooms with a small bathroom from two to five square metres. Some had a tub, but very few had built-in hot water supply. In the cities, over 50 per cent of the people showered or bathed at their workplace. Another 25 per cent used a public bath and paid RMB 1 to RMB 5 for a bath or shower. The rest would heat water, pour it into a tub or a wooden barrel and bathe at home. Very few people showered at home. In the workplace and public bath, the change areas were usually small, humid and cold, making a rapid towel-dry the norm. For surfactant to give the best moisturizing effect, it is better to dry naturally in open air. All of these conditions limited the use of shower cream.

During the summer, however, some people showered at home using tap water, sometimes twice a day. But, rather than seeking a moisturizing feeling, people valued the dryness of soap and associated "dry" skin with a clean feeling. Some even perceived the silky feeling of existing moisturizing soaps and shower creams as "sticky," and "unclean."

LIUSHEN BRAND

Jahwa registered the Liushen brand name in the late 1980s for its eau de toilette products. When translated directly, Liushen stands for "six spirits." In traditional Chinese belief, human organs such as heart and liver are all internal "spirits" that determine the health of the body. Liushen is the name of a traditional prescription made of pearl powder, musk and several other ingredients, usually sold in the form of a tiny tablet with a very strong mint flavor. Liushen tablets had been widely used in the summer season for relieving all kinds of heat induced ailments, including prickly heat and sunburn. Many families stocked the tablet at home.

In the early 1990s, the market for Chinese eau de toilette was estimated at RMB 100 million. The product was used mostly during the summer season, not for its fragrance, but for its refreshing qualities. Mothers put a few drops in the water when bathing their babies, and adults simply sprayed it on to relieve itchiness or soothe prickly heat. Others rubbed it on their temples or pulse points to relieve stress or drowsiness brought on by the summer heat.

Jahwa had two leading brands of Chinese eau de toilette on the market, which together captured a 25 per cent share of the market, and competed with a dozen other locally manufactured brands. These products were widely distributed, primarily in department stores, drugstores, and convenience shops and retailed for approximately RMB 2 for a 200 ml bottle. There was very little advertising, and price differentials across brands were narrow. It was considered a mature product that was hard to differentiate. Jahwa had been looking for opportunities to increase its 25 per cent share of this market. At the same time, the company was also trying to launch a new natural line of personal care products associated with traditional Chinese therapies. Jahwa registered the Liushen brand name and launched the new eau de toilette nationwide at a 100 per cent price premium over its existing entries in the market. Liushen eau de toilette was positioned as an improved product targeted at mainstream households. The company invested in intensive advertising on television, radio and in newspapers to promote Liushen as a natural and refreshing eau de toilette. The association with traditional therapy was strong and instant. Liushen became the preferred solution to summer heat-related ailments. Jahwa withdrew its previous brands from the market. Sales of Liushen eau de toilette grew from RMB 20 million in 1991 to RMB 60 million in 1992, and it was estimated they would reach RMB 80 million in 1993, capturing close to a 60 per cent market share.

LIUSHEN SHOWER CREAM

Mr. Qing, the Liushen brand manager, and Mr. Chang from R&D, had been closely following the development of Lux shower cream for the past year. The idea of developing a Liushen shower cream intrigued them. Mr. Chang collected and analysed dozens of samples of competitive shower creams from around the world. By the end of 1992, he had completed development on three prototypes of Liushen shower cream. They were standard shower cream formulations blended with different proportions of Liushen extract. Tests on the prototypes showed they matched international products on key specifications.

After the peak summer season in 1992, Mr. Qing commissioned a market research report on Liushen eau de toilette. Consumers identified the brand as traditional and reliable. When compared with competing Chinese eau de toilette brands, Liushen by far led the rest in terms of perceptions of quality and reliability. When compared with other personal care brands, Liushen was strongly associated with "freshness," "Chinese therapy," "summer" and "natural." Brand awareness was high, ranging from 40 per cent to 70 per cent depending on the region. After reviewing the findings,

Mr. Qing felt the strength of the brand and its associations might allow an extension to shower cream. He was further encouraged by a recent research study, which showed that people showered 10 times more in the summer season (May to September) than in the winter season (October to February), and that showers were replacing baths.

Mr. Qing also knew that there would be more showers at home as well as more running hot water as living standards improved. Commercialization of the real estate sector had initiated a new wave of residential development in which the new buildings being built were more spacious and included larger, integrated bathrooms. While these new apartments were fairly expensive, the government was experimenting with mortgage plans. Another interesting development was the popularity of household water-heating units. These five-litre to eight-litre electric or gas-fired units, which sold for between RMB 800 and RMB 2,000, had become extremely popular since their recent introduction. Reports indicated that, driven by increasing demand, producers of water-heating units were increasing production capacity.

In January, Jahwa carried out focus-group and in-home tests in Shanghai, Beijing and Guangzhou. The feedback on the brand, the concept of a shower cream and the three prototypes was encouraging but not overwhelming. Half the group indicated that Liushen is for summer use only, another 25 per cent believed it had medicinal properties effective for skin rashes. Over 80 per cent of the respondents said the brand name reminded them of the refreshing, mint fragrance of the Chinese prescription. Only 20 per cent had heard of shower cream, mainly through the Lux advertisement. Most of them perceived it to be a luxury cosmetic item for young women. Although over 40 per cent indicated they would like to try it, 70 per cent said RMB 40/350 ml was too expensive, and they would continue to use soap. A few agreed that shower cream was more convenient to carry and use than soap. Consumers testing the three prototypes confirmed that most people associate the "silky" feeling with "stickiness" and "not clean." The typical comment was that it was difficult to rinse off. There was consensus on the right proportion of Liushen extract.

Mr. Chang believed the "stickiness" problem could be solved by reverting to a soap-based formulation or a blend, although this would reduce the moisturizing effect. Armed with the results from market research, and confirmation from R&D that they could make a less "sticky" version of the product, Mr. Qing turned his attention to the positioning of Liushen shower cream. Lux clearly dominated the market. Unilever was expected to increase its 1993 marketing budget for the product. Other multinationals in China might also enter the market. Both J&J and P&G had been in China for over five years, and had invested heavily in production facilities and building marketing capabilities. J&J's Baby brand of products had been successful. Women used Baby products for their perceived "mildness," "softness" and "safe" image. Rejoice and Pantene from P&G had become the two dominant shampoo brands in China. There were indications that P&G might launch a Safeguard shower cream to complete its line. Its "antibacterial" positioning would be very attractive to urban Chinese consumers. Kao, though a late-comer compared with the Americans, had done well with its Kao and Biore brands. The company aggressively promoted its "beauty" positioning through billboard advertisements. Outside of China, prices of the shower creams carried by these brands were very close to those of Lux.

More broadly, traditional beauty soap was also considered a competitive product. There are mainly four positionings in the soap category: skin type, beauty, natural ingredient and fragrance. Traditionally, soap is purchased either on price or fragrance. However, with the growth of international brands, consumers were starting to pay attention to the other criteria also. At the same time, the retail price of soap at the top end was increasing and the range was widening.

The manufacturing division estimated that the unit cost of the 350 ml would be around RMB 12. Mr. Qing knew that the marketing budget of Unilever or other multinationals would dwarf the budget he could get. But before he went any further with the project, he needed Mr. Ge's approval and support, based on a well-thought-out launch plan.

The Richard Ivey School of Business gratefully acknowledges the generous support of The Richard and Jean Ivey Fund in the development of this case as part of the RICHARD AND JEAN IVEY FUND ASIAN CASE SERIES.

Exhibit 1 Major economic indices

	1980	1985	1990	1992
GDP (RMB Billion)	452	896	1,854	2,400
Retail Price Index (Previous Year = 100)	106	108	102	108
Retail Sales (RMB Billion)	179	380	725	1,099
Import (US$ Billion)	20	42	53	83
Export (US$ Billion)	18	27	62	86
Exchange Rate RMB = US$1	3.5	5.3	5.7	8.6
Foreign Direct Investment (US$ Billion)	1	6	7	58

Exhibit 2(a) Population (million)

	1953	1964	1982	1990
Total Population	582	691	1,003	1,130
Male	301	354	515	581
Female	281	337	488	549
Urban	71	130	193	301
Rural	511	561	810	829
Natural Growth Rate	2%	2.80%	1.20%	1.40%

Exhibit 2(b) Population by age group (million)

	0–9	10–19	20–34	35–50	50+	Total
Male	100.0	90.0	145.0	110.0	136.0	581
Female	85.0	75.0	145.0	100.0	144.0	549
Total	185.0	165.0	290.0	210.0	280.0	1,130.0

Exhibit 3 Per capita consumption (RMB)

	Urban	Rural	National Average
1980	496	178	236
1985	802	347	437
1990	1,686	571	803
1991	1,925	621	896
1992	2,356	718	1,070

Exhibit 4 Import tariff and consumption taxes for cosmetics and personal care products (per cent)

	MFN*	GPN**	Consumption Tax***
Lipsticks	55	150	30
Eye Shadow	55	150	30
Nail Enamel	55	150	30
Powder	55	150	30
Shampoo	55	150	17
Styling Gel	55	150	17
Shower Gel/Cream	55	150	0
Soap	45	130	0

*Most Favored Nation; **General Preference Nation; ***Applies also to locally manufactured products.

Exhibit 5 Multinationals in China

	Year of Establishment	Sales (1992) RMB Million	Products
S.C. Johnson & Son, Shanghai	1987	453	Shampoo, cream
P&G, Guangzhou	1988	490	Shampoo
Unilever, Shanghai	1989	286	Cream
Johnson & Johnson, Shanghai	1989	145	Baby Series
Avon, Guangzhou	1989	60	Cream
Shiseido, Beijing	1992	6	Cream

Exhibit 6 Per capita consumption in major cities in 1992

	Population (Million)		Annual Income	Annual Consumption
	Male	Female	RMB	RMB
Beijing	5.5	5.3	3,507	3,154
Shenyang	2.7	2.7	2,112	1,833

(Continued)

(*Continued*)

	Population (Million)		Annual Income	Annual Consumption
	Male	Female	RMB	RMB
Harbin	1.8	1.7	1,791	1,545
Fuzhou	0.3	0.3	2,535	2,178
Wuhan	2.3	2.2	2,316	2,003
Guangzhou	3.3	3.1	4,397	3,918
Chongqing	4.9	4.5	2,284	1,987

Exhibit 7 Per capita cosmetics and personal care products consumption by region (1992) (RMB)

Coastal		Inland			
Beijing	68	Heilong Jiang	13	Yunnan	4
Shanghai	39	Xingjiang	10	Guangxi	4
Zhejiang	22	Ninxia	9	Qinghai	4
Tianjing	19	Shanxi	8	Jiangxi	4
Jiangsu	18	Jiling	8	Anhui	3
Liaoning	16	Hebei	7	Shanxi	3
Guangdong	14	Hubei	6	Henan	3
Fujian	12	Neimeng	5	Sichuan	3
Hainan	10	Gansu	5	Guizhou	2
Shandong	6	Hunan	4	Tibet	

Exhibit 8 Jahwa income statement (RMB million)

	1985	1989	1990	1991*	1992
Revenue	125.92	450	300.48	70.8	260
COGS	100.67	396	233.69	38.48	206
Gross Profit	25.25	54	66.79	32.32	54
Marketing Expense	1.2592	22.5	7.58	5.34	20.8
Other Expense	5.81	22.5	27.5	12.15	19
Profit	18.1808	9	31.71	14.83	14.2
Gross Profit Ratio	20%	12%	22%	46%	21%

*In 1991, a large chunk of Shanghai Jahwa was incorporated into a separate joint venture with S. C. Johnson and Son, called the Ruby Johnson Cosmetics Co. Ltd.

Exhibit 9 Jahwa organization chart

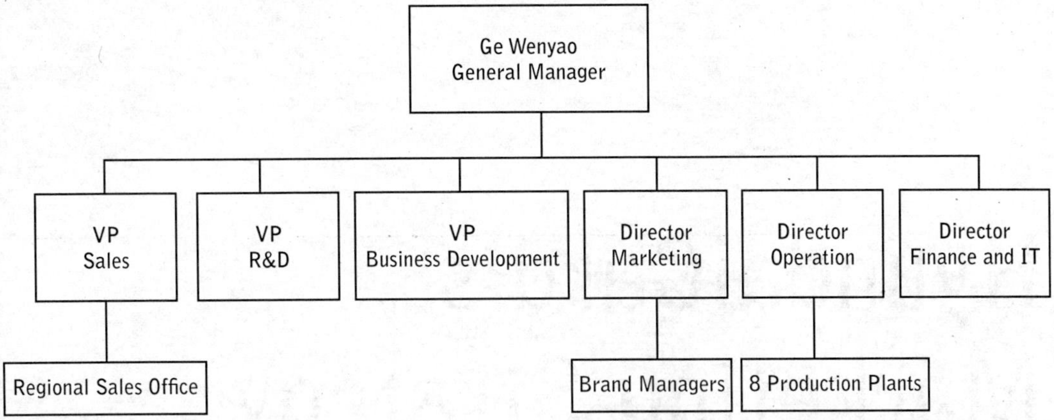

Exhibit 10 Jahwa brands

Brands	Products	Launch Date	Partnership
Shuangmei	Chinese eau de toilette	1915	
Youyi	Facial cream	1960	
Yashuang	Skin care products	1960	
Maxam	Shampoo	1962	
	Styling mousse		
	Hand cream		
	Moisturizing cream		
Ruby	Skin care products	1981	
	Color cosmetics		
Voila Paris*	Perfume	1987	L'Oreal, France
Kanebo*	Skin care products	1987	Kanebo company, Japan
Liushen	Chinese eau de toilette	1989	
Mingxing	Skin care products	1989	
Chinf de Chinf	Skin care products	1989	L'Oreal, France
	Color cosmetics		
	Perfume		
G.LF	Men's series	1992	
Lion*	Home care products	1993	Lion, Japan
Fumakilla*	Household insecticide	1995	Fumakilla, Japan

*brands owned by partners.

2

HyundaiCard's Marketing Strategy

Chan Soo Park and Ronald D. Camp II wrote this case solely to provide material for class discussion. The authors do not intend to illustrate either effective or ineffective handling of a managerial situation. The authors may have disguised certain names and other identifying information to protect confidentiality.

In January 2009, the vice-president of HyundaiCard's marketing division (see Exhibit 1), Jae-Woo Park, and several marketing managers discussed the marketing strategies of HyundaiCard in Korea. Following a review of HyundaiCard's marketing plans, the marketing managers put forward many ideas for marketing strategies and anticipated possible difficulties for HyundaiCard as a market follower in the competitive Korean credit card market. Jae-Woo reported the marketing strategies to Ted Chung, president of HyundaiCard.

HyundaiCard entered the competitive Korean credit card industry in 1999 and branded itself as "Hyundai M Card" (see Exhibit 2). Its creative business model forecasted HyundaiCard holders would be pre-discounted as much as 2,000,000 won (US$1,800) for buying Hyundai automobiles when paying with the HyundaiCard. They could then pay the discount back with credit card point mileage within five years. Although this creative business model achieved tremendous success within the Korean market, the company's performance had not progressed since 2002. HyundaiCard suffered from minimal customer count (i.e. number of cards distributed) and had difficulty relating its creative business model to the strong personas of leading players in the credit card industry. As a result of the innovative marketing strategy, however, HyundaiCard successfully positioned itself as a market leader.

Yet challenges remained for senior management. How could HyundaiCard, a market follower, successfully position itself as a market leader? Could HyundaiCard's marketing strategy keep enhancing its competitive edge in the market? What future strategy would be best for HyundaiCard?

HYUNDAICARD CO., LTD.

HyundaiCard was the country's fourth largest credit card company. HyundaiCard, sponsored by Hyundai Kia Automotive Group, was established in 1999 when the Hyundai Motor Group acquired Diners Card as a subsidiary and changed the card's name in 2001 to "HyundaiCard" (see Exhibit 3), thereby challenging the highly competitive credit card industry. Hyundai Motor Group prepared a long-term strategy in order to transform itself from an automobile manufacturer into the world's leading provider of additional services related to automobile businesses. The company's goal was to strengthen its financial services, retail businesses and Internet fields, etc.

In 2005, HyundaiCard strengthened its funding base through the formation of a strategic alliance with GE Consumer Finance (GECF), a unit of General Electric (GE). GECF invested 678.3 billion won in the firm, thus becoming the largest shareholder. HyundaiCard's largest shareholders became Hyundai Motor and GE Consumer Finance (see Exhibit 4). After years of gaining cumulative expertise and know-how, through its association with GE Consumer Finance, HyundaiCard made efforts to become a market leader in the credit card industry by initiating a unique, customized service via alphabet card marketing activities. HyundaiCard secured a more stable financial base with this alliance; the BIS capital adequacy ratio increased to 43 per cent from 11.3 per cent, addressing a significant improvement in the company's risk profile. HyundaiCard upgraded creditability and reinforced financial stability through the formation of the strategic alliance. A sustainable growth base was firmly laid by introducing GE's advanced financial product planning and risk management systems. The partnership formed a solid foundation upon which HyundaiCard could become a market leader in South Korea.

"HyundaiCard M," a HyundaiCard representative product, had enjoyed yearly high performance. It secured more than one million subscribers within the first year of its launch. As a single credit card brand, it had the largest subscriber base of any credit card in Korea. In addition to "HyundaiCard M," which created a huge sensation among male customers, HyundaiCard released the "M Lady" card, designed to offer additional beneficial services to female customers. The "M Lady" credit card brand also gained a favorable response from the Korean market (see Exhibit 5).

THE CREDIT CARD MARKET IN SOUTH KOREA

South Korea Credit Card History

The concept of paying merchants by using a credit card was invented in 1950 by Frank X. McNamara, an American businessman who left cash in his hotel room and, as a result, was unable to pay his bill at a restaurant. The Diners Club produced the first general purpose credit card; shortly thereafter, it was followed by American Express and Carte Blanche. The Bank of America created the BankAmericard in 1958, which evolved into the VISA card. MasterCard appeared in 1966.

In Korea, the concept of the credit card was introduced in 1969 by a Korean department store, Shinsaegae. In 1978, Korean Exchange Bank launched its first credit card under a joint venture with VISA International, issuing the credit card to its clients who travelled frequently (see Exhibit 6). In the 1980s, bank and non-bank credit card companies began to do business in Korea. It was not until the year 2000 that the market saw an annual growth rate of 80 per cent and more than 100 million cards issued.

Credit Card Consumption Patterns and Trends

Between the 1990s and 2002, the number of credit cards issued in South Korea increased tenfold, from 10 million to 100 million. Bank of Korea records show the credit card usage amount at that time was 40 per cent or higher of private final consumption. Koreans paid for many purchases with credit cards, even small purchases of a few dollars at convenience stores. Private consumption with credit cards amounted to approximately $210 billion in 2006. According to the Bank of Korea (BOK), Korea ranked 34th in per capita income in the world, but the credit card penetration in South Korea was quite high, with the world's second highest per capita card issuance. The average South Korean cardholder held 3.78 credit cards in 2008, trailing only the United States with 5.3 cards. Trailing behind were Singapore with per capita card issuance of 2.98 cards, followed by the United Kingdom (2.36), the Netherlands (1.92) and Belgium (1.57).

A unique characteristic of the Korean credit card was its multi-functionality. South Korea's credit card companies offered competitive incentives in order to entice credit card customers to use their products frequently (see Exhibit 7). A great deal of credit card use was tied to retail chains or conglomerates. For example, consumers who had a HyundaiCard bought products at the Hyundai Internet shopping mall (www.Hmall.com) and at Hyundai department stores run by the Hyundai conglomerate. Similarly, consumers who had a Samsung credit card bought products at the Samsung Internet shopping mall (www.samsungmall.com) and Samsung department stores run by the Samsung conglomerate. The online and offline stores used incentives such as a five per cent discount or interest-free installments over three months or airline mileage points to increase consumer loyalty. In order to survive in the competitive credit card industry, companies needed to keep up with new and creative marketing incentives and promotions.

IT Developments in South Korea

Information technology was an important growth engine for the South Korean economy and had expanded rapidly since the early 1990s. In particular, South Korea was a technology-savvy country in which electronic payment was easy and popular. The number of people using the Internet regularly was about 30.7 million as of March 2007.[1] Korea's rate of Internet usage by those above the age of six, as of June 2007, reached 75.5 per cent,[2] showing a rapid growth in the number of people who were very comfortable using the Internet. The use of credit cards was the most common mode utilized by South Koreans to pay for products and services, followed by cash and online banking services[3] (see Exhibit 8).

---

[1] www.koreanclick.com, 2007, accessed May 22, 2008.

[2] Whitepaper of Korean Ministry of Information and Communication, 2007.

[3] Korean Credit Finance Association, 2005.

Korean credit card web sites had gained nationwide popularity (see Exhibit 9), resulting in various new services and goods appearing on the Internet. Generally, credit card holders checked their transaction history and processed some transactions related to products and services with their accumulated mileage points. However, credit card consumers had qualms about being treated as simply a part of a large mass, either while on the Internet or on offline channels. Korean credit card web sites had been working hard to pack web pages with as many features as possible. They were spending millions of dollars on aspects of customer relation management vital to consumers. Therefore, credit card companies had taken a customer-focused view and retreated from the mass marketing approach.

In the U.S. market, many affiliated merchants were not equipped with electronic authorization and settlement technologies. Usually, it took one or two weeks to get reimbursed from the credit card companies after giving signed payment slips to the banks. This created a major inconvenience. On the other hand, Korean credit card companies, using the VAN service, developed high-end technologies and finally automated the entire process. The affiliated member stores were then reimbursed within three days. This convenience helped the issuers attract more affiliated stores.

Active Support from the Korean Government

South Korea was one of the world's most dynamic countries encouraging credit card use (see Exhibit 10), thanks to the support and an encouraging policy by the Korean government since 2000. The Korean government encouraged consumers to use credit cards to stimulate private spending and secure more taxes. The Korean government made the acceptance of the credit card mandatory and penalized stores not accepting the credit card. There were sensational credit card lottery events and tax incentives for credit card usage. With the above-mentioned active support, the non-bank, specialized companies such as Samsung, LG (Shinhan) and Hyundai endeavored to increase their market shares through proactive marketing such as ardent sales promotions (i.e. street promotions and sales), improvement of CRM systems, and interest-free installment payments on purchases.

Credit Card Issuers in South Korea

The Korean credit card market was characterized by rapid growth and intensified competition. The major monoline credit card issuers were Samsung Card, LG (Shinhan) Card and HyundaiCard. The aforementioned companies issued credit cards customized for Korean individuals. There were cards such as the "Lady Card," the "Cellular Phone Card," the "Teen Group Card," the "Revolving Card" and the "Transportation Card." Another variety was credit cards issued by banks. Several banks were cooperating with BC card (a bank credit card established by several member banks). Some of these banks were with Kookmin Card and Hana Card; Gwangju was cooperating with the Korean Exchange Bank Credit Service (see Exhibit 11).

In the M&A credit card market in South Korea, Shinhan Financial Group Co. bought South Korea's largest credit card company, LG Card. LG Card was South Korea's largest credit card company, consisting of approximately 10 million card holders, which meant that approximately one out of every four and a half people in the country held an LG card. Shinhan offered at least 65,000 won ($67.30) per share for LG Card. The deal to create the credit card firm exceeded $7.25 billion. It was the largest business deal in Korean financial history.

One of the notable competences of the Korean credit card industry was its product development ability. "LG Lady Card," "Kookmin Pass Card" and "Hyundai M Card" were benchmarked even by global issuers such as JCB. These cards developed a variety of membership programs which provided benefits associated with retail stores, popular services, etc. The diversity of the card products met the needs of the different customer segmentation groups. The proactive marketing program played a major role in the rapid growth of the Korean credit card industry.

Kookmin Card

Kookmin Bank, the country's largest bank, launched its credit card business in 1980. With 9.3 million cardholders and total card sales of W57.3 trillion in 2008, Kookmin Card established its leadership position in the industry. Kookmin Card launched innovative cards which represented a new source of revenues. Furthermore, the Kookmin Bank worked aggressively to capture a larger share of the high-growth check card and corporate card markets, recording high growth in card usage in South Korea.

Kookmin broadened its lineup of credit cards that met customers' diverse needs, launching "SK LPG Save KB Card," "S-Oil KB Card," "KB Fn Save Card" and others. Kookmin Bank also provided enhanced services for its mainstay card product, "KB Star Card." Kookmin Card introduced a series of social service voucher cards including the "Senior Citizen Support Voucher Card," the "Housekeeping/ Nursing Voucher Card," and the "Beautiful Mommy Card" for expectant mothers. Kookmin Card had its credit cards designed by renowned Korean fashion designer Andre Kim.

Samsung Card

Established in 1988, Samsung Card was Korea's third largest card issuer. Samsung Card had launched innovative products and services, and won several awards in many customer satisfaction surveys. In 2004, Samsung Card merged with Samsung Capital, Samsung Group's financial affiliate, and expanded into commercial financing markets. In 2007, Samsung Card was listed on the Korea Exchange and was the first listing among Korean credit card issuers.

Samsung Card's core competence included its size and breadth of product offerings, advanced customer relationship management system, and extensive business network based on partnerships with Samsung Group affiliates.

Samsung Card developed new products such as the Samsung Blue American Express Card and the Shinsaegae-Samsung Card (Shinsaegae was one of the biggest Korean department stores).

The company's social contribution activities set Samsung Card apart from its peers in the industry. The company had been very active in community service, providing volunteer services and other charitable work by forming relationships with local communities. All employees joined at least one volunteer activity under the company's 365 Volunteering program.

Shinhan (LG) Card

Shinhan Card had the strong customer base of its parent company, Shinhan Financial Group, the nation's second largest financial holding company. In 2007, Shinhan Card and LG Card were integrated as the new Shinhan Card. The integration of two card issuers resulted in a strong customer base—at the end of 2008, the number of active cardholders reached 13.6 million and market share reached 24 per cent. Shinhan Card was the largest card issuer in Asia and No. 10 in the world.

Under the umbrella of the financial group, there were two kinds of distribution channels by which Shinhan Card attracted new customers — 1,052 branches of Shinhan Bank and 30 credit card branches. Shinhan Card had the infrastructure of the product sales network and merchant. This great infrastructure allowed customers to easily use its credit cards almost anywhere they went. Shinhan Card boosted cross-selling between subsidiaries of the financial group, and optimized product mixture.

HYUNDAICARD'S MARKETING STRATEGY IN SOUTH KOREA

The importance of the customer segmentation strategy and the use of websites was even greater for HyundaiCard. HyundaiCard focused on its customers' needs, developed new credit card products, and provided different online marketing campaigns in order to actively prevent the loss of customers. HyundaiCard utilized a diverse segmentation strategy using online and offline channels to create a multi-stage roadmap. The company also strengthened its internal administration regarding customer service and guaranteed safe online business. The company provided the highest level of services by utilizing customer segmentation and diverse marketing strategies to compete with other credit card companies.

In order to increase profits, credit card companies focused on the fact that customers had to be willing to use their cards often. The key to profits was frequent card usage. To achieve the goal of increasing profits, marketing strategies were employed to convert customers with low usage frequency into customers with high usage frequency.

Customer Segmentation

The innovative marketing strategy focused on customers' lifestyles. HyundaiCard divided its card members into four categories (general, low, middle, high) according to credit card payments. Customer segmentation filtered each group's usage status and purchasing methods and helped in collecting data according to their age, gender and the main location of purchase (shops, gas station, restaurants, etc.). Through the use of a strategic homepage and e-mail, various information and benefits (such as discount rates and bonus points) could also be offered for special cards, according to the customer's traits (gender, age, level, card type) and main usage contents. Region and location of use, usage count, and the monetary amount for which the card was used all provided more refined discrepancy data services.

HyundaiCard formulated "Alphabet Marketing." Alphabet marketing meant differentiated marketing named M, S, W, U, K and A, based on consumer lifestyle. HyundaiCard executed the company's alphabet marketing strategy by launching HyundaiCard M, S, W, U, K and A. For example, HyundaiCard discovered that women in their thirties represented the largest consumer group using credit cards via Internet and offline channels. Thus, the company issued the new "HyundaiCard S" for women in their thirties. Features such as "more enjoyable shopping" and "more purchases lead to more bonus points and benefits" were adopted with an aim to dramatically increase new membership. The customized marketing approaches included "Alphabet Credit Cards" having unique and creative designs.

To distinguish its services from those of its competitors, HyundaiCard diversified its product line and expanded into the premium market via the introduction of "the Black" and "the Purple" cards. HyundaiCard had moved beyond its earlier premium-level credit cards to concentrate on VIP customers. Powerful efforts were made to advance into the niche market by establishing alliances with various financial partners. HyundaiCard targeted the top 0.05 per cent of credit card holders, limiting its issue to 9,999 extremely important clients.

eCRM Strategy

Electronic Customer Relationship Management (eCRM) was introduced in the most widely used credit card websites in Korea. HyundaiCard upgraded its Internet system environments and integrated customer relationship management (CRM) capabilities to fully satisfy the ever-increasing needs and expectations of customers. To raise the eCRM quality to a higher level, HyundaiCard intended to (1) provide effective tailor-made services through its website for HyundaiCard consumers; (2) promote marketing campaigns with suitable online business strategies and competitive online services; and (3) upgrade e-mail solutions. To achieve the company's objectives, the following activities were implemented:

- Strengthened customer relationship management: HyundaiCard discovered and analyzed customer tendencies to provide customized services for individual credit card holders.
- Established themed malls in the website: mall themes, such as shopping, insurance and travel products, were based on card members' tendencies.
- Design and GUI upgraded: The company upgraded designs to connect the HyundaiCard website, family site services, and contents with ease.

The eCRM collected HyundaiCard customer information. It accurately collected and analyzed data regarding HyundaiCard customers on its family site. It analyzed customers' online activities in categories such as anonymous members, royal members and special card members and loaded every customer's online usage information into the database. It provided data on content preferences, banner ads, and e-mail marketing. The database provided useful, accurate information about Internet customers and their transactions. Establishing an effective eCRM system could potentially strengthen Internet services and allow the company to execute effective Internet marketing strategies (see Exhibit 12).

Promotion Development

The finance shop (see Exhibit 13) was the place that enabled HyundaiCard customers to enjoy all-in-one service, getting financial consultation services and enjoying an ambience created by world-famous designers. HyundaiCard's first finance shop opened for business in 2006 in Seoul, South Korea, and, by 2009, the company had doubled the size of the network to 12 shops nationwide. HyundaiCard also brought a paradigm shift to culture marketing by hosting the Super Concert series with big celebrities such as musical stars Billy Joel and Placido Domingo.

Integration of Customer Information

To capture the attention of consumers, HyundaiCard broke from tradition by deploying a unique marketing plan. HyundaiCard integrated online and offline customer data and maximized the potential of marketing campaigns. HyundaiCard had long known of the importance of this process. It maximized the two channels (online and offline channels) to increase customer profits and strengthen customer relationships. HyundaiCard enjoyed the synergy effect of online and offline channels for customer information. Online, HyundaiCard improved customer relationships and familiarity. The recent website usage duration, frequency of visits, and history with HyundaiCard provided metrics[4] for assessing online familiarity, such as last log-in date, frequency, etc. The above evaluation of familiarity determined various stages of customer status. Thus, to carry out an effective marketing strategy and increase profits, HyundaiCard focused on customer value and online interaction.

The integration of online and offline information provided accurate customer data to CRM Business departments and related administrators. The integrated information could then be shared by the whole

[4] Number of cards distributed = [(total login number/customer period) × 100].

company. For example, after CRM department representatives produced analysis reports, every department was able to access the resources. In addition, by integrating the data analysis environment, a variety of marketing data could be shared using web log and actual channel customer data. This assisted marketers with decisions on strategies.

HyundaiCard's customer information had been converted into a marketing database available for anyone within the company to easily use and expand. Integration of customer data created new card products suitable for customer needs. Connecting marketing programs with their targets helped provide more diverse data for financial services and added value. In addition, cross-selling mechanisms for shopping, travel, insurance and financial products could be established.

HYUNDAICARD'S PERFORMANCE

After surpassing three million members in August 2005, with the introduction of "HyundaiCard M" in the same year, the company set new standards. HyundaiCard M had the largest subscriber base of any credit card in Korea. HyundaiCard's market share increased more than five-fold, from 1.8 per cent in 2001 to 9.96 per cent in 2006 (see Exhibit 14), and its business grew six-fold in five years while posting the highest sales volume per cardholder in the domestic cards market. In 2006, the number of HyundaiCard members grew to 5.3 million (see Exhibit 15), and its Alphabet Cards continued to lead the domestic credit card market. In 2007, through an innovative marketing strategy, HyundaiCard was named Korea's Most Admired Company for the second consecutive year out of all Korean credit card companies. HyundaiCard ranked number one in the National Customer Satisfaction Index (NCSI) for the third consecutive year (2005, 2006 and 2007). HyundaiCard was also selected number one in the Credit Card category of Net Promoter Score (NPS) surveyed by Bain & Company in 2006. HyundaiCard joined Samsung Card, Kookmin Card and LG Card (merged with Shinhan in 2007) as one of the four leading enterprises within the credit card market.

According to analysis reports in 2002 and 2005 by MediaChannel Inc, a professional research and consulting company based on Internet users' behaviour analysis[5], the web traffic of the HyundaiCard website was low in comparison with several competitors in spite of an aggressive marketing campaign in 2003 and 2004. But its web traffic almost caught up with the top three credit card companies in 2005 and 2006. Backed by its stable financial results (see Exhibit 16), HyundaiCard was slowly becoming a brand name in the international markets.

MARKET COMPETITION AND CHALLENGES

Compared to other major credit card companies, HyundaiCard entered the Korean credit card market late. As a latecomer, HyundaiCard sustained a very low customer count. HyundaiCard, as a market follower, had to generate an aggressive marketing strategy to catch up with the market leaders. But HyundaiCard suffered a few problems such as low brand awareness, weak marketing communication and weak card services. To cover these strategic problems and to increase its membership and credit card usage rate, HyundaiCard had to adopt a differentiated marketing strategy. However, under the strict control of the Korean government, adding new members swiftly and redistributing cards to expired members proved very difficult.

[5] Rankey Monthly Report (MediaChannel Inc., 2002, 2005), www.rankey.com, accessed December 15, 2007.

The Korean credit card market experienced a period of overheating due to a rapid expansion in the number of cards, reduced standards for issuing cards, etc. In the loan services, credit card companies began witnessing an alarming growth in the number of late payments and users with bad credit history. There was an indication that the Korean economy would face a so-called "Korean Credit Card Crisis." The Korean credit card industry was a bubble on the verge of foaming and bursting.

The industry underwent an adjustment period, with many credit card companies forced to change the way they did business. To avoid mounting losses, numerous credit card companies decided to downsize their operations and undergo reconstruction to lower their burden. HyundaiCard was no exception. In comparison to its competitors, HyundaiCard had fewer customers and sustained moderate losses.

WHAT NEXT?

HyundaiCard will face tough competition from Kookmin Card, Samsung Card and Shinhan (LG) Card, all of whom are leading players in the South Korean credit card industry. HyundaiCard will have to realize sustainable growth by further developing its differentiated marketing strategies. It will be important for HyundaiCard to continuously develop advanced marketing strategies to maintain current customer relations and attract potential customers. HyundaiCard will have to increase efforts to create new, additional value in the constantly changing domestic market.

In the auto financing sector, HyundaiCard will have to create additional value by promoting cross-selling and expand customized services that will perfectly address each customer's lifestyle and needs. Strong efforts should also be made to maintain the company's leading position in the auto financing market. HyundaiCard will also have to extend its network of alliances with major players in various industries, and strengthen its "M point"-based marketing activities.

Internationally, HyundaiCard will have to break into the foreign financial markets, thereby solidifying a base from which it can become a global player. HyundaiCard is expanding its business territory into North America, Europe and Asia, and aligning itself with well-known global brands such as VISA, Coca-Cola, Wal-Mart and Google. As a new brand in the international market, raising the status of the company by solidifying with GE will be vital.

The authors would like to acknowledge the helpful discussions with Professor Ilan Vertinsky (The University of British Columbia), Professor Jack Ito (University of Regina) and Professor Chol Lee (Sogang University). The authors also appreciate the interview time given by the HyundaiCard Marketing Managers.

Exhibit 1 HyundaiCard's organization

President & CEO	Strategic Planning Division	Strategic Planning Dept. Process Innovation Dept.
Risk Management Committee	Finance Division	Corporate Planning Dept. Finance Dept.
Customer Protection Committee	Corporate Service Division	Public Relations Dept. Corporate Service Dept. IT Dept. Customer Satisfaction Dept. Business Legal Dept.
Audit Committee		

Risk Management Division	Collection Management Dept.
	Early Collection Dept.
	Risk Management Dept.
	Underwriting Dept.
Sales Division	Personal Sales Dept.
	Corporate Sales Dept.
Marketing Division	**CRM Dept.**
	Marketing Dept.
	Brand Marketing Dept.
	PRIVIA Dept.
	Financial Business Dept.
Integrated Marketing Division	Alliance Sales Dept.
	SME Business Dept.
Finance Business	Cross-Sell Business Dept.
Finance Business Division	Cross-Sell Business Dept.

Exhibit 2 HyundaiCard M, as a HyundaiCard representative product

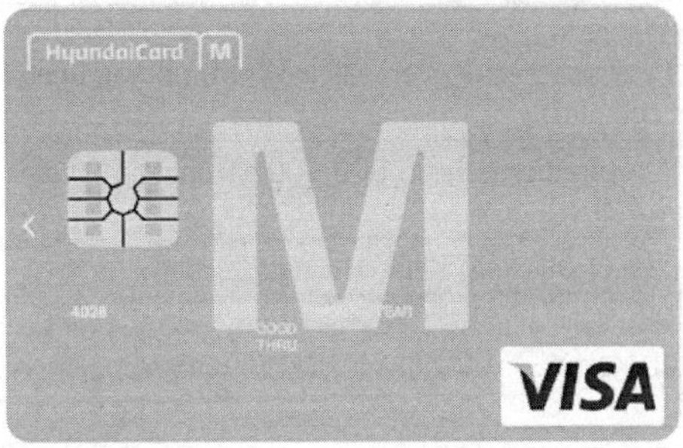

Source: Company files.

Exhibit 3 Corporate milestones

1967		Diners Club Card, the world's first credit card, launched in Korea by its agent, Korea National Tourism Organization
1984	June	Citi Corp. opened the Korean branch of Diners Card
1993	Feb.	Daewoo Group took over the management of Diners Club Korea
1994	Sept.	Launched prepaid cards
1996	June	Launched overseas travel supporting services
1997	Dec.	Began overseas ATM cash withdrawal service
1998	July	Increased capital to W100 billion
2001	Oct.	Changed company name to HyundaiCard Co., Ltd.

(*Continued*)

(*Continued*)

	Nov.	Became an affiliated company of Hyundai Motor Group
2002	Jan.	Released Hyundai "M" Card
	Oct.	Opened wireless Internet site
2003	March	Increased capital to W180 billion
	April	Remodeled and opened Internet shopping mall site (http://shop.hyundaicard.com)
	June	Increased capital to W310 billion
2004	Jan.	Disclosed HyundaiCard's corporate identity
	June	Selected as Korea's most respected enterprise
	Sept.	Won first place in Service Quality Index for the Credit Card
	Oct.	Opened customized travel site
2005	May	Opened HyundaiCard VIP Lounge at Incheon International Airport
	Aug.	Established a strategic alliance with GE Consumer Finance
2006	April	Renewed Alphabet Card marketing
	Dec.	Selected top in the Credit Card category of National Consumer Satisfaction Index (NCSI)
2007	Jan.	Released HyundaiCard M Lady
	Apr.	Released HyundaiCard V Completed first successful overseas US$400 million bond by an Asian card company
	July	Attainment of an impressive 5,000,000 cardholders under HyundaiCard M
2008	Feb.	Released Family Discount Card, HyundaiCard H

Exhibit 4 Ownership structure (%)

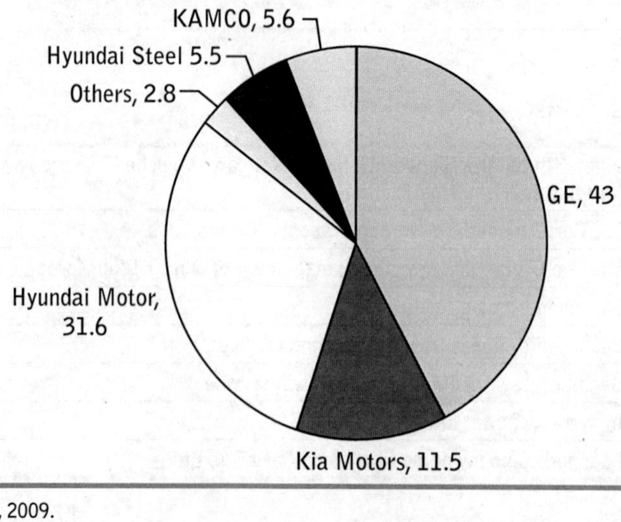

Source: HyundaiCard, 2009.

Exhibit 5 Hyundaicard's products

Products	Target Customers	Main Services
HyundaiCard M	The all-around, all-purpose multi-point card for driving, dining out, flying or even shopping.	Clients earn up to three per cent of their purchase in points each time they use their card and in turn save points to redeem a discount voucher worth up to US$2,000 on a Hyundai/Kia car, or redeem points at a growing list of locations including GS Caltex gas station, CJ Home Shopping, Lotte Cinema and more.
HyundaiCard M Lady	The multi-point card and service exclusively for women.	Clients benefit from multi-rewards points when buying a car, filling up their gas tank, dining out, flying or shopping. They acquire additional movie discounts and interest-free payments on purchases made at alliance stores.
HyundaiCard S	A serious shopping card for serious shoppers.	Clients receive a five per cent discount on all purchases at Hyundai Department Stores and 80 points per liter of gas purchased during weekends at four major fuel gas stations. Clients can earn points to save five per cent on cell phone charges and get additional discounts for movies and dining out.
HyundaiCard W	The weekend travel card that earns free travel benefits while you travel.	Clients spend US$12,000 and receive one Travel Ticket redeemable for airline tickets at all airlines. They also enjoy a variety of complimentary travel services.
HyundaiCard U	The value card made for university students.	Clients earn up to one per cent in U points on all purchases. They also trade points for points at cooperative partner businesses.
HyundaiCard K	A premium mileage card doubling as a Korean Air SKYPASS Membership card.	Clients earn and save up to three miles on every purchase. Discount vouchers worth up to 10 per cent off airfare are also offered and clients may receive up to 15 per cent off purchases at major duty-free shops.
HyundaiCard K VIP	An ultra-premium card doubling as a Korean Air SKYPASS Membership card.	Clients receive all the benefits of HyundaiCard K, plus free round trip ticket vouchers for a travel companion around South Korea.
HyundaiCard A	A premium mileage card doubling as an Asiana Club Membership card.	Clients earn and save up to three miles on every purchase. Clients also receive discount vouchers worth up to 10 per cent off airfare and up to 15 per cent off purchases at major duty-free shops.
The Black	The first VIP card made exclusively for the top 0.019 per cent of South Korea. High-class benefits for high-class customers.	Clients may receive free upgrades to first class on Korean Air and Asiana Airlines. They may also receive 10 per cent off coupons for air travel and US$300 gift vouchers for use at top hotels, beauty shops and more. Full access to Club Services.
The Purple	A VIP card made for the top five per cent of South Korea, including medical doctors, pharmacists, successfully self-employed individuals and CEOs.	Double Rewards are offered on M points and airline mileage. A free airfare voucher may be redeemed for a companion on trips to Hong Kong, China, Japan and most countries in Asia.

Source: HyundaiCard IR, 2007.

Exhibit 6 Timeline of the Korean credit card market

Year	Development	Credit Card Service Companies
1960s	In 1969, the first card was issued by the Shinsaegae Department Store to Samsung Corporation employees.	Shinsaegae Department Store
1970s	The first VISA card was introduced by the Korean Exchange Bank Credit Service Co., LTD (KEBCS), in a joint venture with VISA International.	KEBCS and VISA International
1980s	In 1987, the credit laws were amended and the credit card market began to develop more aggressively. Four mono-line credit companies were established.	Four mono-line credit companies: LG in 1987, Kookmin in 1987, the Korean Exchange Bank Credit Service (KEBCS) in 1988 and Samsung in 1988.
1990s	Tax laws were modified at the end of 1999. A tax deductible system was introduced—a portion of credit card purchases could be deducted from income before tax.	I: Department stores II: Bank: BC, Suhyup, Kwangju III: Mono-line credit card companies: LG, Samsung IV: Automobile and oil companies
2000s	Private consumption with credit cards was approximately $210 billion annually. The average South Korean had at least four credit cards.	64 types of credit card service products by 2002. Distribution industry: 38 Mono-line issuers: 10 Banks: 16

Source: Financial Supervisory Committee and Credit Finance Association.

Exhibit 7 Various incentives provided by dynamic Korean credit card companies

Credit Card Services	Incentives
Cash discounts	Five to 10 per cent discount to consumers who purchase products with their credit cards
Interest-free installments	Several online shopping websites provide credit card consumers with the option of interest-free installments over three to twelve months
Air mileage service	Give consumers a certain number of free miles on airlines for every W1,000 (US$1) they spend
Point cash	A small percentage of each settlement saved in the card user's account can be spent the same as cash, which could be used in more than two million shops This point money could be used to make political contributions or donated to a nonprofit organization
Pre auto financing service	HyundaiCard provides Hyundai car purchasers with a nominal discount on the price of a car. Card users must pay this amount back with accumulated mileage points.

Exhibit 8 The preference of payments

1	Credit Card	38.70
2	Cash	27.76
3	Transmitting with Cash machine	9.89

4	Internet Banking	6.98
5	Debit Card	6.78
6	Telephone Banking	4.97
7	Giro	4.32
8	Mobile Banking	0.4
9	Electronic Cash	0.2

Source: Korea Credit Finance Association, 2005.

Exhibit 9 The usage rate of Korean financial web sites

Domain	Unique Online Visitor	Total Page View
Bank	19,931,102	2,120,305,390
Credit Card	14,038,598	664,025,739
Insurance	8,860,826	327,639,548
Investment	7,532,188	877,177,163
Other Financial Service	4,809,701	51,705,433
Real Estate	4,754,289	424,377,102
Security	4,181,004	320,381,728
Financial Service in Portal	5,445,323	50,604,349

Notes: Unique Online Visitor: a statistic describing a unit of traffic to a web site, counting each visitor only once in the time frame of the report.
Total Page View: a total request to load a single page of a web site.
Source: Korean Click, 2005, www.koreanclick.com, accessed December 15, 2007.

Exhibit 10 Korean population and the number of cards issued

Unit: 1,000

Year	Population	Economically Productive Population	Number of Credit Cards Issued	Number of Credit Cards per Person	Membership Stores
1995	45,093	20,845	33,278 (31.5)	1.6	2,760 (34.3)
1997	45,954	21,782	45,705 (11.2)	2.1	4,257 (23.0)
1999	46,617	21,666	38,993 (–7.2)	1.8	6,192 (33.2)
2000	47,008	22,069	57,881 (48.4)	2.6	8,611 (39.1)
2001	47,343	22,417	89,330 (54.3)	4.0	12,627 (46.6)
2002	47,640	22,877	104,807 (17.3)	4.6	15,612 (23.6)

(*Continued*)

(*Continued*)

Year	Population	Economically Productive Population	Number of Credit Cards Issued	Number of Credit Cards per Person	Membership Stores
2003	47,925	22,916	95,517 (–8.9)	4.1	16,949 (8.6)
2004	48,082	23,370	83,456 (–16.0)	3.6	17,095 (8.6)
2005	48,294	23,743	82,905 (–0.7)	3.5	16,124 (–5.7)
2006	48,497	23,978	91,149 (9.9)	3.8	17,037 (5.7)
2007	48,692	24,216	89,565	3.7	14,701
1/4 2008		23,852	90,673	3.8	14,851
2/4 2008		24,638	93,481	3.8	15,145
3/4 2008		24,503	97,519	4.0	15,364

Source: The Credit Card Finance Association, 2008.

Exhibit 11 Korean credit card companies

Type of Credit Card	Number of Businesses	Company Names
Credit Cards	7	
– Pure Bank	3	BC, Shinhan, Industry Bank Capital
– Mono-line	4	Samsung, LG, Hyundai, Lotte
Bank with Credit Card Service	15	
– BC affiliates	11	Kyongnam, etc.
– Koomin Bank	3	Koomin, etc.
– Korean Exchange	1	Korean Exchange
– Shinhan Bank	4	Jeju, etc.
Retailers and Distributors	13	Department Stores, etc.
Total	35	

Source: Credit Finance Association of Korea.

Exhibit 12 An example of 1:1 marketing

Gender	Age	Content			
		Area A	Area B	Area C	Area D
Female	20-29	a1, a2	b1	c1	d1
Male	20-29	a2	b2	c2, c5	d2

Female	30-39	a3	b3, b5	c3	d3
Male	30-39	a4, a5	b4	c4	d4

HyundaiCard defined the marketing rules appropriate for 1:1 marketing. According to the rules, it provided different content to different customer segment groups.

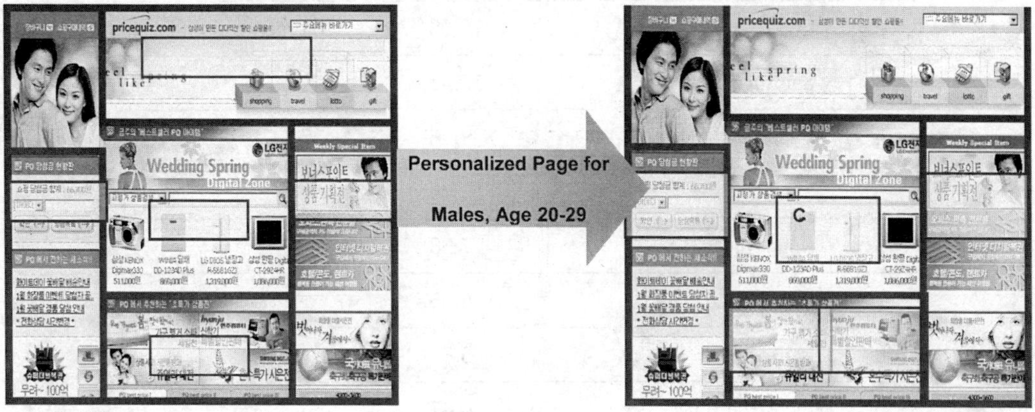

Source: Company files.

Exhibit 13 A finance shop in South Korea

Source: HyundaiCard, 2009.

Exhibit 14 Market share of Korean credit card companies

Rank	Company	Market Share	Remarks
1	Koomin	16.21	
2	LG	16.08	Merged with Shinhan
3	Samsung	12.33	
4	Hyundai	9.96	
5	Shinhan	8.70	
6	Nonghyup	7.58	
7	Woori Bank	6.35	
8	Lotte Card	5.82	
9	Industrial Bank	4.47	
10	Korean Exchange Bank	4.46	
11	Hana Bank	3.61	
12	SC Bank	1.33	
	Others	3.11	

Source: www.Hankyung.com, May 2007.

Exhibit 15 Sales volume and number of valid cardholders

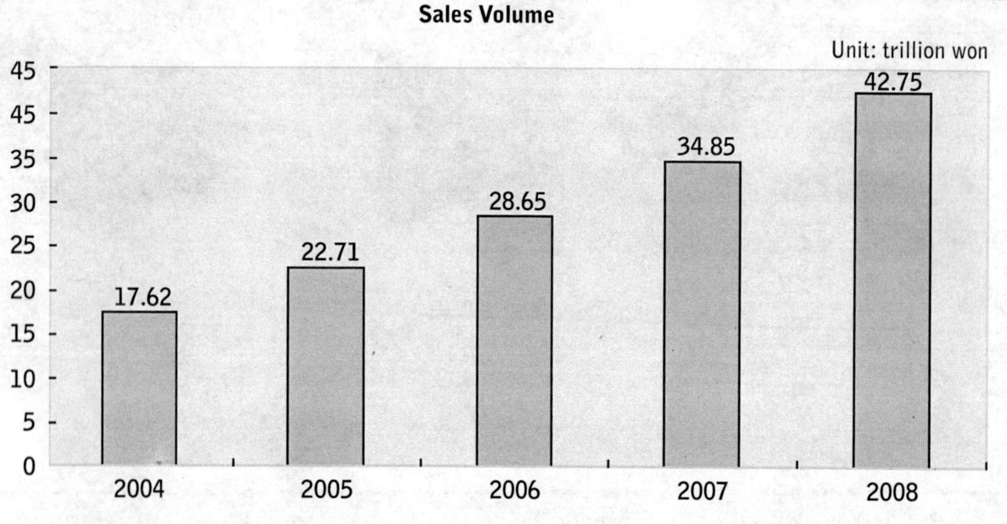

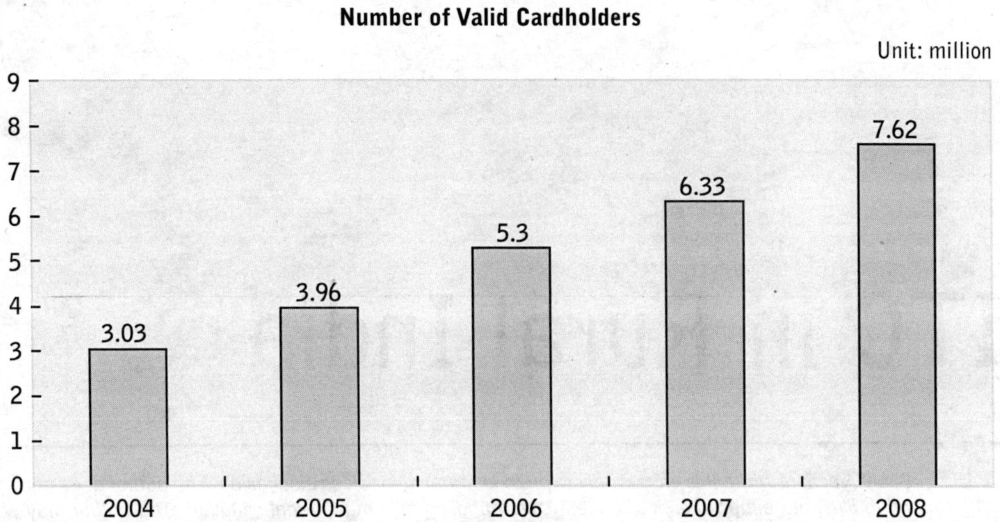

Source: HyundaiCard, 2009.

Exhibit 16 HyundaiCard's financial highlights

	2007		2006		2005		2004		2003	
Operating Revenue	11,213	11,952	11,095	11,826	7,333	7,816	5,877	6,284	4,950	5,276
Net income	2,344	2,498	2,810	2,995	863	920	−2,184	−2,328	−6,273	−6,686
Total Assets	46,452	49,512	33,834	36,063	28,968	30,876	24,584	26,203	24,707	26,334
Total Liabilities	35,222	37,542	25,527	27,208	26,619	28,372	23,207	24,736	23,602	25,157
Total Share-holders' Equity	11,230	11,970	8,307	8,854	2,349	2,504	1,377	1,468	1,105	1,178

Note: First column for each year is in 100 millions of Korean won. Second column is in 100 thousands of U.S. dollars.
Source: HyundaiCard 2007 Annual Report.

3

ITC in Rural India

In summer 2007, ITC was poised for expansion into rural India. While it was one of two large companies with a rural beachhead, the market was far from secure. Multinationals like Wal-Mart (United States) and Carrefour (France) were pressing the Indian government to open the retail sector to foreign investors. If the government relented, there could be a tsunami of foreign investment. The retailing opportunity had also attracted the attention of the giant Indian business group Reliance Industries.

INDIAN ENVIRONMENT

Early History

The Indian sub-continent was known to have been inhabited since the Stone Age. Its first major civilization, the Indus Valley civilization, lasted a thousand years till 1550 BC and covered 500,000 square miles. It was followed by numerous kingdoms. In 1526, Muslim invaders came from Central Asia and created the Mughal Empire. This was soon after Vasco da Gama discovered the sea route from Europe to India, south of Africa's Cape of Good Hope. British, French, Dutch and Portuguese companies began trading in India and colonized parts of it. The British East India Company became the most influential among them and, in 1757, as the Mughal dynasty withered, it won the right to administer Bengal (in Eastern India). In 1857, the British East India Company removed the last Mughal emperor. The British government immediately acquired control of India from the company, making it the jewel of the British empire.[1]

India became free on August 15, 1947, after a long non-violent independence struggle led by Mohandas Gandhi, revered as "Mahatma" Gandhi. (Mahatma meant great soul.) The British split undivided India into two countries: mainly Hindu India and predominantly Muslim Pakistan. Partition was accompanied by religious violence in which 500,000 people were killed. In 1950, India adopted a new constitution making it a secular, democratic republic. In 1971, East Pakistan became Bangladesh.

The Land and the People

Physically, India was a third of the size of the United States. In 2006, 81 per cent of India's 1.1 billion people were Hindus, followed by Muslims (13 per cent), Christians (two per cent) and Sikhs (two per cent). They spoke 15 languages and many dialects. While Hinduism was a unifying force, its caste system created tensions. Religious violence erupted periodically. Disputes over the Muslim state Jammu and Kashmir caused tension between India and Pakistan, both nuclear powers.

Politics and Government

Until 1989, the Congress Party, which was instrumental in securing freedom, dominated politics. Jawaharlal Nehru, his daughter, Indira Gandhi (no relation of Mahatma Gandhi), and grandson Rajiv Gandhi served as prime ministers during most of that period. In 1989, Congress lost elections amid corruption scandals. After 1990, governments relied on multi-party coalitions, causing political uncertainty. It was not uncommon for members of Parliament to be accused of corruption. Some had criminal records. Indians valued their voting rights and periodically dismissed governments at both the state and national level. In 2004, rural voters, disenchanted because India's spectacular economic growth was disproportionately benefiting urban areas, voted out the incumbents.

Civil Society

Indian civil society, comprising thousands of non-governmental organizations (NGOs), was one of the largest and most vibrant in the world. NGOs of all kinds provided assistance to the poor and voiceless. Some campaigned for human rights and sustainable growth, sometimes blocking the acquisition of land for industrial use. Some worked closely with government and the private sector. Self-help groups organized village women into cooperatives that obtained credit from banks.

Economy

In 1947, when Nehru became prime minister, India had been declining economically for three decades. In the early 1940s, the Great Bengal Famine had killed three million people. There was enough food, but the poor could not afford it. Life expectancy was 33 years.[2] There had been little encouragement of local industry; cotton would be shipped to England, spun and woven into cloth and sold in India, rather than being processed in India. (Gandhi's freedom struggle included the boycott of British textiles.)

---

[1] This paragraph draws from Geoffrey Barraclough, The Times Atlas of World History, third edition, Times Books, New York, NY, 1989 and Economist intelligence Unit, India: Country Profile, Economist Intelligence Unit London, UK, 2006.

[2] Amartya Sen, "How is India Doing?" in R.A. Choudhury, S. Gamkhar and Aurobindo Ghose, The Indian Economy and its Performance Since Independence, Oxford University Press, New York, NY, 1990.

India's proud leadership vowed not to let the country be shackled economically by foreign powers. Their economic strategy favored the production of capital goods to develop an industrial base. The seventeen most important industries, the "commanding heights," were reserved for state ownership, as in the former Soviet Union. The private sector had to obtain manufacturing licenses for the remaining industries. Job creation was encouraged by promoting small firms using labor-intensive techniques. Imports were limited to encourage local production. Foreign investment was discouraged.

By the eighties, India had a well-developed industrial environment by developing country standards, but its companies rarely competed abroad. Most were content with the protected domestic market. Without licenses and foreign exchange to import technology and inputs available to international competitors they could not compete, except in labor-intensive products like textiles. High government control encouraged the black market.

Agriculture

Great effort was devoted to improve agriculture, through the use of new seeds, fertilizer, pesticide and irrigation. Defying predictions that millions would starve, India became self-sufficient in food. Agricultural production was entirely private, taking place in small, fragmented farms. Distribution was mostly private, though the government managed a public distribution system to provide essential goods to lower income segments at controlled prices.

Informal Sector

A good deal of business took place in the "informal" or "unorganized" sector comprising small "cottage" firms, which were exempt from many restrictions applicable to large firms in the "formal," "organized" sector. With its socialist ideology, India had done more than most countries to nurture small firms. It reserved some industries for them and provided tax breaks in others.

Labor

Organized sector labor was privileged compared to the poorest people. Labor-management relations were often contentious. Unions were politically active and during major industrial disputes the government intervened. It was difficult to lay off workers. When companies became economically unviable, the government sometimes took them over as "sick" companies.

Foreign Direct Investment (FDI)

At independence, there were several multinationals in India. In 1973, the government asked all multinationals to dilute foreign equity in their subsidiary to 40 per cent unless they were in a high-technology industry or undertook export commitments. Companies with less than 40 per cent foreign equity were treated as Indian companies. Some multinationals, like IBM and Coca-Cola, sold their assets and left. Others, such as Colgate Palmolive and Unilever, diluted equity and creatively used benefits provided by the government, such as tax breaks and protected markets, to diversify and grow. They sold stock to thousands of individuals and retained control with less than 40 per cent ownership.[3]

While multinationals were irked by India's bureaucracy, they liked some other factors. They could do business in English, there was an abundance of low-wage, well-qualified personnel, distribution systems were in place even though infrastructure was very poor, and services such as advertising and market research were readily available. India had a functioning stock market though not as well-

---

[3] D. J. Encarnation and S. Vachani, "Foreign ownership: when hosts change the rules," Harvard Business Review, September-October 1985, pp. 152-60.

developed as developed country markets. Unfortunately, contracts could be difficult to enforce. Some multinationals used the country's large supply of engineers to develop software. In the eighties, Texas Instruments began transmitting software to the United States via satellite from Bangalore. By the 2000s, software exports had grown significantly. Some of the leading IT companies, like Tata Consultancy Services (TCS) and Infosys, were home-grown.

Economic Liberalization

By 1990, the economy was in trouble. Government control had limited economic growth to the "Hindu rate of growth" of 3.5 per cent per year, while China surged ahead. Exports could not cover imports, and with little investment inflow India relied on foreign debt. Short-term liquidity was severely hurt by the 1990-91 Gulf War. As oil prices rose, exports to West Asia fell and remittances from the Indian diaspora in the Middle East dropped. Inflation exceeded 15 per cent. India's foreign debt rose to $70 billion and its foreign currency reserves dried. It requested help from the International Monetary Fund (IMF), which sought economic liberalization.

India needed a strong leader. Fortunately, Rajiv Gandhi was staging a comeback. However, a young Sri Lankan woman strapped dynamite around her waist, walked up to Rajiv Gandhi at a political rally and killed him. This was payback for his abortive effort to send the Indian army to help the Sri Lankan government suppress the Tamil Tigers, who were fighting for an independent homeland in northern Sri Lanka. Narasimha Rao, a less-known Congress loyalist, became prime minister. He stunned both his party and the opposition with quiet and firm actions that, in the words of the news magazine *India Today*, "took the country by the scruff of the neck and said move or we all die."[4] He appointed a bright, politically-neutral, Sikh finance minister, Manmohan Singh.

Singh was a respected international economist and former governor of the Reserve Bank of India (India's "Fed"). He was also scrupulously honest. He instituted a liberalization program that significantly reduced economic controls and opened the economy to imports and FDI. Congress lost elections in 1996, and when it returned to power in 2004, the president of the Congress Party, Sonia Gandhi (Italian-born wife of Rajiv Gandhi), appointed Manmohan Singh as prime minister rather than assume the position herself. While Singh's commitment to reform was strong, it was tempered by his socialist partners. The Congress-led coalition comprised more than 10 parties which held only 41 per cent of seats in Parliament and relied on the Left Front (which included two communist parties and held 11 per cent) to form the government.

Economic Performance

In the early 2000s, the Indian economy finally took off (see Exhibit 1). Between 2003 and 2006, growth averaged 8.4 per cent. The information technology (IT) sector grew rapidly as foreign companies aggressively outsourced services to India. The combination of low wages and a pool of relatively highly-skilled workers helped Indian companies compete for value-added services. GE's Jack Welch R&D center in Bangalore employed 1,500 researchers and conducted as much as 40 per cent of GE's (R&D) for some divisions. Engineers in India designed auto components for U.S. companies, and technicians analyzed X-rays for U.S. hospitals. FDI inflow rose to $8.3 billion in 2005-06 and was expected to touch $12 billion in 2006-07. While overseas borrowing by companies rose, foreign reserves grew significantly.

---

[4] Edward A. Gargan, "India's New Premier Challenges the System, and the Reaction is Predictable," New York Times, August 6, 1991.

Rural India

About 70 per cent of Indians lived in its 638,000 villages. An overwhelming number lived in poverty. A staggering 88 per cent of the rural population lived on less than $2 per day (see Exhibit 2). Rural access was severely hampered by poor road, rail and telecommunications links. In February 2006, concerned about poverty alleviation, the government announced a rural jobs program to lift 60 million people out of poverty. It launched schemes to improve rural electrification. The postal system, whose 139,000 rural post offices comprised the largest rural presence of any Indian organization, was expanding services (for example, selling insurance products of private companies). Most rural post offices operated out of franchisees' homes.

Indian Retailing

Retail sales in India, estimated at around $250 billion in 2006, primarily took place in small, family-owned stores. Only three per cent were accounted for by the "organized" sector, comprising retail chains, most of which were set up in the 2000s.[5] Chains' share was 65 per cent in the United States, 40 per cent in Thailand and 10 per cent in China. By 2016, the organized sector's share of Indian retail sales was expected to rise to 15 to 18 per cent.[6]

Government Control

The government restricted the entry of foreign retailers. It allowed wholly-owned FDI in trading companies if they were exporters. In 2006, it began granting approvals for 51 per cent foreign-owned operations in domestic retail trade provided the company engaged in single-brand trading, the branding occurred at the manufacturing stage and the product was sold with the same brand internationally.[7] FDI was also allowed in wholesale "cash-and-carry" businesses. The Left Front adamantly opposed FDI in retailing. The government also controlled prices of selected products, such as sugar and some cereals, at multiple distribution stages: the factory, wholesale and retail.

Rural Markets

Despite widespread poverty, the poor provided significant markets for products like tea, cooking oil, electric bulbs, footwear, bicycles and radios. For some products, as early as the mid-90s, rural demand exceeded urban demand (see Exhibits 3 and 4). In 2005, rural markets accounted for 56 per cent of demand for fast moving consumer goods (FMCG), which included products such as food, household and personal care products, confectionary and tobacco. FMCG accounted for 80 per cent of all Indian consumer spending.

Most products bought by rural consumers were manufactured, distributed and sold by the informal sector. Village shops were often located in shopkeepers' homes. Large companies' distribution chains generally did not extend beyond wholesalers located in small towns that had a population of 100,000. Village shopkeepers came to these towns and bought products on a "cash-and-carry" basis

---

[5] A. Jain, "A dramatic change in shopping," Financial Times, June 28, 2006.

[6] EIU, India: Country Profile, 2006.

[7] EIU, India: Country Commerce, November 2006.

and transported them in hired vehicles. HUL and ITC had greater rural penetration than most large companies.

HINDUSTAN UNILEVER LIMITED (HUL)[8]

HUL was the Indian subsidiary of the European FMCG giant Unilever, known globally for brands such as Lipton, Ponds, Sunsilk and Surf. Unilever began manufacturing in India in 1931. In 2006, it held 51.4 per cent of the stock in HUL, which had long been a dominant player in the Indian FMCG market. In 2006, HUL had revenues of $3 billion and net profits of $460 million. About 71 per cent of its sales were derived from non-food FMCG (soap, detergent and personal products like toothpaste, cosmetics and deodorants) and 16 per cent from foods.[9] In 2001, HUL launched "Project Shakti" to strengthen its rural presence. This had three components.

The Shakti Entrepreneur program appointed village women, who were members of self-help groups, as agents who sold HUL products directly to homes in clusters of three to five villages. Company distributors brought products from district warehouses to the village entrepreneur's home.[10] The average entrepreneur earned about $16 per month in sales commissions, which helped supplement family income. A field force of 1,000 helped train the 30,800 Shakti entrepreneurs, who covered 100,000 villages in fifteen states. By 2010, HUL expected to have 100,000 Shakti entrepreneurs servicing 500,000 villages with a population of 600 million.

The Shakti Vani program provided valuable health and hygiene information, which helped promote the company's products, such as toothpaste. It trained women to communicate with fellow villagers using specially designed materials provided by HUL.

IShakti was a more recent program to provide broader information through a rural community web portal. Villagers accessed information on a variety of topics including agriculture, education, veterinary services and entertainment through kiosks installed in partnership with the state government. The web interface used voice-over design to make information accessible to the illiterate. When the cursor moved over an icon, a voice announced the topic, and when the icon was clicked, a voice provided information in the local language. At the end of 2006, HUL had 200 IShakti kiosks in the state of Andhra Pradesh in South India.

HUL had a large range of FMCG products and did not sell others' brands. It was laying the foundation for deeper rural penetration as incomes rose and consumption increased.

ITC Limited

ITC was established in India by British American Tobacco (BAT) as the Imperial Tobacco Company in 1910. In 2007, BAT owned 31 per cent of ITC's stock and foreign institutional investors owned about 13 per cent. Indian financial institutions (including banks, insurance companies and mutual funds) collectively owned the largest chunk of ITC's stock, about 37 per cent. Over the years, ITC had diversified into multiple businesses; for example, its highly regarded five-star hotel chain known as Welcomgroup. ITC's 2006-07 revenues of $3.1 billion (excluding excise collected) were dominated by cigarettes, which accounted for 46 per cent of revenues (see Exhibit 5).

---

[8] The company's name was changed from Hindustan Lever Limited (HLL) to HUL in 2007.

[9] HUL Annual Report, 2006.

[10] Administratively, India was divided into 28 states and nine union territories, and sub-divided into 604 districts.

FMCG

ITC's major FMCG product, cigarettes, contributed significantly to its profits despite continued pressure from substitutes (crude rolled tobacco products called bidis, chewing tobacco, snuff, etc.) produced by the informal sector. Taxes on cigarettes were much higher than those on the informal sector's products. Though cigarettes accounted for only 15 per cent of tobacco sales, they generated 86 per cent of taxes. Domestically produced cigarettes also faced competition from smuggled foreign cigarettes that avoided taxes.

ITC was bullish about the future of its more recently launched FMCG products like branded packaged foods (for example, flour, candy, salt, pasta and ready-to-eat food products) and apparel (launched in 2001). It had a hundred distinct food products sold under five brands. It expected demand for these to increase with income. Some products (e.g. incense sticks and safety matches) were sourced from small-scale firms. The revenues of the "FMCG - others" segment grew 68 per cent in the last year to $425 million. While segment losses rose from $38 million to $51 million, they fell as a percentage of revenues from 17 per cent to 12 per cent (see Exhibit 6). The performance was affected by "gestation costs… associated with brand building, product development and infrastructure creation."[11]

Agri-commodities

ITC's agri-business division sourced commodities for sale in India and abroad, as well as supplying them to its branded foods division. Domestic sales grew by 56 per cent and exports by 45 per cent in 2006-07. A critical component of ITC's agri-commodities strategy was to leverage its unique procurement system, the purchases through which were almost a million metric tons in 2006-07. Wheat procurement through the system doubled over the previous year.

Traditional Commodity Procurement

Typically, small farmers brought their produce, such as soya bean, to the mandi (pronounced "mun-dee"), a state-sanctioned wholesale marketplace where traders bid for the produce. Given that most farmers sold small quantities and quality varied across farms, the mandi provided a convenient place for price discovery. Each farmer was offered a price for the commodity, depending on its weight and quality grade (adjustments were made for moisture, foreign matter, broken seeds, etc.). The farmers' bargaining position was weak. They lacked accurate information on prices being offered in other transactions at that mandi, and at other regional mandis, were unable to verify weighing accuracy, and were discouraged from turning down an offer because they had already incurred the cost of bringing produce to the market and would need to incur additional costs to take it back and return. Essentially, farmers earned less income than would be possible if there were ways to ensure accurate weighing and grading, and if they had information that gave them better options on when and where to sell.

Itc's It-enabled Procurement

ITC, which previously bought commodities from traders who procured them from farmers at the mandi, set up a system that empowered farmers in two ways: by providing them with real-time information on prices, and giving them an alternative selling channel, direct to ITC. It did this by setting up computer kiosks, called e-Choupals, in villages. (Choupal meant village gathering place in Hindi. The pronunciation of "ou" in choupal was similar to that in "out.") In each village it recruited

[11] ITC Annual Reports, 2006 and 2007.

a farmer to serve as its representative, called a sanchalak (pronounced "sun-chaa-luck"). ITC set up a computer in each sanchalak's home and through its web portal provided information on commodity prices from the previous day at each mandi in the state and at its own procurement center. It also presented information on prices in international markets such as the Chicago commodities exchange, which influenced local prices. Each evening the portal announced the minimum price ITC would offer the following day at its procurement center.

Given that many villages lacked Internet connectivity, ITC set up a satellite dish on the roof of each farmer's home to ensure web access. Since electric supply was erratic, it installed a solar panel and battery to provide enough electricity for two hours of uninterrupted computer operation. ITC's hardware investment in e-Choupals had fallen from about $4,000 in 2000 to around $3,200 in 2006 as the cost of satellite dishes fell because it bought in larger volume, and because the company's exports allowed it to waive import taxes (see Exhibit 7). The investment was depreciated over about five years. In May 2007, ITC had nearly 6,500 e-Choupal kiosks, each servicing six villages on average. Together, they were estimated to reach about 3.5 million farmers in nine states (Andhra Pradesh, Haryana, Karnataka, Kerala, Madhya Pradesh, Maharashtra, Rajasthan, Uttar Pradesh and Uttaranchal). The system procured a variety of commodities: soya bean, wheat, coffee, pulses, shrimp, etc. If farmers chose to sell their produce to ITC, the sanchalak graded it, gave them a tentative price and sent them to the company's procurement hub, which was three to 20 miles away.

Procurement Hub

ITC had reconfigured the traditional procurement system, which had four components: price discovery, selling, delivery and cash payment, all of which previously occurred at the mandi. It had introduced a hub and spoke system, unbundling the transaction components and dispersing them. At the spokes were the e-Choupals, which enabled decentralized price discovery and selling in the village. Delivery and payment were centralized at procurement hubs, which included storage warehouses. ITC's procurement hubs were large, clean and well-maintained. Farmers were able to wait in the shade rather than in the open sun and had access to cool drinking water and toilets. They used electronic weighing systems, which reduced inaccuracy. Farmers were given cash for their produce rather than deferred payments as sometimes happened at the mandi. If prices at the nearby mandi turned out to be higher that day, ITC raised its procurement price to match them. However, if prices at the mandi were lower it maintained the price commitment made the previous evening on its web portal, on which the farmers based their decision to bring produce to market. The reconfiguration eliminated the need for ITC's commission agents at the mandis, some of whom were contracted to assist with operations at the hub. They were called samyojaks, or coordinators. (Samyojak was pronounced sum-yo-juck.) The reconfiguration resulted in savings for farmers and ITC (see Exhibit 8). These were significant given the low income of the typical small farmer, whose farm was a hectare or less and produced one metric ton (MT[12]) of soya per hectare (2.47 acres). This required about $150 of inputs (seed, fertilizer, pesticide and diesel), not counting labor. In 2007, soya sold for around $300 per MT.

Activities in Villages

In addition to assisting the procurement of produce from farmers, ITC's sanchalaks sold a host of products and services to villagers, earning a commission on sales. The bulk of the goods were FMCG, but ranged all the way from insurance to motorcycles. During 2006-07, ITC's rural distribution

---

[12] One MT equals 1,000 kilograms or 2,204.6 pounds.

network sold a little over $42 million of goods produced by 100 companies. (The previous year it had sold goods worth $20 million produced by 45 companies.) Marketing strategies were adapted for rural consumers who were not easily convinced that it was worth paying significantly higher for large companies' branded products. ITC and the sanchalaks also contributed toward enhancing farm productivity through the provision of extension services (in partnership with the government) to demonstrate agricultural best practices.

Sanchalaks' Earnings

The sanchalaks earned commissions of 0.5 per cent to two per cent on the value of commodities procured. The sanchalaks also earned two per cent to 15 per cent on sales of goods and services to villagers. The typical sanchalak earned a total of about $1,500 to $1,750 per year in commissions. Low performers made $250 to $500 per year and stars took in as much as $7,500 to $10,000.

Rural Mini-malls

In August 2004, ITC broadened its rural distribution scope by building mini-malls at some of its hubs to sell a wide variety of products and services, including packaged consumer goods, white goods, diesel, agricultural inputs, and health, insurance and banking services. These were called "Choupal Saagars." (Saagar was pronounced "saa-gur." See Exhibit 9.) ITC had partnerships for the provision of goods and services at these mini-malls. For example, Apollo Hospital, which had a chain of hospitals around India, was a partner in providing health services. An Apollo-affiliated general physician was available for consultation and to conduct basic diagnostic tests. The physician could access specialists via the Internet and telephone as necessary.

Each Saagar was built on about seven acres of company-owned land with $1 million to $1.5 million of investment. This included a warehouse, food court, training facility, medical clinic and hypermarket, where goods were displayed and sold. There were savings in putting different activities at one site. The total investment in building separate units would probably have been 40 per cent higher. In addition, shared jobs reduced wages by about 20 per cent. In May 2007, ITC had 18 Saagars in three states. Ten were in the state of MP (Madhya Pradesh) in central India, and four each in UP (Uttar Pradesh) and Maharashtra.

ITC was aware that it would take significant time to build sales at the Saagars. At one of the older ones, sales in 2005-06 (after 18 months of operation) were estimated by analysts to be around half a million dollars. A year later, they had risen to about three-quarters of a million dollars. Sales were seasonal, with three months accounting for half the annual sales. Margins were about 12 per cent on average and varied considerably across products. For apparel, they were as high as 20 per cent, while for fertilizer, as low as two to three per cent (see Exhibit 10). The company priced agricultural inputs aggressively to convince farmers that they got excellent value at ITC's stores. For example, the government sold subsidized bags of urea to retailers for $5.40 per bag, stipulating a maximum resale price of $5.55. While some retailers sold at the maximum price and made a profit of 15 cents a bag, ITC restricted its margin to about 10 cents. The company expected that sales at most Saagars would rise to about $2 million each.

The annual cost of operating the retail store at the Choupal Saagar was about $60,000 (60 per cent manpower and 15 per cent electricity). A few key positions were filled by ITC employees; for example, the Saagar manager and the chemist who tested the quality of commodities procured. The manager cost the company about $15,000 per year and the chemist about $4,500. In addition, there was labor provided by the samyojak for tasks such as loading goods and maintenance of the premises. The samyojak received a small commission based on the Saagar's revenues.

The Saagars were located on the highway, three to five miles outside a small town (like Mhow in MP) with a population of about 100,000, and aimed to draw customers from 100 to 200 villages close by as well as from the town. Prices of some products, such as apparel, were sometimes as low as 30 to 40 per cent of comparable products in large cities. In such cases, manufacturers gave them different brand names to facilitate differential pricing across markets. In addition to contribution margins on products sold at the store, ITC earned rent for space provided to manufacturers for special displays inside and outside the store. It also provided space for tractor servicing on which was earned a basic rental fee plus a percentage of sales over a benchmark.

Not all procurement hubs were suitable for conversion into Saagars, owing to geographic variation in the potential for commodity procurement and sale of goods and services through a mini-mall. In MP, for example, the company expected that eventually 25 of the 40 procurement hubs would be developed into Saagars. When the company decided to develop a procurement hub into a Saagar it was expected to be located in a cluster of 40 e-Choupals. Typically, standalone procurement hubs that were not upgraded to Saagars were located on leased premises and required little investment.

Network Support

The integrated network of sanchalaks, procurement hubs and Saagars was supported by a central management group of around 1,200 people (including company personnel deployed at the Saagars), whose annual cost (salaries, travel, office administration, etc.) amounted to $12.5 million. This group designed and maintained the systems, provided training and logistical support, negotiated with suppliers, liaised with the government, managed mini-mall operations and provided oversight over e-Choupal operations.

ITC'S CORPORATE SOCIAL RESPONSIBILITY (CSR) INITIATIVES

> It is my firm belief that business enterprises can and must make a difference towards achieving greater social equity... your Company today is instrumental in creating and sustaining livelihoods for nearly five million people, many of whom represent the weakest sections in rural India... We have constantly strived to meaningfully blend our social responsibilities with business competitiveness, so that we can continue to create shareholder value even as we enhance the benefits that accrue to rural communities.
>
> Y.C. Deveshwar, chairman, ITC Limited

ITC's rural engagement dovetailed with its CSR initiatives, for which it worked closely with a number of NGOs, helping alleviate rural poverty. ITC was proud of its Triple Bottom Line performance. It had been a "water positive" organization for five consecutive years through conservation, recycling and rainwater harvesting on its property and in the communities it operated in. The watershed projects promoted by ITC had the potential for harvesting rainwater four times its net consumption. As part of its "Sunehra kal" (golden tomorrow) program, ITC worked with an NGO to form water users associations, building NGOs' capacity to analyze problems and take decisions, and then partially funding programs for building water harvesting structures. Another initiative aimed to improve livestock through artificial insemination and better dairy farming practices. This activity tended to benefit the poorest rural families and the value generated was especially beneficial for women and children.

Some of the funds for CSR activities were raised as part of marketing programs that promised consumers that a small percentage of the company's FMCG sales would be devoted to charity. Total annual expenditure on CSR activities was around $25 million.

THE FUTURE OF ITC'S RURAL BUSINESS

Over the next 15 years, India was expected to account for 12 per cent of global growth (see Exhibit 11). Multinationals were impatient to enter. Meanwhile, Reliance Industries Limited (RIL), the aggressive Indian petrochemicals and textiles giant, was integrating forward into gas stations in cities and highways, and had begun expanding into retail. Reliance was exceptionally adept at government relations, and with annual revenues of $27.2 billion and profits of $2.7 billion, it had deep pockets. It launched its retail effort in 2006 with a $750 million budget, and expected to ramp up investment to $5.6 billion to set up a range of formats: convenience stores, supermarkets and hypermarkets. It had hired 2,000 professionals and planned to raise that to 10,000 in five years. Its first "Reliance Fresh" convenience store was opened in the city of Hyderabad in November 2006. By March 2007, it had 90 stores in several cities.

As S. Sivakumar (known as Shiv), chief executive of ITC's agri-business division, reviewed the company's rural expansion plans, he was well-aware of the opportunities and risks. The rural distribution platform could open up new opportunities; for example, the network made it possible to trace and certify the origin of commodities. This could enable growth of organic product sales, which accounted for less than a per cent of sales in 2007. Direct interaction with farmers also made it easier for the company to inform them of the market's needs and influence them to grow high-value strains of commodities. The company was accumulating valuable rural market information.

Expansion Plans

By 2012, ITC planned to add 10,000 e-Choupals to extend its network to 15 states and reach 10 million farmers in 100,000 villages. Eighty per cent of the company's procurement of soya and wheat flowed through the e-Choupal network. Network expansion would increase the range of commodities. The company also planned to increase the number of Saagars to 100 by 2010.

As the company expanded its e-Choupal network it needed to recruit able sanchalaks, who were key to the preservation of competitive advantage. Sivakumar really did not view them as company representatives:

> In the current Indian context, with its serious infrastructural limitations, it is difficult to access rural markets simply with physical investment. If there is one sustainable advantage we have in the face of an avalanche of impending competition it is the network of sanchalaks with the unique relationship they forge with the village as one of their own. Our sanchalaks build valuable social capital, based on trust and relationship, which secures two-way access between ITC and the villages, and enables endorsement of the wide range of products and services that villagers are unfamiliar with. Sanchalaks' influence would be lost the moment they are seen as company agents rather than independent entrepreneurs who are vested with certain power and knowledge that they use to facilitate transactions between villagers and the company. Sanchalaks represent the interests of villagers as much as those of ITC; by design they are equidistant from ITC and the villagers.

Government

The government had made the e-Choupal initiative possible by amending laws to permit trade outside mandis. It was difficult to predict the future impact of public policy on ITC's business. The government had the power to shut out companies, provide competition, and introduce onerous regulations. As companies increased rural market penetration, it was possible that politicians, NGOs and others might question their social impact and demand controls to discourage the potential abuse of market power.

Exhibit 1 India—basic economic indicators

	2002	2003	2004	2005	2006	2007*
GDP ($ billion)	506	596	692	806	923	1,131
Real GDP growth (%)	3.6	8.4	8.3	9.2	9.4	7.8
Consumer price inflation (%)	4.3	3.8	3.8	4.2	6.2	6.4
Population (millions)	1,034	1,050	1,065	1,080	1,095	1,110
Exports of goods ($ billion)	51	61	78	102	122	148
Imports of good ($ billion)	–61	–76	–106	–149	–185	–222
Current account balance ($ billion)	7	9	1	–10	–9	–15
Foreign exchange reserves ($ billion)**	68	102	130	136	176	275
Total external debt ($ billion)	105	113	124	123	135	147
Exchange rate (avg.) Rs/$	48.6	46.6	45.3	44.1	45.3	41.3

*Estimated. **Excluding gold.
Source: EIU, India: Country Report, 2006 & 2007.

Exhibit 2 India population (millions), 2001

	Total	With Income Below $2/day
Rural	744	658
Urban	289	175
Total	1,033	833

Source: World Bank Povcal data.

Exhibit 3 Sales of consumable products in India

Product	Units	1985–86	1992–93	1998–99	CAGR* 19'92–99	Rural Share 19'85–86	Rural Share 19'98–99
Cigarettes	Billion	97	65	85	4.6%	53%	58%
Cooking oil	Millions MT**	2.3	3.8	5.3	5.7%	66%	66%
Electric bulbs	Millions nos.	200	252	460	10.6%	32%	42%
Footwear	Millions pairs	127	289	516	10.1%	64%	61%

(*Continued*)

(*Continued*)

Product	Units	1985–86	1992–93	1998–99	CAGR* 19'92–99	Rural Share 19'85–86	Rural Share 19'98–99
Tea	'000 MT	215	334	580	9.6%	57%	60%
Toilet soap	'000 MT	227	434	659	7.2%	51%	58%
Toothpaste	'000 MT	16	40	96	15.7%	29%	47%
Washing cake	'000 MT	830	1,204	1,540	4.2%	61%	67%
Washing powder	'000 MT	515	872	1,312	7.0%	43%	58%

*CAGR: Cumulative annual growth rate. **MT: Metric ton equals 1,000 kilograms or 2,204.6 pounds.
Source: NCAER, Indian Market Demographics Report, 2002.

Exhibit 4 Sales of durable products in India (millions)

Product	1985–86	1992–93	1998–99	CAGR 19'92–99	Rural Share 19'85–86	Rural Share 19'98–99
Bicycle	4.7	7.1	10.4	6.6%	82%	78%
Motorcycle	0.20	0.36	1.24	22.9%	52%	51%
Pressure cooker	2.20	3.39	5.66	8.9%	34%	52%
Radio	3.20	4.73	6.17	4.5%	79%	81%
Refrigerator	0.56	1.19	3.07	17.1%	14%	28%
Sewing machine	0.98	0.55	0.99	10.3%	60%	74%
TV (B&W)	1.4	3.39	6.11	10.3%	26%	81%
TV (color)	0.60	0.83	3.87	29.3%	11%	37%

Source: NCAER, Indian Market Demographics Report, 2002.

Exhibit 5 ITC—financial statements ($ million)

Profit & Loss Account, 2006-07		
Gross revenue		**4,876**
Less excise & other taxes		1,784
Revenue (without taxes)		3,092
Other income		84
Net revenue		**3,176**
Expenditure		
Raw material	1,346	
Manufacturing, selling, etc.	758	
Depreciation	91	
Cost of goods sold		**2,195**

Balance Sheet (ending March 31, 2007)		
ASSETS		
Fixed assets		1,403
Investments		767
Current assets		1,572
Total assets		**3,742**
LIABILITIES		
Current liab. & provisions		965
Stockholders funds		
Capital	94	

Profit before tax (PBT)	**981**	Reserves & surplus	2,515	
Tax provision	307	Total stockholders funds		2,609
Profit after tax (PAT)	**674**	Debt		50
		Deferred taxes		118
Dividends	**284**	**Total liabilities**		**3,742**

Source: ITC Annual Report, 2007.

Exhibit 6 ITC segment data, 2006-07

	Revenue		**PBT***	
Segment	**$ million**	**%**	**$ million**	**%**
FMGC: cigarettes	1,425	46	793	82
FMCG: others	425	14	–51	–5
Hotels	245	8	88	9
Agri-business	680	22	31	3
Paper & packaging	318	10	104	11
Total	3,093	100	965	100

*Before allocation of corporate expenses.
Source: ITC Annual Report, 2007.

Exhibit 7 ITC's investment per e-Choupal ($)

Component	**$**
Satellite dish	1,500
Personal computer	650
Solar panel	400
Battery/power supply	280
Printer	120
Misc. hardware	250
Total	3,200

Source: ITC.

Exhibit 8 Transaction costs in soya procurement* via alternative chains

Dollars per metric ton (MT)			
Mandi Chain		**Choupal Chain**	
Farmer's cost	**$/MT**	**Farmer's cost**	**$/MT**
Transport to mandi	3.00	Transport to ITC hub	3.00
Labor	1.25		

(*Continued*)

(*Continued*)

Mandi Chain		**Choupal Chain**	
Agent's commission	3.75		
Handling loss	1.25		
Farmer's total cost	9.25	**Farmer's total cost**	3.00
ITC's cost		**ITC's cost**	
Agent's commission	2.50	Sanchalak's commission	1.25
Farmer's cost	**$/MT**	**Farmer's cost**	**$/MT**
Cost of bags	1.88	Cost of bags	1.88
Handling at mandi	1.00	Samyojak's commission	1.25
ITC's total cost	8.38	**ITC's total cost**	5.38
Total transactions cost	17.63	**Total transactions cost**	8.38

*Costs could vary with commodity since commissions were different.
Source: ITC.

Exhibit 9 Layout of a typical Choupal saagar

Source: ITC.

Exhibit 10 Saagar: category shares and margins

Product Category	Share of Sales (%)	Margin (%)
Apparel and footwear	20	30
Agricultural inputs	30	3
FMCG	20	15
Consumer durables	10	6

Source: ITC.

Exhibit 11 Comparative economic data and projections—India and others

	GDP Annual Growth, 2000-05 %	GNI,[13] 2005 $b	GNI per Capita $	GNI (PPP), 2005 $b	GNI (PPP) per Capita, 2005 $	Projected Real GDP Growth,[14] 2006-20 %	Projected Contribution to Global Growth,[14] 2006-20 %	Share of World GDP[14] (PPP), 2005 %	Share of World GDP[14] (PPP), 2020 %
China	9.6	2,264	1,740	8,610	6,600	6.0	26.7	13.7	19.4
Germany	0.7	2,853	34,580	2,409	29,210	1.9	1.9	NA	NA
India	6.9	793	720	3,787	3,460	5.9	12.2	6.2	8.8
Japan	1.3	4,988	38,980	4,019	31,410	0.7	1.1	6.7	4.5
South Korea	4.6	765	15,830	1,055	21,850	4.0	2.1	1.8	1.9
United States	2.8	12,970	43,740	12,438	41,950	2.9	15.9	20.8	19.0

Source: World Bank, World Development Report, World Bank, Washington D.C., 2007, unless otherwise noted.

[13] GNI: Gross National Income. Equals GDP plus net receipts of primary income from foreign sources.
[14] Economist Intelligence Unit, Foresight 2020, London, U.K., 2006.

4

Ontario Machinery Ring (A)

Problem Definition

Jack Janzen, general manager of the Ontario Machinery Ring (OMR) was optimistic about the prospects of his organization. Since joining the Machinery Ring two years ago, Janzen spent most of his time developing a prototype operation in Huron County. This operation was now working smoothly, with over 300 farmers using the matchmaking services of the Machinery Ring. With a successful prototype developed, Janzen now turned his attention to expanding the Machinery Ring to the entire province. In this context, he developed a long-term business plan for the operation, which included the requirement for a sizable short-term loan to facilitate expansion. Because of the company's status as a non-profit co-operative, Janzen felt that the Ministry of Agriculture and Food might be interested in providing the required assistance. Initial contacts with the Ministry revealed that a third-party assessment of demand and a business plan would be required to be submitted prior to approving this type of loan. It was for this reason Janzen was considering doing some marketing research.

MACHINERY RING CONCEPT

The Ontario Machinery Ring was a non-profit, member-owned co-operative that had been established to provide a matchmaking service between farmers who wanted custom work done and farmers who wanted to do this type of work. The Machinery Ring concept was very popular in Europe where an estimated 80 per cent of all farmers were members and used the matchmaking services extensively.

Modern farming was a very capital intensive business. Many farmers had an investment in crop production equipment alone that exceeded $250,000. Interest, depreciation and maintenance on this equipment represented a major cost item for most farmers.

The seasonal nature of farming, where a high proportion of field work must be done in a very short period of time, together with the fact that much of the equipment is capable of doing more work than is available on many individual farms, has led to a situation where farmers with excess time and equipment sell their service to farmers needing additional time and equipment. In agriculture, this was referred to as "custom work." Current estimates in Ontario put the annual value of custom work at nearly $145 million (see Appendix 1 for details).

Custom work was mainly used in crop production and consisted of the following activities: cultivating, seeding, spraying, hay baling, combining and plowing. Traditionally, custom work was done between neighbors and relatives. A good example: was one farmer invested in a combine that had the capacity to do 4,000 acres of harvesting in a season, yet the owner may have only 1,000 acres of his own crops. Other farmers may be aware of this and would ask the farmer with the large combine to harvest their crops on a custom basis, and, therefore avoid making a large investment in a major piece of equipment. Rates for custom work would be negotiated between buyers and sellers, but were fairly standard in any community. They varied depending upon the time of year, field conditions, urgency of getting the work done and type and condition of equipment involved.

In the absence of a service such as the Machinery Ring, custom work arrangements among farmers were very informal. Farmers needing custom work done usually approached neighbors, friends or relatives who had excess capacity and asked them to consider doing custom work. Rates were negotiated using guidelines published by the Ministry of Agriculture and Food. The person doing the custom work had to establish a schedule that allowed him to get his own work done as well as that of his customers. This was a potential problem with custom work because of the importance of timeliness in crop production. If work was delayed even a week, it could result in lower yields for many crops. A second potential problem with custom work was the difficulty that custom operators sometimes experience in collecting their fees.

The concept of the Machinery Ring was to bring more order to the custom work market. It was intended to work in the following manner. Farmers who were potential sellers of custom work became members of the Machinery Ring by registering and paying an annual fee of $50. When registering, these farmers completed a form that listed the following information: name, address and details of all the equipment they owned that could be used for custom work. The equipment was then visually inspected by a representative of the Machinery Ring to make sure it was in good operating condition. Farmers who wanted custom work done also registered and paid an annual membership fee of $50. When registering, they provided the following information: name, address, banking information, number of acres, farm location, type of crops, time frame involved and any special requests (e.g. John Deere combine with a straw chopper). Potential buyers and sellers of custom work were then entered into a large computer database, which had been developed specifically for the Machinery Ring. This database not only listed potential buyers and sellers, but also contained a program that could match the closest seller with a potential buyer. This program was developed specifically for the OMR at a cost of over $300,000 and was considered state-of-the-art. As a matter of fact, Janzen couldn't wait to show it off to some of his Machinery Ring friends in Europe when he attended the International Machinery Ring Congress in Sweden next year. Appendix 2 provides a detailed description of how the database works.

When a farmer needed custom work done, he phoned the OMR to place an order. The OMR inputted this request into the computer database and found the closest available farmer with the required equipment. The OMR provided this information to the farmer buying custom work who then contacted the farmer selling custom work to arrange the details of the transaction. These details included time, type of equipment and cost. After the work had been completed, the OMR billed the buying farmer, collected the prearranged fee, and provided payment to the selling farmer. The OMR charged a two per cent service fee to the buyer and to the seller. As noted earlier, this model had been successfully used in Europe for many years.

BUSINESS PLAN

Over the past few months, Janzen had spent a considerable amount of time developing plans to expand the Machinery Ring to other areas of Ontario. His current thinking was to add five new counties each year until the entire province was served. He planned to do this by expanding to the western region first, followed in turn by the southern, central and eastern regions.

In each county, Janzen planned to hire an area manager who would have the following responsibilities: recruit new members, visit each new "selling" member to inspect the condition of his equipment, visit each new "buying" member to inspect the condition of his fields, manage quality control and handle any complaints. Janzen felt that retired farmers would be ideal candidates for this position. He thought in many cases the area manager's wife would also be involved in some of the activities. He allocated $72,000 in salary and expenses for each area manager. Although using area managers was an expensive proposition, Janzen wasn't sure how he could operate without them.

In order to create awareness and interest in the Machinery Ring, Janzen planned to continue advertising in farm publications and manning booths at agricultural trade shows such as the International Plowing Match and the Royal Winter Fair. He felt these were very effective means of reaching sizable numbers of farmers with information about the OMR. Janzen's proposed annual promotional budget was $80,000. Exhibit 1 shows an example of the type of ad used by the OMR. An ad similar to this had appeared each month in the *Western Ontario Farmer* over the past year. In the future, Janzen planned to continue with the same format, but he wanted to put more emphasis on the Machinery Ring as a way for farmers to save money by avoiding the purchase of new machinery and/or spreading the fixed costs of machinery over more units of output.

Janzen was convinced the joint effect of the overall promotional program, together with the appeal of the concept itself, would rapidly gain customers for the OMR. Based on the European experience, he felt a 25 per cent penetration in each county in the first year was quite possible, followed by a 50 per cent penetration in the second year. Even though penetration reached as high as 80 per cent in many European countries, Janzen was not sure whether penetration beyond 50 per cent was possible in Ontario.

In addition to the cost of area managers, there was also a head office cost of running the business. This included the general manager, secretary, communications, insurance, professional fees, supplies and travel. This cost was estimated at $400,000 per year for the first year of expanded operations. Janzen expected this cost to increase by about $50,000 per year over the next five years.

Based on the above business plan, Janzen made some financial projections for the next five years. In making these projections, Janzen used the following assumptions:

- He would add five new counties per year.
- An average county had 2,000 farms.

- The average custom work per farm was $2,250 ($144,777,000 spent on custom work/64.412 farms in Ontario).
- The first year the Machinery Ring was in a county, it would capture 25 per cent of the farms.
- The second year the Machinery Ring was in a county, it would capture 50 per cent of the farms.
- Each county would be serviced by an area manager.

The projections that are provided in Exhibit 2 show that it would take three years before the Machinery Ring would turn a profit and five years before the cumulative profit was positive.

THE NEED FOR RESEARCH

Janzen was anxious to start implementing his business plan, but he needed up to $700,000 in short-term funds to finance his projected losses in the first couple of years of expanded operations. Because of the company's status as a non-profit co-operative, Janzen felt the Ministry of Agriculture and Food might be interested in providing the required assistance. Initial contacts with the Ministry revealed they would required a third-party assessment of demand and a business plan prior to providing any financial assistance.

Janzen began to contact a number of marketing research companies to discuss his situation. He was particularly impressed with Agri Studies Inc., a small marketing research firm specializing in agriculture. Janzen felt it was important that the company who was doing the marketing research should understand the agricultural market. He also felt this would add to the credibility of research results with the Ministry of Agriculture and Food.

After a few meeting with Agri Studies, Janzen asked Tom Wilson, the general manager of the research firm, to prepare a preliminary proposal for a project designed to assess demand for the matchmaking concept and the validity of the current marketing plan. At this stage, Janzen was primarily interested in the type of information needed and specific research objectives. He was also interested in Wilson's initial thoughts about how data could be collected and a rough idea of required sample size.

Exhibit 1 Ontario machinery ring AD in western ontario farmer

ONTARIO MACHINERY RING CO-OPERATIVE CORPORATION

Report found in a car accident insurance form: "I pulled away from the side of the road, glanced at my mother-in-law, and headed over the embankment".

Who establishes the "Suggested Custom Rates"?

* The "Suggested Custom Rates for 1992 were compiled by averaging the rates presently charged by customer operators and the "1992 Custom Farmwork rates charged in Ontario" submitted by OMAF.

* The "Suggested Custom Rates" guides are intended to be just that. It is impossible for us to set fixed prices since individual circumstances, quantity of work, field topography and operating conditions vary considerably.

* The Ring matches the customer and the custom operator, then leave the two to negotiate prices and work details using our "Suggested Rates" as a guide.

* Members are encouraged to utilize their available machine capacity through the Machinery Ring and to cover their own custom work requirements through the Ring.

Machinery Ring Customers Requesting Summer Work:
North 1/2 of Bruce County area–wanted to purchase, approximately 200 acres of standing barley.

Dave Dalzell
Area Manager
519-228-6904

Jack Janzen
General Manager
Toll Free **1-800-668-0399**

Source: Western Ontario Farmer.

Exhibit 2 Financial projections

Data and Assumptions					
	Year 1	**Year 2**	**Year 3**	**Year 4**	**Year 5**
New Counties	5	5	5	5	5
Mature Counties	–	5	10	15	20
Total Counties	5	10	15	20	25
New County Penetration	25%	25%	25%	25%	25%
Mature County Penetration	50%	50%	50%	50%	50%
Average Farms/ County	2,000	2,000	2,000	2,000	2,000
OMR Farms in New Counties	2,500	2,500	2,500	2,500	2,500
OMR Farms in Mature Counties	–	5,000	10,000	15,000	20,000
Total OMR Farms	2,500	7,500	12,500	17,500	22,500
Average Custom Work/Farm	$2,250	$2,250	$2,250	$2,250	$2,250
Average Custom Work/County	$4,500,000	$4,500,000	$,500,000	$4,500,000	$4,500,000
OMR Co-ordinated Custom Work	$5,625,000	$16,875,000	$28,125,000	$39,375,000	$50,625,000
Membership Fee/Farm	$50	$50	$50	$50	$50
Buyer/Seller Service Fee	4%	4%	4%	4%	4%
Cost/Area Manager	$72,000	$72,000	$72,000	$72,000	$72,000

Financial Summar					
	Year 1	**Year 2**	**Year 3**	**Year 4**	**Year 5**
Revenue					
Membership Fees	$125,000	$375,000	$625,000	$875,000	$1,125,000
Service Fees	$225,000	$675,000	$1,125,000	$1,575,000	$2,025,000
Total Revenue Costs	$350,000	$1,050,000	$1,750,000	$2,450,000	$3,150,000

Head Office	$400,000	$450,000	$500,000	$550,000	$600,000
Advertising & Promotion	$80,000	$80,000	$80,000	$80,000	$80,000
Area Managers	$360,000	$720,000	$1,080,000	$1,440,000	$1,800,000
Total Costs	$840,000	$1,250,000	$1,660,000	$2,070,000	$2,480,000
Profitability					
Profit(Loss)	$(490,000)	$(200,000)	$90,000	$380,000	$670,000
Cumulative Profit(Loss)	$(490,000)	$(690,000)	$(600,000)	$(220,000)	$450,000

Appendix 1 Custom work statistics

Ontario Ministry of Agriculture & Food		
County	**Total # of Farms**	**$ Value of Custom Work**
Southern		
Hamilton Wentworth	1,225	$2,525,000
Niagara	2,706	$4,126,000
Haldimand Norfolk	3,066	$7,817,000
Brant	1,010	$2,833,000
Oxford	2,382	$9,205,000
Elgin	1,764	$4,986,000
Kent	2,822	$7,908,000
Essex	2,215	$4,231,000
Lambton	2,682	$5,848,000
Middlesex	3,162	$11,189,000
Total Southern	23,034	$60,668,000
County Average (Southern)	2,303	$6,066,800
Western		
Peel Halton	1,455	$4,465,000
Dufferin	1,023	$1,760,000
Wellington	2,849	$6,186,000
Waterloo	1,618	$5,019,000
Perth	2,894	$9,740,000
Huron	3,260	$10,334,000
Bruce	2,613	$5,265,000
Grey	3,146	$4,159,000
Simcoe	2,709	$4,846,000

(Continued)

(Continued)

Ontario Ministry of Agriculture & Food		
County	**Total # of Farms**	**$ Value of Custom Work**
Total Western	21,567	$51,774,000
County Average (Western)	2,396	$5,752,667
Central		
Hastings	1,244	$1,487,000
Northumberland	1,514	$2,586,000
Peterborough	1,430	$1,943,000
Victoria	1,668	$2,474,000
Durham	2,090	$4,231,000
York	1,210	$2,609,000
Total Central	9,156	$15,330,000
County Average (Central)	1,526	$2,555,000
Eastern		
Stormont Dundas Glengarry	2,203	$5,479,000
Prescott Russell	1,337	$3,136,000
Ottawa Carleton	1,606	$2,869,000
Leeds Granville	1,492	$1,720,000
Lanark	1,053	$1,130,000
Frontnenac Lennox Addington	1,459	$1,434,000
Renfrew	1,505	$1,237,000
Total Eastern	10,655	$17,005,000
County Average (Eastern)	1,522	$2,429,286
Total Ontario	**64,412**	**$144,777,000**
County Average (Ontario)	**2,013**	**$4,524,281**

Appendix 2 The ontario machinery ring computerized system

The Ontario Machinery Ring was dedicated to the farming industry, to keep up with current and future improvements in efficiency and family farm profitability. The matchmaking system was founded on a database and a geographical grid system, which enabled the operator of the Machinery Ring to select the most suitable candidate for an agricultural custom work job. Accounting and reporting features were also included in the computer system. The system worked in the following manner:

- A database was set up, keeping a record of all members' names and addresses, locations, types of equipment available, telephone numbers and e-mail addresses. The telephone numbers were used in the system as the members' I.D. number.
- A geographical grid system was developed that enabled the location of a field or farmer to be described in axis co-ordinates.
- When a farmer called into the Machinery Ring office to have some custom work done (e.g. plowing), the operator entered the request into the computer.

- The computer then matched the type of request (e.g. plowing) with farmers who had such a piece of equipment available and were willing to do the work.
- The list created by matching equipment to the job was prioritized according to the proximity of the machinery to the location of the field.
- The farmer wanting custom work done then contacted the possible suppliers and made an acceptable deal. The name of the contracted supplier was communicated to the OMR.
- As soon as the farmer contracted to do the work, the computer printed a confirmation of the job to be performed, giving details such as names, locations, acreage, etc.
- After each successful completion of a match, a statement was produced, outlining the financial data such as price per acre, acreage, total amount and the fee to be paid to the Machinery Ring.
- The accounting part of the service was fully automated. Daily transactions were transmitted to the bank for clearing. As well, preauthorization by both customers and custom operators allowed for automatic debiting and crediting of the appropriate accounts.
- Statements for the customer and custom operator were printed for each successful transaction.
- Computer analysis of specific geographical areas could indicate which machinery was needed most and when. This kind of analysis provided a sound financial planning tool for farmers wanting to purchase new equipment.
- At the month end and year end, reports and statistics were produced showing such details as total number of transactions, number of transactions per member and seasonal transaction volume.

5

Cineplex Entertainment

The Loyalty Program

Renée Zatzman wrote this case under the supervision of Professor Kenneth G. Hardy solely to provide material for class discussion. The authors do not intend to illustrate either effective or ineffective handling of a managerial situation. The authors may have disguised certain names and other identifying information to protect confidentiality.

INTRODUCTION

Sarah Lewthwaite, marketing director for Cineplex Entertainment, was approached by chief executive officer (CEO) Ellis Jacob in August 2006 to resume the development of a loyalty program. The movie industry yielded inconsistent revenues each year, and Jacob wanted to increase and stabilize Cineplex's revenues. As chair of the Loyalty Steering Committee (the committee), Lewthwaite was scheduled to present her recommendations to the committee the following week. She would need to make a persuasive argument that included recommendations on program development, the reward structure and the type of promotional campaign that would be most effective under the existing budget constraints. Finally, she needed to suggest whether the program should launch regionally or nationally. Her recommendations would be reviewed by senior Cineplex executives to ensure that the recommendations aligned with their criteria.

CINEPLEX ENTERTAINMENT

Cineplex Entertainment (Cineplex) was founded in 1979 as a small chain of movie theaters under the Cineplex Odeon name. In 2003, under the direction of Onex Corporation, a Canadian private equity firm that held a major ownership claim in the company, Cineplex merged with Galaxy Entertainment Inc. (Galaxy). The CEO of Galaxy, Ellis Jacob, took over the newly merged company. In late 2005, Cineplex Galaxy acquired its largest competitor, Famous Players, and became Cineplex Entertainment — Canada's largest film exhibitor. With a box-office market share of 64 per cent, the chain enjoyed approximately 40 million visits per year under the Cineplex Odeon, Galaxy, Famous Players and Cinema City brands.[1]

Cineplex's corporate mission focused on offering movie-goers "an exceptional entertainment experience." In addition to seeing a movie, customers could eat at various branded concession counters or play in the arcade. In 2005, Cineplex expanded its strategy to focus on developing new markets, using the theaters' large screens to showcase live events, such as major hockey games, wrestling matches and the Metropolitan Opera. These events contributed greatly to Cineplex's success, which was measured primarily on customer traffic and revenue per guest (RPG), which was in turn composed of box-office and concession revenues.

In 2005, weak box-office attendance throughout the movie theater industry had affected Cineplex's operating performance (see Exhibit 1 for Cineplex's income statements for 2003, 2004 and 2005). Following the acquisition of Famous Players in 2005, Cineplex executives adjusted the pricing and products in the food and beverage concessions in 2006. With these moves, Cineplex was able to increase its average box-office RPG to $7.73 and its average concession RPG to $3.44 (see Exhibit 2).

A GROWTH OPPORTUNITY

Like the entire industry, Cineplex faced variable attendance levels depending on the crop of new movies. Additionally, RPG fluctuated based on the film genre. Cineplex executives knew that audiences for action-themed and children's movies purchased a high volume of concession items, which typically resulted in a higher RPG than dramas. From these viewing patterns, Cineplex executives were able to distinguish the groups of customers that were particularly valuable. However, with no actual link to individual customers, they faced challenges targeting customers for specific movies and special events. Although market research was helpful on an aggregate level, Cineplex executives wanted to link box-office and concession purchases to a particular customer. Senior executives were supportive of Lewthwaite and the committee collecting this information through a customer relationship management program.

FILM EXHIBITION

The first Canadian film screening took place in 1896, in Montreal, Quebec, and the earliest cinema opened in 1906.[2] Attending the cinemas, also known as theaters, became a popular social activity; by the 1930s, a variety of independent and studio-owned theaters competed for customer attention. In 1979, Canada's first 18-theater multiplex opened in Toronto, Ontario, with several other multiplexes following in subsequent years. After a series of consolidations, by 2005, only three major theater companies existed in the Canadian movie and event exhibition market.

---

[1] Cineplex Galaxy Income Fund 2005 Annual Report,http://dplus.cineplexgalaxy.com/content/objects/Annual%20Report%202005.pdf, accessed January 3, 2008.

[2] Marcus Robinson, "A History of Film Exhibition in Canada," Playback: Canada's Broadcast and Production Journal (2005), accessed December 30, 2007.

Table 1 Observations on the motivations and frequency of movie attendance by age

Frequency, Reasons for Attendance*	Age Segment Labels					
	13-15	16-19	20-24	25-35	36-54	55+
	"Teenagers"	"Young Adults"	"Young Working"	"Young Families"	"Older Families"	"Retirees"
Low (Special Events)				X	X	
Medium (Special Movies)						X
High (Routine)	X	X	X			

* These observations were drawn from an independent focus group study conducted in 2003.

To showcase films, theaters required licensing from distributors who purchased rights from the production studios. The licensing agreement stipulated the "box-office split," also known as the percentage of proceeds that the theater received from a given film over a specified duration. Although both parties were mutually dependent, distributors held the balance of power and theaters relied heavily on concession revenues, of which they retained 100 per cent of the receipts. The margins on customers' purchases of concession treats and beverages were 65 per cent on average.[3] Table 1 (below) shows one way of characterizing the motivations and frequency of movie-going behavior according to various age segments.

"Teenagers" — Teenagers use the movie theatre and arcade for social gatherings because locations are accessible and movie-viewing is considered by parents to be an appropriate social activity. They are among the highest frequency of visitors.

"Young Adults" — This segment has access to a variety of other social venues because they can drive. Some in this segment are still in high school and others are post-secondary students; this segment visits theatres with high frequency.

"Young Working" — This segment has disposable income and they combine movies with socializing at other venues such as bars and restaurants. This segment has a high frequency of movie visits.

"Young Families" — This segment struggles to balance family and work-related obligations; they take their children to special movies occasionally.

"Older Families" — With a busy work and family life and varying interests within the household, older families attend theatres only for special events, and seldom attend as a family unit.

"Retirees" — This segment has significant free time to attend movies. They attend movies at a medium frequency.

CUSTOMER RELATIONSHIP MANAGEMENT (CRM)

Customer relationship management (CRM) is a marketing approach in which a company collects individual purchasing information to improve its ability to understand and respond to customer desires

---

[3] Janet Wasko, How Hollywood Works, Sage Publications, London, 2003.

and buying patterns. The information is typically stored in a central database from which the company managers can analyse trends and the purchasing behavior of particular market segments. A better understanding of customers enables organizations to develop targeted campaigns to increase marketing effectiveness, such as restructuring its products and services. For Cineplex, a CRM program could also be used to share valuable information with concession suppliers and movie distributors. Through the sharing of this information, partners would be better able to develop products for Cineplex's customer base.

Although several mechanisms were available to collect customer information, the most frequently used systems were point-of-sale systems, which scanned barcodes on wallet-sized cards or key chains. A recent trend for CRM programs was to offer incentives such as discounts or points that could be collected and redeemed for merchandise in return for the customer's permission for the company to collect data on the customer's buying habits. Among the Canadian companies following this trend were Shoppers Drug Mart with the Optimum card program, Air Canada with the Aeroplan rewards program and Office Depot and Boston Pizza which both participated in the Flight Miles card campaign.

CREATING LOYALTY

Even with 65 per cent market share in Canada, Cineplex had to aggressively compete for customer attention. Ongoing film piracy, rental movies, concerts and sporting events, combined with inconsistent box-office revenues encouraged Cineplex managers to explore ways to increase customer spending and frequency, particularly within the lucrative 16- to 24-year-old segment. Before merging with Cineplex Odeon, Galaxy Entertainment had established the Galaxy Elite card, which offered customers the opportunity to accumulate points toward free movie viewing. Although the program had no CRM capabilities, it had been successful in driving customer traffic. During the merger with Cineplex, the program had been disbanded and Galaxy's customer traffic had promptly waned. In a survey of Cineplex customers in May and June 2005, 95 per cent of respondents stated they were interested in joining a movie rewards program (see Exhibit 3).

In 2004, a steering committee composed of different department representatives was established to investigate CRM opportunities for Cineplex. After being put on hold during the acquisition of Famous Players, the committee was anxious to move forward in investigating a joint loyalty/CRM program. Senior managers had several concerns, primarily regarding data control and ownership, which would be relevant if the program were disbanded. Another criterion concerned resource requirements; a program this size would be a costly investment and would likely require new employees to manage it. Lewthwaite would need to prove that it was a worthy financial investment. Finally, the committee needed to consider the length of time required to establish a new database because most committee members believed that conclusive information on customer behavior could be drawn only from a minimum of 500,000 members. Further, although they thought that an investment in such a program could be largely beneficial for Cineplex, if implemented poorly, the organization's image and its ability to deliver customer value could suffer widespread harm. Lewthwaite knew that although the following partner options might not meet all the committee's criteria, she had to evaluate the most important considerations.

LOYALTY PARTNER OPTIONS

Internal Development

Under this option, Cineplex managers would develop and operate the program; they would then know their brand best and would have complete control over the direction of the program and the data ownership. However, the organization would incur the entire cost estimated at $5.5 million in the first year with diminishing costs in subsequent years. The company would also be fully exposed to the financial risk of unredeemed points and could face difficulty in divesting the program if it proved unsuccessful; a new department would need to be created to manage the exit of the program. This option would also require a new database, which, depending on promotional effectiveness, could take several years to create. However, because of the unlimited data access and control, this option appealed to several members of the committee.

Flight Miles Partnership

With 72 per cent of Canadian households as active members, Flight Miles was the top Canadian loyalty program.[4] This program gave cardholders the opportunity to earn leisure and travel rewards by purchasing products at various retailers across the country. Flight Miles executives viewed Cineplex as an opportunity to increase its youth membership, and their executives approached Cineplex executives to propose a special joint program. In this program, traditional Flight Miles cards would be used to collect points. Supplementary key tags would be issued for movie customers who opted to receive additional member benefits and rewards. Although the key tags might confuse other existing Flight Miles members, the proposal seemed to offer numerous benefits to Cineplex, including immediate entrance into a database of seven million people. Cineplex would also have the opportunity to access data from other Flight Miles partners, which would be beneficial in targeting specific retail buyers for niche films.

Lewthwaite estimated that access to the Flight Miles program would cost Cineplex yearly fees of approximately $5 million. Cineplex would also be required to pay $0.09 for each point issued. Lewthwaite thought users of the program would expect each movie transaction to be worth a minimum of 10 Flight Miles points. Cineplex would also be required to pay each time it accessed the data, which Flight Miles would own. A commitment of three years would be required, and if Cineplex decided to leave the program, it would lose all access to accumulated data. Lewthwaite recognized that Cineplex would be required to adhere to the partnership's decisions; no easy out was available if she did not like some aspect of the program after they signed the deal. To make the proposal more attractive, Flight Miles executives offered to contribute $250,000 to launch a Cineplex-designed and -initiated marketing campaign.

Scotiabank Proposal

Just as Lewthwaite and her committee sat down to examine the two options in further detail, Scotiabank executives approached Cineplex as a potential loyalty partner. The bank had a relationship with Cineplex derived from earlier corporate sponsorships. As one of the Big Five banks in Canada, Scotiabank offered a diverse range of financial services, including domestic banking, wholesale banking and wealth management. Through 950 branches, Scotiabank served approximately 6.8 million Canadians in 2005.[5] Because banks competed in an intensely competitive marketplace, many banks aligned their brands with sporting events, venues and other companies through corporate sponsorship.

Scotiabank executives were interested in acquiring new youth accounts and increasing overall transactions, so they viewed a partnership with Cineplex as a means to achieve their objectives while sharing financial risk. Scotiabank, which had prior experience with data management companies

---

[4] "Air Miles Rewards Program," http://www.loyalty.com/what/airmiles/index.html. accessed November 2, 2007.

[5] Scotiabank, 2005 Annual Report, http://cgi.scotiabank.com/annrep2005/en/rbl_ov.html, accessed February 10, 2008.

through its gold credit card program, proposed 50-50 cost-sharing. In return for partnering on the program, Scotiabank expected naming rights on three major theaters and an exclusivity agreement for Scotiabank bank machines in all Cineplex theaters.

Scotiabank proposed a three-card rewards strategy. The basic reward card would be Cineplex-branded and used at theaters; the Scotiabank debit and credit cards would act as reward accelerators that accumulated additional points based on customers' purchasing habits. Any Scotiabank debit- or credit-card user enrolled in this program would be issued the Cineplex card, and holders of basic Cineplex theater cards would not be required to open an account at Scotiabank.

Lewthwaite considered that the multiple card system might discourage some customers who disliked carrying additional cards. Secondly, because it would be a 50-50 partnership, Cineplex's decision-making power would be constrained, and the direction of the program would be subject to mutual agreement. Also, owing to privacy laws, Cineplex executives would not be able to access individual-level banking information on the Scotiabank program users, data that might be helpful in targeting specific retail consumers. However, this program could be promoted in theaters and bank branches across the country. The costs to develop and maintain Cineplex's portion of the partnership were estimated to be \$3 million, \$1.7 million and \$1.9 million in years 1, 2 and 3 respectively.

Lewthwaite had to fully consider the potential benefits and drawbacks of each proposal and weigh them against Cineplex's criteria before recommending which partner to select. She also acknowledged other options were available beyond those that were presented. She knew that this decision could not be made without analysing the potential reward structure of the program because the committee would expect a detailed net benefit analysis to support her recommendation.

STRUCTURING THE REWARD PROGRAM

Lewthwaite believed it was essential to create a program that would appeal to customers. However, creating a program with valuable and easy-to-gain rewards might be too costly to carry out for an extended period of time. If Cineplex went forward with the Flight Miles partnership, an offer of 10 Flight Miles points per transaction would be required to align with cardholder expectations and could be supplemented with Cineplex discounts. If Cineplex went forward with other loyalty partnerships, it would have full design control over the reward structure of the program. Points could be earned based on box-office transactions, concession transactions, or both. The points could then be used towards movies and concession items. Determining the number and value of points to be given per transaction and the required price per transaction were aspects that Lewthwaite needed to determine. She also needed to decide on the number of points required for particular rewards and whether different reward levels should be created.

Among the other options, Cineplex could reward cardholders with a permanent discount on theater tickets or concession items (or both) or possibly provide first access to special events. If Lewthwaite went forward with free or discounted movies and concession items, she would need to estimate the extent to which she would be rewarding customers who would have attended without being offered any rewards,[6] the so-called cannibalization rate (see Exhibit 4). To determine the other potential revenues, Lewthwaite needed to perform a sensitivity analysis around any increases in the concession RPG, which she hoped might increase by five to 15 per cent for loyalty program members. She also had the option of charging a nominal one-time or annual membership fee of \$2 to \$5. Finally, as

[6] Cannibalization refers to the number of free visits redeemed that would have been paid visits in the absence of a loyalty program.

with any loyalty point program, Lewthwaite knew that only 40 per cent of earned points would be redeemed annually. She drafted a preliminary list of four unique reward structures she thought could be effective, but was unsure which, if any, would maximize customer appeal through retail value while minimizing costs (see Exhibit 5).

SELECTING THE DATABASE VENDOR

If a recommendation were made to move forward with program development, the committee would need to select a database vendor to manage customer data and the e-communication site. This vendor would need strong website design capabilities and a technology platform that could collect a variety of data on Cineplex's customers. Because Canada had only a few such vendors, Cineplex released a request for proposal (RFP) to three major companies: Alpha, Kappa, and Gamma. Each company responded with a unique proposal for the project (see Exhibit 6).

THE MARKETING COMMUNICATIONS CAMPAIGN

Cineplex executives wanted to enroll 500,000 customers per year for the first three years in any loyalty program, After the first year, she believed the data bank would be large enough to derive meaningful customer information, and the organization could then focus on customer retention. To meet these targets, Cineplex would need to build substantial awareness of the program, particularly in markets where the Galaxy Elite card had previously existed. Launching the loyalty card would also require a marketing campaign to fit a variety of geographic markets, including Quebec, a province whose official language was French. Lewthwaite had a budget of $300,000, and she needed to make some creative decisions, including the name of the program, the marketing message to customers and the media to be used to deliver the message.

In-Theater Advertising

In 2005, Cineplex served 5.3 million unique visitors annually with an average of 7.5 visits per guest. No costs were associated with in-theater advertising, and Lewthwaite knew it was an excellent way to reach the market but she was unsure which media would be most effective without overwhelming movie-goers. The program could be promoted on concession products, point-of-purchase displays, backlit posters or on the website. The program could also be advertised to a captive audience via the digital pre-show or during the presentation of upcoming attractions.

Newspaper Advertising

Lewthwaite wondered whether the target market would respond to regional newspaper advertisements. She knew that the committee was opposed to advertising in a national newspaper, such as the *Globe and Mail*, because it did not have strong reach in every market in which Cineplex operated. However, Cineplex was accustomed to promoting events through half-page ads in regional papers. Although this option would be more costly than advertising solely in a national paper, several more movie-going markets could be reached. The average weekly cost per half-page ad in the small to medium markets was $1,200, and $3,600 for larger markets, with a development cost of $850 for each advertisement. If this option were selected, Lewthwaite would need to determine in which papers to advertise, and the message and frequency of the insertions (see Exhibit 7).

Radio Advertising

Local radio advertisements could achieve significant coverage in key markets across Canada. The average weekly cost per 30-second commercial was $160 in small-and medium-sized markets and $225 in larger markets. Development of local radio ads would cost approximately $1,100 per city. Because Cineplex had used this medium for other events, particularly in rural theater markets, Lewthwaite was confident Cineplex could also negotiate free advertisement space on many radio station's websites.

Online Advertising

In addition to advertising on the Cineplex website, the program could be promoted through various websites, such as Google, Muchmusic.ca, MTV.ca and canoe.qc.ca, a French-language news site. Costs varied according to advertisement format and site (see Exhibit 8).

Grass Roots Initiatives

Lewthwaite had also considered smaller initiatives with the goal of spreading word-of-mouth publicity. Event teams could promote on college and university campuses or at highly visited attractions, thereby raising awareness for the program. Cineplex could also engage in corporate sponsorships. She was unsure what costs would be associated with these options.

LAUNCH

Launching the program was the final recommendation to be made. Cineplex's head office was located in Toronto, Ontario, and the company operated in six provincial markets — Quebec, Ontario, Manitoba, Saskatchewan, Alberta and British Columbia — but none of the four Atlantic provinces.

Lewthwaite would have to decide whether the program should be launched regionally or across all six provinces. In early 2006, Cineplex had completed the installation of a new point-of-sale platform, which had the technological capability to support a national loyalty rollout. A national launch was appealing to Lewthwaite because it would be cost-efficient and would accrue revenues faster than a regional rollout. However, it was also riskier than a regional rollout: any problem would affect all markets. A regional launch would give Cineplex the opportunity to resolve problems before full implementation. The regional rollout would be more expensive at completion, but it would allow Cineplex to stretch funds over a longer time period. If Lewthwaite recommended the regional option, she would need to decide how the regional launch would be phased in.

Lewthwaite knew several complex decisions needed to be made, and she had little time before the steering committee's meeting the following week. Having a more comprehensive understanding of customer behavior and demographics was important in improving Cineplex's success, but could a loyalty program be implemented in such a way to fit senior management's criteria? If she recommended going ahead with the program, which loyalty partner should she use? How should the rewards be structured and promoted? What would the promotional campaign entail, and how should the launch take place? As she leaned back in her chair, she knew it was going to be a very long week.

Exhibit 1 Cineplex entertainment income statements 2003–2005 (Cdn$ in thousands)

	2005	2004	2003
Total revenue	490,299	315,786	295,540
Cost of operations	421,529	248,818	242,636
Gross income	68,770	66,968	52,904
Amortization	42,948	22,530	18,404
Loss on debt	4,156	–	–
Impairment on assets	4,296	–	–
Loss (gain) on disposal of assets	122	(111)	(92)
Interest on long-term debt	18,401	8,280	4,020
Interest on loan	14,000	14,000	1,381
Interest income	(378)	(473)	(922)
Foreign exchange gain	–	–	(3,696)
Income taxes	(1,463)	(1,149)	366
Income from discontinued operations	28,116	6,357	6,184
Non-controlling interest	1,828	–	304
Net Income	12,976	30,248	39,323

Source: Cineplex Galaxy Income Fund 2005 Annual Report, http://dplus.cineplexgalaxy.com/content/objects/annual% 20rport% 202005.pdf, accessed January 3, 2008.

Exhibit 2 Cineplex entertainment attendance and revenue per guest data

	2006E	2005	2004	2003
Attendance	61,000,000	39,945,000	28,096,000	27,073,000
Box office RPG	–	$7.73	$7.45	$7.28
Concession RPG	–	$3.44	$3.04	$2.91
Film cost as a per cent of box-office revenue	–	51.7%	51.6%	52.1%

Source: Cineplex Galaxy Income Fund 2005 Annual Report, http://dplus.cineplexgalaxy.com/content/objects/annual% 20report%202005.pdf, accessed January 3, 2008.

Exhibit 3 Highlights from Cineplex email survey of current customers

Survey Period: May–June 17, 2005
Respondents: 4,261

- 95 per cent of respondents were interested in joining a Cineplex Entertainment movie rewards program
- 87 per cent of respondents currently belonged to the Flight Miles program, and 39 per cent identified Flight Miles as their "favorite rewards program"
- 31 per cent of respondents were interested in the opportunity to collect Aeroplan points

- 56 per cent of respondents indicated that they would be interested in receiving a 10 per cent discount at concessions
- The majority of respondents suggested that they would be more inclined to join if there were no additional card to carry

Exhibit 4 Summary of revenues and cannibalization rates

- Membership fee possibilities, a one-time fee of $2 to $5
- Increase in concession RPG of from 5 per cent to 15 per cent
- Net increase in attendance (actual incremental attendance times 1- the estimated cannibalization rate)
- Cannibalization rate assumptions
  Worst: 50 per cent
  Most Likely: 25 per cent
  Best: 12.5 per cent

Exhibit 5 Preliminary reward structure options

	Option 1	Option 2	Option 3	Option 4
Membership fee	No	One-time $2	Annually $5	No
Permanent concessions discount	–	10%	15%	10%
Points?	Yes	Yes	No	Yes
Sign-up points	500	100	–	250
Points per adult movie transaction	100	100	–	100
Points per concession combo transaction	–	75	–	–
	Reward Items and Maximum Retail Value			
Points Required				
500	Free child admission $8.50	–	–	–
750	Free concession combo $12.37	–	–	–
1000	Free adult admission $10.95	Free adult admission $10.95	–	Free adult admission $10.95
1500	Free event admission[1] $19.95	Free event admission $19.95	–	Free adult admission/ concession combo ($23.32)
2,000	–	–	–	Free adult/2 children admission $27.95
2,500	–	Night out package[2] $37.47	–	–

[1] Includes admission to the following viewings: the Metropolitan Opera, NHL series, or WWE series.
[2] A Night out package includes two adult movie admissions, two large sodas and one large popcorn.

Exhibit 6 Summary of Cineplex's request for proposal

Program Overview

Cineplex Entertainment is looking into the possibility of creating a new entertainment-focused loyalty program. Members will earn points that can be redeemed for free movies or other entertainment-related rewards. An ongoing marketing program requiring a member database and website is required.

Vendors to Provide

- A proposed approach and high level design concept for the website that is creative and functional
- Pricing for the database and website build

Website Goals

- Acquire new customers and deepen relationships with existing customers by enticing them to sign up, then encouraging them to remain active in the loyalty program
- Provide an easy way to sign up, check status of points earned, get information on rewards that can be earned, redeem points, and interact with other members
- The site will be a major marketing channel to reach members. It will be used for viral and targeted online promotions
- Provide an online community for members

Database Use

- For program administration, analysis and reporting
- For analysis and reporting on moviegoer's behavior and preferences
- For marketing to customers

The Target Market

- Is very comfortable with the online environment, text messaging, downloading, and browsing
- Wants and expects discounts and free offers in an attainable timeframe
- Wants simplicity and convenience

Website Requires

- A public section accessible to all, a member's section accessible with member ID and password and an administrative site to be used for customer support
- Site must connect to program database to collect, maintain, retrieve and report member data including demographic information and points data
- Integration with Cineplex's POS equipment and mobile channels for marketing
- Site will link to and from the sites of main partners and vendors
- Site must be available in English and French

Vendors' Responses to the Cineplex Request for Proposal

Alpha

Alpha was a leading marketing firm specializing in loyalty programs and performance improvement. As a global company, Alpha's clients include American Express, Coca-Cola, Hewlett-Packard, and Microsoft. Alpha has served the Canadian marketplace since 1980, and its focus is helping organizations identify, retain, and build customer relationships in order to maximize profit and drive long-term success. With a history of designing and implementing loyalty programs, Alpha's technology platforms focused on customer behavior tracking and loyalty rewards fulfillment. In preparing its response, Alpha held focus groups to help determine what type of website appealed to Cineplex's target market. These groups indicated the importance of security, easy navigation, and keeping site content up-to-date; they also spoke out against pop-up advertisements. All respondents were familiar with e-newsletters, and noted that loyalty members should have the option to opt in, because they do not want to be overwhelmed with promotional messages. Alpha used this information in conjunction with Cineplex's specifications to present how the website would be designed. The approximate investment cost for the program design was $500,000 with $40,000 per month required for website upkeep.

Kappa

Known for managing data for the Royal Bank of Canada, Kappa was one of the largest global marketing agencies. With a strong focus on customer loyalty programs, Kappa offered a high standard in data privacy and security and was the undisputed industry leader in mobile marketing, which linked strongly to Cineplex's target market. The Kappa proposal focused on creating a youth-driven brand identity that engaged viewers to join the program through program incentives and links to third-party social networking sites, such as MySpace. With a significant portfolio of integrated loyalty program solutions, Kappa also had entertainment industry experience, having previously worked on technology platforms with Famous Players, the Toronto International Film Festival and IMAX. Kappa's main differentiating factor was its proposal to have two distinct sites, one for members and one for non-members. Although similar in nature, one site would focus on member acquisition and program information while the other would focus on member retention through contest promotions and access to personal account activity. Approximate costs would be $1 million.

Gamma

Gamma, a competitor in the Canadian marketplace for four years, had vast experience in information technology strategy and a track record of developing CRM programs for leading organizations, such as Kaplan University and Citi Financial. Gamma's response to the RFP included a proposal to plan, design, and manage Cineplex's marketing and technology programs on its specialized marketing platform that supported all aspects of email management and e-communication campaigns. This platform would also enable Cineplex to track members on an ongoing basis through different promotional mediums, such as web advertisements and search functions, and to respond instantly to member behavior through messaging for those leaving the site. Gamma's offer was appealing because it included a fixed-price, fixed-time model. Gamma was unable to provide costs for data management because it was unsure of Cineplex's technical capabilities, but preliminary planning and design costs were estimated at around $200,000.

Exhibit 7 Large media markets

Market	Newspaper	Radio
Calgary	Calgary Herald	VIBE 98.5
Edmonton	Edmonton Journal	Sonic 102.9
Montreal	Montreal Gazette	Q92
Ottawa	Ottawa Citizen	BOB FM
Toronto	Toronto Star	Mix 99.9
Vancouver	Vancouver Sun	Z95 FM
Small and medium sized media markets		
Barrie	Barrie Examiner	Rock 95 FM
Cornwall	Standard Freeholder	Rock 101.9
Guelph	Guelph Mercury	Magic FM

(Continued)

(Continued)

Market	Newspaper	Radio
Kitchener	Kitchener Record	KOOL FM
London	London Free Press	Fresh FM
North Bay	North Bay Nugget	EZ Rock
Owen Sound	Owen Sound Sun Times	Mix 106
Quebec City	Quebec City Journale	Le 93.3
Regina	Regina Leader Post	Z-99
Saskatoon	The Star Phoenix	C95
Sault Ste. Marie	Sault Ste. Marie Star	EZ Rock 100.5
St. Thomas	St. Thomas Times-Journal	Fresh FM
Sudbury	Sudbury Star	Big Daddy 103.9 FM
Thunderbay	Chronicle Journal	Rock 94
Windsor	Windsor Star	89X
Winnipeg	Winnipeg Free Press	Q94

Exhibit 8 Cost per thousand impressions (in Cdn$)

Website	Big Box Advertisement	Banner Advertisement
google.ca	20	12
mtv.ca	27	35
muchmusic.ca	29	32
yahoo.ca	19	13
imdb.com	17	9
canoe.qc.ca	26	–

6

Super Shampoo Products and the Indian Mass Market

Dr. S. Ramesh Kumar and Nitya Guruvayurappan wrote this case solely to provide material for class discussion. The authors do not intend to illustrate either effective or ineffective handling of a managerial situation. The authors may have disguised certain names and other identifying information to protect confidentiality.

In 2010, Suresh Venkataraman, following a successful period of marketing industrial products in the city of Coimbatore in the Southern part of India (a city known for its textile industries and entrepreneurs), became interested in consumer products. He had always been fascinated with single use packaging, and wondered how shampoo as a category was transformed from an unaffordable product to an affordable one with the invention of sachets (single use packs that had about six to eight millilitres (ml) of shampoo costing about $US 0.10). Venkataraman also had a firm belief that the lower economic strata of consumers, especially in the rural markets, offered a huge potential for consumer products. Though he did not have a management background, he had asked various people why several brands of shampoos (though quite successful in lower price segments and in the rural areas of the country) did not have a brand name that was simple to understand. His aspirations took shape when he decided to launch a product called Super Shampoo for this target segment. He selected the name "Super" as it was easy to pronounce and had an English overtone that was considered a part of the aspirations of rural consumers (who were influenced by the globalized urban markets); more specifically, he chose it because the word "super" was amplified by the media to celebrate film stars by projecting them as "superstars" (India ranks very high on the production of films, and films are a part of the Indian psyche). The word "super" triggered a superior image amongst whatever it was competing against in a specific context. Venkataraman had adequate business experience to know that a name alone cannot create a superior brand: the challenges were indeed quite confounding. How could established brands of shampoos be addressed? Super Shampoo would not have the financial muscle to compete against the advertising blitzkrieg of the megabrands. Were there ways to compete in the war of marketing communication when communication held much sway in such a competitive and glamour-ridden category? Venkataraman decided to consider such issues through a market survey set in a rural market in the Indian context to help analyze marketing communications and its impact on consumer behaviour.

THE INDIAN CONTEXT

In 2010, India contained a diverse array of product categories, brands, prices, lifestyles and cultures.[1] While marketers were upbeat about the consumption of categories and brands stretching from unbranded edible oil to prestigious brands of watches, there were unique challenges to marketers. These unique challenges included the management of marketing mix elements, understanding the diversity of cultures, development of appropriate product lines, localizing global communication and, more specifically, understanding the consumer psyche in a changing environment. While there were quite a few studies undertaken on several aspects of consumer behaviour, one of the most important facets of the Indian cultural environment was the aspiration-based appeals of marketing communication and brands that triggered such marketing communication. This was especially important given the fact that just 14 percent of the world's population lived in countries with a per capita GNP of greater than US$10,000. India was characterized by the unorganized sector[2] in a number of product categories.[3] The mindset of the "have not" with reference to the aspirations created by categories and brands has been largely explored. The shampoo category contained products in single use packs as well as regular packaging. Approximately 60 to 65 per cent of the market was accounted for by such packets, with significant volumes being sold to consumers in lower economic situations. In several fast-moving consumer goods, these lower-level consumers contributed to a significant amount of sales. This begs the questions, how do the non-users perceive the category of shampoos? Are they only influenced by functional attributes? Do they attach symbolic benefits to shampoos?

---

[1] S. Ramesh Kumar, "Addressing Diversity: The Marketing Challenge in India," Wall Street Journal, October 20, 2010.

[2] A term used commonly to denote a sector of labour where production units are a subset of unincorporated enterprises owned by households, i.e., not constituted as separate legal entities independently of the households, and for which no complete sets of accounts (including balance sheets of assets and liabilities) are available, which would permit a clear distinction of production activities of the enterprises from other activities of their owners and the identification of any flows of income and capital between the enterprises and the owners.

[3] S. Ramesh Kumar, Consumer Behavior and Branding: Concepts, Readings and Cases, Pearson, New Delhi, 2009, p. 9.

The high penetration yet low per capita consumption of shampoos in the Indian market was indicative of the available opportunity in the category, as there was a large segment of low frequency users (and non-users) for the category. What attitudes are developed in category non-users or low frequency users in the shampoo category in these low income markets where the key usage barrier is affordability? Which variables—such as their psychographics and lifestyle, media consumption, purchasing power and the brand communication of key players in this category—influence these attitudes? What would it take for a new shampoo entrant to use these attitudes to generate likeability and persuade consumers to try the brand?

INTRODUCTION AND BACKGROUND TO MARKET—BOTTOM OF THE PYRAMID

In 2010, there were about two billion middle-class consumers (annually earning US$13,500 to 113,000) in twelve countries (including the BRIC countries) that spent US$6.9 trillion.[4] The bottom of the pyramid (BoP) in India concerning income classification is defined as the bottom two classes of less than ₹75,000 and between ₹75,000 to ₹150,000 per year.[5] This comprised roughly 150 million households across India, with 25 per cent of this coming from urban India and the remaining 75 per cent from rural (see Exhibit 1).

The rural Indian market has had a slower pace of change in the percentage of households that fall under the BoP classification, and it was expected to take at least 25 years from 2009-10 for rural India to get to the same salience as urban India with respect to the number of BoP households within the total households. Urban BoPs contributed to only 15 per cent of urban income despite comprising almost 40 per cent of the population, and this segment was expected to move upwards very fast. On the other hand, despite being such a large percentage of total rural households (82 per cent), the rural BoPs contributed to about half the total income of rural India.[6]

RURAL INDIA

The rural Indian consumer market consisted of between 720 and 790 million consumers with around 160 million households, and comprised 12.2 per cent of the world's population. The market grew 25 per cent in 2008 and was projected to be around US$425 million in 2010-11: double what it was in 2004-05.[7]

THE FMCG MARKET IN RURAL INDIA

The fast moving consumer goods (FMCG) category can be broadly split into household care, personal care and food and beverages (see Exhibit 2). The FMCG market in India was estimated at between US$15 billion to $18 billion and likely to grow to US$33 billion by 2015. Of the first figures,

---

[4] David Court and Laxman Narasimhan, "Capturing the world's emerging middle class," McKinsey Quarterly, Issue 3 , 2010, pp. 12-17.

[5] "Section Title/Report Name," Indicus Analytics, www.indicus.net/blog/index.php/indian_economy/amit/the-bottom-of-the-indian-pyramid, accessed September 25, 2010.

[6] Ibid.

[7] "Rural Market," India Brand Equity Foundation, www.ibef.org/economy/ruralmarket.aspx, accessed on September 25, 2010.

57 per cent was contributed by rural India. The growth of rural India in the contribution to FMCG is evident from the fact that urban markets were once 50 per cent of total FMCG, and had reduced to 29 per cent (the rest coming from semi-urban), as of 2010.[8]

The BoP market had been seeing a lot of traction with big brands rushing to cash in on the huge opportunities to sell branded products to the estimated 350 million low-income consumers in the country. Below are some examples of how FMCG companies were responding to the traction in the rural markets[9]:

- According to published sources, several brands were conscious of the market for low priced offerings in India. Horlicks Asha, a low cost milk food, Coca Cola's Vittigo, a powder based beverage, Pepsi Co's ongoing work on low priced snacks, and Unilever India's Shaktimaan initiative to cover 150,000 villages that had a population of less than 2,000 through cycle vendors (as a low cost distribution alternative for rural Indian villages or hamlets) were examples of introducing priced cost offerings to rural segments or reaching out to rural segments.[10]

MEDIA TRENDS IN RURAL INDIA[11]

Unlike urban India, rural India was what one might call a significantly dark media market in terms of the most penetrated urban media; for example, television was the media with the highest reach, yet it penetrated only 38 per cent of rural India. Interestingly, radio was ahead of print in terms of reach, likely owing to literacy barriers: it reached 18 per cent while print reached 15 per cent. Cinema had a mere five per cent reach.

Some touchpoints that were used successfully by brands that have penetrated this market were the *melas*, *haats* or *mandis*, which were places where the entire population of a village congregated on a periodic basis to purchase a multitude of essential goods while also seeking a day's entertainment for the family. Outdoor media, such as wall paintings, folk media and fairs, had also been effective in reaching out to a large number of consumers at a time. Influencers were also an important medium of disbursing information and educating the consumer. This could be in the form of individuals such as the educated youth of the village, the local retail store owner, the key decision makers such as the chiefs and landlords or even a collective influence worked by women of similar background like through various self-help groups.

THE RURAL INDIAN CONSUMER

Rural India was a highly heterogeneous consumer market, making it impossible to look at it as a single consumer market. However, within a region, the homogeneity of the consumers was bounded by the traditions, customs and values of that region. Rural India had a lower level of traditional

---

[8] "Fast Moving Consumer Goods," India Brand Equity Foundation Report, www.ibef.org/download/fmcg_sectoral.pdf, accessed on September 25, 2010.

[9] Ratna Bhushan, "Nestle exploring low-cost infant milk market," Economic Times, August 12, 2010, http://economictimes.indiatimes.com/news/news-by-industry/cons-products/food/Nestle-exploring-low-cost-infant-milk-market/articleshow/6296113.cms, accessed on September 25, 2010.

[10] Namrata Singh, "Shaktimaans to Power Rural Reach," Times of India, August 16, 2010, http://timesofindia.indiatimes.com/business/india-business/Shaktimaans-To-Power-Rural-Reach-/articleshow/6316529.cms, accessed on September 25, 2010.

[11] "Lintas Media Guide 2008: Urban and rural reach of advertising media," afaqs!, January 21, 2008, www.afaqs.com/perl news/story.html?sid=20191, accessed September 25, 2010.

education; however, their awareness levels were going up with the increasing penetration of various media, as well as education of the youth and their migration to urban India. Rural Indian consumers were historically believed to be conservative, implying a high-value consciousness. Owing to the comparatively low per capita income levels, the rural consumer was more risk averse to spending when she did not see value clearly. The increasing influx of branded goods indicated that the consumer was willing to spend a little extra for quality and satisfaction, and was not conservative about the absolute outlay per se.

SHAMPOO MARKET IN INDIA—KEY BRANDS, SKUS AND SALIENCES

In 2010, the total hair care market in India was approximately ₹70 billion in value,[12] of which the shampoo category was estimated to be around ₹30 billion. There was a high awareness of the category in both the urban (90 per cent) and rural (80 per cent) markets. The overall shampoo market was growing at 14 per cent a year, and had taken penetration to more than 90 per cent in urban and 80 per cent in rural as well. Consumption, however, was still low for India as an index to other countries; for example, per annum consumption in India was 13 ml per capita, while in other parts of Asia it was much higher (160 ml in Indonesia and 330 ml in Thailand)[13].

The key national players in this category were Hindustan Unilever Ltd. (46 per cent share with brands such as Clinic Plus, Clinic All Clear, Sunsilk and Dove), Procter & Gamble (24 per cent share with brands such as Pantene and Head & Shoulders), Cavin Kare (18 per cent share with brands such as Chik) and Dabur (seven per cent with brands such as Vatika)[14].

The primary stock-keeping units (SKUs) in the shampoo category were bottles and sachets. Bottles ranged from 25 ml to 500 ml, whereas sachets usually contained around five to eight and were priced between 50p and ₹3 depending on the segment. In urban India, the salience split between bottles and sachets was 60:40, whereas in rural India 90 per cent of the shampoo sales occurred as sachets.[15] There was a geographical skew in this too, with the southern market being a strong sachet hold: roughly 70 per cent of the sachet volumes came from the South. The North, on the other hand, contributed to 50 per cent of bottle volumes.[16]

BENEFIT-BASED SEGMENTATION OF THE SHAMPOO MARKET

The biggest consumer hair problem in India was hair fall. However, the fastest growing segment at 12 to 15 per cent growth year-on-year was the anti-dandruff segment, which was around 15 to 20 per cent of the market[17]. The key benefit segments were cosmetic (which refers to shine, strength and lustre), anti-dandruff and herbal (see Exhibit 3).

---

[12] "Hair Care in India," Euromonitor, www.euromonitor.com/Hair_Care_in_India, July 2010, accessed on September 25, 2010.

[13] Rupall Mukherjee, "Turf war: HUL losing share in toothpaste, shampoo market," Times of India, August 3, 2009, http://timesofindia.indiatimes.com/business/india-business/Turf-war-HUL-losing-share-in-toothpaste-shampoo-market/articleshow/4849829.cms, accessed on September 25, 2010.

[14] "Dabur, CavinKare see growth bubbling in shampoos," The Hindu Business Line, March 13, 2010, www.thehindubusinessline.com/2010/03/13/stories/2010031352130500.htm, accessed on September 25, 2010.

[15] "2nd strike P&G cuts shampoo prices," www.dnaindia.com/money/report_2nd-strike-p-and-g-cuts-shampoo-prices 1369108, accessed on September 25, 2010.

[16] "Shampoo Industry," http://sify.com/advertise/industry-shampoo.ppt, accessed on September 25, 2010.

[17] "Preity Zinta to endorse Dabur's anti-dandruff range" The Hindu Business Line, March 24, 2009, www.thehindubusinessline.com/2009/03/24/stories/2009032451681500.htm, accessed on September 25, 2010.

SHAMPOO MARKET IN RURAL SOUTH INDIA

The top three shampoo brands in rural South India (total region encompassing Tamil Nadu, Kerala, Karnataka and Andhra Pradesh) were Clinic Plus, Head & Shoulders and Chik. Below is a summary of each of these players along with an understanding of their consumer segment and positioning.

Clinic Plus—Background

Clinic Plus was a cosmetic shampoo brand of Unilever. It was in the popular/economy tier in terms of pricing and targeted at the low-income consumer (semi-urban and rural). The brand was sold in bottles ranging from 25 ml to 300 ml, sachets of 7.5 ml (₹2) and value packs or multi-sachet bundles. The brand's place in the company's shampoo portfolio seemed to be a "Family Value and Health Foundation" brand.[18] On viewing the Clinic Plus Indian ads, it was possible to establish an understanding regarding its target segment and positioning (see Exhibit 4).

Head & Shoulders—Background

Head and Shoulders was an anti-dandruff shampoo brand of Procter & Gamble. It was in the premium tier in terms of pricing and targeted at consumers who sought a chemically mild yet effective anti-dandruff solution. The brand was sold in bottles ranging from 100 ml to 400 ml, sachets of 7.5 ml (₹3) and value packs or multi-sachet bundles. The brand's place in the company's shampoo portfolio seemed to be the lead anti-dandruff shampoo, which was endorsed by experts.[19] On viewing the Head and Shoulders Indian ads, it was possible to establish an understanding regarding its target segment and positioning (see Exhibit 5).

Chik—Background

Chik was a cosmetic shampoo brand of Cavin Kare. It was in the popular/economy tier in terms of pricing and targeted at the low-income consumer (semi-urban and rural). The brand was sold in bottles ranging from 25 ml to 100 ml and sachets of 7.5 ml (50p to ₹1). The brand's place in the company's shampoo portfolio seemed to be the flagship brand that promised soft, nourished, beautiful hair for the confident Indian woman.[20] On viewing the Chik Indian ads, it was possible to establish an understanding regarding its target segment and positioning (see Exhibit 6).

CONCLUSION

Venkatraman decided to commission a survey to obtain some insights related to the several attitudinal aspects of consumers towards the shampoo category as well as towards the brands. He thought this would enable him to decide on the marketing strategy for his brand. The following details provide the overview of his approach to the survey.

Before launching Super Shampoo, Venkataraman conducted a market survey. For the purposes of sampling, the target population was defined in terms of elements, sampling units, extent and time. The element was as below:

---

[18] Michel Dallemagne, "Unilever Asia Hair Care," Unilever, November 14, 2007, www.unilever.com/Images/ir_Hair-in-Asia_tcm13-114446.pdf, accessed on September 25, 2010.

[19] "Head & Shoulders," Procter & Gamble, www.pg-india.com/hp/hs.htm, accessed on September 25, 2010.

[20] "Chik Shampoo," CavinKare, www.cavinkare.com/chikshampoo.html?reload, accessed on September 25, 2010.

- Females aged 18 to 50, belonging to rural or semi-urban household basis income classification (annual household income of less than ₹75,000 or between ₹75,000 and ₹150,000);
- Category (shampoo) non-users or low frequency users, yet aware of the top three shampoo brands in the market;
- Significant television media consumption and enjoys watching advertisements.

The sampling unit was households, since the income parameter was used at the household level. The second level included individuals fitting the demographics and consumption characteristics above. With regard to sampling frame, the basis of selection of representative elements of the target population were taken as gender, age group, household income, category consumption and media consumption as detailed above.

The extent was rural Karnataka, a state in South India; specifically, two towns (Bidadi and Hoskote) which are part of the Bangalore Rural District and a cluster of adjoining villages (Jigani) were selected for the study. An external agency was used to gather data. The questionnaires formulated in English as well as the brand communication material were translated into the local language of the consumer (i.e. Kannada) while it was administered. The time factor was the period of the survey (i.e. September 2010).

The selection of the towns, which could be treated as the strata, was performed based on the judgment of rural household penetration and category awareness. Within these geographies, probability sampling was the chosen technique, in which simple random sampling was performed to select the elements. The individuals were tested through the filter questionnaire to ensure that they met the demographic and category criteria that was required for the study. Seventy-five respondents were chosen based on the above criteria.

Exhibits 4, 5 and 6 capture the storyboards of the three brands (Clinic Plus, Head & Shoulders and Chik) along with the author's description of the storyboards. Also captured are some print ads that the consumers were exposed to as part of the study.

Exhibit 7 contains the respondent profile. A summary of the respondents' background, lifestyle and aspirations, media consumption and FMCG habits is captured here based on the in-depth interviews mentioned in Exhibit 8. The Attitudes, Interests and Opinions section is captured in a quantitative Likert scale, with mean values summarized in Exhibit 8. Exhibit 9 is the shampoo category questionnaire, whereas Exhibits 10, 11 and 12 are the brand-specific questionnaires for Clinic Plus, Head & Shoulders and Chik respectively. The values on the statements in Exhibits 9 to 12 are mean values of the agreement levels with the statement coded from a Likert scale.

The authors would like to thank Professor Dinesh Kumar, Chairperson, Research and Publications, Indian Institute of Management, Bangalore for funding the field survey associated with the study.

Exhibit 1 Emerging India

Income per Year	Households in Millions
Less than ₹90,000	101.1 (Deprived)
₹90,000 - ₹200,000	91.3 (Aspirers)
₹200,000 - ₹500,000	10.8 (Seekers)
₹500,000 - ₹1,000,000	2.4 (Strivers)
More than ₹1,000,000	1.2 (Global Indians)

Source: "The Marketing Whitebook," Businessworld, 2007-2008, p. 33.

Exhibit 2 FMCG categories

Category	Products
Household care	Laundry soaps and detergents, floor cleaners, dish cleaners, mosquito repellents, etc.
Personal care	Oral care (toothpaste/toothpowder and toothbrushes), hair care (hair oil, shampoo), skin care (soaps), etc.
Food & beverages	Cereals, bakery products, tea, coffee, vegetables, dairy products.

Exhibit 3 Shampoo market benefit segments

Classification	Prominent Brands
Cosmetic (shine, strength, health, lustre, anti-breakage, etc.)	Sunsilk, Pantene, Clinic Plus, Chik
Anti-dandruff	Clinic All Clear, Head and Shoulders
Herbal	Vatika, Nyle, Meera

Exhibit 4 Clinic plus sample storyboards from TV advertisements

*Clinic Plus Ad Understanding Summary	
Central character	Young girl, typically between 8 to 14 years old, school-going.
Personality and attributes of central character	Strong-willed, go-getter, sporty and playful, outdoorsy, will match up to young boys of her age, cherishes her long hair but does not want to be inhibited by the same when it comes to being free.
Setting	Problem-solving approach
Influencer	Mother
Drama	The drama focuses around a situation in which the need for the young girl to get out and be free is inhibited by the dirt and grime that impacts her hair from being clean, healthy and strong. The mother steps in here as a protector and advisor who introduces Clinic Plus to her daughter and gives her back her freedom, while her shampoo takes care of keeping her hair nourished and strong.
Inferred consumer segment	Clinic Plus is aimed at the entire family in low-income households and targets them through the mother who is the decision-maker or key influencer in this category.
Inferred benefit statement	Clinic Plus helps you keep your family's hair healthy and strong and lets them be uninhibited to do what they want.

Storyboard 1: A mother and daughter enter the sports-master's room in school. The mother requests that her daughter be a part of the cricket team, to which the sports-master says that it is for the boys. The mother argues that her daughter is as good or better than the boys, to which he expresses concern over how she will handle all the exposure to dirt and grime that will follow her clothes and her lustrous long hair in the outdoors. The mother requests that he let her on the team and leave the rest for her to worry about. Cuts to scene advocating Clinic Plus and its benefit of keeping hair healthy and strong due to features such as milk protein, so that one need not worry about their hair and can be free in the outdoors. Cuts back to scene where daughter plays for the team and drives them to victory in front of a proud mother.

Storyboard 2: A young girl asks the boys in her playground if she can join them. She is taunted by them when one of them pulls off her hair band and she loses some hair in the same. She goes home to her mother who then consoles her and gives her Clinic Plus, which keeps her long hair lustrous and strong, and encourages her to go out and take on the boys in the field. The daughter does so and enjoys herself uninhibitedly.

Sample Print Advertisements of Clinic Plus

* Authors have used their perception to describe the storyboard of the respective brand.
Source: Advertisements reproduced with the permission of Mukesh Pawar, Senior Brand Manager, Clinic Plus, Hindustan Unilever Ltd., India.

Exhibit 5 Head & Shoulders sample storyboards from TV advertisements

*Head & Shoulders Ad Understanding Summary	
Central character	Young male or female, typically between 18 to 25 years old, attractive and smart. Has used celebrity faces such as Kareena Kapoor and Saif Ali Khan.
Setting	The ads are clinical and pristine in their setting, which is augmented by use of foreign models, lab settings and experts such as dermatologists.
Influencer	Expert (dermatologist) or celebrity
Drama	The drama focuses around a dandruff-related problem like hair fall and explains how Head and Shoulders is superior in dandruff-fighting capability. It explains the problem of dandruff with cause and effect using graphics and explains scientific components in the product (e.g. VitaZinc). It is accompanied by the use of a superiority claim like "95 per cent hair fall reduction" or "9/10 dermatologists recommend H&S." Some ads include an angle of attractiveness to the opposite sex or the courage to get closer without worrying about dandruff showing in some television commercials.
Inferred consumer segment	Targeted at both male and female audiences, aged 18 to 44 and suffering from dandruff problems.
Inferred benefit statement	Head and Shoulders is the expert-recommended brand for dandruff-free healthy hair.

Storyboard 1: A young woman is shown examining distastefully the hair that comes off on her hairbrush when she combs. The celebrity star explains to her that one of the causes of hair fall is dandruff and that is why you need Head & Shoulders. A voiceover goes on to explain how H&S removes dandruff and allows oil to permeate, allowing hair to grow stronger and reduce breakage. It closes with a "95 per cent less hair fall" claim and an endorsement from an "American testing centre."

(*Continued*)

(*Continued*)

Storyboard 2: An expert in a white coat says that he will demonstrate how Head & Shoulders is more effective than ordinary anti-dandruff shampoos in dandruff removal. There is the use of a dandruff-testing strip and a side-by-side comparison of scalp washed with ordinary anti-dandruff shampoo and with Head & Shoulders, and it says that while ordinary shampoos takes three washes to remove dandruff, Head & Shoulders does it in one. It uses the strip to compare the residual dandruff and show the difference. It ends with a claim that Head & Shoulders is endorsed by experts.

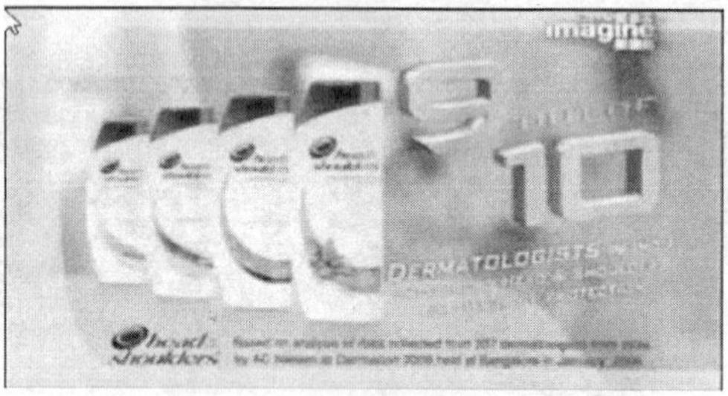

* Authors have used their perception to describe the storyboard of the respective brand.
Source: Advertisements reproduced with the permission of Anupam Chaudhury, Assistant Brand Manager, Head & Shoulders, Procter & Gamble, India.

Exhibit 6 Chik sample storyboards from TV advertisements

*Chik Ad Understanding Summary	
Central character	Young woman, typically between 18 to 25 years old.
Personality and attributes of central character	Beautiful, assured of herself, pays attention to her looks, feels comfortable letting her hair down, progressive and outgoing.
Setting	Problem-solving approach
Influencer	Mother
Drama	The drama focuses around a situation in which the woman is out in the open and her hair gets tangled due to a natural circumstance. However, owing to the double conditioners in Chik shampoo, she simply smoothes her hair out and it is back to looking perfectly detangled and healthy with shine. Furthermore, Chik also has variants in different fragrances, such as jasmine, that appeal strongly to markets like the South, and trade up variants, such as satin for existing Chik consumers, which have an even more modern feel to the ad and the central character.
Inferred consumer segment	Chik is aimed at women in the age range of 18-44 in semi-urban and rural areas.
Inferred benefit statement	Chik keeps your hair soft, nourished and beautiful all the time so you do not have to worry about tangles and can look and feel your confident best.

Storyboard 1: Two young women dressed for the occasion enter a wedding hall. As the table fan next to them blows their hair, one of the women is concerned and distressed about her hairstyle being impacted and not looking her best with her hair tangled. The other woman, a Chik consumer, waits to pass the fan and smoothes out her hair with her hand, only for it to be perfectly set and looking soft and healthy. The product attribute of double conditioners is explained to establish the benefit.

Storyboard 2: A young attractive woman heading to work is standing on a railway platform and there is a young man watching her from the other side. As a train passes by, it blows through her hair and disturbs it completely, making it unruly as the young man watches in consternation. The young woman seems unconcerned and simply smoothes her hair back into shape. This benefit is then explained with the active double conditioners in Chik shampoo.

*Authors have used their perception to describe the storyboard of the respective brand.
Source: Advertisements reproduced with the permission of C. K. Ranganathan, Managing Director, Cavinkare Pvt. Ltd., India.

Exhibit 7 Respondent profile

Respondent Background

The respondents were typically from families of four to five members in which the husband was predominantly the earning member of the household. The other members were usually one to two children or aged parents. Occupations of the main income provider included farming, sales jobs and working in a factory (manufacturing unit) on the job floor. The respondent was usually the wife, in the age group of 25-40, for the purpose of the depth interviews.

Identity, Aspirations and Dreams

Almost all of the respondents, when asked about themselves, described themselves with respect to the roles they play in the household and their relationships with each member of the family. Their identities were ingrained with their family.

These respondents belonged to the low-income households and a lot of their aspirations and dreams were on the lines of a better position in terms of wealth. However, equally important was to earn societal respect for their family, and their need to be seen as people-in-the-know among their friends and neighbours. They associated this with owning their own businesses or working for large corporations. They foresaw themselves as setting an example for others, and defining lifestyles for people of their kind. Some of these women aspired to work themselves and add to the household income, and they even had clear careers of their choice in mind. They saw the route to achieving their dreams as hard work, saving and compromising on current non-essential things in life.

Media Habits

TV Viewing: The respondents were unanimously regular TV viewers. Typical TV viewing occurred in mid-morning when the household chores were done, and in the night with the rest of the family. A significant proportion of the programs watched were entertainment-related, including serials, movies and cinema-related shows. However, there was some information-seeking related viewing, primarily of the categories of shows that were women-specific and gave advice and lifestyle tips (i.e. cooking programs and the regional news channels). Health was another category of active information gathering as these respondents watched programs that provided advice on taking care of themselves and their family's health and fitness.

(*Continued*)

(*Continued*)

Advertisement Involvement: Advertisements were watched and enjoyed by all these respondents with heightened levels of attention to certain categories, such as detergents, fairness creams and mobile phones. The reasons quoted for greater attention for certain categories of advertising was communication which addressed a current problem (e.g. detergents), use of celebrities (e.g. soap and fairness creams) and distinctiveness of communication (e.g. mobile phones and service providers).

Celebrity Influence: Celebrities were seen as adding trust to an ad or product; however, it was not necessarily a reason to buy. Some regional movie celebrities were looked up to as role models, and this was explained with awareness of their associations with some social causes.

Other Media: Radio was also a fairly popular media in two slots. The first was the early morning slot in which the program content was primarily devotional music. The second was morning to mid-morning, when the respondents said that cinema music would play on radio accompanying their household chores. Select radio show hosts were remembered by name and were liked for their styles and the kind of information they provided on their shows. Newspapers and magazines, however, were less popular forms of media. On occasion, coupons in newspapers were noticed and retained for promotional offers, and the classified section was an area of interest for jobs, depending on the life-cycle stage of the respondent; otherwise, it was a low-involvement media for women.

FMCG Buying Patterns

Categories and Purchase Behaviour: The monthly expenditure of these respondent households was primarily across the categories of groceries and cosmetics as the two broad heads. The food and beverages expenditure was around ₹2,000 to 2,500 per month, whereas the personal products and cosmetics would add up to ₹500. Purchase frequency was usually weekly. The standard place of purchase was the kirana stores close to home or sometimes ration shops.

Source of Awareness: The shopper in the household was typically the one with more time, and hence the wife. She also usually decided what brands were to be bought on most household categories, unless asked specifically for something by the family members. She got her knowledge of new brands from three key sources. The first and most common was TV advertisements. They also remembered some brands due to program sponsorships, wherein the brand name was tied to the program name. In-store was another source of awareness of new brands and products. The third was through friends, neighbours and relatives. Although in-store created more awareness of brand, it was word of mouth that generated more trial.

***New Brand Trials*:** Some of the most recent trials of new brands were initiated through word of mouth; for example, sensitive toothpaste because of a similar oral care problem affecting a relative. Products like hair oils (which were perceived as low risk) were tried out in small-sized bottles after having seen them on TV. Mobile phone was another category in which a new brand was tried; however, this was after TV awareness and retailer guidance. The retailer was usually asked for advice on medical products or new cosmetics regarding side effects of usage, but most other categories were not enquired about at the kirana.

Source: Based on actual respondents in field who were interviewed. Criteria for selection was provided by the authors.

Exhibit 8 Respondent interview questionnaire

Introduction

We'd like to know more about you. Could you please tell us the following details about yourself?

- Name
- Age
- How many members in the family and what do they do
- Occupation of main income earner
- Occupation of respondent (if different from above)
- Please tell us more about your daily routine. What is a typical weekday like? What is a typical weekend like?

Aspirations and Ambitions

- If you had to tell someone who doesn't know you about yourself, how would you describe yourself?
- What are your aspirations and dreams?
- If you were given a chance to look into the future, what do you see yourself as?
- What do you want to achieve? Why is that important? How different is that from the state you are in now?
- What do you think you need to do to achieve your dreams?

Media Habits and Attitudes

- Do you watch TV regularly? How often do you watch TV and when in the day do you watch?
- What do you watch on TV and why?
- What information do you seek from TV?
- Do you consider any TV celebrities as role models?
- Do you like watching advertisements? Can you tell us any advertisement you liked recently? Why did you like it?
- Do you listen to the radio? When in the day and how often do you listen to radio?
- What programs do you listen to and why?
- Do you read any newspaper or magazine regularly? Which ones? When in the day do you read?
- What kind of information do you seek from a newspaper/magazine?
- What sections of the newspaper/magazine do you read? Which is your favorite section in the newspaper? What do you like about it?
- Do you recall any advertisements in the newspaper/magazine? Do you spend time reading advertisements?

FMCG Buying Patterns

- What products do you buy for your household? How often do you buy them?
- Where do you buy these products?
- How much of your monthly expenditure is spent on food and beverages like rice, dal, milk, tea, coffee, etc., and how much is spent on personal care products like soap, detergent, toothpaste, shampoo, etc.?
- Who goes to buy these products?
- Who decides what brands to buy?
- Where do you learn about different brands?
- When did you last buy a new product or new brand? Why did you decide to try the new brand?
- Have you tried something new after seeing it on TV?
- Have you tried something new because you heard from a friend or relative?
- Have you asked the retailer's advice on what to buy?

Attitudes, Interests and Opinions

For each of the statements below, express your agreement or disagreement by marking the appropriate box on the side.

Statement	Mean Value
I enjoy watching TV	**4.5**
I enjoy spending time talking to my friends and neighbours	**4.2**
I do the shopping for my family's daily needs	**4.2**
I spend time every day on taking care of my hair and skin	**3.1**
I try out new products when I see them advertised on TV	**3.2**
I am interested in new products that come in the market	**3.0**
I always try new products in small quantities first	**3.8**

(*Continued*)

(Continued)

Statement	Mean Value
I always try to find out more information on beauty tips	**2.3**
I always look out for offers or promotions while shopping	**3.8**
I ask my retailer for his opinion when I am trying something new	**3.4**
I don't mind paying a little extra for branded goods	**3.4**
I ask my friends and neighbours before buying something new	**4.0**
I am the decision-maker for household products for the family	**3.7**
I believe it is important to be well-groomed all the time	**4.0**
If celebrities are endorsing a product, then it must be good	**4.0**

Mean Value Explanation:
The above set of statements were measured on a Likert scale for each respondent ranging from Strongly Agree to Strongly Disagree, and the values were coded as Strongly Agree–5, Agree–4, Neither Agree nor Disagree–3, Disagree–2, Strongly Disagree–1. The mean values are the average of the same across all respondents.

Source: Questions were created by the authors. Results are based on actual field interviews.

Exhibit 9 Shampoo Category Questionnaire

1. How often do you wash your hair?
   - Once in 2 weeks—**7 per cent**
   - Once a week—**48 per cent**
   - Twice a week—**43 per cent**
   - Thrice a week—**3 per cent**
   - Daily—**0 per cent**
2. What do you use to wash your hair? (can be a combination of more than one product)
   - Soap—**37 per cent**
   - Shampoo—**24 per cent**
   - Shikakai—**67 per cent**
   - Others **(please specify)**
3. Where did you learn about shampoos?
   - TV—96 per cent
   - Radio—**4 per cent**
   - Newspapers or magazines—**4 per cent**
   - Friends or relatives—**32 per cent**
   - Store—**31 per cent**
   - Others **(please specify)**
4. Please name some of the shampoo brand names you have heard of ____________

Top Unaided Awareness Brands

	Unaided Awareness (in per cent)
Clinic Plus	93
Chik	76
Head & Shoulders	53
Sunsilk	37
Clinic All Clear	20

5. How often do you use shampoo to wash your hair?
   - Every time—0 per cent
   - Mostly use other products, occasionally use shampoo—**71 per cent**

- Have used shampoo once or twice—**16 per cent**
- Never—**12 per cent**

6. What brands of shampoo have you used?

- Clinic Plus—**61 per cent**
- Chik—**49 per cent**
- Pantene—**1 per cent**
- Meera—**2 per cent**
- Nyle—**0 per cent**
- Vatika—**0 per cent**
- Any other **(please specify)** ________
- Head and Shoulders—**35 per cent**
- Sunsilk—**5 per cent**
- Rejoice—**0 per cent**
- Clinic All Clear—**5 per cent**
- Ayur—**0 per cent**
- Dove—**0 per cent**

7. Have you seen advertisements of any of the below brands?

- Clinic Plus—**75 per cent**
- Chik—**59 per cent**
- Pantene—**5 per cent**
- Meera—**1 per cent**
- Nyle—**0 per cent**
- Vatika—**0 per cent**
- Any other **(please specify)**
- Head and Shoulders—**47 per cent**
- Sunsilk—**12 per cent**
- Rejoice—**0 per cent**
- Clinic All Clear—**10 per cent**
- Ayur—**0 per cent**
- Dove—**0 per cent**

If so, please describe in brief for any 2 brands remembered
Brand 1 – <brand name> <description> ________
Brand 2 – <brand name> <description>________

8. What pack type of shampoo have you used?

- Bottle—**1 per cent**
- Sachet—**99 per cent**

9. How did you choose the brand of shampoo?

- Saw on TV and liked—**51 per cent**
- Saw in store and liked—**4 per cent**
- Recommended by friend/neighbour—**37 per cent**
- Recommended by retailer—**8 per cent**

For each of the statements, express your agreement or disagreement by marking the appropriate box on the side

Statement	Mean Value
Shampoos are not good for my hair since they have chemicals	3.2
Shampoo can be used for occasional wash but not for daily wash	3.2
I try out a shampoo that my friend or relative has recommended	3.7
Shampoo cleans my hair better than soap	3.9
Washing with shampoo makes my hair look beautiful	4.1
I feel more confident when I use shampoo	3.9
I use shampoo only when I have to wash oil from my hair	4.0
Shampoo is very expensive	2.5
Shampoo is a luxury that I use only for special occasions	2.6
I always buy shampoo in sachets only	4.1
Shampoo makes my hair strong and healthy	4.0

(Continued)

(*Continued*)

Mean Value Explanation:
The above set of statements were measured on a Likert scale for each respondent ranging from Strongly Agree to Strongly Disagree, and the values were coded as Strongly Agree–5, Agree–4, Neither Agree nor Disagree–3, Disagree–2, Strongly Disagree–1. The mean values are the average of the same across all respondents.

Source: Questions were created by the authors. Results are based on actual field interviews.

Exhibit 10 Clinic plus shampoo questionnaire

For each of the statements, express your agreement or disagreement for the statement with respect to Clinic Plus Shampoo by marking the appropriate box on the side.

Statement	Mean Value
It has a lot of chemicals in it	3.1
It prevents my hair from getting dandruff	3.8
It makes my hair smell fresh	3.9
It keeps my hair healthy and strong	4.0
It has a great fragrance	3.9
It is not different from any other shampoo	3.2
It is an expensive shampoo	2.3
It is recommended by hair experts	3.2
It is for people with long hair	2.4
It keeps hair untangled and smooth	3.3
It is used by celebrities	3.2
It is a brand for my family	3.6
It is a shampoo I can trust for my hair	3.7
It makes me look beautiful	4.1
It makes me feel confident	3.4
It is a brand for those who are in the outdoors	2.6
It allows me to feel free and unworried	3.4
It is a brand for the youngsters	2.6
It is a shampoo for special occasions	2.5
It reminds me of my childhood	2.7
It makes me feel in control	3.4
The person in this advertisement reminds me of myself	3.5
It will make me refreshed and revived	3.5
It will make me feel like everyone's eyes are on me	3.4
It makes me feel taken care of by an expert	3.2
I will ask my friends or neighbours about this brand	3.9

Which of these statements best describes the chance that you will buy Clinic Plus Shampoo next time?–3.9

- I will definitely buy it
- I will probably buy it
- I am uncertain if I will buy it

- I will probably not buy it
- I will definitely not buy it

If the answer to above is "definitely buy" or "probably buy," then continue with below table, else move to next section.

Statement	Mean Value
I will search for this brand when I go shopping next time	4.5
I will buy shampoo only if I find this brand, else I will not buy	3.3
I will compare prices of different brands before I buy	3.3
I will buy the brand because I like its advertisement	3.9
I will buy the brand only if I like its packaging	3.4
I will buy the shampoo in sachet only	4.1
I will ask the retailer about it before buying	4.1
I will tell my friends and neighbours about my experience with the brand	4.1

Mean Value Explanation:

The above set of statements were measured on a Likert scale for each respondent ranging from Strongly Agree to Strongly Disagree, and the values were coded as Strongly Agree – 5, Agree – 4, Neither Agree nor Disagree – 3, Disagree – 2, Strongly Disagree – 1. The coding for the likelihood to buy assessment was similar with "definitely buy" being 5 and "definitely not buy" being 1. The mean values are the average of the same across all respondents.

Source: Questions were created by the authors. Results are based on actual field interviews.

Exhibit 11 Head & Shoulders shampoo questionnaire

For each of the statements, express your agreement or disagreement for the statement with respect to Head and Shoulders Shampoo by marking the appropriate box on the side.

Statement	Mean Value
It has a lot of chemicals in it	3.2
It prevents my hair from getting dandruff	3.9
It makes my hair smell fresh	3.9
It keeps my hair healthy and strong	3.8
It has a great fragrance	3.9
It is not different from any other shampoo	3.0
It is an expensive shampoo	2.5
It is recommended by hair experts	3.8
It is for people with long hair	2.5
It keeps hair untangled and smooth	3.1
It is used by celebrities	3.1
It is a brand for my family	2.6
It is a shampoo I can trust for my hair	3.1

(*Continued*)

(Continued)

Statement	Mean Value
It makes me look beautiful	3.2
It makes me feel confident	3.1
It is a brand for those who are in the outdoors	2.5
It allows me to feel free and unworried	3.0
It is a brand for the youngsters	2.4
It is a shampoo for special occasions	2.4
It reminds me of my childhood	2.4
It makes me feel in control	3.2
The person in this advertisement reminds me of myself	3.3
It will make me refreshed and revived	3.4
It will make me feel like everyone's eyes are on me	3.3
It makes me feel taken care of by an expert	3.8
I will ask my friends or neighbours about this brand	3.7

Which of these statements best describes the chance that you will buy Head and Shoulders Shampoo next time? –2.7

- I will definitely buy it
- I will probably buy it
- I am uncertain if I will buy it
- I will probably not buy it
- I will definitely not buy it

If the answer to above is "definitely buy" or "probably buy," then continue with below table, else move to next section.

Statement	Mean Value
I will search for this brand when I go shopping next time	4.2
I will buy shampoo only if I find this brand, else I will not buy	3.1
I will compare prices of different brands before I buy	3.9
I will buy the brand because I like its advertisement	3.9
I will buy the brand only if I like its packaging	3.8
I will buy the shampoo in sachet only	4.1
I will ask the retailer about it before buying	4.0
I will tell my friends and neighbours about my experience with the brand	4.0

Mean Value Explanation:

The above set of statements were measured on a Likert scale for each respondent ranging from Strongly Agree to Strongly Disagree, and the values were coded as Strongly Agree–5, Agree–4, Neither Agree nor Disagree–3, Disagree–2, Strongly Disagree–1. The coding for the likelihood to buy assessment was similar with "definitely buy" being 5 and "definitely not buy" being 1. The mean values are the average of the same across all respondents.

Source: Questions were created by the authors. Results are based on actual field interviews.

Exhibit 12 Chik shampoo questionnaire

For each of the statements, express your agreement or disagreement for the statement with respect to Chik Shampoo by marking the appropriate box on the side.

Statement	Mean Value
It has a lot of chemicals in it	3.1
It prevents my hair from getting dandruff	3.3
It makes my hair smell fresh	3.9
It keeps my hair healthy and strong	3.8
It has a great fragrance	3.8
It is not different from any other shampoo	3.2
It is an expensive shampoo	2.1
It is recommended by hair experts	3.5
It is for people with long hair	2.4
It keeps hair untangled and smooth	3.8
It is used by celebrities	3.0
It is a brand for my family	2.6
It is a shampoo I can trust for my hair	3.3
It makes me look beautiful	3.3
It makes me feel confident	3.2
It is a brand for those who are in the outdoors	2.9
It allows me to feel free and unworried	3.2
It is a brand for the youngsters	2.2
It is a shampoo for special occasions	2.6
It reminds me of my childhood	2.2
It makes me feel in control	3.3
The person in this advertisement reminds me of myself	3.3
It will make me refreshed and revived	3.4
It will make me feel like everyone's eyes are on me	3.2
It makes me feel taken care of by an expert	3.4
I will ask my friends or neighbours about this brand	3.8

Which of these statements best describes the chance that you will buy CHIK SHAMPOO next time?–3.0

- I will definitely buy it
- I will probably buy it
- I am uncertain if I will buy it
- I will probably not buy it
- I will definitely not buy it

If the answer to above is "definitely buy" or "probably buy," then continue with below table, else move to next section.

Statement	Mean Value
I will search for this brand when I go shopping next time	4.5
I will buy shampoo only if I find this brand, else I will not buy	3.3
I will compare prices of different brands before I buy	3.9
I will buy the brand because I like its advertisement	3.7
I will buy the brand only if I like its packaging	3.4
I will buy the shampoo in sachet only	4.4
I will ask the retailer about it before buying	4.2
I will tell my friends and neighbours about my experience with the brand	4.2

Mean Value Explanation:

The above set of statements were measured on a Likert scale for each respondent ranging from Strongly Agree to Strongly Disagree, and the values were coded as Strongly Agree–5, Agree–4, Neither Agree nor Disagree–3, Disagree–2, Strongly Disagree–1. The coding for the likelihood to buy assessment was similar with "definitely buy" being 5 and "definitely not buy" being 1. The mean values are the average of the same across all respondents.

Source: Questions were created by the authors. Results are based on actual field interviews.

7

Tinplate Company of India

Need for a Conceptual Focus

THE COMPANY

The Tinplate Company of India Ltd. (TCIL) was established in 1922, in Jamshedpur, India, in order to manufacture tinplate to meet the demand for 15-litre tin cans for packing kerosene. The company was jointly held by three companies making tinplate cans: Burmah Shell, Shaw Wallace and Tata Steel. In 1981, two years after the commissioning of the new electrolytic tinning line, Tata Iron and Steel Company stepped in, actively acquiring a 34 per cent sharehold. TCIL increased its involvement in the packaging industry by adding a facility to manufacture tinplate with thicknesses that could range from 0.17 millimetres to 0.30 millimetres. The company started addressing the requirements of the metal packaging industry, which required imported tinplate for the production of cans for baby food, processed food and tinplate for battery jackets.

The raw material for manufacturing tinplate, Tin Mill Black Plate (TMBP), continued to be entirely imported. TCIL faced inherent disadvantages: they were continuing to import TMBP, while all major steel mills worldwide were making both their own TMBP and their own tinplate. In 1997, TCIL established a new cold rolling facility. Combined with the supply of hot rolled coils from Tata Iron and Steel Company (TISC) (a sister concern), TCIL was now in a position to receive an uninterrupted supply of raw material to meet the tinplate product demands. TCIL supplied tinplate to manufacturers in four major product segments: edible oil cans, soft drink crowns, processed food and batteries. While the first three manufacturers were food related, they were viewed as distinct segments, due to the buying behavior of their end users, brand equity related to their end products and the nature of competition in the food market.

THE PRODUCT, MARKET AND COMPETITION

Tinplate is a low-carbon steel, coated with tin and used primarily for packaging. It was a versatile alternative material suitable for any food or non-food product requiring packaging. Despite being a preferred alternative, tinplate had to contend with competition from other materials such as plastic, PET (polyethylene terephthalate), aluminum, blackplate, Tetra Pak and paper.

Classification of Tinplate

Prime grade tinplate, characterized by being "free from any visual defects," found an application in food packaging, where the customer had high-speed can-making equipment. Secondary grade tinplate, on the other hand, was banned for food packaging in a number of countries, as it could cause food to become carcinogenic. This lesser grade tinplate was used for packaging non-food products, such as paints and lubricants, but was unsuitable for battery jackets, which demanded a high degree of adherence to specifications.

The import duty structure for tinplate gave credence to the view of liberalization. The downward revision of customs duty resulted in foreign companies entering the tinplate market. A review of the content of the imports (see Exhibit 1(a)) revealed that a large portion of the product being imported under the low customs tariff were secondaries, which were not prescribed for food packaging. The differential duty structure, which mandated a higher duty for secondaries, was withdrawn in 1994 to 1995. This coincided with an increase in imported secondaries, a large portion of which were used for food packaging in India.

Applications of Tinplate

The tinplate used to manufacture cans for edible oils was procured by the edible oil manufacturers themselves. The manufacturers sold the packed cans to distributors, to reach the consumer through retailers (see Figure 1). A distinguishing feature of the edible oil market was the buying behavior of consumers. They bought in loose quantities that were not standardized by size and were not branded. A major portion of the market was considered "loose" and was highly price sensitive. The reduction of customs duty for imported tinplate (see Exhibit 1(a)), changing environmental trends and the lack of monitoring mechanisms (see Exhibit 2) led to the import and use of non-food grade tinplate (secondaries) in the edible oil industry. A number of unorganized and small companies (not registered with government authorities) tended to use the prohibited imported tinplate. As a result, those who marketed loose edible oil products were in a position to compete in a price-sensitive environment. Consumers were unaware of the negative consequences of the sub-standard material being used in

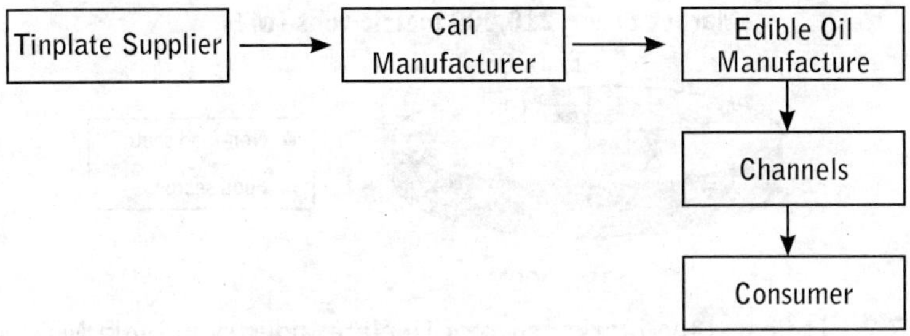

Figure 7.1 Supply Chain Participants

the packaging of the edible oil products they purchased. This lack of knowledge can be attributed to India's low literacy levels.

Edible Oil Vis-a-Vis Other Segments

Coca-Cola and Pepsi were the two brands that dominated the Indian soft drink industry. These multinationals demanded a high standard to product parameters (see Exhibit 3) and even sample tested the crowns in Japan and Atlanta, Georgia. Due to such stringent focus on specifications, the companies that catered to Coca-Cola and Pepsi purchased their requirements from foreign companies, such as Fritz, Sukai and TMN (see Exhibit 3), forcing a number of the Coca-Cola and Pepsi competitors to fold in the past decade.

Battery manufacturers bought about 90 per cent of their tinplate from foreign companies (see Exhibit 5), as even a minor flaw in the tinplate quality (which could cause difficulties in printing the battery label, and thus affect the brand image) could lead to rejection of their product.

The processed food industry used tinplate for packaging foods such as fruit pulp and juices, mushrooms, meats, coffee and cashews. The food market included well-known companies such as Nestle and Brooke Bond. Traditionally, these brands have had a business relationship with the Tinplate Company of India, buying 22 per cent of their cans from this supplier (see Exhibit 5).

The edible oil industry differed from the other industries in the willingness of their can manufacturers to waive the specification required for products made from tinplate. In other sectors, manufacturers were not in a position to waive specifications, due to the brand equity built up over a period of time and manufacturing complexities.

Competition to Tinplate Company of India in the edible oil segment was largely from the unorganized companies. In other segments, competition came from foreign companies (see Exhibit 5). SAIL was a company that made significant inroads into the edible oil segment by positioning itself as a company that was better than the unorganized sector (see Exhibits 3 and 6(a)). Tinplate Company of India and SAIL catered to organizations in the edible oil segment that were more sensitive to specific product parameters, rather than just price. Even these customers may not have exhibit loyalty because of the price-sensitive nature of end users of edible oil.

In other segments, namely battery, crown and processed foods, foreign companies owned the majority of the market. Despite buying centres influences belief that Tinplate Company of India had the capabilities to cater to the technical requirements of their customers, the company was not capable of responding to the changing and sensitive needs of customers. (Market demands for more fizz in soft drinks could require a change in the tinplate specifications or tinplate with new specifications might be required to accommodate a new line of equipment in the battery industry.) Tinplate Company of India was caught between the highly price-sensitive lower-end customers and the high-service expectations of the high-end customers. These high-end customers also seemed to have a more

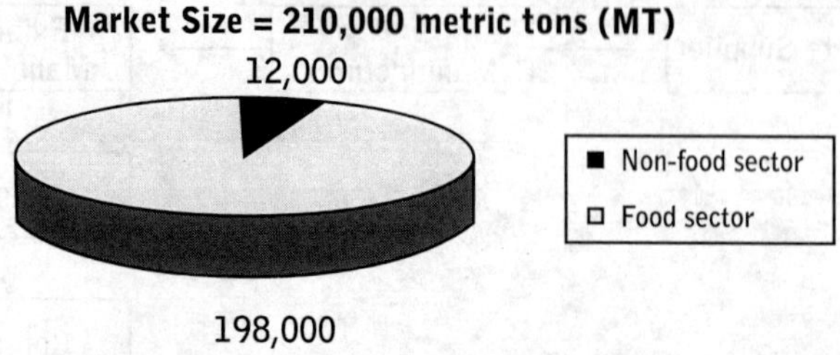

Figure 7.2 Indicates the Market Size of Tinplate Industry in India MT= Metric Tons. Food Sector Includes Edible Oil/Vanaspati, Processed Food and Soft-drink Crowns

favorable perception of foreign companies, as reflected in the market shares of companies in different segments (see Exhibit 5).

The high profitability of Tinplate Company of India in the battery segment was, to a certain extent, dampened by the high cost of credit in this segment (see Exhibit 6(a)). This was understandable, as the company seemed to be making an effort to gain market share in this segment, and credit may have been one of the factors required to make these inroads. Fritz, Sukai and TMN were able to charge higher prices, due to the high-quality perception they were able to cultivate in the battery segment, as well as in the processed food and crown segments (see Exhibit 6).

Distribution and Promotion

TCIL had a factory in Jamshedpur, India, and distributed its products through a network of 15 agents throughout the country. These agents conducted business with the producers of edible oil cans. A sales team of 20 personnel interacted with customers in other segments. There were four producers of batteries, four crown manufacturers and about 15 customers in the processed food industry. The sales personnel also interacted with the agents and customers in the edible oil segment. SAIL had its major share of the edible oil market in the southern region and distributed directly to consumers (see Exhibit 5). Fritz and Sukai had Indian agents to book orders, which had not penetrated the edible oil segment (see Exhibit 5). Unorganized companies marketed to local edible oil manufacturers who sold in loose quantities. Personal selling was the dominant promotion method used by all companies in all segments.

The Dominance of the Food Sector

The Tinplate market was about 210,000 metric tons per annum, of which the food sector, including edible oil, processed foods and crowns, consumed about 94 per cent of tinplate for packaging see (Figure 3). The edible oil industry was the single largest driver of tinplate demand in the country, consuming almost 148,000 metric tons or about 70 per cent of total tinplate demand (see Figure 3).

The domestic industry comprised of only two suppliers, with a combined installed capacity of 240,000 metric tons per annum, sufficient to meet the domestic demand. TCIL produced about 60,000 metric tons of tinplate per annum, and SAIL produced about 20,000 metric tons per annum. Both producers operated much below their installed capacity, mainly because of the quantity of sub-standard secondaries imported and used in the edible oil segment (see Exhibit 1(b)). SAIL marketed tinplate to the edible oil segment (see Exhibit 5) and priced its products just above the prices offered by the unorganized sector (see Exhibit 6(b)). SAIL, therefore, did not compete directly with TCIL in any segment. The middlemen supplying to the end customers in a price-sensitive market, wielded a powerful influence in deciding on the company from which they would source their tinplate.

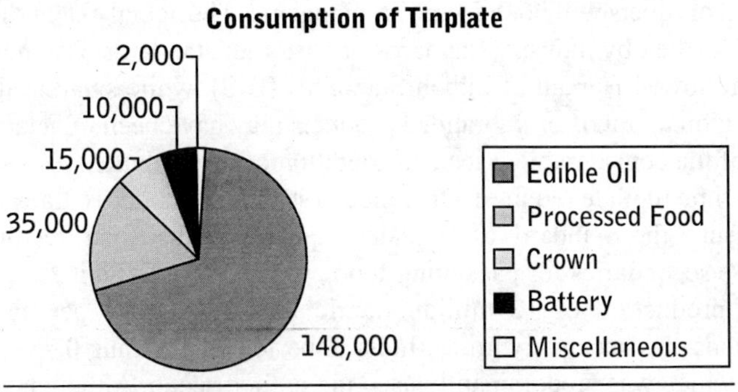

Figure 7.3 Tinplate Used in Packaging Food Product (in Metric Tons). This Figure Also Includes the Soft-drink Crown Segment Though It Has Been Categorized as Distinctive Segment

The Buying Influence

Typically, a tinplate manufacturer supplied tinplate to a can fabricator, who in turn supplied the product to the manufacturer of packaged goods that reached end consumers (see Figure 1). Major influences in the buying process differed for the various segments (see Exhibit 7). The varied buying influences reflected different factors at work in different segments. In the edible oil segment, for example, the middlemen (distributors or retailers) exerted a major influence on the price of edible oil, therefore the marketing personnel of the edible oil manufacturing unit exerted pressure on the tinplate manufacturer through the can manufacturer. In other segments, however, the research and development department, packaging department or quality control department (depending on the product) exerted pressure on the tinplate manufacturer, with a focus on specifications and speed of flexibility to deliver the specifications when needed.

IMPORTANCE OF CUSTOMER SATISFACTION

Customer satisfaction of tinplate from different manufacturers across different segments reflected the customer perception of specific product parameters (see Exhibit 3). Although TCIL scored well on most parameters in the edible oil segment, customers may have preferred alternate suppliers if their prices are lower. Customers may even waive the prerequisites on specific parameters in favor of a lower price with a competitor.

Vigorous competition in the edible oil segment may have resulted in a kind of price war, as SAIL and the unorganized sector were able to offer their products at lower rates in a price-conscious market. Even with customers who are not price conscious, SAIL was likely to gain ground in the edible oil segment by charging a lower selling price (see Exhibits 3 and 6(b)). In other segments, customer satisfaction was important. Compared to TCIL, foreign companies had a major portion of the market, mainly due to higher customer satisfaction on product parameters.

STANDARDS REQUIRED FOR THE FOOD SECTOR

Standards required in the food sector, ethically and legally, made it mandatory to use prime tinplate. Packaging materials used in the food sector should have specifications to ensure that they are free from defects and that food products will not become carcinogenic. The actual extent of standards, however, was determined more often by industry standards or customer standards. Can manufacturers catering to national brands followed Bureau of Indian Standards (BIS), while small scale units supplying to manufacturers of regional brands or unbranded products may have been reluctant to produce to these standards because of the considerable price consideration of these markets.

Manufacturing prime tinplate required adherence to stringent standards. Lack of proper monitoring mechanisms to ensure the standard of tinplate required in the food sector, encouraged some manufacturers to use secondaries for packaging food products (see Exhibit 2).

Of total global production of 12 million metric tons of tinplate per annum, approximately 1.8 million metric tons was secondary grade. India imported an alarming 0.75 million metric tons of secondary tinplate, which was predominantly used in the food sector. Although alternative packaging (in the form of PET and plastic containers) was entering into the edible oil sector and food processing industry, there are not addressed as reliable data was not available. In the other sectors, threat from alternative packaging was almost non-existent.

AT ISSUE

It was time for TCIL to make some strategic decisions. Should it continue in the edible oil segment? How can TCIL compete with foreign companies? What strategies can TCIL formulate based on organizational buying behavior concepts?

Exhibit 1(a) Customs duty structure on Tinplate imports 1992 to 1993 and 1997 to 1998

Year	Tinplate Prime	Tinplate Secondaries
1992-93	85%	110%
1993-94	75%	85%
1994-95	50%	50%
1995-96	40%	40%
1996-97	32%	32%

Exhibit 1(b) Tinplate prime primary and secondary tinplate imports, 1992 to 1993 and 1998 to 1999 (MT = in metric tons)

Financial Year	Tinplate Prime	Tinplate Secondaries	Total
1992-93	31,543	71,110	102,653
1993-94	35,953	74,300	110,253
1994-95	38,712	76,065	114,777
1995-96	40,654	79,751	120,405
1996-97	41,189	81,432	122,621
1997-98	43,976	84,323	128,299
1998-99	44,496	86,756	131,252

Exhibit 2 Threats, opportunities and its implications in the tinplate industry

Threats	**Implications?**
Lowering of customs tariff	Global tinplate manufacturers compete aggressively
Household units becoming smaller	Demand for smaller packaging with increased buying frequency (tinplate manufacturers rely heavily on bulk container units)
Regulating standards lacking enforcement	Widespread use of defective tinplate
Opportunity Trends	
Growth in the hotel industry	Sustained demand for bulk packs
Political climate showing signs of continuity in policies towards industries	Survival of strongly focused, customer-oriented companies
High industrial growth (9%)	Increased demand for branded/packed products, the driving force would continue to remain buoyant

Exhibit 3 Customer satisfaction on the product (tinplate) across segments (competitors of TCIL have been named for each segment)

	Product Parameter	**TCIL**	**FRITZ**	**SUKAI**
Battery	Temper	2	5	4
	Size	2	5	5
	Dimension (Tolerance)	2	5	5
	Productivity	3	5	4
	Service (Pre & Post)	3	4	3
	Price	5	4	4
	Delivery	3	5	5
		TCIL	**SAIL**	**Unorganised Supplier**
Edible Oil	Price	3	4	5
	Brightness	5	4	2
	Delivery	5	3	2
	Service (Pre & Post)	5	3	2
		TCIL	**FRITZ**	**SUKAI**
Soft Drink Crowns	Size	2	5	5
	Dimensional Tolerance	2	5	5
	Price	3	5	5
	Delivery	5	4	4
	Temper	3	5	5

(Continued)

(*Continued*)

	Product Parameter	TCIL	FRITZ	SUKAI
Processed Food (In order of customer rating)	Delivery	5	4	4
	Lacquer adhesion	4	5	4
	Temper	3	5	4
	Price	5	4	4
	Dimensional tolerance	3	5	4

*The higher the rating, the better.

Note: "Unorganized" sector is ranked between 0-2 on all parameters except price by customers in this sector in the processed food segment. Price is ranked as 4.

Exhibits 3 to 8 give inference on customer satisfaction on TCIL's and competitors' products, growth rate of tinplate industry, break-up of segments with regard to sales volumes of companies, profits and buying influences involved in various segments.

Source: TCIL – sponsored survey.

Exhibit 4 Growth of Tinplate in specific segments 1993 to 1997 (in percentage)

	(1993–1997)				
	1993	1994	1995	1996	1997
Battery	5	8	10	15	20
Edible Oil	7	7	6	6	5
Crown	9	10	12	12	15
Processed Food	8	7	8	9	10

Source: Internal records of TCIL.

Exhibit 5 Market share of companies across segments by volume (as percentage of the total market)

	TCIL	FRITZ	SUKAI	TMN	Unorganized Supplier	SAIL
Battery	10	45	45	—		
Edible Oil	28	—	—	—	54	18
Crown	10	45	45	—	—	—
Processed Food	22	—	—	78	—	—

Source: Internal records of TCIL.

Exhibit 6(a) TCIL's costs by segment

	Segment 1 Battery (₹ per MT)	Segment 2 Edible Oil (₹ per MT)	Segment 3 Crown (₹ per MT)	Segment 4 Processed Food (₹ per MT)
Manufacturing Cost	27,000	22,000	25,000	26,000
Selling Cost	800	200	700	600

Distribution Cost	250	250	250	250
Cost of credit	1,400	450	1,000	1,350
Profit	6,000	3,000	3,000	5,500

Source: Internal records of TCIL.

Exhibit 6(b) Selling prices of TCIL and competitors (in Indian ₹ per metric ton)

Segment	TCIL	SAIL	FRITZ	SUKAI	TMN
Crowns	29,950	—	35,560	34,990	—
Battery	35,450	—	44,500	46,000	—
Processed foods	33,700	24,000	40,100	41,300	43,000
Edible oil	25,850	20,000	—	—	

Current rate US$1 is approximately equivalent to ₹36.
The "unorganized" sector in the edible oil/vanaspati segment quotes a selling price in the range of ₹13,000 to ₹17,000 per MT; in the processed food segment the "unorganized sector" quotes a selling price in the range of ₹16,000 to ₹19,000.
Source: Internal records of TCIL.

Exhibit 7 Buying influences in Tinplate purchases (buying center influences)

	Buying Centre Influences			
	Purchaser	**Decision-maker**	**Influences**	**User**
Battery	Purchaser	CEO	Production/ Marketing/ R&D	Production/ Quality Control
Edible Oil	Purchaser/owner of the edible oil/vanaspati company	CEO/owner of the edible oil/vanaspati company	Middleman/ Marketing	Production/Quality Control
Crown	Purchaser	CEO	Production/ Marketing/Quality Control	Production/Quality Control
Processed Food	Purchaser/owner of the company	CEO/owner of the company	Marketing/ Packaging division/ Production/ Quality Control	Production/ Quality Control/ Packaging division

Source: Internal records of TCIL.

8

Shoppers Stop

Targeting the Young

R. Chandrasekhar wrote this case under the supervision of Professor Shanker Krishnan solely to provide material for class discussion. The authors do not intend to illustrate either effective or ineffective handling of a managerial situation. The authors may have disguised certain names and other identifying information to protect confidentiality.

In June 2006, Govind Shrikhande, chief executive officer (CEO) of Shoppers Stop, India's biggest chain of large-format department stores (in terms of retail space), was reviewing the Brand Navigator study that had landed on his desk. This study was conducted periodically to measure customer perceptions of the Shoppers Stop brand compared with its closest competitors. According to the 2006 study, Shoppers Stop was perceived as a "caring" brand. This perception seemed to harmonize with the characteristics of its core customer group, adults aged 25 to 45. But the study also showed disengagement with younger customers. The lack of connection was evident in how customers perceived the three competitors' brands: Lifestyle, Pantaloon and Central, which were described as "fashionable," "trendy," "flashy," "modern," "sporty" and "lively" (see Exhibit 1).

Shrikhande had been appointed CEO two months earlier, after having joined Shoppers Stop in April 2001 as director of Buying and Merchandising. Previously, he had worked at Bombay Dyeing & Manufacturing Co. Ltd., a branded apparel maker and a Shoppers Stop vendor. Since Shoppers Stop's inception 15 years earlier, the company had sustained its focus on the department store format. The retailer had also built up a loyal customer base, which had become a source of competitive advantage over its peers.

Shrikhande needed to establish a fit between the company's strategic goals and the necessity to connect with younger consumers. The company's major competitors were all weighing their options for pursuing the youth market although none had yet formulated any specific, long-term plans. Shrikhande had to ensure that any attempt on the part of Shoppers Stop to connect with younger consumers would neither detract from the Shoppers Stop's business focus, dilute its brand identity nor alienate existing customers.

INDIAN RETAILING

The Indian retail market was valued at INR12,781 billion[1] (see Exhibit 2). With approximately 12 million retail outlets spread across the country, India was home to the world's highest number of retail outlets per capita. The fragmented nature of the Indian retail industry was evident in Pantaloon, an apparel retailer that opened in 1993. Pantaloon, despite having sales of INR35.63 billion (US$ 0.87 billion) in 2006, the highest revenue among retailers on India's stock exchange, had a national market share of only 0.3 per cent. More than 85 per cent of India's retail outlets were so-called mom-and-pop establishments.

In 2006, India's share of organized retail—characterized by customer requirements being met by trained staff in an ambience of comfort, style and speed[2]—was INR530 billion. At 4.1 per cent of total retail, the percentage of organized retail contrasted sharply with not only the United States (at 80 per cent) but also with neighboring markets, such as China (at 20 per cent), Indonesia (at 30 per cent), Thailand (at 40 per cent), Malaysia (at 55 per cent) and Taiwan (at 81 per cent).[3] India's share of organized retail was expected to grow to 10 per cent by 2010 and 20 per cent by 2020. The imminent rise was mainly because India was in the middle of a retail revolution that had no parallel in economic history.

Elsewhere in the world, the development of a country's retail industry was usually spread over 30 to 40 years, with customers savoring each experience methodically, as it was introduced. Thus, consumers first became accustomed to convenience stores, which were followed by department stores and shopping centers, then large shopping malls. Big-box retailers, hypermarkets, discounters and specialty stores followed at their own pace. In India, however, all retail development was coming together at the same time. All retail formats, which were commonplace in the developed markets of Europe and North America, were appearing simultaneously in India. The retail phenomenon, already evident in Tier 1 and Tier 2 cities, which comprised the major and mainstream cities of India, was percolating progressively into Tier 3 and Tier 4 towns (see Exhibit 3) and further into India's vast rural areas. Simultaneously, consumers themselves were undergoing a change in profile, which was as sudden and dramatic as the changes in external environment. Indian consumers were becoming rich, youthful and aspirational, all at the same time. They now also had an unprecedented choice of product offerings.

---

[1] US$1 was equivalent to INR44.95 in June 2006, http://www.economywatch.com/exchange-rate/rupee.html, accessed April 28, 2009.

[2] An interview by "Business Barons" magazine with Sundara Rajan, CEO, Market Search, http://www.market-search.com/news01.html, accessed April 28, 2009.

[3] The figures pertained to 2004/05. See "Retail — Market and Opportunities," Ernst & Young and India Brand Equity Foundation. www.ibef.org/download/Retail_220708.pdf.

At a more basic level, four factors were driving the retail revolution in India: changing demographics, an upward migration of income, easy availability of credit and government impetus.

Changing Demographics

India had the second-highest population of all countries in the world. Against the backdrop of an aging world, however, India had the advantage of a large young population. For example, 35 per cent of Indians were younger than 15 years of age, and 70 per cent were younger than 35 years of age (see Exhibit 4). Because young customers had a high propensity to consume, the lucrative consumer base had positioned India as a promising destination for global retailers.

Upward Migration of Income

Of India's 204 million households, 22.0 million households (amounting to 10.8 per cent) were defined as "rich" because they had annual incomes greater than INR180,000. Just below the rich households was a population of 50 million households that formed the consuming class who earned between INR90,000 and INR180,000.This middle-income class, known as the real consumers, currently comprised 24.5 per cent of the total households, but was expected to increase to 32 per cent of the total households by 2010 (see Exhibit 5). This large and growing consumer class was also witnessing a shift in attitude from saving money to spending money. As a result, a consumption boom was in the offing in India, fueling the growth of Indian retail for the next few decades.

Easy Credit

Indian consumers had been under-leveraged for decades, having financed all their purchases through cash payments. During the mid-1990s, leading commercial banks, led by Citibank, started promoting credit cards. Going forward, with falling or stable interest rates, consumer credit was expected to grow, providing an impetus for both consumer spending and the growth of organized retail. Penetration of credit cards was low, at 18 to 20 cards per 1,000 consumers, which indicated a major opportunity for expansion.

Government Impetus

A major driver for retail revolution was the Indian government's decision in February 2006 to allow 51 per cent ownership by a foreign enterprise in a local retail venture of a "single" brand. Thus, "multi-brand" retailers, such as Wal-Mart, did not have an easy time establishing a direct presence in India. Global apparel brands, however, could now enter India and establish a local business with majority ownership.

From the perspective of global retailers seeking new markets, retail businesses in India fell into three categories: Ready-to-Go, Shape/Adapt and Wait-and-Watch (see Exhibit 6). The first category, Ready-to-Go, consisted of several sub-categories in which determined retailers could quickly build their positions. New entrants did not need to make a major investment. Ease of sourcing, proliferation of brands and consumer acceptance in this category had reached levels that permitted, from day one, the exploitation of both economies of scale and economies of scope. The second category, Shape/Adapt, required investments both in back-end operations, such as building the supply chain, and in front-end operations, such as developing the sales force. The third category, Wait-and-Watch, consisted of underdeveloped businesses that provided no immediate opportunities for market development. The businesses were largely regulated by federal and provincial governments, making market entry difficult for a foreign company.

DEMOGRAPHIC DIVIDEND

The population of India was forecast to stay young for the next two decades (see Exhibit 7). The country was on the cusp of what economists referred to as "a demographic dividend." This rare social phenomenon led to opportunities for economic growth because of a confluence of factors, such as a decline in the birth rate, an increase in the number of working adults and a decrease in the dependent population. Demographic dividend would provide India with a competitive advantage over not only the developed countries of the world but also emerging economies in Brazil, Russia and China. Experts widely acknowledged that the Indian economy could achieve consistent growth of approximately 9 per cent each year for the next two decades.

The concept was explained by economist Kaushik Basu:

> Consider that in the year 2004, India had a population of 1,080 million, of whom 672 million people were in the age-group 15 to 64 years. This is usually treated as the "working age population." Since outside of this age group very few people work, it is reasonable to think of the remainder, that is, 408 million people, as the "dependent population." A nation's "dependency ratio" is the ratio of the dependent population to the working-age population. In the case of India, this turns out to be 0.6. On this score, India does not look too different from many other developing countries. Bangladesh's dependency ratio is 0.7, Pakistan's 0.8, Brazil's 0.5.
>
> What is different about India is the prediction that it will see a sharp decline in this ratio over the next 30 years or so. This is what constitutes the demographic dividend. India's fertility rate—that is, the average number of children a woman expects to have in her life time—used to be 3.8 in 1990. This has fallen to 2.9 and is expected to fall further. Since women had high fertility earlier, we now have a sizeable number of people in the age-group 0–15 years. But since fertility is falling, some 10 or 15 years down the road, this bulge of young people would have moved into the working-age category. And, since, at that time, the relative number of children will be small (thanks to the lowered fertility), India's dependency ratio would be lower.
>
> It is expected that, in 2020, the average age of an Indian will be 29 years, compared to 37 for China and 48 for Japan. By 2030, India's dependency ratio should be just over 0.4.[4]

By increasing the percentage of young people in the population, the demographic dividend would bring additional benefits: a rise in the relative number of breadwinners, an increase in the number of women joining the workforce and a decline in the dependency ratio. Together, these benefits would lead to higher savings. The rate of savings in India as a percentage of gross domestic product (GDP), was already much higher than developed countries at 33 per cent and would increase further over the next few decades.

---

[4] Kaushik Basu, "India's Demographic Divide," BBC News, July 25, 2007, http://news.bbc.co.uk/1/hi/world/south_asia/6911544.stm, accessed January 12, 2009.

The demographic dividend would come into play only for a period of time. In a progressive cycle, each demographic dividend phase would be followed by a "demographic echo," characterized by a rise in the dependency ratio as the working population moved into retirement. Therefore, reaping as much as possible from the demographic dividend and investing in social capital would ensure the social foundation of a community (i.e. education, skill levels, employability, health care and civic infrastructure) was robust enough to withstand the effects of an echo (see Exhibit 8).

CUSTOMER SEGMENTATION

When identifying customer target groups, Indian companies relied on data from two basic sources: the periodic analysis of consumers' income levels by the National Council of Applied Economic Research, an Indian market research agency (see Exhibit 9) and the socio-economic classification (SEC) of consumers, provided by the Market Research Society of India, another premier market research agency (see Exhibit 10).

The SEC system, India's most widely used consumer classification system, had two categories: urban and rural. SEC Urban used demographics as a combination of occupation and education, both of which shaped not only the earning capacity of the "chief wage earner" (the term used for the purpose of classification) in an urban household but also the self-image and social status of the household (see Exhibit 11). The system was based on the assumption that consumption behavior of an executive with a professional qualification working in the corporate sector differed from the consumption behavior of a self-employed store owner even when both shared the same income level. SEC Urban comprised eight segments (A1, A2, B1, B2, C, D, E1 and E2), whereas SEC Rural comprised four segments (R1, R2, R3 and R4).

The retail advisory group of Ernst & Young India, a management consultancy firm, published a study of Indian youth, whom it referred to as "the main architects of Indian retail." The study classified India's youth into three segments: Dabblers, aged 13 to 21; Aspirers, aged 22 to 28; and Thrivers, aged 29 to 35 (see Exhibit 12).[5]

COMPANY BACKGROUND

Promoted by K Raheja Corp., a real estate and hospitality enterprise based in western India, Shoppers Stop pioneered modern retailing in India when it opened its first, 2,800 square foot store in suburban Mumbai in 1991. By 2006, its operations had grown to 20 stores across 10 cities, covering a total retail space of 950,000 square feet. Sixteen stores were located in the Tier 1 cities of Mumbai (seven stores), Bangalore (two stores), Kolkatta (two stores), Pune (two stores) and Hyderabad, Chennai and Delhi (one store each). For the year ending March 2006, the company had a sales turnover of INR6.6 billion and after-tax profit of INR271 million (see Exhibit 13).

Shoppers Stop's target was to cover 22 cities with 39 stores by March 2008, occupying an area of 2.5 million square feet. The company was also planning to extend its footprint into the country's Tier 2 and Tier 3 cities. By regularly expanding its vendor portfolio, the company had partnered with more than 200 brands, both local and global, for distribution in India. Shoppers Stop also had an active

---

[5] "YouSumerism: Youth in India—Opportunity Knocks," Ernst & Young India Retail Advisory Group, 2007, www.ey.com/Global/Assets.nsf/India/Youth_Final/$file/Youth_Final.pdf, accessed March 9, 2009.

private-label program that in 2006 contributed 23 per cent of its overall revenues and approximately 40 per cent of its overall margins. The pursuit of private labels conflicted with the need for recognition as a national-branded retailer that stocked the best of brands.

Driven by the vision of "being India's number one global retailer in the Department Store category,"[6] the company's strategy had three elements:

> Delivering higher levels of sensory experience by offering fashionable merchandise, great store layout and ambience, educated staff, food, and events for a complete shopping experience; contemporizing the product basket to offer premium value; and sustaining leadership in the department store format through pan-India presence, efficient processes and excellent service standards.

For more than a decade, Shoppers Stop's focus on a single format had led to better operational metrics and higher profitability than its competitors, which were not only late entrants but were experimenting with different formats simultaneously. Of late, Shoppers Stop had begun to leverage its learning to new formats, such as hypermarkets and specialty stores. Each new format, however, was being planned and executed as a separate strategic business unit (SBU) within the group. The diversification had not led to any shift in the positioning of Shoppers Stop, which had not only remained as a premium, lifestyle departmental store but had continued to contribute the maximum to the company's revenues and margins. Within each Shoppers Stop store, however, a progressive list of offerings was available, from apparel (for men, women and children) to non-apparel (e.g. personal accessories, perfumes, cosmetics, home leather, watches, jewelry and electronics).

The majority Shoppers Stop offerings were standardized, and the scope for customization was limited. In 2005, however, the company had launched a "do-it-yourself" program as a special service: customers could purchase fabric from the store and in-house fashion designers, who were recruited from leading fashion schools, could design an outfit according to individual requirements.

As of March 2006, the company had 2,509 employees. Nearly 65 per cent of the front-end sales staff comprised university graduates who received higher than average pay. This remuneration was in contrast to the North American retail industry, where most front-end jobs were held by high-school graduates receiving minimum hourly rates.

Shoppers Stop was a conservative retailer, wary of the risks of inventory pile-up (which would increase costs) and low inventory turns (which would reduce cash flow). The risk aversion stemmed from its grounding as an apparel retailer that purchased goods largely on an as-needed, consignment basis. The company had an initial public offering (IPO) in May 2005, which raised INR1.53 billion. Unlike other listed retailers in the country, Shoppers Stop believed in funding expansion from internal accruals. Some analysts believed the company could "easily leverage its balance sheet to fund expansion plans without impacting cash flow in a significant manner" and that it could be more aggressive in pursuing growth.[7]

Shoppers Stop's strong back-end systems provided real-time information to managers and had helped them to achieve operating metrics often considered the benchmarks for Indian retail (see Exhibit 14). Shoppers Stop was becoming a preferred partner for global brands seeking to do business in India. It had also become a poaching ground for new entrants to Indian retail seeking managerial talent.

---

[6] Shoppers Stop draft Red Herring prospectus p. 46.

[7] Shoppers Stop Equity Research Report, B&K Securities, February 2007, p. 5.

The company had adopted a customer-centric marketing campaign as opposed to the conventional product-based campaign (see Exhibit 15). Together with promotions that coincided with the seasonal fashions, the advertisements had helped to drive footfalls (i.e. the number of people entering the stores) at a compounded annual rate of 16 per cent and to maintain the conversion rate (i.e. the number of customers making a purchase) at about 27 per cent.

Shoppers Stop had contrasting experiences with men's and women's clothing. Men's clothing was a growth area. Valued at US$3.5 billion in 2006, the men's clothing segment was growing at 30 per cent per annum. The branded ready-to-wear category, in which Shoppers Stop led its competitors, comprised 40 per cent of the market for men's clothing. However, the market for women's clothing in India was uncertain, particularly outside two particular outfits distinctive to Indian women: the sari and the salwar kameez. Western clothing was likely to remain a niche market, restricted to college students in urban markets and a relatively small number of women executives. Standardization, which was typical of ready-to-wear dresses, was not favored by Indian woman, who preferred the cloth, cut and finish of their clothing to be unique. Thus, the manufacture of women's clothing in India was dominated by small-scale businesses offering an array of fabric designs and patterns and an army of tailors who catered to individual tastes. The difficulty of building a strong retail business in women's clothing was the single largest bottleneck in the development of clothing superstores and of department stores in general because women were often the main buyers of all clothing, including men's clothing and accessories.

Shoppers Stop viewed the young adult apparel category to be medium on supply chain sophistication and very high on consumer readiness. This category included not only casualwear that young adults wore to college—T-shirts, jeans, denims and casual shirts—but also partywear. The fashion quotient was high among the young adult target group. Their clothing was most likely to feature colors, patterns and designs that were the latest in vogue. The company had also found that young adults were high consumers of accessories. Although young adult rarely splurged on high-end apparel, they preferred to have the best brands of fashion accessories, such as sunglasses, shoes and handbags.

CUSTOMERS

Shoppers Stop had one of the most successful loyalty programs among Indian retailers. First Citizen, which was introduced in 1994, had enrolled 630,000 members by March 2006. Membership had been growing by 10 to 15 per cent every year. The amount spent by the First Citizen card members was approximately twice the amount spent by other customers. The loyalty program provided the company with the competitive edge of a solid customer base and business certainty. The loyalty program had also generated a perception, strengthened over time, that Shoppers Stop was a "caring" brand, more reminiscent of a mature adult than a young adult.

Internal data had generated a demographic profile of First Citizen members: 75 per cent were in the 25- to 45-year-old age group, 70 per cent were married, 30 per cent were independent, working women and 90 per cent belonged to the SEC-A classification of the Indian urban consumer. Most were high net-worth individuals (HNWs) with high disposable income in terms of their shopping habits. Of all Shoppers Stop's revenue, 65 per cent came from its First Citizens. The number of First Citizens was approaching one million, of a total number of 20 million customers. First Citizens were the most valued among Shoppers Stop customers.

A common characteristic of Shoppers Stop customers was their aspiration quotient. They wanted to see themselves shopping with others of the same ilk and mindset. This characteristic was in contrast to typical luxury customers in India, who, based on the belief of having arrived in life, wanted to differentiate themselves from people around them. Shoppers Stop catered to the high-end consumers but saw itself as a bridge to luxury.

The loyalty card was available in three categories: Classic, Silver and Gold as shown in Table 1.

Table 1 Shoppers stop loyalty cards

Tier	Number of Visits per Year	Average Spend per Year (INR)
Classic	2	6,000
Silver	5	25,000
Gold	7	45,000
Overall	4	15,000

The typical Shoppers Stop customer belonged to SEC A urban, was between 15 and 40 years of age, earned a household income of INR30,000 per month, owned a car, shopped in groups (with family or friends), visited Shoppers Stop at least once a month and spent between INR2,000 and 2,500 per month on apparel and accessories.

On the basis of the findings of a sample survey by Customer Satisfaction Management & Measurement (CSMM), an independent, specialist unit of IMRB International, the company had classified its existing customers into three categories: premium-conscious, value-conscious and time-conscious (see Exhibit 16).

More than half the individuals in the premium-conscious segment earned more than INR50,000 a month. The time-conscious and value-conscious segments were predominantly male and single. Half of the individuals in the value-conscious segment were walk-in customers; in contrast, the other two segments had a high proportion of loyal customers.

NET GENERATION

The United States and other countries had classified their ongoing demographic pool into four broad categories: the Baby Boom Generation, Generation X, the Net Generation and Generation Next. The Baby Boom Generation consisted of those born between January 1946 and December 1964. Generation X comprised those born between January 1965 and December 1976. The Net Generation, the focus of most youth marketing initiatives, consisted of those born between January 1977 and December 1997. The most recent generation, born after January 1998, was called Generation Next.[8]

Each generation had been exposed to a set of events that characterized its place in history and varied with each country. For example, the Vietnam War was a defining moment for the Baby Boom Generation in the United States. However, some universal forces shaped the Net Generation's outlook in most countries, including India. The three most common drivers were the rise of the personal computer, the arrival of the Internet and the availability of digital technologies. These drivers cut across geographies. In India, the Net Generation had an additional stimulus—they had grown up with the process of economic liberalization begun in early 1980s. The Net Generation comprised a large share of the population in most economies although its rate of growth varied with each country. India had topped the list on both indices (see Exhibit 17).

[8] Don Tapscott, Grown up Digital: How the Net Generation Is Changing Your World, McGraw-Hill, Columbus, OH, 2009.

Net Geners, as the members of the Net Generation were called, had unique shopping behaviors, which were common across geographies. Before going to a store, they went online to scrutinize the product they wanted to buy. They were not satisfied with one-size-fits-all items that could be bought only in certain places and at certain times: they wanted something that fit them where, when and how they wanted it. They expected plenty of choice and high-speed service. They believed that fun should be embedded into the product. They were not easily influenced by commercial advertising the way that baby boomers were (see Exhibit 18).

Some people, particularly parents and employers, had expressed concerns and criticisms regarding the general behavior of Net Geners. According to some critics, Net Geners were shallow and distracted, lacking an ability to focus. They lacked social skills and had no time for reading, sports or healthy activities. They had no sense of privacy; instead, freely divulged their personal information online. They regularly violated intellectual property rights on peer-to-peer networks, by sharing anything they could, such as music, with no respect for the rights of its creators. They were violent and narcissistic. They had no work ethic and they didn't care.[9]

According to Mark Bauerlein:

> The 21st century teen, connected and multi-tasked, autonomous yet peer-mindful, makes no great leap forward in human intelligence, global thinking, or netizen-ship. Young users have learned a thousand new things, no doubt. They upload and download, surf and chat, post and design, but they haven't learned to analyze a complex text, store facts in their heads, comprehend a policy decision, take lessons from history or spell correctly. Never having recognized their responsibility to the past, they have opened a fissure in our civic foundations, and it shows in their halting passage into adulthood and citizenship.[10]

ISSUES IN JUNE 2006

As CEO, Govind Shrikhande knew that he had to set the tone for the company's overall strategy. In his mind, the youth market could be the future of the company. Yet, he had seen countless cases where others had failed with this segment because their targeting efforts had been imprecise. Further, Shoppers Stop had limited experience catering to the younger generation and would require a shift in mindset to be able to appeal to this consumer group. In approaching this decision, Shrikhande thought he should run the numbers first and then assess whether any change made sense from a business perspective. Despite having decided how to approach this decision, Shrikhande continued to be preoccupied by the following questions.

- Were young adult Indians a market force that Shoppers Stop needed to factor into its long-term growth plans? Or could Shoppers Stop ignore this segment?
- Although the demographic dividend was a major driver of growth in Indian retail, Shrikhande needed to identify the target audience that was relevant for Shoppers Stop. Because the company catered to premium-end lifestyle products, the addressable audience would be limited to urban centers. How should Shoppers Stop zero in on young adults in the country's tiered cities?

---

9 Ibid.

10 Mark Bauerlein, The Dumbest Generation: How the Digital Age Stupefies Young Americans and Jeopardizes Our Future (or Don't Trust Anyone Under 30), Penguin Books, New York, 2008.

- After it had decided to focus on the young consumer, Shoppers Stop needed to create new categories, discover new segments, unfold new formats, develop new distribution channels, experiment with new media and advertising vehicles, form new stores structures and rewire the entire organization to make it more responsive to younger customers. How could this enormous task be implemented?
- Given the shopping behavior of Net Geners on eight different attributes, how should Shoppers Stop reorient its retailing to be relevant to the young?

Exhibit 1 Brand perception study of shoppers stop compared with lifestyle, pantaloon and central

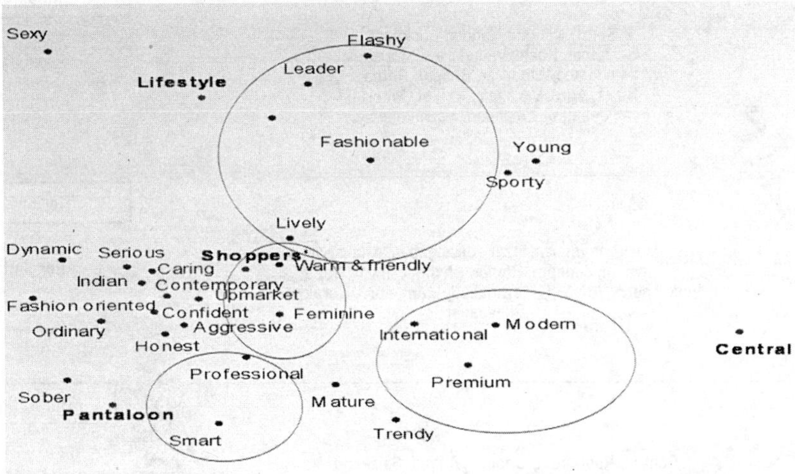

Source: Company.

Exhibit 2 Indian retail industry, 2006

	(in INR Billion)		%
Category	**Total Retail Sales**	**Organized Retail Sales**	**Share of Total Organized Retail**
Food and beverages	9,510	93	0.98
Clothing and textiles	1,190	195	16.39
Consumer durables	622	106	17.04
Home décor and furnishing	388	34	8.76
Jewelry and watches	549	34	6.19
Beauty care	281	10	3.86
Footwear	134	44	32.84
Books, music and gifts	107	14	13.08
Total	12,781	530	99.14

Source: "Retail–Market and Opportunities," by Ernst & Young for India Brand Equity Foundation, 2008, p. 4.

Exhibit 3 India's tiered cities

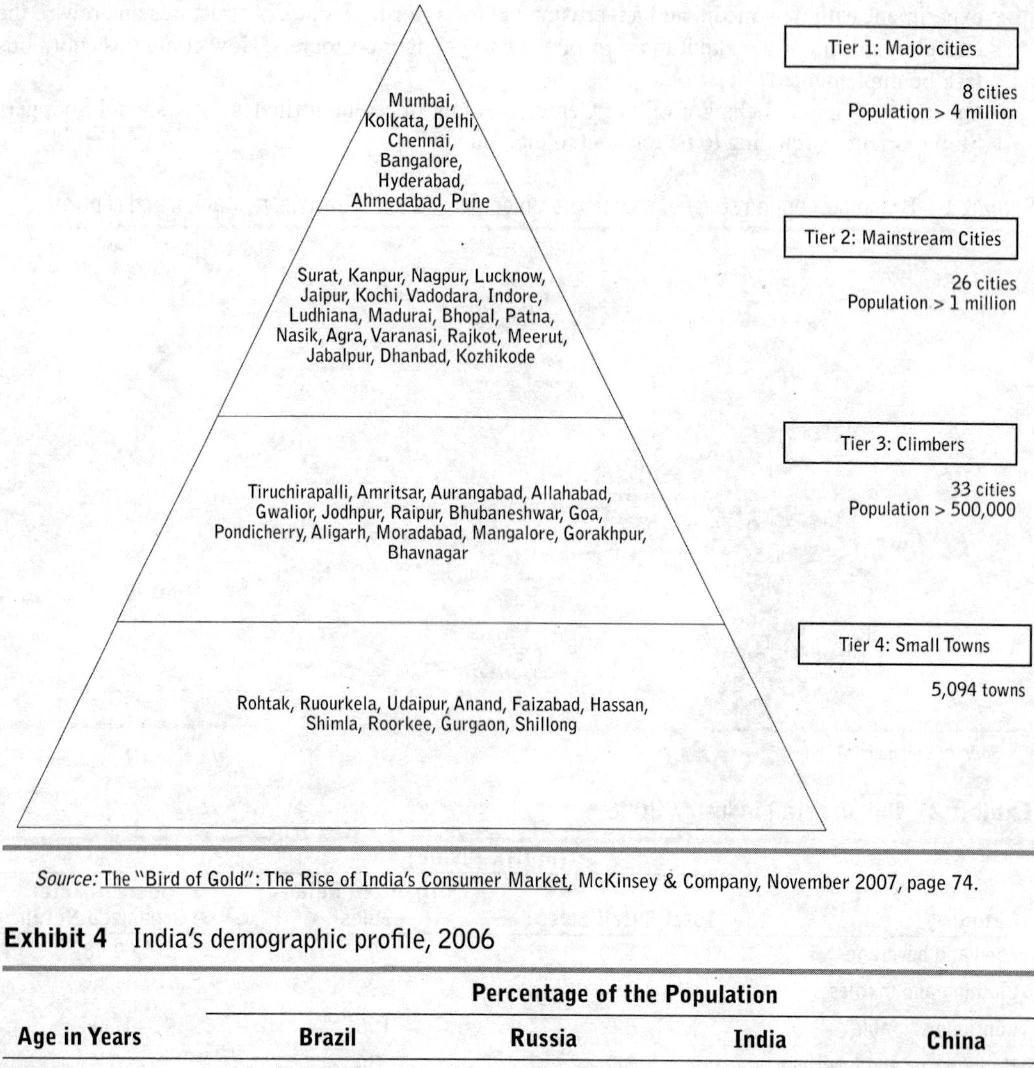

Source: The "Bird of Gold": The Rise of India's Consumer Market, McKinsey & Company, November 2007, page 74.

Exhibit 4 India's demographic profile, 2006

	Percentage of the Population			
Age in Years	**Brazil**	**Russia**	**India**	**China**
0–14	29	16	35	25
15–34	37	26	35	35
35–59	26	36	23	30
60 and over	8	23	7	10

Source: Shoppers Stop Equity Research Report, B&K Securities, February 2007.

Exhibit 5 India's growing middle class

Annual Household Income (INR)	(Percentage of the Population) 2002	2006	2010 (Estimate)
Up to 45,000	35	26	16
45,000–90,000	37	39	35
90,000–135,000	14	17	22
135,000–180,000	7	8	10
Above 180,000	7	10	17

Source: Shoppers Stop Equity Research Report, B&K Securities. February 2007.

Exhibit 6 Indian retail categories

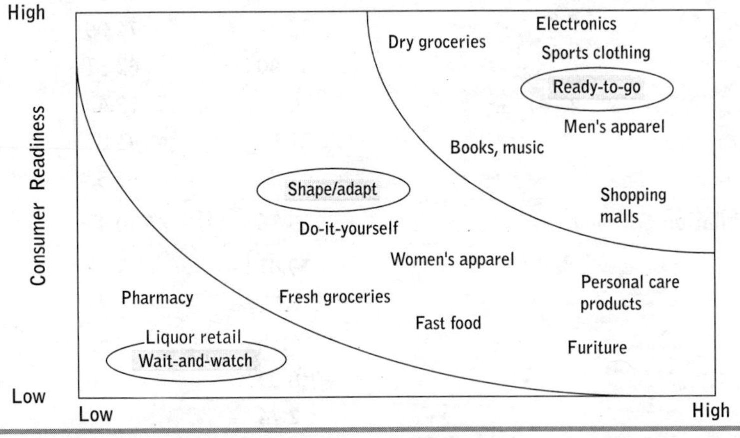

Source: Michael Fernandes et al, "India's Retailing Comes of Age," McKinsey Quarterly, December 2000.

Exhibit 7 Young India

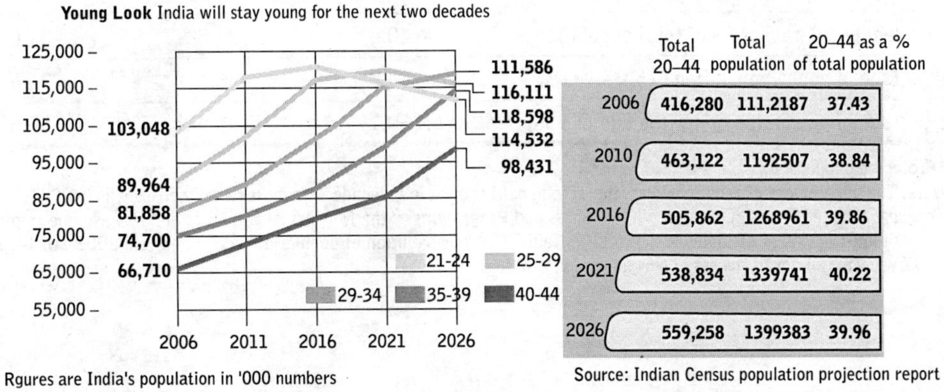

Exhibit 8 India's demographic dividend

	(Population in Millions)		
Age Group in Years	**2001**	**2011***	**2021***
0–4	110.45	115.58	110.96
5–9	128.31	115.43	112.69
10–14	124.85	120.43	113.07
15–19	100.21	119.99	114.31
20–24	89.76	116.21	119.10
25–29	83.44	103.84	118.23
30–34	74.27	92.33	114.23
Young Population (15–34)	**347.68**	**432.38**	**465.88**
35–39	70.57	83.62	101.85
40–44	55.74	74.09	90.19
45–49	47.40	63.51	80.96
50–54	36.58	52.43	70.58
55–59	27.67	41.82	59.03
60–64	27.52	32.58	47.02
Working Population (15–64)	**613.16**	**780.43**	**915.51**
65–69	19.81	24.92	35.56
70–74	14.71	18.74	25.71
75–79	6.55	12.55	17.53
80 plus	8.03	8.46	15.99
Age not stated	2.74	–	–
Total Population	**1,028.61**	**1,196.55**	**1,347.02**
Median age of the population (years)	22.51	25.47	29.33
Working population as % of total population	59.6	65.2	68.0
Dependent population as % of total population	40.4	34.8	32.0
Percentage of young population (15–34 years)	33.8	36.1	34.6
Percentage of population below the age of 35	69.1	65.5	59.6

*Projected population.

Note: The government of India conducts the official census once in a decade. The most recent census was in 2001.

Source: –Adapted from "Youth in India—Profiles and Programmes," the Ministry of Statistics and Programme Implementation of the Government of India, October 2006, Table 2(a) "Distribution of population by age and sex, 2001-2021," page 37, http://www.mospi.gov.in, accessed November 12, 2008.

Exhibit 9 India's income classes and number of households, 2005

	Income Classes	Number of Households (in 000s)	
Category	**Annual Income Range (INR 000s)**	**Urban**	**Rural**
Super rich	>10,001	46	6
Sheer rich	5,001–10,000	87	16
Clear rich	2,001–5,000	360	94
Near rich	1,001–2,000	842	280
Strivers	501–1,000	2,301	911
Seekers	201–500	8,889	4,923
Aspirers	91–200	25,158	28,118
Destitutes	<90	23,156	109,093
Total		60,839	143,441

Source: The Great Indian Middle Class, the National Council of Applied Economic Research, www. ncaer. org_accessed November 12, 2008.

Exhibit 10 India's socio-economic classes and number of households, 2006

Socio-economic Class	Estimated Number of Households (in Millions)
A1	2.2
A2	4.1
B1	5.3
B2	5.3
C	12.8
D	14.2
E1	6.7
E2	10.8
R1	5.8
R2	15.9
R3	56.7
R4	67.3
Total	207.1

Note: The top band of purchasing power in India, Urban A1A2, comprised a little more than 6 million households. The next band, which would qualify for the "middle-class India" label, comprising B1R1B2C, included approximately 30 million households. These two groups together formed the ABCR1 target group, the broadest possible target group for most consumer goods, at approximately 36 million households. The lower middle-class comprised DE1R2 at approximately 37 million households.
Source: Market Research Society of India.

Exhibit 11 India's socio-economic classification (sec)—urban

Education/Occupation of the Chief Wage Earner in a Household	Il-literate	Upto Grade 4	Grade 5–9	Grade 10	Pre-University	Grad/PG (General)	Grad/PG (Professional)
Unskilled workers	E2	E2	E1	D	D	D	D
Skilled workers	E2	E1	D	C	C	B2	B2
Petty traders	E2	D	D	C	C	B2	B2

Shop owners	D	D	C	B2	B1	A2	A2
Entrepreneurs (Nil employees)	D	C	B2	B1	A2	A2	A1
Entrepreneurs (<10 employees)	C	B2	B2	B1	A2	A1	A1
Entrepreneurs (>10 employees)	B1	B1	A2	A2	A1	A1	A1
Self-employed professionals	D	D	D	B2	B1	A2	A1
Clerical/Salesmen	D	D	D	C	B2	B1	B1
Supervisory level	D	D	C	C	B2	B1	A2
Officers/Executives (Jr)	C	C	C	B2	B1	A2	A2
Officers/Executives (Mid and Sr)	B1	B1	B1	B1	A2	A1	A1

Note: Socio-economic classification (SEC) indicates the affluence level of a household. The SEC of an urban household is defined by the education and occupation of the chief wage earner of a household. The classification system has eight categories: A1, A2, B1, B2, C, D, E1 and E2, rated in descending order of affluence.
Source: Market Research Society of India.

Exhibit 12 Indian youth as consumers, 2006

Segments	**Dabblers**	**Aspirers**	**Thrivers**
Age Group	13–21	22–28	29–35
Segment size (in millions) - All India - In Tier 1 and 2 Metros	174.0 17.0	129.0 10.3	105.0 12.2
Consumption Attributes	- Children of liberalizing India - Into their early years of discretionary spending - 10 per cent have graduated and are working - Spend seven hours a day with friends at a movie, gym, class or just "hanging out" where they form consumption-related opinions	- Coming of age with more than 90 per cent receiving their first pay check - 60 per cent get married during this phase - Steady growth in incomes - Driven by middle-class values - Price-conscious but also prone to impulse purchases and a need for instant gratification	- Time is a major constraint - A large part of household expenses is spent on stores providing customization, relationship-based service and flexible hours - Seek efficiency and convenience
Media/Leisure Habits	- Quality time at home limited to commercial breaks on sports or music channels - Although they pay little attention to commercials, dabblers do not forget witty advertising	- Major time spent in commuting, leaving little time for leisure or shopping on week days - Tend to splurge, however, on weekends - Extensive users of the Internet	- TV is the main source of news and entertainment - Drawn to prime-time sitcoms and serials
Monthly Discretionary Spend on Lifestyle Products (Metros)	INR 4,000–5,000	INR 5,000–8,000	INR 6,000–9,000

(*Continued*)

(Continued)

Segments	Dabblers		Aspirers		Thrivers	
Largest Share of Spend	Apparel and footwear		Apparel and eating out		Apparel and health-care products	
Attitude - toward shopping - toward malls	A byproduct of hanging out with friends A place for a bite and to be with friends		"The" purpose, with or without friends Meets all my shopping needs in one place		A necessity A good place for my family to shop	
Sub-segments (Income)	Very well-to-do	Well-to-do	Very well-to-do	Well-to-do	Very well-to-do	Well-to-do
Present in Tier I and Tier 2	3 million	7 million	3 million	6 million	2 million	5 million
SEC classification	A1, A2 and B1		A1, A2 and B1		A1 and A2	

Source: "YouSumerism: Youth in India—Opportunity Knocks," Ernst & Young India Retail Advisory Group, 2007, http://www.ey.com/Global/Assets.nsf/India/Youth_Final/$file/Youth_Final.pdf, accessed April 20, 2009.

Exhibit 13 Shoppers stop income statements, 2002–2006

Year Ending March 31 (in INR Million)	2002	2003	2004	2005	2006
Income	2, 402	2,949	3,953	5,001	6,660
Gross retail sales	9	25	100	114	311
Less: Value-added tax	2,393	2,924	3,854	4,887	6,349
Net retail sales	93	81	91	79	191
Other income	2,486	3,005	3,945	4,966	6,540
Less: Cost of goods sold	1,757	2,077	2,712	3,421	4,322
Employee costs	158	172	224	288	403
Operating and administrative	467	560	764	920	1,249
expenses	54	32	40	39	24
Interest and finance charges	49	58	75	90	139
Depreciation	1	106	130	207	402
Profit before tax	1	106	120	190	271
Profit after tax					

Source: Company annual reports.

Exhibit 14 Shoppers stop performance indices, 2003–2006

	2002	2003	2004	2005	2006
Number of Stores	9	12	14	16	20
Operating Profit (%)	4.2	6.5	6.1	6.6	8.4
Dividend Payout (%)	Nil	Nil	Nil	10.0	15.0
Retail Space (millions of square feet)		0.56	0.67	0.77	0.95
Inventory Holding Period (number of days)				107	94

Gross Margin Return on Inventory (INR/Inventory)	2.69	2.41	2.41	2.23	2.35
Gross Margin Return on Floor Space (INR/Unit of retail space)	1,775	1,910	2,000	2,330	2,353
Gross Margin Return on Labor (INR/Employee)	594,971	676,509	636,690	899,045	1,046,768
Same Store Growth (%)	(4)	9.1	12.0	9.1	17.0
Footfalls[1]	6.5	7.1	12.2	14.6	18.3
Conversion Ratio[2] (%)	33	34	26	27	27
Sales per Square Foot[3] (INR)	5,923	6,238	6,898	6,903	7,576
Sales Mix[4] (%)	70.5	70.1	67.6	64.7	61.0[5]
	29.5	29.9	32.4	35.3	39.0
Average Selling Price[6] (INR)	477	535	591	605	647
Transaction Size[7] (INR)	1,109	1,280	1,258	1,278	1,366
Shrinkage[8] (%)	0.66	0.54	0.41	0.41	0.41
Associate Satisfaction Index	–	–	4.0	4.03	–
Customer Satisfaction Index	–	–	–	61	60
Number of First Citizens			254,000	429,000	632,000

Source: Company annual reports.

[1] Number of people entering the stores.

[2] Number of entrants making a buy.

[3] Sales per square foot of built-up area.

[4] Consists of Apparel and non-apparel.

[5] In 2006, apparel sales were further divided into men's apparel (35.5%), women's apparel (18.8%) and kids' apparel (6.7%).

[6] Sales divided by the number of units sold.

[7] Sales divided by the number of invoices.

[8] Loss of inventory (due to pilferage).

Exhibit 15 Shoppers stop print advertisements

(*Continued*)

(Continued)

Source: Company files.

Exhibit 16 Shoppers stop customer segmentation

	Premium-Conscious	Value-Conscious	Time-Conscious
Percentage of Shoppers	26	46	28
Socio-economic Classification	A1	A1 and A2	A1
Age Group (years)	15–40	15–35	15–40
Profile	Males and females in almost equal numbers; married and single people in almost equal numbers	Single males	Single males
Shopping Habits	Visits with family and friends, 80 per cent are First Citizens	Visits with friends and family; most likely walk-in customers	Visits with friends and family, 70 per cent are First Citizens
Spend	High	Average	Average
Shopping Statements	* Shopping helps me buy the latest * I want to be the first to buy the latest	* I do most of my shopping during the sales	* I don't care about the ambience as long as the store is conveniently located
	* I buy only brands* I do not mind paying extra for quality * I don't like designs which are common * I like to check out new outlets * I prefer a mall because you can do other things as well * I prefer exclusive outlets offering premium products * I often buy on impulse * I don't mind spending time while shopping * Shopping is like an outing with friends * We don't just shop, we also like to eat and drink at the mall * Shopping is a way of spending quality time with the family	* I shop where there are special offers or sales * I like to browse around and may not always buy * I don't think brands are worth the price * When I buy items at full price, I feel I am paying too much	* I like to finish my shopping quickly * I do not like sales people disturbing me * I compare prices before deciding to buy * Shopping frees me from daily tensions of life * I first buy what was planned and then, if I have time, browse

Source: Company.

Exhibit 17 The net generation's share of population, 2005

Country	Population Younger than Age 25	Percentage of Population Younger than Age 25	Growth in Population Younger than Age 25 since 1980
India	593,293	52	46
China	501,558	38	(9)
United States	105,246	35	11
Brazil	87,437	47	22
Mexico	50,986	49	14
Russia	46,209	32	(15)
Japan	31,846	25	(27)
Germany	21,655	26	(20)
France	19,029	31	(7)
United Kingdom	18,676	31	(10)
Spain	11,500	27	(27)
Canada	10,004	31	(4)

Source: UN Department sof Economic and Social Affairs, Population Division World Population Prospects: The 2006 Revision; and World Urbanization Prospects: The 2005 Revision, http://esa.un.org.unpp, accessed December 10, 2008.

Exhibit 18 Net generation's buying behavior

Attribute	Underlying Statement	Articulation
1 Freedom	"Give me choice."	They value the freedom to be who they are. They are not overwhelmed by the proliferation of sales channels, product types and brands. They leverage technology to cut through the clutter and find the marketing message that fits their needs. They love the freedom of choice and the challenge of finding the perfect fit.
2 Customization	"Make it my own."	They have grown up receiving the kind of media they want, when they want it, how they want it and being able to change media for greater customization. They want to customize everything in the world around them — their desktop, their website, their ring tone, their screen saver, their news sources, their entertainment.
3 Scrutiny	"Let me check out."	They are skeptical, scrutinizing what they see and read in the media, including the Internet. They turn to their friends for advice on shopping instead of trusting company executives or advertisements.
4 Integrity	"Do you deserve my money?"	They see through public relations and "spin." They are honest, considerate and abide by their commitments. Whether they are researching a future employer or exposing a flawed viral campaign, Net Geners ensure the company's values align with their own. Transparency, in the form of gaining access to pertinent information about companies and their offerings, seems natural to them.

(Continued)

(*Continued*)

Attribute	Underlying Statement	Articulation
5 Collaboration	"Let us talk. Let me help."	They are great collaborators, both with friends online and at work. They develop what is called N-Fluence networks via the Internet, especially through social media channels.
6 Entertainment	"Make it fun."	Having fun with the product is as important as using it. From their experience with video games, they know there is always more than one way to achieve a goal. They are less structured. The interactive experiences they are exposed to help them both to think outside the box and to be irreverent.
7 Speed	"Serve me now."	They are quick on the uptake. Net Geners assume that companies can respond with the same kind of simplicity, speed and directness that they respond with when they exchange instant messages with their friends.
8 Innovation	"Give me the latest."	They want to be current and contemporary with whatever they buy. Buying the latest is their way of indulgence and self-gratification.

Source: Adapted from Don Tapscott, Grown up Digital: How the Net Generation Is Changing Your World, McGraw-Hill, Columbus, OH, 2009.

9

Air Miles Canada

Rebranding the Air Miles Reward Program

R. Chandrasekhar wrote this case under the supervision of Professor Niraj Dawar solely to provide material for class discussion. The authors do not intend to illustrate either effective or ineffective handling of a managerial situation. The authors may have disguised certain names and other identifying information to protect confidentiality.

Towards the end of September 2005, Caroline Papadatos, vice-president of marketing for the AIR MILES Reward Program (the Program) was reviewing a campaign, undertaken a year earlier by her team, to rebrand the Program. The campaign was to be launched nationally the following week. The anticipation was building because the rebranding campaign was more than a routine TV commercial and a radio spot. It was intended to re-energize the brand and the Program's more than nine million active household accounts, representing more than 14 million Canadians. The campaign was also meant to refocus the brand's premier position in the loyalty industry.

The rebranding campaign featured two approaches that were new for a company known for its direct marketing and data-driven loyalty strategies. The background consumer research had not followed the conventional route of focus groups, and the campaign had strong emotive elements in its design and execution. These strategies were a departure, even at a personal level, for a database-marketing career professional, such as Papadatos. "Can a campaign build on behavioral loyalty to secure a deeper emotional connection between the brand and its consumers?" she wondered.

Said Papadatos:

> There are, of course, several parts of the campaign which are aligned with our corporate DNA. There is documentation at each stage of the run-up to the campaign. There is consistency in the methodology. The campaign is targeted at a specific customer sub-segment. There is organizational commitment to the goals and measurement metrics. They give us confidence in managing the uncertainties of the campaign. But, at the end of the day, a creative strategy driven by non-traditional consumer research is a new territory for us.

THE COMPANY

The Program was owned and operated by Loyalty and Marketing Services, a wholly owned subsidiary of Alliance Data Systems Corp. (ADS), which was based in Dallas, Texas. ADS had three different business segments: transaction services, credit services and marketing services (see Exhibit 1). Managing more than 105 million consumer relationships for some of North America's leading companies, ADS employed approximately 8,000 associates at more than 40 locations worldwide. Papadatos had joined the company in 1998, and assumed the marketing leadership role in 2004.

Said Papadatos:

> Our business is to help clients build long-term relationships with their customers and reward consumers for loyalty. We develop insights into consumer behavior, create customized solutions for individual companies and manage all aspects of the loyalty program for them. With re-branding, we are deepening the emotional engagement that consumers have with the AIR MILES brand.

THE CUSTOMERS

The Program had two sets of customers: Sponsors and Collectors.

The Sponsors

More than 100 brand-name business partners, representing thousands of retail, service, marketing and promotion opportunities, utilized the coalition loyalty platform offered by the Program, by issuing reward miles to shoppers for their everyday purchases. The Sponsors included supermarkets, financial services providers, a national petroleum retailer, specialty retailers, pharmaceutical retailers, consumer services and business-to-business services, together forming the largest coalition offering a common loyalty platform and a common currency. Canada Safeway, Bank of Montreal, Shell Canada and Amex Bank of Canada were the four largest Sponsors, representing 44.6 per cent of the Program's revenues in 2005.[1] Each AIR MILES reward mile was both a reward to the consumer for shopping at a Sponsor's location and an incentive to shop again with the same retailer. Each transaction helped Collectors accumulate reward miles that could be redeemed for rewards.

The Program offered category exclusivity to Sponsors on a regional or segment basis. For example, in the grocery category, A&P Dominion had sponsorship rights in Ontario, IGA in Quebec and Sobey's in Atlantic Canada.

---

[1] Page 7 of the company's Form 10–K filing, dated March 3, 2006.

For Sponsors, the benefits of participation were many. Most important, the Program contributed to a Sponsor's effort to change consumer behavior in a manner that was beneficial to the consumer and increased the Sponsor's market share and profitability. It also provided a Sponsor with a turnkey loyalty program, enabling the business to operate a loyalty program at a lower cost than if it were implemented as a stand-alone program. In addition, the Program assigned, for each Sponsor, a dedicated account team led by a relationship manager. The team included marketing and analytical professionals focused on guiding and servicing each account.

The Collectors

The Program's reach in Canadian households was unparalleled. Individual consumers and households signed on as Collectors and accumulated reward miles based on their purchases at Sponsor locations or by using one of the Program's credit-card partners. The reward structure facilitated a quick and easy manner for Collectors to earn a broad selection of rewards. The Program had issued about 17 billion reward miles since inception in 1992.[2]

The Suppliers

Suppliers included airlines, leisure and entertainment providers, and manufacturers of consumer electronics that provided the products and services that Collectors could receive in exchange for their accumulated AIR MILES reward miles. The Program featured more than 300 suppliers, offering more than 800 reward opportunities, in multiple categories of products and services.

THE BUSINESS MODEL

Most of the Sponsors were in non-discretionary staple categories, such as grocery, petroleum and banking services.

The Revenue Stream

The Program collected fees from the Sponsors based on the number of reward miles issued. However, issuance fees were not immediately recognized as revenue. The issuance fees became recognized as revenue when the reward miles were redeemed, or at 42 months, whichever occurred earlier.[3]

A second component of revenue was the fee for marketing and administrative services provided to Sponsors. This fee was recognized as revenue pro-rata over the estimated life of a reward mile. It was shown on the balance sheet as "deferred revenue–service."

Some reward miles went unredeemed by Collectors. The percentage of unredeemed reward miles was known as "breakage" in the loyalty industry. Breakage could occur for several reasons: a Collector moved out of the Program area, death of a Collector or loss of interest in the Program or in the Sponsors. Breakage was factored into the revenue and cost models. If actual redemptions were greater than the estimates, the cost of "excess" redemptions (however notional) would affect the profitability of the Program. AIR MILES reward miles never expired. Some Collectors thus chose to save for big-ticket items, such as a family trip, which would take longer to accumulate.

---

[2] Page 8 of the company's Form 100-K filing, dated March 3, 2006.

[3] Page 31 of the company's Form 10-K filing, dated March 3, 2006.

ADS estimated the average life of a reward mile at 42 months. The provision for breakages based on historical analysis was 33 per cent.[4] These two measures had remained constant over the years and had been independently validated. As of December 31, 2005, the Program had $610.5 million[5] in deferred revenue related to the reward program. It had issued 3.25 billion reward miles in 2005 (see Exhibit 2).

THE COMPETITION

The Program competed with advertising and other promotional programs, both traditional and online, for a portion of the Sponsor's total marketing budget. It also competed against loyalty programs and services created by other companies in the market. Crucial to staying competitive was an ability to remain partnered with Sponsors that were desirable to consumers and that offered rewards consumers perceived to be both attainable and attractive. Also crucial was the Program's ability to sustain a large number of active Collectors. A reduction in Collectors' use of the Program would undermine the Program's ability to attract new Sponsors and consumers, and to generate revenue from current Sponsors and consumers. As loyalty programs became more prevalent in the Canadian market, loyalty was becoming an increasingly commoditized industry. Maintaining differentiation was therefore crucial.

Said Papadatos:

> AIR MILES has had a strong differentiation since the beginning. Before AIR MILES, the dominant loyalty model was frequent flyer programs that rewarded frequent travelers for choosing one airline over another. AIR MILES was the first to open up an opportunity to collect to all Canadians, by offering AIR MILES for all of their key shopping categories. Unlike other loyalty cards which are specific to a Sponsor or category, AIR MILES offers everyday rewards for everyone on every purchase. The "democratization" of loyalty rewards has always been the main plank of differentiation for AIR MILES. That has remained unchanged as the core value proposition. Rebranding is meant to reinforce the brand proposition with an emotional connection.

REBRANDING

The Program ranked among the top-three loyalty brands in the world.[6] AIR MILES was a well-known brand in Canada, with 97 per cent awareness among Canadians. But the Canadian loyalty market, already limited in size because of low population density, was becoming saturated. Credit-card loyalty programs were growing in popularity: 97 per cent of Canadian households participated in at least one loyalty program, 73 per cent had three or more loyalty cards and 53 per cent had four or more loyalty cards.[7] Countless coffee-club cards, sandwich cards, bookstore cards and discount programs were moving in and out of the consumer mindspace. Papadatos had to find ways to sustain Collectors' activity levels in the Program, but more importantly, she had to keep the Program relevant to their needs. She also had to preserve the distinctiveness of the AIR MILES brand and communicate it in such a way as to motivate consumers.

---

[4] Ibid.

[5] All funds in Canadian dollars unless specified otherwise.

[6] Caroline Papadatos, "The Art of Storytelling," Journal of Consumer Marketing, vol. 23, no. 7, 2006, pp, 382–384.

[7] "Loyalty Program Participation Rate on the Rise According to New ACNielsen Study," PanelTrack Loyalty Card Study 2005, ACNeilsen Canada, September 16, 2005, available at http://www.acnielsen.ca/news/20050916.shtml, accessed August 30 2006.

The Program had segmented Collectors into four groups based on the intensity of their engagement with the brand: The Best, Next Best, Maintain and Low.

Said Papadatos:

> The Best segment comprises those who are strong advocates for the brand. They collect reward miles regularly, visit the company's website, respond to its surveys and pull out their AIR MILES card at the checkout counter without a prompt. They are highly profitable, contributing significantly to the Program's bottom line. The rebranding is not targeted at them. Instead, it is targeted at the Next Best Collectors. We need to get them to lift their activity level to that of The Best segment. The Next Best will of course happily pull out their card but only on a prompt. It is not top-of-mind. That would happen when the collection of reward miles, rendered mechanical through everyday activities like buying groceries and gasoline, acquires an aspirational ring to it. The aspiration is created, not by the reward per se, but by the emotional experience that Collectors go through while spending their reward miles.

There were two other reasons for rebranding. First, Collectors were diversifying their collection across multiple categories. The Program was thus no longer earning a bulk of its revenue from air travelers; however, Collectors had limited awareness that the Program went beyond the flight reward. Second, Aeroplan, the Air Canada frequent flyer program, was indicating that its goal was to replicate the AIR MILES model.

THE REBRANDING METHODOLOGY

The Basics

In developing a rebranding strategy, Papadatos first examined the two traditional approaches to rebranding: Look outwards at the competitive scenario, ascertain the gaps in the market offerings and seek differentiation by filling one or more of them; and look inwards, get to the heart of what the company stands for and adjust the positioning to reflect that deeper insight. The latter, thought Papadatos, would be an opportunity for the Program to reconnect with what had made the AIR MILES Reward Program successful as an organization. Such an approach, she felt, would also provide an opportunity for AIR MILES, as a brand, to become more meaningful to consumers.

Papadatos and her team were clear about their expectations from rebranding. The rebranding campaign was not targeted at Sponsors or suppliers. Customer acquisition was not a goal, neither was creating consumer awareness. Nor were they looking for a direct increase in the issuance of reward miles or their redemption. The goal was to change the attitudes of a specific Collector segment—the Next Best—from neutral (or negative) to positive.

Focus groups had been a key source of consumer insight in past years at AIR MILES. The focus group format—in which a direct question yielded little more than a direct answer—was seen as unsuitable for an exercise aimed at exploring the basis for an emotional connection to the brand. The company looked at alternative forms of research. Storytelling emerged as a possible format.[8]

---

[8] Caroline Papadatos, "The Art of Storytelling," Journal of Consumer Marketing, vol. 23, no. 7, 2006, pp, 382–384.

Storytelling

The company brought together groups of about 20 Collectors for in-depth research in key consumer markets across Canada. It enlisted the help of a consultancy firm that specialized in storytelling methodology. The consultancy's chief executive officer (CEO), Edward Wachtman, acted as the facilitator. Rather than focusing on consumers' experiences with an AIR MILES card, as might have been expected in a focus group setting, consumers participated in a series of storytelling exercises that centered on the theme of "feeling rewarded."

As the members of each group shared their individual experiences of being rewarded, a commonality emerged in the participants' use of specific terms and the meanings they associated with those terms, such as *gifts*. Each group was randomly split into teams, and each team was asked to develop a story about "feeling rewarded," written as a play, a poster or a narrative. A team member was then asked to present the story in an interactive session with the group. As a wrap-up, each participant was invited to write a personal story about feeling rewarded. At that stage, the participants were free to leave but, invariably, everyone preferred to stay. The storytelling exercise—taking on the form of icebreakers, group activities and solo play—lasted three to four hours for each group. By the end of the session, the company had accumulated a portfolio of about 120 stories.

Said Edward Wachtman:

> We know from a generation of neurological research that many of our so-called rational decisions are, in fact, driven by deep and powerful emotions. These emotions are difficult, if not impossible, to identify through conventional focus group methods. The StoryTellings™ process helps individuals let go of their logical guards so that they have better access to their emotions. Although the process itself never varies; the prompt—what individuals create stories about—changes from client to client. The AIR MILES prompt was "Feeling Rewarded." AIR MILES believed that understanding and repositioning its brand around a deep-seated motivation would help create enduring bonds with Collectors and provide the brand with a strong competitive advantage.

Collectors from one end of Canada to the other opened up with strikingly similar stories about the reward experience. Although each story was personal and different, they all followed the same plot. Every story Papadatos and her team heard was built around common elements. Each story began with a sense of hope for the future. A baby was born, a young woman moved to a new town to take a new job, a young man went to school to earn his degree. Then there was crisis. An unexpected, life-altering event happened. The newborn was diagnosed as being deaf. The woman who left her family behind lost her job. The university student lost his scholarship and had to drop out. In every story, the feeling of anticipation was followed inevitably by a period of despair. And then, a helping hand came along. A nurse gave a referral to a pediatric surgeon who might help restore the baby's hearing. A friendly neighbor gave the young woman a job lead. A guidance counselor suggested that the student apply for a work-study program. The arrival of unexpected help was followed immediately by goal setting and a period of hard work. The parents found time and money to find the surgeon, the young woman interviewed for jobs and the young man balanced classes with a night job.

After a period of trial and tribulation, each story ended with a resolution. The goal was achieved. That was the reward. The baby's operation restored some of her hearing. The woman landed a higher paying job than she had before. The student stood on the podium to receive his degree. And then interestingly, in every story, there was a second level of reward. The mother saw the child from her kitchen responding to the neighbor's query. The young woman brought her family to where she was now located. The student came home to share his pride in his degree with his parents.

There were many lessons from the storytelling research but a couple of insights stood out. First, a reward that came out of the blue was not as valuable as a reward that one had worked hard to earn. Second, the work of collecting had intrinsic value. Third, an equal exchange of value was critical to the feeling of being rewarded, in recognition of the give and take in life. Finally, it became clear that the emotions associated with "feeling rewarded" were deep rooted and, in many cases, individuals were marked by these defining moments that gave real meaning to their day-to-day lives.

Said Papadatos:

> One of the biggest lessons was the notion of the double reward. It has a lot of relevance to the direction we took with our re-branding. In each of our stories, the protagonist enjoys the extrinsic achievement of the goal. But there is also an intrinsic, emotional connection to the reward. For the mother of the deaf child, the real reward comes long after the operation, when she looks out of the kitchen to see her daughter playing with the neighborhood kids. For the young man, the real reward occurs after he takes the midnight bus to his hometown to sit at the dining table, degree in hand, and celebrates with his family. The lesson here is that the material reward matters little in and of itself. It is what you do with it and with whom you share it that does. Interestingly, the consumer research echoes the hundreds of letters that we at AIR MILES receive from Collectors every year, thanking us for the experiences they have had with people who matter most to them.

That learning was a defining moment, in its own right, for Papadatos and her team. They realized that the AIR MILES reward experience, although effective from a functional and service perspective, was not celebratory. The company was congratulating Collectors for earning their rewards but was not addressing the inherent possibilities for celebration. It was this realization that marked the beginning of a new journey for the brand, from a functional experience to one that is emotionally engaging.

The findings of the research formed the basis for developing a new creative platform. The company hired a new brand agency to work on a two-minute brand manifesto that would serve as a talking piece to employees and Sponsors. In fact, this video became the catalyst for every employee to "participate" in the development of the new brand, and Papadatos met with all 600 call-center employees in small group settings to ascertain that the "voice of the brand" was consistent with "the voice of the Collector." The agency developed TV commercials, radio spots, employee launch materials, direct marketing materials and a video message from the company's president to Sponsors and their employees.

Papadatos was keen that the campaign should be monitored to ascertain not only whether it was delivering results but whether there was need for mid-course corrections. She decided upon some metrics of performance to track the progress of the campaign (see Exhibit 3).

The campaign was set to launch in early October 2005. As she looked out of her office at Yonge Street in Toronto and at the greenery extending into the Don Valley Golf Course, Papadatos wondered, "Will this be the platform for building lasting engagement with Collectors?"

Exhibit 1 Alliance Data Systems, Inc.'s business segments

Business Segment	Products and Services	Target Markets
Transaction services	Issuer services	Specialty retail
	– Card processing	
	– Billing and payment processing	
	– Customer care	
	Utility services	Utilities
	– Hosting customer information systems	
	– Billing and payment processing	

	Merchant services – Point-of-sales services – Merchant bankcard services	Petroleum retail
Credit services	Private-label receivables financing – Underwriting and risk management – Merchant processing – Receivable funding	Specialty retail
Marketing services	Loyalty programs – Coalition loyalty – One-to-One loyalty Marketing programs – Database marketing – E-mail communication solutions	Financial services Supermarkets Petroleum retail Specialty retail Utilities Pharmaceuticals

Source: Company reports.

Exhibit 2 Alliance Data Systems, Inc.–income statement

In US$ Millions	2005	2004	2003	2002	2001
Revenue					
Transaction services	699.89	681.74	614.45	538.36	503.17
Credit services	561.41	513.99	433.70	342.13	289.42
Marketing services	**604.14**	**375.63**	**289.76**	**231.72**	**201.65**
Others	(313.00)	(313.92)	(291.37)	(245.63)	(220.52)
Total	1,552.44	1,257.44	1,046.54	866.58	773.72
Operating Income					
Transaction services	28.78	30.42	34.53	32.14	25.35
Credit services	151.12	112.52	69.41	31.18	25.69
Marketing services	**56.71**	**29.15**	**26.85**	**12.45**	**3.18**
Total	236.61	172.09	130.79	75.77	54.22
Rewards miles issued (mn)	3,246.55	2,834.12	2,571.50	2,348.10	2,153.55
Reward miles redeemed (mn)	2,023.22	1,782.18	1,512.79	1,260.00	984.92

Source: Alliance Data Systems, Inc. annual reports.

Exhibit 3 Performance metrics
Air miles brand study 2005-06
Supporting numbers for the brand re-launch

Awareness and Recall Section	Lift
AIR MILES Unaided awareness (total sample)	5%
Best	15%

(*Continued*)

(*Continued*)

Awareness and Recall Section	**Lift**
Next Best	5%
Maintain	5%
AIR MILES - Measuring Attitude, Action, Engagement	
Best (Top Box) % Strongly Agree	
I'd rather use an AM coupon than a cents off coupon	7%
I've set a goal to collect AMRM towards a specific reward	4%
I plan to increase the number of AMRM I collect over the next 12 months	6%
AIR MILES is making a strong effort to earn my loyalty	4%
The rewards or experiences I can earn with AIR MILES are things that can be used in a meaningful way	4%
I always recommend AM to friends and neighbours	4%
Next Best (Top Box) % Strongly Agree	
I'd rather use an AM coupon than a cents off coupon	7%
I've set a goal to collect AMRM towards a specific reward	6%
I choose to shop at/use an AM Sponsor over a competing retailer/ service	4%
AIR MILES is making a strong effort to earn my loyalty	5%
The rewards or experiences I can earn with AIR MILES are things that can be used in a meaningful way	8%
I trust AM and its product and services	4%
AIR MILES is the perfect program for people like me	6%
I always recommend AM to friends and neighbours	4%
Competitive Assessment (Personality, Attributes)	
For AMRP	
Exciting	4%
Makes time to be with family	12%
A good storyteller	14%
Fun	6%
Could get along with anyone	11%
Optimistic	6%
Feminine	6%

It's simple and straightforward to be part of this program	5%
I'm proud to use this program	5%
Has unique rewards	6%
It's a program set up to help everyday people	5%

Notes: AMRP is the Air Miles Rewards Program; Lift refers to the increase over prior baseline measurement.
Source: Air Miles Canada.

10

Kids Market Consulting

KIDS MARKET CONSULTING

Kids have a lot of bright ideas that adults can not know.

Natalia Berezovskaya

In May 2004, Natalia Berezovskaya, founder of Kids Market Consulting (KMC) in Kyiv, Ukraine, was pleased with the success of her business to date. Her niche market research company had enjoyed solid growth and profitability since it began two years ago, and it had developed a strong customer base. Now, Berezovskaya had been presented with last quarter's results, which showed slowing corporate growth. The competition among Ukrainian market research firms was fierce, and Berezovskaya knew that protecting her niche would be increasingly difficult. She had to determine the strategic direction of her company.

UKRAINIAN ECONOMY

The Ukrainian economy expanded by four per cent to eight per cent annually since 2000, due to solid domestic demand, low inflation, and strong investor and consumer confidence. Per capita gross domestic product (GDP) in 2003 was $5,300.[1] The official living minimum for 2004 was $64 per month, and the average monthly wage per employee was $86. Unemployment in Ukraine was four per cent for officially registered workers, but the country had a high number of unregistered or underemployed workers. An estimated 29 per cent of the population lived below the poverty line.

UKRAINIAN MARKET RESEARCH INDUSTRY

Market research in Ukraine was a developing industry in the 15 years after the country's independence from the former Union of Soviet Socialist Republics (USSR). Fast moving consumer goods (FMCG), pharmaceutical products, alcohol and tobacco were the most popular market research areas. The most significant development in the industry took place in the past seven years. Opinions about the size of the industry varied. As of 2004, the Ukrainian market research industry was estimated to range from $5 million to $20 million, while the Russian industry was estimated to be at least 10 times larger.

Accurate estimation of the total market size was complicated by poor tax accounting in Ukraine. In 2004, there were three types of companies: white, gray and black market businesses.

The companies that fully reported their revenues in the Ukrainian market research industry were considered part of the "white market," which was estimated to be $5 million to $8 million. The "black market" referred to those businesses disguising their revenue for tax purposes, while the "gray market" consisted of companies whose business practices straddled both areas. The exact size of the black and gray markets was unknown, but experts estimated them to be $8 million to $10 million altogether. As legislative changes began to take place, over time, the black and gray market companies were expected to join the white market.

Most domestic firms tended to focus their marketing strategies on advertising efforts, rather than on market research. As a result, spending on advertising was significantly more than spending on market research. However, the market research industry in Ukraine had made much progress over the past years. The sophistication of the industry could be seen through the development of self-regulating organizations. For example, the Ukrainian Marketing Association (UMA) developed an ethical code and regulations that were designed to stabilize pricing policies in market research, diminish unfair competition and promote legal companies. White market firms adhered to these regulations and tended both to be more professional and to deliver better quality work.

There were approximately 30 market research companies operating in Ukraine. The major firms included Gfk-USM, ACNielson Ukraine LLC, IPSOS S.A., Consumer Insights Ukraine (CIU) and Comcon Ukraine. Gfk, a German-based firm, had global sales of $747 million and net income of $41.8 million in 2003. Revenue for the French-based IPSOS S.A. was $564.3 million, and its net income was $7.5 million for the same year. ACNielson was part of VNU N.V. from the Netherlands, the largest market research firm in the world. VNU N.V. had revenue of $4.9 billion in 2003, and net income of $163.1 million. The largest firms were all part of the prestigious European Society for Opinion and Marketing Research (ESOMAR), a global community of market research professionals which was founded in 1948. While there were many niche players, none of the firms operating in Ukraine was solely dedicated to market research focusing on children.

There were several sources of competition in market research. Traditionally, advertising agencies contracted market research work to a separate firm, but they had begun conducting their own market research in response to their customers' demands. There was increasingly less and less differentiation between advertising, branding and marketing agencies, as they each worked to satisfy all of their clients' needs.

[1] All monies in US$ unless otherwise specified.

Other competition in the market research industry existed besides the large firms competing for contracts, such as independent consultants who were soliciting market research work. In between election periods, companies that conducted research for political blocs would conduct commercial market research as well. The quality of work among these firms tended to be poorer than that of full-time consumer market research firms.

KIDS, TWEENS AND TEENS IN UKRAINE

The segment of the population that ranged from birth to 19 years of age was identified by KMC as an unserved niche. None of the other market research firms in Ukraine focused on this particular niche. Brands oriented toward kids were relatively new to local companies as they had largely ignored the purchasing power possessed by this segment. Panel research conducted by KMC, in 2004, showed that disposable income was, in fact, available to kids, tweens and teens (see Exhibit 1). Furthermore, owners of adult brands began to recognize that the kids, tweens and teens segments would eventually become their target consumers, and were, therefore, an important audience.

The Ukrainian population was centered in seven major cities, including Kyiv, the capital of Ukraine, with a population of 3.5 million. These cities were called "millionniki" since they each had populations in excess of one million, and they accounted for approximately 20 per cent of the Ukrainian population. Kids, tweens and teens made up roughly 25 per cent of the total population of 47 million (see Exhibit 2). Studies by KMC showed that the kids, tweens and teens in Kyiv were representative of these segments in most of the other Ukrainian urban centres. Advertisers and marketers in Ukraine generally ignored the rural areas of the country.

GETTING STARTED

Natalia Berezovskaya started KMC in September 2002 with her partner, Vitaly Ocheretyanyi. Her studies in mass media and communications at Dnipropetrovsky State University sparked her interest in the advertising and marketing industries. With more than 10 years' experience as a radio anchor and author for youth programs, director of programming at a national radio station and coordinator at a Ukrainian advertising agency, Berezovskaya was able to identify kids, tweens and teens as unserved segments in the Ukrainian marketplace.

Prior to starting at KMC, Berezovskaya made contact with market research firms serving the kids, tweens and teens segments in other countries, such as Yeladim, Teenage Research Unlimited and Doyle Research. Along with this research, Berezovskaya monitored media sources, such as magazines, the Internet and business publications, to determine the value of such a niche market research firm in Ukraine. The presence of Western children's brands, the appearance of low-quality national Ukrainian brands, as well as the general lack of information regarding the consumer psychology of children were encouraging indications of the success of such a niche business. Berezovskaya's contacts in the Ukrainian advertising community further helped to ensure the success of KMC.

KIDS MARKET CONSULTING

The agency was formed as part of Dynamic Development and Innovation Group (DDI), a 100 per cent Ukrainian-owned business, co-founded in 1995, by Vitaly Ocheretyanyi. DDI consisted of five specialized companies representing the entire scope of marketing services. In 2004, SC-DOM, a market research firm focusing on adult consumers, accounted for 50 per cent of DDI's revenue, KMC represented 40 per cent, with the other businesses representing the remaining 10 per cent (see Exhibit 3).

Being a part of DDI provided many advantages for KMC. Berezovskaya has commented that "being a part of DDI is very comfortable for KMC." A variety of corporate resources were available to KMC from other DDI businesses at significantly reduced rates. These resources included access to both DDI's network of interviewers for market research and their tools to collect sociological, market and consumer behavior information. KMC was able to enter the market with access to DDI's customer base and experience. A further advantage was the cost-efficiency of sharing physical office space with SC-DOM in Kyiv. Rental costs accounted for 10 per cent of KMC's total expenses, utilities and web hosting were 12 per cent, and miscellaneous office expenses were three per cent. The cost savings of shared advertising to promote DDI's collection of businesses as well as leveraging the well-known DDI brand have proven significant for KMC over the past two years. KMC's expenses for promoting the business were five per cent of its overall expenses. DDI benefited from KMC because it expanded DDI's area of specialization and became another source of customers for all of DDI's companies.

Challenges arose for KMC in the beginning, due to its first-mover position in the kids, tweens and teens niche. There was initially a low level of acknowledgement from potential clients, due to the lack of information surrounding this specific segment in Ukraine. In order to promote the business, KMC worked to increase prospects' knowledge about the advantages of marketing to children and addressing segmentation in general. KMC organized seminars and presentations and introduced information at various meetings, including free specialized workshops called "Child-targeted Marketing." The company promoted consolidated research, whereby it offered one package of market research to several buyers. It was important to educate Ukrainian businesses of the value of market research, and to emphasize the varying levels of research, in terms of quality. Traditional market research services were offered, with the focus of each service on kids, tweens and teens. Services included:

- Surveys and questionnaires for quantitative studies
- "Delicate Age" study, a regular investigation of lifestyles and consumer preferences of children and teenagers
- Focus group discussions
- One-on-one, in-depth interviews (IDI) with children to better understand their feelings towards brands
- Child-and-parent pair interviews to understand the psychology of child-parent interaction in purchasing
- Creative groups (brainstorming groups with children to develop ideas about names, heroes, slogans, etc.)
- Observation and immersion experiences
- Desktop studies (analysis of secondary information and its assessment by different experts)
- Hall-test and home-test (assessment of the target group's reaction to the product at its point of sale, or practical use of the study subject in the target group's routine life)

KMC's customers included both Ukrainian and international firms seeking to better target kids, tweens and teens. Project costs for KMC varied, based on the type of project and customer requirements. KMC's Kyiv-based operation provided a competitive advantage because of its close proximity to Ukraine's largest market. Non-Ukraine-based firms that specialized in the kids, tweens and teens segment could not offer the same level of expertise for the Ukrainian business environment.

Difficulties involved in working in this niche included collecting information from children, who were often unable to clearly articulate their thoughts. With the use of child psychologists specially trained by KMC in concepts of marketing and market research, KMC was able to study the market awareness of kids, tweens and teens in Ukraine. KMC was the only market research company in both Ukraine and the former U.S.S.R. that focused exclusively on kids, tweens and teens.

By 2004, KMC was a relatively small business compared to its global competitors, with annual revenues of approximately $100,000. The company had five full-time employees in Kyiv, including Berezovskaya, and their salaries accounted for 70 per cent of KMC's expenses. The company hired freelance workers to fulfill the demands of its larger projects. KMC's relationship with DDI Group enabled the business to be profitable by controlling costs and to provide the best services at competitive rates for the loyal customer base it had developed. In its first year, KMC used 50 per cent of its revenue for new computer equipment and project planning activities. Re-investment in the business was 15 per cent to 20 per cent of revenue in subsequent years.

NEXT STEPS AT KMC

Increasingly the non-specialized Ukrainian firms began competing for KMC's niche business. KMC's growth appeared to have stabilized (see Exhibit 4), and the expected growth of the children's market was uncertain.

Berezovskaya had told Ocheretyanyi that she would brainstorm ideas to take KMC forward to protect its niche or expand its business. Was it a viable option to expand to other geographical areas? Were there additional services KMC could offer its clients? Could another niche be targeted? Berezovskaya had to make a decision and let him know by the end of the week, and there seemed to be a large range of possibilities she had yet to consider.

Exhibit 1 Weekly disposable funds available to each group

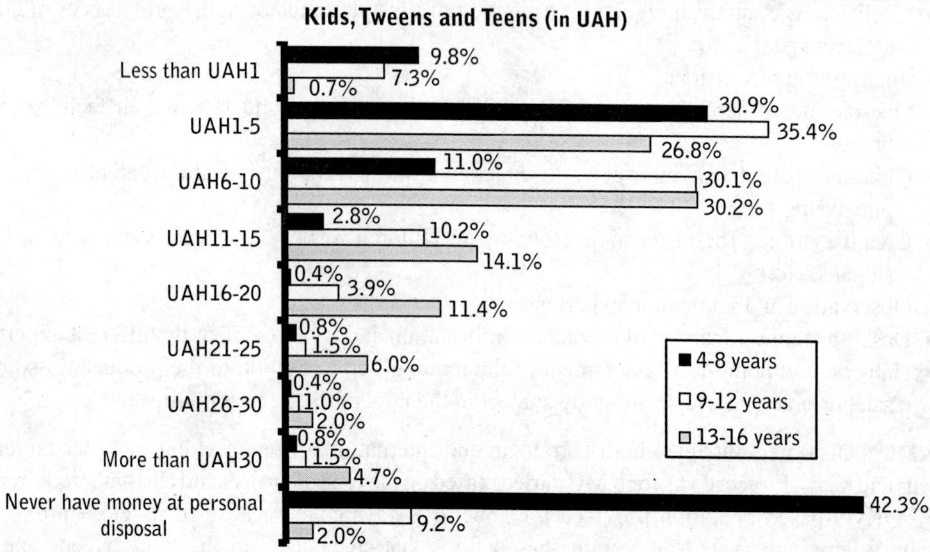

US$1 = UAH5.31 (Hryvnya).

Exhibit 2 Kids, tweens and teens population in ukraine 2001

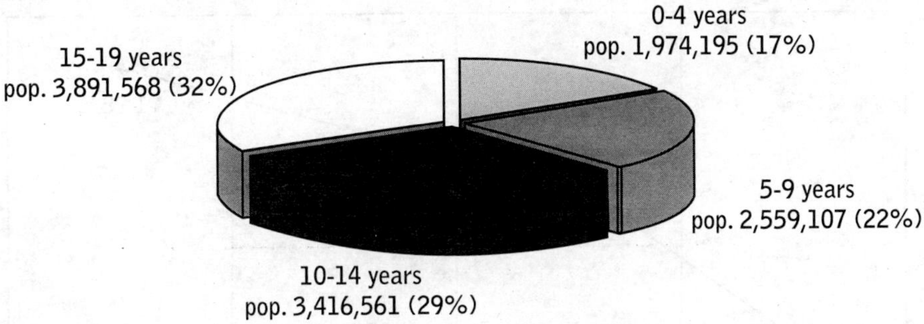

Source: "Goscomstat," National Committee of Statistics, population census 2001.

Exhibit 3 DDI group's companies

SC-DOM	• Marketing Consulting
Kids Market Consulting	• Marketing research and consulting for the age segments "kids/ tweens/teens"
Media Box	• Advertising Monitoring and Press Publications
Main Stream	• Promo-agency
~Ing Division	• All-Ukrainian network for primary data collection

Exhibit 4 Revenue growth at KMC 2003 to 2004

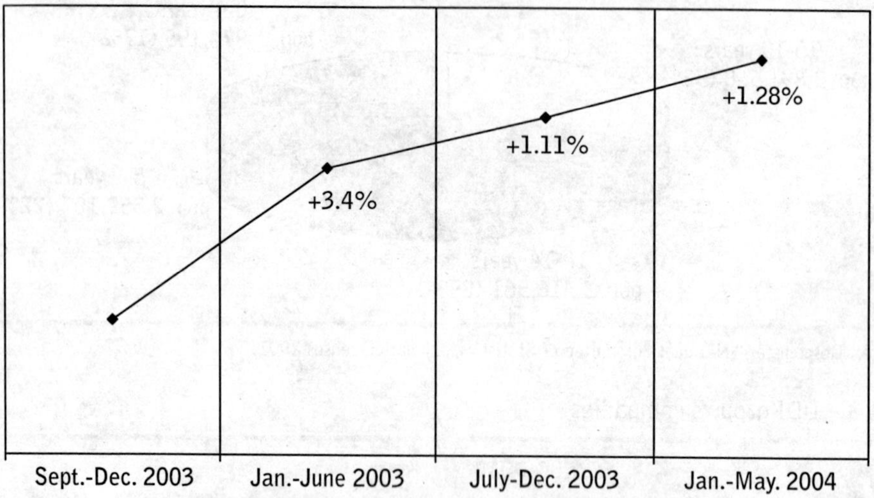

Source: Company files.

11

The Wii

Nintendo's Video Game Revolution[1]

George Harrison was in an enviable position. As senior vice president of marketing for Nintendo of America, he had overseen the reemergence of Nintendo as the leading video game console maker in the United States. Both of the company's recent product launches were phenomenal successes. The most recent, a home video game console known as the Wii, had surpassed the company's most optimistic sales projections. However, months after the launch of the Wii, Nintendo experienced chronic product shortages despite an increase in manufacturing capacity.

As the holiday season approached, Harrison became increasingly concerned about the potential for a repeat of the shortages in Japan when the company launched its popular handheld console, known as the DS. Like the Wii, the DS handheld console took the Japanese market by storm. As soon as new supplies arrived at retail stores, they sold out. Smaller retailers complained that all the supply went to large retailers and consumers complained that they had to pay exorbitant prices on the grey market.[2]

---

[1] This case has been written on the basis of published sources only. Consequently, the interpretation and perspectives presented in this case are not necessarily those of Nintendo of America or any of its employees.

[2] Grey Market: The legal sale of merchandise through retail channels that have not been authorized by the manufacturer. In the United States, flea markets and online auction sites, such as eBay, were popular venues for the sale of grey market merchandise.

"There is no guarantee that we are not going to have 'out-of-stocks' this holiday season," Harrison explained. "We're trying to figure out what is a reasonable monthly level, but as we have seen, every time we ship product to the market, whether it is in Japan or here in the U.S., it sells out in a matter of days."[3] Although Harrison advised consumers to purchase a console early in anticipation of holiday season shortages, he knew that many would wait until the last minute.

COMPANY BACKGROUND

Nintendo was founded in 1889 in Kyoto, Japan, where it produced elaborate handmade playing cards. After World War II, the company expanded into toys and games. In the late 1970s, company president Hiroshi Yamauchi became concerned about a perceived shift away from traditional toys toward electronic entertainment. Japan had already witnessed a shortage in coins following the rise of coin-operated arcade games. To take advantage of this shift, Yamauchi secured an agreement with Magnavox to become the Japanese distributor of the Odyssey, one of the first home video gaming consoles. Nintendo also began designing its own arcade games, which it rented to arcade centers, shopping malls, and taverns.

For Yamauchi, the Magnavox Odyssey distribution agreement gave Nintendo an opportunity to learn about the video games market and to build relationships with key customers, game developers, and electronics suppliers. In the early 1980s, Nintendo released its own home console, which became an instant success. Nintendo went on to dominate the video games market, both in home video game consoles and in handheld consoles. In 2007, more than 99 per cent of its revenues came from electronic entertainment products, earning the company \$1.5 billion on revenues of \$8.2 billion (see Exhibit 1).[4] The company employed 3,000 people worldwide.

Shigeru Miyamoto and the Art of Donkey Kong

Much of Nintendo's success could be attributed to Shigeru Miyamoto, universally recognized as the father of modern video games. Miyamoto began his career with Nintendo in the late 1970s. At first, the struggling art school graduate did not impress Yamauchi. When Miyamoto arrived for a job interview with a bag full of toys he had designed, Yamauchi protested that Nintendo needed engineers, not artists. Yet, because Miyamoto's father was a childhood friend of the Nintendo president, Yamauchi offered Miyamoto a position as the company's first staff artist.

Miyamoto spent the first years of his career at Nintendo designing artwork for arcade game cabinets. Then, in 1980, Yamauchi called Miyamoto into his office to get his opinion on a poorly selling arcade game. Miyamoto believed that games generally suffered from overly simplistic gameplay and excessive violence. Games could be improved, he suggested, if only they would follow the examples of classical literature and offer interesting story lines and complex characters.[5]

---

[3] Nintendo Wii may be scarce for holidays, Reuters, July 11, 2007 (reuters.com/article/technology-media-telco-SP/idUSN11400220070711 Accessed July 23, 2007).

[4] Financial data for the fiscal year ending March 31, 2007.
Source: nintendo.com/corp/report/FY07FinancialResults.pdf Accessed July 6, 2007. Currency converted to U.S. dollars from Japanese yen at a rate of US\$0.0085 per yen. Source: Oanda Currency Converter (oanda.com/convert/classic Accessed July 6, 2007).

[5] Chaplin, Heather & Aaron Ruby, Smartbomb: The Quest for Art, Entertainment, and Big Bucks in the Videogame Revolution, Algonquin Books, 2005, p. 73.

Miyamoto's ideas fascinated Yamauchi, who gave the young artist responsibility for redesigning the arcade game. The result was Donkey Kong. The new game featured a hero, known as Jumpman, who had to rescue a damsel in distress from a giant ape known as Donkey Kong. When Nintendo's U.S. sales force learned of Donkey Kong, they were dismayed. The game not only lacked proven features, such as bombs and missiles, it "had more in common with a Bugs Bunny cartoon than an apocalyptic science-fiction saga."[6] Even so, upon its release in 1981, Donkey Kong quickly became a best-seller, with first year sales of more than $100 million.[7]

Nintendo licensed Donkey Kong to Coleco, an American toy manufacturer and one of the first companies to offer a home video game console. Coleco went on to sell more than 6 million units. Nintendo reinvested the earnings from its fledgling video game business into developing its own video gaming console. Meanwhile, Miyamoto was hard at work developing new video game adventures, including Super Mario Brothers, The Legend of Zelda, and a sequel to Donkey Kong.

In 1983, the home video gaming market experienced a precipitous decline as consumers grew tired of simplistic arcade games and diverted their attention to the newly emerging home computer market. Most console manufacturers exited the market either through bankruptcy or by refocusing on other product lines. One of the few survivors was Atari, which saved itself through drastic cost-cutting measures. Between 1983 and 1984, it reduced its staff from 10,000 to only 200.[8] Former Atari developer Chris Crawford reflected on the situation in 1984.

> The videogame industry died in 1983; home computer sales boomed in Christmas 1983. The damage was greatest in those areas of computer gaming that were closest to video gaming. Most of the smaller publishers, and all of those who had specialized in skill-and-action games, went out of business. Those that did survive did so by cutting costs and having something other than games, or at least something more serious, to keep them going.[9]

The Nintendo Entertainment System

It was into this environment that Nintendo decided to launch its own home video gaming console, the Nintendo Entertainment System (NES). Although some could not understand why Nintendo would enter a "dead" market, others believed the collapse helped Nintendo establish itself as the undisputed market leader. "Out of the ashes of the industry collapse of 1984, a new entertainment software industry began to emerge," Crawford observed.

> The videogames business had been so thoroughly discredited, Nintendo was able to enter the market with no competition and rebuild the videogame industry in its own desired image.[10]

That image was one of imaginative worlds and tales of adventure inspired by religious fables, Homeric adventures, and Shakespearean plays. Gone were the simplistic shooting games of the late 1970s and early 1980s. Those games had "relied too much on violence," Miyamoto explained.

---

[6] Ibid., p. 75.

[7] Gardiner, Roy, Games for Business and Economics, Wiley, 2003, p. 230.

[8] The History of Computer Games: The Atari Years, The Journal of Computer Game Design, Volume 5, 1992, www.erasmatazz.com/library/JCGD_Volume_5/The_Atari_Years.html (Accessed June 1, 2007).

[9] Ibid.

[10] Ibid.

Instead, he envisioned electronic worlds that reflected "good and evil, honor and disgrace, beauty and horror."[11]

A truism within the gaming industry was that a good game was "easy to learn, but difficult to master." Whereas early gaming consoles offered games that were easy to learn, they were also easy to master. The NES was different. Consumer satisfaction surveys undertaken by Nintendo showed that the most compelling selling attribute of the NES was its ability to maintain interest with challenging games.[12]

In 1989, Nintendo launched a portable version of the NES, known as the Game Boy. The original Game Boy contained a 2.6-inch monochrome screen and played many of the same games made popular by the NES, such as Mario Brothers and Donkey Kong. By 1992, Nintendo had captured an 80 per cent share of the market for video games, earning it $1.25 billion on more than $4.3 billion in revenues.[13]

Sony and the 32-bit Revolution

As early as 1993, critics had begun to complain that the NES was "dull." By this time, Sega Corporation of Japan and 3DO Company of the United States had each announced more advanced consoles priced at $300 and $700, respectively. The new consoles would offer greater graphics capabilities and more adult-oriented games.[14]

However, Nintendo's greatest challenge came in 1995 when Sony introduced its PlayStation console. Sony, as a major supplier of components for the NES, knew the market for computer games. When Nintendo chose to ignore new threats to its market, Sony saw an opportunity to launch its own console. Although the $299 PlayStation was more than twice the price of the Nintendo console, it proved to be an instant hit.

In 1996, Sony, Sega, and 3DO dropped the price of their consoles to $199. Nintendo responded to the challenge by introducing an advanced system of its own, the Nintendo 64 (N64). Still, for most consumers, Nintendo's offering was too little, too late. When all its competitors had modern CD-based systems that could also play music, Nintendo chose to continue using bulky cartridges.

By 1998, the Sony PlayStation outsold the N64 by a ratio of 10 to 1. In addition, whereas Nintendo did much of its software development in-house, Sony used its status within the electronics industry to establish strong relationships with independent developers. As a result, Sony was able to offer PlayStation customers a constant stream of new game titles. In 1998 alone, the PlayStation had 500 new software titles, compared to only 40 for the Nintendo 64.[15]

The Decline of Nintendo

In 2000, Nintendo's situation deteriorated further. That year, Sony released its PlayStation 2 (PS2) console. The PS2 offered improved graphics, a built-in DVD player, and, most importantly, backwards compatibility. That meant that owners of the original PlayStation could continue playing their existing

---

[11] Chaplin, Heather & Aaron Ruby, Smartbomb: The Quest for Art, Entertainment, and Big Bucks in the Videogame Revolution, Algonquin Books, 2005, p. 73.

[12] Video Games Are Enjoying A Resurgence in Popularity, The Washington Post, June 21, 1987.

[13] Game Over: How Nintendo Zapped an American Industry, Captured Your Dollars, and Enslaved Your Children, Kirkus Reviews, February 1, 1993.

[14] Nintendo; Game over? The Economist, November 20, 1993.

[15] Marketing Focus: Market raider: How Sony won the console game, Marketing, September 10, 1998.

games, while gradually upgrading to newer titles. By the time Nintendo's next generation game console, called the Gamecube, was released one year later, the PS2 was already well entrenched, with more than 5 million units sold.[16]

Initially priced at $199, the Gamecube was $100 cheaper than the PS2. However, it did not play DVDs or CDs, and it could not play N64 games. Instead, it used a new proprietary minidisk format that was incompatible with games designed for previous generation consoles. Between purchasing new games at $50 each and purchasing a separate DVD player for $150 or more,[17] many customers saw the PS2 as the better value.[18]

Nintendo also faced stiff competition from Microsoft, which released its Xbox console three days before the Gamecube. Although Microsoft was new to video game consoles, it was the leader in computer games. The Xbox reflected Microsoft's PC heritage, with hardware and software that closely mirrored existing personal computers, and like the PS2, it came with a built-in DVD player.

Gamers who compared the Gamecube to the PlayStation 2 and Xbox consoles saw it as an underpowered toy with too many games oriented to small children. They wanted realistic graphics, more violence and more action. Titles such as Grand Theft Auto for the Sony PlayStation 2 became all the rage.[19] Miyamoto, however, was unapologetic. Nintendo was more about "making good games that sell well," than seeking a holy grail of realism and performance. "If you look back at what we've done in the past," he explained, "Nintendo has a unique strength in that it is very good at making games that kids enjoy."

> But these are also games that everyone can enjoy, and I think that by focusing effort on our development you're going to see that there are going to be a lot of games that are going to appeal to people of all ages.
>
> Gradually over the years, very simple gameplay and very simple rules weren't enough to keep gamers satisfied, and so the games got more complicated. With the evolution in hardware and graphics the worlds got more complicated and the graphics got more incredible, and so in one sense the games got better, but at the same time they got less simplistic and so fewer people were really able to get in and play them.
>
> At Nintendo, what we want to do is show to other developers and our third-party partners that you don't have to just make games more complicated or more beautiful, you an actually have very simple gameplay that will be fun and very exciting for people.[20]

Satoru Iwata, president and CEO of Nintendo, believed that games needed to be innovative, intuitive, and inviting. "Photorealism is not the only means of improving the game experience," he asserted. "It's just one path."[21]

---

[16] Restocking keeps Xbox rockin', Video Business, December 17, 2001.

[17] In 2001, the average price for a single disc DVD player was between $150 and $200. Source: DVD Players, Consumer Reports, December 2001.

[18] Winners are many in war of consoles, Video Business, November 26, 2001.

[19] Chaplin, Heather & Aaron Ruby, Smartbomb: The Quest for Art, Entertainment, and Big Bucks in the Videogame Revolution, Algonquin Books, 2005, p. 85.

[20] Adapted from an interview published on www.miyamotoshrine.com, May 16, 2003, accessed March 20, 2007.

[21] Chaplin, Heather and Aaron, Ruby, Smartbomb: The Quest for Art, Entertainment, and Big Bucks in the Videogame Revolution, Algonquin, 2005, p. 254.

Nevertheless, Nintendo continued to lose market share to both Sony and Microsoft. By 2003, Nintendo had to cut production of the Gamecube in order to clear out 5 million units of excess inventory, as its market share slipped to 16 per cent. Meanwhile, Sony and Microsoft increased their market shares to 55 per cent and 22 per cent, respectively.[22] Miyamoto confessed that he worried about the future of Nintendo. "Of course my biggest concern is always that people's impression of Nintendo is going to decline, or that people will stop thinking about us," he said.[23]

The Nintendo DS: Reaching Non-Gamers

Nintendo recognized that it faced a "difficult environment," one in which competitors were willing to suffer major financial losses to gain market share.[24] Although gamers benefited when companies subsidized their console purchases, Miyamoto felt that such behavior was harmful to the industry.

> We've reached an era that's almost a dream come true for gamers, because they're able to buy these high powered games consoles at less than cost. It's obviously not good for the companies that are doing it, because they're bleeding money, and it's going to raise questions as to whether or not they can survive as a business.[25]

Instead of continuing to battle Sony and Microsoft for an increasingly limited market of core gamers, Nintendo sought to expand its market with less complicated and more versatile gaming systems. The first of these was a handheld device known as the Nintendo DS. The DS was equipped with dual screens, a touch screen interface, wireless network capabilities, and a microphone port (see Exhibit 2).

Nintendo complemented the device with new software aimed at an older audience. One such title was Nintendogs, a pet simulator in which players raised virtual puppies. Players used voice recognition to issue commands to their dogs and they used the stylus to pet, wash, and play with their puppies. By 2007, Nintendo sold more than 13 million copies of Nintendogs.[26]

Another popular title was Brain Age, a puzzle game that, if used daily, promised to stimulate brain activity and increase mental acuity (see Exhibit 3). Nintendo marketed Brain Age to middle aged and older players who enjoyed puzzle games and related activities. By the end of 2006, Nintendo had sold more than 8 million copies of Brain Age worldwide.[27]

Traditionally, the United States adopted new video game technology before other regions of the world. Yet, it was the last major video games market to embrace the DS. "Although we launched Brain Training software in Europe and in the Americas almost simultaneously," Iwata noted, "Europe was constantly selling significantly more DS hardware on a weekly basis."

> It was taken for granted that American markets would easily sell twice the number as Europe, but Europe was first in blooming and the Americas are yet to show their real

---

[22] *Source:* The NPD Group, TRSTS Reports, December 2005 Projected, cited in Emerging Trends In Computer Entertainment, PowerPoint presentation by Sony Computer Entertainment America, January 2006.

[23] A Developing Revolution, Nintendo Power, June 2007, pp. 74-77.

[24] Analysis of Operations and Financial Review, Nintendo 2005 Annual Report, p. 36.

[25] Nintendo Interviews: Miyamoto speaks! Computer and Video Games, May 13, 2003, computerandvideogames.com/article.php?id=91537, accessed July 6, 2007.

[26] Nintendo Full Year Results Show Rapid Gain, Gamasutra Industry News, April 26, 2007, gamasutra.com/php-bin/news_index.php?story=13682, accessed July 9, 2007.

[27] Nintendo posts $456.6 million profit, GameSpot News, October 26, 2006, gamespot.com/news/6160557.html, accessed July 9, 2007.

> strength. Of course, we anticipate the expansion of DS there thanks to Pokémon and other titles. We will be glad as more Pokémon are sold, but it is not enough when we want to expand the gaming population.
>
> When I received a report from the U.S. that they sold 1 million Pokémon games already, I asked them, "Why did you sell only 10,000 Brain Age last week, when Europe sold 30,000?" This is a typical example of how I communicate with our people in the U.S. We need constantly to make an effort to appeal to the new audiences.[28]

To appeal to new audiences, Nintendo focused its development efforts on discovering new uses for the DS. For example, Tokyo art museums began using the DS to provide interactive tours of exhibitions. One screen displayed compositions, while the other provided detailed explanations of the art. At the same time, users could access an audio tour using the console's headphone jack.[29] In Kyoto, public high schools used the DS to teach English using special character recognition software. In one school, students achieved 80 per cent English proficiency, compared to only 18 per cent for students who did not use the DS.[30]

Iwata also believed that gaming consoles could become productivity tools. "Modern human beings have less time and energy to spend on any activity," he observed.

> A great many things are changing with incredible speed. The energy one can spend on entertainment has never been very big in the first place. We have a very unusual software program for DS, which tells you how to prepare a meal. I love to use this cooking software to help me prepare meals at home on my days off. I think it important for us to create this type of software that will keep the owners' interests for a long time. . .
>
> As the number of consoles with a single architecture increase, there will be a variety of different possibilities for the machine to benefit society, and they can be steps toward making the DS the machine that enriches the owners' daily lives.[31]

In Japan, Nintendo sold between 600,000 and 700,000 DS consoles per month, with a production rate that continued to be insufficient to meet market demand. Although the console had been on the market for more than two years, retail outlets continued to sell out as soon as new stock arrived. During peak holiday periods, supply shortages in Japan were critical enough to prompt Nintendo to issue a public apology to its customers.[32]

By early 2007, Nintendo had sold more than 40 million DS consoles worldwide. It also began to phase out its Game Boy consoles to focus strictly on the DS platform (see Exhibit 4). Although the

---

[28] Adapted from Q&A from Nintendo Analyst Meeting, April 27, 2007,press.nintendo.com/object?id=7657, accessed July 9, 2007.

[29] TAB Event - "Super Escher" Exhibition, Tokyo Art Beat, December 2006, tokyoartbeat.com/tablog/entries.en/2006/12/super_escher_at_bunkamura_muse.html, accessed July 10, 2007, Nintendo DS museum guide, plasticbamboo.com/2006/10/31/nintendo-ds-museum-guide/, accessed July 13, 2007.

[30] Beyond Pokémon: Nintendo DS Goes To School in Japan, The Wall Street Journal, July 11, 2007, p. A1.

[31] Adapted from Q&A from Nintendo Analyst Meeting, April 27, 2007, press.nintendo.com/object?id=7657, accessed July 9, 2007.

[32] Nintendo DS Shortage Strikes Japan, Leads to $300 Prices, GamePro News, January 10, 2006, gamepro.com/news.cfm?article_id=51053, accessed July 13, 2007.

Game Boy had enjoyed a life span of more than 15 years in its various iterations, Iwata hoped for even better results with the DS. "If we can continue our efforts with DS, to the extent it can be used as a social infrastructure," he noted, "it may be able to enjoy a far longer lifespan than any hardware in the past."[33]

THE WII: NINTENDO'S REVOLUTIONARY CONSOLE

By 2003, analysts began to wonder if Nintendo could ever hope "to recover from what appears to be a withering defeat at the hands of Sony."[34] Nintendo president Satoru Iwata remained unfazed by the criticism. "We are preparing a new product which will give a fresh surprise to consumers," he explained in a 2003 conference.[35] That "surprise" was an early prototype of the Wii, codenamed Revolution.

Nintendo executives already realized that they could not hope to win back market share with faster processors and better graphics while continuing to make a profit on consoles. They also knew that lower prices could not sustain sales if consoles continued to perform poorly relative to competitor consoles. Customers, it appeared, were willing to pay a slight premium for better performance. Nintendo's dilemma was how to increase performance while keeping costs low. Iwata and Miyamoto decided to focus the company's design efforts on one of the console's least expensive components, the controller.

The basic design of a video game controller had not changed in nearly two decades (see Exhibit 5). Iwata and Miyamoto believed that current game pads with their arrays of buttons were intimidating to most non-gamers. If Nintendo could design a controller that looked more like a television remote, the company might be able to attract new customers who have never played video games. Rather than compete directly with Sony and Microsoft for the core 18 to 35 year-old male gamer, the Nintendo Revolution would be targeted to a broader audience that included young children, parents, and even senior citizens.[36] Noted Iwata,

> We decided that Nintendo was going to take another route—game expansion. We are not competing against Sony or Microsoft. We are battling the indifference of people who have no interest in videogames.[37]

Robert Kotick, CEO of Activision, a leading game publisher, was one of several industry leaders to support Nintendo's new approach. "In the past I would have said that the 360 and the PlayStation 3 are likely to take leading market share and that Nintendo would have a very tough time competing," he said.

> But we've grown increasingly excited about Revolution and we do think that it will present some interesting opportunities for the future. The controller is so innovative that I actually think you'll see the potential for application development and genre development that is markedly different and will be a good point of differentiation.[38]

---

[33] Ibid.

[34] Earnings Roundup: Software Up, Hardware Down, Prospects Mixed for Sony, Nintendo, and Atari, Electronic Gaming Business, August 13, 2003.

[35] Ibid.

[36] How the Wii is creaming the competition, Business 2.0 Magazine, April 25, 2007.

[37] Wii will rock you, Fortune, June 1, 2007.

[38] Ibid.

Software Development

Software publishers also welcomed the simplicity of the Revolution, relative to other consoles. They often complained that game system complexity had become increasingly unmanageable. By 2005, the cost to develop a single game often surpassed $20 million,[39] and development times increased to almost 3 years.[40]

The Nintendo Revolution, which was based on much of the same technology as the Gamecube, was simpler than other game consoles. As a result, the development cost for a Nintendo game ranged from 25 to 50 per cent of the cost of a similar Xbox 360 or PlayStation 3 title. Development cycles were also significantly shorter, allowing publishers to produce more games in the same amount of time.[41] That was "good news for Nintendo," noted one video games analyst. "Top game publishers are already developing content for the Revolution, and it's ultimately the software that drives hardware sales."[42]

E3 Unveiling

> Introducing . . . Wii. As in "we."
>
> While the code-name "Revolution" expressed our direction, Wii represents the answer. Wii will break down that wall that separates video game players from everybody else. Wii will put people more in touch with their games . . . and each other.
>
> But you're probably asking: What does the name mean? Wii sounds like "we," which emphasizes this console is for everyone. Wii can easily be remembered by people around the world, no matter what language they speak. No confusion. No need to abbreviate. Just Wii. Wii has a distinctive "ii" spelling that symbolizes both the unique controllers and the image of people gathering to play. And Wii, as a name and a console, brings something revolutionary to the world of video games that sets it apart from the crowd.
>
> So that's Wii. But now Nintendo needs you. Because, it's really not about you or me. It's about Wii. And together, Wii will change everything.[43]

The Nintendo Wii was first unveiled on May 9, 2006, at the Electronic Entertainment Expo (E3), an annual video game trade show. Gamers scoffed at the name chosen by Nintendo, which seemed unusual and less aggressive than "Revolution." "Months of positive hype, a genuine competitive advantage, and they named the thing Wii?" complained one gamer. "If consumers don't even want to say the name of the product, they're not going to buy it."[44]

In reply to the flurry of criticism, Matt Atwood, Nintendo of America's public relations manager observed, "Anytime you announce a new name you're going to get a lot of questions."

> We wanted a name that represented the fact that this system was really for everyone to play. There were thoughts of sticking with Revolution, then there were thoughts

[39] Microsoft Xbox 360; Game prices rise, reflecting advancements, St. Petersburg Times, November 21, 2005.
[40] Product Development, THQ 2006 Annual Report, June 7, 2006.
[41] Wii dev costs fraction of PS3's, 360's, GameSpot.com, May 5, 2006, accessed February 20, 2007.
[42] Don't Write Off Nintendo's 'Revolution,' Analysts Say, Consumer Electronics Daily, March 10, 2006.
[43] Nintendo Press Release, cited in Are Wii Ready? Nintendo's Revolution Renamed, 1up.com news, April 27, 2006, 1up.com/do/newsStory?cId=3150013, accessed June 18, 2007.
[44] The Revolution Has A Name: Nintendo Wii, MTV News, April 27, 2006, www.mtv.com/news/articles/1529658/20060427/index.jhtml, accessed June 18, 2007.

> of a completely different name, but once everything came together this was the name decided. I think Nintendo wanted a name that was very unique, because this system is about an entirely new way to play, an entirely new type of system.[45]

Unlike gamers, analysts attending E3 focused more on the Wii's new motion-sensing controller that redefined the way people played games. Unlike traditional controllers, which required players to manipulate an array of buttons and sticks, the Wii controller often required no button pushing at all (see Exhibit 6). The Wii controller was "a multifunctional device, limited only by the game designer's imagination," Nintendo announced.

> In a tennis game, it serves as a racket you swing with your arm. In a driving game, it serves as your steering wheel. For first-person shooters, the Wii Remote acts as a weapon that you point at an enemy. The list of potential uses goes on and on. In addition to its pointing and motion-sensing abilities, the Wii Remote also includes a speaker, a rumble feature[46] and an expansion port for additional input devices.[47]

Trade show attendees, enamored with Nintendo's new device, queued for up to three hours for a hands-on demonstration at one of the company's 75 console booths.

E3 2006 was also Sony's opportunity to display its new PlayStation 3 console, which, like the Nintendo Wii, was to be released in November 2006. In the months leading up to the trade show, Sony publicized the PlayStation 3 as the only console offering "supercomputer-like power and performance."[48] Yet when Sony revealed its pricing strategy, analysts were dismayed. At $599, it was higher than an Xbox 360 and Wii combined, they observed. At Sony's news conference, Ken Kutaragi, president of Sony Computer Entertainment, became an object of ridicule for suggesting that the PS3 was "probably too cheap."[49] "Although the PS3 does have better graphics," wrote one gaming analyst, "we're really looking forward to the Nintendo Wii and all its titles."

> We feel the fun aspect the Wii will deliver is going to be difficult to beat with better graphics alone. Of course, this is solely based on personal opinion, so we would like to see how far both the Xbox 360 and PS3 can push the limits of console gaming.[50]

The Wii also impressed investment analysts. Noted one,

> Nintendo accomplished the task of convincing publishers, developers, retailers, and the investment community that they have a compelling system. While some critics might say the Wii is a Gamecube with a motion-sensing controller and not much in addition to that, the fact is the other hardware manufacturers are moving toward much more costly platforms—development costs are doubling for the PS3 and Xbox. Nintendo has something that is differentiated, and people are going to like that.[51]

---

[45] The Revolution Gets A Name: Wii, Game Informer News, April 27, 2006, gameinformer.com/News/Story/200604/N06.0427.1154.38678.htm, accessed June 18, 2007.

[46] Rumble was a feedback mechanism within the controller that caused it to vibrate in response to certain game actions, such as weapons fire, crashes, road vibrations, etc.

[47] What is Wii?: Wii Remote, wii.nintendo.com/controller.jsp, accessed June 6, 2007.

[48] PlayStation 3 System Fact Sheet, Sony Computer Entertainment of America Press Release, December 18, 2006.

[49] E3 2006: Kutaragi Claims PS3 Too Cheap?, IGN E3 Expo Coverage, ign.com, May 9, 2006, accessed June 20, 2007.

[50] E3 2006: PlayStation 3 and Nintendo Wii, anantech.com, May 16, 2006, accessed June 6, 2007.

[51] E3 06: Analysts react swiftly to console news, GameSpot.com, May 11, 2006, accessed June 6, 2007.

By the end of E3 2006, Nintendo had won more awards than any other company, including the coveted "Best of Show" award, and "Best Hardware" award.[52] Reginald Fils-Aime, president and COO for Nintendo of America, went away from the show with renewed confidence in his company's strategy. "Our competitors are both going down the same path," he observed.

> Both believe that more and more performance with higher and higher price tags are their keys to success. So what do I see? I think our two competitors will trade share between them, while we go off and grab share in a completely different way.[53]

Marketing Campaign

Viral Marketing

Instead of following a traditional print and television campaign, Nintendo initially supported the wii with viral marketing efforts. It set up consoles in shopping malls and other venues, where people could try the console and then talk about their experiences with friends, acquaintances, and family members. "There is going to be massive amounts of hands-on activity," explained Fils-Aime, "as well as showcasing exactly how Wii games are different.

> We are going to create advocacy. We are going to make it so that everyone who tries the Wii experience talks to their friends and neighbors. It is going to be a really provocative sight to be seeing teens and 20-year-olds and 40-year-olds and 50-year-olds talking about how different this experience is.[54]

In an effort to expand beyond its traditional target market of 9 to 24-year-old males, Nintendo identified key community influencers in major U.S. cities, including gamers, mothers, and multi-generational families, and invited them to company-hosted events. Participants, from children to grandparents, were asked to take turns with the console. Afterwards, attendees were to go to their communities and talk about their experiences. "Our core presumption is if we could get someone to put their hands on the controller, they would be hooked," explained Harrison.

> Most were not video game players, or had potentially a negative attitude about video games, but we identified them as people who were influential in their community. One of the things we were concerned about was if we started advertising on television to this audience, they wouldn't pay attention. We felt like we had to open up the audience's willingness to hear from us before we started the TV advertising.[55]

The company also showed up at non-traditional venues. One that caught the attention of the media was the American Association of Retired Persons Annual Meeting. Nintendo was the first video games company to participate in the conference. Articles about Nintendo's courting of "grey gamers" appeared in dozens of newspapers, including the front page of the New York Times.[56]

Nintendo benefited from the media's extensive coverage of the Wii, which was invariably positive (see Exhibit 7). The majority of the more than 300 newspaper articles published each month about the Wii focused mainly on the console's motion controller, its ability to help tackle obesity and improve

---

[52] Wii tops Game Critics' Best of E3 2006, GameSpot.com, May 31, 2006, accessed June 6, 2007.

[53] Nintendo hopes Wii spells winner, USA Today, August 15, 2006, p. 3B.

[54] Ibid.

[55] Marketing moms, Los Angeles Times, December 25, 2006, p. C-1.

[56] As Minds Age, What's Next? Brain Calisthenics, The New York Times, December 27, 2006, p. 1.

fitness, and its success against the Xbox 360 and PlayStation 3, while the relatively few negative articles centered on sports injury cases and property damage caused by controllers flying out of users' hands.

Advertising

Traditional game advertising typically emphasized the technical qualities of a console. Television commercials displayed scenes from games that demonstrated the more advanced qualities of the system. Sony, for example, demonstrated the advanced graphical capabilities of the PlayStation 3 through a combination of game play scenes and narration (see Exhibit 8).

For the Wii, Nintendo took a decidedly different path. Instead of showing games, commercials focused on users. In one television spot, titled "Wii for all," two Japanese Nintendo representatives dressed in black suits arrived at American homes. After bowing to their hosts, they announced, "Wii would like to play." These were the only words spoken during the commercial, followed by scenes of regular people swinging their arms, jumping, and running as the two Nintendo representatives watched quietly from the back of the room (see Exhibit 9). "One thing that is very important in entertainment," explained Miyamoto, "is that when one person is doing something, it has to be entertaining in a way that when other people see that person playing a game, they want to play it too."

> That was one of the concepts of the Wii. We not only wanted it to be fun, we wanted it to look fun so that it would be inviting to other people, who would then want to pick it up and play it.[57]

Pricing

Priced at $249, the Wii was the least expensive next generation console. Unlike the Xbox 360 and PS3, both of which required the purchase of additional content in order to play games, the Wii included a collection of five sports games in the standard retail package. The games were chosen carefully by Nintendo to demonstrate the motion sensing capabilities of the Wii Remote. For example, in Wii Tennis, users used the controller as a tennis racket, while in Wii Baseball it was used as a bat.

Despite the Wii's lower price relative to competitors, Nintendo earned about $50 on each console sold. The acclaimed Wii Remote controller cost Nintendo approximately $10 to manufacture, including a motion sensing chip, rumble feature, and Bluetooth wireless communications.[58]

Online Gaming

Although Microsoft was the undisputed leader in online gaming with more than 6 million subscribers to its Xbox Live service, Nintendo offered its own free service, known as the Wii Channel. As Nintendo extended its online service, it hoped to generate revenue from online advertising and from subscription fees for access to the site's advanced features.

One of the more popular features of Nintendo's online service was the Virtual Console (VC), a section of Nintendo's online store where Wii owners could purchase and download classic video games originally released for Nintendo 64, the Super Nintendo Entertainment System and the NES. Nintendo also struck deals with Sega Corporation and 24 other software developers to offer third party

---

[57] Shigeru Miyamoto Interview, GameSpot.com, July 12, 2007. (gamespot.com/video/942009/6174769/shigeru-miyamoto-interview, accessed July 16, 2007.

[58] Wii will rock you, Fortune, June 4, 2007.

classic game titles, including many that had never before appeared on a Nintendo console.[59] Titles were priced between $5.00 and $10.00 each.

Another popular feature was the Mii Channel, which included an art program for creating personalized avatars (digital representations of a player), known as Miis. Once players created their Miis, they could use them in multiplayer games such as Wii Sports (see Exhibit 10).

Lastly, the Wii could also function as a full-fledged Internet browser with access to the latest weather, news, and sports, as well as e-mail and other standard Internet services.

Third Party Support

The early success of the Wii also surprised game developers, many of whom shifted more resources to the development of Wii titles. In particular, the popularity of sports games prompted some developers to announce new sports-related game titles exclusively for the Wii platform. For many, it was a godsend. The lower development costs and faster turnaround times meant that developers could produce new titles quickly and earn higher margins. David Zucker, president and CEO of Midway Games, explained,

> Since the typical development cost for a Wii title is significantly less than it is for a PS3 or Xbox 360, it allows you to continue to invest efficiently in that platform. We have plans to continue to pursue and support the Wii with three more titles this year. And we will have more next year.[60]

Even games that were not exclusive to the platform often functioned differently on the Wii. For instance, THQ Inc., modified the controls on its popular wrestling game, WWE SmackDown, to take advantage of the Wii's motion controls. Specific motions with the Wii Remote controlled corresponding punches, throws, and slams against virtual opponents. On other platforms, users pressed buttons to control on-screen action.[61]

Just as the success of the PlayStation and PlayStation 2 depended on the thousands of software titles available for those systems, a steady stream of new Nintendo titles ensured that interest in the Wii would remain strong. By the end of June 2007, the Wii had more than 400 available or announced game titles, compared to less than 300 for the PS3.[62] Robust console sales and strong launch titles translated into healthy game sales. Seven of the top ten selling titles were for Nintendo systems, including four for the Wii and three for the DS.[63]

Although new content was critical to a gaming console's success, too much new content could confuse customers and lead to poorer sales of key titles. With thousands of titles available for various gaming platforms, retail stores had a difficult time displaying games effectively. Often games had to be stacked together in such a way that only the spine of the display box was visible. Only the most popular titles received proper display space. Iwata was concerned that many of those titles did not represent the best gaming experiences, but they received better promotion because of motion picture tie-ins. "If a person is disappointed by the software he or she has chosen," Iwata explained, "they may say, 'I won't play games anymore.'"

---

[59] 24 Wii VC devs ID'd, GameSpot News, September 14, 2006 (gamespot.com/news/6157639.html, accessed July 10, 2007.

[60] Q1 2007 Midway Games Earnings Conference Call, FD (Fair Disclosure) Wire, May 3, 2007.

[61] WWE SmackDown! vs. RAW 2008 First-Look, gamespot.com/wii/action/smackdownvsraw2008/news.html, March 30, 2007, accessed July 2, 2007.

[62] *Source:* gamespot.com, accessed July 2, 2007.

[63] Nintendo Throws Down Again, New York Times, July 23, 2007, bits.blogs.nytimes.com/2007/07/23/nintendo-throws-down-again-not-the-way-you-think, accessed July 24, 2007.

> The increase in software titles per se is good, but we cannot be content with the situation. We have to recognize that our customers have a limited amount of attention, we have to struggle to find out a way to communicate what they really want to know and we have to be considerate so that we will not betray our customers' expectations. This is going to be an increasingly important mission for us.[64]

Sony and Microsoft Respond

Sony responded to the Nintendo juggernaut by lowering the price of its PlayStation 3 and PlayStation Portable consoles to $499 and $169, respectively. Microsoft followed Sony with price reductions of between $20 and $50 for its Xbox 360 systems. This placed the base Xbox 360 within the same price range as the Nintendo Wii, with base Xbox 360 systems selling for a suggest retail price of $279.[65]

Both companies also tried to put a bold face on the situation by emphasizing the value added features of their consoles. Compared to the Wii, they offered significantly better graphics. In addition, the PS3 included a Blu-Ray DVD drive for watching high definition movies, while Xbox 360 owners benefited from the most advanced online experience available. To take full advantage of these features, users needed to connect their consoles to high definition television (HDTV) sets and to broadband Internet. Although HDTV penetration rates remained low at 30 per cent of U.S. homes, that number was set to increase substantially with average annual growth of more than 50 per cent.[66] Broadband penetration was considerably higher at 53 per cent of US households and more than 70 per cent of Internet subscribers.[67]

Sony and Microsoft also took direct aim at Nintendo by introducing new games for casual gamers. "Scene-It?" for the Xbox 360 required players to respond to trivia questions and puzzle challenges. The retail package also included a simplified controller designed to imitate a game show buzzer (see Exhibit 11). Sony offered Echochrome for the PlayStation 3 and PSP, a downloadable puzzle game in which a stick figure tries to cross a rotating 3D platform (see Exhibit 12).

All the same, Nintendo continued to dominate console sales heading into the 2007 holiday season (see Exhibit 13). Projected cumulative deliveries of Wii consoles were expected to reach 20 million units worldwide by April 2008,[68] compared to 10 million units for the Sony PlayStation 3[69] and 18 million units for the Xbox 360.[70]

Managing Supply Shortages

In the United States, the holiday season was critical to the success of a new game system. Although console sales invariably declined after the holidays, demand for the Wii unexpectedly accelerated,

---

[64] Q&A from Nintendo Analyst Meeting, April 27, 2007, press.nintendo.com/object?id=7657, accessed July 9, 2007.

[65] Microsoft to cut $50 off price of Xbox 360, The Seattle Post-Intelligencer, August 6, 2007, seattlepi.nwsource.com/business/326586_msftxbox07.html, accessed August 17, 2007.

[66] Report Shows HDTV Sets Likely to See Major Growth, TMCnet, June 28, 2007, tmcnet.com/voip/ip-communications/articles/8029-report-shows-hdtv-sets-likely-see-major-growth.htm, accessed July 24, 2007.

[67] Over Half of U.S. Households Subscribe to Broadband Internet, Leichtman Research Group Press Release, June 7, 2007, eichtmanresearch.com/press/060707release.html, accessed July 24, 2007.

[68] Console makers setting new parameters for game market, The Nikkei Weekly, May 7, 2007.

[69] Analyst: Sony Missing Sales Goal By 25%, Gamasutra Industry News, January 15, 2007, gamasutra.com/php-bin/news_index.php?story=12397, accessed July 2, 2007.

[70] Case writer estimates based on cumulative sales of 12 million units through June 2007 and average quarterly sales of 1.5 million units.

leaving Nintendo scrambling to increase production. When new stock arrived at retail stores, it sold out within a few hours. By the summer, Nintendo was still struggling to make enough units to meet demand. At the Nintendo store in New York City, approximately 100 customers stood in line every morning hoping to obtain one of the consoles that arrived nightly, something normally seen during the first few days after a popular product launch.[71]

Many new Wii owners became advocates, spreading the word through social networking and blog websites. Even Nintendo was unprepared for such a response. "We have no recollection of a time when our products were being talked about this much in non-business situations," Nintendo of America executives told Iwata.[72]

Although Nintendo admitted that it was unprepared for the popularity of the Wii, some accused the company of deliberately withholding stock. Dan DeMatteo, COO of GameStop, a leading video game retailer, believed that "Nintendo intentionally dried up their supply," to meet certain financial objectives. Mike Wolf, research director for Digital Home magazine, felt the shortage was an attempt to create demand for the Wii. "Intentional scarcity is nothing new," he explained.

> It can be a great demand-creation tool as the buzz builds for consumers who hear great things about a new product and yet, cannot get one themselves. Whether or not this shortage of Wiis in the market was happenstance or calculated, Nintendo needs to realize that consumers are fickle and the well of Wii-mania they are drinking from may not be entirely bottomless.[73]

Harrison, however, was adamant that the shortages were unintentional.

> We have worldwide territories that are all competing over the available production. The Japan and European markets are doing extremely well with the Wii. People in Nintendo Japan are making the best decisions that they can about which products get shipped to which market and when.[74]

One way retailers attempted to manage demand was to bundle accessories and games with the console. Many retailers offered Wii packages for between $350 and $600, depending on the number of included accessories. Miyamoto was concerned that expensive bundles would place the Wii out of reach of many families. "When the peripheral is bundled together, it makes it all more expensive and people aren't willing to spend the money on it," he explained.[75] Nevertheless, retail bundles appeared to do little to soften demand, with most packages going out-of-stock within hours.

Harrison knew that if shortages were to continue into the 2007 holiday season, the ranks of discontented retailers and consumers would grow. Unfortunately, components suppliers were unable to increase production sufficiently to meet Nintendo's needs until well into 2008.[76] Accordingly, most

---

[71] Want a Wii? Get in line, USA Today, June 29, 2007,usatoday.com/tech/gaming/2007-06-29-wii-demand_N.htm Accessed July 2, 2007.

[72] Q&A from Nintendo Analyst Meeting, April 27, 2007, press.nintendo.com/object?id=7657, accessed July 9, 2007.

[73] Intentional Scarcity: For Nintendo, how long is the lack of Wii's a good thing?, ABI Research, April 27, 2007, abiresearch.com/Blog/Digital_Home_Blog/338, accessed August 1, 2007.

[74] Nintendo Rejects Wii Shortage Plot, Next Generation, March 28, 2007, next-gen.biz/index2.php?option=com_content&task=view&id=5050, accessed August 1, 2007.

[75] An interview with Nintendo's super game designer Shigeru Miyamoto, San Jose Mercury News, July 29, 2007, blogs.mercurynews.com/aei/2007/07/an_interview_with_nintendos_super_game_designer_shigeru_miyamoto.html, accessed August 1, 2007.

[76] Nintendo delays plan to increase Wii production, Virgin Media, August 17, 2007, virginmedia.com/games/gamingnews/news-story.php?storyid=11677902, accessed August 17, 2007.

analysts predicted a significant deterioration in Wii availability for the remainder of 2007. However, unlike the 2006 holiday season, which saw console prices soar on grey markets, such as eBay, consumers could turn to alternative consoles. Neither the Xbox 360 nor the PlayStation 3 was in short supply, and both cost significantly less than they did in 2006.

Exhibit 1 Nintendo company, limited

			Consolidated Sales Information (US$ '000)[1]	
Business Category	**Main Products**		**Year Ended March 31, 2006**	**Year Ended March 31, 2007**
		Handheld	1,902,887	3,179,536
	Hardware	Console	209,678	1,330,063
		Others	280,050	461,193
Electronic entertainment products	Hardware total		2,392,614	4,970,792
		Handheld	1,467,619	2,481,286
	Software	Console Royalties,	429,276	700,069
		content income, etc.	20,596	45,059
	Software total		1,917,490	3,226,413
	Electronic entertainment products		4,310,104	8,197,205
Other	Playing cards		18,496	18,309
Total			4,328,600	8,215,514

Source: Nintendo Co. Ltd.

[1] Currency converted to U.S. dollars from Japanese yen at a rate of US$0.0085 per yen. Source: Oanda Currency Converter, oanda.com/convert/classic, accessed July 6, 2007.

Exhibit 2 The Nintendo DS

Exhibit 3 Brain age for the nintendo DS

Source: Nintendo.

Exhibit 4 Nintendo company, limited

Sales Units in Ten Thousands

Consolidated Sales Units, Number of New Titles, and Sales Unit Forecast[1]						
			Year Ended Apr.-Mar. '06	**Year Ended Apr.-Mar. '07**	**Life-To-Date Mar. '07**	**Foreeast Apr. '07-Mar. '08**
Game Boy Advance	Hardware	Japan	100	11	1,666	
		The Americas	472	300	4,110	
		Other	261	122	2,171	
		Total	833	434	7,946	–
of which Game Boy Advance SP		Japan	42	8	650	
		The Americas	426	252	2,347	
		Other	176	109	1,195	
		Total	644	369	4,192	
of which Game Boy Micro		Japan	58	3	61	
		The America	47	48	95	
		other	79	8	87	
		Total	183	59	242	
	Software	Japan	728	255	7,236	
		The Americas	3,534	2,599	20,857	
		other	1,674	999	8,532	
		Total	5,939	3,853	36, 625	800
Nintendo DS	Hardware	Japan	478	912	1,602	
		The Americas	292	663	1,174	
		Other	376	781	1,252	
		Total	1,146	2,356	4,029	2,200

(*Continued*)

(*Continued*)

			Year Ended Apr.-Mar. '06	Year Ended Apr.-Mar. '07	Life-To-Date Mar. '07	Foreeast Apr. '07-Mar. '08
of which Nintedo DS Lite		Japan	58	890	948	
		The Americas	—	641	641	
		Other	—	569	596	
		Total	58	2,128	2,185	
	Software	Japan	2,152	4,977	7,511	
		The Americas	1,608	3,720	5,803	
		Other	1,235	3,658	5,085	
		Total	4,995	12,355	18,398	13,000
Ninetendo Game Cube	Hardware	Japan	20	2	402	
		The Americas	172	63	1,281	
		Other	44	8	476	
		Total	235	73	2,159	
	Software	Japan	298	44	2,741	
		The Americas	2,388	1,448	13,613	
		Other	592	188	4,234	
		Total	3,279	1,680	20,588	350
Wii	Hardware	Japan	–	200	200	
		The Americas	–	237	237	
		Other	–	147	147	
		Total	–	584	584	1,400
	Software	Japan	–	612	612	
		The Americas	–	1,449	1,449	
		Other	–	823	823	
		Total	–	2,884	2884	5,500

[1] *Source:* Nintendo Consolidated Financial Statements, April 26, 2007.

Exhibit 5 Game controllers (1983 to 2001)

Nintendo Family Entertainment System (1983)

Super Nintendo (1990)

Sony PlayStation (1995)

Nintendo Gamecube (2001)

Source: Wikipedia.org, accessed June 18, 2007.

Exhibit 6 Wii remote

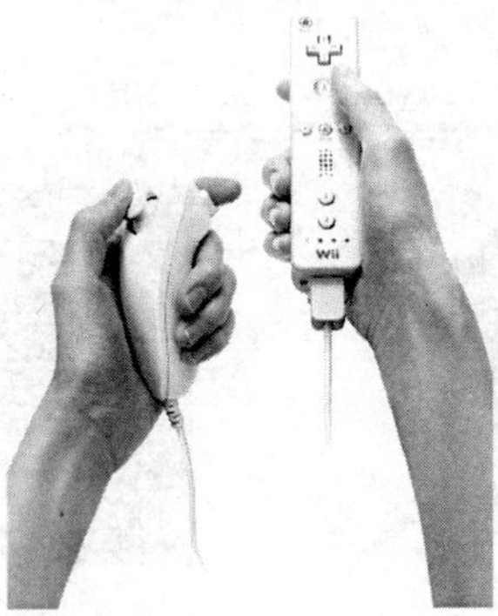

Source: Nintendo.com.

Exhibit 7 Sample of newspaper headlines (January – July 2007)

1. Wii needs more games; Developers push to meet demand on popular box, The San Francisco Chronicle, May 18, 2007
2. COVER STORY: Getting off the couch; Wii's sports games are scoring points as a way to work out, Newsday (New York), March 13, 2007
3. Nintendo's Wii, Radiating Fun, Is Eclipsing Sony, The New York Times, January 31, 2007
4. Wii are the champions Video-game system lets couch spuds mimic the motions of their favorite sports, Arkansas Democrat-Gazette (Little Rock), July 9, 2007
5. Hackers take remote beyond video games; What WON'T a Wii-mote do?, The Seattle Times, May 1, 2007
6. Wii wins big among casual gamers; Group could be huge, untapped mass market, USA Today, May 25, 2007
7. Fitness; Take that, body fat!; Nintendo's Wii is getting video game players off the couch and into a mini-workout., Los Angeles Times, March 5, 2007
8. Games Seek To Bring Seniors To Their Feet — Nintendo marketing the Wii in retirement communities, The Boston Globe, June 16, 2007
9. Game-makers underestimated appeal of Wii; Companies are now scrambling to produce titles for the hit console owned by more than three million fans, writes Michael White from New York., Ottawa Citizen, April 10, 2007

(Continued)

(*Continued*)

10. Waiting Game; Nintendo's Popular Wii System Remains Hard to Find, Pittsburgh Post-Gazette (Pennsylvania), June 15, 2007
11. For gamers, Wii is No. 1; Low price, unique controller make Nintendo most popular, The San Francisco Chronicle, March 17, 2007
12. Channels, Classic Games Draw Older Audience to Wii, Pittsburgh Post-Gazette (Pennsylvania), March 10, 2007
13. Wii-markable; Nintendo's gaming system entrenched as a cultural phenomenon, Ottawa Citizen, May 31, 2007
14. Nintendo Wii steers virtual route toward youth fitness — Game systems offered as exercise equipment, The Boston Globe, May 14, 2007
15. 'Wii Play' completes gaming package; Shipping extra controller shows folks at Nintendo know business, Grand Rapid Press (Michigan), March 5, 2007
16. Nintendo Says Its Wii Game Will Remain in Short Supply, The New York Times, July 12, 2007

Source: LexisNexis (sorted by relevance).

Exhibit 8 "Higher definition: play beyond" PS3 trailer

Scene 1: Opening Scene

Scene 2: "This is a pixel"

Scene 3: "Image that is 10X the quality"

Scene 5: "Every vivid detail is rendered"

Scene 6: RSX "100 billion operations a second"

Scene 7: HDMI "highest quality video & audio"

Scene 4: Blu-ray – 50GB High Definition

Scene 8: Closing Scene

Source: Playb3yond.com.

Exhibit 9 Nintendo "Wii for All" Trailer

Scene 1: "Wii would like to play!"

Scene 5: Urban professionals–Adventure game

Scene 2: Suburban Family–Wii Sports

Scene 6: Farmers–Football and Action games

Scene 3: Mexican American Family–Fitness

Scene 7: Farmer shows his gratitude

(*Continued*)

(*Continued*)

Scene 4: Mexican American Family-Boxing

Scene 8: Wii Ambassadors Drive into Sunset

Source: wii.nintendo.com.

Exhibit 10 Mii channel

Source: ign.com.

Exhibit 11 Scene-T for the XBox 360

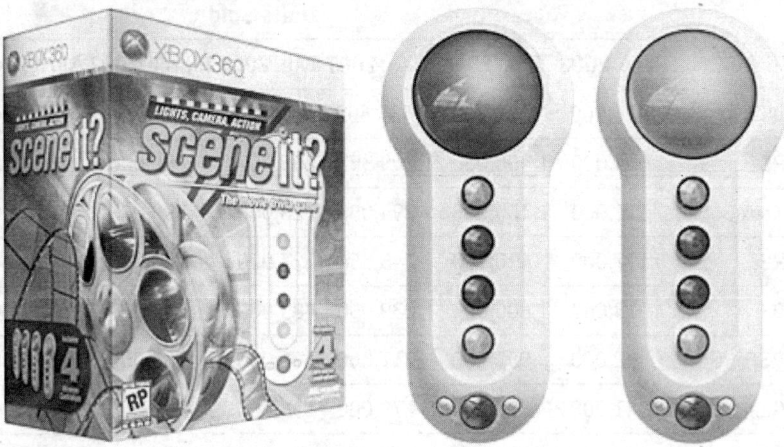

Source: ign.com.

Exhibit 12 Echochrome for the PS3 and PSP

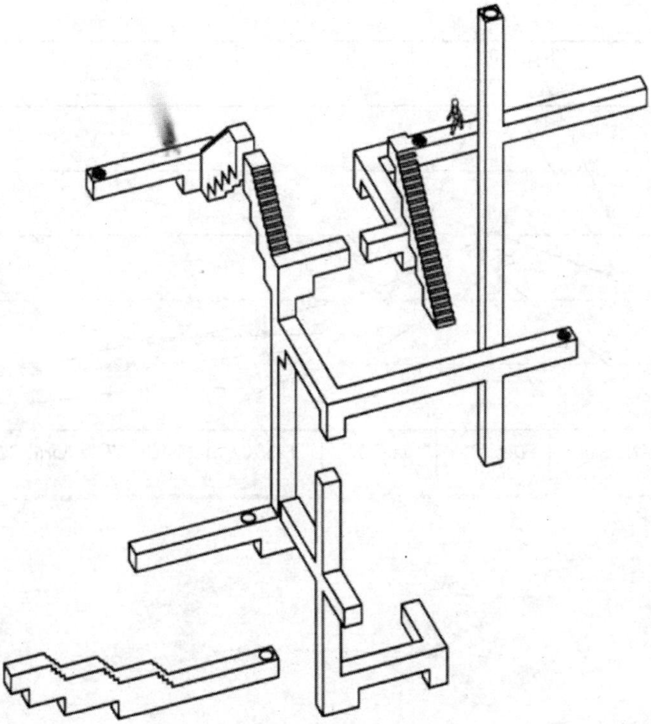

Source: Gamespot.com.

Exhibit 13 Monthly US sales of video game hardware

		Units Sold						
Company	**Platform**	**Nov. 2006**	**Dec. 2006**	**Jan. 2007**	**Feb. 2007**	**March 2007**	**April 2007**	**May 2007**
Nintendo	Wii	476,000	604,200	435,503	335,000	259,000	360,000	338,000
Sony	PS2	664,000	1,400,000	299,352	295,000	280,000	194,000	187,000
Microsoft	Xbox 360	511,000	1,100,000	294,000	228,000	199,000	174,000	154,900
Sony	PS3	197,000	490,700	243,554	127,000	130,000	82,000	81,600
Nintendo	DS	918,000	1,600,000	239,000	485,000	508,000	471,000	423,000
Sony	PSP	412,000	953,200	211,000	176,000	180,000	183,000	221,120
Nintendo	Game Boy	641,000	850,000	179,000	136,000	148,000	84,000	80,554
Nintendo	Game Cube	70,000	64,000	24,000	24,000	22,000	13,000	10,728

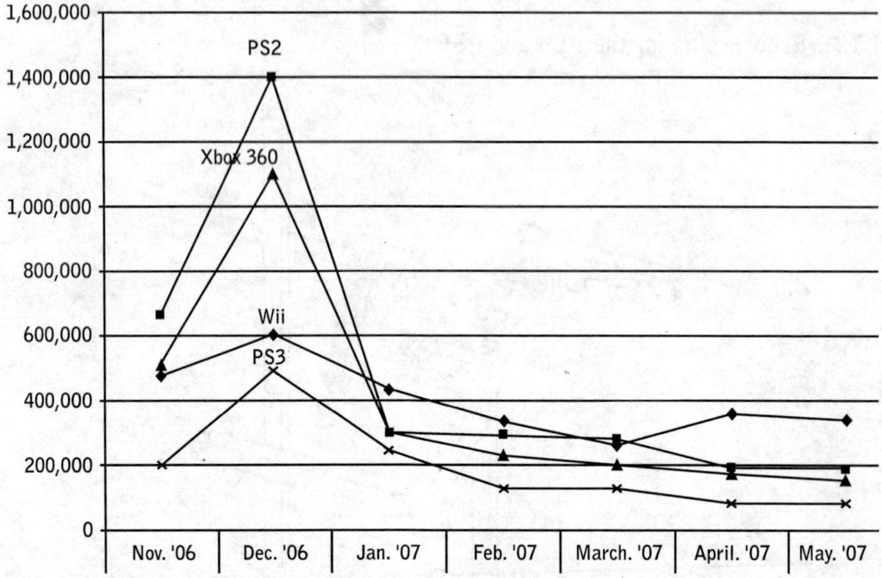

Source: NPD Funworld.

12

SaskTel

Marsha Watson prepared this case under the supervision of Elizabeth M.A. Grasby solely to provide material for class discussion. The authors do not intend to illustrate either effective or ineffective handling of a managerial situation. The authors may have disguised certain names and other identifying information to protect confidentiality.

It was January 2007. Pat Tulloch, senior director of marketing at SaskTel, was in her Regina, Saskatchewan, office reviewing product information for the LifeState™ health monitoring system. SaskTel's executive committee had recently approved a proposal to launch this system into the Canadian marketplace. In preparation for the proposed July 1, 2007, product launch, Tulloch had been given the task of developing a marketing plan, which she would have to present to the executive committee in two weeks' time. To create this plan, Tulloch would need to quickly make some distribution and promotion decisions and conduct a financial analysis of the product's potential profitability.

CANADA'S HEALTH-CARE SYSTEM

History

Canada's health-care system, introduced more than 40 years ago, provided universal, comprehensive coverage for medically necessary hospital and physician services. These services were provided on the basis of need rather than on the patients' ability to pay. This health insurance program, known to Canadians as "Medicare," was best described as an interlocking set of 10 provincial and three territorial health insurance plans, all of which shared certain common features and basic standards of coverage.[1] This universal health-care system was funded primarily through personal and corporate taxation, with private donations accounting for about a quarter of the funding. Roles and responsibilities for Canada's health-care system were shared between the federal and provincial-territorial governments. Under the Canada Health Act (CHA), federal health insurance legislation, criteria and conditions had to be satisfied by the provincial and territorial health-care insurance plans in order for them to qualify for funding. Health Canada was the federal department responsible for helping Canadians maintain and improve their health, while respecting individual choices and circumstances. Provincial and territorial governments were responsible for the management, organization and delivery of health services for their residents.[2]

2000–2007

The costs of illness in Canada were expected to exceed $140 billion dollars due to an aging population. To control costs, the number of hospital beds had been decreased by over 11.5 per cent from 1999 to 2004. As well, Health Canada had adopted a preventative vision and an active role in health-care across the country,[3] subscribing to the belief that an active role in prevention by all Canadians could help lower the costs of health care, increase quality of life and reduce wait times. With wait times and overcrowded emergency rooms, many Canadians began to look at other options for faster treatment. One of these options was private clinics where services were paid for by the patient.

With chronic diseases among the costliest to the health-care system, Health Canada had been forced to consider alternatives to acute care and had begun funding programs that provided patients with the ability to manage their own condition. In 2006, three per cent of Canada's health-care spending (approximately $3.9 billion) was spent on information technology. This market was expected to grow by approximately 15 per cent for the next five years,[4] with software and services growing the most rapidly, followed by mobile health care.

SASKATCHEWAN

With a population of 968,157,[5] Saskatchewan was Canada's sixth largest province and the birthplace of Medicare.[6] Because of its large land mass, many of Saskatchewan's population lived in rural communities that focused on agriculture, forestry and mining. Almost 95 per cent of the goods produced in the province were dependent on natural resources. With China's need for potash and commodity prices on the rise, Saskatchewan's economy had been booming, and the province had become one of the world's top producers of uranium. Oil and natural gas production were also important industries, attracting Canadians from across Canada to the province. Saskatchewan had the highest proportion of citizens over the age of 65 in Canada, and 14.88 per cent of the population was of aboriginal descent.

---

[1] Health Canada, http://www.hc-sc.gc.ca/hcs-sss/medi-assur/index-eng.php, accessed August 18, 2008.
[2] Health Canada, http://www.hc-sc.gc.ca/hcs-sss/medi-assur/index-eng.php, accessed August 18, 2008.
[3] Health Canada, http://www.hc-sc.gc.ca, accessed August 18, 2008.
[4] Among developed nations, Canadians were the highest users of the Internet and computer technology.
[5] Government of Saskatchewan, http://www.gov.sk.ca, accessed August 19, 2008.
[6] The Canadian universal health-care system was modelled on Saskatchewan's public hospital insurance program and Medicare program. The program, enacting hospital coverage in 1947 and medical coverage in 1962, was the first of its kind in Canada. Envisioned and promoted by Thomas C. Douglas (1904-1986) a politician from Saskatchewan. (*Source:* http://www.mta.ca/about_canada/study_guide/doctors/delivery.html)

SASKTEL

Company Background

SaskTel, in operation for nearly 100 years, was a provincial Crown corporation[7] that specialized in full-service communication to the province of Saskatchewan. Its service offerings ranged from voice, data and dial-up high-speed Internet, entertainment, web hosting, text messaging, cellular, wireless, home phone, business solutions and multimedia data services. Through its subsidiaries, Sasktel offered security monitoring, directory assistance, hospital-room communications to the health care sector and international telecommunications consulting.[8]

SaskTel had posted a consolidated net income of $64.4 million in 2005, and the company had exceeded $1 billion in operating revenue in 2006, resulting in a consolidated net income of $72.2 million. SaskTel and its subsidiaries employed 5,200 people, had been ranked by Maclean's magazine as one of Canada's top 100 employers six years in a row, had won the human resources award from the International Association for Native Employment and had been deemed by J.D. Power and Associates[9] to have the highest customer satisfaction levels for contracted wireless providers of any service provider in Canada.

Robert Watson

In late 2004, Robert Watson, a telecommunications veteran, assumed the position of president and chief executive officer at SaskTel. Watson had held executive positions in many telecommunications companies across Canada, was the recipient of the Saskatchewan Centennial Medal and had served on the boards for the Information Technology Association of Canada and the Canadian Prostate Cancer Network.

Pat Tulloch

Upon graduating from the University of Regina's marketing program, Pat Tulloch was immediately hired by SaskTel as a marketing associate. She progressed within the company where she had worked on many projects for various products, including the launch of Max Entertainment Service, merchandising programs for the SaskTel stores and promotional activities for the 2006 Juno Awards[10] in Saskatoon. Tulloch was promoted to senior director of marketing in 2005.

LIFESTAT™

Product Description

The LifeStat™ service was a monitoring device that enabled the communication of a client's health information and could be used by the client, a direct relative (or a loved one) or a professional caregiver. Clients used tools such as blood pressure monitors, scales, glucose meters and heart rate monitors (see Exhibit 1) to collect information, which was then transmitted to SaskTel's secure data

---

[7] A Crown corporation was a government-owned business that did not pay income tax. Most Crown corporations operated at arm's length from the government, with control exercised on budgeting and appointments only.

[8] Sasktel, http://www.sasktel.ca/about-us/company-information/corporate-profile.html, accessed August 16, 2008.

[9] J.D Power and Associates was a global marketing service company known for its customer satisfaction research.

[10] The Juno Awards are presented annually to Canadian music artists acknowledged for their achievements in aspects of music.

centre. Thus, the service linked the communication gap between patients and their caregivers to ensure personal health and well-being was maintained. LifeStat™ also provided a means for the patient to be monitored around the clock by health-care professionals who would contact the client in the event of an emergency (see Exhibit 2).

Sasktel had trademarked LifeStat™ with the Canadian Intellectual Properties Office and had a patent on the technology for Canada. To date, the system has undergone three successful trials (seven First Nations reserves with the Battleford, Saskatchewan, Tribal Council, St. Paul's Hospital in Saskatoon, and the Diabetes Education Centre at the Royal University Hospital in Saskatoon) and was showing promising results for its public launch.

Potential Customers

Tulloch had identified two potential customer segments that would benefit from the LifeStat™ technology: individuals with diabetes and individuals with hypertension.

Diabetes Customers

The LifeStat™ system had recently gained attention from the Diabetes Association of Canada and was being promoted as a resource to aid in the self-management of blood sugar levels. There are two main types of diabetes. Type 1 diabetes occurs when the pancreas is unable to produce insulin, and Type 2 diabetes occurs when the pancreas does not produce enough insulin or the body does not use the insulin it produces. If blood sugar levels are not properly controlled through monitoring and regulation, complications could lead to long-term health problems ranging from vascular disease, coronary artery disease, stroke, gangrene and dementia. Typically, monitoring was performed by the individual at home or at work through a small monitoring device; however, no data was transferred to the patient's caregiver, so it was left to the individual to ensure that their own glucose levels were within the normal range and to administer self-treatment when needed.

Approximately 8.3 per cent of the Canadian population[11] had been diagnosed with diabetes,[12] and, in an independent survey, eight per cent of individuals diagnosed with diabetes indicated they would purchase LifeStat™ at a monthly cost of between $50 and $65 to help monitor their blood glucose levels. In Saskatchewan, 8.1 per cent of the population had reported being diagnosed with diabetes, with a high prevalence in aboriginals.

Hypertension Customers

Hypertension is the persistence of high blood pressure and is the No. 1 cause of strokes. Blood pressure measures the force of blood against the walls of the blood vessels, and readings consistently higher than 140/90 mm HG are considered high. In Canada, 14.9 per cent of the population had been diagnosed with hypertension, and this number was expected to grow to close to 20 per cent by 2011. Self monitoring was the primary doctor-recommended preventative action for hypertension patients. In Saskatchewan, 15.9 per cent of the population has been diagnosed with hypertension and, in an independent survey, two per cent of those diagnosed said they would purchase LifeStat™ at a monthly cost of between $50 and $65.

When managing their health, both hypertension and diabetes patients searched for products that were reasonably priced, convenient, easy to use and added to the patient's independence.

---

[11] Canada's population in 2006 was 31,612,897.

[12] 2005: Statistics Canada, Canadian Community Health Survey, 2005.

Competition

There were three major technology and communications companies, CyberNet Medical, Philips Medical Systems and AMD Telemedicine, that posed potential competition for LifeStat™.

CyberNet Medical

CyberNet Medical Corporation was a division of CyberNet Systems Corporation, which was located in Ann Arbor, Michigan. Founded in 1988, CyberNet Systems focused on robotics technology with developments in commercial web devices and national defence robotics. CyberNet's medical monitoring system offered to the public was called MedStar. Users collected physiological information from in-home devices and sent the information, via the Internet, to a data management system where medical reports could be compiled to individual specifications. The MedStar unit retailed in the United States for $975 to $2,946, depending on the specific devices needed for the unit. There was also a $37.50 monthly account monitoring fee.

Philips Medical Systems

Philips Medical Systems, a division of Philips Electronics, operated in 63 countries, including Canada, with over 6,000 sales professionals and service technicians. As of 2004, Philips Electronics had yearly revenues of US$30 billion and assets exceeding US$4.4 billion. In 2006, Philips purchased LifeLine Inc., a medical alarm company that serviced over 500,000 Canadians. This service included telephone reminders, personal help buttons and speaker phone devices. Philips' medical monitoring device was called the Motiva Interactive, which used broadband television, along with home vital sign measurement devices, to connect individuals to a health-care provider and monitoring system. The monitoring service cost $140 per month. This fee did not include a one-time cost for the specific devices needed to take physiological measurements.

AMD Telemedicine, Inc.

AMD Telemedicine, Inc. (AMD) had over 4,000 installations in 58 countries and was considered to be the leader in the telemedicine industry. In 2006, AMD signed a contract with the Visiting Nurses Association, the oldest home care agency in the United States. U.S. home care nurses cared for over 24,000 patients and made more than 400,000 home visits a year. AMD's health monitoring system, the CareCompanion, provided event reminders and medication prompts and measured vital signs through the user's peripheral monitoring equipment. This information was then transmitted over the Internet to the patient's health-care professional for monitoring. This service was currently available only in the United States and retailed for US$125 per month plus a one-time cost for the specific devices needed to take physiological measurements.

Distribution Options

Market research indicated that 70 per cent of respondents would prefer to purchase LifeStat™ through their local pharmacy, while the majority of the remainder of the respondents preferred to be able to purchase the product online. After discussions with a number of pharmaceutical representatives, Tulloch narrowed her distribution options to three possible retail chains: Shoppers Drug Mart, London Drugs and Safeway Pharmacy. She would have to choose which of the retailers should be offered the product to ensure its success.

Shoppers Drug Mart

Shoppers Drug Mart (Shoppers) represented a large portion of the pharmaceutical retail market. A well-known brand with more than 1,055 stores across Canada, Shoppers presented a significant opportunity to LifeStat^{TM} for national sales. Although Shoppers was the best option for national distribution, Tulloch wondered whether a nationwide launch would be too aggressive so early in the product's life cycle. Shoppers maintained margins of 45 per cent on all hardware and expected a \$75 commission on all one-year contracts sold.

London Drugs

A leader in Western Canada, London Drugs had not yet entered the Eastern Canada market. With more than 45 million customers across British Columbia, Alberta, Saskatchewan and Manitoba, London Drug's pharmacy was still the centre of the business, despite the company's having diversified into small appliances, furniture, computers and cosmetics. London Drugs maintained a 48 per cent margin on all hardware sold in-store and expected a \$75 commission on all one-year contracts sold.

Safeway Pharmacy

Safeway Pharmacy was a division within the Safeway grocery stores that were prevalent across Western Canada and the United States. With over 1,775 locations, this option had the greatest potential for diversification into the United States. Within Canada, Safeway had 182 stores west of Thunder Bay, Ontario. Safeway Pharmacy offered a focus on diabetes health and wellness through education and preventative education. On all hardware, Safeway expected margins of 40 per cent and a \$75 commission on each one-year contract signed.

Promotion

Tulloch needed to determine LifeStat^{TM}'s promotional plan for fiscal 2007. The 2007 marketing budget was set at \$300,000 for a Saskatchewan-only launch and at \$1.2 million for a national launch, and she would have to effectively allocate these resources to various promotional activities. After the first year, the promotional budget would be eight per cent of sales. It was critical that the promotional campaign should create awareness and interest to foster sales and profitability. See Exhibit 3 for a breakdown of prices for various promotional alternatives.

Projected Costs

SaskTel's goal to achieve profits in the first year was an aggressive one. Upfront costs for the project's development were \$2,200,000. Annual research and development was projected at \$47,000, and technical support per subscriber was projected at \$25 per month. Due to the risk involved with medical monitoring, insurance would need to be purchased for \$71,000 annually, and Internet security would cost \$3,500 every two months. Other additional annual costs included: hiring of five more employees at a cost of \$200,000 (including benefits), server costs of \$53,000, a \$167,000 licensing fee, and \$150,000 for general and administration expenses.

CONCLUSION

Although LifeStatTM had shown promising results in clinical trials, Tulloch knew she faced a challenging task to get this product "off the ground" in six months. Tulloch wondered what the campaign should entail, which distribution and pricing strategy would be best, how to maximize the current marketing budget and how many units would need to be sold in order to recoup the costs. Tulloch knew the success of LifeStatTM would rely on an effective marketing campaign, and she would have to decide quickly on an appropriate marketing mix to meet the expectations.

Exhibit 1 Hardware cost to retailer

Hardware Needed	Purchase Price
Glucometer BT* accessory	$48
Landline BT access point	$120
Blood pressure monitor	$120
Cell phone	$150
Glucometer	$51

Source: Company files.

Exhibit 2 LifeStat^{TM} service breakdown

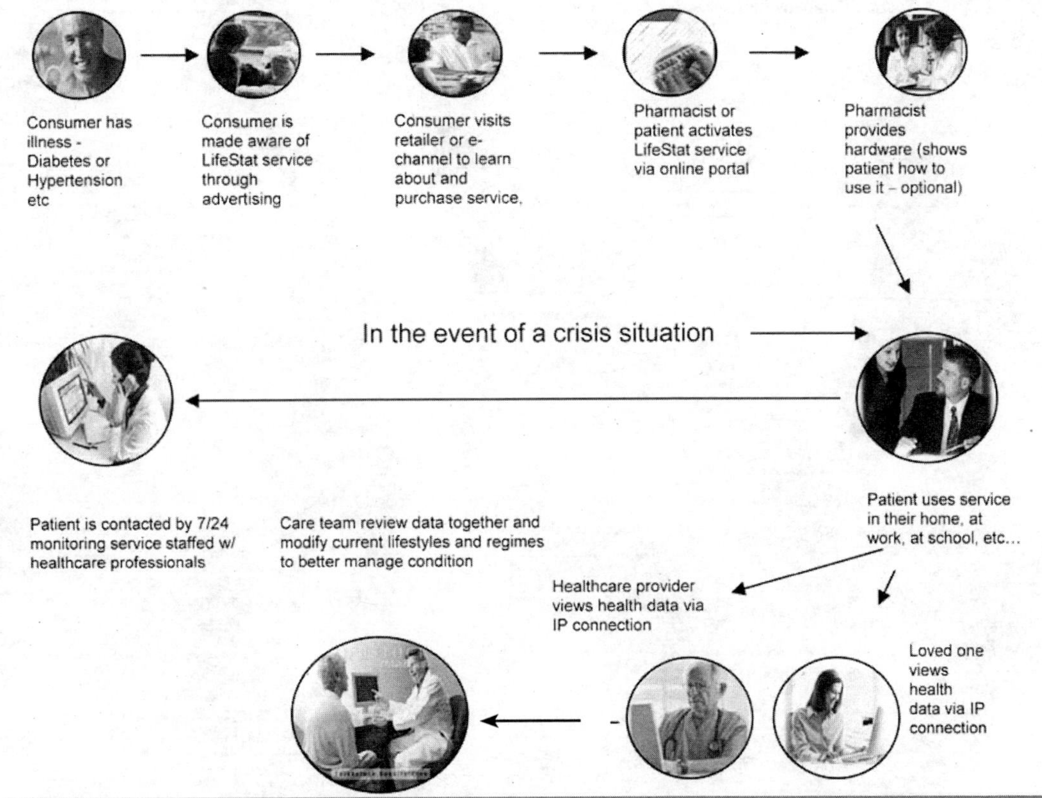

Source: Company files.

Exhibit 3 Sample costs for promotional alternatives

Promotional Channel	Cost
Television	$420 per 30-second spot
Discovery Health Channel	
Diva/Showcase	$100 per 30-second spot
Radio	$350 per 30-second spot
In-store Demonstration	$5,000 for 10 in-store demos
Direct Mail	$10,000 per 50,000 pieces
Trade Show	
Canadian Diabetes Association	$4,500
E-Health conference	$2,500
Newspaper	
The Globe and Mail (1/8 of page)	$300 per weekday
	$500 Saturday
Canadian Health magazin	$6,200 per issue
Direct Sales Team	$10 per hour per employee

Source: Company files.

13

Hanson Production

Pricing For Opening Day

Dr. S. Ramesh Kumar and Radhika Vishvas wrote this case solely to provide material for class discussion. The authors do not intend to illustrate either effective or ineffective handling of a managerial situation. The authors may have disguised certain names and other identifying information to protect confidentiality.

Joanne Shen arrived home to her Central Park West apartment late on a wet October night in 2008, after overseeing work on her company's most recent production of a revival of a Broadway musical. As she boiled water for some tea, she noticed the clock on the microwave showed 1:30 a.m. She sighed; tonight was the 12th consecutive night she had arrived home after midnight. As she dropped the tea bag into her cup and looked out the window to see the Manhattan skyline, she considered her challenges: she suddenly had to decide on a new theatre for the play, and she still needed to decide on ticket pricing structure. Shen lamented "How am I going to recoup this investment?"

JOANNE SHEN

Shen had worked for Hanson Productions (Hanson) for 12 years. She started as an intern while she was a student at New York University (NYU) and steadily worked her way up to President of Production, a title she had held for the past two years. She grasped the world of Broadway immediately:

> From the first time I saw Cats with my grandmother, I knew I wanted a career within the industry. The city, the atmosphere, the production, the costumes—audience members have no choice but to be captivated by the stage and performances.

Hanson Productions was a well-established Broadway production company. Since Shen had joined Hanson, the company had won much acclaim, including numerous Tony awards for both musicals and plays. Although Shen would never admit it, the industry considered her a rising star with a serious future in the business. Shen had a keen eye and ear for a script and, at any time, could recall all the vacant theatres and their seating capacity. She was well-connected in the industry and had terrific relationships with agents and managers. She also had close ties with the artistic directors at the various regional theaters across the country, where she discovered emerging work and new talent. Also, she kept in contact with her friends at some of the nation's foremost university theater programs, which allowed her to tap into worthy newcomers. Shen was currently quite concerned about the viability of Hanson's newest production.

HANSON PRODUCTIONS

Formed in the mid-1950s by a husband and wife team, Hanson Productions had earned acclaim with its off-Broadway shows. The company's goal was to further the advancement of the arts in New York City. Hanson's first show had been a small production of *Cat on a Hot Tin Roof*, which had played off-off Broadway to an audience of 50 people, most of whom were friends and relatives of the cast. Over time, the quality and scope of Hanson Productions' shows outgrew the off-off Broadway model, and the company began opening at some respected off-Broadway venues.

The company achieved its first major success in the 1970s, when a well-known Academy Award–winner had fallen in love with a script that the Hansons had under option. The script was a musical based on the Old West and had several great musical numbers for the two leads. The Oscar-winning actor had made an offer to purchase the script himself but the Hansons, recognizing his passion for the material (and hoping to entice him into the show), offered him a role as an executive producer. Their bet paid off, and the high-profile star helped the Hanson to secure a major theatre on Broadway. This move was the beginning of a successful production that opened to remarkable reviews and a healthy advance. The show went on to win a Tony for Best Musical.

From that moment forward, the Hansons grew their name and reach as a production company. They continued to option material and to commission new work. At any one time, the company was in development on up to a dozen projects in the United States and in the West End (in London). With shows in Chicago, San Francisco and London, the company had grown to become a global production force. Although the company grew consistently each year, the work force had expanded at a much slower pace. George Hanson recounted:

> The company goal was simple; continue to develop the Arts in urban locations. We wanted quality, not quantity, so we were deliberately rigorous about developing the material. We would tolerate some of the more temperamental writers or eccentric directors because of their good work. Our sense of material was the key and there were countless story meetings where we locked horns over even the smallest of details. In the end, I think that's what set us apart. We weren't the easiest place but we certainly displayed a work ethic that showed we cared. Artists, at the end of the day, appreciated that and so it was not so difficult to work with them again on future shows. Some of my best friends in the theater are people I've screamed at and who've screamed right back at me.

CURRENT PRODUCTION

Shen's biggest concern was what to do with her current production, a large-scale musical with a cast of 20 (see Exhibit 1 for a list of all the shows on Broadway at the time of the case). Set in 1967 Detroit, this rarely seen revival boasted some of the most beloved songs in the show-tunes canon. The musical was in development, and opening night was slated for first week in the coming March. In the meantime, a considerable amount of work still needed to be done to finalize the show: the composer had agreed to contribute two new numbers but they weren't working yet; some rewrites to the book required additional massaging; marketing materials had to be reconceived after research showed the initial materials did not successfully sell the show as a "fun night at the theater"; the costumes needed to be overhauled because the director had decided late in the game that he wanted a wind machine and real rain for the Act I finale. Shen had to revise the budget and pull funds from other areas without dipping too deeply into the contingency fund. She had decided that the natural target audience was baby boomers not only because of the familiar music from the 1960s but also because the female lead had been a child star on the Disney Channel; Shen wisely had the audience in her crosshairs.

A big question remained of whether this play would appeal to the tourist crowd because the subject matter presented its fair share of challenges. Shen wanted to attract the widest possible audience to the show but she could not afford to alienate parents, the typical the ticket buyers, due to the relative high prices for Broadway shows. The highest weekly grossing shows in New York are included in Exhibit 2. Typical ticket prices for New York on Broadway plays and musicals is included in Exhibits 3 and 4.

Shen always conducted market research with test audiences, despite her extremely hectic daily activities. Shen stated:

> A typical day during development would start at the office around 7 a.m. just so I could get some work done before the phone rang.
>
> By about 8 a.m., I would start getting calls about the state of the set design and the orchestra selection or [would need to] deal with a "crisis" regarding an actor who was photographed in an undesirable environment that may hurt the draw of the show. Then I'd be off to the venue to sit through a tech rehearsal; meet with the director, conductor, union stewards and give them updates on ticket projections or critic concerns with the script.
>
> In the afternoon I would meet with my boss and explain where we were in relation to the budget. By the time the evening rolled around I would have to follow up on the eight other projects either in development or production or go see other shows that we might have investments in. It was always satisfying to launch a show, but the next day it was back to the drawing board to make sure my show was still on course.

The story was centered on the riots in Detroit in 1967 and shared a common racial thread with the upcoming 2008 American presidential election. The script had been purchased several years ago, but the announcement of the Democratic nomination had created a new relevance to the subject matter. Timing, after all, was everything; and, according to the talk, if the Democrats should win the November 2008 election, Shen's show was poised to be a hot ticket. Should the Republicans win, however, the undertones would still exist but they would not be nearly as loud.

The cast was a coup for Hanson Productions. The lead actors were splashed all over the tabloids but they hadn't yet flamed out from over-exposure. The rest of the ensemble was played by solid performers, some of whom had television experience. Their worth to the show was indicative of their projected weekly salaries, as presented in Exhibit 5. The venue had still not been secured, which was not a catastrophe because Shen was in talks with three possible theatres: the Longacre Theater, the St. James Theater and the Hilton Theatre. Regardless of the theatre, revenue expectations were expected to be between $830,000 and $1.03 million per week. The weekly costs incurred by the production are included in Exhibit 6, the royalty schedule in Exhibit 7.

RECENT DEVELOPMENTS

Hanson Productions had been in extensive talks with the three theaters and had handshake deals — conditional offers — that followed the customary provision that the theater owner could enact an early termination clause if theatre revenue (based on 6 per cent of gross) fell to less than $50,000 per week. Each theater presented its own unique values and drawbacks. Shen's choice of venue would influence the pricing strategy for the show. Shen commented:

> The great balancing act is to find a venue that perfectly suits the audience and the production. We could save money with a smaller theatre, but fewer seats make it much tougher to recoup in a timely manner. Conversely, having empty seats in too large a theater would also be less than ideal. I wanted to be careful not to be forced into offering hefty ticket discounts during the first six months from opening. Critics are not the only ones who hate to see empty seats and the actors don't draw the same energy from a half-filled house.

The three venues that could accommodate the production were the Hilton Theatre, the Longacre Theater and the St. James Theater (see Exhibit 8). The owners of these theatres demanded the industry standard 6 per cent rental fee, based on gross ticket sales. The owners of the Hilton Theatre were willing to invest 10 per cent of total costs in the production, which would entitle them to 6 per cent of the gross revenue in addition to 10 per cent of the profits after tax (pre-recoupment) and 10 per cent of 50 per cent of the adjusted net profits post-recoupment.

Regardless of the theatre chosen, Hanson Productions would need to enter into agreement with the theatre owner regarding a termination clause. Typically, if the gross receipts of the show dipped below the weekly operating costs (including rent) for two consecutive weeks, the theatre owner had the option to cancel the contract. If the contract were canceled, the show's chances of launching a national tour would be seriously impinged. Shen appreciated the potential for a national tour, but this possibility was secondary to her desire for a long run on Broadway.

TICKET PRICING

Setting the price correctly could influence the success of a production. Setting the price too low left money on the table and forestalled recoupment, which was the goal of any show. On the other hand, setting the price too high risked alienating a large portion of the paying audience and offending the all-powerful critics who could be unforgiving if the on-stage performance was not commensurate with the ticket price. Rolling prices back, after setting the initial ticket price, was often interpreted as admitting failure, and, thus, created negative publicity for the show. Worse, dropping the ticket price meant the road to recoupment would be that much longer. After a show started to discount its ticket prices, climbing back up to full-price tickets was almost impossible unless a major change in casting created a surge in the demand at the box office.

Shen was weighing the potential rate of return, on the basis of an average ticket price. If Shen charged at the average show price ($79.10),[1] and demand was intense, she would have left too much money on the table. If, however, she priced too high, and demand was low, audience perceptions would be lowered if the show later had to lower its prices. See Exhibit 9 for a list of typical seating for a New York show.

Shen knew she had to consider the financial situation of *The Detroit Riots* production (see Exhibits 5, 6, 7 and 8), choose a theatre and make a final pricing decision. She needed to do make these decisions fast—opening day was only eight weeks away, and the play still had no home!

Exhibit 1 Theatre venues and capacity

Theatre	Current Show	Address	Capacity	Opening Date	Closing Date
Ambassador Theatre	*Chicago**	219 West 49th Street	1,125	November 14, 1996	Open-ended
American Airlines Theatre	*Hedda Gabler*	229 West 42nd Street	740	January 25, 2009	March 28, 2009
Brooks Atkinson Theatre	*Rock of Ages**	256 West 47th Street	1,044	April 7, 2009	Open-ended
Ethel Barrymore Theatre	*Speed-the-Plow*	243 West 47th Street	1,096	October 23, 2008	February 22, 2009
Vivian Beaumont Theatre (at Lincoln Center)	*South Pacific**	150 West 65th Street	1,080	April 3, 2008	Open-ended
Belasco Theatre	*Joe Turner's Come and Gone*	111 West 44th Street	1,018	April 16, 2009	Open-ended
Booth Theatre	*The Story of My Life*	222 West 45th Street	785	February 19, 2009	Open-ended
Broadhurst Theatre	*Equus*	235 West 44th Street	1,186	September 25, 2008	February 8, 2009
The Broadway Theatre	*Shrek**	1681 Broadway	1,752	December 14, 2008	Open-ended
Circle in the Square Theatre		235 West 50th Street	623	—	—
Cort Theatre	*You're Welcome America. A Final Night With George W Bush*	138 West 48th Street	1,084	February 1, 2009	March 15, 2009
Samuel J. Friedman Theatre	*The American Plan*	261 West 47th Street	650	January 22, 2009	March 15, 2009
George Gershwin Theatre	*Wicked**	222 West 51st Street	1,933	October 30, 2003	Open-ended

(*Continued*)

[1] www.broadwayworld.com/shows/tickets/ (calculated average), accessed December 18, 2008.

(*Continued*)

Theatre	Current Show	Address	Capacity	Opening Date	Closing Date
Hilton Theatre		213 West 42nd Street	1,813		
Al Hirschfeld Theatre	*Hair**	302 West 45th Street	1,437	March 31, 2009	Open-ended
Imperial Theatre	*Billy Elliot the Musical**	249 West 45th Street	1,421	November 13, 2008	Open-ended
Bernard B. Jacobs Theatre	*God of Carnage*	242 West 45th Street	1,078	March 22, 2009	Open-ended
Walter Kerr Theatre	*IreAria's Vow*	219 West 48th Street	947	March 29, 2009	Open-ended
Longacre Theater		220 West 48th Street	1,096		
Lunt-Fontanne Theatre	*The Little Mermaid**	205 West 46th Street	1,475	January 10, 2008	Open-ended
Lyceum Theatre	*Reasons to be Pretty*	149 West 45th Street	924	April 2, 2009	Open-ended
Majestic Theatre	*The Phantom of the Opera**	247 West 44th Street	1,655	January 26, 1988	Open-ended
Minskoff Theatre	*The Lion King**	200 West 45th Street	1,710	November 13, 1997	Open-ended
Music Box Theatre	*August: Osage County*	239 West 45th Street	1,010	December 4, 2007	Open-ended
Nederlander Theatre	*Guys and Dolls**	208 West 41st Street	1,203	March 1, 2009	Open-ended
New Amsterdam Theatre	*Mary Poppins**	214 West 42nd Street	1,747	November 16, 2006	Open-ended
Palace Theatre	*West Side Story**	1564 Broadway	1,784	March 19, 2009	Open-ended
Richard Rodgers Theatre	*In the Heights**	226 West 46th Street	1,368	March 9, 2008	Open-ended
Shubert Theatre	*Blithe Spirit*	225 West 44th Street	1,521	March 15, 2009	Open-ended
Neil Simon Theatre	OCCUPIED December 10	250 West 52nd Street	1,297		
St. James Theater		246 West 44th Street	1,623		
Studio 54	*Pal Joey**	254 West 54th Street	920	December 18, 2008	March 1, 2009
August Wilson Theatre	*Jersey Boys**	245 West 52nd Street	1,275	November 6, 2005	Open-ended
Winter Garden Theatre	*Mamma Mia!**	1634 Broadway	1,513	October 18, 2001	Open-ended

*Denotes musical performance.
Source: www.en.wikipedia.org/wiki/Broadway_theatre, as of December 18, 2009.

Exhibit 2 Attendance and weekly gross revenue–highest grossing new york shows

Rank	Title	Theatre	Average Attendance	Gross
1	*Wicked*	George Gershwin Theatre	100.0%	$1,769,489
2	*The Lion King*	Minskoff Theatre	100.0%	$1,555,984
3	*Billy Elliot the Musical*	Imperial Theater	99.9%	$1,358,454
4	*Shrek the Musical*	The Broadway Theatre	90.2%	$1,268,342
5	*Mamma Mia!*	Winter Garden Theatre	99.5%	$1,261,939
6	*Jersey Boys*	August Wilson Theatre	101.1%	$1,248,236
7	*Mary Poppins*	New Amsterdam Theatre	97.6%	$1,225,467
8	*The Phantom of the Opera*	Majestic Theatre	100.4%	$1,188,823
9	*The Little Mermaid*	Lunt-Fontanne Theatre	96.7%	$1,159,724
10	*In the Heights*	Richard Rodgers Theatre	92.4%	$1,136,062

Note: Some venues rendered as vacant in Exhibit 1 for case illustration only.
Source: www.broadway.com/buzz/broadway-grosses, accessed December 18, 2008.

Exhibit 3 New York city average ticket prices for plays

Seat Area	Regular	Group	Cap	Notes
Price Code: A	STANDARD			
ORCHESTRA 20+	110.00	**69.50**	0	
MEZZ A-J 20+	110.00	**69.50**	0	
ORCH O-P 20+	110.00	**49.50**	0	STUDENT/SENIOR ONLY
MEZZ K-L 20+	76.50	**49.50**	0	STUDENT/SENIOR ONLY
COPM 1/20	0.00	**0.00**	0	ONE PER 20 PAID
ORCHESTRA 10+	11.00	**92.40**	0	
MEZZ A-J 10+	11.00	**92.40**	0	
MEZZ K-J 10+	76.50	**49.50**	0	
Price Code: B	FRIDAY(E)			
ORCHESTRA 20+	110.00	**69.50**	0	
MEZZ A-J 20+	110.00	**69.50**	0	
COMP 1/20	0.00	**0.00**	0	ONE COMP PER 20 PAID
Rrice Code: X	SATURDAY(E)			
ORCHESTRA	110.00	**120.85**	0	NO DISCOUNT SERVICE FEE APPLIES
MEZZ A-J	110.00	**120.85**	0	NO DISCOUNT SERVICE FEE APPLIES
MEZZ K-L	76.50	**84.00**	0	NO DISCOUNT SERVICE FEE APPLIES

Source: www.broadway.com/shows/august-osage-county/, ticket prices for August Osage County, accessed December 18, 2008.

Exhibit 4 New York city average ticket prices for a musical

Seat Area	Regular	Group	Cap	Notes
Price Code: A	TUESDAY-THURSDAY			
ORCHESTRA	111.25	**100.25**	1176	
LIGE AA-CC	111.25	**100.25**	46	
FRONT MEZZ A-E	111.25	**100.25**	299	
REAR MEZZ F-G	76.50	**68.75**	104	
REAR MEZZ H-H	51.25	**46.25**	138	
ORCHESTRA (STUDENT)	111.25	**56.25**	100	STUDENTS ONLY: ROWSYZZ
REAR MEZZ (STUDENT)	76.25	**41.25**	200	STUDENTS ONLY: BEST AVAIL IN RMEZZ
Price Code: B	FRIDAY			
ORCHESTRA	126.25	**113.75**	1176	
LIGE AA-CC	126.25	**113.75**	46	
FRONT MEZZ A-E	126.25	**113.75**	229	
REAR MEZZ F-G	91.25	**82.25**	104	
REAR MEZZ H-M	66.25	**59.75**	138	
Price Code: C	SATURDAY, SUNDAY MATINEE			
ORCHESTRA	126.25	**138.75**	1176	NO DISCOUNT/SERVICE FEE APPLIES
LIGE AA-CC	126.25	**138.75**	46	NO DISCOUNT/SERVICE FEE APPLIES
FRONT MEZZ A-E	126.25	**138.75**	229	NO DISCOUNT/SERVICE FEE APPLIES
REAR MEZZ F-G	92.25	**100.25**	104	NO DISCOUNT/SERVICE FEE APPLIES
REAR MEZZ H-M	67.26	**72.75**	138	NO DISCOUNT/SERVICE FEE APPLIES

Source: www.broadway.com/shows/wicked/, ticket prices for Wicked, accessed December 18, 2008.

Exhibit 5 Production costs for a broadway production (Musical)

October 4, 2008

"THE DETROIT RIOTS" *Estimated Production Budget - Draft* *For Discussion Only-Subject to Change*

Physical Production		**Fees**		**Rehearsal Salaries**		
Scenery	750,000	Executive producer	30,000	Principals	8	225,000
Motors/hardware/ paint	105,000	Directors	50,000	Ensemble	12	225,000
Automation	120,000	Choreographer	30,000	Swings	6	98,000

Trussing	40,000	Scene design	25,000	Standbys	4	25,000
Props	100,000	Costume design	20,000	Stage managers	2	70,000
Costumes/shoes	800,000	Lighting design	30,000	Company managers		60,000
Hair/makeup	60,000	Sound design	30,000	Associate director		50,000
Lighting	120,000	Projection/video design	20,000	Pa to the director		6,000
Set electrics	25,000	Hair/makeup design	25,000	Design assistants	Scenic-4	140,000
Special effects	50,000	Special effects design	10,000	Design assistants	Costume-6	120,000
Projections/video	20,000	General manager	40,000	Design assistants	Lighting-2	44,000
Sound	80,000	Technical supervisor	60,000	Design assistants	Sound-2	50,000
Production reserve	500,000	Production supervisor	5,000	Design assistants	Sfx-2	50,000
Musical instruments	25,000	Casting director	25,000	Tutors/ chaperones		44,500
Theatre refurbished	20,000	Musical supervisor	7,500	Production crew		527,650
	$2,815,000	Musical director	12,000	Wardrobe		217,525
		Musical coordinator	5,000	Prod. Assistants	2	10,000
Audition/rehearsal halls	30,000	Orchestration	200,000	Musical director		52,500
Scenery/props/ costumes	22,475	Vocal arrangements	10,000	Rehearsal musicians		63,000
Script blueprints/ models	23,750	Dance arrangements	10,000	Orchestra musicians		42,000
Stage manager	12,000	Vocal coach	2,500			2,120,175
Casting expense	9,656	Press agent	8,000			
Miscellaneous	5,000	Marketing director	10,000			
	$102,881	Internet marketing	See ad budget	Subtotal carried forward		5,703,056
	$2,917,881		**$665,000**			

(Continued)

(*Continued*)

October 4, 2008

"THE DETROIT RIOTS" *Estimated Production Budget-Draft* *For Discussion Only-Subject to Change*

Advertising Marketing & Publicity	
Newspaper/outdoor	
Television/radio commercial	
Photography/printing/signs	
Artwork & mechanicals	
Direct mail	
Group sales/tourism	
Educational programs	
Promotions/marketing	
Website/internet marketing/email blast	
Press agent expense	
Press video	
Tony award show campaign	
Post opening advertising	
Miscellaneous	
	$1,500,000
Union bonds & deposits	
AEA	
IATSE	40,000
ATPAM	
AFM	15,000
Local 764	40,000
Theatre	
Misc	25,000
	$ 120,000
	1,620,000

Administration & General	
Producer office	18000
GM office	10000
Legal	125000
Immigration attorney	15000
Accounting	12000
Payroll taxes (13%)	275619
Insurance	225000
Pension/welfare/ 401k (20%)	424030
Vacation/sick pay	45000
Transportation	111545
Relocation fees	7500
Star housing	27000
Star expenses	32000
Hauling-local	68547
Payroll service	12375
Telephone/fax/xerox	25000
Opening night gifts/etc	75000
	$ 1,508,616

Out of Town-Production Period	
Theatre expenses	
Local musicians	
AEA per diems	
Per diems - crew	
Transportation	
Hauling	
Storage	
Advertising	
Misc	
	$3,000,000
Reserves	
Closing costs	
Potential contingencies	
	$1,250,000
Subtotal carried forward (page1)	$5,703,056
Advertising	$1,500,000
Union bonds	$120,000
Administration	$1,508,616
Out of town	$3,000,000
Reserves	$1,250,000
Total Capital Required	**$13,081,672**

Note: PA = personal assistant; SFX = special effects; GM = general manager; AEA = Actors' Equity Association; IATSE = International Alliance of Theatrical Stage Employees; ATPAM = Association of Theatrical Press Agents and Managers; AFM = American Federation of Musicians.

Source: Case Writer's Estimates.

Exhibit 6 Weekly operating costs for a broadway production (musical)

October 4, 2008

"THE DETROIT RIOTS" *Estimated Weekly Operating Budget* *For Discussion Only-Subject to Change*

Salaries			**Department Expenses**		**Fixed Fees/Royalties**		**General Administration**	
Principals	8	90,000	General managers	500	Executive producer	3,500	Producer's office	1,225
Ensemble	12	18,000	Carpenter	450	Marketing consulting	1,200	GM office	575
Swings	6	12,000	Props	475	Hair design	500	Legal	900
Standbys	4	8,000	Electrics	1,750	Makeup design	200	Accounting	1,500
Child standbys	2	2,000	Projections	800	Special effects design	300	Payroll taxes	13,437
Tutor	1	700	Special effects	175	Orchestrator	900	Insurance	7,500
Stage managers	4	8,000	Wardrobe/ cleaning	2,750	Dance arranger	500	Pension/ welfare/401	20,672
Musical director		3,000	Physio	800	Vocal arranger	500	Vacation pay	4,134
Company crew	8	14,400	Music	-	Music rights	400	Star expenses	4,750
Wardrobe super	2	3,350	Rehearsal calls	1,000	Music contractor	635	Per diems	1,000
Star dresses		1,800	Costume accrual	1,000	Synth programmer	250	Misc	4,000
Hair/ makeup super	2	3,270	Closing cost accrual	5,000	Casting director	1,250		$59,693
Stylist	2	2,850		$14,700	Technical supervision	1,225		
Associate director		1,800			Electrician	300	**Rentals**	
General manager		4,000	**Advertising & Publicity**		Misc fees	1,500	Automation	7,000
Company manager		2,000	Print/outdoor			$13,160	Electrics	9,525
Press agent		2,135	Television/ radio				Projections	1,100
Marketing director		1,550	Talent payments				Music rights	2,000
		$178,855	Playbill				Sound	11,000
			Website				Instruments	750
			Tony award accrual				Props	125

(*Continued*)

(*Continued*)

Salaries	Department Expenses		Fixed Fees/Royalties	General Administration	
	Press agent expenses			Special effects	900
	Marketing expenses			Misc	500
	Production costs				$ 32,900
	Misc				
		$115,000			

Source: Case Writer's Estimates.

Exhibit 7 Royalty fee schedule for Typical New York Musical (based on profit)

	Points	Royalties	Minimums
Authors	7.90	13.28%	6,000
Underlying Rights	2.63	4.43%	2,000
Director	2.00	3.36%	2,000
Choreographer	1.50	2.52%	1,500
Set and Costume Designers	1.00	1.68%	1,000
Lighting Designer	1.20	2.02%	1,000
Sound Designer	0.50	0.84%	500
Producers	3.50	5.88%	3,000
TOTAL Weekly Royalties	20.23	34.01%	$17,000

Source: Case Writer's Estimates.

Exhibit 8 Theatre budgets for three New York Theaters

"THE DETROIT RIOTS" Theatre Budget-Weekly October 4, 2008

Longacre Theater		St James Theater		Hilton Theatre	
Operating budget	$ 414,308	Operating budget	$ 414,308	operating budget	$ 414,308
Theatre Expenses		Theatre Expenses		Theatre Expenses	
Fixed expense	11,500	Fixed expense	27,500	fixed expense	31,250
Fixed rent	6% of gross	Fixed rent	6% of gross	fixed rent	6% of gross
House Payroll		House Payroll		House Payroll	
15 Local One Crew	52,605	15 Local One Crew	52,605	16 Local One Crew	56,112
13 musicians	49,257	17 musicians	64,413	17 musicians	64,413

House manager Box office Ushers Cleaners	26,815	House manager Box office Ushers Cleaners	39,709	House manager Box office Ushers Cleaners	44,358
Other (taxes, energy, etc)	21,952	Other (taxes, energy, etc)	24,763	Other (taxes, energy, etc)	26,584
Total Fixed Weekly	**576,437**	**Total Fixed Weekly**	**$623,298**	**Total Fixed Weekly**	**$ 637,025**

Source: Case Writer's Estimates.

Exhibit 9 Theatre seating charts for three New York Theaters

Scale: Tuesday through Saturday at 8 p.m.
Wednesday and Saturday at 2 p.m.
Sunday at 3 p.m.
(8 performances per week)

Longacre		**St James**		**Hilton**	
Seats*		Seats*		Seats*	
Orchestra	530	Orchestra	734	Orchestra	852
Front Mezzanine	300	Mezzanine (A-K)	212	Mezzanine (A-K)	325
Rear Mezzanine	266	Mezzanine (L-P)	208	Mezzanine (L-P)	104
	1,096	Rear Mezzanine	98	Rear Mezzanine	92
		Balcony A-D	243	Balcony A-D	259
		Balcony E-H	114	Balcony E-H	169
		Boxes	14	Boxes	12
			1,623		1,813

Note: Seat layouts may require modifications due to placement and size of orchestra, lighting, set design, curtain adjustments. Some numbers have been modified for case purposes.

Source: www.nytheatre.com/nytheatre/chartweb/plan_lon.htm and www.newyorkcitytheatre.com/theaters/stjamestheater/seatingchart.php and www.hiltontheatre.com/seating.php, accessed December 18, 2008, as well as Case Writer's Estimates.

14

Synnex International

Transforming Distribution of High-tech Products

Professor Shih-Fen Chen (Richard Ivey School of Business, University of Western Ontario) and Professor Lien-Ti Bei (College of Commerce, National Chengchi University) co-authored this case solely to provide material for class discussion. The authors do not intend to illustrate either effective or ineffective handling of a managerial situation. The authors may have disguised certain names and other identifying information to protect confidentiality.

INTRODUCTION

In June 2005, the world's third largest electronic products distributor, Synnex Technology International Corporation (Synnex), was celebrating the completion of an automated logistic centre near Shanghai, its first of 30 such centres planned in China. In two decades, Synnex had transformed itself from a local agent selling electronic parts and components in Taiwan to a channel management conglomerate that distributed information and communication products worldwide. At Synnex headquarters in Taipei, Chief Executive Officer (CEO) Evans Tu, who had masterminded the growth of the firm, was pondering the company's opportunities for future expansion into foreign nations, unrelated industries and even other business formats (e.g. Internet marketing).

HISTORY OF SYNNEX

Synnex was started in 1975 as a division of MiTAC, one of the two pioneer makers of personal computers (PCs) in Taiwan (the other was Acer). The division was created to distribute Intel CPUs (central processing units) to Taiwanese manufacturers who cloned IBM PCs. It also generated a small percentage of business from institutional clients such as research organizations. Thanks to the explosive growth of the PC industry, the division grew rapidly and, in 1985, it was big enough to be separated from the parent as an independent firm with its own identity, Micro Electronics Corp. (see Exhibit 1). At that time, the annual billing was only 500 million New Taiwan Dollars (NT$), about US$20 million. The fledgling company had 20 employees inherited from its parent and occupied an office not much bigger than a regular apartment in Taipei.

Micro Electronics continued its rapid growth by representing more vendors of hardware and software, such as chip sets, disk drives, printers, monitors, operation systems, and so on. Eventually, its product lines had been extended to also include consumer electronics and its customer base to cover retail outlets serving individual end-users.

The founding president of Micro Electronics was Evans Tu, who joined MiTAC after graduating from National Chiao Tung University, a top engineering school in Taiwan that sent a large number of technicians and entrepreneurs to the high-tech industries. Unlike his peers, who pursued engineering careers in research and development (R&D) and production, Tu started as a field application engineer and was also involved in sales and marketing divisions. He became an administrator later, rising at 29 to be the third highest ranked executive at MiTAC, administrative vice-president.

The rapid development of the information sector in Taiwan provided fertile ground for the growth of Micro Electronics. Tu was keen to find a niche for this newly independent company, positioning it as the "bridge of high-tech products" that could link to vendors on one side of the business and to users on the other. He did not mean to run the firm the same way as many distributors, who added little value to the products that they carried. Instead, he started building the firm on two pillars: the first, an advanced management information system (MIS) that filled orders electronically, and the second, a corporate identity system (CIS), rarely used as a marketing tool by electronic product distributors (see Exhibit 2).

The management style of Tu was well reflected in his appearance. He wore a dark suit with a white shirt and a brightly colored tie to work everyday, and kept his hair and moustache neatly trimmed. His office looked tidy all the time, as if it had just been freshly cleaned. He set up a performance-oriented reward system for the young company's staff and instilled in employees a hard-working ethos. He paid relentless attention to the details of almost all aspects of the company's operations, even to the format of the slides used in his weekly and monthly meetings with the sales team.

The business of Micro Electronics took off rapidly, with record-breaking sales being celebrated monthly, quarterly and annually. In 1988, the firm was incorporated into a new company called Synnex Technology International Corporation. Good sales figures helped Synnex attract more upstream vendors, which further boosted its market power vis-à-vis downstream customers. It was in the constant state of hiring more workers and seeking more office space. Managing double-digit growth and insatiable capital demand became Tu's biggest challenges. (see Exhibit 3).

It did not take long for Synnex to venture out of the capital city, Taipei, and to establish branch offices in central and southern Taiwan in 1989. In 1993, it built a fully automated warehouse facility near Taipei that represented the single biggest capital commitment in the history of the firm. In addition to product distribution, it established a fleet of trucks to shorten delivery time to a mere half day in the greater Taipei area and began providing after-sales services for some consumer electronics.

Synnex became a full-range channel management company covering inventory control, sales, distribution, transportation and after-sales services. In 1995, it became the first (and the only) distribution company listed on the Taiwan Stock Exchange. The price of its stock soared by 152.33 per cent the next year, marking the biggest jump in value among the 362 companies listed. (See Exhibit 4 for financial reports of Synnex from 2001 to 2007.)

In 1997, Synnex began its overseas expansion through an acquisition of a distribution company in Hong Kong, which it used as the springboard to serve mainland China. Synnex created an Australian subsidiary (which also covered New Zealand) the next year, then acquired a local distributor in Thailand in 1999. In addition to these company-owned subsidiaries, Synnex took equity shares in several distribution companies in the United States, India and elsewhere (see Exhibit 5).

The operations of Synnex were divided into three areas: products (multi-brand, multi-category and multi-field), channels (sales and distribution) and logistics (warehousing and transportation). The company represented 300 brands that covered more than 7,000 items in four categories: integrated circuit (IC) components, information products, communication devices and consumer electronics. It served 181 cities in 29 countries, and had more than 35,000 clients ranging from manufacturers (e.g. PC makers) and institutional buyers (e.g. research organizations) to retail outlets (e.g. national chains and specialty stores). In 2006 alone, the firm filled over 1 million orders and made more than 6,400,000 deliveries in Taiwan. See Exhibit 6 for the business structure of Synnex.

In 2007, Synnex had a turnover of more than NT$171 billion (close to US$6 billion) in Taiwan, China, Thailand and Australia. Further adding in the turnover from North America, India and Middle East, the worldwide revenue of the Synnex Group had reached more than NT$4,943 billion (close to US$170 billion), of which about 70 per cent was generated from overseas markets. It was the third largest electronic products distributor worldwide. Its success attracted admiration from a wide variety of audiences. *Business Week*, for instance, repeatedly ranked Synnex among the top 100 information technology companies in the world, and *Interbrand* ranked the corporate name one of the 10 most valuable global brands from Taiwan (see Exhibit 7).

DISTRIBUTION OF HIGH-TECH PRODUCTS

According to *Business Week*, Taiwan was the world's market leader in a wide range of high-tech products: 72 per cent market share in notebook computers; 70 per cent in chip foundry services; 68 per cent in LCD monitors, 33 per cent in computer servers, 34 per cent in digital cameras and 79 per cent in PDAs (personal digital assistants). Taiwan's technology clout had earned it the nickname "Silicon Island." The emergence of a booming information industry had attracted many high-tech companies to Taiwan. Unfamiliar with the local environment, most information-technology suppliers chose to delegate product distribution to indigenous firms that were often small in size and weak in capability.

Distribution of information-technology products could be divided into two chains: supply and demand (see Exhibit 8). Sitting between the two sides of the distribution chain were a large number of manufacturers, who outsourced parts and components from suppliers on the one hand and sold final products to customers on the other.

The supply side of the distribution chain handled two types of products: parts/components (e.g. memory chips) and system products (e.g. mother boards). Some vendors sold only parts/components (part makers), while others went one step further to assemble sub-modules (system assemblers). The two categories of vendors were not necessarily mutually exclusive. Intel, for instance, sold not only parts/components but also delivered system products to its clients.

The demand side of the distribution chain carries mostly computer peripherals (e.g. printers) and consumer electronics (e.g. cell phones and other hand-held gadgets) purchased by individual end-users. A big portion of the products were also sold to corporate customers (PCs sold to business buyers). A relatively small portion of the final products are sold to government-sponsored organizations, such as research institutions.

Distributors played a key role on both ends of the distribution chain. A distribution business in high-tech industries was easy to start in Taiwan. All one needed was an office, a few salespersons, a phone line and perhaps a truck. The biggest challenge was to secure distribution rights. The operation was often rudimentary and required limited capital commitment. Many distributors carried a single product and possessed little bargaining power vis-à-vis their vendors. Many of these distribution businesses were family-owned and their distribution rights could be forfeited at any time without warning.

The role of distributors on the supply side was often difficult. They frequently faced big hardware and software manufacturers such as Intel and Microsoft. The distribution relationship evolved over time. Initially, such vendors relied heavily on local distributors to serve the market. Later, they established branch offices in Taiwan to provide technical support. As the market became mature and stable, some would even add a sales team to take over direct accounts (e.g. clients with a high business volume) from their distributors. Such big-name vendors possessed strong bargaining power and very much dictated the terms of the distribution relationship. They usually had multiple agents in Taiwan, although most agents were banned from carrying products of their rivals, for example, Intel's distributors were not allowed to carry CPUs made by Advanced Micro Devices (AMD).

What made the position of distributors even tougher was that they were serving makers of final products that were quite big in size. They included, for instance, a large number of manufacturers who served as subcontractors in supplying Western firms with electronic gadgets, such as desktops, notebooks, digital cameras and so on. Some of them also marketed products in Taiwan under their own brand names. In this case, such clients would become vendors themselves feeding final products into the demand side of the distribution chain.

On the demand side of the distribution chain, distributors could be classified into two categories. First, there was a large number of channel operators distributing products to a wide range of retail outlets patronized by individual end-users. Distributors in the category varied in the products they carried and the size of their operation. They could be a small family operation or a huge conglomerate such as Synnex. Second, there was a relatively small number of the so-called value-added distributors, who sold computer hardware bundled with their service packages, mostly to business clients or other government-sponsored institutions.

The vendors on the demand side of the distribution chain included those manufacturers who appealed directly to end-users in selling computer peripherals and consumer electronics. For instance, there were close to 10 suppliers competing in the computer printer market, including Hewlett-Packard (HP), Epson, NEC, Canon, Oki, Lexmark, Kodak, Brother, Samsung and Panasonic. Another big item under this category was cellphones (e.g. Nokia, Samsung, Sony Ericsson, Motorola, LG Electronics). While the majority of these vendors are foreign companies, there was an increasing number of Taiwanese manufacturers, who served mostly as subcontractors of Western firms but later turned their attention to the domestic market.

On both sides of the distribution chain, one could also find startups with innovative solutions to various information-technology problems. Their products could be sold to individual end-users (e.g. Research in Motion's BlackBerry), or distributed to business buyers (e.g. NVIDIA's graphic cards). Whereas some of the manufacturers kept rolling out better products (for instance, Seagate with its hard disk drives), others faded quickly after their initial success (for example, Chips and Technologies with its chipsets). It was relatively easy to secure distribution rights from such vendors; the big challenge distributors faced was to identify the product that had real market potential. However, after such startups had achieved initial success and the market power that followed, they would usually expand their distribution networks by adding more agents or establishing their own sales forces (just as the big-name vendors did).

Generally speaking, most distributors created little value for the products that they carried. Their scope of operations varied from case to case. Some simply collected orders from clients and passed them over to vendors. Others might cover a wide range of functions, such as warehousing, advertising, promotion, transportation and pre- and after-sales services. The business model was to chase big clients by offering volume discounts, particularly in cases where a manufacturer signed up multiple agents to distribute the same product. Small clients were often neglected because their business volume was not big enough to justify the service cost.

In high-tech industries, manufacturers on both supply and demand sides tended to put distribution issues on the back burner. To begin with, most high-tech companies put more effort into R&D than into distribution. They lacked a strong incentive to cut distribution costs, since the potential savings accounted for a tiny portion of their fat profit margin. Further, the low value that a distributor added to high-tech products made it even harder for the distributor to attract high-quality personnel, who tended to pursue careers in development or production.

By the early 1990s, several trends had emerged to alter the channel structures of high-tech products. High labor costs in Taiwan had triggered a mass exodus of manufacturers to China, a trend that had substantially cut the market size of computer parts and components. Consolidation in the retail industry had also given rise to chain stores that had the capacity to appeal directly to end-users as well as the power to deal directly with manufacturers. Rapid innovations were drastically shortening the life cycles of new products and writing off outdated items became a big issue in the industry. Lastly, intensive market competition had driven retail prices down quickly, which led distributors to seek compensation from upstream vendors or to reimburse downstream clients for the loss in the value of unsold stock.

THE SYNNEX WAY

Immediately after its separation from MiTAC in 1985, Synnex (called Micro Electronics then) did not differ much from other distributors of electronic products in Taiwan, except that its operation scale was bigger than most rivals'. Its income was generated mainly from sales of parts and components to PC manufacturers (on the supply side of the distribution chain), and then from sales of system products to institutional clients (on the demand side of the distribution chain).

In 1987, Synnex established a division to distribute computer peripherals to retail outlets by carrying such products as Epson printers and NEC monitors, further expanding its operation into the demand side of the distribution chain. The extension of its distribution network to computer peripherals (and to such consumer electronics as cellphones and digital cameras in 1995) allowed the firm to reduce its reliance on computer parts and components (supply side). This turned out to be a fitting response to the exodus of PC makers to China and the booming market for consumer electronics in Taiwan.

Unconventional Practices

As a newcomer in consumer electronics distribution, Synnex adopted three practices that were considered unconventional in Taiwan: it catered to a broad client base, it refused to fill unrealistically high volume orders and it would not reimburse customers for unsold stock.

1. **Broad client base:** The retail industry in Taiwan was highly fragmented, featuring thousands of street-side electronics stores operated by individual entrepreneurs. Most of them were small shops that popped up from nowhere and could disappear without any warning. While competing with its rivals in chasing big stores with volume, Synnex was also very keen to cater to small outlets that were neglected by others. This violated the business norm in the industry, as the profit generated from small clients was usually not big enough to offset the service cost.

2. **No push for volume sales:** Maximizing sales volume was one of the business guidelines in consumer electronics distribution in Taiwan. On the one hand, retailers could use a big volume to negotiate a better deal with the distributor. On the other hand, the high-volume order helped distributors reduce delivery frequency and lower the service cost. More important, high-volume sales raised the retailer's inventory level, which pressured the retailer to promote the product more aggressively to shoppers and increase its market share. To the surprise of its peers and especially of its clients, Synnex discouraged small stores from placing orders that were apparently bigger than their capacity. Instead, it increased delivery frequency to meet higher-than-expected turnovers, which in turn reduced inventory risk and lowered bad debt.

3. **No reimbursements for unsold stock:** By pushing high-volume sales to raise the inventory level at the retail store, distributors had also transferred the risk of carrying inventory to their clients. This risk was particularly high in the information-technology industry where the retail price of a new product dropped rapidly and frequently. As such, most manufacturers allowed distributors to reimburse retailers the loss yin the value of unsold stock caused by pricing changes in the retail market. Facing strong resistance from its downstream clients (even from some of its upstream vendors), Synnex decided to discard this practice and refused to reimburse retail outlets for unsold stock even when market prices dropped significantly.

The three practices were unconventional and counterintuitive. Catering to small accounts, for instance, put Synnex at a cost disadvantage vis-à-vis those rivals who served only big clients. To most distributors, it was unimaginable (if not crazy) that Synnex would refuse to fill big orders but chose instead to increase delivery frequency. Eliminating price reimbursements for unsold stock was also considered infeasible in an industry where new products came and went in short life cycles marked by rapid drops in retail prices.

Behind the three unconventional practices lay an ambitious agenda that Tu had conceived to transform electronic products distribution in Taiwan. With the customer base expanded to cover small clients the average order size became smaller, and hence it became less harmful for Synnex to curb volume sales. With low-volume sales plus frequent delivery, Synnex actually centralized inventory control and thereby reduced the likelihood that one store would be out of inventory while another had unsold stock. A lower risk of bad debt was another side benefit of low-volume sales. Because retail outlets no longer carried inventory, Synnex did not need to reimburse them for the loss in inventory value caused by price changes. This, in turn, eliminated the nightmare experienced by all distributors in verifying the quantity of unsold stock, as their clients (or even their own sale representatives) might have incentives to provide fictitious figures.

Full-Range Logistics Operations

By linking the three unconventional practices, Synnex could potentially enhance the efficiency of the distribution chain. Filling up small orders at high delivery-frequency, however, would put Synnex at a cost disadvantage vis-à-vis its rivals who cherry-picked big clients and advocated volume sales. In adopting these unconventional practices to transform electronic products distribution, Synnex had serious cost issues that had to be addressed to keep its business profitable. "We fill all orders even if they contain only a low-price item," Tu explained. "Since small clients cannot order in large quantities, their business volume tends to be small, especially when an order covers only a single item. Filling such orders will cause us to lose money."

While small retailers tended to order in low quantities, they carried a wide variety of items in their stores. This meant that Synnex could boost the efficiency of serving this client group by bundling multiple items in one shipment. Even if the quantity of each item was small, the overall order size could be substantial. "We need to carry more products," Tu continued; "if small clients place a multiple-item order, the overall sales volume will be quite big, although they only order a small quantity for each item."

To achieve this goal, Synnex made extra efforts to sign up more vendors and positioned itself as a one-stop distributor for small clients. It raised the total number of vendors from 28 in 1992 to 300 in 2008 and the number of items it distributed from less than 1,000 to 7,000. It paid special attention to those products marked by a high retail price and speedy turnover (e.g. cellphones). In the first quarter of 2008, for instance, the average order size from small clients at Synnex was about NT$4,000 (roughly US$120) and the average number of items in each shipment was only three.

Shipping information-technology products to retail outlets was a tricky business. Many of the products were sophisticated electronics that could be easily damaged. Mishandling of such high-value items could be costly to all parties involved. Even though most distributors owned trucks, they also relied on delivery services provided by outside shipping companies. To exert tighter control over the shipping process, Synnex established a fleet of trucks that numbered in the hundreds. Its internal trucking operation handled millions of deliveries every year (about 97 per cent of total shipments), but the company kept shipping errors at or below 0.004 per cent. The few errors that did occur were mostly due to clients providing incorrect business hours or a wrong address.

One missing piece in this distribution business was a logistics centre to handle all aspects of inventory management, such as unpacking, repacking, assorting, shipping and so on. In the early 1990s, Tu was promoting the idea of building a logistics centre to the shareholders of Synnex, and he finally got the green light. This fully automated warehousing facility represented the single biggest capital outlay in the history of the firm. It went into full operation in October 1993 and was expanded in 1998 and again in 2000. Creating this logistics centre was a trial-and-error process that contributed to the core competency of Synnex. Similar facilities were later built in central Taiwan and foreign markets such as Australia, China and Thailand.

Synnex was no longer just a distributor of electronics products but a logistics management company that provided a wide range of distribution services built on an internal trucking operation and a network of warehousing facilities. It used a "half-day" as the scheduling unit in setting operation benchmarks. All orders, for example, had to be delivered in two half-days (i.e. orders placed in the morning would be delivered in the afternoon; those placed in the afternoon would be delivered the next morning). In Taiwan alone, Synnex could fill and deliver 3,400 orders on a daily basis.

Management Information System (MIS)

Serving thousands of street-side stores, each ordering many products in small quantities (out of more than 7,000 items), was a demanding job for any distributor. To ensure the accuracy of order contents and lower the cost of processing orders, Synnex embarked on an ambitious journey of office automation. It created from scratch an in-house management information system (MIS) that linked all operational units.

Inventory Control

It was a daunting challenge for Synnex to stock over 7,000 items that were mostly high-price products with a short life cycle, of which more than 5,000 were distributed to downstream retailers. Based on the current inventory level and historical sales data, Synnex designed an information system that could automatically classify all products into five categories—shortage, normal, overstock, slow-moving and dead items. The life cycle of each product (mature versus new) was also marked in the computer. When a mature product was classified as slow-moving, the computer would alert the product manager to take necessary actions to clear inventory (e.g. lowering its price). Further, by tracking the sales volume of all products, the system could prompt the automatic warehousing equipment to move popular items to more accessible areas during the night, so that during the day the robotic packing equipment could work more efficiently. This information system normally took about six minutes to fill an order, and the ordered items would be ready for shipment within 30 minutes.

Customer Management

Serving 35,000 clients of various sizes and backgrounds (from giant PC makers to tiny roadside stores) was another challenge to Synnex. The computer system could track all clients based on their business size, transaction volume, order frequency and the number of items in each order. If a big client was always ordering in a small quantity or at a low frequency, for instance, the system would alert the sales manager to find out the reason for the gap between the market potential and actual sales. If a client constantly ordered a single item, the sales team would try to find other products to bundle with the ordered item. The policy was to keep a long-term relationship with all clients. If a client were to never order more than a single item, this business relationship would be broken if Synnex stopped carrying the item or failed to maintain its competitiveness. However, if a client often ordered more than one item, the business relationship would continue no matter what happened to a single product in the marketplace.

Express Delivery

As Synnex added more items to its product offerings, it found out that delivering multiple-item orders to a client was very time-consuming. When a truck arrived at the store, the driver and the store owner would have to count all items in the shipment to verify the correctness of the order. The truck was parked along the street with its engine idling, rather than running on the road delivering other clients' shipments. To speed up this process, Synnex created a new delivery system that pooled all small items in one big box. The warehouse videotaped the packing process and assigned a computer number to each box. When the truck arrived at the client site, the driver just dropped the box and left the verification of the order to the store owner who alone counted all ordered items. The truck could move on to serve the next client. In cases of disputes, the warehouse would simply key in the box number to pull out the videotape and identify the errors made in the packing process. This innovative system substantially increased the efficiency of Synnex's shipping operations.

Telephone Sales

While Synnex tried to bundle as many items as possible in those orders placed by small clients, serving them still posed a cost disadvantage versus other distributors who cherry-picked only big customers. To address this cost issue, many firms had attempted to replace personal sales with telephone sales, but most of these attempts failed, for a wide range of reasons. Face-to-face business dealings were considered necessary in Taiwan. Even if some clients were willing to order through telephone calls, they insisted on talking each time to the same sales representative, who knew their business well. Yet, when the clients picked up the phone to call, the salesperson they wanted was often visiting clients elsewhere and could only call back the next day to fill the order.

Synnex quickly figured out that the key to the success of telephone sales lay in an information system that made customer data available to any telemarketer who answered the phone call. Synnex first assigned its clients to small groups of telemarketers who were trained to recognize a caller through his or her voice. This allowed the sales team to create a personal touch with the customers that they served. After picking up the phone, they keyed in the client name and the computer screen would display all information about prior transactions. With the help of the computer system, any members of a sales team could answer any incoming phone call, which not only reduced customer wait time but also boosted the productivity of the team. A customer could place orders with one telemarketer but make corrections with another later without causing any confusion.

The MIS department at Synnex was bigger than some information service companies. At the headquarters, the software centre supporting all of the subsidiaries accounted for four per cent to six per cent of the headcounts and the system required more than 100 staff members to keep it running. This information system turned out to be a strategic asset to the core competency of Synnex. For instance, the automatic warehousing equipment was always running at 120 per cent capacity at Synnex, while the same system usually had an idle capacity of 20 per cent in other firms. Most amazingly, sales representatives (who were much more expensive to recruit and retain than telemarketers) accounted for merely 30 per cent of the total headcount at Synnex, although the corresponding figure was about 70 per cent in other distribution companies.

Service Differentiation

The creation of a corporate identity system (CIS) right after Synnex gained independence from its parent company signaled its ambition to appeal directly to individual end-users, which was unimaginable to most distributors of electronic products. Synnex had achieved this unprecedented task through differentiation of its distribution services, namely, by providing after-sales services to end-users for their vendors.

Quality warranty and reliable after-sales services were both critical to the success of a high-tech product. Most manufacturers had to incur high costs to fulfill their quality promise and had great difficulty meeting the expectations of end-users (e.g. short wait time). In Taiwan, distributors of electronic products did not hold a stake in the quality reputation of the products that they stocked and were reluctant to provide after-sales services for their vendors. They often saw the provision of repair and maintenance services as a cost drain rather than a revenue source.

It turned out that Synnex was in an excellent position to take over the service function from some of its vendors. Its logistics centres possessed all necessary capacity (e.g. space and personnel) to offer repair and maintenance services; its information system could accurately track the flow of all items under repair and its trucking operation could pick up and return such items promptly. More important, Synnex could carry out these service tasks as new revenue sources with limited cost increases.

Nonetheless, after-sales services could not be a public good available to all of the distributors who carried the same product. Instead, Synnex made them a differentiator of their distribution services. Beginning in 1997, Synnex attached a service label to the products that it distributed, and in 2000 it went further by offering an additional year of quality assurance on top of the original manufacturer warranty. This practice gained approval from retail outlets and end-users alike. The term "Synnex goods" emerged in the market and the distribution services provided by Synnex were no longer homogenous to those offered by rivals. Such a differentiator allowed Synnex to appeal directly to end-users and strengthened its position vis-à-vis downstream outlets as well as upstream vendors.

With its advanced logistics system, Synnex could pick up a broken item from a retail outlet, send it to the maintenance centre and return the item to the store in four half-days (i.e. two full days). It soon became obvious to Synnex that most items required less than 30 minutes to repair and the two turnaround days were indeed unnecessary wait time to consumers. To push service quality to the next level, Synnex selected some retail outlets and helped them set up a service stand. These "partner stores" also carried the Synnex logo and offered repair and maintenance services for "Synnex goods" only. This arrangement not only increased consumer exposure to the Synnex name but also reinforced its relationship with retailers.

Successful Transformation

The market position that Tu carved out for Synnex—a bridge of high-tech products—worked out beautifully. While its unconventional business practices originally faced strong resistance from retail outlets, most of them eventually came to appreciate the benefits of the Synnex way. The portfolio of the products carried by Synnex made one-stop shopping possible at the wholesale level, which allowed retail outlets to curtail administrative hassles. The overall size of a multiple-item order was big enough to justify service costs, and yet the quantity of each item was small enough to keep the inventory level low. Thanks to frequent deliveries made by Synnex, retail outlets rarely lost sales on out-of-stock items. They could further leverage the reliable and prompt after-sales services provided by Synnex to make existing shoppers happy or to attract new clientele.

The logistics system created by Synnex had become an open platform that benefited all of its vendors. The indiscriminate reach of Synnex to all retail outlets (big and small) had eliminated unnecessary layers from the supply chain and flattened the distribution channel for its vendors. This meant that Synnex was closer to end-users and hence could project market trends more accurately. More important, the practice of not pushing for big orders allowed Synnex to control the actual sales figures at the retail level, which in turn helped manufacturers avoid the over-production problem and reduced the subsequent inventory risk. Most vendors could also delegate after-sales services to Synnex, a big headache that was costly and difficult to cure in the high-tech sector. Certain vendors even shut down their own warehouses and subcontracted logistics management to Synnex. To keep this platform open and efficient to all, some big-name manufacturers gradually dropped the exclusive-dealing policy and allowed Synnex to carry products of their competitors (e.g. it could now carry CPUs supplied by Intel and by AMD or cellphones from both Nokia and Motorola).

INTERNATIONAL EXPANSIONS

In Taiwan, the power structure in a traditional distribution channel resembled an upside-down pyramid, where upstream manufacturers held the most power and downstream retailers the least. The distribution chain created by Synnex looked more like a beer barrel, where power was concentrated in the middle. While Synnex had garnered tremendous power over clients and vendors, Tu took great care in exercising this power and would never use it unilaterally for short-term gain.

The restraint that Synnex took in exercising its power had earned trust from many vendors, who played a role in advocating "the Synnex way" outside Taiwan. Witnessing the efficiency of the logistics system created by Synnex in Taiwan, some of its vendors became increasingly unsatisfied with the distribution setup of their products elsewhere. Such vendors tried to convince their agents to imitate the Synnex way, but the operation system turned out to be proprietary and thus hard for others to copy. To avoid possible logistics nightmares in other nations, they began pushing Synnex to expand abroad. Such vendor-driven expansion into foreign countries was unique but served Synnex very well.

Synnex had created in Taiwan an operational template that could handily be replicated in foreign markets. Its core competency was built not only on deep pockets and advanced technologies, but also on its logistics system and managerial know-how. Indeed, Tu saw similarity between Synnex's overseas expansion and the expansion of McDonald's restaurants into a worldwide chain. Synnex took a two-step process to replicate its logistics systems in foreign markets. The first was to implement the MIS in the foreign subsidiary, be it a newly created entity or an acquired unit. As it grew business volume and accumulated local knowledge in the host country, it made plans to build a logistics centre there, usually opening it a few years after the initial entry.

In 1997, Synnex acquired an electronic products distributor in Hong Kong and used it as a springboard to enter the mainland China market. The acquired unit contributed 23 per cent of Synnex's revenues in its first year of operation. In the same year, together with its parent MiTAC, Synnex took an equity stake in the third largest distribution company in the United States, which also covered Canada and Mexico. In 1998, it created its Australian subsidiary (serving New Zealand as well), then expanded into Thailand the next year. In 2004, Synnex took a partial stake (36.3 per cent) in an Indian distributor called Redington that also ran operations in several Arab and African markets.

By 2006, Synnex had reached 141 cities in 16 nations worldwide. It served more than 16,000 retail outlets on a monthly basis and generated 56 per cent of its total income from overseas operations. It was the third largest distributor of electronic, information and communication products in the world. Its foreign subsidiaries were ranked first in Thailand; second in China, Australia, India and the Middle East; and third in the United States.

LOOKING AHEAD

Synnex had had the right formula to take advantage of rapid and incessant growth in the high-tech industry in the past two decades. With minor adjustments, its operational template had been successfully replicated in foreign nations. The challenge to Tu was no longer the viability of the Synnex way, but its extension to new frontiers. Before establishing the first logistics centre in Taiwan in 1992, he had made more than 10 presentations before he got the green light from the board of directors. Now similar logistics centres were being erected at an increasing rate in multiple markets and no one was questioning the necessity of these hugely expensive facilities. Nonetheless, in ushering the growth of the company to the next stage, he still needed to monitor capital commitments closely and carefully.

Without any doubt in his mind, Tu would continue the expansion of Synnex to more foreign markets. At the top of the list was China, which still lacked efficient distribution networks to meet insatiable consumer demands for information and communication products. Synnex put its first logistics centre in China into operation in 2005, and had three under construction and 26 more on the drawing board. The expansion into India had thus far been a success, with the value of the acquired firm appreciating about 600 per cent. India was indeed a hidden gem that had been brought to the attention of Synnex by its vendors. Thus, the challenge that Tu faced was to correctly identify the next foreign market to enter (perhaps neighboring Asian nations such as Malaysia or even Europe).

Synnex created its logistics system specifically to distribute high-tech products. These products featured a high unit value, a short life cycle and rapid drops in retail prices. The question was whether this open platform could be extended to other products with similar features. Synnex had evaluated the possibility of uploading more products into its system, but so far it had taken no action in this regard.

In 2000, Synnex began marketing products directly to end-users through a website called Synnex e-City. Tu had long ago decided that Synnex would not operate its own retail stores. Its logistics system, nevertheless, could be easily redeployed to serve end-users. While overseas expansion remained the top priority of the firm at this moment, excursion into other product categories or channel setups was still a possibility in the future.

The success of Synnex was based mainly on its extremely high level of operational accuracy. The firm handled millions of orders yearly, each containing only a few products out of the more than 7,000 items that it carried. The margin was about three per cent and any mistakes along the distribution chain (e.g. shipping errors) could easily turn a profitable order into a losing transaction. Synnex had to maintain this level of operational accuracy as the company kept growing and its geographic coverage kept expanding. Even if the opportunities for Synnex to grow were abundant, Tu needed to watch capital commitments closely and carefully, a situation best reflected through a metaphor that he used to describe his mission:

> I am running a huge earth-moving machine and must be extremely careful. I ask my managers to monitor every step in building a logistics centre. To protect our ROE [return on equity], we cannot commit too much capital at once, but we are also planning to build so many logistics centres at the same time. This is a huge challenge to us.

The Richard Ivey School of Business gratefully acknowledges the generous support of Bureau of Foreign Trade, Ministry of Economic Affairs, R.O.C. and Taiwan External Trade Development Council in the development of these learning materials.

Exhibit 1 Organization chart of synnex group

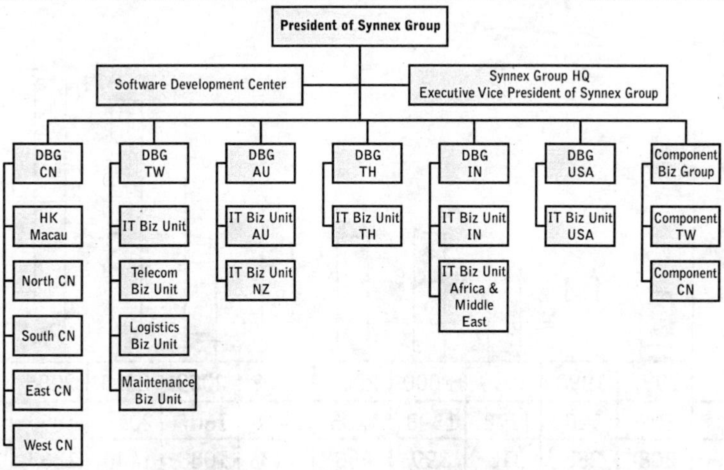

Note: In 1985 the MiTAC–Synnex Group divided into three companies: MiTAC Inc., Micro Electronics Corp, and MiTAC International.
DBG: Distribution Business Group; IT: information technology; CN:China; HK: Hong Kong; TW: Taiwan; AU: Australia; NZ: New Zealand; TH: Thailand; IN: India; USA: United States of America.
Source: Company files.

Exhibit 2 Synnex Logo and Business concepts

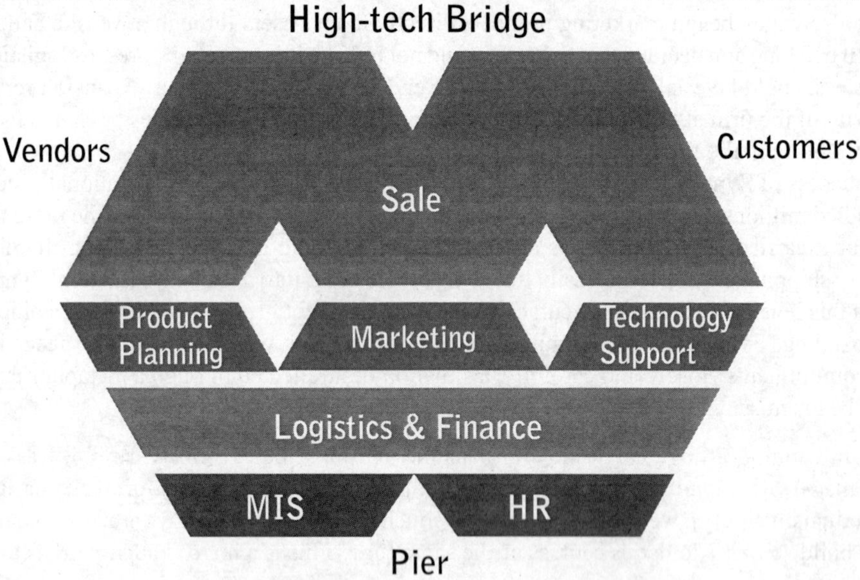

Source: Company files.

Exhibit 3 Synnex consolidated and breakdown sales revenue, 1997 to 2007

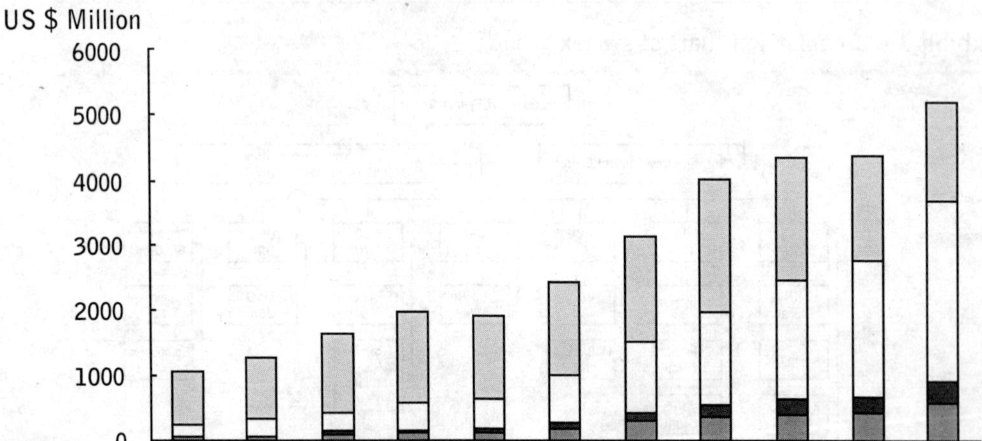

	1997	1998	1999	2000	2001	2002	2003	2004	2005	2006	2007
Taiwan	809	920	1178	1398	1285	1431	1607	2013	1850	1608	1534
HK&China	208	268	316	399	458	713	1088	1440	1863	2087	2752
Thailand	0	0	37	51	65	95	148	194	227	252	331
AUS&NZ	35	71	96	118	118	185	296	361	391	423	583

Regions: Taiwan, China, Hong Kong, Thailand, Australia, New Zealand.
Source: Company files.

Exhibit 4A Financial reports—income statement (in US$)

	2007	2006	2005	2004	2003	2002
Operating revenues	5,621,108	4,638,001	4,495,827	4,491,785	3,728,708	2,912,568
Cost of sales	(5,353,467)	(4,414,812)	(4,283,007)	(4,279,015)	(3,542,539)	(2,758,485)
Gross profit	267,641	223,189	212,821	212,770	186,168	154,083
Operating expenses	(163,806)	(138,426)	(123,684)	(120,500)	(96,109)	(86,360)
Operating income	103,835	84,762	89,136	92,270	90,059	67,723
Non-operating income	60,491	45,064	38,810	27,311	22,924	39,771
Non-operating expenses	(19,129)	(28,488)	(15,040)	(14,756)	(7,045)	(7,137)
Income before income tax	145,197	101,338	112,906	104,825	105,938	100,357
Income tax expense	(17,846)	(16,358)	(20,501)	(22,016)	(22,502)	(15,433)
Minority interest income					(613)	(286)
Cumulative effect of changes in accounting principles		3,184				
Net Income	127,351	88,165	92,405	82,809	82,823	84,638

Source: Company files.

Exhibit 4B Balance sheets—2001 to 2007

Assets	**2007**	**2006**	**2005**	**2004**	**2003**	**2002**	**2001**
Current assets (*cash, accounts receivable, inventories*)	$1,514,973	$1,196,039	$1,186,640	$1,201,067	$1,175,187	$850,203	$645,369
Long-term investment	$278,172	$246,735	$220,180	$208,122	$184,316	$173,326	$128,429
Fixed assets (*land, buildings, tools*)	$90,287	$92,874	$77,219	$78,968	$72,393	$68,136	$64,432
Intangible assets (*good will, trademark*)	$19,657	$22,818	$24,116	$21,748	$16,886	$18,519	$19,555
Other assets	$36,846	$24,139	$21,744	$6,018	$5,947	$3,791	$7,135
Total	$1,939,935	$1,582,605	$1,529,900	$1,515,923	$1,454,728	$1,113,975	$864,921

(*Continued*)

(*Continued*)

Liabilities and Stockholders' Equity

	2007	2006	2005	2004	2003	2002	2001		
Current liabilities (*short-term loans, commercial paper payable, accounts payable*)	$938,053.86	$714,524.03	$723,893.33	$749,778.48	$767,746.04	$508,492.89	$355,958.35		
Long-term liabilities	$102,851.96		$98,819.15	$97,632.61	$102,299.74		$2,887.72	$2,197.55	$1,381.35
Other liabilities	$8,591.67		$3,504.64	$3,206.18	$12,831.20		$40,162.40	$7,401.63	$6,125.31
Total liabilities	$1,049,497.49		$816,847.82	$824,732.12	$864,909.42		$810,796.17	$518,092.07	$363,465.02
Stockholders' equity (*common stock, capital reserve, retained earnings*)	$890,437.48		$765,756.78	$705,167.77	$651,013.94		$643,932.26	$595,882.55	$501,456.11
Total	$1,939,934.97		$1,582,604.60	$1,529,899.88	$1,515,923.37		$1,454,728.42	$1,113,974.63	$864,921.13

All figures are in million US dollar.
Source: Company files.

Exhibit 5 Global reach of synnex

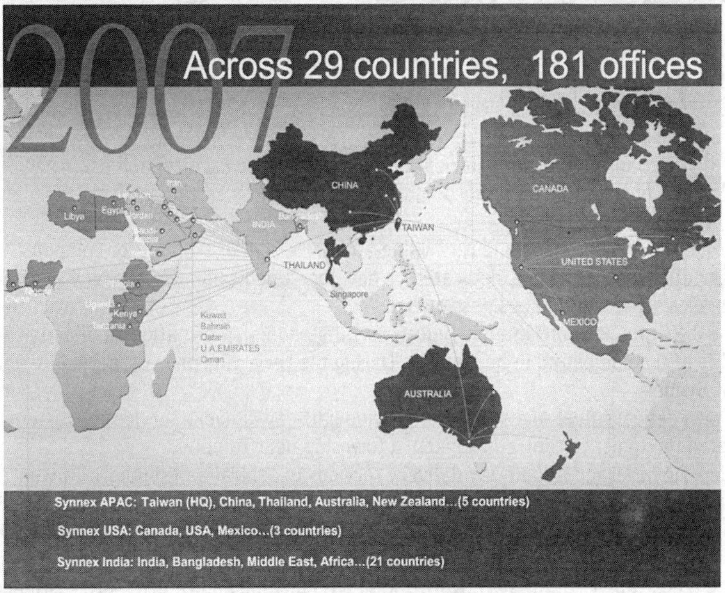

Source: Company files.

Exhibit 6 Operational structures of synnex

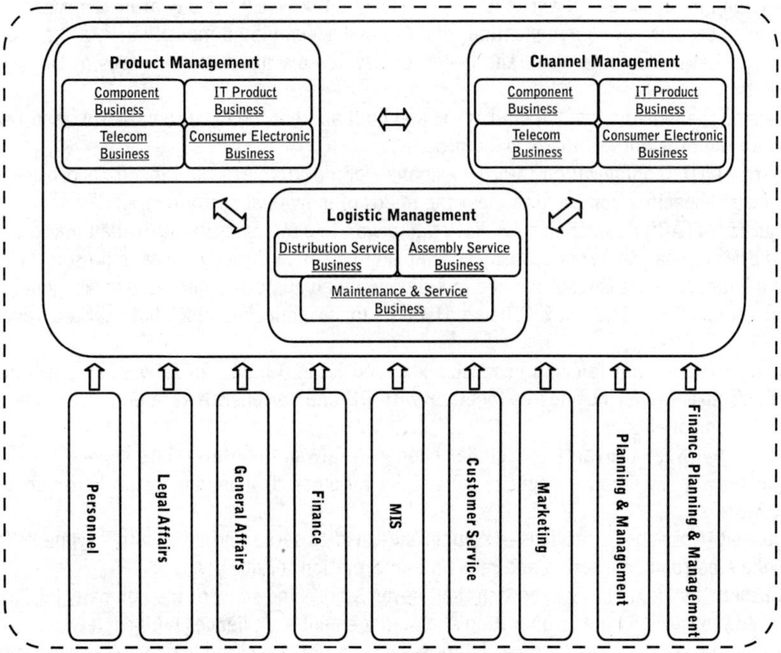

Source: Company files.

Exhibit 7 Chronicles of synnex

1988
- Established with capital of NT$200 million, with Matthew Feng-Chiang Miau as Chairman and Evans S.W. Tu as President.
- Upgraded the in-house MIS (management information system) to create a real-time operations system.

1989
- Launched own IT product brand: Lemel.
- Invested NT$20 million in computerization to upgrade hardware capacities.
- Expanded the business into southern and central Taiwan by setting up Kaohsiung and Taichung branch offices.

1990
- Transformed the business model into a value-added channel distributor for computer/communication and consumer electronic products, dedicated to develop "Open Channel" strategy and "Sales, Delivery and Maintenance" three-in-one business model.

1991
- Won the Institute for Information Industry's Outstanding Information Application Award, proving the capability of the company's in-house MIS. During the reviewing process, all judges voted unanimously in favor of Synnex.

1992
- Set up own delivery fleet and started to provide half-day delivery services to customers in Taipei.

1993
- Completed the logistics centre in Linkou, a township near Taipei.
- Extended the coverage of half-day delivery services to central and southern Taiwan.
- Initiated "small volume with variety products and one-stop shopping" services—enabling customers to minimize inventory levels and increase the ease of purchasing products from Synnex.
- Launched Lemel PC systems in the market.

1994
- Initiated quick repair services—"two working days pick-up and return"—to customer site.
- Published the "Synnex Shopping Mall," a monthly purchasing handbook for Synnex customers only.

1995
- Listed in the Taiwan stock market, and became the first publicly owned distributor in Taiwan.

1996
- Ranked the best performing stock among 362 listed companies in Taiwan during the first half year due to its outstanding operation performance.

1997
- Promoted new service—"Send it for repair tonight, take back the day after tomorrow"—for end-users.
- Expanded the base of communication retailers and accumulated more than 3,000 customers.
- Acquired Laser Computer Ltd. and began to develop distribution businesses in Hong Kong and China markets.

1998
- Expanded the logistics capacity in Linkou and built another highly automatic sort-and-retrieve system to improve the efficiency of the packing process.
- Initiated CTO (configuration-to-order) centre for desktop PCs in Linkou to provide time-to-market pricing and specifications, and to meet the needs of individual customers.
- Acquired MiTAC's Australian subsidiary and began to penetrate the Australian market.

1999
- Set up Maintenance Service Business Unit and began to directly serve end-users in Taiwan, initiated "30 minutes handset repair" service to build up a leading position in after-service quality.
- Joint ventured with Compex (Thailand) Co., Ltd. to penetrate the Thai market, renamed Synnex in 2002.
- Annual revenue from Telecom products exceeded NT$10 billion in Taiwan, as telecom became one of Synnex's three major businesses together with PC and peripherals-related products and IC (integrated circuit) components.

2000
- Initiated two-year warranty for cellular phones in Taiwan to differentiate service.
- Expanded the warehouse capacity by a fully automated, unmanned warehouse in Linkou Logistics Centre.
- Launched two website services—"Synnex's e-City" to serve end-users and "Synnex's Dealers Only" to provide electronic marketing and real-time information services.
- Published "Synnex: The Stagecoach that Never Stops," the story of the company by Shang-Xun Culture Co., Ltd., to share Synnex's operating and management experiences with society.

2001
- Completed Taichung Logistic Center with space of 7,300 pings (24,132 square metres). Its capacity was 1.3 times that of Linkou.

- Completed Melbourne Logistic Center in Australia with space of 5,200 pings (17,190 square meters).
- Extended the range of service from products offered through the Service & Repair Center to all computers, communications and consumer-electronics products sold by Synnex, and established relations with third-party repair service contract business vendors.
- Started up LSP (Logistics Service Provider), an integration with Warehousing/Delivery/ Repair/CTO services business, and contracted with vendors.

2002
- Completed Bangkok Logistic Center in Thailand with space of 2,700 pings (8,926 square meters).
- Planned designs for logistic centres in Beijing and Shanghai to expand into the China market.
- Visitors to "Synnex e-City" website exceeded 9.5 million over the year, as site was linked to more than 120 other websites. Website became an ICP (Internet content provider) for 3C product-related content.
- Engaged in strategic alliance with BESTCOM Infotech Corp., thus indirectly penetrating the commercial segment of IT-related products sectors.

2003
- Introduced CTO system to logistic centres in Bangkok and Melbourne to manufacture customized PCs.
- Initiated service brand marketing programs by focusing on the distinguished service symbolized by "Synnex's service."
- Total consolidated revenue reached NT$108.2 billion, surmounting NT$100 billion for the first time.

2004
- Acquired Yung Kang and Teampo to expand the components business scale.
- Invested in Redington Group in India to extend the distribution scope to India, the Middle East and Africa.

2005
- Completed Shanghai Logistics Center in China.
- Set up a subsidiary in New Zealand.

2006
- Expanded warehouse operations in the Linkou Logistics Center. The storage capacity was approaching twice the original.
- Set up the Consumer Business Unit, a new business marketing field in addition to the components, IT and telecom products businesses.

2007
- Started to distribute Nokia cellular phones in China and stepped into overseas telecom markets.
- Introduced Automatic Storage Retrieval System fully automated warehousing system into the Bangkok Logistics Center in Thailand.

Source: Company files.

Exhibit 8 Operational structures of synnex

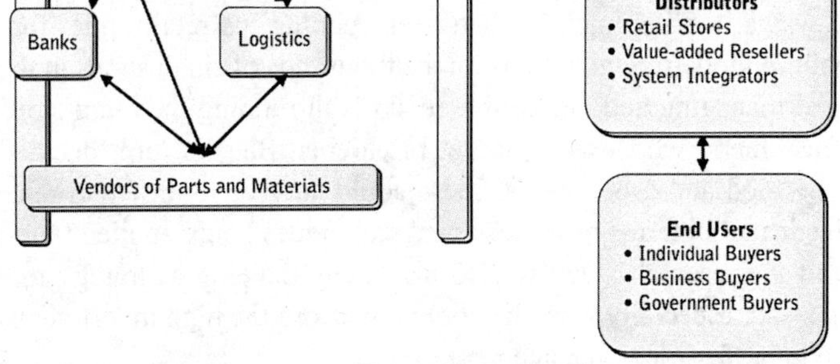

Source: Company files.

15

Shiny Provision Store

Retailing Challenges in the Indian Context

Dr. S. Ramesh Kumar and Radhika Vishvas wrote this case solely to provide material for class discussion. The authors do not intend to illustrate either effective or ineffective handling of a managerial situation. The authors may have disguised certain names and other identifying information to protect confidentiality.

Imbranghattin Madhavan Anandan, the owner of Shiny Provision Store in one of the suburbs of Bangalore, India, was a worried man. He had been running his retail outlet for several years, well before the onslaught of modern retail outlets on the thousands of small shops in the city. He wondered about his traditional managing and market-based skills in running the retail store and discussed this with one of his customers, who was a market researcher. She, in turn, decided to explore how a small retailer in the food and groceries business could survive in an environment that was getting increasingly sophisticated in terms of professional techniques being applied to modern retailing.

The objective of the research study was to ultimately develop a strategy to assist Anandan and stand him in good stead, especially when he could not afford the high investments that multinationals were able to make in professional management.

INDIA

The unique challenges in the Indian marketing and retail context emerged from its diversity as reflected through the country's geographic, demographic, cultural and psychographic diversity.[1] The country had 28 states and seven union territories as geographic territories. Consumer segments differed significantly in terms of lifestyle, income, religious practices and customs. Seventy-two per cent of the population lived in hamlets or villages that numbered about 638,596 (with only 100,000 having a population of more than 3,500 people).[2] There were eight cities with a population of more than four million people, 26 cities with a population of more than one million and 33 cities with a population of more than 500,000 people. There were 5,094 towns in the country. Urban India accounted for 64 per cent of consumption. According to the National Council of Applied Economic Research (2005), 22 million households earned about US$5,377 per annum (US$1 = ₹45 (Indian Rupees)). Sixteen million households earn in the range of US$4,693 to $5,377 per annum. About 34 million households earned US$2,970 to $4,693 per annum. Eighty million households earned US$1,584 to $2,970 per annum and 53 million households earned less than US$1,584 per annum.[3]

INDIAN RETAILING SCENARIO

An Historical Perspective

Retailing was not a new chapter in the business history of India. The existence of trade and commerce in India could be traced back to the beginnings of India with the birth of the Indus Valley Civilization, one of the largest among the four ancient urban civilizations of Egypt, Mesopotamia, India and China. The ancient cities Harappa and Mohenjo-Daro traded cereals, vegetables, fruits, eggs, mutton, pork, pottery, cotton and woolen clothes, baked bricks, weapons, etc.[4] India's ancient scriptures, called *Vedas*, considered trading activity to be the pillar of society.[5] The Indian grocers (traders) were perhaps among the earliest in the world to acquire professional retailing skills.[6]

The following are some of the major traditional retail formats that prevailed in the country:

- **Fairs:** Fairs were annually conducted markets at one place on a specific auspicious day of the year. They attracted thousands of people from nearby geographical areas. The retailers sold goods such as clothes, ornaments, spices, toys, sweets and other ready-to-eat foods, fruits, vegetables and even livestock (cattle, camels and goats).
- **Shandies:** These were regularly organized weekly markets that were held on a particular day of the week. The retailers and farmers sold their goods and produced throughout the day. The pricing was not fixed and bargaining was quite common.
- **Village shopkeepers:** These were the individual merchants who went about selling textiles, spices and ornamental items door-to-door. Such practices were prevalent in villages and semi-urban areas.

---

[1] S. Ramesh Kumar, "Addressing Diversity: The Marketing Challenge in India," The Wall Street Journal, Oct 29, 2009

[2] Dipta Joshi, "Indian Cities Coming of Age," Urban Development, www.ibef.org/download/URBAN_DEVELOPMENT.pdf, www.ibef.org/Archives/Overview.aspx?cat_Id=584, accessed on Aug 31, 2010.

[3] "The Marketing White Book 2010-2011 One Stop Guide for Marketers," Businessworld, New Delhi, 2010, pp. 250-251 and 289-291.

[4] http://india.gov.in/knowindia/ancient_history.php, accessed July 23, 2009.

[5] R. K. Singh, Restrictive Trade Practices and Public Interest, Mittal Publications, pp. 16-20.

[6] Gibson G. Vedamani, Retail Management: Functional Principles and Practices, Second Edition, Jaico Publishing House, Mumbai, 2004.

- **Public Distribution Shops (PDS):** These shops were government-run chains of stores started under the government's economic policy of ensuring the availability of food grains (e.g. wheat and rice), sugar, kerosene, etc. to the public at affordable prices, as well as of enhancing food security for the poor[7] (456 million or about 42 per cent of the population earned about $1.25 per day[8]).

GROWTH OF RETAILING

India, at the time of independence in 1947, was in the clutches of a vicious circle of poverty characterized by very low per capita consumption and one of the lowest income levels in the world. Retailing was focused more on basic necessities rather than luxury.[9] In the 1950s, there were only 0.25 million retail outlets in India.[10] Even in the early 1960s, it was reported, "there is not a single supermarket in all of India."[11] In 1978, the country had just 2.335 million retail outlets stocking fast moving consumer goods (FMCGs), or 3.7 shops per 1,000 persons. In 1997, the total number of shops, at 5.13 million, translated into 5.55 shops per 1,000 persons. In 2005, retail density was 10.51 shops per 1,000 persons.[12] There was about a tenfold increase in retail density as a result of the liberalization of the economy.

Kirana stores were somewhat comparable to the "mom and pop" shops of the West. But given the diversity of the Indian market, it might be difficult to provide a definition that would convey a degree of standardization. A kirana store could normally range from 25 to 400 square feet, with a range of product categories associated with the daily requirements of the masses. These categories included branded or unbranded offerings like coffee, tea, biscuits, toffees, shampoos, soaps, hair oils, edible oils and small quantities of rice and wheat. Some kirana stores might also carry a few vegetables and fruits. Most of the millions of kirana shops catered to the mass market and hence carried offerings that had limited stock keeping units (SKUs). Low-priced SKUs were popular among kirana shops. Several of the kirana shops also carried unbranded offerings that might be priced 20 to 30 per cent lower than branded offerings but might be of inferior quality to branded offerings (biscuits, edible oil, rice and washing powder are a few examples). Kirana shops predominantly dealt with food and grocery merchandise. According to KPMG, the food and grocery market in India was valued at US$236 billion in 2008. It contributed about 60 per cent of retail sales in India and comprised mostly the unorganized sector.[13]

The Indian retailing industry was dominated by kirana stores[14] and this unorganized retail trade (as distinct from modern retail) had created employment opportunities for nearly 39.5 million people, or nearly 9.2 per cent of the country's population.[15] More than 80 per cent of the retail outlets were run

---

[7] http://fcamin.nic.in/dfpd/EventListing.asp?Section=PDS&id_pk=1&ParentID=0, accessed July 24, 2009.

[8] http://timesofindia.indiatimes.com/India/One-third_of_worlds_poor_in_India/articleshow/3409374.cms, accessed July 24, 2009.

[9] Sengupta Anirban, "Emergence of modern Indian retail: an historical perspective," International Journal of Retail and Distribution Management, 36:9, 2008.

[10] http://fcamin.nic.in/dfpd/EventListing.asp?Section=PDS&id_pk=1&ParentID=0, accessed July 24, 2009.

[11] R. Westfall and H.W. Boyd, Jr., "Marketing in India," Journal of Marketing, 25:2, 1960, pp. 11-17.

[12] Singhal Arvind, "A Strong Pillar of Indian Economy," 1999, www.ksa-technopak.com.

[13] Chaterjee Purvita, "On a quest for value — food and grocery retailers take a leaf out of the Kirana model to stick it out in recessionary times," The Hindu Business Line, July 2, 2009, p. 3.

[14] N. Jones, P. Lasserre and C. Gehlen, "Mass retailing in Asia (A) — the markets," INSEAD case study, February 2005, Paris, 5261.

[15] Jayanthi Iyengar, "China, India Confront the Wal-Marts," Asia Times Online, January 31, 2004, www.atimes.com.

and managed by individuals or family members.[16] Their very existence in local neighbourhoods acted as a competitive advantage. In contrast, modern retail outlets were not present in every locality of a large city. India had about 15 million kirana shops.[17]

In several non-urban markets of the country, the retailer had informal interactions with consumers and could even influence purchase and brand decisions. This aspect of Indian retailing culture had significant implications for the consumer's perception of modern retailing versus kirana shops.

Modern Retailing Formats

In India, retail trade was primarily divided into two segments, which could be defined as follows:

> **Modern/organized retailing**: Any retail outlet chain (not a one-shop outlet/standalone) that was professionally managed and had transparency in accounting (with correct usage of MIS and accounting standards) and organized supply chain management, along with centralized quality control and sourcing, could be described as an organized retailer in India.
>
> **Unorganized retailing:** This included any retail outlet that was operated locally by a single owner or the caretaker of the shop. These outlets usually lacked technical and accounting standardization. Kirana shops fell under the category of unorganized retailing.

Organized modern retailing in the country was expected to reach $30 billion by 2010, up from $14 billion.[18] The following are some of the modern retail formats that were popular in the country:

According to Technopack Analysis, Crisil Research,[19] there were four types of modern retail formats that operated in India. Supermarkets included food and household products (for example, Food World, More and Nilgiris). Departmental stores had multiple categories usually lifestyle driven with apparel accessories predominating (for example, Lifestyle, Shoppers Stop and Westside). Hypermarkets/discount stores were large volume driven discount based stores (for example, Reliance Fresh and Big Bazar). Specialized/category killer stores had an extensive range of products under a single category (for example, Croma for household durables product categories, Vasant &Co and Vivek &Co in durable categories). In addition to these four types of retail outlets there were factory outlets in urban areas where offerings that were out of vogue were sold at discounted rates (for example, Van Heusen, Louis Philippe and Allen Solly in apparel, and Reebok and Nike in footwear).

Exhibit 1 provides information on the shopping habits of Indian consumers. Exhibits 2 and 3 give an impression of the appearance of a modern retail outlet and a kirana store.

KIRANA SHOPS VERSUS MODERN RETAIL OUTLETS—FOCUS OF RESEARCH STUDY

The study attempted to provide conceptual insights into the comparison between shoppers in a modern retail outlet and those in a kirana outlet. The objective of the study was to highlight the importance of

---

[16] http://fcamin.nic.in/dfpd/EventListing.asp?Section=PDS&id_pk=1&ParentID=0, accessed July 24, 2009.

[17] S. Ramesh Kumar, Consumer Behaviour and Branding — Concepts, Readings and Cases, Dorling Kindersley (India) Pvt. Ltd., Pearson Education (South Asia), 2009, p. 291.

[18] Guruswamy Mohan et al., "FDI in India's Retail Sector — More Bad than Good?" Economic and Political Weekly, February 12, 2005, pp. 619-623.

[19] "The Marketing White Book 2010-2011 One Stop Guide for Marketers," Businessworld, New Delhi, 2010, p. 291.

analyzing the retail strategies of kirana outlets. Such a perspective might also be useful to marketing managers managing modern retail outlets.

The required information for the research study was collected from 100 respondents. The respondents were 50 shoppers from Reliance Fresh (a modern retail outlet) and 50 from Shiny Provision Store (a kirana store) located in BTM Layout (a locality in the city of Bangalore). Reliance Fresh's store area was in the range of 3,000 to 3,500 square feet, while Shiny Provision Store's area was in the range of 600 to 1,000 square feet. There were nearly 38 traditional kirana stores in the vicinity of BTM Layout and 11 were similar to Shiny Provision Store in size, SKUs and the trading of both vegetables and fruits along with groceries. Shiny Provision Store was selected for the study for the following reasons:

1. Shiny Provision Store and Reliance Fresh were located in the main area of BTM Layout and were situated two kilometres apart (a two-kilometre vicinity was considered for this study).
2. Shiny Provision Store stocked several kinds of groceries and fast moving consumer goods. It also had a mix of branded and unbranded offerings like a typical kirana store.
3. Shiny Provision Store carried several categories that were carried by Reliance Fresh. This ensured an appropriate comparison between a kirana store and a modern outlet in terms of consumer choice.
4. Shiny Provision Store provided door delivery service and mobile/phone order delivery in the neighbourhood, like a typical kirana store.

Some of the assumptions that were made during the study are as given below:

1. Households in the two-kilometre vicinity had more or less the same kind of demographic and lifestyle preferences.
2. Consumer loyalty: Those consumers who had bought monthly groceries at least three times either from a local kirana or from Reliance Fresh were termed as loyal consumers for the purpose of this study.

The survey was conducted using a questionnaire with the following parts (see Exhibits 4 and 5).

Section I: **Retail store image** carried five different sub-dimensions, namely aesthetic image (AI), product/brand image (PI), merchandising/stocks/variety (M), store service (SS) and store personnel (SP). In turn, each of these five sub-dimensions carried different questions (see Exhibit 4) that were ranked on five-point Likert scales, where higher ratings were better.

Section II: The questions related to the **demographics** of the respondents were the focus of this section, which concerned information such as name, age, sex, marital status, family size/type, income, education and occupation details.

Section III: This section carried questions on the **psychographics** of the respondents, which were grouped together under three sub-headings: activities (A), interests (I), and opinions (O).

Exhibits 6 to 9 provide information on relevant factors associated with this study area and Reliance Fresh and Shiny Provision Store. The focus of the study was two-dimensional:

1. Several factors of retailing that contributed to retail image (a modern retail format or a traditional kirana outlet)
2. The changing lifestyles of consumers that were reflected through activities (A), interests (I), and opinions (O) (referred to as AIO)

Exhibits 10 and 11 provide the average ratings of the retail image of Reliance Fresh and Shiny Provision Store, respectively. Exhibits 12 and 13 provide the average ratings of the psychographics (AIO) of the respondents of Reliance Fresh and Shiny Provision Store, respectively.

With all the data in hand, it was now time to analyze it and provide recommendations to Anandan.

The authors would like to thank P. Seshagiri Rao and P. Srinivasan, managing partners, and the former franchises of Nilgiris of Rutun Enterprises for their support in providing the photographs of a modern retail outlet, and Imbranghattin Madhavan Anandan, owner of Shiny Provision Store (Kirana), for providing support to the study.

Exhibit 1 Shopping habits of Indian consumers

- Most shop daily
- Most cook everyday without using microwaves or storing food in refrigerators.
- Most would like to touch and feel a product before buying it.
- Most are highly price sensitive when it comes to fast moving consumer goods (FMCG).
- Most families have a budget for spending on basic necessities. Given the diversity of incomes, it may be a daily/weekly/monthly budget.
- Most consumers may alternate between branded and unbranded offerings in several categories.
- It is not uncommon to find small kirana shop owners providing monthly credit to their consumers. Such an arrangement with regard to modern retailing may be possible only with consumers using credit cards. Credit card penetration in the country is dismally low.
- Even in geographical areas where modern retailing exists, consumers normally mix their purchases between modern retailing formats and kirana shops in neighbourhoods.

Source: Observations of the authors, who have been part of the Indian shopping context; S. Ramesh Kumar, Consumer Behavior and Branding—Concepts, Cases and Readings, Pearson Education, 2009.

Exhibit 2 Photographs of Indian traditional and modern retailing

Frontage of the kirana store

Frontage of the morden retail outlet

Merchandise display at a kirana store

Merchandise display in a modern retail outlet

Source: Field survey interviews with store personnel.

Exhibit 2 Shopkeeper transacting with customer

The owner/shopkeeper of the kirana store does business with the consumer without the consumer being allowed inside the store.
Source: Field survey interviews with store personnel.

Exhibit 4 Retail image dimensions

Dimension	Attributes
Aesthetic image/physical settings/display	The store has a pleasant atmosphere.
	The store has an attractive layout.
	The store has informative advertising.
	It is very easy to find the products in the shop.
	Products on the shelves are messy.
	The outlet has well-spaced merchandise.
	The outlet has exhibited good displays all over.
	The shop has attractive and informative displays.
	Shop signage is very good.
Product/brand image	The store has well-known brands.
	The store has low-quality products.
Merchandise/stocks/variety	The store has an unlimited selection of products.
	The store has both private and manufacturer brands.
	I get better prices by buying private label groceries.
	The store has exclusive product assortments.
Store personnel/service/behavior	The store's sales clerks are well-dressed.
	The store has knowledgeable sales clerks.
	The store has helpful sales clerks.

Exhibit 5 Psychographics—AIO dimensions

Dimension	Attributes
Activities (A)	When I shop, I tend to go with my friends.
	Buying vegetables is on the top list of my routine shopping activities.
	I prefer watching TV to going shopping.
	I do not mind shopping for groceries even on weekdays.
	I normally shop in the evening for groceries.
	I get opinions and information about retail outlets and prices from my friends.
	I do not mind skipping going to a movie for shopping.
	I spend a lot of time in cleaning groceries that I buy.
	I buy vegetables on a day-to-day basis.
	I feel cleaned vegetables would save me cooking time.
	I enjoy bargaining while shopping.
	Sales promotions by the retailer incent me to buy more.
	I always read point of purchase advertisements while shopping.
	I do not mind traveling a kilometre extra for shopping at my favourite grocery shop.
	I will save a lot of time if home delivery is provided by my retailer.
	Loyalty programs incent me to shop with a particular retailer.
	I would choose a retailer who provides clean and convenient packaging of groceries.
	I prefer to get fresh stocks all the time from the retailer.
	I prefer to get a credit facility from my favourite retailer.
Interests (I)	Shopping for me is more like entertainment amid my everyday routine.
	I wish I could win some prize in "event marketing," which is conducted for shoppers while shopping in the outlet.
	I am excited to see the radio jockeys (RJs) and television jockeys (VJs) conducting some events in the shopping area.
	Friends/colleagues are the best shopping mates for me.
	I prefer to spend as much time as possible while shopping.
	Unplanned buys interest me and make me browse more.
	The new product arrival counter is what I always look at in the outlet.
	It makes me happy that my favourite retailers have started providing mobile recharge and electricity bill payment facilities.
	I am drawn to the retailer because he stocks ready-to-eat food.
	Special offers by marketers tempt me to buy more quantity.

(*Continued*)

(*Continued*)

Dimension	Attributes
	Clear sign boards make my shopping easier.
	Restrooms enable me to spend more time shopping.
	I prefer to have a lot of assistance from the sales personnel while shopping.
	I consider any kind of shopping as a choir (pleasing).
	I prefer to shop with different retailers for better offers that save me money.
Opinions (O)	I like shopping areas that have good lighting and space and a soothing environment.
	I look at the displays before buying new products.
	Seeing too many brands at the retailer confuses me.
	I prefer to pay with cash for my shopping activities.
	Stores with no availability of stocks make me seek other outlets.
	I shop for vegetables along with groceries.
	I would like to get credit card points on every shopping transaction.
	In-shop announcements make me buy more.
	The retailer should not compromise on quality of products.
	Checkouts without queues attract me to the retailer.
	I prefer the retailer whose billing does not have mistakes.
	I feel modern retailers offer exclusive sales promotion offers.
	I feel private label (retailers' own brand) brands offer more value.
	I would prefer to shop with a retailer who accepts credit cards.
	I feel retailers cheat customers on sales promotional gifts.
	Shopping with familiar retailers is less time consuming.
	Going to a large department store is a waste of time as I do not get adequate returns.
	Shopping in a modern retail outlet gives me a thrill.
	People shopping in modern stores are high-income people.
	For me convenience means everything in shopping.

Exhibit 6 No. of households in 2-km vicinity of Reliance Fresh and Shiny Provision Store

Income Range in INR	No. of Households	% of Households in BTM Layout
<10,000	3,000	35
10,000-20,000	2,300	27
20,000-30,000	1,100	13

30,000-40,000	900	11
40,000-50,000	700	08
>50,000	500	06
Total	8,500 (34,500 voters)	100

Note: INR - Indian rupees; US$1 is approximately equal to INR48.
Source: Mr. K. Devdas, Ex-Corporator, Bangalore Mahanagara Palike, Ward No. 65 (old), 136 (new), 2008.

Exhibit 7 Average monthly expenditure on groceries/vegetables/fruits

Income Range in INR	Reliance Fresh: Average Monthly Expenditure on Groceries/Vegetables/Fruits in INR per Household	Shiny Provision Store: Average Monthly Expenditure on Groceries/Vegetables/Fruits in INR per Household
<10,000	2,000	2,000
10,000-20,000	3,500	3,100
20,000-30,000	4,600	3,300
30,000-40,000	4,700	3,700
40,000-50,000	5,600	4,900
>50,000	7,200	6,000
Total	27,600	23,000

Note: INR - Indian rupees; US$1 is approximately equal to INR48.
Source: Field survey.

Exhibit 8 Consumer consumption pattern (based on average consumption of consumers)

		Reliance Fresh		Shiny Provision Store	
Products	**% of Total Consumption**	**Branded %**	**Unbranded/ Store Brands %**	**Branded %**	**Unbranded/ Store Brands %**
Rice	40	100			100
Wheat	20	100		100	–
Rawa	10	100		–	100
Sugar	5	100		–	100
Spices	3	–	100	–	100
Oil	5	100		100	–
Poha (beaten rice)	5	–	100	–	100
Raagi	10	100		–	100
Total	100				

Note: This exhibit refers to the unbranded offerings of Shiny. Unbranded offerings are those that have no identification with any brand, and are generally sold with loose packaging, meaning that they get packed as and when the consumer wants to buy them. They are very often sold in small quantities (such as 250 grams of rice, sugar or wheat). These are not consistent private labels, though some of these packs in small quantities may carry some names.
Source: Field survey.

Exhibit 9 Average percentages of expenditure on groceries/vegetables/fruits as given by the respondents

Outlets	Reliance Fresh	Shiny Provision Store
Income Range in INR	**Average % of Monthly Expenditure on Groceries/ Vegetables/Fruits Out of the Total Retail (Consumables) Expenses**	**Average % of Monthly Expenditure on Groceries/ Vegetables/Fruits Out of the Total Retail (Consumables) Expenses**
<10,000	90	85
10,000-20,000	85	86
20,000-30,000	80	84
30,000-40,000	82	84
40,000-50,000	75	78
>50,000	80	80

Note: INR-Indian rupees; US$1 is approximately equal to INR48.
As an illustration of how to read the table, in the income range INR <10,000 for Reliance Fresh, groceries, vegetables and fruits make up 90 per cent of total monthly retail expenditure. Apart from these expenses, consumers will also be spending on other retail expenses like personal care products, cosmetics and any other offerings relevant to them in a retail outlet.
Source: Field survey.

Exhibit 10 Reliance fresh (average ratings of retail image)

Income in INR	Aesthetic Image (AI)	Product/Brand Image (PI)	Merchandising/ Stocks/Variety (M)	Store Service (SS)	Store Personnel (SP)
<10,000	4.30	4.33	4.42	4.00	3.78
10,000-20,000	3.80	3.38	3.52	3.56	3.89
20,000-30,000	3.51	3.25	3.68	3.73	3.83
30,000-40,000	3.81	3.75	3.78	3.66	3.92
40,000-50,000	3.74	3.58	3.81	3.83	3.62
>50,000	4.06	3.42	3.96	4.29	3.89
Total	3.87	3.62	3.86	3.84	3.82

Note: INR-Indian rupees; US$1 is approximately equal to INR48.
Source: Field survey.

Exhibit 11 Shiny provision store (average ratings of retail image)

Income in INR	Aesthetic Image (AI)	Product/Brand Image (PI)	Merchandising/ Stocks/Variety (M)	Store Service (SS)	Store Personnel (SP)
<10,000	3.00	4.43	3.39	3.29	3.38
10,000-20,000	3.12	4.65	3.21	3.34	3.20
20,000-30,000	2.90	4.94	2.97	2.39	3.11

30,000-40,000	2.96	4.38	3.53	3.34	3.67
40,000-50,000	3.76	4.64	3.18	3.61	3.57
>50,000	3.08	4.63	3.44	3.75	3.08
Total	3.14	4.61	3.29	3.29	3.33

Note: INR-Indian rupees; US$1 is approximately equal to INR48.
Source: Field survey.

Exhibit 12 Reliance fresh (average ratings of AIO)—psychographics

Income in INR	**Activities (A)**	**Interests (I)**	**Opinions (O)**
<10,000	3.74	3.87	3.78
10,000-20,000	3.54	3.57	3.60
20,000-30,000	3.32	3.44	3.47
30,000-40,000	3.43	3.38	3.61
40,000-50,000	3.72	3.61	3.69
>50,000	3.52	3.81	3.77
Total	3.54	3.61	3.65

Note: INR-Indian Rupees; US$1 is approximately equal to INR48.
Source: From the field survey.

Exhibit 13 Shiny provision store (average ratings of AIO)—psychographics

Income in INR	**Activities (A)**	**Interests (I)**	**Opinions (O)**
<10,000	3.24	2.88	3.14
10,000-20,000	3.11	3.25	3.32
20,000-30,000	2.93	3.13	2.99
30,000-40,000	3.19	3.33	3.39
40,000-50,000	3.67	3.52	3.65
>50,000	3.03	3.25	3.54
Total	3.19	3.22	3.37

Note: INR-Indian Rupees; US$1 is approximately equal to INR48.
Source: Field survey.

16

The Brand in the Hand

Mobile Marketing at Adidas

David Wesley prepared this case under the supervision of Professors Andy Rohm and Fareena Sultan solely to provide material for class discussion. The authors do not intend to illustrate either effective or ineffective handling of a managerial situation. The authors may have disguised certain names and other identifying information to protect confidentiality.

Nick Drake, Global Media manager (Global Media Group) for adidas, arrived at the company's headquarters to present a bold new marketing strategy, based around mobile phones. "We call it the Brand in the Hand," he told the senior marketing executives who had gathered to present their strategy for the upcoming year. The Global Media Group had been arguing that mobile marketing was the surest, and perhaps only, way for adidas to break free from the advertising clutter and fragmentation of traditional media. "Mobile is the most personal medium available," Drake explained. "People run their whole lives off of mobile. It's business, it's personal, it's information gathering. It's on 24/7. With mobile, you have the customer's complete attention."

The Global Media Group predicted that mobile media would eventually replace most forms of print media, and by taking advantage of this trend early, adidas had a chance to surpass its competitors. Uli Becker, adidas head of Global Communications, was not so sure. "Prove it to me," he said. He gave the Global Media Group one year to test various mobile marketing concepts in order to demonstrate how handheld devices could provide a positive brand experience without annoying potential customers by intruding into their personal lives.

A few months later, adidas entered into a promising agreement to market a new line of footwear and clothing by Missy Elliott, hip-hop's leading female artist. The Global Media Group proposed a mobile component that would appeal to "hundreds of thousands" of young Americans and provide a long-term connection between the adidas brand and Missy Elliott fans.

COMPANY BACKGROUND

Adidas was founded in Germany in 1920, by Adolf Dassler. Following the Second World War, it became an important supplier of footwear to German soccer teams. Later, the company expanded its footwear line to include "fringe sports," such as high jumping, weight lifting and bobsledding, all of which featured prominently in the Olympics. In 1974, the brand achieved international prominence when the adidas-sponsored German national team won the World Cup soccer championship.

In the 1990s, the company increasingly outsourced production to third-party suppliers in order to focus more on marketing. Adidas became a public company in 1995, as global sales of its performance footwear continued to increase and it secured its position as the leading supplier of soccer footwear worldwide.

In 1998, adidas began to focus more on the U.S. market, which had been dominated by Nike and Reebok, by sponsoring basketball icons, such as Kobe Bryant. Within a year, adidas more than doubled its U.S. market share. The company hoped to continue making inroads into the U.S. basketball market with the 2004 launch of the T-MAC 4, the world's first laceless basketball shoe. In 2004, adidas was the largest supplier of sportswear in Europe, with consolidated global revenues of more than $6 billion.

The company's global media division was part of adidas International B.V., a Netherlands-based subsidiary responsible for the company's trademarks, sports promotion, and global communications and advertising. In 2004, it launched the "Impossible is Nothing" campaign, featuring sports legends, such as Mohammed Ali and David Beckham, as well as lesser known heroes, such as Fauja Singh, a 92-year-old Indian marathon runner who began running when he was 89. "Impossible is Nothing" aimed to associate the adidas brand with the ability of individuals to go beyond conventional limits for athletic performance.

Execution of marketing campaigns was the responsibility of regional subsidiaries, which had their own marketing departments. Regional offices localized advertising messages to suit national markets, based on guidelines and principles developed by adidas International in the Netherlands.

Competition

Nike was the global leader in athletic footwear. In the U.S. market, it had a 40 per cent market share, compared to approximately 16 per cent each for adidas and Reebok. Nike's dominance of the basketball segment began with the 1985 signing of basketball star Michael Jordan, and the introduction of the Air Jordan line of basketball shoes. By 2003, Nike's share of the basketball segment was approximately 60 per cent versus 20 per cent for adidas and 15 per cent for Reebok.

In addition to basketball, Nike's top products were running, children's, cross-training and women's shoes. Nike also began to aggressively pursue adidas' traditional market of soccer footwear and accessories by sponsoring the Manchester United[1] soccer team in 2002. The company likewise

---

[1] Arguably the United Kingdom's top professional soccer team, as well as its best known; Manchester United has consistently been one of the top 10 teams in the world since the 1950s.

increased advertising spending for important soccer events, such as the World Cup. In 2003, Nike edged out adidas for the first time in the European soccer market with a 34 per cent market share, compared to 30 per cent for adidas.[2]

In 2004, Nike spent a total of $1.4 billion on advertising and promotion, compared to approximately $900 million by adidas. Therefore, adidas had to be more effective and focused in its advertising spending. "Our goal is to be the leading sport brand," explained Rich Prenderville, head of Global Media. "And that means we have to use our money in smarter ways."

BREAKING THROUGH THE CLUTTER

For adidas, television remained the primary communications medium. While the company was gradually moving away from print media and replacing it with online and mobile advertising, digital advertising remained a lesser component of larger integrated campaigns. Noted Prenderville:

> Print for us has become a poor environment in regard to clutter. If you look at the magazine *FHM*, for example, in some issues you need to go to page 48 before you get any editorial. Unless you have the inside front or back covers, you just become part of the clutter.

Adidas traditionally advertised at sporting events and through sponsorship of sports teams and players. These events reinforced the brand's value to an existing customer base, but did little to attract consumers outside the sporting sphere. Meanwhile, urban environments were fast becoming saturated with advertising messages as companies vied for attention. Not only were consumers harder to reach, but clutter had made many people hostile to the perceived intrusions that advertising made in their lives. In an effort to break free of clutter, consumers sought refuge in new technologies, such as digital video recorders and popup blockers that offered ways to avoid unwanted messages.

In this environment, consumers on average received no more than eight minutes of adidas advertising per year through all forms of broadcast media. Given the scarcity of time available to directly address consumers, adidas had to ensure that its messages were meaningful and memorable. Grabbing the attention of potential consumers meant seeking innovative ways to deliver advertising. For example, in 2002, the company created a special billboard for the World Cup soccer tournament in Japan, featuring a giant foot extended toward a large boulevard. Half way down the boulevard a giant soccer ball sat atop a crushed car. The advertisement received extensive coverage by international news media as part of their World Cup coverage.

Another early attempt to penetrate clutter was the "living billboard." In September 2003, adidas Japan created a vertical soccer field where two "players" were suspended on bungee cords down the side of the billboard five times a day for 20 minutes. According to one observer:

> Hundreds of people stopped to take photos and cheer the two players on. Then, by talking about the event to others, the bystanders spread the word about it. The resulting buzz just got bigger and bigger.[3]

For a time, the living billboard received coverage on local and international news media, and drew millions of visitors.

[2] "Nike Tackles Adidas at Home," News24.com, November 30, 2004.
[3] "Welcome to the Matrix," Asia Inc., December 2003.

The Role of Digital Media

A more pressing dilemma was the move away from traditional media forms, in favor of digital media, such as mobile devices, video games and the Internet. As late as 2003, adidas devoted its entire marketing budget to traditional media. Based on the assumption that more than half of all media consumption would be digital by 2007 (see Exhibit 1), adidas decided to gradually shift its marketing efforts toward new media. In particular, 12- to 24-year-olds, who made up the core of adidas's target audience, devoted a large portion of their time to using online instant messengers, downloading music and communicating with friends via e-mail. "We're not walking away from TV," noted Prenderville. "We're still spending about three-quarters of our budget on traditional media, such as TV, out of home (billboards), and cinema." The Global Media Group saw new media as offering richer, more personal, transactional experiences than television or print. "It is an environment in which consumers are entirely focused and want to receive a message," Drake explained.

By 2005, adidas was spending between 15 and 25 per cent of its marketing budget on new media, more than any of its competitors. Regional subsidiaries were required to spend at least 10 per cent of their budgets on new media. Production for online was relatively inexpensive, since it often adapted existing creative from traditional media. At the same time, online costs for website takeovers and banner advertising increased substantially and, as a result, consumed a larger portion of new media advertising budgets.

Reaching Internet users with an impactful message became increasingly difficult amid the clutter of banner ads and popup windows. One way to stand out was to "take over" a popular web portal. For between $200,000 and $500,000 a day, advertisers could rent the Yahoo homepage. In early 2004, adidas took over the Yahoo portal to promote its "Impossible is Nothing Campaign" featuring female boxing star, Laila Ali, daughter of Muhammad Ali (see Exhibit 2). Users could stream a short film to their computer featuring Laila Ali and her father.

According to Tara Moss of adidas America:

> Our objective was to extend the "Impossible Is Nothing" adidas brand campaign online to effectively increase our reach to 12- to 24-year-old consumers. We sought to harness the emotional concepts of improvement, challenge and achievement, bringing them to life in an inspirational narrative.[4]

The Yahoo takeover far exceeded expectations, reaching more than twice the number of customers initially hoped for. It was also one of the most successful advertisements placed on Yahoo with more than 5 million downloads. Of those downloads, the average user viewed more than 22 seconds of the 30 second clip. Visitors to the site were directed to adidas's online retail representative (finishline.com), but the site was unable to handle the unexpectedly high number of visitors and crashed part way through the day. As a direct result of the takeover, adidas sold several thousand pairs of shoes.[5]

At adidas, the failure of some competitors to adapt to rapid technological change created opportunities to deliver advertising messages through "softer points," such as mobile devices. In the words of one analyst, "Advertisers will have to keep moving if they want to reach young people who wait at the corner, playing with the keypads on their mobile phones."[6]

[4] "Like Father, Like Daughter," iMedia Connection, April 07, 2004.

[5] Sales were directly traceable to the Yahoo takeover, and did not include indirect sales or longer term trends from increased brand awareness.

[6] "Ad Agencies Sound Alert over the Mobile Phone Generation," Financial Times, November 8, 2004.

According to the Global Media Group, adidas needed to invest heavily in interactive media in order to gain an advantage over better funded competitors, such as Nike. "The ideal scenario," Drake explained, "is to have intuitive marketing, where you completely understand what consumers want, when they want it and how they want it. And the only way to do that is to collect data. The amount of data that we are talking about is phenomenal."

Pushing unwanted content (popularly known as spam) on users proved unpopular when it was tested in Korea and Europe using SMS advertising.[7] "We have to be careful," explained Drake.

> To me, the phone is sacrosanct. If your personal life can appear in the same manner as a business question can, it can be intrusive. With computers you are more prepared to receive messages like this. You can read the heading, and choose to disregard it. In terms of consumer reaction to messages like this, people are very aware of what is intrusive.

After its Korea experience, adidas adopted an "opt-in" policy for all Internet and mobile advertising. In order to receive communications from adidas, users had to request it. The most challenging aspect of such a policy was developing compelling content that would attract users.

Personal Mobile Gateway

Personal mobile gateways (PMGs) allowed cellular phone users to manage personal data, such as addresses, e-mail, etc. Analysts expected PMGs to quickly replace personal digital assistants, such as Palm Pilots and Pocket PCs, by allowing everything to run off a single platform. PMGs on cellular phones would also add functionality to control household devices such as TVs, Internet, refrigerators and heart rate monitors. Adidas envisioned a platform that would allow users to manage a variety of fitness and sports programs, such as tracking exercise activity or accessing professional sports statistics.

In its current form, a PMG allowed content, such as news, music, games and applications, to be delivered directly to cellular telephones. Adidas divided content into three tiers, based on production cost and user value. Free content provided an incentive for consumers to interact with the adidas brand and usually included inexpensive media, such as wallpapers. Any production costs associated with free content were viewed as advertising expense. Cost-plus content charged a small fee to cover the expense of creating the content, such as ring tones. Finally, fee-based content provided extra value that customers were willing to pay for, such as an interview with a sports celebrity. In contrast, Nike charged users for all content downloaded to cellular phones, including wallpapers sporting the Nike logo as their central feature (see Exhibit 3). The Global Media Group debated whether or not adidas should follow the same model as Nike. "Usually marketing is about giving something for free," Drake explained. "Should marketers be selling marketing content? It's still an open debate."

THE BRAND IN THE HAND

When Drake joined the adidas Global Media Group in 2003, he was already convinced that wireless information services were quickly becoming the primary communication and entertainment medium for younger consumers. Drake had just finished working on the Vodafone account for a U.K.-based

---

[7] SMS: Short Message Service was a feature available with some wireless phones that allowed users to send and receive short text messages.

media agency, where his task had been to re-brand Vodafone's J-Sky service as Vodafone Live, an early attempt to develop a global third-generation (3G) brand.[8]

Japan was the first to implement 3G cellular telephony in 2001, with transfer speeds as high as 2 megabits per second. Such speeds were comparable to cable modems and wireless broadband.[9] With the advent of 3G in Europe, wireless providers prepared to deliver rich content to phones. Users would be able to browse the web, watch movie clips and sporting events, download music and play games. For adidas, advanced mobile technology created new opportunities to have its brand in the hands of consumers.

By 2003, 70 per cent of Europeans owned cellular phones. The majority of these phones provided basic voice and text features. Beyond portability, most provided little beyond traditional landline phones. However, some 28 per cent of mobile phone users were equipped with a newer technology, known as 2.5G, and the number of subscribers with access to advanced features continued to increase at a steady pace. Although 2.5G phones often included color screens and enhanced audio, they were still too slow to provide delivery of rich multimedia content. They could, however, allow users to download wallpaper, ringtones, and stripped-down Internet text, as well as send picture messages using built-in digital cameras.

With the implementation of 3G, the situation had begun to change dramatically, especially among younger consumers. While the number of Europeans with cellular phones was not expected to increase much over time, subscribers were trading in older phones for newer ones with 2.5G or 3G capabilities. By 2006, most cellular phones in Europe would be either 2.5G or 3G equipped (see Exhibit 4).

For the Global Media Group, mobile media offered several advantages over traditional media. For one, advertising could be delivered directly to a targeted audience in much the same way as direct mail. And while mobile media devices had the portability of print, they were much more time-sensitive, providing continuous on-time delivery of content. Furthermore, as the technology progressed, it began to approach the richness of TV and some wireless providers had already begun delivering television content to 3G-equipped cellular telephones.

Nevertheless, measuring the effectiveness of mobile marketing in a rapidly changing technology environment was a challenge. Without solid evidence to support the transition to new technologies, advocates found it difficult to convince other managers that Internet and mobile marketing was not just hype, particularly after the dot-com-inspired stock market decline of 2000.[10] Without strong company backing, supporters of new media had to be willing to take greater risks. The Global Media Group wanted adidas to break free of the idea that television was the center of marketing communications and embrace the potential of mobile technology.

The Global Media Group viewed Coca-Cola's Flaschenpost[11] campaign in Europe as an example of the potential of mobile marketing. In Germany, Austria and Hungary, customers who purchased Coca-Cola products received unique codes imprinted on product boxes, cans and bottles

---

[8] Vodafone was the world's largest cellular phone carrier with more than 150 million subscribers in 39 countries. J-Sky was the cellular brand for Japan-based J-Phone, the world's first wireless carrier to provide 3G. The company was acquired by Vodafone in 2001.

[9] Regulatory delays and diverging standards delayed the introduction of 3G technology in the United States. However, by the end of 2004, all three major U.S. carriers had announced plans to make broadband cellular service available in urban centers. By 2008, most of the country would be linked to broadband cellular phone services.

[10] In early 2000, the failure of prominent Internet companies, such as E-toys and Value America, caused many investors to reevaluate the market. As bearish sentiment began to take hold, the technology shares entered into an extended downward spiral. In March 2000, the technology laden NASDAQ exchange peaked at 5,000. By year's end, approximately half of that index's value had been erased.

[11] Flaschenpost: German for "message in a bottle."

(see Exhibit 5). The codes could then be used to download free mobile content. During the campaign, more than six million free wallpapers and ringtones were downloaded to mobile phones. "That's the kind of number we're interested in," explained Drake.

> They put their entire marketing budget into this (€8 million) and it was hugely impactful and very successful. That's where we have to take adidas. The small steps we are taking now must show our chief marketing officer that we can achieve this.

When adidas announced its mobile marketing initiative to regional subsidiaries, most were enthusiastic. Only the company's U.S. subsidiary was reluctant, due to the relative paucity of spending on mobile media by American youth compared to other regions of the world (see Table 1). However, once adidas Global Media presented its strategy, along with growth projections by medium, adidas America agreed to support the plan.

Table 1 Youth spending on mobile media by region

	2003 (Actual)		2008 (Projected)	
Region	**Total Spending ($ Millions)**	**% Leiure Spending**	**Total Spending ($ Millions)**	**% Leiure Spending**
North America	250	<0.1	4,500	5
Asia-Pacific	6,250	13.5	16,000	7.5
Europe	6,900	9.2	8,500	9

Source: w2forum Mobile Youth 2003.

Global Brands vs. Regional Preferences

Technology adoption among developed countries varied from region to region, with the Far East (particularly Japan) leading the world in mobile technology, followed by Europe, and finally North America. The lag in technology adoption in the U.S. cellular phone market provided an opportunity for adidas to test new products in Europe before launching them in North America. Noted Drake:

> The U.S. is our key market. Everything that we test in Europe is done so that we have a better practice for the U.S. The battle can be won or lost in the U.S.

While consumers around the world enjoyed sports, movies and music, advertising had to be tailored to the regional tastes reflected through these forms of entertainment. For instance, the endorsement of soccer superstar David Beckham[12] had a major impact on sports fans in Europe, but had little impact on Americans, who were more interested in baseball and basketball, or on Canadians obsessed with hockey.

With that in mind, adidas partnered with MTV, the most well-known music entertainment channel on television. With its vast audience and global reach, MTV became an important part of the adidas campaign. "MTV is a source of cool," Drake explained.

> We can try to integrate adidas into MTV programming, but we also need an element where consumers can react and take action. For example, we can mix songs and tones with mobile applications.

---

[12] As soccer's best-known icon, David Beckham was renowned for his long curving kicks. He helped lead the Manchester United soccer team to championship wins in 1996, 1997, 2000, 2001, and 2003. In 2003, Beckham was traded to the Real Madrid team. His personal fortune was estimated to be greater than the Queen of England.

Mobile messaging had to be both fun and interactive in order to compel people to use it. Therefore, adidas sought methods that gave customers a "hook," and then relied on viral marketing to convince others to use the service or product.[13]

Moving Beyond Text Messages

Ringtones and Wallpaper

Adidas's first attempt at interactive mobile marketing was in Sweden in 2002, with a campaign called "Colours." Using very simple banners and wallpaper, users could click on an icon to download to their phones wallpaper that featured the adidas logo. The wallpaper was collectable and enabled discounts in stores, which proved to be the main driver for consumers. By tracking the number of clicks, adidas was able to determine that campaign had been more effective than anticipated. From that experience, adidas marketing executives came to believe that mobile marketing could be an effective weapon.

Another pilot involved a ring tone[14] program in the United Kingdom, in which users could download ring tones to their cell phones for a small fee. Adidas advertised the ring tones on interactive TV for 10 days, which resulted in 600,000 downloads. While the profit from the ring tones was miniscule, it helped create brand awareness and helped establish the effectiveness of such tools in reaching consumers.

As a first step, adidas wanted consumers to feel comfortable with the company logo on their cellular phones. Ultimately, adidas envisioned its own broadband channel that could be accessed through an adidas icon. Once accessed, subscribers would enter a virtual "adidas world" that would include a number of multimedia services aimed at increasing brand awareness and product purchases.

Video Games

According to the Global Media Group's research, video games were one of the few ways that adidas could provide a brand experience specifically aimed at the 12- to 24-year-old demographic. "Gaming is the biggest growth area among youth consumers," Drake observed. In response, mobile companies and mobile handset manufacturers invested more in developing gaming technology than any other service area.

In recognition of the trends, adidas hired a software development firm to create an arcade-style soccer game applet that could be downloaded for a fee of €1.99. The game offered three areas of play: trick play, in which a player kicks the ball in the air and tries to prevent it from hitting the ground, free kicks, which require players to bend the ball around a wall of opposing players, and penalties. As players completed each level of play, they progressed to increasingly difficult levels.

The intent of the game applet was to create a complete brand experience for users by linking brand icons, such as David Beckham, to company products. Moreover, the acquisition of virtual equivalents of certain products, such as particular styles of soccer shoe, allowed players to improve their performance in certain areas. As a result, adidas hoped that players would realize the benefits offered by the real products represented in the game. Finally, Vodafone Live subscribers could post high scores or exchange scores with other subscribers.

---

[13] Viral marketing referred to "network-enhanced word-of-mouth." Users accessed content voluntarily and then solicited their friends to do the same, often through e-mails (viral e-mail) or text messages.

[14] A ring tone is a music clip that plays when receiving phone calls. Ring tones could be customized to identify specific callers, or they could be used to help distinguish one phone from other nearby devices. Finally, ring tones added a personal element that reflected a sense of individuality.

The Road to Lisbon

One of the more important sporting events in Europe was the Union of European Football Associations (UEFA) Championship, a soccer event also known as the European Cup. Once every four years, the European Cup brought 16 of Europe's national teams together to compete for the title of European champion. In 2004, Portugal played host to the largest ever UEFA event and the largest sporting event ever hosted by Portugal. More than one million event tickets were sold to fans in 100 countries, and television broadcasts of the 31 games reached a cumulative audience of approximately seven billion viewers.[15]

Adidas sponsored the event with its "Road to Lisbon" (R2L) campaign, featuring 13 of Europe's greatest soccer stars as they travelled together across Europe on motorized scooters to their final destination, the European Cup (Euro 2004) in Lisbon. The centerpiece of the campaign was a short film that featured the soccer greats as they stopped in various locations along the way.

The company also invested heavily in television ads to build awareness, complemented by an Internet site from which the company promoted the mobile component. Although advertising was prohibited within one square mile of the stadium, adidas sent out "scooter squads" to other areas of Lisbon to remind people of the campaign.

The success of the R2L campaign was rounded out with an upset win by the adidas-sponsored Greek team at the Euro 2004 championship. In addition to the publicity generated by the event, sales of adidas-licensed sales of replica jerseys and Euro 2004 jerseys surpassed 2.5 million units.

Adidas's media campaigns were designed to follow three steps: impact, involvement and activation. The first step, "impact," meant that the campaign had to be relevant to its target audience. In this respect, R2L tapped into the affinity Europeans had for soccer. Second, "involvement" meant that the advertising had personal relevance and interactivity for the consumer. For instance, by downloading wallpaper or ring tones, consumers received a benefit that made them want to participate in the marketing campaign. However, neither of these prerequisites were any benefit to adidas if they did not increase sales. "Activation," the final and most important step, involved purchases of adidas products as a direct result of advertising and promotion.

R2L Mobile Marketing

To complement the campaign, the company created a Road to Lisbon website that included downloaded polyphonic ringtones featuring music from the company's television commercial. Adidas charged less than $1 per ringtone, which included a small profit margin. In its first month, 10,000 ringtones were downloaded.

Members of Club Nokia[16] in Germany were sent text messages advertising clips from the Road to Lisbon commercial that could be inserted into conversations. Of the 120,000 messages sent, 10 per cent responded by downloading clips, such as crowds cheering or booing.

Adidas created a more useful and interactive product with its Euro 2004 Java ticker applet.[17] The ticker could be downloaded to cellular phones and offered real-time scores for the championship matches (see Exhibit 6). The applet was promoted through soccer websites across Europe, such as

---

[15] This figure represents the cumulative number of viewers, including repeat viewers. Therefore, one person viewing all 31 games would be counted as 31 viewers.

[16] Club Nokia was a marketing program in which subscribers agreed to receive promotional messages on their cellular phones in exchange for benefits such as product discounts and free cellular phone content or services.

[17] An applet is a small self-contained computer application written in the Java programming language developed by Sun Microsystems, Inc. An applet has limited connectivity and can usually only interact with the site from which the applet originated. A ticker applet downloads and displays simple information, such as weather, news headlines and sports data.

football365.com in the United Kingdom, and it was available in five languages (English, French, German, Spanish and Swedish). Additionally, some phone service providers, such as Vodafone, promoted the applet on their websites in order to encourage subscribers to use newer forms of multimedia services.

The applet could be downloaded to 2.5G phones using an advertised code at a cost of €5.00 for two months' use, which was charged directly to the user's monthly mobile phone bill. The applet then connected with a third-party information provider that adidas had hired to feed scores and other information to users for a flat fee. Any earnings generated from subscription fees also went to the information provider rather than adidas.

Actual subscriptions to the Euro 2004 applet far exceeded pre-launch projections of 30,000 subscribers. When the mobile provider's tracking site failed halfway through the campaign, the company already had more than 63,000 subscribers. Although users could still download the applet, the mobile phone provider was never able to restore tracking or collect additional subscription fees. Nevertheless, adidas viewed this early effort in branded cellular phone services as a qualified success. Although user profiles were not collected, the Global Media Group was concerned about the lack of focus on the key 12- to 24-year-old consumer. "From the testing we did," Drake explained, "the applet was too factual and appealed mainly to hardcore football geeks. Kids want something that is more lighthearted; something that's a bit cooler; something that will give them an advantage over their friends."

Some believed that the R2L mobile effort could have been even more successful had it been cross-promoted on food and beverage containers, for example. The cost of such promotion, however, was very high. With R2L, adidas was "testing the waters" to see what could be achieved on mobile devices, without spending a significant amount of money. According to Prenderville, new media had to be approached cautiously. "We will continue to migrate to digital media, such as mobile devices," he explained. "However, for senior management to have faith in new media, we need to have a gradual transition. We have to make sure that the tools we are using have critical mass before we invest money in them."

A second generation program called "Match Centre" provided up-to-date regional league scores for the Italian, French, German, Spanish and U.K. leagues. The applet was promoted on sports websites (see Exhibit 7). By clicking on a banner ad, users were taken to an instruction page that explained how to enter a text code into their phone (see Exhibit 8). Once the code was entered, a download link was sent to the phone, and any associated fees were automatically charged to the user's phone bill.

Although Match Centre appeared to be popular among soccer fans, the Global Media Group was unsure how much the service would appeal to younger consumers. According to Drake:

> We have found a way to impart information; we have found a way to demonstrate products, and we can align it all with the current brand concept. We've achieved all of that. Has it made a positive impact on the football fan? We think yes, as future research will demonstrate. But we still haven't been able to engage youth in a meaningful way.
>
> We are only interested in the 12- to 24-year-olds, which is an age in which we can make a favorable impression. Although they have greater spending power, we are less interested in older consumers because they already have brand loyalty.

In future generations of Match Centre, adidas planned to incorporate "cooler" elements, such as photos and video.

URBAN COOL

Basketball

Basketball had traditionally been dominated by Nike and its affiliation with basketball star Michael Jordan. The affinity American urban youth had for basketball resulted in a large market share for Nike among American teens. For adidas, breaking into this market was a critical part of its U.S. product strategy. The Global Media Group sought to adjust the R2L tools to provide the same benefits to basketball fans in the United States, such as real-time basketball scores and other basketball data on a mobile Java ticker. Drake explained:

> Right now we are limited by the bandwidth in the U.S., which means that we can only deliver text. But it is only a matter of time before the technology will allow us to deliver more information. The problem for us is not delivering information to the consumer, but combining it with product and brand messaging.

Drake believed that mobile phones could prove to be an important way to deliver marketing messages to basketball fans in American cities:

> In my opinion, the basketball fan is inclined to look for personalization and for the latest technology, something that can demonstrate urban cool. And we think the mobile phone is a cool item. Therefore, an investment in that will be a big part of their income.

One option involved creating an adidas-branded mobile phone. To realize the concept, adidas would have to work with cellular phone manufacturers to include features important to its target market. Secondly, it had to develop appealing add-on content, such as sports tickers, games and ringtones.

Hip-Hop Music

Adidas based its U.S. brand strategy around "urban centers of cool," where hip-hop (rap) music stars strongly influenced style fashion trends. Although Reebok was arguably the most aggressive company when it came to sponsoring hip-hop, the first music group to endorse a line of footwear was Run DMC with its 1986 hit song "My adidas." At the time, marketers were only beginning to look at the cultural phenomenon of hip-hop, so when Run DMC subsequently asked adidas to underwrite a concert tour, company executives were hesitant. One observer noted:

> They were skeptical about the marketing potential of rap musicians until they were convinced to attend a Run DMC concert. At a crucial moment, while the rap group was performing the song, one of the members yelled out, "Okay, everybody in the house, rock your adidas!" and three thousand pairs of sneakers shot into the air. The adidas executives couldn't reach for their checkbooks fast enough.[18]

By 2003, the hip-hop cultural phenomenon had reached 45 million Americans, who spent more than $10 billion on hip-hop music and related merchandise. Of this number, an estimated 80 per cent were Caucasian between the ages of 13 and 34, with a total spending power of roughly $1 trillion.[19]

---

[18] "Simmons' Rush for Profits," Black Enterprise, December, 1992.

[19] "Hip-hop's Bling Culture is Wooing Corporate America," Marketing Week, June 24, 2004.

The influence of hip-hop even extended to other countries, particularly the United Kingdom, Germany and Japan, where fans imitated the clothing and lifestyle choices of their favorite hip-hop stars.

Respect M.E.: The Missy Elliott Campaign

Five-time Grammy nominee Missy Elliott was the best-selling female hip-hop star of all time with more than 7 million albums sold. In 2001, she signed a one-year deal to promote Reebok shoes before appearing in television commercials for the Gap and Sprite. After her contract with Reebok expired, she signed a deal with adidas to create her own line of adidas-branded clothing and footwear.

Known as Respect M.E., the line ranged from "Run DMC style" sneakers priced at $70 to Missy Elliott "Remix" boots for $120. Adidas even set aside its long-standing guidelines for style and color in order to accommodate Missy's unique fashion.

The Missy Elliot line was launched well into the fiscal year, when advertising budgets had already been allocated to various campaigns. With limited marketing support available to Respect M.E., adidas decided to promote the line in three ways: mobile, online and a face-to-face event at the music awards in Miami, Florida. Mobile was viewed as a particularly inexpensive media that would allow adidas to "stretch the budget" while reaching a wide audience.

The objectives of the mobile campaign were to:

- Show the product line,
- Create consumer demand,
- Drive traffic to retail outlets,
- Help consumers locate the products,
- Grow the existing database of Missy fans and capture SMS data,
- Alert fans to product line activity, such as Missy press updates and appearances, and
- Enable users to download exclusive Respect M.E. mobile content onto their handsets for viral promotion.

The Missy Elliott campaign was adidas's most ambitious mobile effort yet, one that the Global Media Group hoped would attract "hundreds of thousands" of potential customers. It included a broad variety of content, such as monophonic, polyphonic and true-tone ringtones, voice tones[20] and adidas-branded wallpapers. Adidas decided to initially price content at $1.99 (except true tones, which sold for $2.99). Users were required to register on the Respect M.E. website by entering personal data and a valid credit card number (see Exhibit 9). Once registered, any downloads were charged to the user's credit card. Finally, any profits generated from the site would be donated to Missy Elliott's "Break the Cycle" charity.[21]

Cell phones that accessed the site could also be used to browse the Respect M.E. collection, find the nearest adidas store by inputting a postal code, sign up for product and content alerts, chat with Missy Elliott once a week, send a notification to another cell phone about Respect M.E., and enter a contest to win a vacation with Missy Elliott.

The delivery of exclusive product previews of the new Respect M.E. line was a key component of the campaign. "People generally like to show their friends what's coming and what's new," Drake

---

[20] Unlike ringtones, which used music to notify subscribers of incoming calls, voice tones utilized voice messages from Missy Elliott, such as "Yo, this is Missy Elliott. Why don't you show me some respect and pick up your phone." True tones were digital music samples similar to MP3 audio recordings.

[21] "Break the Cycle" offered programs aimed at reducing domestic violence in the United States.

reasoned. "And if brands are considered cool, they definitely want to show their friends before it becomes available."

To encourage traffic to the site during its initial launch, adidas offered for free the first 10,000 wallpapers downloaded from the site. Also, for each message sent to a friend about the Missy Elliott site, members received credits that could be used to download content, also for free. Finally, Missy Elliot created an exclusive track for adidas, which was advertised on various blogging sites.

Exhibit 1 Media consumption trends

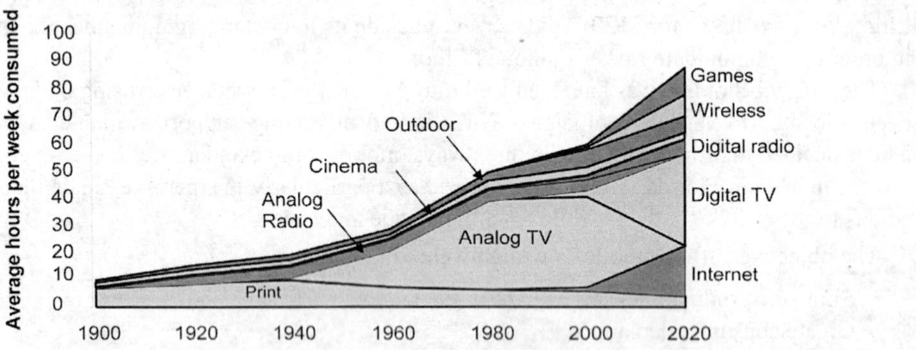

Source: Adidas Global Media.

Exhibit 2 Yahoo web portal takeover

Source: Yahoo.com web archive.

Exhibit 3 Nike mobile downloads

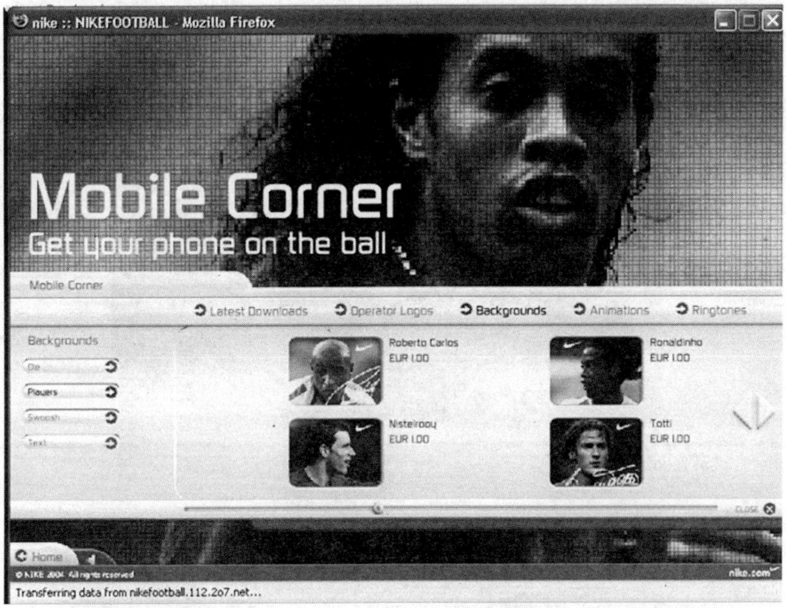

Source: nikefootball.com, December 2004.

Exhibit 4 European mobile phone penetration by country 2003 (actual) and 2006 (estimated)

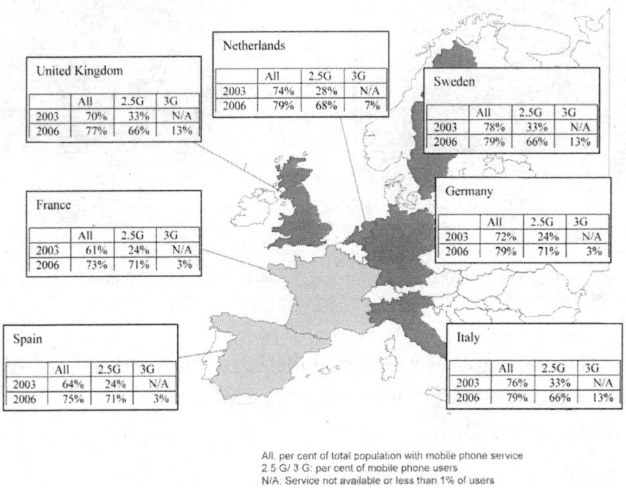

Source: adidas Global Media (based on Forrester Research data).

Exhibit 5 "Flaschenpost" for Coca-cola

Source: adidas Global Media.

Exhibit 6 Adidas match centre

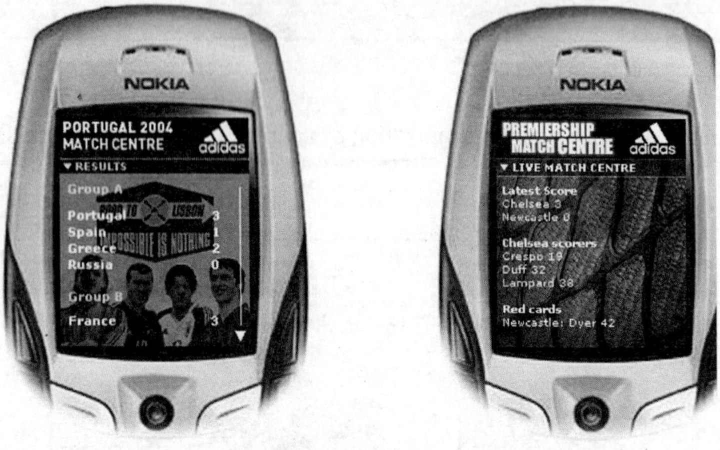

Road to Lisbon Match Centre 2.0

Source: company files.

To get the adidas Match Centre, users entered the keyword "adidas." The Match Centre provided users with live scores, statistics and European soccer news.

A simple menu structure included:

- *Live Scores*
- *Results of Previous Matches*
- *Group Tables*
- *News*
- *adidas Zone*

Exhibit 7 U.K. soccer website with adidas match centre advertisement

Source: rivals.net, February 2005.

Exhibit 8 Adidas match centre sign-up webpage

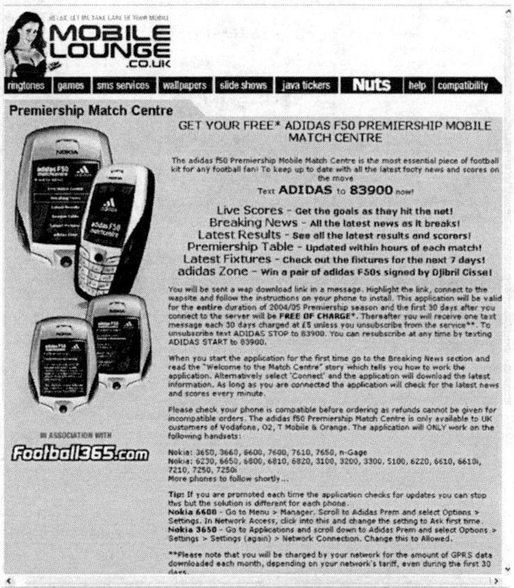

Source: www.mobilelounge.co.uk.

Exhibit 9 Respect M.E. registration site and sample wallpaper

Source: company files.

17

Nike Inc.

Developing an Effective Public Relations Strategy

"Nike is a company of people rooted in our responsibility to be good corporate citizens. We have improved labor practice throughout Southeast Asia by paying decent wages, adhering to a Code of Conduct, and having it monitored by independent parties.

In many cases, critics will tell you that Nike is doing a good job, but people target Nike because it's the market leader, and they believe other companies will change their labor practices."

Vada Manager
Global Director of Issues Management

It had been almost a decade since the media first alleged that Nike-aligned factories in China and Indonesia were forcing employees to work long hours for low pay under harsh working conditions, and for utilizing physically and verbally abusive managers. At that time, these allegations seemed so absurd to Nike managers, no response was deemed necessary. The article however, would be the seed of a global media campaign that was to gather such momentum, that by the mid-1990s, it had created a public relations nightmare for the company. By 1998, after three years of record performance, the financial crisis in Asia (a region that accounted for one-quarter of Nike's sales) and intense competition in the domestic market (which accounted for one-half of their sales) had contributed to a decline in Nike's revenue and market share. Though no direct correlation could be proven between the consumer's negative perceptions of Nike and the company's decline in market share and stock price, it certainly did not help in their efforts to more solidly establish themselves as the global leader in a hotly competitive industry.

THE ATHLETIC FOOTWEAR AND SPORTSWEAR APPAREL INDUSTRY

Nike Inc., based in Beaverton, Oregon, created authentic athletic footwear, apparel, equipment and accessories for sports and fitness enthusiasts. By 1998, Nike's revenue had exceeded US$9 billion (see Exhibit 1). The company was the undisputed market leader in the athletic shoe market in the U.S., selling four out of every 10 pairs of athletic shoes sold in the world's largest athletic shoe market. Nike was also the world's number one athletic shoemaker—commanding the market leadership position in many of the 110 countries where Nike goods were sold. Reebok placed a distant second with sales of approximately US$3.5 billion, followed by Adidas and Fila.

In 1997, the athletic shoe industry had been characterized by poor sales, lower gross margins brought about by greater close-out sales in the U.S. and Asia, and high inventory levels. Sales had declined in both Asia (attributable to the Asian financial crisis) and the U.S., partly due to a shift of consumer tastes away from traditional white sneakers to darker, all-purpose footwear. Though many of these issues would remain a challenge throughout 1998, there was more optimism throughout the industry for the remainder of the year, into the next millennium. Nike was keen to be well poised to ride the wave of increased market opportunities.

NIKE—COMPANY LEGENDS

Nike began as a venture between Nike's CEO, Phil Knight, a student at the University of Oregon (U of O) (widely regarded as the most prestigious university in the U.S. for track and field) and Bill Bowerman, a U of O track and field coach. Knight went on to do an MBA at Stanford, where he wrote a paper on how to break Germany's domination of the U.S. athletic shoe industry, identifying a niche for affordable, high-tech athletic shoes.

Upon graduation from Stanford in 1964, Knight and Bowerman founded Blue Ribbon Sports, Nike's predecessor. After a trip to Japan, to source a supplier of high-tech athletic shoes based on Bowerman's designs, which had helped U of O runners break track and field records, Knight began distributing shoes at local track meets (selling the first versions out of the trunk of his 1963 Plymouth Valiant). During these venturesome times, Knight practiced as a certified public accountant and taught at Portland State University until 1969. Three years later the "Cortez"—the first athletic shoe to appear under the Nike brand name—was launched, and became an immediate success. Crowned with their first triumph, Knight took an increasingly active role in launching innovative products and implementing groundbreaking marketing strategies in the industry to promote brand awareness, including the use of sponsorships to reinforce ties between product performance and athletes (including such high profile names as John McEnroe and Michael Jordan). (See Exhibit 2 for a chronology of Nike's development.)

Other innovative ideas included futures-based ordering, substantial investment in research and development and a dynamic organizational culture. Another key success factor was Nike's use of offshore manufacturing. Though Nike had begun manufacturing athletic shoes in Japan, their international manufacturing focus shifted in a major way to Taiwan and Korea in the mid-1980s until the early 1990s, following the industry trend of shifting domestic production to Southeast Asia (see Exhibit 2). Instead of losing the management skills and partnerships that Nike had forged with Taiwanese and Korean factory managers and owners, those stakeholders moved with Nike and built factories in China from scratch when the manufacturing base shifted once again. With another shift of the global manufacturing base to Indonesia and Vietnam, Nike followed the same strategy of working with the Korean and Taiwanese owners and managers with whom they had forged relationships. According to Knight, the benefits of international trade had become apparent in all the regions where Nike had sub-contracted manufacturing—"economic advancement of impoverished people, better values for consumers in developed countries and increased cross-cultural understanding." Global expansion of Nike's manufacturing base, combined with their international marketing efforts, resulted in Nike becoming one of the world's most recognized brands, with millions of people around the world identifying the "Nike swoosh" as a highly sought-after label.

However, the globally recognized "swoosh" had become increasingly difficult to defend in the face of negative publicity that had become a big part of Nike's story throughout the 1990s. During that period, allegations of worker abuse and exploitation in Nike-aligned factories gained such momentum, that it had shaken the company to the core. Company spokespeople constantly reaffirmed that worker abuse occurred infrequently among Nike's global workforce, and that when it was apparent, quick and decisive action was taken to eradicate it. Nike had conscientiously drafted a corporate code of ethics and was highly committed to enforcing it; it was well understood that the risk of not backing up their promises to improve factory conditions was to add hypocrisy to the charges already mounted against them. However, credibility was not easily achieved—western consumers had more faith in the activists than in Nike. Adding to the challenge was the fact that detractors had seemingly endless access to the media who were keen to provide their readers with scandalous headlines and tantalizing soundbites.

GUILTY UNTIL PROVEN INNOCENT

Fair labor practices had been a core value at Nike since it was founded, and Nike prided itself in playing a leadership role around the globe in this respect. Though several incidents of improper labor practices had indeed occurred, the 450,000 workers employed at the 150 Nike-aligned factories throughout Southeast Asia were often the best treated in the region, according to Manager. Nevertheless, with hundreds of thousands of workers throughout the region, ensuring that individual plant managers strictly adhered to corporate standards regarding labor practices was a formidable challenge.[1] Additionally, an entrenched history of deep animosity between the Vietnamese workers and their Korean and Taiwanese managers added a layer of sensitivity to the entire issue.

In 1998, Nike's communications strategy in dealing with the negative publicity was marked by a distinct shift from their original approach. For a three-year period, from the beginning of the negative press that began as a trickle in 1989 and lasted until 1992, Nike's policy was to largely disregard the issues, saying that the subcontractors were in charge. In an early 1990 issue of *The Oregonian* (the local paper where Nike world headquarters was located) David Taylor, Nike's vice-president in

[1] In Vietnam alone for example, Nike employed 38,000 Vietnamese in their five factories—more than any other foreign business, and accounted for five per cent of the total exports for the country.

charge of production was quoted as saying that "we don't pay anybody at the factories, and we don't set policy within the factories. It's their business to run."

However, with increasingly rapid speed, the trickle seen in 1989 had become a torrent, and the media began running weekly and even daily accounts describing supposedly harsh factory conditions, low pay and instances of management abuse. Watchdog groups, including such high-profile groups as the Washington, D.C.-based Campaign for Labor Rights and San Francisco's Global Exchange accused managers at Nike's subcontracted factories of forcing factory workers to work excessively long hours, in unsatisfactory working conditions, for below average wages. These and other activists groups authored numerous articles outlining several particular incidences of worker abuses throughout Southeast Asia, targeting Nike-aligned facilities specifically. Their articles included stories depicting alleged humiliation and intimidation, and physical abuse of workers (the vast majority of whom were female) by their (male, foreign) managers—in an environment of record profits for Nike and high-profile multimillion dollar endorsement contracts. Watchdog groups accused Nike of worker exploitation through low pay, stating that a worker's pay was not only inadequate, but was spent mainly on feeding and housing themselves and their families, leaving them no chance to save money. Yet other accusations involved excess levels of toxic fumes in the workplace and forced overtime.

Specific incidents of abuse circulating on the international newswires included several incidents in Nike-aligned factories in Vietnam. Allegedly, as punishment for not wearing regulation (Nike) shoes to work, workers were forced to run laps in the 100-degree heat, causing several of them to faint. At another Nike plant, there were reports that 125 assembly-line workers were lined up and slapped with the sole of a Nike sneaker. At a third Nike-aligned facility, workers were allegedly forced to lick the factory floor for misdemeanors.

The media seemed only too willing to disseminate anti-Nike stories to aid the activist's campaigns. Numerous watchdog groups pursued Nike with a dogged determination, seemingly endless zeal and caustic, well-organized, media campaigns. And it did not end there. Several events were organized by unrelated groups that were not designed in collusion, but nonetheless served to synergistically fuel the attack on Nike.

The group Campaign Labor for Rights organized "National Days of Consciousness," which involved the distribution of leaflets outside Nike stores across the U.S. Activists met with officials at various universities throughout the country, attempting to persuade them of Nike's alleged unfair labor practices.[2] The irony of such a campaign did not escape Manager. Nike's competitors, who were also using off-shore manufacturing in Asia, were not subjected to the extent that Nike was, as an industry leader, and, thus, were often less circumspect in the monitoring and enforcement of the labor practices of their subcontracted factories. Nonetheless, by mid-1997, the campaign had rallied the participation of Nike's key target markets and had gone mainstream.

New Jersey schoolchildren staged an anti-Nike play on Broadway in October 1997. More than 40 members of Congress signed a letter—which circulated through the Capitol—calling on the company to improve conditions in the factories. Earlier that month, an "International Nike Day of Protest" was organized to "educate people on the deplorable working conditions in Nike's Asian manufacturing plants, and to get more people involved in global employment issues" according to organizers. Demonstrators in 28 states and 12 countries including Canada, Switzerland, Australia and

---

[2] One example occurred when Campaign for Labor Rights issued a statement that they had successfully lobbied team officials of the University of California at Irvine's women's basketball team to switch to Converse athletic products. A UC spokesman consequently issued a statement saying that the switch was due to personal ties that the new coach had with Converse. The spokesperson continued saying that "while we were sympathetic to the issues, it was purely a business decision" and "our men's basketball and track and field teams continue to wear Nike products."

Malaysia gathered to "encourage Nike to clean up its Asian sweatshops and to pay workers decent salaries." Admitting that Nike was not the only company accused of allowing poor working conditions in subcontracted factories, organizers said they had valid reasons for targeting Nike:

> Nike is one of the few companies that has great influence over the entire industry. If they changed and raised their human rights standards, it could set a precedent for the entire apparel and garment industries. We didn't call them a leader—they did. And they're not doing what a leader would do.

Medea Benjamin, director of Global Exchange,[3] and one of Nike's harshest critics, constantly denounced Nike for ineffective monitoring of the working conditions in their subcontracted factories, and for not exerting more control over the conditions in those factories. Almost daily, damning statements such as "the only reason that Nike started to show any desire to clean up labor abuses is the media exposure generated by watchdog groups such as ours (Global Exchange)" were printed in national and international editions of the *New York Times*, the *Wall Street Journal*, and the *International Herald Tribune*.

High-profile critics included the iconoclastic filmmaker Michael Moore, who gained fame by satirizing General Motors in his film *Roger & Me*, and for his irreverent style of ambushing CEOs while filming documentary-style. In his book, *Downsize This*, Moore labelled Knight "Corporate Crook No. 3." While promoting his film *The Big One* on CNBC, Moore stated that Nike had "14-year-old girls in Indonesia making shoes for 40 cents an hour." Knight—the only CEO to respond to Moore when accosted by him—did so in a genuine attempt to answer some of Moore's accusations with facts regarding Nike's labor initiatives. However, this move backfired, as much of Moore's arguments never made it on released film (see Exhibit 3). From the perspective of Nike's senior management, statements such as these were just a few examples among hundreds of how Nike's critics distorted or ignored the facts and the complexity of Nike's human resources, wage policy and labor practices.

Despite the company's persistant efforts to clear the record on this, and many other contentious issues, facts were being lost in activists' rhetoric, and it was becoming increasingly challenging for Nike to defend their commitment to workers' rights in their subcontracted factories. In light of the importance to Nike to resolve these issues, a separate division—the Corporate Responsibility Division—was formed.

NIKE'S CORPORATE RESPONSIBILITY DIVISION

In 1998, Nike consolidated their community affairs, labor practices, environmental action groups into the Corporate Responsibility Division. One of the key players was Maria Eitel, Nike's vice-president of corporate responsibility. Reporting directly to Knight, Eitel was responsible for ensuring compliance of Nike's labor practices and environmental affairs, according to a Code of Conduct developed in 1992, as well as deepening the company's global community involvement. Though only 38, Eitel had gained valuable experience in public relations before joining Nike. She had behind-the-scenes experience as a reporter and producer for several large news stations, had been the White House deputy director of Media Relations and special assistant to past president George Bush from 1989 to 1992. Eitel had also held several top management positions in public and corporate affairs departments of various multinationals, including MCI Communications and Microsoft.

---

[3] Based in San Francisco, Global Exchange was a human rights organization (and the only one that had a full-time staff person devoted to the Nike anti-sweatshop campaign).

Eitel had been hired as part of Nike's efforts to improve their image as a good corporate citizen through real and tangible improvements in their labor, human resource and environmental practices. The use of a so-called "ethics manager" was an increasingly popular strategic move for corporations facing similar challenges. For example, Reebok International Ltd. had hired Sharon Cohen to act in the same capacity as Eitel. However, according to Benjamin:

> Yes, Cohen has been more effective in crafting a corporate image than Nike; however, she's had less to deal with. The only reason Reebok has escaped such extensive international criticism is because the focus has been on Nike. Also, though Cohen is effective on the PR front, I consider her less successful in making real changes on the ground.

In response to Nike's detractors, who remained either cautiously optimistic or overtly cynical, stating that Eitel had been hired as a public relations move as opposed to an instrument of true change (referring to her as "more of a lapdog than a watch dog") Eitel responded:

> I'm really being given responsibility, and Nike is really very committed to these issues and doing the right thing. This is in no way a public relations exercise. I'm here to look at programs and policies and to work with our critics. I wouldn't have taken the job if the desire to do the right thing wasn't there.

Another key player in the implementation of Nike's commitment to fair labor practice and corporate communications strategy was Dusty Kidd, Nike's director of labor practices. Kidd's mandate was one of tremendous importance and enormous scope. Specifically, he was responsible for the management and training of contract labor managers, trainers and inspectors in key production countries including China, Vietnam and Indonesia. To manage information on Nike's initiatives on this front, and for any other potentially contentious issues, Vada Manager was hired in 1997 in the capacity of Senior Manager, Corporate Communication. Manager had come directly from another market leader of the apparel industry, Levi Strauss, where he acted in a similar capacity. Within a short time, Manager was promoted to Director, Issues Management, Global. Despite Manager's determined efforts to educate the public on Nike's efforts, and resultant successes, in improving the conditions at their subcontracted factories abroad, the media's relentless attack on Nike seemed to be gathering momentum—both externally and internally.

EMPLOYEE MORALE

Simon Pestridge, Nike's labor practices manager, was responsible for managing corporate programs at post-secondary institutions throughout the US. Pestridge explained that over the years, he had seen a change in the type of interaction he had with students that he encountered on campus. For years, Pestridge would often be approached by students who were very interested in working at Nike. However, he was now more frequently questioned (and often reproached) for Nike's perceived labor practices in developing countries, finding that he had to defend Nike's position on such issues. In order to do so, he felt that it was critical that he visit some of the factories in Asia, and witness the conditions there first-hand.

During his tour of several Asian factories, Pestridge was encouraged by what he saw. After speaking with several workers on an informal basis, his pride to be associated with Nike was reaffirmed, and he was eager to correct erroneous perceptions of Nike's labor policies—both externally and internally. He explained:

> Several of my colleagues explained that they had been repeatedly put in the difficult position among their peer group, friends and relatives of defending their employment at Nike in light of the perceptions of Nike's labor policies in subcontracted factories in Southeast Asia.
>
> I heard stories that at parties, when our employees began small talk about their hobbies and careers, lively discussions would ensue. Soon, many employees began to demand our position on various moral issues. We saw emotional discussions emerge on our intranet.
>
> Nike has always encouraged questioning and freedom of speech, because we had nothing to hide. Over time, we have discovered that we need to address this issue internally in a systematic way to ensure that our employees are aware of the extent of our efforts to safeguard the well being of our employees everywhere.

Defending the brand internally, and externally, was becoming an increasingly difficult mandate for the Corporate Responsibility team. A major thrust toward this end was the establishment of Corporate Standards and Practices programs.

NIKE CORPORATE STANDARDS AND PRACTICES

To ensure that Nike's partners "shared their commitment to the promotion of best practices and continuous improvement in occupational safety and health, compensation, hours of work and benefits standards," Nike implemented their Corporate Standards programs, which included MESH (Manufacturing-Environment-Safety-Health), Manufacturing Leadership Standards, and a Code of Conduct and Corporate Practices, including outside monitoring and a compliance system (ensuring compliance to the Code of Conduct).

A key component of their Corporate Standards was Nike's Code of Conduct, drafted in 1992. The Code of Conduct was designed as a quantifiable way to ensure Nike's responsibility to their workers and to demonstrate their commitment to this responsibility (see Exhibit 4). According to a Nike press release, the Code of Conduct was universal in its application:

> Wherever Nike operates around the globe, we are guided by this Code of Conduct. We bind our manufacturing partners to these principles. Our manufacturing partners must post this Code in all major workspaces, translated into the language of the worker, and must endeavor to train workers on their rights and obligations as defined by this Code and applicable labor laws.

When press reports and watchdog groups continued to fervently accuse Nike of allowing poor conditions in their subcontracted factories, senior management continually referred to the Code to substantiate their serious commitment to improving the situation. Another key component of Nike's corporate standards was their MESH program.

Launched in June 1998, MESH was designed to ensure best practices in human resource management, protection of the environment and compliance on health and safety policies. Moreover, every Nike subcontracted manufacturing facility was obligated to adhere to these Manufacturing Leadership Standards, which included:

- Nike's stance against fines for disciplinary shortcomings and deposits as a condition of employment
- Protection from discrimination against pregnant workers, to ensure equal opportunity for female workers
- The strict requirement for all contractors to have a "simple, clear, written and mandatory Personal Protective Equipment (PPE) policy" and all applicable PPE available where appropriate
- The provision of annual leave at the worker's request (accompanied by an encouragement of taking the time off versus working for additional bonus pay)
- Strict monitoring of time-keeping, through the use of time clocks, and pay documentation through clear payment records, which must accompany a worker's wage
- The compensation of workers during their training period and a fair wage structure
- The agreement of the subcontracted factory to undergo a Price Waterhouse Coopers Labor Practices Assessment Audit, and a Nike SHAPE (Safety-Health-Attitude of Management-Environment) inspection before approval

Manager explained that Nike was committed to ensuring that the principles behind their Corporate Standards programs were applied in reality. When deficiencies were found, Nike and the factory in question worked together on plans of action to bring the factory into compliance. If the factory management team was unwilling or unable to meet Nike's standards, the contractor was "formally fined, put on probation and given specific time lines and target actions to accomplish, or face losing the business," according to a Nike corporate document outlining their policy on enforcement of the Code of Conduct. If that failed, the relationship would be terminated—a move Nike had resorted to only 10 times since 1996, given the adverse impact such a step would have on the workers and their dependents.

According to Manager, Nike's Corporate Standards and Practices programs ensured a comprehensive and groundbreaking crusade for a deepening commitment to improved conditions at subcontracted factories. Manager pointed out the irony did not escape him or his colleagues in the Social Responsibility Department of having to constantly defend labor practices when the company had led labor responsible practice throughout its history. Nonetheless, given the growing public protests and stories in the press depicting Nike in a negative light, it was clear that Nike was not perceived to be a responsible corporate citizen.

However, despite the breadth and scope of Nike's Standards and Practices programs, they were ultimately ineffective in persuading the public that Nike was serious in eradicating poor labor conditions in their subcontracted factories throughout Southeast Asia. Critics relentlessly contended that the Code actually meant little, if anything, to the average factory worker, and remained highly cynical that the Code was making any real impact on the working environment. The deluge of damaging press continued. If anything, perceived shortcomings in Nike's plan to improve conditions had increased the anti-Nike sentiment among watchdog groups and consumers. Nike consistently drew their critic's attention back to the Code of Conduct, as well as their extensive use of independent monitoring.

NIKE'S AUDITING AND INDEPENDENT MONITORING

According to Manager, Nike had been the first company in the apparel industry to use ongoing independent monitoring. With a view to improving corporate practices where necessary, Nike commissioned Dartmouth College's Tuck School of Business and the former U.N. Ambassador Andrew Young to visit 15 Nike factories and to subjectively report on conditions. The Tuck students reported that "workers earned above the local minimum wage, and with special allowances such as meals, housing and health care, as well as the opportunity to work overtime, the workers were earning more than enough to cover their basic needs."

The Young report, released by Nike in the summer of 1997, was similarly encouraging and Nike felt that it presented an accurate appraisal of factory conditions. Young's conclusion; "Nike is doing a good job—but can do better." Young went on to say that "though Nike's performance was positive overall, the Code of Conduct is not visible on the factory floors and (is) not well understood by the factory workers." In response, Nike issued each worker with a laminated pocket-sized card, printed in the local language, which outlined acceptable corporate labor practices. Nike also launched training programs in factories to ensure the Code was well understood by all workers at every level. In the report, Young also stated that it was his "sincere belief that Nike is doing a good job in the application of its Code of Conduct, but Nike can—and should—do better."

The study was widely criticized by human rights groups as lacking objectivity. Benjamin was quoted as saying, "Nike has spent millions of dollars buying off major athletes—now it's bought off Andrew Young." In response, Nike printed a full-page ad in seven major newspapers, including the *New York Times* (see Exhibit 5); however, the negative press was relentless—within a matter of hours, national newswires had nine headlines on Nike, and Garry Trudeau had created a whole series of *Doonesbury* comic strip[4] ridiculing Nike for its labor practices. It seemed that despite Nike's well-organized and genuine efforts to improve conditions, their actions were misconstrued by their critics' well-oiled anti-Nike machine. According to Manager, there were innumerable examples of how Nike's detractors ignored the larger, far-reaching implications of many issues.

NIKE'S POSITION

Wages at Nike subcontracted factories, for example, were a hotly debated issue. According to a Nike press release, many activists chose to "disregard the growing body of data regarding our contribution to workers in developing countries." Nike's position on wages was clear—Manager found it illogical to draw a comparison between factory wages in Vietnam, China or Indonesia and the U.S. where the cost of living was exponentially higher. Complicating the issue was the fact that often wages were described as "below-sustenance"; however, the "facts" would vary.

Wage figures from approximately US$30 per month, to over US$45 monthly for Vietnamese factory workers, were available depending on the source and date of the study, as well as the factory surveyed (see Exhibit 6). Often, these wages would be directly contrasted to Knight's standing as the sixth richest man in America, noting his net worth of more than US$5 billion, or for dramatic effect Michael Jordan's US$40 million sponsorship deal.

Manager stated that information distributed by various watchdog groups, even if correct, presented Nike in the harshest light, often with an isolated statistic presented out of context, ignoring the larger issues. Activists would state that "a factory worker's wages, accounting for just US$5 for a shoe selling for over US$100, could be doubled resulting in only marginally increased costs for Nike." However, though roughly accurate, this figure ignored all other factors in the cost structure of Nike products, including design, research and development, duties and shipping, personnel as well as the sales and marketing expenses, overhead and profit margins of both Nike and the retailer.

Other critics stated that a "mere 10 per cent of Nike's US$650 million marketing campaign would be enough to double the wages of 100,000 young women in Indonesia, putting them over the poverty line." This argument however, disregarded the macroeconomic consequences of such a move. Stephen

[4] A popular political satire in the form of a comic strip with national circulation in hundreds of American dailies and with wide reproduction in leading local papers in countries around the world.

Parker, chief economist at the Asia Foundation in San Francisco told the Boston Globe in an September, 1988 article, "A lot of economists believe wages shouldn't be set higher than the local market." The article also added: "Parker, who hasn't studied Nike specifically, said that although Asian workers might not live well on their salaries, they usually won't work for starvation wages. The fact that Nike's contractors can find people willing to work for the wages they offer now is proof enough that the pay is in line with the going rate in the local market.

This perspective about the correlation of wages to the local market was also reflected by James Rockwell, president of Vatico, the first American company licensed to do business in Vietnam by the U.S. and Vietnamese governments. In an article, Rockwell wrote, "if Nike were to double its salary as suggested, those in the employment line at Nike will include surgeons, teachers, engineers and key government officials. But does not Vietnam need her surgeons, engineers and teachers?"

Nike's position on the issue of wages was that multinational factories had a responsibility to pay competitive wages but not to change the living standards of a nation. Newspaper articles would quote human rights activists who said that "Nike workers made a *whopping* $2.46 a day as mandated by minimum-wage law." Manager argued that implicit comparison of the wage in a developing country to that of a worker in the U.S. ignored that often a worker in a Nike-aligned factory made at least minimum wage, and often more, surpassing wages in many other factories in the region. In their press releases, Nike officials would often reiterate their commitment to offering workers in their subcontracted plants a "living wage"—a salary that afforded them a minimum standard of living, based on the cost of living in that particular region.

Nike consistently reinforced in all their media communications that in each and every developing country, the wage that workers at Nike subcontracted factories received was at least the minimum wage as dictated by the regional governments. According to Manager, "activist groups have spread false statements that obscure Nike's commitment to human rights." Nike's commitment to their workers and sanctified in their Code of Conduct was lost: a worker would be guaranteed "the prevailing or legal minimum wage, whichever was higher". Manager continued, saying "the fact that Nike is the only shoe manufacturer in the Far East paying more than minimum wage, for instance, is lost in their rhetoric."

Manager further explained that with little or no social security programs, factory jobs were highly valued throughout developing countries in Southeast Asia. For millions of unskilled workers and their families, a factory job was a valuable prize—a chance to send money back to their home to support an entire family, and to "retire" after several years with enough money to begin their own business in their village. Manager pointed to the fact that average annual employee turnover in Vietnam was around one per cent.

Nike officials claimed that Global Exchange, as well as other activist groups, had been extreme in their approach. He insisted that Nike had taken several key steps in ensuring fair wages and in improving the conditions at their subcontracted factories; however, consumers had not received this message, which was obscured by a savvy, well-organized, global anti-Nike campaign. The labor issues Nike faced were to come to a head in late 1997.

MERRY CHRISTMAS

In December of 1997, Nike managers didn't even need to open the morning edition of the *New York Times* to discover yet another story on Nike. On the front page were some strategically chosen excerpts of an internal audit that Nike had commissioned Ernst & Young to conduct on a subcontracted plant near Ho Chi Minh City in Vietnam. The article had been leaked by a former

Nike employee to Dara O'Rourke,[5] a research associate with the Transnational Resource and Action Centre (TRAC). The audit reported various factory conditions and violations in Nike's stated overtime policies, and that:

> more than half the employees in several departments who use chemicals do not wear protective equipment (mask and gloves)—even in highly hazardous places where the concentration of chemical dust and fumes exceeded the standard frequently.

According to a New York Times article on November 8, 1997,

> The Ernst & Young report painted a dismal picture of thousands of young women, most under age 25, laboring 10½ hours a day, six-days-a-week, in excessive heat and noise and in foul air, for slightly more than $10 a week.

The leak and the ensuing media coverage prompted Nike to take immediate action.

A press conference was called—a response rarely taken but deemed necessary at this juncture. Manager reiterated that the audit was conducted so that Nike could "make meaningful changes to factory conditions, and the very fact that it was conducted pointed to our determination to improve practices." Manager continued:

> This audit demonstrated the integrity and stringency of our third-party monitoring process. A select few have criticized us for not paying them to conduct our monitoring, and challenged the independence of auditing firms like Ernst & Young and Price Waterhouse. Clearly, this report is not a whitewash. By the recommendations cited in this audit and the steps that Nike has taken to improve the working conditions, it is clear that our system works.

Within several days, Nike had also released details of the audit to the media—a departure from past policy. Since the audit had already been released, however, senior management decided to take the opportunity to fully detail its monitoring process, the results of this particular audit, and importantly, the steps they had taken to ensure a safe, comfortable workplace and sufficient wages for their employees.

According to Nike, the audit reported that the factory was "generally in compliance with Vietnamese law and applicable health and safety standards." The audit examined the factory's compliance with Vietnamese labor requirements and practices, production facility compliance and waste tracking system, chemical storage, and employee and safety measures. Some of the highlights included:

- the average wage exceeded the local minimum wage by US$5
- chemicals were stored in isolated positions away from working places that were well ventilated, and
- health and safety measures were adequate (including clearly posted instructions on machines and general safety policies).

And where actual practices fell short of acceptable standards, Nike also outlined in their press release the immediate steps they had taken based on the results of the audit. For example, upon receiving the Ernst & Young report, Nike immediately:

- reduced overtime hours and restricted the maximum work week to 60 hours
- materially upgraded the ventilation system

[5] O'Rourke was also a consultant to the United Nations Industrial Development Organization. His research focused on strategies for preventing adverse environmental and social impacts on industrial activities in Vietnam.

- increased worker access to protective equipment (e.g. safety goggles, gloves, earplugs and masks), and
- tripled the capacity of the medical facility, doubled the size of the medical staff, and instituted health-care training

According to Manager, the development of this action plan "showed that the system of monitoring really worked," stating that Nike "uncovered these issues clearly before anyone else, and have moved fairly expeditiously to correct them."

However, according to a critique of the audit by TRAC

> Though the Ernst & Young report was flawed in a number of ways, it reports continuing violations of labor laws on maximum working hours, unprotected chemical exposure, poor treatment of workers, and management control of the trade union.

In an increasingly open-door policy, Knight invited congressional critics to visit Nike factories. Also, Nike announced that they would fly several students from the University of North Carolina—where students were particularly vocal about Nike's labor practices—to inspect overseas working conditions first-hand. Nonetheless, critics remained highly skeptical, accusing Nike of cherry-picking those factories that were to be monitored and audited.

By 1998, beyond independent auditing, Nike had taken several other pro-active measures to manage their brand image, including:

- purchasing full-page ads in the U.S. major newspapers
- conducting press conferences and press releases outlining the steps that Nike had taken to ensure compliance around the world with its Code of Conduct
- posting progress on improving labor conditions on the corporate Web site
- responding to each inquiry from the media or watchdog groups and trying to openly communicate with them
- establishing of an extensive Web site specifically addressing labor issues

The last initiative was a particularly integral part of Nike's communication strategy. With the increased adoption of the Internet in the 1990s came the ability—for virtuous and less than virtuous ends—to reach mass audiences and to disseminate information instantly around the globe, regardless of its accuracy or source. Indeed, a well-designed Web site could be perceived as an authoritative source of information.

Nike's detractors had deftly used the World Wide Web to instantly disseminate information to thousands of users visiting chat rooms and Web sites devoted to challenging Nike's labor practices. Within seconds, thousands of people around the globe could instantly become aware of defamatory statements and criticisms of Nike's policies and actions—regardless of the truth of the material. In an effort to combat this and to use the Internet to their advantage, Nike created a corporate Web site to disseminate facts regarding the improved working conditions in their subcontracted factories, their labor Standards and Practices programs, and the myriad of initiatives they had undertaken to improve conditions. The site also invited response from visitors and addressed each of their e-mailed concerns with a response.

Nonetheless, despite Nike's extensive efforts at informing the public of the improvements in the conditions at their subcontracted factories, Nike's own surveys demonstrated that the company's image continued to be tarnished through a seemingly endless barrage of negative publicity. However, Manager had the irrefutable results of several other surveys that implicitly confirmed that consumers' purchasing decisions were not affected by their views of Nike's labor practices. Manager however, felt that though there was little adverse effect to consumers' brand loyalty at present, there was a danger of erosion of Nike's brand equity among younger consumers if the issue was not dealt with deftly and swiftly.

THE $9.2 BILLION QUESTION

Manager remained adamant that there was no proven correlation between Nike's decline in stock price in 1997 and the adverse publicity that they had received over the past several years. However, though it was clear that the publicity had not yet affected Nike's stock price, a key question was the degree to which it could adversely impact future revenue streams.

Manager attributed a recent decline in revenue to several external factors, including the hyper-competitive industry, various changes in consumer purchasing patterns, and the Asian financial crisis. Revenue from Nike's Asian operations had soared from almost US$300 million in 1994 to US$1.2 billion in 1997; however, the Asian economic crisis had adversely affected revenues, and regional layoffs were inevitable. Nike's market position, firmly established over the last six years or so, was sure to be a competitive advantage once the region rebounded (and in 1998 there were increasing signs that Asian economic conditions were gradually improving). Moreover, Nike's success in other regions meant that they were well positioned to ride out the economic storm in Asia, to emerge once again to capitalize on the lucrative opportunities there.

Though Nike was the market leader in most countries throughout the world, they competed with highly talented, resourceful and powerful companies that had not been subjected to negative press to the extent Nike had. In 1998, the company had performed well in the European market (accounting for about US$2 billion in sales) and good growth momentum was expected; however, parts of Europe were only slowly recovering from an economic downturn. The Americas (Canada and Latin America), accounting for approximately half a billion in revenue, had experienced a growth period of several quarters, although the Latin American market was exposed to economic volatility of late. Nonetheless, Nike saw Latin America as another market with "great potential for the future" and was well positioned to capitalize on that growth. Nike's largest market by far was the U.S., which accounted for approximately US$5 billion in sales. If Nike were to remain the world's leading supplier of athletic footwear and apparel, the company would have to actualize the full market potential of the U.S. and other regions around the globe. To do so, they would need to address their public profile and design an effective and comprehensive public relations strategy.

Manager explained:

> There is a growing recognition that issues, left unchecked and unanswered, can have a long-term negative connotation. We need to be more aggressive communicating the positive things that Nike has done over the last few years.

The question that remained was how would Manager and the Corporate Responsibility team accomplish this goal?

The Richard Ivey School of Business gratefully acknowledges the generous support of The Richard and Jean Ivey Fund in the development of this case as part of the RICHARD AND JEAN IVEY FUND ASIAN CASE SERIES.

Exhibit 1 Nike's financial data (in millions, except per share data and financial ratios)

Year Ended May 31	1998*	1997	1996	1995	1994	1993	1992	1991	1990	1989
Revenues	$9,553.1	$9,186.5	$6,470.6	4,760.8	$3,789.7	$3,931.0	$3,405.2	$3,003.6	$2,235.2	$1,710.8
Gross Margin	3,487.6	3,683.5	2,563.9	1,895.6	1,488.2	1,544.0	1,316.1	1,153.1	851.1	636.0
Gross margin %	36.5%	40.1%	39.6%	39.8%	39.3%	39.3%	38.7%	38.4%	38.1%	37.2%
Net income	399.6	795.8	553.2	399.7	298.8	365.0	329.2	287.0	243.0	167.0
Year-end stock price	46.000	57.500	50.188	19.719	14.750	18.125	14.500	9.938	9.813	4.750
Market capitalization	13,201.1	16,633.0	14,416.8	5,635.2	4,318.8	5,499.3	4,379.6	2,993.0	2,942.7	1,417.4
FINANCIAL RATIOS										
Return on equity	12.5%	28.5%	25.2%	21.6%	17.7%	24.5%	27.9%	31.7%	36.3%	34.5%
GEOGRAPHIC REVENUES										
United States	$5,452.5	$5,529.1	$3,964.7	$2,997.9	$2,432.7	$2,528.8	$2,270.9	$2,141.5	$1,755.5	$1,362.2
Europe	2,143.7	1,833.7	1,334.3	980.4	927.3	1,085.7	919.8	664.7	334.3	241.4
Asia-Pacific	1,255.7	1,245.2	735.1	515.6	283.4	178.2	75.7	56.2	29.3	32.0
Canada, Latin America, and other	701.2	578.5	436.5	266.9	146.3	138.3	138.8	141.2	116.1	75.2
Total Revenues	$9,553.1	$9,186.5	$6,470.6	$4,760.8	$3,789.7	$3,931.0	$3,405.2	$3,003.6	$2,235.2	$1,710.8

* = forecasted.

Source: Nike website: www.nike.com., October 2, 1999.

Exhibit 2 A Chronology of nike's development and major milestones

1998	• Corporate Responsibility Division formed (Labor, NEAT, Community Affairs)
1997	• Nike Asia takes off, pushing revenues from $300 million in 1996 to $800 million in 1997.
	• China becomes both a source country and a vital market for Nike.
	• Nike revenues reach more than $9 billion.
1996	• Nike footwear production expands to the Philippines.
	• Nike begins working with non-governmental organizations to develop factory/worker programs. First project: improved worker health/factory clinics.
	• NEAT begins first factory environmental/indoor air quality screening.
	• Nike joins the White House Apparel Industry Partnership anti-sweatshop coalition.
	• Nike Labor Practices division established.
1995	• Nike footwear production expands to Vietnam and Italy.
1992	• International revenues increase 32 per cent to more than $1 billion for the first time, making up 33 per cent of total Nike revenues.
1990	• The burgeoning international market helps Nike surpass $2 billion in consolidated revenue.
	• Employees number 5,300 worldwide.
1989	• The Just Do It campaign enters its second year.
	• Nike sales grow through athlete endorsements.
	• Nike's net income reaches a high of $167 million.
1986	• Revenues pass the landmark billion-dollar mark, reaching $1.07 billion.
1982	• The apparel line grows to nearly 200 styles and $70 million as Nike undergoes massive growth.
1981	• Nike footwear sourcing expands to China and Thailand.
1980	• Nike offers two million shares of common stock to the public.
1979	• The Tailwind shoe introduces Nike-Air cushioning. The first Nike apparel line appears.
	• With nearly 50 per cent of the U.S. market revenues, Nike is the No. 1 running shoe. Nike-shod runners hold every record from 800 to 10,000 metres.
1978	• Nike begins to produce apparel in the Far East. Nike begins producing shoes in own factories in New Hampshire and Maine.
1969	• Knight quits his day job.
	• With 20 employees and several retail outlets, BRS approaches $ 300,000 in revenues.
1964	• Knight and Bowerman each contribute $ 500 to BRS.

Source: www.nike.com., April 28, 1999.

Exhibit 3 Nike and Michael Moore—answers about The Big One

As a heralded maverick athletic company, we thought *Roger & Me* was both funny and entertaining when it came out years ago.

So when New York City resident filmmaker Michael Moore came to Portland, Ore., we invited him out to meet with Nike founder and chief executive officer Phil Knight. Why? Moore had undeservedly labelled Knight "Corporate Crook #3" in his book *Downsize This.* We wanted a chance to change his point of view.

We honestly thought that during our two meetings we found some common ground. You wouldn't know it from watching this documentary.

But Moore, in promoting his new documentary, was using Nike to garner publicity for himself and to sell movie tickets.

In the interest of feeding the viewer what he thought was funny, Moore left out the facts, even facts he acknowledged when he spoke with Phil Knight. As a result, a huge pile of film for this documentary was left on the editing room floor. For example, you miss:

- The part where Michael states, "I honestly think you're the good guy. I honestly think that Nike is the good guy here; you're not General Motors. . ."
- Phil's comments from the second interview on the minimum age of workers in Indonesian factories where our shoes are made. A shame. Moore could have enlightened the viewing audience.
- Phil's offer to join him on a tour of our Indonesian factories. Although Phil couldn't accept Moore's invitation to accompany him that weekend following the first interview, Phil did go to Indonesia in January. Michael declined the invitation to join Phil. Too bad. He might have learned something.

- Moore, in promoting his film on CNBC's *Equal Time* program on September 22, stated that Nike had "14-year-old girls in Indonesia making these shoes for 40 cents an hour." Moore was wrong. And he knew it. Nike's standard on this issue was unequivocal. The legal age in Indonesia was 14, an age at which compulsory schooling has ended. The factories we worked with assured us that no person under their voluntary age limit of 16 years old worked at a factory in any capacity, and Nike worked with local governments to ensure compliance.

Source: Nike Press Release, 1997.

Exhibit 4 Nike's code of conduct

Nike Inc. was founded on a handshake.

Implicit in that act was the determination that we would build our business with all of our partners based on trust, team work, honesty and mutual respect. We expect all of our business partners to operate on the same principles. Wherever Nike operates around the globe, we are guided by this Code of Conduct. We bind our manufacturing partners to these principles. Our manufacturing partners must post this Code in all major workspaces, translated into the language of the worker, and must endeavor to train workers on their rights and obligations as defined by this Code and applicable labor laws.

While these principles establish the spirit of our partnerships, we also bind these partners to specific standards of conduct. These standards are set forth below.

1. **Forced Labor:** The manufacturer does not use forced labor in any form—prison, indentured, bonded or otherwise.
2. **Child Labor:** The manufacturer does not employ any person below the age of 18 to produce footwear. The manufacturer does not employ any person below the age of 16 to produce apparel, accessories or equipment. Where local standards are higher, no person under the legal minimum age will be employed.
3. **Compensation:** The manufacturer provides each employee at least the minimum wage, or the prevailing industry wage, whichever is higher; provides each employee a clear, written accounting for every pay period; and does not deduct from worker pay for disciplinary infractions, in accordance with the Nike Manufacturing Leadership Standard on financial penalties.
4. **Benefits:** The manufacturer provides each employee all legally mandated benefits. Benefits vary by country, but may include meals or meal subsidies; transportation or transportation subsidies; other cash allowances; health care; child care; emergency, pregnancy or sick leave; vacation, religious, bereavement or holiday leave; and contributions for social security and other insurance, including life, health and workers' compensation.
5. **Hours of Work/Overtime:** The manufacturer complies with legally mandated work hours; uses overtime only when each employee is fully compensated according to local law; informs each employee at the time of hiring if mandatory overtime is a condition of employment; and, on a regularly scheduled basis, provides one day off in seven, and requires no more than 60 hours of work per week, or complies with local limits if they are lower.
6. **Management of Environment, Safety and Health (MESH):** The manufacturer has written health and safety guidelines, including those applying to employee residential facilities, where applicable; has a factory safety committee; complies with Nike's environmental, safety and health standards; limits organic vapor concentrations at or below the Permissible Exposure Limits mandated by the U.S. Occupational Safety and Health Administration (OSHA); provides Personal Protective Equipment (PPE) free of charge, and mandates its use; and complies with all applicable local environmental, safety and health regulations.
7. **Documentation and Inspection:** The manufacturer maintains on file all documentation needed to demonstrate compliance with this Code of Conduct; agrees to make these documents available for Nike or its designated auditor to inspect upon request; and agrees to submit to labor practices audits or inspections with or without prior notice.

Minimum Age Requirements

"Nike has zero tolerance for under-age labor."
Nike CEO Phil Knight

Source: www.nike.com., October 7, 1999.

Exhibit 5 Nike's full-page ad in the *New York Times*—A response to the andrew young report June 25, 1997

"It is my sincere belief that Nike is doing a good job. . . but Nike can and should do better"

Ambassador Andrew Young
Good Works International, LLC

After six months of investigation, visiting twelve Asian factories and interviewing hundreds of workers in Indonesia, China, and Vietnam about Nikes's overseas labor practices, this was how Andrew Young concluded his independent 75-page report, released yesterday. Nike agrees. Good isn't good enough in anything we do. We can and will do better. For details on exactly how—and for a complete copy of Ambassador Young's report and recommendations—Please call 1-800-501-6295 go to www.nike.com/report, or go directy to Good Works at www.digitalrelease.com and enter the keyword: Good Works

Source: Nike.

Exhibit 6 Comparisons of reported annual wage for nike workers in vietnam

Source	Reported Wage	Comments
Ernst & Young Audit	• "Over US$40/month" • basic salary was US$45 / month.	• Nike-sponsored study • Random selection of 50 workers (by payroll) at one Nike-subcontracted factory in Vietnam
Tuck School of Business, Dartmouth report	• Average monthly income—US$32/ month	• Nike-sponsored study
Transnational Resource and Action Centre (TRAC)	• One-third of the workforce at one Nike factory reported pay below legal minimum wage (US$35/month)	• Survey conducted in early 1998 • Interviews with Nike workers outside factories (many of whom remained anonymous)
Vietnam Labor Watch	• Average monthly income—US $32/month	• March 1997 • Interviews with Nike workers outside factories (many of whom remained anonymous)
Ministry of Planning and Investment, Vietnam	• Nike subcontracted factories pay "competitive wages" as compared to foreign shoemakers in the country • US$3 per month over minimum wage	• Government sponsored survey conducted in early 1998

18

Spectrum Brands, Inc.

The Sales Force Dilemma

Joe Falconi wrote this case under the supervision of Professor Don Barclay solely to provide material for class discussion. The authors do not intend to illustrate either effective or ineffective handling of a managerial situation. The authors may have disguised certain names and other identifying information to protect confidentiality.

"We are in the business of building our strengths by managing brands. . . as retailers get bigger. . . we get bigger to fight fire with fire. I'm now in the business of managing BRANDS, not simply PRODUCTS!"

It was November 2005, and Bob Falconi, vice-president of sales and marketing for the Canadian division of Spectrum Brands Inc., was sitting in his new Brantford, Ontario office, pondering his next steps regarding his sales force. During the course of the last year, the company had gone through a number of changes at the global level. Spectrum Brands (Spectrum), a global consumer products company formerly known as Rayovac Corporation, had made a number of acquisitions to diversify and expand its product and brand portfolio. With these changes, Spectrum had become a leading supplier of consumer batteries, lawn and garden care products, specialty pet supplies, and shaving and grooming products.

Falconi, charged with the task of creating a national sales force from the teams of the newly merged companies, sat in his office trying to make sense of the new business. He knew that creating an effective sales team—one which would capitalize on the synergies across the various businesses—would be very difficult, since these companies each operated differently with regards to the role of their sales forces, customers targeted and products sold. Knowing the importance of the sales function to each of these companies, Falconi wanted to ensure, despite the differences amongst the diverse groups, that he still maintained a team that would effectively and efficiently continue to increase the sales of each business unit.

The task ahead of him was big, but Falconi knew that a plan needed to be implemented immediately to avoid disrupting the growth momentum of the company's individual brands, to maintain customer relationships, and to preclude competition from taking advantage of any perceived disruptions during this time of change.

THE CONTEXT

The consumer brands industry had become highly competitive on a global basis. Numerous acquisitions and mergers had taken place over the past decade, resulting in a select group of large companies with extensive brand portfolios. These companies had developed numerous product lines that allowed them to compete in a variety of markets and product categories, and also strengthened their relationships with retailers.

With the growth of large retail chains across North America through retail consolidation, the balance of power had shifted away from manufacturers. Small players could no longer compete effectively, as strong relationships with retailers had become essential in order to compete for limited and valuable shelf space within stores. Manufacturers built alliances with other consumer brand companies in order to gain strength and power in the retail market. As a result, companies such as Procter & Gamble (P&G), Unilever, S.C. Johnson, and others with large portfolios of popular consumer brands, dominated the shelves in traditional retail channels including Grocery (e.g. Loblaw, Dominion), Drug stores (e.g. Shoppers Drug Mart, Katz Group), Hardware retailers (e.g. Home Hardware), Home and Garden retailers (e.g. RONA, The Home Depot) and Mass Merchandisers (e.g. Wal-Mart). Internet and direct-to-consumer sales had not proven to be valuable alternate channels for these companies, as retailers would retaliate by de-listing products of those manufacturers who tried to go in this direction.

Companies competing against the brands under the umbrellas of these large companies continued to struggle for position and, ultimately, for market share, mainly because of the established relationships that these large firms had with the retailers. The trend was towards companies such as Spectrum Brands who had a presence in batteries, shaving and grooming products, lawn and garden products, and specialty pet supplies.

CONSUMER BRANDS MARKETS

Battery Market

North American consumers of household batteries (AAA, AA, C, D and 9-volt standard batteries) sought convenience and quality when purchasing batteries and tended to gravitate towards the brand names they knew and trusted. Duracell and Energizer continued to dominate the market due to their brand recognition, their relationships with distributors and retailers, and their established presence in the large one-time-use alkaline battery category. These two firms were leaders in this market for decades because of their ability to adapt to consumer needs and to merge with other consumer goods companies to create brand portfolios, thus gaining valuable negotiating power with retailers. For example, the Duracell battery brand was owned by the largest and most recognized consumer products company in the world—Procter & Gamble (P&G)—while the Energizer battery brand was owned by Energizer Holdings Inc., which also owned the Shick Razors brand. Each company held a 40 per cent market share within the battery industry.

Household batteries were sold through wholesalers, distributors, professionals and OEMs, but the large majority were sold through traditional retail channels. Of these retailers, mass merchandisers, home and garden centers and niche electronic stores accounted for more than 60 per cent of sales.

As of 2005, the alkaline battery was the predominant type of household battery in North America, and was offered by all major competitors in all sizes. The growth within this segment had become relatively flat, at only one to two per cent annually, yet, due to its size, it was expected to dominate the market for the next five to 10 years. In 2005, the overall battery market in Canada was estimated to be $300[1] million, with the alkaline category representing 70 per cent, the rechargeable category making up 10 per cent, and other battery chemistries, including zinc, representing 20 per cent.

The market for household batteries was highly seasonal. The large majority of sales occurred during the months leading up to and following Christmas sales of electronics and other battery-operated devices. Close to 70 per cent of battery sales occurred during this period.

Shaving and Grooming Products Market

The shaving and grooming products industry was dominated by a select group of companies selling electric shavers and accessories, electric grooming products and hair care appliances. Electric shavers included both rotary and foil designs for men and women, and accessories included replacement parts, pre-shave products and cleaning agents for shavers. Electric grooming products included beard/moustache trimmers, nose and ear trimmers, haircut kits and related accessories. Hair care appliances included hair dryers, setters, curling irons, crimpers, straighteners and hot air brushes.

The shaving and grooming products market was growing at a rate of three to four per cent annually, and this trend was likely to continue. The market for electronic shaving and grooming products was highly seasonal with peaks during the months leading up to and following the Christmas holiday season and around Father's Day and Mother's Day weekends. The majority of these products were purchased as gifts, and thus the sales cycle followed these gift-giving seasons.

The primary competitors in the shaving market included: Norelco, Braun and Remington. Norelco was a division of Koninklijke Philips Electronics (Philips), which was one of the world's biggest electronics companies and the largest one in Europe. Braun was a member of the Gillette family of products which was now part of P&G, while Remington was part of Spectrum. Norelco only sold rotary shavers, Braun only offered foil shavers, while Remington was the only company competing in both segments. Quality, price and brand awareness were the main factors influencing sales in this segment.

The major competitors in the hair care market were Remington, Norelco, Conair Corporation and Helen of Troy Limited. Each company offered a complete line of hair care products and accessories and competed on quality and price within this category.

Competitors within both of these segments sold their products largely through traditional retail channels with a heavy emphasis on mass merchandisers and specialty retailers such as salons and hair and body care shops. Like all consumer product companies, those firms able to maintain or increase

[1] All funds are in Canadian dollars unless otherwise indicated.

the amount of retail shelf space allocated to their respective products could gain share of mind and, potentially, a share of the market.

Lawn and Garden Market

The lawn and garden market was a US$4 billion industry in North America, with an additional US$1 billion in sales of household insect control products. Companies manufactured and marketed fertilizers, herbicides, outdoor insect control products, rodenticides, plant foods, potting soil, grass seeds and other growing media. The lawn and garden industry had been driven largely by affluent baby boomers who enjoyed gardening and also by increasing home ownership levels. Growth in this market had been between four and five per cent annually and was expected to continue at this pace. In North America, more than 80 per cent of households were participating in at least one lawn and garden activity in 2004.

The main competitors within the lawn and garden segment included: United Industries (United)/ Nu-Gro, Scotts Miracle-Gro Company (Scotts) and Central Garden & Pet Company (CGPC). Scotts marketed products under the Scotts and Miracle-Gro brand names. They led this market with a 30 per cent market share. CGPC sat behind United with a 17 per cent market share. They sold garden products under the Amdro, Image and Pennington Seed brand names.

Growth in the insect control market had been generated by population growth in the insect-prone Sunbelt region and the heightened awareness of insect-borne diseases such as West Nile virus. Growth in this market had been slightly higher than historical levels since 2002 with a seven to eight per cent annual growth rate.

In the insect control market, the major competitors included United, Scotts and S.C. Johnson & Son, Inc. Scotts, once again the market leader, sold products under the Ortho and Roundup brand names, while S.C. Johnson marketed their insecticide and repellent products under the Raid and OFF! brands.

Competitors within both of these markets sold mainly through mass merchandisers, home centers, independent nurseries and hardware stores. Home centers and mass merchandisers typically carried one or two premium brands and one value brand on their shelves. Obtaining and maintaining share of shelf within these retailers was critical as 50 to 60 per cent of sales passed through these two channels.

The lawn and garden market was also highly seasonal. Products were shipped to distributors and retailers beginning as early as March in preparation for the spring season. Demand for products typically peaked during the first six months of the calendar year. This seasonality created a major risk within this industry, as there was a heavy dependence on weather to drive sales. A poor season greatly hindered the bottom line.

Specialty Pet Supply Market

The specialty pet supply industry had historically been one of the fastest growing consumer product categories with annual growth between six and eight per cent. This category consisted of aquatic equipment (i.e. aquariums, filters, pumps), aquatic consumables (i.e. fish food, water treatments, conditioners) and specialty pet products for dogs, cats, birds and other small domestic animals. In North America, this was an US$8 billion market in 2004, and was expected to grow to over US$11 billion by 2007.

Much of this growth could be attributed to the increasing levels of pet ownership. On average, households with children under the age of 18, and adults over 55 (who were typically "empty nesters"), tended to keep pets as companions and had more disposable income and leisure time to spend with them. In North America, both of these categories have expanded rapidly with the aging of the baby boomer population. As of 2004, 62 per cent of households in the United States owned a pet, and 46 per cent owned two or more pets. In addition to these trends, the growing movement towards pet humanization—the tendency of pet owners to treat pets like cherished members of the family—had also factored greatly into this market expansion.

The specialty pet supply industry was highly fragmented. There were over 500 manufacturers in North America, consisting of both small companies with limited product lines and larger firms. No company held a market share of greater than 10 per cent. The largest competitors included: CGPC, United Pet Group/Tetra and the Hartz Mountain Corporation. CGPC led the market with a nine per cent market share.

Products within this segment were sold through specialty pet stores, independent pet retailers, mass merchants, grocery stores and through various professional outlets. Mass merchandisers, supermarkets and discounters increasingly supplied pet products, but they focused mainly on a limited selection of items such as pet food. The majority of sales were made through pet supply stores, of which there were over 15,000 in the United States and more than 5,000 in Canada. There were only two national retailers in this industry: PetsMart and PetCo. PetsMart accounted for 10 per cent of North American pet product net sales in fiscal 2004. PetCo reflected similar statistics, but no other retailer accounted for more than eight per cent of industry retail sales.

Sales in this segment remained fairly stable throughout the year since pets needed to be maintained continuously.

COMPETITIVE CONTEXT

In all of these industries, some competitors had gained significant market share and had explicitly committed significant resources to protecting share and/or stealing share from others. In some product lines, competitors had lower production costs and higher profit margins, enabling them to compete more aggressively through advertising and by offering retail discounts and other promotional incentives to retailers, distributors and wholesalers. This aggressive strategy obviously provided additional strength in attracting retailers and consumers. The ability to retain or increase the amount of retail shelf space allocated to their respective products provided competitive advantages in each of these market spaces.

SPECTRUM BRANDS, INC.

Spectrum brands products were available through the world's top 25 retailers, in over one million stores throughout North America, Europe, Asia Pacific, the Middle East, Africa, Latin America and Brazil. Overall, the company was generating US$2.8 billion in annualized revenues from its brand portfolio (see Exhibits 1 and 2 for Spectrum pre-merger and consolidated financial information).

Similar to its competitors, Rayovac had acquired other consumer brand companies to enhance its ability to gain retail presence. Beginning in 2003, Rayovac acquired Remington Products Inc., a company specializing in consumer shaving and grooming products.In February 2005, Spectrum Brands was created when the Rayovac Corporation acquired United Industries Corporation (a leading U.S. manufacturer of consumer lawn and garden care, and insect control products), Nu-Gro Corporation (the Canadian subsidiary of United, specializing in lawn and garden care products) and Tetra Holdings Inc. (a leading supplier of fish and aquatics supplies). Continued growth and strategic acquisitions allowed the company to leverage global distribution channels, purchasing power and operational processes. These mergers provided the company with an extended brand portfolio. This allowed all of the brands to access a number of new retailers where they had not previously been able to gain shelf space. In turn, this increased the ability for each brand to compete within its given markets. Spectrum became the global leader in aquatic supplies; the number two player in the lawn and garden industry, the household insect control market, and the shaving and grooming supplies industry; and the third largest global company in the battery industry (see Exhibit 3 for a list of brand names under the Spectrum label).

Rayovac

Rayovac was the third largest global consumer battery manufacturer in the world—third largest in North America and second largest in Europe. The company sold batteries and flashlights for various household and industrial uses and was the largest worldwide seller of hearing aid batteries. Their battery product line included one-time-use alkaline and Nickel Metal Hydride (NiMH) rechargeable batteries available in all standard sizes (AAA, AA, C, D, 9-Volt) to compete in the highly saturated but lucrative household market. Globally, Rayovac held a 14 per cent market share, with a 20 per cent share of the Canadian market. The division generated US$1.5 billion in annual global revenues in 2004.

The company began operations in 1906, but did not introduce the Rayovac name until the 1930s. Their initial focus was on manufacturing specialty batteries for use in such devices as their patented vacuum tube hearing aids. The company expanded and grew through their continued development of state-of-the-art flashlights and non-traditional batteries, including their successful hearing aid battery line. They eventually entered the competitive household battery market through key acquisitions and by capitalizing on existing distributor and retailer relationships. This was long after the market leaders, Duracell and Energizer, had become well-established within this market. Rayovac made great strides over its last few years in an attempt to gain ground. Acquisitions had been made to gain access to international markets including Europe (Varta Battery Corporation acquired in 2002), China (Ningbo Baowang acquired in 2004) and Brazil (Microlite acquired in 2004).

The leaders in this industry had leading brands and thus greater control over distribution channels, retailers and prices. Rayovac had only been able to secure shelf space in a small number of retailers, including Wal-Mart (making up 40 per cent of sales), Canadian Tire (15 per cent of sales), Home Hardware (10 per cent of sales), and other chains and smaller niche retailers such as Toys R' Us, Radio Shack and others (35 per cent of sales).

Remington Products Company

Remington was a leading designer and distributor of consumer shaving and personal care products in North America and the United Kingdom. They marketed a broad line of electric shaving and grooming products for both men and women, as well as hair care products and other personal care items.

Beginning operations in 1936 as a division of Remington Rand, Remington captured a strong position as a global player in the market by developing new innovative shaving products. Before being bought by Rayovac Corporation in 2003, the Remington Electric Shaver Division had been involved in various mergers: merging with the Sperry Corporation in 1955; being bought by entrepreneur Victor Kiam in 1979; and then acquiring Clairol Inc.'s worldwide personal care appliance business in 1993. Through all of these moves, Remington was able to command a 30 per cent market share in North America and a 21 per cent share in the United Kingdom, with the number one position in men's foil shavers, women's foil shavers, and men's grooming products, and the number two position in men's rotary shavers globally. Remington had become an established name in the industry, achieving global revenues of US$350 million in 2003.

Remington, like Rayovac, sold its products largely through traditional retail channels. The breakdown of retailers was similar to that of Rayovac, with the niche retailers being salons and specialty hair and body care shops.

United Industries Corporation

United Industries Corporation was a leading manufacturer and marketer of professional and consumer lawn and garden care and insect control products. It produced a wide variety of products, including brand name items and private label products for individual retail chains. United also produced and distributed controlled release nitrogen and other fertilizer technologies to the consumer, professional and golf industries worldwide under various brand names.

United competed in the United States under the United name. In Canada, the company operated under the Nu-Gro Corporation (Nu-Gro) name. United, which began operations in the early 1950s, acquired Nu-Gro in April 2004 to serve as the Canadian arm of the company. Nu-Gro was established in 1988 as an exclusively Canadian lawn and garden company. Both were leaders within their marketplaces, maintaining a number of top-selling brands including Vigoro, Shultz and CIL.

Within the lawn and garden industry in North America, United/Nu-Gro was the number two company, holding a 23 per cent market share. The company targeted consumers who wanted products comparable to and at lower prices than premium-priced brands, and thus positioned their brands as the value alternatives. In 2004, United/Nu-Gro together generated sales of US$550 million in this market.

In the household insect control industry, United/Nu-Gro generated US$150 million in sales in 2004. With their insect control brands, it was again the number two company, with 24 per cent market share in North America.

The consumer division for both of these categories sold its products through various retail outlets, including home and garden centers, large home supply retailers, and general mass merchandisers. The sales breakdown was as follows: Canadian Tire (13 per cent), Home Depot (nine per cent), Rona (seven per cent), Lowe's (six per cent), Home Hardware (five per cent), Wal-Mart (three per cent), independent garden retailers (five per cent), other small retailers and garden stores (12 per cent) and their professional division made up 40 per cent.

The United/Nu-Gro professional division served two major markets: Professional Turf Care Products for golf courses and lawn care companies, and Professional Pest Control Products and Animal Health Products for pest control operators and farms (making up 25 and 15 per cent respectively of the company's overall sales). This division had its own dedicated sales force and marketing team to manage the diverse needs of the professional customers.

United was also a leading supplier of quality products to the pet supply industry in the United States, under the United Pet Group (UPG) name. UPG operated in the fragmented U.S. pet supply market, manufacturing and marketing premium-branded pet supplies for dogs, cats, fish, birds and other small animals. Products included: aquarium kits, stand-alone tanks, filters and related items, and other aquarium supplies and accessories, as well as pet treats and supplies. This division was number two in North America, with an eight per cent market share and annual revenues in 2004 totalling US$250 million (figure includes Tetra sales). This division sold its products through large mass merchandisers, while also targeting the larger pet supply chains of PetsMart and PetCo, and the considerable number of independent pet supplies stores.

Tetra Holdings

Tetra Holdings was a global supplier of fish and aquatic supplies, operating in over 90 countries worldwide and holding leading market positions in Germany, Japan, the United States and the United Kingdom. They manufactured, distributed and marketed a comprehensive premier line of foods, equipment and care products for fish and reptiles, along with accessories for home aquariums and ponds.

Tetra was founded in Germany in the early 1950s, pioneering the development of flake fish foods. The company grew into one of the most recognized global brand names in the pet supplies industry. In addition to the products they offered, they also published hundreds of books on aquarium fish keeping, reptile and amphibian keeping, and water gardening.

Tetra was acquired by United Industries in early 2004, joining the UPG division. Despite the merger, United maintained separate operations for each brand with the exception of combining administrative functions. UPG only operated in the United States, while Tetra operated globally. These groups together held the number two position in the North American pet supply market, with eight per cent market share. Like UPG, Tetra sold its products through large mass merchandisers, while also targeting the larger pet supply chains (PetsMart and PetCo) and smaller pet supplies stores in the countries in which it operated.

BOB FALCONI

Bob Falconi completed his Executive MBA program at the Richard Ivey School of Business in 1990. He had been involved in the battery business for 27 years, working his first 16 with Duracell, where he became vice-president of sales. He left Duracell in 1995 for a new start-up battery company, Pure Energy Battery Corporation, which introduced a revolutionary new rechargeable alkaline battery system. He left Pure Energy in 1999 to serve as country manager for Rayovac Canada, and had then taken on the role of vice-president of sales and marketing for Spectrum. Throughout his career, he had developed a keen understanding of brand management, and had been given the responsibility within Spectrum to leverage his experiences.

REASONS FOR THE ACQUISITIONS

Through the evolution into Spectrum Brands, Rayovac had become a channel marketer, and purveyor of specialty brands. The Rayovac Corporation had been painted into a corner in the competitive battery market due to its lack of retail strength. In order to compete on a larger scale, greater power within retail channels was required. The company had continually looked for potential acquisitions where it felt that it could add value to the company's operations while at the same time creating a larger and more powerful combined company. Rayovac's goal was to grow through acquisitions that diversified and increased its revenue base while leveraging its strengths and capabilities in global merchandising and distribution.

With the Remington merger, there were many similarities between the two companies in terms of marketing and channel strategies. However, the systems Remington had in place to manage logistic processes were outdated and inefficient. Rayovac saw this as an opportunity to add value to this company through the sharing of best practices. Rayovac acquired Remington and was able to update the company's logistic processes and systems and improve the overall operations of the firm. Through this merger, Rayovac was able to drive US$35million in annual costs out of the combined enterprise while adding the Remington revenues to Rayovac's top line.

With the recent United/Nu-Gro/Tetra acquisitions, Rayovac was looking to continue its growth and expand into new product categories. New products would provide increased negotiating strength with the larger retailers while diversifying the company's revenue base. For example, with this merger, worldwide battery sales represented approximately 40 per cent of revenue as compared to the 2004 level of 67 per cent. More importantly, the merger served to balance out the sales cycle for the firm given the different seasonalities of the various categories—this meant no down time for the sales force. Finally, Spectrum Brands had at least one brand in all of the major retailers in the world, a situation they hoped to leverage into having other brands in many retailers (see Exhibit 4 for annualized revenues by product category).

THE ISSUE

As Falconi looked through his notes on his individual Canadian business units and their competitive markets, he questioned how best to organize the new sales force in order to capitalize on the strengths of each brand, given the similarities and differences between them. He knew that with the recent acquisitions, the company was looking to leverage any synergies created and reduce costs where possible. However, as overarching objectives, he wanted to make sure that customers would be serviced in the same fashion, if not better, and that sales would not be affected. Falconi decided to take a look at how each business unit currently operated, and how some of their major competitors were organized (see Exhibit 5 for a post-merger organizational chart).

THE CURRENT SALES FORCES

Rayovac and Remington

In Canada, the Rayovac/Remington sales force was currently organized by distribution channel. The eight sales representatives serving this division were responsible for selling all products under both the Rayovac and Remington brand names to their assigned retailers. This was a small sales team, but it had tremendous support from the U.S. office for large accounts, as well as for marketing and trade promotion campaign design. Sales targeted towards hearing aid professionals and industrial and OEM distributors were handled from the U.S. office.

These sales representatives were organized geographically as well. The allocation was as follows: six in Toronto, and one in each of Vancouver and Montreal. Each representative was responsible for the retailers in their regions. Toronto had a greater number of corporate head offices, thus requiring more representatives to service these accounts.

The average base salary for these sales reps was approximately $70,000, with an overall employee expenditure budget of around $900,000 annually, including bonuses. With these representatives, this division was able to generate a 2004 sales volume of over $50 million in Canada.

Overall, this sales force had worked well for the company. The division had been able to minimize the size of the sales force while still achieving their sales goals in an effective and efficient manner.

Nu-Gro

In a similar fashion, Nu-Gro operated customer-focused teams made up of 30 consumer sales reps. Logistics were a very important element within the lawn and garden industry, as shipping costs for these products were significant. For example, a trailer shipment of fertilizer could have a maximum of 1,500 bags valued at $3 a bag, while the same trailer could ship $1 million worth of batteries. As a result, sales reps for Nu-Gro needed to plan carefully with customers in order to minimize costs by ensuring full truck shipments.

As with Rayovac/Remington, sales representative were distributed geographically to service key Canadian locations: 17 in Ontario, six in Vancouver, three in Montreal, and two in each of Calgary and Winnipeg.

The average base salary for these sales reps was slightly lower than for Rayovac/Remington representatives at $60,000, with an overall employee expenditure budget of approximately $2 million annually, including bonuses. With these sales reps, this division was able to generate a 2004 sales volume of more than $105 million in Canada.

Nu-Gro, however, had been struggling as the company's operations and product offerings were extremely unfocused. Over the past five years, the company had acquired a large number of their smaller competitors and had accumulated their associated brands under the Nu-Gro umbrella. As a result, Nu-Gro experienced a proliferation of products and brands (see Exhibit 6). There were strong arguments to stay in under-performing categories, including contribution toward fixed manufacturing costs, improved transportation economics and account control. On the other hand, the significant working capital required to support these under-performing products could not justify keeping them. Brand and SKU rationalization was needed, and a target of up to a 50 per cent reduction over a one year period was being considered. Ultimately, a more focused product portfolio would facilitate the efforts of the sales force.

In addition to the large SKU offerings, the sales team was forced to target a wide variety and large number of customers with these brands, including both the large mass retailers and the small "mom and pop" garden stores. These efforts were very time-consuming and uneconomical for the sales team, as the majority of stores were of the smaller garden shop variety that ordered limited quantities.

The professional division that served the two major lawn and garden markets had been fairly successful in the past through its strong established relationships. The sales force for this division had and would continue to remain independent from Spectrum's consumer (retail) sales division. Nu-Gro maintained a separate sales force beyond the 30 consumer representatives exclusive to this division.

Overall, Nu-Gro's consumer sales operations needed adjustment. A strategy that refocused the sales team's efforts on their large and more important areas, while still finding a way to reach their current customer base, was required to turn this division around.

Tetra/United Pet Group

The sales force for this division in the United States was regionally based so that each sales rep could ensure an ample supply of product for their distributors and dealers. These sales representatives were responsible for the large accounts such as PetsMart and PetCo, mass merchandisers such as Wal-Mart, and the large number of smaller specialty retailers.

However, in Canada, sales for this division were handled by distributors. These distributors were responsible for the sales to the highly fragmented Canadian specialty pet retailer market. They offered the same services that an internal sales force could provide, including organizing special promotions and setting up in-store displays. Ultimately, they were able to generate sales from a large number of smaller players more economically than a small internal sales team could. The sales managers for Rayovac/Remington and Nu-Gro were responsible for managing these distributors. The larger retail accounts were managed by the U.S. sales team but serviced by these distributors.

Sales Management

Of the 38 sales reps between the Rayovac/Remington and Nu-Gro divisions, four of them filled the roles of sales manager, two managers for each division. Each rep/manager was responsible for the various representatives in their specific geographic regions. They spent 65 per cent of their time selling to their own individual accounts. The remaining 35 per cent was spent managing reps, managing distributors, forecasting, strategic planning and analysing their market. For each division, one rep/manager was responsible for the sales reps in the large Ontario market, while the other managed the sales reps in the rest of the country. Regardless of structure of the sales operation going forward, Falconi would likely organize around three regions: the West, Ontario and the East, with one manager responsible for the sales reps within each region. This, of course, raised the issue of the surplus manager and would provide an opportunity to reconsider the incumbents.

COMPETITOR ORGANIZATIONS

Falconi wanted to look at how some of Spectrum's competitors organized their sales forces within Canada. He decided to select a few of the major players from each industry as comparison points. Koninklijke Philips Electronics and P&G operated their sales divisions by product category. Each category had its own dedicated sales force further divided by specific retail channels and/or customer, depending on the size of the retailer. For example, Norelco's sales force was responsible exclusively for shaving and grooming products and did not cross-sell other Philips brands such as televisions. Similarly, Braun sales reps would sell both the Braun and Gillette shaving brands, Duracell would have its own sales team, but neither group would cross-sell other P&G brands. In certain circumstances, one purchasing manager for a retailer such as Wal-Mart might deal with a sales rep from each product category but these sales reps would deal exclusively with Wal-Mart as a customer. In other circumstances, the sales reps would interface with different purchasing managers in those retailers where the purchasing function was organized by category.

Both Scotts and CGPC operated their sales divisions in a different manner. Their sales forces were organized by product category, but covered all retail channels. Thus, they had specific sales reps for categories such as fertilizers, soils and seeds, insect control products, and pet supplies (CGPC only), but each sales rep would service clients across multiple channels. Like Philips and P&G, these companies had developed a sales force with product category expertise, yet they did not concentrate an individual sales rep on a specific retailer.

Due to the size and strength of each of these companies, they had been successful at developing a "pull" strategy with the consumers. Retailers were almost mandated to support and sell these companies' products because of the consumer demand created. In addition, the sales forces had developed strong relationships with retailers, the "push" component.

SALES FORCE OPTIONS

Looking forward, Falconi wanted to evaluate his options regarding how to organize his sales force to see what alternatives or combinations made sense to Spectrum's operations and the market characteristics.

Separate Sales forces

Maintaining a separate sales force for each brand line would offer Spectrum the greatest degree of expertise on each brand. These sales reps were already familiar with, and had extensive knowledge about, their brands and would require little, if any, additional training. Sales reps could continue to operate as they already did, and maintain the momentum they had already generated for their product lines. Ultimately, such an organization would allow for a more focused sales force in that representatives would be in a better position to answer product-related questions and offer product educational services.

On the other hand, maintaining separate sales forces would not take advantage of the synergies that the recent merger had created for the company. There would be little to no expense reduction, as the existing sales rep levels would likely be maintained. In addition, this organization would not offer any efficiency improvements in the use of sales reps during slower seasonal periods. Finally, there would be a significant duplication of efforts as Spectrum would have multiple sales reps calling on the same retailer at any given time.

Merged Sales force

With a merged sales force, Spectrum would essentially move to a "one bag" sales rep approach, in that each representative would be responsible for becoming an expert on all product lines and selling every brand to their specified customers. With this option, Falconi would have to define each sales rep's responsibilities relating to whether or not the representative would cover all customers in a geographic area, or be responsible for a specific retail group or nationwide chain.

As with the separate sales force option, the "one bag" sales rep would offer Spectrum numerous benefits. First, Spectrum would be able to capitalize on the potential synergies of the merger as Rayovac did with the Remington acquisition and integration. With each representative selling the entire Spectrum product line, there would be the opportunity to cross-promote brands, leveraging the strong relationships that certain brands have with particular retailers to sell and promote the other lines. This is especially important as Spectrum tries to gain presence for all their lines within each major retailer across the country.

Additionally, Falconi would be able to consolidate the existing teams into a smaller unit. Responsibilities for individual retailers could be handled by one or two sales reps selling the entire portfolio of brands, rather than one representative for each individual brand. For example, there are certain customers to whom each business unit has been selling products, including Wal-Mart, The Home Depot, RONA, Canadian Tire, as well as many others across the country. Overall, by merging the sales force, it is estimated that Spectrum would be able to reduce the salaries and bonus expense to approximately $2 million for the entire Canadian sales division.

Finally, a merged sales force would create a more efficient team to cope with the seasonality issues inherent in the industries in which Spectrum operates. Sales reps would always have something going on with one of the portfolio brands, allowing them to be in constant contact with retail purchasers.

While there are many benefits to this approach for a diversified company like Spectrum, there could be great difficulty in creating an effective and efficient merged team. First, with the addition of numerous new brands to the company's portfolio, sales reps would need to develop an expertise for a large number of brands and products. In addition, the new products they would be selling are completely different from the current brand category they have experience with (i.e. a battery sales rep selling fertilizer). Additional training would be required for all sales reps to educate them on the unfamiliar brands. This training could ultimately be costly and take a substantial amount of time.

Given the variety of products and brands under the Spectrum name, a merged sales force may prove to be highly unfocused. A representative may be incapable of attaining a sufficient knowledge base about every product line, or have too much going on to give each brand the necessary focus needed to sustain its current sales levels. This could hinder sales and effectively kill the existing momentum of the brands.

Distributors

Distributors provide sales and logistic services to firms in exchange for commission fees. Such firms are typically hired by smaller companies with limited sales reach, or by companies who are entering new geographic markets but do not yet have a sales team in place. They usually have an advantage over these types of companies as they are well-established, they have existing relationships with retailers, and they operate large sales groups that can service a large number of customers. They typically serve a variety of manufacturers, and thus are able to operate such a sales process in an efficient manner. As a result, distributors are typically given the task of reaching the large number of smaller retailers that prove to be too costly for a small sales force to target, while the manufacturer's internal sales team targets the smaller number of large customers that contribute greater individual sales.

Though there are many benefits to using professional distributors as the company's sales force, there are drawbacks as well. The costs associated with these services can be substantial relative to an internal sales force. The cost of sales through a distributor is approximately 15 per cent against revenues, while it is two to three per cent with an internal sales person. As a result, successful firms that are able to establish large sales teams can ultimately generate sales at a lower cost.

Other Alternatives and Considerations

While each of these alternatives would provide Spectrum with benefits in particular areas, Falconi knew that creating a sales force based on a combination of one or more of these elements might generate greater returns for the company. For example, one option would be to use a combination of a merged sales force and distributors in order to reach both large and small retailers more effectively. Another option could be to create "platform teams," where one business manager would be responsible for maintaining the relationships with the retailers, while a group of product experts support the manager during sales pitches. Falconi wanted to further explore these opportunities, and others, to see what benefits might be derived.

Falconi knew that before any changes could be made to the sales strategy, selecting his sales managers would be the first essential step. He would need to ensure that he had the right people in this role, whether they were the current managers or new ones. These individuals would serve as the leaders for the overall sales force, ensuring continued momentum and performance of the representatives. They would also be the "change agents" responsible for implementing the plans developed by Falconi for any reorganization. If there was a new strategy implemented, Falconi would have to decide how to judge these managers and how best to use them given the chosen system.

Falconi realized he would have to consider the impact that this major change would have on the current employees. The employees recognized that, with such a merger, the company would look for potential synergies to reduce overall company expenses. Other companies in similar situations have typically looked to consolidate employee positions as one option to reduce costs. If there was to be a merger of the sales teams, Falconi would be responsible for selecting the best candidates for the new organization, meaning that nobody's job was safe. As a result, employees from both the Rayovac/Remington and Nu-Gro divisions would be feeling very apprehensive at this point. People are often averse to change and the sales reps would be concerned about their future employment status and the implications of any forthcoming changes to the company.

Falconi knew that dealing with the sensitivities of his employees would be crucial to achieving a successful implementation of a new sales strategy, if, indeed, the company chose to proceed with that option. Changes would need to be made while the company was still in operation; thus, care needed to be given to these issues in order to avoid potential disturbances and to preserve the current momentum of the business. Falconi realized that change management skills would definitely be required to implement a new structure, or to alleviate concerns if no changes were planned, but he wondered how best to deal with these issues moving forward.

Finally, Falconi needed to decide how many sales reps should be kept if a new strategy was to be implemented and by what criteria he should be judging his representatives. He knew that the sufficient number of sales reps would depend on the chosen direction of the sales force strategy, but he wondered what his team would look like once the dust had settled.

DECISION

Given the nature of the new company, and the industries each business unit competed in, Falconi was unsure what sales force structure would offer the company the greatest benefits, at the same time allowing it to grow its sales and gain a greater retail presence for the entire Spectrum brand portfolio. How should the new company be structured in terms of reporting, responsibilities and the size of the sales force? Should Spectrum try to structure itself similarly to its competitors, or did their operation require a different approach?

Additionally, depending on which sales force structure was selected, Falconi would have to consider how to organize the teams relative to Spectrum's retail customers. He could organize them by geography, by retail channel, by individual retailers, by some combination of these or by another method altogether. Falconi would have to explore the benefits of the options and determine what made the most sense.

The board of directors was meeting next week and Falconi wanted to present them with a full report outlining his proposed strategy regarding the sales force, and why the other alternatives were dismissed. Overall, Falconi knew that a decision would need to be made quickly in hopes that the new sales force strategy could be implemented prior to the peak period for the lawn and garden industry. Falconi knew that sufficient time would be needed to implement changes and initiate any training that might be required for the sales team.

Exhibit 1 (Numbers based on fiscal year ending september) rayovac corporation net sales breakdown

Consolidated Net Sales by Product Line (US$ Millions)	2005	2004*
Batteries	$968	$939
Lights	$94	$90
Shaving & Grooming	$271	$272

(Continued)

(Continued)

Consolidated Net Sales by Product line (US$ millions)	**2005**	**2004***
Personal Care	$143	$116
Lawn and Garden	$447	N/A
Household Insect Control	$150	N/A
Pet Products	$286	N/A
Totals	$2,359	$1,417

*United/Nu-Gro was acquired by Rayovac mid 2005.

Rayovac & Remington

(US$ millions)	**Rayovac**		**Remington**	
	2004	**2003**	**2004**	**2003**
Net Sales	$1,029	$922	$388	N/A
Gross Profit	42.8%	38.1%	47.0%	N/A
Operating Income	$109	$60	$47	N/A
Net Income	$39	$15	$ 17	N/A

*Remington was acquired by Rayovac mid 2003.

United Industries and Tetra

	United	**Tetra**
North America (US$ millions)	**2005**	**2005**
Net Sales from External customers	$787	$96
Segment Profit	$79	$10
SP as % of Net Sales	10.0%	10.4%

Exhibit 2 Spectrum brands, Inc. and subsidiaries consolidated statements of operations (years ended septemeber 30, 2005, 2004) (US$ 000s)

	2005	**2004**
Net Sales	$2,359,447	$1,417,186
Cost of goods sold	$1,465,096	$811,894
Restructuring and related charges	$10,496	$(781)
Gross Profit	$883,855	$606,073
Operating Expenses		
Selling	$473,834	$293,118
General and Administration	$160,382	$121,319
Research and Development	$29,339	$ 23,192

Restructuring and related charges	$15,820	$12,224
	$679,375	$449,853
Operating Income	$204,480	$156,220
Interest expense	$134,053	$65,702
Other income, net	$(856)	$(14)
Income from continuing operations before taxes	$71,283	$90,532
Income tax expense	$24,451	$34,372
Income from continuing operations	$46,832	$56,160
Loss from discontinuded operations, net of tax benefits	$	$380
Net Income	$46,832	$55,780

Source: 2005 Spectrum Brands Inc. Annual Report.

	2005	2004
Assets		
Current Assets:		
Cash and cash equivalents	$29,852	$13,971
Receivables:		
Trade A/R, net of allowances	$362,399	$ 269,977
Other	$10,996	$19,655
Inventories	$451,553	$264,726
Deferred income taxes	$39,231	$19,233
Assets held for sale	$108,174	$9,870
Prepaid expenses and other	$45,762	$ 51,262
Total Current Assets	$1,047,967	$648,694
Property, plant and equipment, net	$304,323	$182,396
Deferred charges and other	$47,375	$35,079
Goodwill	$1,429,017	$320,577
Intangible assets, net	$1,154,397	$422,106
Debt issuance costs	$39,012	$25,299
Total Assets	$4,022,091	$1,634,151
Liabilities and Shareholder's Equity		
Current Liabilities:		
Current maturities of LT debt	$39,308	$23,895
Accounts payable	$281,954	$226,234
Accrued liabilities:		
Wages and benefits	$47,910	$40,138

(Continued)

(*Continued*)

	2005	2004
Income taxes payable	$40,468	$21,672
Restructuring and related charges	$16,978	$8,505
Accrued interest	$31,529	$16,302
Liabilities held for sale	$22,294	$ -
Other	$76,935	$60,094
Total Current Liabilities	$557,376	$396,840
Long-term debt, net of current maturities	$2,268,025	$806,002
Employee benefit obligations, net of current portion	$78,510	$69,246
Deferred income taxes	$208,251	$7,272
Other	$67,199	$37,368
Total Liabilities	$3,179,361	$1,316,728
Minority interest in equity of consolidated subsidiary	$-	$1,379
Shareholders' equity:		
Common Stock	$666	$642
Additional paid-in capital	$671,378	$224,962
Retained earnings	$267,315	$220,483
Accumulated other comprehensive income (loss)	$10,260	$10,621
Notes receivable from officers/shareholders	$-	$(3,605)
	$949,619	$453,103
Less treasury stock, at cost	$(70,820)	$(130,070)
Less unearned restricted stock compensation	$(36,069)	$(6,989)
Total Shareholders' equity	$842,730	$316,044
Total Liabilities and Shareholders' equity	$4,022,091	$1,634,151

Source: 2005 Spectrum Brands Inc. Annual Report.

Exhibit 3

Spectrum BRANDS

BATTERY & LIGHTING PRODUCTS

RAYOVAC

VARTA

SHAVING, GROOMING & HAIR CARE PRODUCTS

REMINGTON

LAWN & GARDEN CARE

INSECT CONTROL PRODUCTS

AQUARIUM PRODUCTS & SUPPLIES

PET PRODUCTS & SUPPLIES

Exhibit 4 Annualized revenues by product line

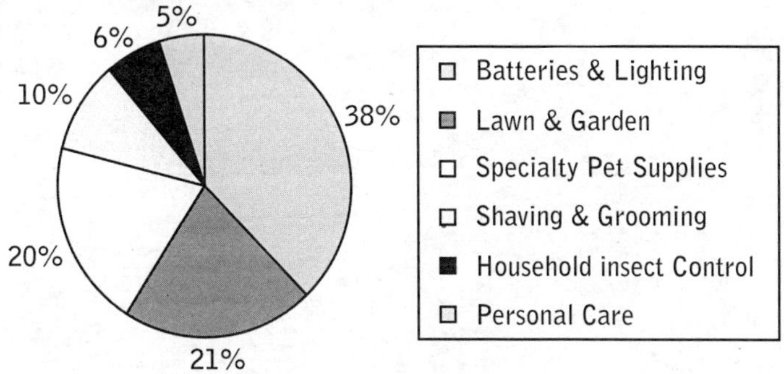

Exhibit 5 Spectrum brands sales division organizational chart

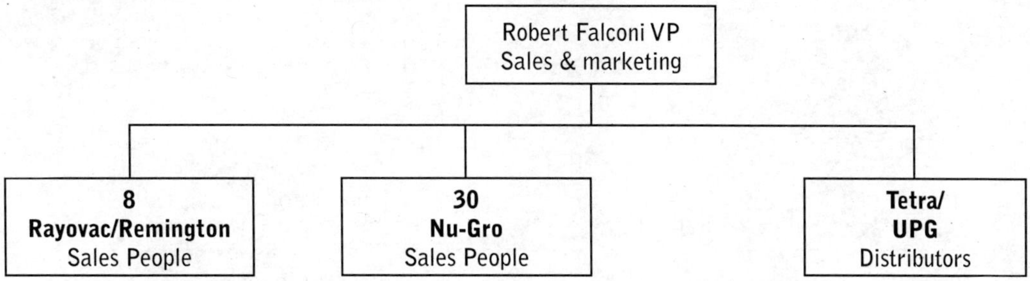

Exhibit 6

		Revenue By Type/Category		Contribution Margin %	
Major	**#SKU's**	**$M**	**% Total**	**$M**	**% Sales**
Fertilizers	752	29.8	36.40%	3.9	13.20%
Pesticides	234	21.9	26.80%	5.5	25.20%
Soils	176	12.3	15.00%	0.2	1.30%
Seed	143	9	11.00%	0.2	1.80%
Other	92	8.8	10.80%	0.3	10.40%
Grand Total	**1,397**	**$82**	**100.00%**	**$10**	**12.30%**

19

Launch of the Ford Fiesta Diesel

The World's Most Efficient Car[1]

David Wesley wrote this case under the supervision of Professor Francis Spital solely to provide material for class discussion. The authors do not intend to illustrate either effective or ineffective handling of a managerial situation. The authors may have disguised certain names and other identifying information to protect confidentiality.

In November 2008, Ford Motor Company (Ford) launched its highly anticipated Fiesta Diesel (Fiesta). At 65 miles per gallon (mpg), the Fiesta was one of the most fuel-efficient cars in the world.[2] Yet, Ford had little to celebrate as sales of new automobiles in the United States "declined to their lowest level in 17 years" amid one of the worst financial crises in history.[3] "It's clearly a very very tough environment," explained Alan Mulally, Ford's president and chief executive officer.

[1] This case has been written on the basis of published sources only. Consequently, the interpretation and perspectives presented in this case are not necessarily those of the Ford Motor Company or any of its employees.

[2] Ben Wojdyla, "Diesel Ford Fiesta Smokes Prius, Gets 62.5 MPG," Jalopnik.com, July 2, 2008; http://jalopnik.com/397712/diesel-ford-fiesta-smokes-prius-gets-625-mpg, accessed November 7, 2008.

[3] "Automakers Want $25 Billion in US Aid," Boston Globe, November 7, 2008, p. B12.

> We have made great progress on our plan for the transformation of our product line and restructuring to operate profitably. Around the world we did very well. South America is very profitable for us, as well as Europe and Asia Pacific. So the real issue is the United States. The sales rate we are looking at is the lowest in 35 years.[4]

Despite Fiesta's groundbreaking performance, Ford had no plans to introduce the model in North America. At a press conference earlier in the year, journalists had been left scratching their heads in wonder. The Fiesta's performance far surpassed the popular Toyota Prius hybrid, which was all the rage in America. So why wouldn't Ford bring the Fiesta to the United States? Mark Fields, executive vice president of Ford Motor Company, explained:

> We know it's an awesome vehicle, but there are business reasons why we can't sell it in the US. . . . We just don't think North and South America would buy that many diesel cars.[5]

Fields then reached into his briefcase and held up a document. The consultants' report was very clear, he explained. "Americans won't buy diesel." The results of a market research study that relied heavily on focus groups had concluded that, in consumers' minds, "Diesel is noisy, smoky and smelly."[6]

Denise McCluggage, senior editor of *Autoweek*, the automobile industry's leading trade journal, was dismayed by what she was hearing.[7] Why hadn't the consultants bothered to correct the focus group's impressions of diesel? True, diesel was once noisy and dirty, but that was no longer the case. In fact, diesel had become one of the cleanest fuels on the market. Modern diesel vehicles offered what every American wanted, namely torque, range and fuel economy. In her mind, Ford was simply unwilling to take the risks necessary to challenge its Japanese competitors. "Mark Fields is a wuss," McCluggage later declared in *Autoweek*.

> Ford will, of course, have diesel cars in Europe "ready to bring here should the market in the U.S. change,"[but] consider the financial loss people are taking to dump a guzzler and [pay] a premium for hybrids, hybrids that can't touch a diesel for economy.[8]

Other journalists who attended the news briefing agreed. David Kiley, senior correspondent for *Business Week* responded:

> If ever there was a car made for the times, this would seem to be it. . . . The risk to Ford is that the fuel takes off, and the carmaker finds itself playing catch-up—despite having a serious diesel contender in its arsenal.[9]

On November 7, 2008, as economic conditions continued to deteriorate, Mulally arrived in Washington to ask the U.S. Congress for $25 billion in low-interest loans. The automobile industry was vital to the U.S. economy, he argued, and loans were needed to ensure the industry's continued

---

[4] "Alan Mulally on the State of the Auto Industry," FoxBusiness.com, November 7, 2008.

[5] David Kiley, "The 65 mpg Ford the U.S. Can't Have," Business Week, September 15, 2008, p. 60.

[6] Denise McCluggage, "A Lack of Leadership," Autoweek, October 13, 2008, p. 11.

[7] Denise McCluggage was a leading figure in the automotive industry. A former world-class race-car driver, she went on to found Competition Press, which eventually became Autoweek, "the largest weekly automotive magazine in the world." *Source:* Matt Stone, "A Racer Named Denise: The Fastest Woman on Four Wheels," Road and Travel Magazine, http://www.roadandtravel.com/celebrities/denise_mccluggage.html, accessed November 14, 2008.

[8] Denise McCluggage, "A Lack of Leadership," Autoweek, October 13, 2008, p. 11.

[9] David Kiley, "The 65 mpg Ford the U.S. Can't Have," Business Week, September 15, 2008, p. 60.

viability.[10] That day, Ford announced a third quarter operating loss of $2.7 billion on revenues of $32.1 billion, after burning through more than $7 billion of its available cash reserve.

COMPANY BACKGROUND

Henry Ford founded the Ford Motor Company in 1903. He was widely credited with having invented the assembly line in 1913, a process that allowed Ford to become the first mass producer of automobiles. Within a few years, the Ford Motor Company was making half the automobiles sold in the United States, and Henry Ford had become one of the richest people in the world.

Ford, like other U.S. automakers, was hit hard by the Oil Crisis of 1973, which resulted in a doubling of oil prices, widespread gasoline shortages and the introduction of government price controls. To deal with the crisis, the U.S. government imposed fuel-efficiency standards on the automotive industry. Ford resisted the government regulations, converting its production only as necessary to comply with the law.

When another oil crisis hit the United States in 1979, Ford found itself unprepared as new Japanese competitors entered the market with small, inexpensive and fuel-efficient cars that quickly gained a 20 per cent share of the market. By the 1980s, U.S.-produced automobiles had declined in quality, while Japanese carmakers had embarked on programs for continuous improvement. The contrast between well-built imports and shoddy domestic cars turned into a "national disgrace," which left the U.S. automotive industry "down and gasping." However, "it did not receive much sympathy. To the contrary, it was scorned for arrogance or sloth for failing to keep up with new trends in automaking."[11]

American carmakers responded by instituting their own quality-improvement programs. Ford also began work on more efficient automobiles. In 1989, Ford announced plans to "step up its development work on low-displacement engines and more efficient automatic transmissions as a means of achieving higher fuel economy levels in the late 1990s and responding to growing concern about global warming."[12]

For the next two decades, Ford led the industry in developing technologies that made cars more fuel-efficient. In 2000, it demonstrated a concept car capable of 72 mpg; and in 2008, it unveiled a sport utility vehicle (SUV) capable of 120 mpg. Yet each time Ford's engineers developed new fuel-saving technologies, they were overruled by managers who believed that consumers wanted large comfortable vehicles, or that the cost of retooling factories was too high. As late as 2004, Ford's average fuel-efficiency rating remained "the worst of all manufacturers selling in the U.S." at 18.8 mpg, according to a report from the U.S. Environmental Protection Agency (EPA).[13] Ford argued that it was merely meeting customer demand. Ford's F-series pickup truck, for example, was the best-selling vehicle in the United States, despite a fuel-efficiency rating of only 16 mpg.[14]

---

10 "Alan Mulally on the State of the Auto Industry," FoxBusiness.com, November 7, 2008.

11 Douglas Brinkley, Wheels for the World: Henry Ford, His Company, and a Century of Progress, 1903–2003, Viking, New York, 2003, pp. 590, 666–667.

12 "Ford Responds to Global Warming Concerns," Metalworking News, May 22, 1989, p. 5.

13 Kari Lydersen, "Ford Gets an 'F' for Fuel Efficiency," Alternet.org, July 2, 2004, www.alternet.org/story/19148/ford_gets_an_'f'_for_fuel_efficiency, accessed November 7, 2008.

14 Natalie Neff, "Lousy Economy, Pricey Fuel Challenge New Ford F-Series to Take Back Its Sales Crown," Autoweek, October 20, 2008, http://www.autoweek.com/apps/pbcs.dll/article?AID=/20081020/FREE/310209997/1023, accessed November 7, 2008.

In 2002, Standard & Poor's downgraded Ford's debt rating to BBB on a "slowing economy and stiff competition from imports." Ford promised "that the company will earn $7 billion a year in operating profit by 2005."[15]

Although some were quick to blame "a weaker car market" for Ford's problems, Japanese automakers posted record revenues during the same time period. Toyota's growth was particularly impressive, allowing it to surpass Chrysler for the first time in 2002, to become the number three automaker in the United States. Fuel efficiency and quality were keys to Toyota's success, observed one analyst. With more than $30 billion in cash, Toyota had "an advantage in developing new models, a process that requires large investments, and has led to a company lineup of more than 60 models."[16]

By May 2005, it had become clear that Ford would not be able to keep its promise to increase profitability, leading S&P to further downgrade its corporate debt to "junk." In the face of steadily rising gas prices, Ford's dependence on the truck and SUV market had become a serious liability (see Exhibits 1 and 2).[17]

Almost the entire decline in Ford's profitability was the result of losses in the United States. In Europe, Ford's profits had been growing consistently year over year; and in the first half of 2008, for the first time, Ford sold more than one million automobiles in the European market (see Exhibit 3).

In September 2008, as the U.S. economy fell into recession, President George W. Bush signed into law an emergency financing package of $25 billion for the Big Three automakers. However, Mulally and other senior automotive executives argued that the aid package was insufficient to meet the challenges of a sustained economic downturn. "It's really tough out there," Mulally pleaded, as he asked Washington to consider an additional $25 billion in aid.[18]

GASOLINE ENGINES

When motor cars were first popularized at the end of the 19th century, those with gasoline engines were deemed the least desirable. Electric cars that ran on rechargeable batteries were popular in cities, where speed was less a concern than comfort, noise and pollution. Automotive enthusiasts preferred steam-driven cars that could be driven faster and farther than electric cars. "Gasoline-powered vehicles came in a sorry third with American consumers, who rightly deemed them dirty, noisy, unreliable, and uncomfortable from the vibration of the firing cylinders."[19]

When engines improved a few years later, gasoline quickly became the most popular fuel for passenger automobiles in North America. In recent years, approximately 40 per cent of crude oil imports in the United States were used in the production of gasoline for use in automobiles and light trucks.[20]

---

[15] Micheline Maynard, "S.&P. Cuts Its Rating of Ford Debt to Record Low," New York Times, October 26, 2002. http://www.nytimes.com/2002/10/26/business/s-p-cuts-its-rating-of-ford-debt-to-record-low.html Accessed April 26, 2010

[16] "Toyota Races Ahead of Rivals," The Daily Yomiuri (Tokyo), November 7, 2003, p. 8.

[17] Greg Schneider, "GM, Ford Bond Ratings Cut to Junk Status," The Washington Post, May 6, 2005, http://www.washingtonpost.com/wp-dyn/articles/A41573-2005May6.html, accessed November 10, 2008.

[18] Jeff Bennett, "Ford CEO Mulally Says Lawmakers Back Auto Makers," The Wall Street Journal, September 8, 2008.

[19] Douglas, Brinkley, Wheels for the World: Henry Ford, His Company, and a Century of Progress, 1903–2003, Viking, New York, 2003, p. 29.

[20] "Reducing America's Energy Dependence," The Natural Resources Defense Council (Policy Paper), July 2, 2004, http://www.nrdc.org/air/transportation/gasprices.asp, accessed November 13, 2008.

Following the oil embargo of 1973, which caused a sharp rise in gasoline prices, the U.S. Congress enacted Corporate Average Fuel Economy (CAFE) regulations, which for the first time regulated the minimum average fuel economy of vehicles sold in the United States. As a result, during the late 1970s and early 1980s, the fuel economy of gasoline vehicles made by U.S. manufacturers improved markedly.

CAFE standards were different for cars and trucks and were based on calculated average fuel efficiency for the vehicles sold by each manufacturer. Thus, a carmaker could use a very efficient vehicle to offset a less efficient vehicle. Carmakers also earned credits if the average fuel efficiency exceeded the minimum standards in a given year, allowing it to offset production of less efficient vehicles in future years.

> Failure to comply with CAFE regulations resulted in fines of "$5.50 per tenth of a MPG under the target value times the total volume of those vehicles in the affected fleet manufactured for a given model year." Since 1983, manufacturers have paid more than $675 million in CAFE civil penalties. Most European manufacturers [paid] CAFE civil penalties ranging from less than $1 million to more than $20 million annually. Asian and most of the big domestic manufacturers have never paid a civil penalty.[21]

When oil prices declined in the late 1980s and 1990s, engine efficiency was redirected to improving performance rather than fuel economy; as a result, U.S. automakers were able to build larger, heavier and more luxurious vehicles that still met CAFE standards. The dichotomy was that, although U.S. manufacturers had the highest fuel efficiency per pound of vehicle weight of any country in the world, the average fuel economy of American cars remained among the lowest in the world due to the extra weight.[22]

The end of the oil crisis provided carmakers with a temporary reprieve. However, everyone agreed that the world's supply of oil was finite and that alternatives to oil were needed. "Peak oil" was the term used to describe the point in time when maximum oil production would be achieved. One of the more accepted models for peak oil was developed by the late Marion King Hubbert, a geologist for Shell Oil. In a seminal paper presented to the American Petroleum Institute in 1956, Hubbert predicted:

> [The] maximum rate of production will be about two and one-half times the present rate, which places the date of the peak at about the year 2000. As in the case of coal, variations of this assumed maximum rate will advance or retard the date of the culmination (see Exhibit 4).[23]

In 2008 as oil prices neared $150 per barrel, Hubbert's predictions seemed prescient. Then, as the economic crisis of 2008 began to take hold, prices fell as quick as they had risen. Within a few months, prices fell to less than $40 per barrel. Some felt that the 2008 price peak was caused by a speculative bubble, while others claimed that the peak properly reflected rising demand in developing countries,

---

[21] "CAFE Overview," National Highway Traffic Safety Administration, United States Department of Transportation, http://www.nhtsa.dot.gov, accessed October 27, 2008.

[22] Amory B. Lovins et al., Winning the Oil End Game, Rocky Mountain Institute, Snowmass, CO, 2004.

[23] Marion King Hubbert, "Nuclear Energy and the Fossil Fuels," Paper presented before the Spring Meeting of the Southern District, American Petroleum Institute, Plaza Hotel, San Antonio, Texas, March 7–9, 1956, p. 22.

which had been temporarily suspended by across-the-board declines in consumption and industrial production. Nobody could be sure when prices would peak again. In the meantime, conservation and efficiency were the best ways of preserving the world's energy supplies and ensuring price stability.

DIESEL ENGINES

Diesel was the fuel of choice throughout most of the world, primarily because of its ability to provide more power than gasoline. Diesel was a natural fit for large trucks, which needed to carry heavy loads over long distances, although smaller vehicles also benefited from diesel's greater efficiency. In Europe and parts of Asia, high government taxes made fuel relatively expensive. Consumers wanting to lower their fuel expenditures often did so by purchasing smaller cars equipped with diesel engines. In Europe, for example, diesel engines were found in more than half of all passenger cars sold.[24] On average, diesel engines were 30 to 35 per cent more fuel efficient than their gasoline counterparts.[25]

Traditionally, the price of diesel had been lower than gasoline; but, beginning in 2004, diesel prices began rising faster than gasoline prices. In the United States, a lack of refining capacity and higher fuel taxes contributed to the increase; however, the main driver was global demand. Rapid growth in less developed countries, such as India and China, led to an increase in orders for construction vehicles, trucks and tractors, the vast majority of which ran on diesel.[26]

In the United States, many consumers held negative opinions of the fuel, which had long been associated with noisy engines and smog. In 2006, U.S. refineries began to produce clean diesel through a process that eliminated 97 per cent of the sulfur commonly found in less refined diesel. The extra cost to produce clean diesel was estimated to be between 5 and 8 cents per gallon.[27] Finally, strict emission standards in some states had discouraged most automakers from launching diesel vehicles in the U.S. market.[28]

Meanwhile, German automakers were at work developing technologies that captured smog-producing nitrogen oxides (NO_x).[29] When the Volkswagen and Mercedes models were launched in 2008, they were the first vehicles to meet emission standards in all 50 states.[30] Steve Purdy, a Detroit-based automobile analyst who reviewed Volkswagen's new diesel explained:

> Modern diesels are no longer dirty, smoky, smelly or slow. . . . Independent engineers have told me that the air coming out of the exhaust pipe is cleaner than the air going

---

24 "Demand for Diesel Fuel: Perspectives and Future Considerations on Prices and Supply for Diesel Car and Truck Fuel Users," Diesel Technology Forum, October 2008, http://www.dieselforum.org/diesel-spotlight/DTF/news-center/pdfs/Diesel Fuel Update - Oct 2008.pdf, accessed November 5, 2008.

25 US Department of Energy, Fuel Economy, 2007 http://fueleconomy.gov/feg/FEG2007_AltFuelVehicles.pdf, accessed November 6, 2008.

26 Steve Purdy, "2009 Volkswagen Jetta TDI Review," The Auto Channel News, November 2, 2008, http://theautochannel.com/news/2008/11/02/214387.html, accessed November 5, 2008.

27 "Demand for Diesel Fuel: Perspectives and Future Considerations on Prices and Supply for Diesel Car and Truck Fuel Users," Diesel Technology Forum, October 2008, http://wwwdieselforum.org/diesel-spotlight/DTF/news-center/pdfs/Diesel Fuel Update - Oct 2008.pdf, accessed November 5, 2008.

28 Ann Job, "Don't Be Fueled: Gas vs. Diesel vs. Hybrid Power," MSN Autos, http://editorial.autos.msn.com/article.aspx?cp-documentid=435228, accessed November 6, 2008.

29 "Two Paths to Clean Diesel, Hybrid Cars," HybridCars.com, October 27, 2008, http://www.hybridcars.com/fuels/two-paths-clean-diesel-25198.html, accessed October 28, 2008.

30 Steve Purdy, "2009 Volkswagen Jetta TDI Review," The Auto Channel News, November 2, 2008, http://theautochannel.com/news/2008/11/02/214387.html, accessed November 5, 2008.

into the engine's intake. They don't even have to vent the exhaust when working on the engine indoors.[31]

New diesel models were also more fuel efficient. Independent road tests in mixed urban and highway settings found that some diesels surpassed the Toyota Prius hybrid in fuel efficiency. In Europe, the *Times* newspaper compared the gas mileage of a BMW 520d Executive Saloon diesel sedan and a Toyota Prius hybrid on a trip from London to Geneva. The BMW sedan, despite being more than 500 pounds heavier than the Prius, proved to be more efficient at 50 mpg, compared with 48 mpg for the hybrid.[32]

HYBRID ENGINES

A hybrid engine used a gasoline engine to provide power to the vehicle, while simultaneously charging an electric battery to provide additional power when needed. Ferdinand Porsche built the first hybrid engine in 1899. The Porsche hybrid used a gasoline engine to provide power to small electric generators in the wheels.[33] In 1900, the Pieper car company of Belgium designed a hybrid engine called the Voiturette that was based on principles similar to modern hybrids. When cruising, a small gasoline engine charged a battery under the seat. The battery then provided supplementary power when climbing hills.[34] These early hybrids achieved some success; however, they were relatively expensive to manufacture, and after Henry Ford introduced the mass-produced Model T in 1908, interest quickly dropped off.

In the late 1990s, Toyota and Honda launched hybrid vehicles that used computers to automatically adjust the power needed from the gasoline engine and electric motor. Hybrids also captured energy generated from braking and coasting, converted that energy to electricity and then stored it in a large onboard battery for later use. The combined benefits of these technologies allowed hybrids to far outperform their non-hybrid equivalents. For example, the 2007 Honda Civic hybrid was rated at 40 mpg in the city and 45 mpg on the highway, whereas the standard Honda Civic had a rating of only 20 mpg in the city and 29 mpg on the highway.[35]

Larger vehicles benefited less from hybrid technology. A good example was the Honda Accord hybrid, which achieved a fuel economy rating of 32 mpg, only one mile per gallon better than the non-hybrid Accord (see Exhibit 5).[36] Honda emphasized the Accord's more potent power train, but its relatively poor fuel economy discouraged most car buyers.[37] In 2007, after two years of disappointing sales, Honda discontinued the Accord hybrid and planned to replace it with a clean diesel version.[38]

---

[31] Ibid.

[32] Nicholas Rufford and Jason Dawe, "Toyota Prius Proves a Gas Guzzler in a Race with the BMW 520d," The Sunday Times, March 16, 2008, http://www.timesonline.co.uk/tol/driving/used_car_reviews/article3552994.ece, accessed November 13, 2008.

[33] "The First Hybrid Vehicle by Dr. Ferdinand Porsche," http://www.hybrid-vehicle.org/hybrid-vehicle-porsche.html, accessed October 27, 2008.

[34] "History of Hybrid Vehicles," HybridCars.com, March 27, 2006, http://www.hybridcars.com/history/history-of-hybrid-vehicles.html accessed October 27, 2008.

[35] U.S. Department of Energy, "Gas Mileage of 2007 Honda Civic," http://fueleconomy.gov/feg/bymodel/2007_Honda_Civic.shtml, accessed November 13, 2008.

[36] U.S. Department of Energy, "Gas Mileage of 2007 Honda Civic," http://www.fueleconomy.gov/feg/bymodel/2007_Honda_Accord.shtml, accessed November 25, 2008.

[37] Don Hammonds, "Honda Accord Hybrid's Sales Run out of Gas," Pittsburg Post Gazette, June 6, 2007, http://post-gazette.com/pg/07157/791702-185.stm, accessed November 25, 2008.

[38] John Brus, "*Beyond the Prius," letter to the editor, The Economist, June 16, 2007.*

In many countries, hybrids benefited from government incentives, ranging from tax rebates to the use of car pool lanes. In the United States, the government offered purchasers of new hybrid vehicles a tax credit of up to $3,000 depending on the make and model. In Europe, hybrids also qualified for tax credits and discounts, and many were exempt from highway tolls.[39]

Hybrid vehicles also posed numerous challenges, such as the loss of fuel efficiency due to the added weight of vehicle's dual power source. The Honda Civic hybrid, for instance, weighed between 200 and 300 pounds more than its non-hybrid sibling. A key area of hybrid research was the development of smaller and lighter batteries.

THE SUPERCAR PROJECT

During the 1970s oil crisis, the U.S. government began to show interest in alternative-fuel vehicles, including models with electric and hybrid engines, and provided various research grants to carmakers to develop more efficient vehicles. After the United States restored relations with the Middle East, however, oil prices returned to normal, and interest in the program waned.

The most significant shift in policy came in 1993, when the U.S. government created the Partnership for a New Generation of Vehicles (PNGV), dubbed the Supercar. That year, President Bill Clinton and Vice President Al Gore met with the chief executive officers (CEOs) of Ford, Chrysler and General Motors on the White House lawn to announce $1.5 billion in federal grants to U.S. automakers to develop clean fuel-efficient vehicles. In exchange, the government agreed to postpone any increase in CAFE standards.[40]

Over the next 10 years, the U.S. government and the American auto industry combined the full weight of their resources—billions of dollars, the best scientific minds and previously secret Cold War technologies—to build an invention simple in concept yet critical in importance: a family car that could achieve 80 miles per gallon. The Supercar project was promoted for its environmental benefits and its ability to cut the nation's reliance on oil imports from volatile Middle Eastern countries.[41]

The PNGV timetable was ambitious. By 1998, government and industry representatives would choose the most promising technology; by 2000, each automaker would present a concept car; and by 2004, each would have a production prototype.

The Big Three focused on diesel hybrids as the best technology for achieving mass-market fuel efficiency. "They were the ones officially building Supercar, and they told their government partners that diesels were their choice." [42] However, Vice President Al Gore was skeptical. After all, diesel vehicles were known to be noisy and to produce high levels of smog. Automotive executives and government administrators tried to assuage Gore's fears by underlining technology improvements that placed diesel engines on the same level as gasoline, in terms of both performance and emissions. In the end, the Big Three prevailed, and diesel became the fuel of choice for the Supercar.[43]

---

[39] Nicholas Rufford and Jason Dawe, "Toyota Prius Proves a Gas Guzzler in a Race with the BMW 520d," The Sunday Times, March 16, 2008, http://www.timesonline.co.uk/tol/driving/used_car_reviews/article3552994.ece, accessed November 13, 2008.

[40] "History of Hybrid Vehicles," HybridCars.com, March 27, 2006, http://www.hybridcars.com/history/history-of-hybrid-vehicles.html, accessed October 27, 2008.

[41] "SuperCar: Part 1: Starting Up," Chicago Tribune, December 2002, http://www.chicagotribune.com/news/watchdog/chi-startingup-special,0,4716734.special, accessed April 21, 2010.

[42] Ibid.

[43] "SuperCar: Part 2: Shifting into Gear," Chicago Tribune, December 2002, chicagotribune http://www.chicagotribune.com/news/watchdog/chi-scoverview-story,0,652329.story, accessed April 21, 2010.

In 2000, the U.S. Department of Energy announced that GM, Ford and Chrysler had each reached the "first milestone," producing concept cars with fuel efficiency that ranged from 72 mpg to 80 mpg (see Exhibit 6). Behind the scenes, however, executives from the Big Three (GM, Ford and Chrysler) were telling government officials that expectations for a production vehicle were unrealistic. The retail cost for each car would be at least $7,500 more than a comparably equipped vehicle with a standard gasoline engine. They did not believe that enough consumers would be willing to pay more to achieve better gas mileage, especially when gas-guzzling pickups and SUVs were more popular than ever. Shortly after George W. Bush was inaugurated as President of the United States in January 2001, the government killed the Supercar project, noting that it was "inconsistent with where the market is headed."[44]

THE TOYOTA PRIUS: JAPAN'S ANSWER TO THE SUPERCAR

In 1993, Toyota petitioned the U.S. government to be made a participant in the Supercar project, but was promptly rebuffed. PNGV was about making U.S. automakers more competitive. As such, any sharing of information with the Japanese was viewed as counterproductive.[45]

The Japanese saw the Supercar as a serious threat to their market leadership in fuel-efficient automobiles. Shortly after Toyota executives met with U.S. officials, they authorized work on a hybrid engine at the Higashi-Fuji Technical Center near Tokyo. Over the next several years, Toyota, Honda and other Japanese automakers spent almost US$2 billion annually on fuel-efficiency research.[46] From the outset, Toyota's goals were more modest than those of the Supercar project. Toyota hoped to produce a commercially viable passenger car that exceeded 55 miles per gallon. The result was the Prius, which Toyota unveiled with great fanfare at the 1997 Tokyo Motor Show.

In 1997, some questioned Toyota's dedication to fuel efficiency at a time when oil prices were near (inflation-adjusted) all-time lows. In the United States, according to a survey of car owners, fuel efficiency ranked 19th in importance. Toyota was convinced, however, that rising automobile ownership in developing countries, such as India and China, would eventually strain world oil supplies, resulting in rising fuel prices. Meanwhile, concern was growing about the impact of oil consumption on the environment. Under the circumstances, Toyota unsurprisingly emphasized the Prius's "green" credentials over its potential to save money.[47]

To maintain a price point of approximately $20,000, Toyota virtually eliminated the advertising budget normally associated with new product launches and reduced dealer margins from 14 per cent to 10 per cent. Nevertheless, the Prius quickly rose to prominence after several Hollywood celebrities became outspoken advocates.[48] The success of the Prius caught Toyota off guard, and it struggled to keep up with demand.

Sales of the Prius remained strong throughout the 2000s. Although Toyota initially lost money on every Prius it sold, economies of scale eventually helped make the car profitable. A major milestone

---

[44] SuperCar: Toyota is Rebuffed, Chicago Tribune, December 2002, http://www.chicagotribune.com/news/watchdog/chi-super2part4,0,5881122.story, accessed April 21, 2010.

[45] "SuperCar: Part 2: Shifting into Gear," Chicago Tribune, December 2002, http://www.chicagotribune.com/news/watchdog/chi-scoverview-story,0,652329.story, accessed April 21, 2010.

[46] Emily Thornton et al., "Japan's Hybrid Cars," Business Week (International Edition), *December 15, 1997, p. 26.*

[47] Emily Thornton et al., "Japan's Hybrid Cars," Business Week (International Edition), *December 15, 1997, p. 26.*

[48] Jorn Madslien, "How Hybrid Power Surprised the Car Industry," BBC News, November 16, 2004, http://www.news.bbc.co.uk/1/hi/business/4015831.stm, accessed October 30, 2008.

was reached in April 2008, when cumulative Prius sales surpassed one million units worldwide (see Exhibit 7). In 2007, Toyota also surpassed General Motors as the largest carmaker in the world.[49]

FORD'S ESCAPE

The surprise success of the Prius also caught Ford off guard. Having scrapped its 72 mpg Prodigy hybrid in 2001, Ford scrambled to be the first U.S. carmaker to launch a hybrid vehicle. Instead of resurrecting the Supercar project, which had been years away from production when the project was killed, Ford decided to enter into a licensing agreement with Toyota.

Ford decided to capitalize on the still popular SUV market by being the first company in the world to produce a hybrid SUV. When the Ford Escape (also branded as the Mercury Mariner) was launched in 2004, it had a fuel-efficiency rating of approximately 30 mpg, a 10 mpg improvement over the standard Escape.[50]

Ford purchased hybrid motors from Aisin Seiki, a Toyota subsidiary located outside of Nagoya, Japan. However, when Ford underestimated demand for the Escape hybrid, it had a difficult time procuring more hybrid motors from its Japanese suppliers. To auto analyst Lindsay Brooke, Ford's procurement problems were no surprise: "There's a small universe of suppliers of key hybrid components, and many have [business group] relationships with Honda and Toyota. They're going to get served first."[51]

Although Ford was able to deliver more than 20,000 Escape hybrids in 2006 and nearly 40,000 in 2007, it was unable to keep up with demand, estimated at five times Ford's maximum production capacity. In subsequent years, Ford's competitors launched several hybrid SUV models, although the Escape remained the leader in fuel efficiency (see Exhibit 8).

THE FORD FIESTA

When Ford launched the 2009 Fiesta Diesel, this model led the industry in fuel efficiency. At 65 miles per U.S. gallon, the Fiesta trumped the Toyota Prius, which had a highway fuel-efficiency rating of 51 mpg.[52] However, due to the longstanding resistance to diesel in America, Ford decided to limit production of the Fiesta Diesel to Europe, where the Fiesta retailed for approximately US$20,000. Steven O'Dell, chief operating officer for Ford Europe commented:

> I had to check the facts, because I couldn't believe it when I first heard it. That's 76.3 miles to the [Imperial] gallon,[53] average consumption. That's fantastic and that's available today.[54]

---

[49] "Toyota 'World's Largest Carmaker'," BBC News, April 24, 2007, http://www.news.bbc.co.uk/2/hi/business/6586679.stm, accessed November 25, 2008.

[50] U.S. Department of Energy, "Gas Mileage of 2006 Vehicles by Ford," http://fueleconomy.gov/feg/bymake/Ford2006.shtml, accessed October 30, 2008.

[51] Devlin, Mark, Japanese Tradition and Loyalties: Forcing Ford into a Corner?, Industry Market Trends, August 16, 2005, http://news.thomasnet.com/IMT/archives/2005/08/japanese_tradit.html, accessed April 26, 2010.

[52] John Gartner, "Hybrid Cars' Fantasy Mileage Ratings Drive into the Sunset," Wired, May 14, 2007, http://www.wired.com/cars/futuretransport/news/2007/05/hybrid_mpg, accessed October 27, 2008.

[53] 1.0 Imperial gallon = 1.2 U.S. gallons.

[54] Ford Press Conference at the 2008 British Motor Show, July 23, 2008.

"This is the lowest CO_2 [carbon dioxide emissions] and best fuel economy car that money can buy in the UK today," explained Roelant de Waard, managing director for Ford of Britain. The new Fiesta Diesel was well positioned in the market. Not only was the Fiesta already the best-selling car in Britain, Ford customers were increasingly selecting fuel efficiency over styling. "Sales [of our fuel efficient engines] have gone up 40 percent in the last year," de Waard added. He was convinced that the Fiesta Diesel would take the market by storm.

> What do you need to be successful? You need good value, which we believe the Fiesta will deliver. You need good fuel economy. You need very [low CO_2 emissions]. But you need to add to that, that you need very good looks.[55]

In 2008, Ford Europe launched 20 new models, several of which were based on the same fuel-efficient ECOnetic technology that had been used in the Fiesta.[56] Other fuel-efficient models launched in 2008 included the Ford Focus ECOnetic, which achieved 54 mpg and the full-sized Mondeo ECOnetic, rated at 44 mpg.[57]

However, Ford's decision to keep the technology out of the United States for the foreseeable future left some scratching their heads. *Business Week* journalist David Kiley, commented:

> Despite the car's potential to transform Ford's image and help it compete with Toyota Motor and Honda Motor in its home market, the company will sell the little fuel sipper only in Europe. . . . Diesel vehicles now hitting the market with pollution-fighting technology are as clean, or cleaner, than gasoline and at least 30 percent more fuel-efficient. Yet while half of all cars sold in Europe last year ran on diesel, the U.S. market remains relatively unfriendly to the fuel. Taxes aimed at commercial trucks mean diesel costs anywhere from 40 cents to $1 more per gallon than gasoline. Add to this the success of the Toyota Prius, and you can see why only 3 percent of cars in the U.S. use diesel. . . . None of this is stopping European and Japanese automakers, which are betting they can jump-start the U.S. market with new diesel models. . . . But Ford, whose Fiesta ECOnetic compares favorably with European diesels, can't make a business case for bringing the car to the U.S.[58]

Ford argued that it was too expensive to export the car from Europe and to make the modifications necessary to pass U.S. emission standards. Building the car in the United States would require an investment of at least $350 million, which required sales of 350,000 cars a year to break even. Instead, Ford planned to introduce a less efficient gasoline engine model in the United States as early as 2010 to compete against similar-sized cars that were already available from Ford's competitors.[59] Scott Monty, head of social media for Ford's Global Digital Communications, responded:

> The situation is a little more complicated than some make it out to be. It's not as simple as dropping a diesel engine into an existing vehicle. The factors include emissions

---

[55] Ibid.

[56] Ford Press Conference at the 2008 Geneva Motor Show, March 14, 2008, http://theautochannel.com/news/2008/09/22/124163.html, accessed November 12, 2008.

[57] Figures in miles per gallon figures have been converted to U.S. equivalent units, except where noted.

[58] David Kiley, "The 65 mpg Ford the U.S. Can't Have," Business Week, September 15, 2008, p. 60.

[59] The similar-sized cars already available included the BMW *Mini, Honda Fit, Chevrolet Aveo, Toyota Yaris, Kia Rio and Nissan Versa. As a whole, the category increased by 30 per cent in 2007 and by 60 per cent in early 2008. P. Vettraino, "Ford's Coming Fiesta, a Small B-car, Could Be the Start of Something Big for American Buyers", AutoWeek, April 21, 2008, p. 21.*

> standards in all 50 states that are far more stringent than Europe's, the cost of building plants to make diesel engines, uncertain demand, and the future price of diesel with respect to gasoline—given the likelihood that the price would rise if demand did. All this means that the payback to the customer wouldn't be realized for years. While it's too early to discuss what power trains will be in the Fiesta when it debuts in the U.S. in 2010, we're confident the car will be a fuel-economy leader.[60]

For the U.S. market, Ford planned to introduce a new hybrid version of the Ford Fusion mid-sized sedan, also marketed as the Mercury Milan with a slightly different body configuration. The gasoline version of the Fusion was first introduced in 2005 (2006 model year), winning immediate favor among car reviewers. *Car and Driver* magazine, for example, ranked the Fusion second, after the Honda Accord, in a comparison with similar vehicles that also included the Toyota Camry and Hyundai Sonata.[61] Despite the Ford Fusion's favorable reviews, the Honda Accord and Toyota Camry outsold it in the United States by more than three to one.[62]

The hybrid version of the Fusion was introduced in early 2009 (2010 model year) and was powered by an Aisin Power Split engine produced by Aisin Seiki,[63] the same technology employed in the Toyota Prius Hybrid Synergy Drive and the Ford Escape continuously variable transmission (CVT).[64] *Car and Driver* magazine gave the Fusion high marks both in fuel efficiency and driving enjoyment. The reviewer likened most hybrids to "supremely boring torture chambers, the vehicular equivalent of watching a documentary on the color brown while sitting on a giant-ass cactus." Not so for Ford's new hybrid. It offered a "driving experience . . . beyond that of the Toyota Camry and Honda Civic hybrids."[65] It was also 5 mpg more efficient than the Toyota and Honda offerings.

Still, the Fusion was not without its faults. For one, it was priced nearly $10,000 more than the popular Toyota Prius, and although it compared favorably to the larger Toyota Camry, mid-sized sedans such as the Camry and Civic did not sell as well as their smaller cousins. The Prius, for example, outsold Camry by three to one.[66]

Ford had several options for the Fiesta: launch it in North America, launch it in another region of the world or continue selling it exclusively in the European market.

Exhibit 1 Ford motor company income statement (in millions of U.S. dollars)

	12 Months Ending December 31,			
	2004	**2005**	**2006**	**2007**
Revenue	172,316	176,835	160,065	172,455
Cost of Revenue, Total	144,226	153,337	157,649	153,514

---

60 "Feedback: Ford's Diesel Fiesta: Steering Clear of the U.S.," Business Week, September 29, 2008, p. 92.

61 Patrick Bedard, "2006 Ford Fusion, vs. Honda Accord, Hyundai Sonata, Toyota Camry — Comparison Tests," Car and Driver, December 2005, http://www.caranddriver.com/reviews/comparison_test/sedans/2006_ford_fusion_vs_honda_accord_hyundai_sonata_toyota_camry_comparison_test, accessed May 12, 2009.

62 "2007 My-Registrations," www.automotive-fleet.com, Stats Viewer application, accessed May 12, 2009.

63 "2010 Ford Fusion Packages & Options," Automobile Magazine, http://www.automobilemag.com/am/2010/ford/fusion/packages_options.html, accessed May 12, 2009.

64 Interim Report: New Powertrain Technologies and Their Projected Costs, U.S. Environmental Protection Agency, October 2005, EPA420-R-05-012, p. 39.

65 Erik Johnson, "2010 Mercury Milan Hybrid — Short Take Road Test," Car and Driver, April 2009.

66 "Hybrid Camry Outsold V6 Camry in March," Hybrid Cars, April 2, 2008, http://www.hybridcars.com/news/hybrid-camry-outsold-v6-camry-march.html, accessed May 12, 2009.

Gross Profit	**28,090**	**23,498**	**2,416**	**18,941**
Selling/General/Admin. Expenses, Total	25,224	25,071	19,389	21,837
Unusual Expense (Income)	–	0	0	2,400
Total Operating Expense	**169,450**	**178,408**	**177,038**	**177,751**
Operating Income	**2,866**	**(1,573)**	**(16,973)**	**(5,296)**
Interest Income(Expense), Net Non-Operating	1,243	1,532	1,899	1,550
Gain (Loss) on Sale of Assets	0	1,095	0	0
Income Before Tax	**4,109**	**1,054**	**(15,074)**	**(3,746)**
Income After Tax	**3,466**	**1,909**	**(12,419)**	**(2,452)**
Minority Interest	(282)	(280)	(210)	(312)
Net Income	**3,184**	**1,629**	**(12,629)**	**(2,764)**

Source: Thompson Reuters.

Exhibit 2 Comparison of crude oil price and ford common share price

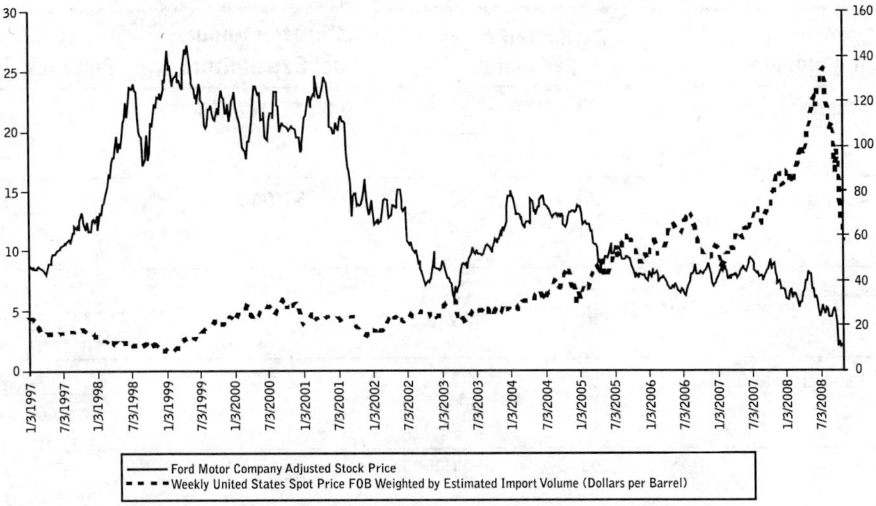

Sources: U.S. Energy Information Administration, Yahoo Finance.

Exhibit 3 Pre-tax quarterly operational earnings by region

In Millions of US$	2006	2007				2008		
	4th QTR	1st QTR	2nd QTR	3rd QTR	4th QTR	1st QTR	2nd QTR	3rd QTR
North America	(2,700)	(645)	(279)	(1,000)	(1,600)	(45)	(1,300)	(2,600)
South America	114	113	255	386	446	250	388	480
Europe	218	219	262	313	223	740	582	69
Asia Pacific	(185)	22	26	30	40	50	153	4

Note: Results have been compiled from various earnings call transcripts and are approximate.
Source: seekingalpha.com.

Exhibit 4 Graph of hubbert's peak oil model (1956)

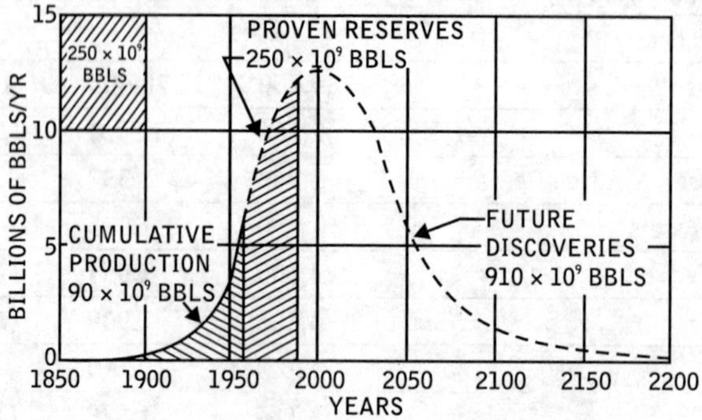

Source: Marion King Hubbert, "Nuclear Energy and the Fossil Fuels," Paper presented before the Spring Meeting of the Southern District, American Petroleum Institute, Plaza Hotel, San Antonio, Texas, March 7–9, 1956, p. 22.

Exhibit 5 Annual fuel cost comparison table (2007 model year)

Make and Model	Estimated Miles per Gallon		Estimated Annual Fuel Expenditure	Pollution Score
Honda Accord	23 city	31 hwy	$1,091	Best 6 (0–10)
Honda Accord Hybrid	24 city	32 hwy	$1,049	Best 9 (0–10)
Ford Escape 4WD	20 city	25 hwy	$1,290	Best 6 (0–10)
Ford Escape Hybrid 4WD	28 city	27 hwy	$1,049	Best 8 (0–10)
Toyota Camry	21 city	31 hwy	$1,134	Best 6 (0–10)
Toyota Camry Hybrid	33 city	34 hwy	$833	Best 8 (0–10)
Toyota Prius Hybrid	48 city	45 hwy	$615	Best 8 (0–10)
Mercedes-Benz E320 Bluetec, Diesel	23 city	32 hwy	$1,536	N/A
Mercedes-Benz E350, Gasoline	17 city	24 hwy	$1,704	N/A

Nissan Altima	23 city	26 hwy	$1,091	Best 6 0 10
Nissan Altima Hybrid	35 city	33 hwy	$833	N/A

Note: Fuel cost estimates are based on 45 per cent highway driving, 55 per cent city driving, 15,000 annual miles and a fuel cost of $1.89 per gallon. Pollution score is based on greenhouse gas emissions emitted by motor vehicles, including carbon dioxide, nitrous oxide and methane. (U.S. Department of Energy, GREET Model 1.7, Argonne National Laboratory)

Source: Fuel Economy Guide, fueleconomy.gov/feg/sbs.htm, accessed April 26, 2010.

Exhibit 6 Supercar announcement

New concept cars demonstrate clean, efficient transportation technologies

OAAT ACCOMPLISHMENTS

High-Powered Partnership Achieves First Milestone

Challenge

In 1993, the Partnership for a New Generation of Vehicles (PNGV) established a goal of developing a vehicle which could achieve fuel efficiencies up to three times those of 1994 family sedans or 80 miles per gallon gasoline equivalent (mpgge). The vehicle was to keep the same level of cost, performance and comfort that consumers have come to expect. Production prototypes were to be developed by 2004, with concept vehicles that demonstrated technical feasibility developed by 2000.

General Motors Precept.

Technology Description

Researchers are looking at every vehicle component and system to determine how it can be improved to meet the PNGV goals. Areas of study include improved aerodynamics, lightweight materials, and advanced propulsion systems.

Accomplishments

This unprecedented partnership among government, industry, and academia has resulted in three concept cars that demonstrate the feasibility of a variety of new automotive technologies. Each of the Big Three auto manufacturers took a different approach in building their hybrid electric concepts and unveiling them in 2000.

Dodge ESX3.

Dodge ESX3

- The combination of an all-aluminum diesel engine, electric motor, and lithium-ion battery achieves 72 mpgge and a 400-mile driving range.
- At 2,250 pounds, body weight is 46% less than that of comparable five-passenger car.
- Lightweight injection-molded body costs 15% less than a conventional steel body.
- New transmission shifts gears as smoothly as an automatic but is as efficient as a manual.
- Advanced lithium-ion battery pack is integrated with cooling and control system to save space.

Ford Prodigy

Ford Prodigy

- Hybrid powertrain based on the new DIATA (direct-injection aluminum through-bolt assembly) diesel engine delivers 72 mpgge and a 600-mile driving range.
- Advanced engine improves efficiency by 35% over conventional diesel engines.

Contact

Robert A. Kost
Leader, Vehicle Systems Team
202-586-2334
Robert.Kost@hq.doe.gov

April 2001

http://www.ott.doe.gov/success.html

Exhibit 7 Toyota prius sales

(Unit = 1,000 vehicles)

	1997	1998	1999	2000	2001	2002	2003	2004	2005	2006	2007	Jan.-Apr. 2008	Total
Total	**0.3**	**17.7**	**15.2**	**19.5**	**29.0**	**28.1**	**43.2**	**125.7**	**175.2**	**185.6**	**281.3**	**107.1**	**1,027.7**
Japan	0.3	17.7	15.2	12.5	11.0	6.7	17.0	59.8	43.7	48.6	58.3	24.2	315.0
Overseas	0	0	0	6.5	18.5	21.4	26.1	66.0	131.5	137.0	223.0	82.9	712.7
North America				5.8	16.0	20.3	24.9	55.9	109.9	109.0	183.8	66.1	591.6
Europe				0.7	2.3	0.8	0.9	8.1	18.8	22.8	32.2	14.2	100.7
Other				0.01	0.2	0.2	0.4	1.9	2.9	5.3	7.0	2.6	20.4

Source: Worldwide Prius Sales Top 1 Million Mark, May 15, 2008, http://www2.toyota.co.jp/en/news/08/0515.html, accessed April 26, 2010).

Exhibit 8 Hybrid vehicles in the United States (2007)

	Trans Type / Speeds	Eng Size / Cylinders	MPG City / Hwy	Annual Fuel Cost	Battery Size / Type
COMPACT CARS					
HONDA Civic Hybrid	AV	1.3/4	49/51	$795	158 V, Ni-MH
LEXUS GS 450h	A-S6	3.5/6	25/28	$1,646	288 V, Ni-MH
MIDSIZE CARS					
HONDA Accord Hybrid	A-5	3.0/6	28/35	$1,284	144 V, Ni-MH
NISSAN Altima Hybird	AV	2.5/4	42/36	$1,018	245 V, Ni-MH
SATURN Aura Hybrid	A-4	2.4/4	28/35	$1,324	42 V, Lead-Acid
TOYOTA Camry Hybrid	AV	2.4/4	40/38	$1,018	245 V, Ni-MH
TOYOTA Prius	AV	1.5/4	60/51	$723	202 V, Ni-MH
STANDARD PICKUP TRUCKS 2WD					
CHEVROLET C15 Silverado Classic Hybrid 2WD	A-4	5.3/8	18/21	$2,091	42 V, Lead-Acid
GMC C15 Sierra Classic Hybrid 2WD	A-4	5.3/8	18/21	$2,091	42 V, Lead-Acid
STANDARD PICKUP TRUCKS 4WD					
CHEVROLET K15 Silverado Classic Hybrid 4WD	A-4	5.3/8	17/19	$2,210	42 V, Lead-Acid
GMC K15 Sierra Classic Hybrid 4WD	A-4	5.3/8	17/19	$2,210	42 V, Lead-Acid
SPORT UTILITY VEHICLES 2WD					
FORD Escape Hybrid FWD	AV	2.3/4	36/31	$1,169	330 V, Ni-MH
LEXUS RX 400h 2WD	AV	3.3/6	32/27	$1,475	288 V, Ni-MH
SATURN Vue Hybrid	A-4	2.4/4	27/32	$1,371	36 V, Ni-MH
TOYOTA Highlander Hybrid 2WD	AV	3.3/6	32/27	$1,371	288 V, Ni-MH
SPORT UTILITY VEHICLES 4WD					
FORD Escape Hybrid 4WD	AV	2.3/4	32/29	$1,284	330 V, Ni-MH
LEXUS RX 400h 4WD	AV	3.3/6	31/27	$1,475	288 V, Ni-MH
MERCURY Mariner Hybrid 4WD	AV	2.3/4	32/29	$1,284	330 V, Ni-MH
TOYOTA Highlander Hybrid 4WD	AV	3.3/6	31/27	$1,371	288 V, Ni-MH

Source: Fuel Economy Guide, fueleconomy.gov, accessed April 26, 2010.

20

Dabur India Ltd.

Globalization

R. Chandrasekhar wrote this case under the supervision of Professor Niraj Dawar solely to provide material for class discussion. The authors do not intend to illustrate either effective or ineffective handling of a managerial situation. The authors may have disguised certain names and other identifying information to protect confidentiality.

INTRODUCTION

In June 2007, consumer packaged goods (CPG) companies around the world were optimistically betting on growth in India. Dabur India Ltd. (Dabur) was among the top 10 CPG[1] companies in India by revenue (see Exhibit 1). Dabur's chief executive officer (CEO), Sunil Duggal, was bullish on the Indian market, yet he was also convinced of the imperative to internationalize. Scheduled to meet soon with a group of institutional investors to brief them on the company's growth strategy, Duggal had to factor in concerns about the priorities of the company's international business division, and, in particular, he needed to address the concerns expressed among foreign institutional investors.

---

[1] Marketing branded and packaged consumer goods through retail outlets, they were more popularly known in India as FMCG (Fast Moving Consumer Goods) companies.

Duggal anticipated their questions: Shouldn't Dabur first build scale in the fast growing domestic market before attempting to go global? Wouldn't a strategy of pursuing new global markets detract from the company's core market in India, where it was beginning to face growing competition from international players, a fast changing retail landscape and an ever more fastidious consumer? Wasn't the growth pattern within the international business division skewed, and likely to be further skewed (see Exhibit 2)?

Duggal was keenly aware of the detractors' arguments:

> Whenever an Indian company announces a domestic expansion, through an alliance or acquisition, its stock price goes up. But on news of an overseas expansion, the stock price falls. That is because of investor apprehensions about integration, product fit and the alien nature of the market. In addition, India is an exciting geography in terms of size and growth, diversity and opportunity, and will remain so in the coming decades. This offers its own rationale for some to expect that managers in a quintessentially Indian enterprise like Dabur must focus their time and energy on the home market they know best. But the reasons to go beyond Indian shores are compelling for us. They outweigh the reasons to concentrate solely on India.

Duggal's task was to present a plan that would convince FIIs that the compulsions were sound, that the strategy being followed by Dabur International Limited (DIL), a newly formed subsidiary, was on track, and that the ongoing globalization plan would indeed boost volumes and margins.

CONSUMER PACKAGED GOODS–INDUSTRY BACKGROUND

CPGs were packaged household groceries and supplies consumed readily and regularly, including foods, personal care products and detergents, among others. The CPG industry comprised manufacturers, wholesalers and retailers. A broad spectrum of competitors prevailed, from standalones occupying niches to integrated firms straddling the continuum. Globally, profit margins were generally low for CPG companies, and their business models emphasized cutting costs, and chasing volumes and elusive top-line growth. Three factors usually influenced a consumer's decision to buy a CPG: price, brand loyalty and impulse.

In most developing countries, including India, CPG was a local business dominated by small indigenous players at provincial levels. Very few graduated to national status. Manufacturing was generally outsourced and retail channels were shared. Distribution was a key success factor in the business. In the developing markets, there were almost no CPG firms that played on the global stage. It was not easy to create universally appealing brand positions or product assortments and run far-flung, people-intensive retail operations. Having acquired a place among the top 10 CPG companies in India, Dabur was attempting what few other CPG companies from emerging markets had attempted to do: become an international company.

The global CPG industry grew by 2.5 per cent in 2006, up from the 1.5 per cent growth in 2005. Growth was driven largely by price increases rather than by volume. Despite low growth rates and low margins, CPG was an attractive industry to manufacturers and investors because demand was stable. Beverages continued to be CPG growth leaders in 2006. Home care products, snack food products and health-care products were also growth categories.

The CPG industry in India had a total market size in 2006 of $13.1 billion (not including soft drinks and tobacco products)[2]. Foods (including groceries) comprised 44 per cent of CPG sales. Unlike the North American market, which was dominated by a few global players, the Indian CPG market was fragmented, with over half the sales accounted for by mom-and-pop outfits making and selling unbranded and unpackaged goods. This presented an opportunity for consolidation through economies of scale for makers of branded products. But building brands was challenging in the Indian context. National coverage was difficult, particularly for new entrants. There were over six million retail outlets in the country–two million urban and four million rural. The supply chain was underdeveloped, and logistics were costly and challenging. Although, overall, CPG transactions accounted for a significant part of the consumer's budget, they were of small individual value, making them unremunerative for marketers.

But what made India attractive was that its CPG market was among the fastest growing in the world. The Indian economy was poised to grow at 9.2 per cent in 2007-2008, after posting a compound average growth rate of 8.6 per cent over the previous three years. The population was young, dynamic and willing to try new products. Almost half of India's one billion people were under the age of 20. Teens among them numbered about 160 million. The Indian CPG market was projected to grow almost threefold by 2015 to $33.4 billion. Growth was expected in the personal care, food, beverages and household care categories. These were categories in which Dabur had strong brands.

DABUR-COMPANY BACKGROUND

Established in 1884 by Dr. S.K. Burman as a trading company, by 2007, Dabur manufactured over 450 products, which it sold in the domestic market through a network of 1.5 million retail outlets, 47 clearing and forwarding (C&F) locations and 5,000 distributors. The company had a consolidated sales turnover of INR 22.6 billion for the year ending March 2007 (see Exhibit 3). Dabur had four business units: consumer care, consumer healthcare, foods business and international business.

Consumer care offered products in hair care, oral care, health supplements, digestives and candies, and baby and skin care products. Consumer healthcare offered both prescription and over-the-counter (OTC) medicines. Foods Business produced fruit juices, cooking pastes, sauces, and bulk items for institutional customers. The international business division manufactured and marketed products for overseas markets.

The company had eight manufacturing plants in India, organized around two main factories and six support factories, catering to consumer care and health care businesses. The foods business was catered to by two separate manufacturing facilities. The company also had production units outside India at Birganj (Nepal), Dhaka (Bangladesh), Dubai (UAE), Cairo (Egypt), and Lagos (Nigeria).

In India, Dabur's product portfolio consisted of categories that were underpenetrated and high-growth. The company's positioning on the health and wellness platform, backed by its differentiated herbal image, ensured that the company was well placed to capture future growth in the Indian CPG market.

Said Duggal:

> Dabur is unique among its CPG peers in India in three ways. First, its products are derivatives of Ayurveda, an indigenous form of medicine. The raw materials are sourced from natural ingredients such as herbs. Second, its products are priced for and targeted

---

[2] http://ibef.org/artdispview.aspx?in=13&art_id=15223&cat_id=445&page=2, accessed May 23, 2007.

at the mass market. Finally, Dabur is one of the few heritage companies in India that has successfully transitioned from being a family-run company to being fully managed by professionals.

DOMESTIC CAPABILITIES

Dabur's major domestic competence was its ability to identify consumer needs, develop localized products and create niches to drive long-term growth. The niches not only provided differentiation but insulated Dabur from competition. Set up originally as a manufacturer of herbal medicines, Dabur had extended the principles of Ayurveda (traditional Indian Medicine) to personal care. In spite of its long heritage, Dabur was a contemporary enterprise where new products or variants contributed between five per cent and seven per cent of sales revenue every year. The Ayurvedic platform, on which Dabur was launching products, was rooted in strong internal research and development (R&D), which, among others, was **identifying** plants with therapeutic powers and promoting their large-scale farming. The company had built up skills in product engineering and localization. For example, while large players used coconut in hair oils, Dabur used *amla* (gooseberry), which had its roots in traditional medicine.

The company's sales force was focused on channels, not products. Dabur had a sales force dedicated to key grocers, mass grocers, chemists, modern retail outlets and wholesale in towns with a population larger than 500,000.[3] The rural market, which provided 50 per cent of Dabur's sales, had its own dedicated sales team. The company was moving away from one-off discount schemes towards long-term loyalty programs that encouraged channel partners to purchase more throughout the year.[4] Dabur was implementing channel software to capture data on stock levels at stockists and to assess the effectiveness of promotions and design schemes for particular regions and products. Dabur had an independent supply chain for each of its four business segments.

APPROACH TO GLOBALIZATION

It was in 1987, with the setting up of a plant in an export processing zone near New Delhi, in north India, that Dabur began looking beyond Indian shores (see Exhibit 5). The initial momentum came from following its consumers – the Indian Diaspora – to the Persian Gulf region of the Middle East. Indian consumers there were familiar with Dabur as a brand and preferred its traditional products. Over the next 10 years, Dabur exported primarily hair oil to the Gulf markets, but did not yet consider its international business as a focus segment. Sales outside India accounted for less than six per cent of turnover. It was finally in 2003 that the company articulated its vision of becoming "a financially successful and internationally respected corporation by occupying herbal, natural and ayurvedic platforms through successful globalization."

Dabur floated a Dubai-based subsidiary, DIL, as an umbrella organization to provide focus and structure for its global operations. By 2006, the company had established five manufacturing units

[3] While the 'key' grocer (a relatively large mom-and-pop grocery store) was comfortable with two salesmen each visiting the store twice a week, the 'mass' grocer (smaller grocery stores) managed with one visit per week, and the chemist wanted just one visit every 10 days. Modern retail stores, on the other hand, required greater focus on an efficient supply chain, replenishing products with a minimum time lag.

[4] For example, 9,000 wholesalers accounting for 80 per cent of wholesale sales had signed up for the 'Dabur Kings' program, resulting in 20 per cent sales growth through wholesalers.

overseas. Its products were being exported to more than 50 countries around the world, including the Middle East, Southeast Asia, Africa, the European Union and America. These markets were serviced locally by the company's offices and representatives. The international business contributed 11 per cent of consolidated sales for the period 2005-06. The current goal was to step up international sales to 20 per cent of revenues by 2012, and the company had taken some strategic steps towards that goal.

All international operations had been streamlined under DIL, headed by a CEO, and reporting to Duggal and headquartered in Dubai. DIL had seven subsidiaries: Dabur Nepal Pvt Ltd., Weikfield International (UAE) Ltd.; Asian Consumer Care Ltd.; African Consumer Care Ltd.; Dabur Egypt Ltd.; Dabur (UK) Ltd.; and Asian Consumer Care (Pakistan) Ltd. (see Exhibit 6).

Existing international markets were categorized into "strategic" and "opportunistic" markets in order of priority for allocation of managerial time. The strategic markets were further categorized into "focus markets" and "potential markets" in order of priority for allocation of financial and human resources (see Exhibit 7).

Dabur had already identified 20 focus countries in which to establish manufacturing and marketing facilities. These fell into two broad portfolios. The first comprised Asian markets (Pakistan, Bangladesh, Nepal, Sri Lanka Bangladesh and Malaysia) and developed markets (United States and United Kingdom). Also, part of this first set would be the health-care business in CIS countries, with Russia being the largest. This portfolio was to be supported by the company's export oriented unit in India and by the local manufacturing units in Nepal and Bangladesh. The second portfolio included markets in the member-countries of Gulf Cooperation Council (GCC), Africa (Egypt, Nigeria, Sudan and Morocco) other Middle-Eastern countries like Iran and Iraq, and the personal care business in CIS countries. This was to be supported by manufacturing facilities in Dubai, Cairo and Lagos.

Said S. Raghunanandan, CEO, DIL:

> The strategic intent in growing the international business is threefold. The first is geographic expansion. We will use the segmentation model to identify the markets for entry and commit financial investments and human resources in geographies designated as focus markets. Second, we will leverage the "natural" platform. DIL will capitalize on the growing global demand for natural products by occupying differentiated competitive niches in the health-care and the personal care segments. And third, we will grow both organically and inorganically. We will acquire assets and drive alliances to build scale globally.

TEMPLATE FOR GLOBALIZATION

To achieve its goal of securing 20 per cent of its revenues from global operations by 2010, Dabur was designing a new template for international expansion. It had the following elements:

- A new market for entry should not be margin-dilutive, even in the short run.
- A new market should be in the landscape between Nigeria and China. Any market beyond that landscape would raise two basic questions: Is it a developed market? Is the cost of doing business high? If the answer was yes, the market would not be pursued.
- Acquisition–of brands, relationships and other assets–would be considered to jump-start growth.
- The technology on offer at the new geography should be compatible with Dabur's technology. There also had to be opportunities for adapting technology to suit local needs.

- The "herbal" platform would remain the basis for new customer acquisition and brand development.
- The overall brand architecture would be limited to four core brands in an overseas market.

A focus country was to be so identified based on some basic considerations. It should have a large consumer population. The economy had to have long-term prospects for GDP growth. The country should already have been playing host to Dabur brands.

Dabur was uncompromising in sticking to the above template. For example, in entering a "developed" market like the United States (normally facing elimination in Round 1 itself), its foray was cautious at each stage. The business had to be margin accretive even if the long-term prospects –in private labels, to cite an instance–justified losses on initial orders. The company also targeted the mainstream population in the host countries only after gaining ground with the local Diaspora. This was particularly true of the Middle East.

Duggal:

> During the initial days of our export sales, we followed our traditional consumers. But the Indian Diaspora, while important, is not our core international market in our current plans. Its presence gives us a comfort level, no doubt, but is no longer mandatory for market entry. I think the Diaspora is finite. There is also a large grey market operating in that segment, importing products directly from our Indian operations, without our approval through small retailers in foreign markets. Instead of the Diaspora, we are looking at the mainstream population in these countries as our prospect.

Based on the above template, DIL was operating, as of June 2007, a product matrix in its focus markets as shown in Exhibit 8.

GLOBAL CONSUMERS

Dabur had profiled three distinct segments of consumers outside India: Arab consumers, Asian consumers and African consumers. Growth of each segment was driven by core product categories (see Exhibit 9).

GLOBAL COMPETITION

Hair oil: Multi-national corporations (MNCs) were generally absent from the hair oil market, worldwide, because they preferred to stay away from commodity trading and also to focus on the growing grooming segment. Dabur faced competition in hair oils, its flagship category, from three sources: peers in India operating overseas, local players and imports. Local players tended to be me-toos and posed little threat, as did imports. Companies like Marico Ltd., an Indian competitor, were a major source of competition. In that sense, the competitive scenario in hair oils in the overseas market was similar to the home market in India.

Outside of oils, Dabur faced competition in every category in overseas markets, largely from MNCs.

Shampoo: Dabur's equity in the home market stemmed from the therapeutic value of its shampoos, based on traditional Indian ingredients. In an ambience in which customers veered intrinsically towards herbal ingredients, the company was able to hold its own in the Indian shampoo market. But the situation in markets outside India was different. A hair care product was beauty related and cosmetic in its appeal. While this was a barrier for Dabur, it also was an opportunity to build a niche on its unique therapeutic platform.

Toothpaste: MNCs were formidable players in oral care products in overseas markets. Dabur did not have home-grown competencies in the category. It was only when it acquired Balsara Hygiene Products, an Indian CPG company, in 2003 that it gained entry into this category. The integration had been successful, and Dabur was launching Miswak, with toothpaste variants and mouthwash, as a core brand in overseas markets. Miswak was pegged on an herbal platform, which was less crowded.
Soap: Consisting generally of creams, lotions, soaps and whitening products, the skincare category was highly competitive with a multitude of MNC and regional brands. Toilet soaps ruled the soaps segment with about 75 per cent market share. Medicated soaps comprised a growing segment, offering therapeutic value, aimed at treating ailments such as prickly heat and rashes, and were often premium priced. There were MNCs like Reckitt Benckiser (with Dettol) in the medicated soaps segment and also local players, but that segment was less crowded in relation to toilet soaps. Dabur was trying to gain a foothold by building on the therapeutic platform.
Mosquito repellant: This was also a category that Dabur had entered with the acquisition of Balsara. The product had wide appeal in the North African region, which was prone to Malaria. Coils, mats, sprays and vaporizers were the preferred product formats, dominated by MNCs like Reckitt Benckiser and S C Johnson. Dabur, however, had a cream offering, which was non-existent in Africa with no competition. This product posed an opportunity.

NIGERIA

Nigeria was an example of an international market that had turned the spotlight on the debate about the merits of Dabur's globalization. Investors were concerned that the Nigerian market was not drawing upon competencies, built not only in the domestic setting but even in the existing international markets. Their concerns rested on two grounds: Dabur was going beyond the Indian Diaspora (a customer segment it had understood best) into the mainstream African population (a customer segment it was not familiar with). And it was building a market not on a category it understood best–like personal care–but on those in which it did not have traditional strengths, like oral care and home care.

Said Raghunandan:

> Nigeria is a large market for toothpastes, soaps, glucose and mosquito repellants, which are part of Dabur's product portfolio. But in many ways, Nigeria has the makings of a new business, quite different from both domestic and international businesses of Dabur. All our focus markets are driven by hair care products, particularly hair oil. Nigeria is an exception. Oral care is the business driver for DIL in Nigeria. Toothpaste is not a focus product for Dabur in any international market. Nor does the company have home-grown strengths in that category. Hair care products sold in Nigeria are cosmetic. They do not have therapeutic value, in which Dabur's core competence resides. There is demand for mosquito repellants in Nigeria. But consumers are used to electrical coils, not creams, which are Dabur's forte. Nigeria does not have a large Indian Diaspora, unlike the Asian and Arab markets where Dabur has a presence. All these make Nigeria a different play.

Certain issues were thus unique to Nigeria (see Exhibits 10 and 11). Could Dabur successfully target an herbal niche in oral care and establish a strong market presence in toothpaste? Could the company operate in skin care successfully and extend herbal equity to soap? Could Dabur leverage its strengths in hair care to the cosmetic segment? Would Dabur be able to create a new cream category in Nigeria in mosquito coils?

Exhibit 1 Indian CPG–top 10 2005-2006

Rank	Company	Net Sales (INR Million)
1	Hindustan Lever	110,800
2	ITC	97,860
3	Nestle India	24,750
4	Asian Paints	24,410
5	Nirma	19,170
6	Nirma Consumer Care	18,140
7	Britannia Industries	17,130
8	**Dabur India**	**13,430**
9	Johnson & Johnson	13,300
10	Kansai Nerolac Paints	10,610

Source: Business World March 5, 2007- The BW Real 500.

Exhibit 2 Dabur international: share of revenues across regions

Focus Region	% of Global Revenue
GCC countries	32
Egypt	11
Pakistan	9
Bangladesh	6
Nigeria	5
US	5
UK	4
Others	28

Source: Edelweiss Equity Research Report March 2, 2007.

Exhibit 3 Dabur India Ltd.—consolidated income[1] statement

Year Ending March 31 (in INR Million)	2007	2006	2005	2004	2003
Income					
Sales less returns	22,337	18,996	15,369	13,295	13,708

[1] Includes group companies and subsidiaries.

Other income	259	134	92	91	72
Total income	22,596	19,130	15,461	13,386	13,780
Expenditure					
Cost of materials	9,711	8,078	6,594	5,814	5,775
Excise duty	371	337	428	654	735
Manufacturing expenses	743	571	405	347	378
Employee costs	1,666	1,449	1,085	915	1,038
Selling & administrative expenses	6,349	5,652	4,769	3,973	4,205
Financial expenses	154	164	124	153	261
Miscellaneous expenditure written off	65	43	15	39	29
Depreciation	342	269	280	248	292
Total Expenditure	19,401	16,563	13,700	12,143	12,713
Profit Before Tax	3,195	2,567	1,761	1,241	1,067
Profit After Tax	2,822	2,266	1,570		
Sales break-up					
Domestic	19,419	16,835	13,557	11,946	12,544
International	2,918	2,161	1,812	1,349	1,164
Total	22,337	18,996	15,369	13,295	13,708
Margin break-up					
Domestic	2,575	2,080	1,485		
International	247	186	85		
Total	2,822	2,266	1,570		

Source: Company files.

Exhibit 4 Dabur—segment wise market size, market shares and sales turnover (domestic)[1]

Business Unit	Category	Brands	Market Size (INR Million)	Market Shares		Dabur's Sales Turnover (INR Million)	
				Dabur	Major Competitors	2007	2006
1 Consumer Care	Hair Care	Hair Oil: 1. Amla 2. Amla Lite 3. Anmol Sarson Amla 4. Vatika	30,178	17.5	Marico–32.8 Emani–6.0 Bajaj–5.7	3,740.94	3,307.97
		Shampoo: 1.Vatika Anti-Dandruff Shampoo 2. Vatika Henna Conditioning Shampoo 3. Anmol Natural Shine Shampoo 4. Anmol Silky Black Shampoo	20,221	5.0	HLL – 48.0 P&G – 24.3 Cavincare – 12.5	804.44	613.73
	Oral Care	1. Dabur Lal Dant Manjan 2. Dabur Red Toothpaste 3. Dabur Red Gel 4. Babool Toothpaste 5. Meswak Toothpaste 6. Promise Toothpaste 7. Binaca Tooth-brush	38,318	10.9	Colgate–45.0 HLL–23.2	3,143.07	2,690.80
	Health Supplements	1. Dabur Chyawanprash 2. Dabur Chyawanshakti 3. Dabur Honey 4. Dabur Glucose	4,447	38.0[2]	Heinz–31.0 Baidyanath–5.6 Emami–4.2	3,047.30	2,550.48
	Digestives & Confectionery	1. Dabur Hajmola tablets 2. Hajmola Candy 3. Hajmola Candy Fun 4. Hajmola Yumstick 5. Hajmola Mast 6. Masala 7. Anardana 8. Dabur Hingoli 9. Pudin Hara Pearls 10. Pudin Hara Liquid 11. Pudin Hara G	11,697	16.0	Alpenliebe–12.0 Digene–7.2.	1,300.00	1,225.50
	Skin Care & Baby Care	1. Dabur Lal Tail 2. Dabur Baby Olive Oil 3. Dabur Janma Ghunti 4. Gulabari 5. Vatika Fairness Face Pack 6. Vatika Honey 7. Saffron Soap	6,557	6.0	Woodwords–28.0 Johnson–9.5	1,000.02	1,005.90

[1] Based on AC Nielsen and company estimates; [2] Excluding honey category; [3] AC Nielsen data not available.

	Home Care[3]	1. Odonil–Air Freshners 2. Odomos: Mosquito Repellants–(Personal Appln. Products) 3. Odomos: Mosquito Repellants-Coils 4. Sanifresh–Toilet Cleaners 5. Odopic – Dishwash	650 390 8,070 1,500 6,500	73.0 87.0 1.6 10.0 2.0	Premium-20.0 Goodknight-8.0 Goodknight- 20.5 Mortein-39.9 Maxo-19.5 Harpic-78 Domex-5.1 Vim- 56.0 Sabena-10.0 Nirma-8.0	974.63	721.40
Sub-total						**14,010.40**	**12,115.78**
2 Consumer Healthcare	Ethical[4]	The business has 280 brands catering to therapeutic areas and categorized as part of 'lifestyle' drugs. Generic – Classicals & Asavas	6,000		Baidyanath-22.0 Zandu-5.0	642.43	576.02
	OTC[5]	Women's Health Cough & Cold Gastro Intestinal Rejuvenator Medicated Oil Aches Pain & Fever Memory Tonic Lifestyle Ailments Dermatological	1,350 5,500 3,500 2,000 6,000 2,000 150 500 2,750		Baidyanath Benadryl, Vicks Baidyanath Baidyanath Himani, Baidyanath Glaxo Smithkline Baidyanath, Unjha Baidyanath Paras	865.20	818.98
Sub-total						**1,507.63**	**1,395.00**
3 Foods	Fruit juice	1. Real 2. Activ 3. Coolers 4. Real Activ	2,300	55.0	Tropicana-35.0 Others-10.0	2,274.92	1,735.92
Total Domestic						17,792.95	15,246.70
4 Others						109.00	158.50
5 International						2,918.11	2,256.30
Grand Total[6]						**20,820.06**	**17,661.50**

Source: Company files.

[4] Data as per Dabur's estimates; [5] Market shares data not available; [6] Excluding turnover of group companies.

Exhibit 5 Approach to globalization

1987: Set up a unit in an Export Processing Zone in north India to cater to export markets.
1990: Opened warehousing operations in London to service European markets.
1991: Set up Dabur Overseas Ltd. in Cayman Islands to facilitate overseas investment needs.
1993: Made an initial public officer (IPO) of INR 541.5 million to finance expansion and modernization of manufacturing facilities and development of new facilities.
1993: Enlisted AF Ferguson for advice on restructuring. Based on its recommendations, regrouped into seven profit centers. Brought in professionals to head units and functions.
1997: Hired McKinsey & Company for advice on strengthening competitive position.
1998: Burman family steps aside to hand over management to a professional CEO
1999: Implemented a restructuring template prepared by McKinsey. Withdrew from low margin businesses like merchant exports, veterinary drugs and herbal intermediates.
2002: Commissioned Accenture to review sales and distribution system. Demerged, as per its recommendations, the Pharmaceutical business to get a renewed focus on CPG business.
2003: Relooked at strategy with a global perspective. Decided to leverage herbal platform in entering new markets. Created Dabur International Limited, based at Dubai, as an umbrella organization to provide focus and structure for global operations.
2006: By end-2006, Dabur had established five manufacturing units overseas. International business contributed 11 per cent of sales for the period 2005-06. The new goal: International business should contribute 20 per cent to the revenues by 2012.

Source: Company files.

Exhibit 6 Dtabur international subsidiaries

Particulars	**Dabur Nepal Pvt Ltd**		**Weikfield Intl. (UAE) Ltd**		**Asian Consumer Care Ltd**		**African Consumer Care Ltd**		**Dabur Egypt Ltd**		**Dabur UK Ltd**		**Asian Consumer Care (Pak) Ltd**	
Country	Nepal		Dubai		Bangladesh		Nigeria		Egypt		UK		Pakistan	
Currency	Nepalese Rupee		UAE Dirham		Taka		Nigerian Nira		Egyptian Pound		British Pound		Pakistani Rupee	
Financials (in INR million)	**2007**	**2006**	**2007**	**2006**	**2007**	**2006**	**2007**	**2006**	**2007**	**2006**	**2007**	**2006**	**2007**	**2006**

Capital	49.91	49.91	18.94	19.44	9.73	9.59	15.42	15.91	22.85	23.46	21.72	NA	6.74	NA
Reserves	646.33	598.08	27.87	42.47	(16.16)	(9.33)	(30.42)	(13.69)	36.05	3.02	(1.3)		24.74	
Sales	2198.8	1948.1	387.94	334.14	135.68	144.33	91.0	80.20	206.9	132.50			197.2	
Profit Pre-tax	67.89	60.40	(12.39)	(3.18)	(9.77)	(5.6)	(16.19)	(10.54)	32.2	8.59	(0.65)		32.5	
Profit Post-tax	53.29	49.84	(12.39)	(3.18)	(9.77)	(6.18)	(16.19)	(10.54)	32.2	8.59	(0.65)		24.8	

Source: Company files.

Exhibit 7 Dabur international–market segments

	Strategic Markets		
	Focus Markets	**Potential Markets**	**Opportunistic Markets**
Geographies	GCC-Egypt-Nigeria–Bangladesh-Pakistan and Nepal	Morocco-Sudan-Libya Iraq-Yemen-Kenya Syria-Jordan-Malaysia	Canada - Afghanistan- Mauritius – Thailand
	U.S.A. (for health-care products and private labels only)	U.K. (for health-care products and private labels only)	Any other market as and when available
Attributes	* Ability to mobilize INR 500 million in sales by 2009-10	* Should have the potential to be upgraded into a focus market in three years	* Minimum resources would be deployed
	* To be designated as a profit center with its own sales and distribution and, where local laws permit, its own manufacturing	* Dabur International will not immediately invest financial resources in potential markets	* Top management team at Dabur International will not spend time on these markets
	* Provision for localization of products from India	* Products will not be localized till the market is upgraded to Focus	* Top management team at Dabur International will not spend time on these markets
	* Dabur International will allocate financial resources and dedicated teams		
	* Focus markets would be '*Implementation intensive*'	* Potential Markets would be '*Mind Share Intensive*'	* Need to be margins-positive

(*Continued*)

(*Continued*)

	Strategic Markets		
	Focus Markets	**Potential Markets**	**Opportunistic Markets**
Mandate	Invest and Grow	Monitor for upgrade	Accept orders selectively
Growth in 2006 %	34	12	50
Revenue share target (%)	80	15	5

Source: Company files.

Exhibit 8 Product matrix in (a few) focus markets

	Country					
Product	**GCC**	**Egypt**	**Nigeria**	**Bangladesh**	**Pakistan**	**U.S.A.**
Hair oil	Focus product	Focus product		Focus product	Focus product	
Hair cream	Focus product	Focus product				
Shampoo	Support product	Support product				
Ayurvedic						Focus product
Digestives				Support product	Focus product	
Soap			Focus product			
Toothpaste	Support product	Support product	Focus product	Support product	Support product	
Insect repellant		Support product	Focus product	Support product	Support product	
Toilet cleaners				Focus product	Focus product	

Source: Company files.

Exhibit 9 Dabur international–consumer segments

	Arab Consumer	**Asian Consumer**	**African Consumer**
Footprints	Middle East & North Africa	South Asia, United Kingdom and United States	East, West and South Africa
Target customer	Arab female	Asian male	African male & female
Core categories	Hair Oils Hair Creams Shampoos Oral care	Hair Oils Shampoos Digestives Oral care	Oral Care Personal Wash Home Care (Insect repellent)
Core market	Dubai	India	Nigeria
Market size (in INR million)	1,340	1,500	320
Supply markets and market sizes (in INR million)	GCC–760 North Africa–460 Iran, Iraq–60–60	Pakistan–440 Nepal–640 Bangladesh–200 UAE–210	Central Africa–10 East Africa–60 South Africa–10 West Africa–240
Key market attributes	• 80 per cent of the population is Arabic • High purchasing power	• Replicating Indian brand architecture and product portfolio • Leveraging learning from Indian marketing mix and media strategy	• High oral care penetration • English speaking • Medium competitive intensity

Source: Company files.

Exhibit 10 Nigeria–country risk profile

	Nigeria		
Population	130 million – 60 per cent below poverty line		
GDP per capita	US$450 per annum		
Risk Assessment	**Probability of Risk**	**Impact of Risk**	**Overall Risk (Probability + Impact)**
Market risk	Low	High	Medium
Supplier risk	Low	Medium	Low
Competitor risk	High	High	High
Implementation risk	High	High	High
Political & Economic	High	High	High
Regulatory	Low	Medium	Low
Financial	Medium	High	Medium

Source: Company files.

Exhibit 11 Nigeria–business risk profile

	Oral Care	Skin Care	Hair Care	Health Care	Home Care
Market size (INR million)	Rural: 2,000 Urban: 3,000	6,000	NA	350	NA
Products	Toothpaste	Soap	Relaxers Hair pomade	Glucose	Mosquito repellant cream
Comp.intensity	Low-Medium	Low-Medium	Low-Medium	Low	Low
Strategic intent	To become the second largest player	To become the third largest player in soaps	To create a market for hair oils	To become a strong player in glucose market	To replicate the Indian product portfolio
Imperatives	• Become a leader in herbal niche • Launch herbal gel	Launch a herbal soap with localized ingredients		Launch Dabur Glucose	• Leverage India competency • Launch Odomos cream
Strategic issues	• Unilever and P&G strong • Herbal niche not crowded	• Soap market fragmented • Unilever and P&G strong • Small players and imports have > 50% market share • Soap is not a core category for Dabur	• Hair care is beauty related and cosmetic • Dabur has therapeutic and not cosmetic equity	A one player play	• Coil is the predominant product form. • No market for cream
Challenge	Can Dabur successfully target herbal niche and establish a strong market presence?	Can Dabur operate in soap successfully? Can it extend herbal equity to soap?	Can Dabur leverage its strengths?	Can Dabur become No. 2 player?	Should Dabur create a new cream category in Nigeria?

Source: Company files.

21

Sat & Co.

Market Orientation

In early 2006, poor management of resources and lack of market orientation hit machine tool manufacturer Sat & Co. and led it to a loss of 50 per cent of sales. The company consisted of two divisions: the lathe division that manufactured the lathe machines, and the computer numerical control (CNC) division that assembled CNC machines. Both divisions were operating at barely half of their capacity and even struggling to achieve that. The lathe division manufactured very basic lathes, whereas the CNC division assembled very technologically advanced machines. Yet both divisions had failed to satisfy their customers' needs. The chairperson of the board of directors, Sat Cartland, was adamant that both divisions must survive, which meant that he was faced with making some harsh decisions. Directors also thought that recovery could only be achieved through the implementation of a market orientation strategy; i.e., the company must meet the customers' needs. Following this decision, John McGuire was hired as marketing director to implement the concept of market orientation. McGuire had a master's degree in new product development and an MBA in marketing and had significant experience in conducting market research as well as developing industrial products. He was a fellow of the Institute of Mechanical Engineers, England, which was the United Kingdom's qualifying body for mechanical engineers with about 83,000 members worldwide. McGuire was faced with several challenges: first, he must increase the plant utilization and second, develop and/or modify the current range of products/machines to meet the customers' needs, and thus regain the lost market share. McGuire was required to see Cartland in about six months with his recommendations.

THE MACHINE TOOL INDUSTRY

Operating a conventional machine tool was a task requiring a high skill level. The operator positioned the work piece, selected the appropriate tools in their correct sequences for each job, and manually operated the handles and levers that controlled the relative position and speed of the tool and work piece to produce parts with the required dimensions and features. The degree of automation of machine tools was as varied as their area of application. One of the major areas of the operation of machine tools was cutting. Innovation in the machine tool design was only limited by the degree of technological development. The automation and flexibility of machines depended on the nature of the components and the quantities to be produced. For example, single-purpose or special-purpose machines were available to the user, as were universal machines offering a wide range of applications.

In the 1940s, it became possible to make machine tools that could carry out a sequence of operations automatically by employing complex arrangements of cams and gears. It was therefore no longer necessary to have one operator at each machine. The operator's job was reduced to loading the work piece, switching on the machine, removing the finished part, and replacing dull tools. Removing dull tools and resetting the machine to carry different sequences of operations was a demanding and time-consuming job. Although these machines could be altered to carry out a wide range of different functions, the long set-up times and high costs of new hardware programs meant that they were only effective with comparatively long production runs or with job order applications where each job required different configurations of tools.

In the 1950s, the computerization of machine tools took place. To make the task of setting and resetting the machine tools easier and quicker, the automatic mechanical controls were replaced with electronic logic circuits. Beside the machine tool stood a plug board (like a telephonist's switchboard) into which the operator plugged the required sequence of operations. This was the first version and it was called a numeric control (NC) machine.

In the early 1960s, machine tools were joined to small computers. The sequence of instructions that the machine followed was stored on a paper tape. To change the sequence of operations, the operator had to change the tape prepared by a programmer. The increased demands in both the performance and precision of machine tools saw further automation of the machine tools, which resulted in the development of a wide range of alternative controls. For example, the development of electronics and computer programs had a marked effect on machine tool controls. The arrival of the microprocessor chip made control techniques even easier than before.

During the 1970s, the machine tool contained a built-in, programmable computer with a conversational video display unit and keyboard. This removed the need for paper tape. The availability of small, reliable computer components in the form of a microprocessor expedited the development of computer numeric control machines. These machines were equipped with adaptive controlling devices which could adjust their speeds and other operating characteristics by taking into account any adverse working conditions that could arise during the manufacturing process such as tool wear, torque deflection, etc. Human intervention at this stage was reduced to loading and removing work pieces and replacing dulled tools. If each machine tool could be operated and controlled by its own computer, it was possible to schedule and control the work of several machines from one central computer, which indicated to the operator through a video screen which work pieces to fit on to which machines. This technology was commercialized in the 1980s. Exhibit 1 shows the development and level of mechanization of machine tools.

Clearly, without the development of these types of machines, the high living standards of the present time would be unthinkable. In some of the most developed countries, approximately 10 per cent of all machines built were machine tools and about 10 per cent of the workforce in machine manufacturing was concerned with machine tools. In the United Kingdom, the machine tool industry was a small but important sector of the manufacturing industry. Machine tools were essential for reproducing the technologies required in an industrialized economy. As machine tool manufacturers typically sold their products worldwide, a weak domestic machine tool industry meant that manufacturers risked losing access to the latest manufacturing technologies. Further, as the machine tool industry supplied capital goods to other capital goods industries, it suffered from the cycles of economic demand (see Exhibit 2). In addition, this industry helped foster innovation in manufacturing processes and played a key role in defence production and the automotive industry. Exhibit 3 shows trends for the machine tool industry in the United Kingdom from 1995 till 2005.

GEOGRAPHICAL LOCATION, EMPLOYMENT AND CONCENTRATION

Machine tool manufacturers were spread across the United Kingdom, particularly located in West Yorkshire, the West and East Midlands, and to a lesser extent in the southeast regions. Differences in skill levels or employment conditions had created employment fluctuations that had been substantially sharper in the machine tool sector than in the durable goods sector of the country. Average changes in employment in the machine tool industry were more than average changes in employment in the durable goods sectors. Industry observers cited this pattern as one of the reasons for the industry's conservative management and the inability of many machine tool firms to attract and retain the brightest engineering, managerial and technical talent. Employment fluctuations caused by market turbulence were seen as a factor that was detrimental to developing new machines. Also, most companies in the United Kingdom had been traditionally small and closely held with narrow product lines. Thus, this industry could not be characterized by firm concentration; it was rather fragmented.

DEFINITION OF MACHINE TOOL

A machine tool was defined as a power-driven machine, not portable by hand when in operation, which worked metal by cutting, forming, physio-chemical (or non-contact) machining, or a combination of these techniques. Metal-cutting machines included lathes, grinding machines, milling machines, and machining centres. Typical metal-forming machines were presses, forges, and punching, shearing, and bending machines. Modern machine tools were controlled by computers and were referred to as CNC machine tools. These machines conformed to the Standard Industrial Classification Codes 3541 (metal-cutting) and 3542 (metal-forming).

COMPANY BACKGROUND

Lathes for turning wood have been in use since 1650 but it was not till the end of the 19th century that lathes for turning metals were invented. Sat & Co. was one of the companies that set up a small factory to manufacture small machine tools. As time passed, the company progressed. In 1966, Sat & Co. set up a lathe machine tool division and manufactured basic manually-operated lathe machines. Ten years later, the company expanded and began manufacturing single and multi-spindle automatic lathes, copy and multi-tool lathes, grinding machines, transfer lines and broaching machineries. In the early 1990s, with the arrival of the electronic age, this company set up another division—CNC—responsible for manufacturing a range of CNC machines and selling them globally. Continuous development of the product range led to the addition of extra features, enhancing further the capabilities of these machines. Although it was a small company, it strived for improving its products continually, and for providing modern and better manufacturing technology throughout the world. All of the company's products had been manufactured to International Standard Organization standards of quality to ensure that customers received consistently high quality products. In fact, all the products were guaranteed to be of premium build using the latest technology. The company employed personnel in design, production, sales and services to market a comprehensive range of machines. Additionally, it provided turnkey engineering solutions to suit specific customer requirements. The company had been supplying machine tools and providing support to customers for over 100 years in over 100 countries through a combination of owned and independent distributors worldwide.

This company took pride in its ability to service machines and in its readiness to provide full customer support in the event of machine breakdown. To maintain the high level of customer support and service, the company held a significant number of spare parts in stock all the time, and dispatched over 90 per cent of orders received before noon of the same working day. Another aspect of customer support was taking care of potential customers' needs prior to sales. The sales personnel of the company would begin by evaluating the buyer's needs and would continue with the offer of various financing packages, if needed. Overall, the company acquired a good reputation for its quality of machines and services and had customers from around the world. Certainly, the company was market-oriented as it had market-led skills necessary to meet customer needs.

However, from 1996 onwards, the company saw a constant drop in sales in both the lathe and CNC divisions of the company. Cartland suspected that the company was focusing too much on technology to improve the productivity and efficiency of the CNC machines. The constant addition of extra features to the CNC machines was not only making these machines more expensive, but also more complicated to operate. Moreover, not all customers wanted those extra features. For example, it was unnecessary to offer a three-axis spindle as a standard attachment when customers wanted only one, or in some cases only a two-axis spindle. At the same time, no attention was paid to upgrading the lathe division. The lathes were still very basic and functional in nature, and thus had low efficiency. Even though these basic lathe machines were inexpensive and workers required no extensive training to operate them, there were few buyers. As a result of the company's failure to focus on the market, sales from both divisions declined to a point where it was absolutely necessary to turn around the divisions.

Being an international company, Sat & Co. had customers from the United States, the United Kingdom, the rest of Europe, and the rest of the world in the proportion of 35 per cent, 25 per cent, 25 per cent and 15 per cent, respectively. Although these numbers looked impressive, Cartland wanted to venture into the markets of developing countries such as India and China, where approximately 10 per cent growth rates in their GDPs were expected. Cartland thought that his company could compete with Indian machine tool manufacturers over quality even if Indian machines were cheaper than British machines. However, Cartland was also aware that Indians were catching up in terms of the technology and quality, and that now they had access to foreign investments capital that they could use to upgrade their production facilities and to distribute their machines globally.

Cartland also knew that the global machine tool market was US$65 billion and that the demand for machine tools was to increase over five per cent per year through 2009 to more than $84 billion. Much of the projected growth was expected to come from within the developed countries, as many existing production facilities needed modernization and upgrades following several years of under investment. Growth was also expected from developing countries such as India, China, Malaysia and Thailand. These countries were expected to experience above-average growth rates along with both South Korea and Taiwan, which had become major producers and consumers of machine tools in the last five years or so. Further, due to the expansion of the European Community and thus the inflow of capital for investments, Eastern European countries were also expected to fuel demands for machine tools because the modernization of their existing plants was needed. Further Japanese investments in Brazil could also give rise to demand for machine tools. Contrarily, in the United Kingdom, where machine tool markets were highly mature and very cyclical, at best only economic recovery was expected.

McGuire had been hired with excellent references for his proven skills in turning around such companies. He was asked to diagnose problems with the divisions, and come up with his recommendations. Cartland said to McGuire, "John, clearly the sky is the limit. We must be market-oriented. Perhaps we were not able to satisfy both sets of customers because we were offering superfluous functions in the CNC lathes and not enough in the basic lathe machines. What do you think?"

EXTERNAL INFORMATION GENERATION PERTAINING TO CUSTOMERS

To diagnose problems with the company, McGuire wanted to conduct market research in order to reveal the needs of the company's customers. While going through previous sales records of the company's customers, McGuire learnt that more than 65 per cent of all engineering shops in the United Kingdom had at least a lathe machine manufactured by the company. So, he wanted to survey the end-users of these machines. The objectives were to discover if the end-users (1) experienced any technical difficulties with the functioning of the machines; (2) would try new efficient machines; and (3) would like the existing machine to be modified.

Motivated by his idea of exploring the end-users' needs, more than 3,500 questionnaires were mailed to these customers to establish specifications and factual details of machines such as size, accuracy, and the number of hours worked on a machine in a week. This was followed by 300 telephone interviews to establish potential users' preferences relating to details such as colour, country of origin, after-sales requirements, preferred methods of programming, and preferred sources of CNC controllers. Respondents were also asked if they would like to recommend any modifications to the existing machines to the R&D department. Two hundred senior level managers were also interviewed to ascertain the price they would be willing to pay for a machine with a particular specification. The focus of the interview was to measure the extent to which Sat & Co. was able to meet the expectations of its customers. Although face-to-face interviews confirmed that the company's good brand name was not associated with the performance of basic lathe machines, it did confirm that the market was willing to try something new. Awareness testing results showed (1) that the company was regarded as a superior lathe supplier in the United Kingdom and abroad; (2) that the company had a reputation for good quality and value-for-money; and (3) that the company's lathes were also considered to offer good resale value in general. Further, the forecasting suggested a demand for at least 1,000 machines on an annual basis. But the difficulty was that this company had a production capacity of only 300 machines annually.

INTERNAL INFORMATION DISSEMINATION PERTAINING TO CUSTOMERS

McGuire took the market research findings seriously, and communicated the customer-related information to all the departments as quickly as possible. To make the information flow freely from the marketing department to the shop floor, he even relocated the marketing department inside the manufacturing plant, and made his office on the same floor of the building as the commercial manager of the sales and service department. This strategy enabled McGuire to conduct internal audits on a regular basis to identify if the key attributes of a machine were being utilized effectively. If they were not, the reasons were discovered and corrective actions were put in place immediately. The unwanted attributes were considered for removal in the development of the next batch of machines and prices were adjusted accordingly. McGuire was determined to achieve market orientation by developing low-cost simple machines with fewer frills. The in-house research team of the company conducted an audit by interviewing end-users of the machines and discovered that the company should also consider manufacturing a Flexible Manufacturing System (FMS) as there was a significant demand for it.

THE PRODUCT SPECIFICATION AND PRICING

Analysis of the data revealed that customers did not find all the functionalities of the CNC machines useful. Eighty-two per cent of the respondents said that they needed only two-axis spindles instead of three-axis spindles in the machines. It was also learned from the R&D department that it was possible to reduce the size of the machine by 15 per cent to achieve the most sought-after specifications in the machines. The data also established precise machine specifications and exact corresponding selling prices. Now it was McGuire's responsibility to develop the product with the technical specifications and the specified price for the market. Because of the competition and the loss of sales for the last few years, there was absolutely no room to deviate either from the established technical specifications or selling prices. It was confirmed that the potential customers were *only* prepared to pay the prices determined by the market research.

END-USERS' PERCEPTIONS OF THE COMPANY

After settling down with the technical specifications and prices for the new machines, McGuire was curious to know the extent to which his company was currently successful in meeting the market orientation expectations of the company's end-users. As a result, 500 customers who used the machines manufactured by the company in the past three years were randomly selected. These customers were asked to give their impressions of the market orientation of Sat & Co. by circling a number on the 7-point Likert scale (1=strongly disagree and 7=strongly agree) corresponding to the items listed in the questionnaire (see Exhibit 4). On the scale, 1 was equivalent to zero per cent whereas 7 represented 100 per cent agreement with the item. For clarity, responses to the questions were converted into percentage points (Exhibit 5). McGuire also completed the same questionnaire *independently* to determine the extent to which he thought his company was practising those market-oriented activities. Comparison of the evaluations between McGuire and his customers confirmed that Sat & Co. had failed to meet its customers' expectations on more than half of the items presented in the questionnaire. Clearly, a gap between the customers' expectations and the company's delivery was detected.

Also, McGuire was wondering if it was the right time to enter in the FMS segment of the machine tool industry. He knew that FMS represented a new application for machine tools in which groups of machine tools were integrated and controlled by a central computer, which in turn controlled robots that moved work pieces from machine to machine and positioned a work piece at each machine. A greater degree of automation than conventional machines could be commercially attractive to his company, given the pressure to reduce the production costs and increase the profit margin. In fact, the prospects for automated factories in the metalworking industry were quite high, as most companies wished to purchase an FMS, which could take care of inventory management, scheduling details and the production process itself. In-house research revealed that the FMS enabled Coma Diesel Engine Company to cut production time by half, reduce annual warranty expenses by an estimated £200,000 and slash the selling price by more than 25 per cent. McGuire was convinced that the specifications of the parts to produce an FMS were not a problem, as he could use the existing in-house computer-aided design (CAD) technology to design an FMS and to connect it to a computer-aided manufacturing (CAM) system. So his task would be to develop a new system that would be based on the integration of information, and electronic and mechanical technologies. Although the design and installation of an FMS were expensive, its efficiency was worth extra costs to customers. But that also meant that McGuire needed extra money to invest in his plant to equip it for the production of FMSs.

Now, McGuire needed to determine reasons as to why this company, once known for high quality machines, was being perceived as a non-market-oriented company. These findings forced him to rethink his strategy for the company and develop a set of recommendations. Time was running out.

Exhibit 1 Level of mechanization

Initiating control source	Type of machine response		Power source	Level of Mechanization
From a variable in the environment	Responds with action	Modifies own action over a range of variation	Mechanical-Non-mechanical	17 Anticipates action required and adjusts to provide it
				16 Corrects performance while operating
				15 Corrects performance after operating
				14 Identifies and selects appropriate set of actions
		Selects from a limited range of possible fixed actions		13 Segregates rejects according to measurement
				12 Changes speed, position, direction according to measurement
				11 Records performance
	Responds with signal			10 Signals pre-selected values of measurement. Includes error detection
				9 Measures characteristics of work
From a control mechanism that directs a predetermined pattern of action	Fixed within the machine			8 Actuated by introduction of work piece or material
				7 Power tool system, remote controlled
				6 Power tool, program control
				5 Power tool, fixed cycle (single function)
From man	Variable			4 Power tool, hand control
				3 Powered hand tool
			Manual	2 Hand tool
				1 Hand

Source: James Bright, Automation and Management, Harvard Business School Publishing, Boston, 1958.

Exhibit 2 Private sector manufacturing business investment in capital equipment 1955-2005 (in £ Billion)

1990	14.4	1998	16.5
1991	13.2	1999	15.1
1992	12.0	2000	14.3
1993	11.2	2001	13.6
1994	12.0	2002	11.4
1995	14.1	2003	11.1
1996	14.1	2004	10.5
1997	15.6	2005	11.7

Source: The Manufacturing Technologies Association, "Basic Facts," 2007, United Kingdom.

Exhibit 3 Trends for machine tools in the UK (in £ million at current prices, 2007)

Year	Sales of U.K. Goods	Export	Import
1995	642	441	563
1996	733	546	642
1997	808	459	707
1998	696	538	698
1999	560	510	520
2000	580	464	574
2001	621	492	543
2002	470	384	452
2003	415	401	389
2004	401	402	381
2005	395	438	404

Source: The Manufacturing Technologies Association, "Basic Facts," 2007, United Kingdom.

Exhibit 4 Questionnaire

With regards to the following items (on the 7-point scale where 1 represents "strongly disagree" and 7 being "strongly agree"), how would you score the following measure of market orientation of Sat & Co., which is the supplier of the machine you have been using for production for the last three years or more?

Items	Relating to Market Orientation Scale:	Strongly Disagree				Strongly Agree		
Q1.	Sat & Co. reveals our needs through customers' research.	1	2	3	4	5	6	7
Q2.	Sat & Co. produces and offers products that are truly satisfying our needs.	1	2	3	4	5	6	7
Q3.	Sat & Co. commits resources in research and development to ensure the quality of the products to suit our needs.	1	2	3	4	5	6	7

Q4. In practice, Sat & Co. avoids conflicts between market orientation and profit orientation.	1	2	3	4	5	6	7
Q5. We are aware of how the entire business of Sat & Co. can contribute towards creating value for us.	1	2	3	4	5	6	7
Q6. Sat & Co. keeps its promises on services after sales, and delivery on time.	1	2	3	4	5	6	7
Q7. Sat & Co. is prepared to disagree with us in order to achieve a better decision for us.	1	2	3	4	5	6	7
Q8. Sat & Co. tries to influence us by information rather than by pressure.	1	2	3	4	5	6	7
Q9. A Sat & Co. representative normally meets us once a year to assess our needs.	1	2	3	4	5	6	7
Q10. Representatives from the manufacturing department of Sat & Co. interact directly with us to assess how best to serve us.	1	2	3	4	5	6	7
Q11. Sat & Co. frequently polls our end-users to assure the quality of its products and services.	1	2	3	4	5	6	7
Q12. Sat & Co. is slow to detect fundamental shifts in the British machine tool industry; e.g., competition, technology regulations.	1	2	3	4	5	6	7
Q13. Sat & Co. tends to ignore changes in the product or services our organization needs.	1	2	3	4	5	6	7
Q14. Sat & Co. reviews its product development efforts to ensure that they are in line with our organizational needs.	1	2	3	4	5	6	7
Q15. Sat & Co. normally takes corrective actions immediately for any complaints.	1	2	3	4	5	6	7
Q16. Sat & Co. is a market-oriented company.	1	2	3	4	5	6	7

Exhibit 5 Market orientation expectations

Items	McGuire's Independent Evaluation of his Company (in Percentage)	End-users' Evaluations of the Company (in Percentage)
Q1.	100	62
Q2.	100	90
Q3.	100	76
Q4.	58	52
Q5.	58	62
Q6.	72	42
Q7.	58	67
Q8.	72	81
Q9.	100	86
Q10.	100	86
Q11.	100	43

(Continued)

(Continued)

Items	McGuire's Independent Evaluation of his Company (in Percentage)	End-users' Evaluations of the Company (in Percentage)
Q12.	15	76
Q13.	100	62
Q14.	100	57
Q15.	71	42
Q16.	100	71

22

Infosys

The Challenge of Global Branding

Padmini Murty and Viren Desai prepared this case under the supervision of Jeff Saperstein solely to provide material for class discussion. The authors do not intend to illustrate either effective or ineffective handling of a managerial situation. The authors may have disguised certain names and other identifying information to protect confidentiality.

In December 2003, Aditi Mishra was appointed head of brand and communications for Infosys. She had been in her job only four months when she was asked to recommend the next phase of the marketing plan. While in the airport terminal in San Francisco, during her trip to client accounts in Seattle, Las Vegas, Houston, New York and London, she reflected on the complex and challenging task. Mishra was asked to not only consider how to increase the visibility of Infosys as a brand, but also to consider how to compete with global players, such as IBM and Accenture, as well as domestic Indian companies, such as Wipro.

The branding challenge for Infosys was not to compete with IBM or Accenture in brand awareness, but to ensure that Infosys, through its reputation for predictable and excellent results, would be included in the short list for major Information Technology (IT) outsource bidding. In that sense, consistently being considered in the number-three slot in requests for proposals would be a great accomplishment. To achieve this status, Infosys needed to rapidly differentiate itself from other IT outsourcing companies.

Management had identified overall company top-line revenue growth as the means to achieve 30 to 40 per cent annual increases but had not allowed for any appreciable budget for marketing communications. The key to the global brand strategy would not be through brand-image advertising, but by communicating its solutions strategy.[1] The marketing goals for Infosys were to be on the short list of providers for the largest, most sophisticated assignments for IT services and to bid against IBM and Accenture, while leapfrogging over other competitors in the fast-growing and fragmented IT outsourcing market.

Mishra was contemplating how she should structure her plan, taking into account that there were four corporate strategies that could define Infosys's future identity:

1. Compete globally for end-to-end services, including high-end consulting, by leveraging the current Global Delivery Model (GDM), which included consulting in IT services.
2. Maintain the status quo.
3. Focus on expanding leadership in the growing domestic Indian market for IT services.
4. Market end-to-end service capabilities to provide vertical industry solutions (such as retail, banking, insurance, etc.).

THE OUTSOURCING OF IT

Outsourcing Information Technologies (IT) was a major trend for multinational companies that were globalizing their business activities in multi-location operations. India was the primary market for IT outsourcing, and revenues had grown from almost \$3 billion in 1997 to 12.5 billion in 2003[2]. As Infosys was the leading IT company headquartered in India, how it charted its future would have a major impact on both the outsourcing industry and the emergence of India as a major global competitor in the innovation economy.

April 13, 2004 marked a historic day for Infosys Technologies Ltd., as it became India's first listed IT firm to exceed \$1 billion in annual revenues. Infosys started in 1981, with seven people, \$250 and a dream.[3] It had grown to become the leading software development company in the country. However, Infosys now faced different challenges. For Infosys to continue its rapid growth, management would need to establish a global brand. Establishing a global identity that would distinguish the company from just another outsourcing vendor was a crucial issue. Senior management needed to address the following considerations:

- How would the solutions strategy be determined for the future growth of Infosys? Would it be geared towards Infosys becoming an end-to-end IT/business process outsourcing (BPO) provider in various industry verticals through the development and acquisition of world-class high-end IT consulting services by leveraging the Global Delivery Model? Or, would the focus be using the Global Delivery Model to hone current distinctive competencies by undertaking penetration of additional industry sectors?
- How would Infosys meet the challenges of creating a global brand that would highlight the uniqueness of the company, while other multinational competitors, such as Accenture and IBM, also operating out of India, were using similar cost and human resource advantages?
- What would be the core positioning strategy for Infosys to enable a global identity for continued growth?

---

[1] Solutions strategy in the IT industry denotes a product as a brand-value proposition.

[2] www.nasscom.org.

[3] www.infy.com/company/billiondollarmilestone.asp.

COMPANY ANALYSIS

Seven professionals, spearheaded by Narayana N.R. Murthy, then chief executive officer (CEO) and chairman, founded Infosys Technologies Ltd. in 1981. The stringent economic policies of the Indian government prior to 1991 made it extremely difficult for companies like Infosys to import computer hardware and other equipment essential for business in the high-tech market. However, by 1991, Infosys was in an ideal position to capitalize on the rationalization of taxes, reductions in import tariffs and incentives to encourage exports. Infosys revenues grew to more than $1 billion in fiscal year 2004.

As business expectations from IT services increased, Infosys grew from being a developer of software programs to being a solution provider for business problems (see Exhibit 1) and successfully managed to align its services to move up the value chain. Infosys services now ranged from consulting (although still in the nascent stage) and IT programming to the development of overall business solutions to increase the competitiveness of its clients in the marketplace (see Exhibit 2). In India, Infosys was one of the top software exporters with more than 97 per cent of its revenues generated by software exports.

The Infosys business model could be readily understood through the Predictability, Sustainability, Profitability, De-risking (PSPD) model for meeting customer satisfaction requirements and achieving growth. Infosys achieved highly predictable results, which had been key to its success (see Exhibit 3). Approximately 85 per cent of Infosys business was from repeat customers, a clear testimony to high customer loyalty and satisfaction.

The Global Delivery Model (GDM), the backbone of Infosys's delivery model, illustrated how division of a project into components that could be developed independently and concurrently, could provide reliable profitability through systematic work processes, while maintaining high quality. Hence, a major part of the project could be executed from cheaper off-shore locations while the balance of the project could be executed from the more expensive on-site client.

A key factor for Infosys's success was that the GDM was not only about cost; it was also about the best quality: doing work where it made the most economic sense with the minimum risk (see Exhibit 4). In addition, this system allowed Infosys to take advantage of the time difference between India and the United States, home to the majority of its clients, creating a virtual 24-hour workday. An important offshoot of reducing the cost of the project was that the savings could be re-invested in the client's business for further business impact.

INDUSTRY ANALYSIS

The Indian IT industry comprised IT software services and exports, domestic IT market, hardware, peripherals and components, and training. Software services and exports was the largest segment, occupying more than 60 per cent of the Indian IT Market.[4] The software services and exports category included:

- Development and maintenance of applications (knowledge management, customer relationship management, enterprise resource planning and security management portals)
- Systems integration or interfacing between two or more applications, such as Oracle and SAP or Peoplesoft and Siebel, for implementation rollouts and upgrades of these packaged applications
- Research and development services and IT-enabled services

---

4 www.nasscom.org.

- Business Process Outsourcing, the other sub-segment of the software exports, comprised all the software services across several industry verticals, which were outsourced across a different geographic domain (see Exhibit 5)

Domestic Indian IT Market

According to Professor Rafiq Dossani, senior research scholar of East Asian studies at Stanford University, the domestic Indian IT market had a great potential for growth and could provide a plethora of opportunities to Indian firms such as Infosys, in various product and service offerings lines. Industries such as insurance, telecommunications and banking services were registering high growth in India and could be lucrative markets for Indian IT players.

The Indian domestic IT industry, which had traditionally lagged behind the IT software and services export segment, continued to increase 11 per cent in 2003, with revenues of US$7.4 billion. The key vertical markets that the domestic Indian IT sector catered to were government, energy, education, small office, banking and finance, manufacturing, IT and telecom (see Exhibit 6).

Infosys's major competitors in India were TCS, Wipro and Satyam, who were building similar consumer bases. However, Infosys's revenue and market capitalization were burgeoning, and the company could be well-positioned with world-class infrastructure, labor and domain expertise to capture the Indian domestic IT market. (see Exhibit 7).

Mishra believed that Indian IT companies shied away from the domestic market because revenues in dollars from the foreign markets provided a more attractive profit margin than those received in rupees in the domestic market. The leaders in the Indian IT industry had grown by earning in dollars and spending in rupees. This strategy was a source of strength as their profit margins were significantly higher than their global competitors.

Indian IT Software Services and Exports

The Indian IT category was the fastest growing segment of the Indian economy (see Exhibit 8). Leading multinationals, such as IBM, were investing in India, capitalizing on the abundant and unique skill sets of India's workforce. The IT software and services market in India had continued to be driven by exports, exhibiting robust growth during the 2003/04 period. The United States and Europe accounted for 86 per cent of all global business outsourcing spending, with the United States being the largest customer of software services from India.[5]

Indian IT Enabled Services and Business Process Outsourcing

The Indian IT enabled services and business process outsourcing (ITES-BPO) market was a crucial sub-segment of the IT Software services and exports and was a key driver of the overall Indian IT software and services sector. In 2003/04, the ITES-BPO category revenues were US$3.6 billion. According to recent studies by the National Association of Software and Services Companies (NASSCOM), the Indian ITES-BPO industry grew at about 54 per cent during 2003/04.

The key trends in the BPO industry were:

- Maturation and consolidation following a large number of mergers and acquisitions during 2002/03.

[5] www.nasscom.org.

- An increase in multi-vendor and build-operate-transfer (BOT) contracts, which through joint ventures, offered services from two vendors and offered advantages such as low risks, scalability and competitive pricing.
- Vendors moving up the value chain to offer high-end services, such as equity research and analytics, insurance, and technology support and development.

Growth within the ITES-BPO segment was focusing on the larger players that could offer clients benefits such as scalability, delivery capability, track record and customer referrals. The industry was also earmarked by service offerings in client locations and setting up facilities in other low-cost ITES-BPO destinations.

India's value proposition was based on its low cost-high quality-scalability model, which gave it an edge over other emerging ITES-BPO destinations, such as Ireland, the Philippines, China and Latin American countries. The Indian ITES-BPO service providers offered higher service and quality levels by implementing industry standards, such as SEI-CMM, ISO and Six Sigma. The average cost saving is 40 to 50 per cent, compared with U.S. service providers, and India had a large pool of skilled knowledge workers.

Global BPO and ITO Trends- Changing Customer Expectations

Global outsourcing spending for business processing outsourcing (BPO) continued to increase by 11 per cent every year. Information technology outsourcing (ITO) accounted for almost 10 per cent of this spending. U.S Fortune 500 companies were the major market for these services.[6] Outsourcing was expected to continue to increase across the developed world economies (see Exhibit 5).

The IT industry had experienced a steep downturn in fund creation because of the dot-com bust and economic recession in 2000/01. These events led to a mass outsourcing binge by many of the companies, primarily to save costs on IT overhead. However, with the exponential growth in the outsourcing market over the past few years, this market was now beginning to mature. Expectations were beginning to change. Many managers no longer simply viewed outsourcing just as a cheaper alternative, but as an enabler of an effective business model to gain value for the company. Infosys could use this opportunity to *establish a global brand*, achieve market penetration and market extension in an increasingly competitive market. Infosys needed to emphasize qualitative advantages, and not just cost-efficiency. Buyer selection criteria, such as "references" and "reputation of the provider," "breadth of skills," "industry expertise" and "prior relationships" were gaining importance over "cost." Cost efficiency was a necessary deliverable for buyers when selecting outsourcing providers, but was no longer the determining factor (see Exhibit 9). While references and reputation had emerged as the most important selection criteria for buyers, providers still ranked cost as the number-one criterion for evaluating their potential as providers. This bridge in perception was a clear indication that the providers did not fully appreciate that buyers were seeking confidence, in addition to cost, as a determining factor for provider selection. The preferences of the buyers and the perceptions of the providers affirmed the importance of branding and positioning for the providers.

As the importance of outsourcing became increasingly evident, so did the need to quantitatively measure the success of an outsourcing venture. Not surprisingly, "timeliness" and "deliverable quality" topped the list of how buyers evaluated the overall success of the outsourcing endeavor. The providers seem to be on track with the overall success initiatives of the buyers.[7]

---

[6] "Business Process Outsourcing - The New Growth Sector", India Info line.

[7] Infosys Technologies company document.

Backlash on Outsourcing from Stakeholders

As more and more jobs were moving offshore from the United States, a major area of concern was the backlash from the various stakeholders. The stakeholders included the government, media and the employees. Election-year politics in the United States had increased pressure on the U.S. government to restrict companies from outsourcing offshore in order to protect jobs within the United States. Furthermore, buyers feared the deterioration of relationships with employees whose jobs were lost and who were forced to work with the offshore partners. Employee backlash was an extremely sensitive topic for companies as it jeopardized employee loyalty that companies had established over a period of time.

Outsourcing Rationale

The two most important questions that a buyer must answer regarding the outsourcing market were:

- Why should a service or product be outsourced?
- What should be outsourced?

Even though reduction of costs remained the prime outsourcing rationale, more and more companies were outsourcing in order to make internal resources available for critical activities. Companies were viewing outsourcing as a catalyst for growth. From the table of Key IT functions outsourced (see Exhibit 10), it was evident that most of the buyers outsourced areas that were exceedingly expensive and lacked internal skill sets. Nearly 25 per cent of the buyers used a structured framework to determine candidates for outsourcing. However, the success of these frameworks was questionable because the buyers relied heavily on cost reduction rather than the value added through the development of beneficial outsourcing strategies. Thus, the key issues for Infosys were to recognize its distinctive competencies in the outsourcing market and then position its brand in order to successfully capitalize on these changing trends.

CHALLENGES FOR INFOSYS

Operating Challenge: Expanding High-End Consulting Across Business Units

On April 8, 2004, Infosys announced the launch of Infosys Consulting Inc., formed by senior leaders from some of the leading consulting firms who had joined Infosys to make their clients more competitive and to add more value with better results and a lower cost proposition (see Exhibit 11). Infosys pioneered this new model of consulting with more than 20 years of expertise in the Global Delivery Model, a demonstrated operational and financial discipline and a commitment to become a strong global powerhouse. This high-end business consulting venture of Infosys had its own challenges, both because it would be initially unprofitable, and there was a high level of competition from the giants who had already established a presence on the Indian turf. Operationally, Infosys had established a reputation as a low-cost operation and a high-efficiency service provider in the IT services field. However, it was now venturing into high-end business consulting, which by definition would be high cost.

However, Mishra believed that by not adopting the partner model (with high hourly rates for senior partners) Infosys could have a better price-value relationship than the major consulting firms. The typical consulting company allocated most of the money to the partners and then reported low profits. Infosys did not have a partner model. She also argued that Infosys Consulting could not be looked at in isolation:

> Consulting defines and designs solutions; they have to be developed and delivered as well. For every dollar in revenue from consulting there would be roughly $3 in revenue from off-shore development. As far as the client is concerned, it's a total package. If the development/delivery is done through GDM, then the total cost of the solution comes down for the customer. Infosys Consulting, with its emphasis on better solution design and definition, and tight coupling with the GDM, would still offer a great value proposition for the customer. Operationally, we are committed to move up to establish expertise in solutions maturity, but it is going to take some time to catch up with IBM.

It could be an uphill battle for Infosys to compete as a global brand with well-known companies, such as IBM and Accenture, for high-end consulting services. IBM and Accenture had already established immense credibility and reputation in the field, and had access to the same cost-effective and rigorous Indian intellectual human capital for IT and BPO services. Clients already had access to the best-known brands along with the needed technical expertise. Infosys, on the other hand, had yet to build its reputation in consulting. Therefore, Infosys management had to decide how to reconcile high-end consulting with a low-cost GDM business model.

Branding Challenge-Developing a Brand without Advertising

Although Infosys ranked high on its Global Delivery Model (see Exhibit 12), it was very low on the other co-ordinates of solution impact, an essential component of high-end consulting, and an area in which IBM and others had already established their supremacy. It was indisputable that Infosys needed to build a global brand; however, the challenge was to do so with a minimal budget for marketing communications.

The consulting market was still in its nascent stage, and various players could still define their unique selling propositions and establish their market share. Global giants, however, had a natural advantage from their years of expertise and from their easy access to Indian human capital by establishing a base in India.

On the flip side, companies such as Infosys had a proven credibility in the Global Delivery Model, which could not be easily replicated or acquired. Infosys had an opportunity to lead the competition at every milestone. Infosys took its first steps towards entering the high-end consulting market by forming Infosys Consulting Group internally in 1999. The company also formed the domain competency group. Both these groups were now embedded into verticals and assisted in the process of solutions being developed for each vertical. The strategy of developing solutions for vertical markets, such as banking, could help Infosys build a brand slowly but steadily. The move to reorganize the company structure in accordance with industry domains such as banking, manufacturing, telecom, energy and utilities was a step in the right direction.

Resources Challenge-Scaling Up for Excellence

How could Infosys continue to significantly add to its global employee base and maintain superior quality performance? Global competitors recruiting from the same Indian talent pool aggravated this challenge. IBM and Accenture were luring top Indian high-tech workers by providing lucrative offers and an opportunity to be associated with a world-class brand; Infosys had to compete for the finite Indian engineer human resource pool.

To meet the challenge, Infosys started the Campus Connect program to attract the talent pool from various engineering colleges in the country. The basic objective was to increase the pool of industry-ready students with courseware aligned for industry needs. Infosys was also visiting various technical institutes to provide seminars and other training session for the faculty. Would that be enough, considering that many knowledge workers would prefer work for a global brand name with an enticing salary and other compensation benefits? Although Infosys already had a strong brand recognition in India, where most of its talent was recruited, it was also recruiting in China, Australia, United States and countries in Europe, where it didn't yet have a strong brand. In addition, Infosys had to deal with the challenge of maintaining excellence while expanding its workforce rapidly. The Infosys branding issue was also tied to the acquisition and orientation of new talent. Furthermore, the company needed to ensure that Infosys values, commitment and processes were embedded into every new Infosys employee hired as the company planned to double its employee base over the next two years.

Solutions Strategy

As Infosys entered the global market, it needed to concentrate on its solutions strategy in order to sustain growth in the highly saturated field of consulting. Developing a solution within the vertical market, which incorporated Infosys's highly sophisticated consulting model, could help Infosys in developing a global brand.

Did Infosys really have a solution it could brand?

Rafiq Dossani posed the problem that Infosys would have to answer in terms of brand creation:

> How to create a product[8] out of a service? When you (Infosys) send your people to write code, it becomes a commodity. Why should one respect it as a product, no matter how good one is at it (writing code). You can only make it (the code) a product if you can provide something to meet a need that is changing rapidly. This can be done only if you have the expertise to respond to those changing needs. If you want to create a product, you have to be able to move higher up (the value chain) and do what an IBM does, i.e., develop capabilities that are very dynamic and flexible. And to do that is very difficult (for Infosys) as they would have to raise their cost structure significantly because the markets in India are not as sophisticated as the U.S. (to provide that flexibility). You can cater to a market overseas provided your internal market is as sophisticated or more than the one you are catering to. Hence Infosys is in a Catch-22. They have skills in something that has already become a commodity and the only way to get out is to provide skills that cater to the clients rapidly changing needs. To do that, you have to be in a rapidly changing environment and that is not available in India.

If Infosys could not move up the value chain, it would not make sense to undertake the costs involved in becoming a branded global company (see Exhibit 13). IBM and Accenture had a big advantage in terms of brand recognition as compared with Infosys. It may not be worth it for Infosys to invest in creating a global brand in order to compete directly with these companies, especially since most of the revenues of Infosys came from the horizontal IT services sector.

On the other hand, Mishra believed that Infosys did have intellectual property in the form of industry solutions. "Clients look for solutions to their business problems. A product may be a part of the solution. But there are other components to a solution as well, like process re-engineering, custom-developed application, etc." Infosys had established proficiency in rolling out sophisticated solutions across different verticals such as banking, insurance and retail. Finacle, a core banking product from Infosys, was widely used by multinational banks, such as ABN Amro, IDBI and ICICI bank in the domestic Indian market.

---

[8] The word product is being used here to define an Infosys-branded suite of services or solutions not software products or goods.

Mishra suggested, "The important thing is to have business and domain expertise, solutions come out of that." The promising solution strategy for Infosys would be to take a solution that included consulting and roll it out into the global market.

Direct Competition with Global Companies for High-end Consulting

Infosys could leverage its advantage as an established firm in India with proven market solutions to compete directly with the new entrants such as IBM and Accenture. Even though Infosys has just begun to build credible expertise, skill and knowledge in the high-end consulting market, it could prove to be a strong player in this market by investing in strategic acquisitions and by hiring seasoned international consultants to augment its consulting team. Infosys made its first acquisition in a year-and-a-half by buying Australian IT firm Expert Information Systems. However, Infosys lags behind rival Wipro in making strategic acquisitions to build vertical and business line expertise; the Expert acquisition was primarily a geographic buy. Infosys could pursue acquisitions more aggressively in order to strengthen its international presence and gain local knowledge in order to be considered competitive with multinational giants such as IBM and Accenture.

The combined impact of IT and BPO, however, was greater than the sum of its parts. Exhibit 14 shows that BPO was highest on the list of areas in which clients planned to extend their outsourcing efforts. Infosys had an advantage over many global players by virtue of launching the BPO subsidiary Progeon, which provided outsourcing solutions to its global clientele, a step that distinguished it from other global solution providers.

Infosys's strategy, built on the cost advantage, propelled the company to reach $1 billion in annual revenue. However, to succeed in high-end consulting Infosys employees had to change their mindset to accept that consulting was crucial to the future growth of the company. BPO, IT outsourcing and package application implementation would be important growth areas going forward for Infosys. The company was trying to change the market perception that it was just an applications services company (application-related services were 78.4 per cent of revenue in 4Q03). BPO revenue was still very small, but it was growing quickly (181 per cent year-to-year).

The Infosys management team believed that one of the advantages Infosys had over the global competitors was the maturity of its GDM model. Exhibit 15 underscores the challenges IBM faced with respect to efficiently implementing an off-shore model and shows the position of IBM with respect to Infosys in terms of GDM maturity. Establishing a base in India was not enough for global consulting companies, such as IBM and Accenture, for the following reasons:

- The complexity of distributed project management with high degree of predictability required processes and methodologies that took time to mature.
- A philosophical commitment to offshoring was required, which would be liable to impact the balance sheets of the global players.

Even after considering the above challenges for the new entrants on the Indian turf, Infosys management realized that it was not realistic to compete in marketing communications (advertising, direct response and trade shows) with IBM or Accenture. These multinational corporations were extremely large and were well established in the field of business consulting. Mishra believed that Infosys could extend the Global Delivery Model that it had perfected over the last 20 years into all aspects and segments of IT services market to leapfrog other consulting companies, such as Deloitte & Touche, Bearing Point, CG, EDS and CSC, to emerge among the top end-to-end players.

Mishra concluded, "Today, the clients want the IT service provider to have consulting/solution capability as well as the ability to leverage the GDM." The Infosys team persistently maintained that IT outsourcing and consulting went hand-in-hand and could not be looked at as separate entities. As Infosys was moving up the value chain, it would continue to use the models that had brought them success in the past and use them effectively in its business ventures. Infosys would continue to try to understand the design problems of customers, develop vertical domain expertise, create industry solutions and implement them quickly by leveraging its well-established processes. Using this strategy Infosys expected to see overall annual company top-line revenue growth achieve the 30 to 40 per cent benchmark identified by management.

Brand Architecture of Infosys

The brand architecture of Infosys relied on its branding and positioning statement "Improve your odds with *Infosys Predictability*."

The business impact that Infosys attracted for its clients was "increased competitiveness." This value was captured in the phrase "Improve your odds" and was achieved through designing business solutions.

The execution of these solutions was accomplished with Infosys Predictability, which was targeted as the Infosys brand identity.

This positioning was meaningful, important and credible in the IT sector where the failure rates of the projects were very high. *Infosys Predictability* (sleeping well at night, peace of mind through transparency and execution excellence—"Getting it done, right") distinguished Infosys from its competitors. This positive customer perception was verified in the research conducted by Infosys (see Exhibit 16).

Infosys Predictability improved the odds for customers to increase their competitiveness due to complete transparency in organizational values, such as total documentation and clarity of commitments. Complete Predictability of Delivery was achieved through processes, tools and methodology with a strong emphasis on software engineering and repeatable optimization of processes, tools and methodologies, strong project management and an ethos of quality. Infosys could build its consulting practice based on high customer confidence in the company for current GDM services.

Mishra strongly believed "Improve your odds" reflected the business impact of the company's solutions. "Infosys Predictability" reflected the peace of mind that Infosys delivered. Today, the center of gravity may be towards the Infosys predictability side, but tomorrow, it could lean towards the business impact side.

Developing the Domestic Market

The present day Indian domestic market provided an opportunity for both global branding and revenue growth.

It was useful for Indian companies to compare Japan and Taiwan as contrasting models to consider in the quest for global branding. One of the key differences between the development of multinational companies in Japan and the lack of global branded companies in Taiwan was that the Japanese companies first established their reputations in their home market. Japan had a large and sophisticated consumer base for companies such as Toyota and Sony to establish their brands in Japan before they expanded to the global market. Taiwan was always export-focused and had not developed any major global brands. The globally branded Japanese firms had amassed far greater market capitalization than the Taiwanese firms, even though both countries had produced excellent companies.

Companies in emerging markets and developing countries can consider whether they want to be the back office of the world—like Taiwan became when it started servicing international brands instead of building domestic brands—or whether they want to become global players. If they wanted to become global players, they needed to build a global brand. Historically, most technology companies, such as IBM, Cisco and HP, which were recognized as international brands, had started locally with a strong domestic focus. Keeping this in mind, should Indian companies like Infosys be looking at strengthening their domestic focus? This was an issue that needed to be addressed in addition to the consideration of the emerging Indian domestic market from an increased revenue opportunity perspective.

Historically, the Indian domestic market was not big enough to support rapid revenue growth. Hence, companies such as Infosys were always export focused and did not establish a brand within the domestic market. In that sense, the Indian market resembled Taiwan. With the entry of the private insurance companies into the Indian domestic market, however, the need for hardware and software services within the domestic market was growing rapidly. In addition, the already growing banking and telecommunication sectors were large consumers of IT services.

Hence, at the corporate level the demand for IT services within India was increasing rapidly, representing a high potential area for Infosys. If Infosys could successfully participate in the growing domestic market, it would not only sustain its growth but it would also be able them to create vertical solutions for the domestic market that could also be adapted globally. Infosys could definitely find new growth opportunities on home turf (see Exhibit 7). The challenge Infosys would face is garnering the resources to work in the domestic market, which would provide considerably less monetary returns.

Was the domestic market attractive for Infosys right now? Did it make sense for Infosys to do business at significantly lower profit margins? Did the domestic IT business, growing but less profitable than foreign markets in the short term, make sense as a strategic imperative for Infosys both for branding and revenue building rationale?

Aditi Mishra now had to prepare for her meeting with Infosys corporate management. She had only three days to develop her recommendation for the next stage of the Infosys marketing plan.

Exhibit 1 Business expectation from IT services

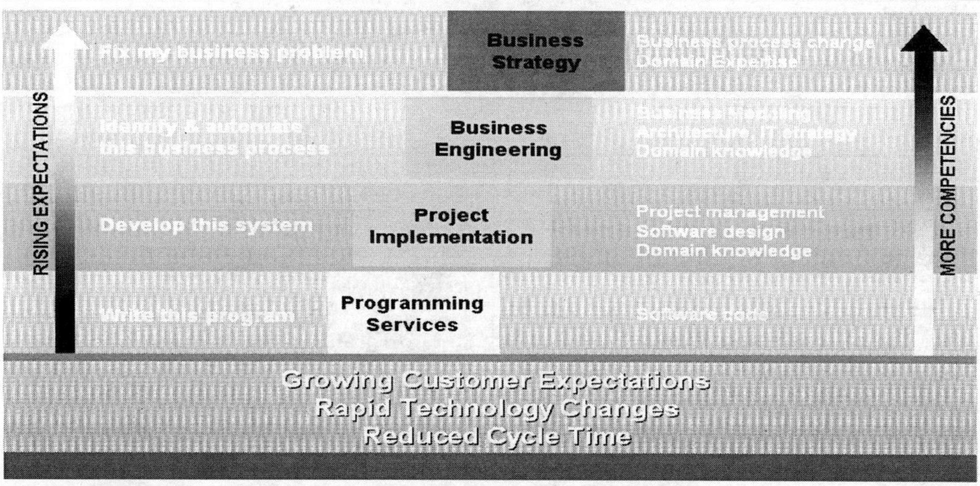

Source: company files.

Exhibit 2 Product and service offerings by Infosys

Consulting and IT

Focuses on aligning client's business strategy with various IT initiatives. With a belief that technology and business go hand in hand, Infosys is able to deliver technology solutions with a competitive advantage.

Product Engineering

Focuses on accelerating the product development and product management life cycles of their clients

Application Product

Infosys enterprise banking solutions, products and services span across the technology requirements of banks, each of which satisfies the needs of stakeholders in the banking enterprise and has a future-proof design. These solutions help enhance a client's customer retention, increase revenue opportunities and create new competitive advantages. Built on Internet technologies, they have been designed with e-commerce components to enable meeting the demands of the new millennium

Source: company files.

Exhibit 3 PSPD model

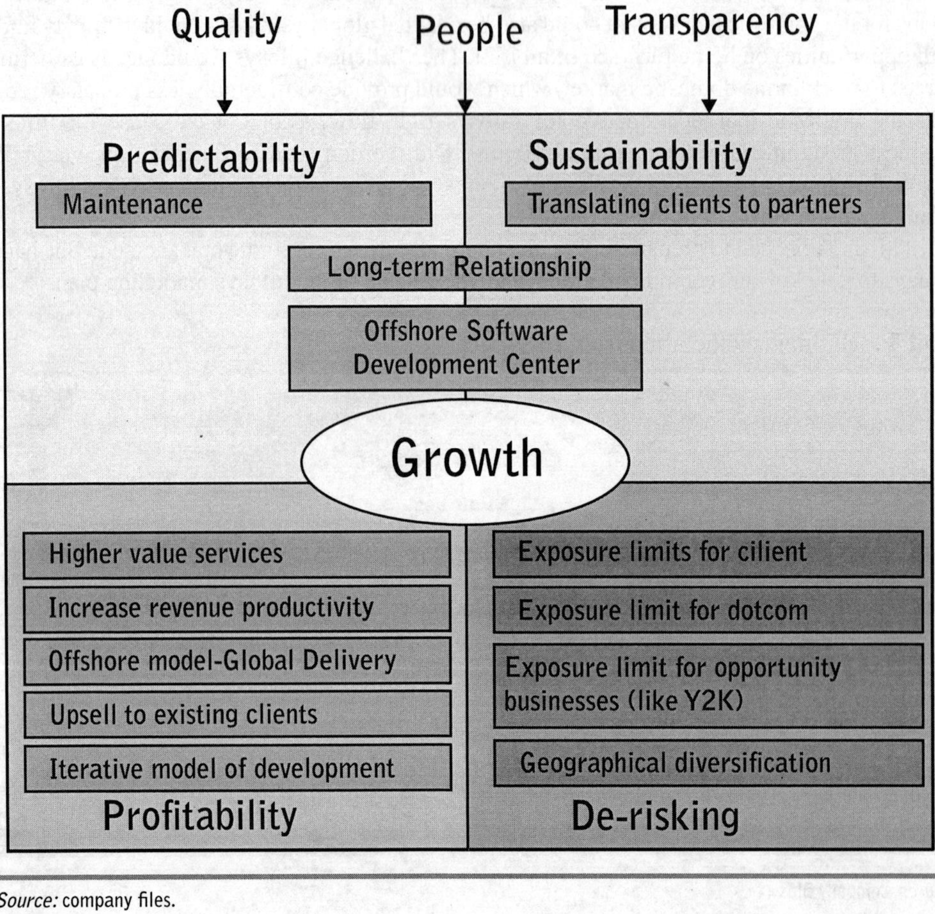

Source: company files.

Exhibit 4 Global delivery model

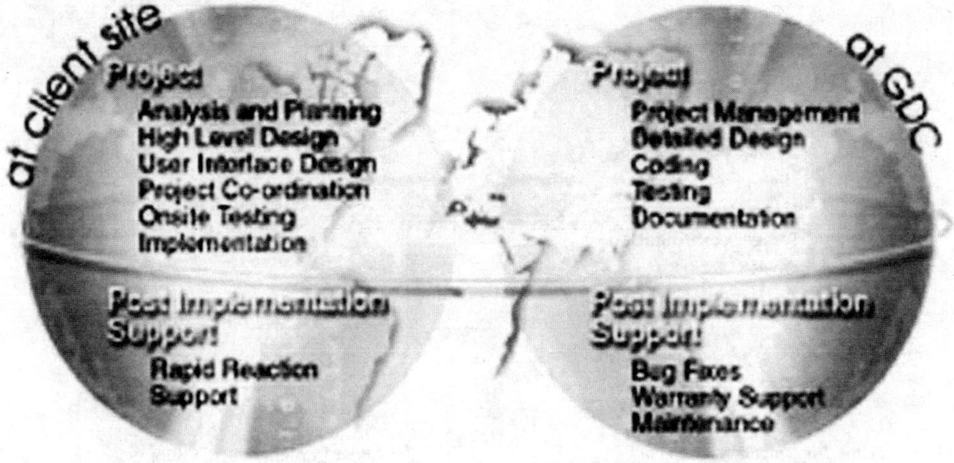

The Infosys global delivery model (GDM) is a framework for distributed project management and multi-location engagement teams. The Global Delivery Model is a key driver of engagement success and value realization for clients. It provides clearly defined process guidelines emphasizing the importance of information flow and communication. The robustness of Global Delivery Model combined with the infrastructure and quality orientation reduces engagement risk for a client compared to conventional delivery models.

GDM and the PSPD

Total Cost of Ownership

Clients expect reduction in total cost of ownership for each type of service. The flexibility offered by GDM saves clients the bother and expense of investing in a huge team. GDM adapts swiftly to a client's changing requirements. For example, a large team can be ramped up for a sudden or short-term requirement, which can be redeployed elsewhere as soon as the project is over.

The high quality and predictability of solutions delivered through this model make them cost-effective.

GDM offers a variable cost for resources, depending on locations, which makes the most economic sense.

De-risking: Clients expect 24*7 availability of services at all times, which translates into providing a delivery model that is robust and resilient to any type of disaster.

Time-to-market: Accelerated demands leading to shrinking cycle times is the order of the day. GDM offers extended workdays across multiple time zones (multiple locations) for faster project completion. Projects are divided into intelligent work pieces that are executed independently and simultaneously at our Global Development Centers, resulting in faster time-to-market.

Quality: Customers not only expect high-quality work products, but also need the products delivered with high degree of predictability. CMM Level 5 is an integral part of Infosys's Global Delivery Model. Infosys is a certified CMM Level 5 organization, which means it is pegged at the highest level of the Capability Maturity Model (CMM) of the Software Engineering Institute (SEI) at Carnegie Mellon. It enables Infosys to institute high levels of quality processes and predictability in work. GDM also provides for a seamless flow of information and access to experts and knowledge bases at multiple places/sites.

Requirements scaling: Monitoring, tracking and quickly reacting to changing requirements and then scaling up where necessary to meet these needs have become critical success factors in a majority of IT engagements.

(*Continued*)

(*Continued*)

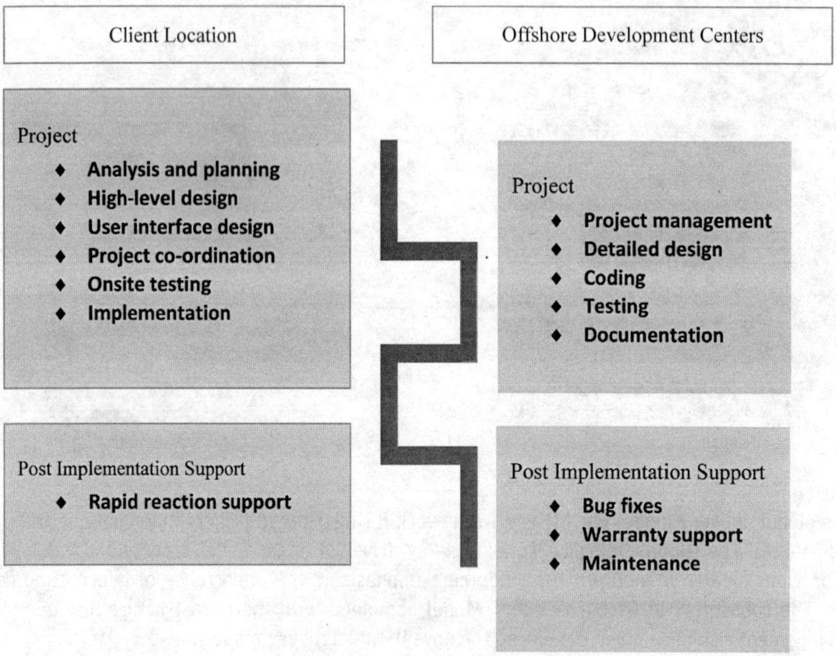

SQA Monitored

Exhibit 5 Key service lines IT software services and IT enabled services/BPO

IT Software Services and Exports	IT Enabled Services/BPO
Custom Application Development	Customer Care
Applications Outsourcing	Web Sales / Marketing
IT Enabled Services	Billing / Accounting
R&D Services	Database Marketing
	Transaction Document Management
	Transcription
	Telemarketing
	Benefits Processing
	Tax Administration
	HR Hiring
	Bio-Tech Research

Source: www.nasscom.org.

Exhibit 6 Growth rates of different vertical segments in India 2002/03 (%)

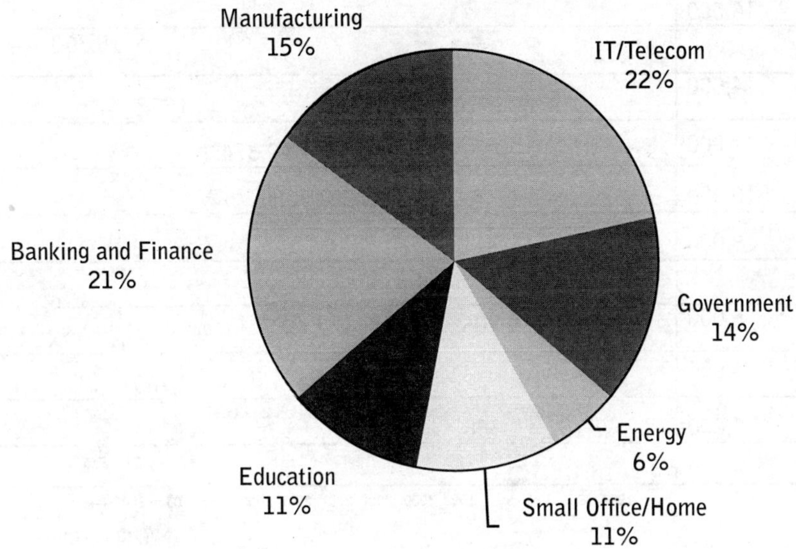

Source: www.nasscom.org.

Exhibit 7 Indian software services and exports 1997-2003

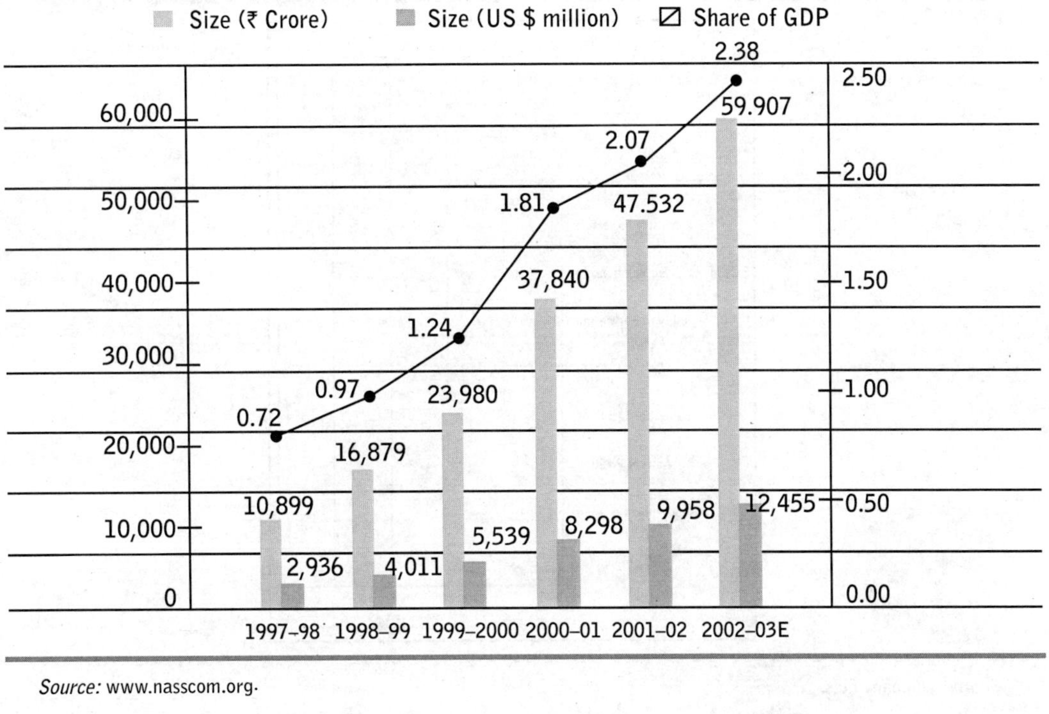

Source: www.nasscom.org.

Exhibit 8 Growth of the domestic IT market in India domestic software and services

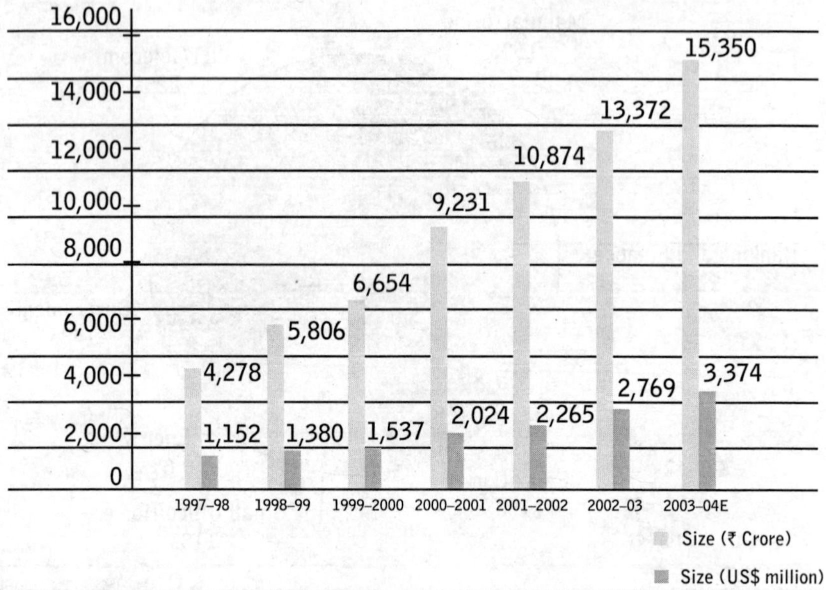

Source: www.nasscom.org.

Exhibit 9 Perceptions of selection criteria between the buyers and the providers

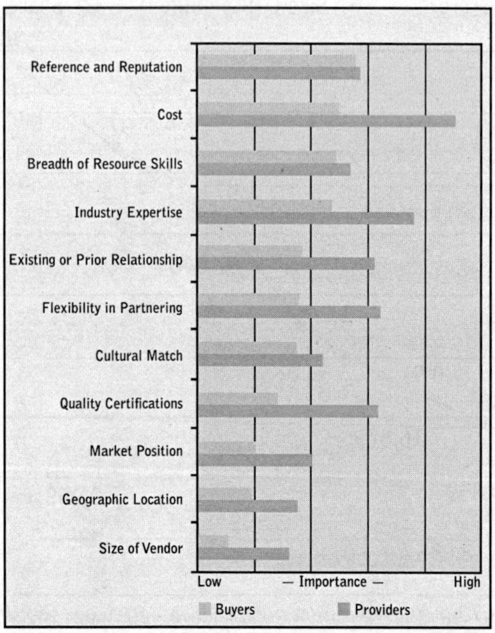

Source: company files.

Exhibit 10 Key IT functions outsourced

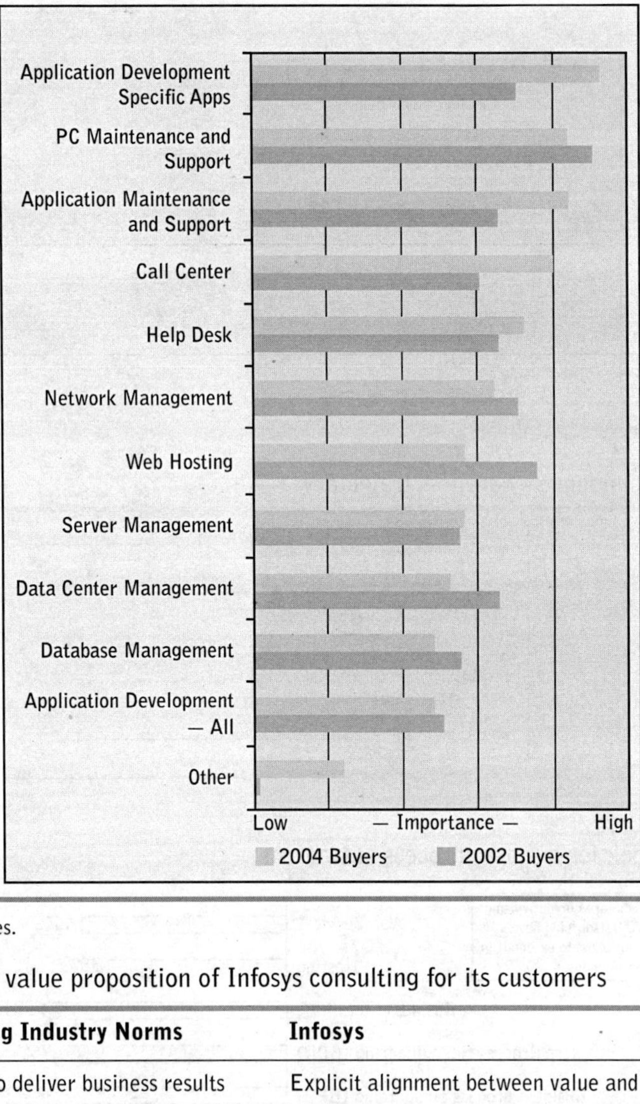

Source: company files.

Exhibit 11 Core value proposition of Infosys consulting for its customers

Current Consulting Industry Norms	Infosys
Projects often fail to deliver business results	Explicit alignment between value and activites
Unnecessary overhead	Operational discipline
Too many bad surprises	Transparent projects
Move the workers to the work	Move the work to the workers
Consultants know everything	Emphasis on constant learning
We are a one-stop shop	We understand that no one has a monopoly on ideas

Source: company files.

Exhibit 12 Challenge for infosys

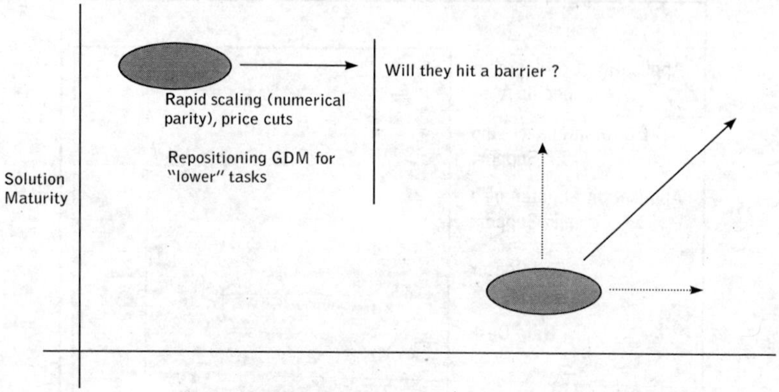

Source: company files.

Exhibit 13 On confidence awareness trajectory

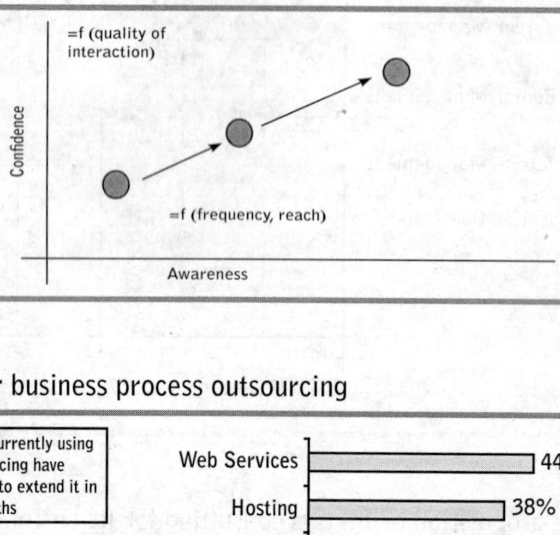

Source: company files.

Exhibit 14 Outlook for business process outsourcing

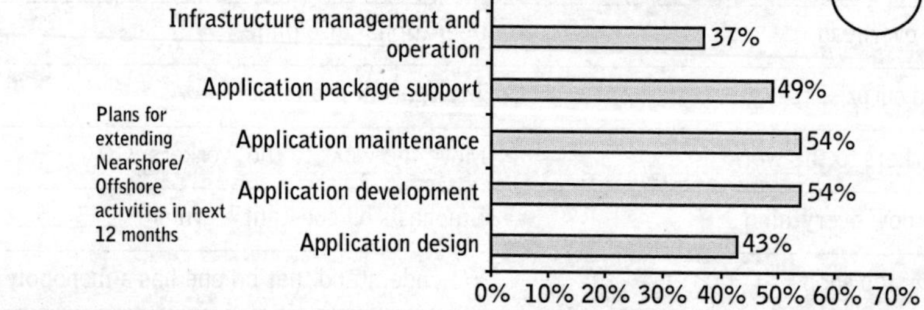

Source: company files.

Exhibit 15 Challenges faced with respect to efficiently implementing an off-shoring model

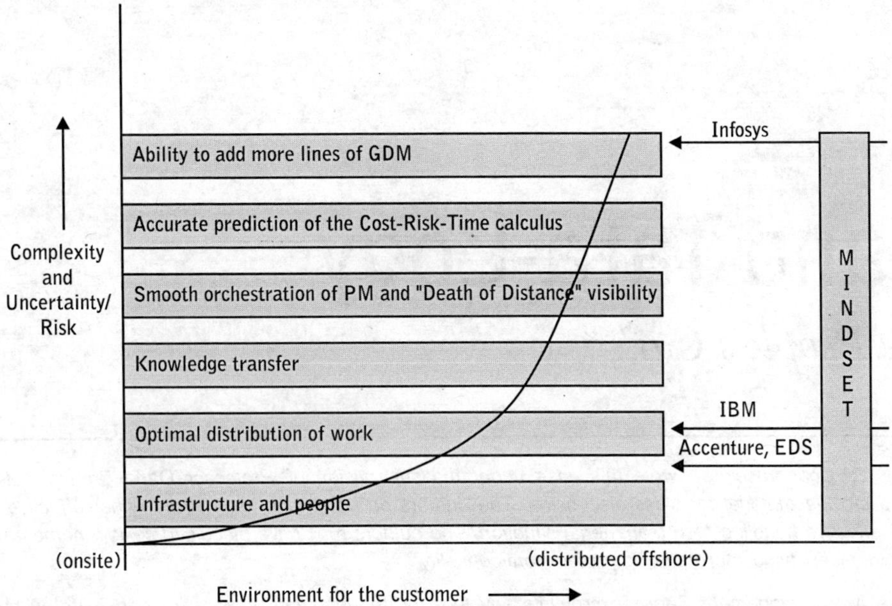

Source: company files.

Exhibit 16 Research conducted by infosys

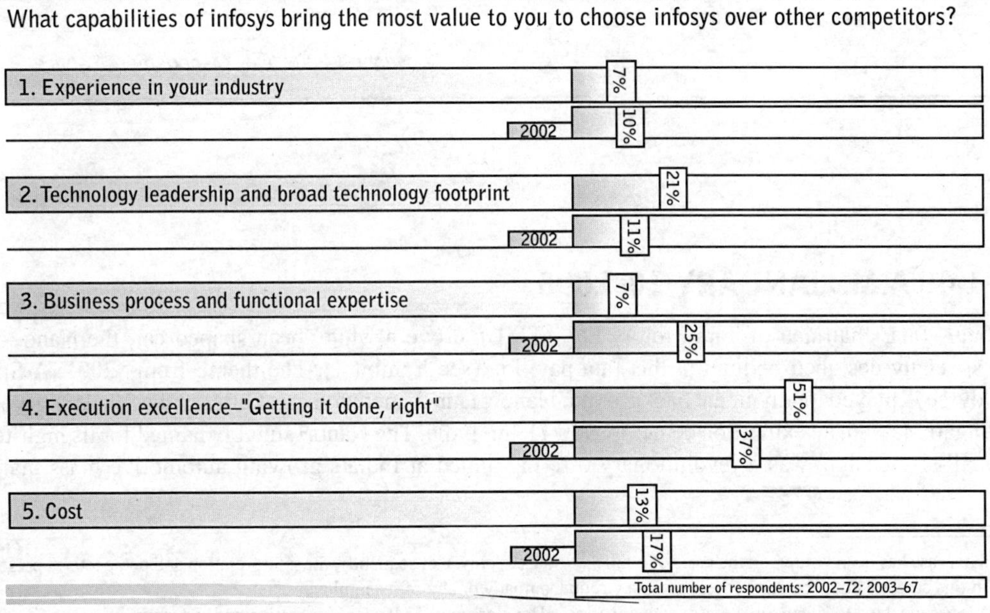

Source: company files.

23

Nano Tata-Logy

The People's Car[1, 2]

R. Chandrasekhar wrote this case under the supervision of Professor Oana Branzei solely to provide material for class discussion. The authors do not intend to illustrate either effective or ineffective handling of a managerial situation. The authors may have disguised certain names and other identifying information to protect confidentiality.

11.40 A.M., JANUARY 10, 2008

Ratan Tata, chairman of Tata Motors Ltd. (TML), drove a white, bean-shaped car, the Nano, onto a specially designed podium at the Tata pavilion (see Exhibit 1). The theme from "2001: A Space Odyssey" played loudly in the background. Nano's launch met with great buzz at the 9th Auto Expo in Pragati Maidan, an exhibition center in New Delhi, India. The Nano,[3] suitably named for its high-tech, small-size design, was a revolutionary offering aimed at India's growing automotive mass market.

---

[1] This case has been written on the basis of published sources only. Consequently, the interpretation and perspectives presented in this case are not necessarily those of Tata Group Company or any of its employees

[2] We are indebted to Ketan Savale, Advanced Business Development, TML. for his creative and suggestive choice of the word Tata-logy.

[3] Nano stands for "small" in Gujarati, the native language of the Tata family, founders of the Tata Group. Its Greek origin means "dwarf."

Sharing the spotlight and joining Ratan Tata on the podium were Girish Wagh, the 34-year-old head of Tata Motors' Small Car Project Team, the group of 500 young engineers charged with the design of the new concept, and Ravi Kant, the company's managing director, who was showcasing two deluxe models of Nano, appealing sights for the more affluent yet environmentally savvy urban dweller in India and globally.

FEBRUARY 13, 2008

In his speech at Nasscom Leadership Summit, Anand Mahindra, vice chairman of Mahindra & Mahindra Ltd, noted:

> A few weeks ago, an Indian car company made a game-changing move. Maybe the Nano will ultimately not retail for a hundred thousand rupees. Maybe it won't have great margins, or replace as many motorcycles as it would like to, but it was a game changing move; it fired a shot that was heard around the world.

FEBRUARY 25, 2008

Newsweek published a special report titled "Small. It's The New Big." According to the article, "Poor countries are getting rich, gas costs are rising and our planet is heating up. The result: a new breed of 21st-century cars that are cooler, cheaper and more compact than ever."[4] The report quoted Global Insight auto analyst John Wolkonowicz saying:

> The Nano is the 21st-century equivalent of the Model T. The Nano will put the Third World on wheels, and that will have far-reaching implications. It's going to affect every citizen of the world.

MAY 22, 2008

AutoObserver reported direct competition to Tata's Nano. The low-cost car, code-named "ULC" for Ultra Low Cost would be produced by a joint venture among Bajaj Auto Ltd., India's second-largest motorcycle manufacturer (50 per cent), Nissan Motor Company of Japan (25 per cent) and Renault SA of France (25 per cent) and was expected to be available to the Indian consumer by 2011.[5] A few months earlier, *The Wall Street Journal* had reported on the growing competition: Ford Motor Co. had announced plans to build a new small car in India with a sticker price of US$7,500; Nissan Motor Co. planned a $7,000 and then a $5,000 model. Fiat SpA, Italy's biggest car maker was to launch five new car models in India in 2008 and German automaker Volkswagen AG was to start production of small cars at a new plant by 2010.[6]

---

[4] "Small: It's the New Big,"http://www.newsweek.com/id/112729/page/1, accessed September 5, 2008. Find out where you stand at "Quiz: A Green Autopia," http://www.newsweek.com/id/111928, accessed September 5, 2008.

[5] Nick Kurczewski, "Renault-Nissan and Bajaj Announce Rival to Tata Nano," AutoObserver, May 22, 2008, http://www.autoobserver.com/2008/05/renault-nissan-and-bajaj-announce-rival-to-tata-nano.html, accessed September 5, 2008.

[6] Eric Bellman, "Tata's High-Stakes Bet on Low-Cost Car," Wall Street Journal, http://online.wsj.com/article/SB119993102461279857.html, accessed September 5, 2008.

AUGUST 23, 2008

The Economic Times[7] commented on the coming of Maruti Suzuki's A-Star, scheduled for launch in Europe and India in October 2008. Made exclusively in India for export to the rest of the world, the fifth-generation Alto sported "a spanking new 1-litre, all aluminium three-cylinder powerplant" generating 60PS of power; its light structure would make it more affordable and also much cleaner to comply with international standards. The youthful and futuristic design showcased in earlier prototypes of the Alto had been toned down to make it more appealing as a family option for the Indian mass market and safer in the eyes of the European regulators, in anticipation of 50,000 units Nissan was expecting to sell under its brand in international markets. The A-star was acclaimed as an important move into the Indian mass market, but its expected price tag of between ₹3 lakh and ₹4 lakh[8] (about US$7,600-10,000) positioned the new car uncomfortably in the rather narrow gap between Maruti Suzuki's two former models, the Zen Estilo and the Suzuki Swift. Industry observers anticipated some cannibalization among Suzuki's offering, especially between the A-Star and its forthcoming Suzuki Splash.

SEPTEMBER 6, 2008

Korean Hyundai, the world's fifth-largest car maker since July 2008, confirmed that it was pressing ahead with the i20, its all new challenger in the super hatch segment, which was expected to make its world debut at the Paris Auto Salon on October 2, on the heels of its earlier chic and trendy i10. The i20 had been designed at Hyundai's European Design Centre in Russelsheim, Germany, but was expected to roll off the production lines of the Hyundai's modern facility in Chennai, India, by October. With a CO_2 output of just 99 grams per kilometer, the i20 would be one of the most eco-friendly cars in its class worldwide and was expected to take the Suzuki Swift head on, according to Adil Jal Darukhanawala, editor-in-chief of *Zigwheels*, the automotive portal of the Times of India Group[9]:

> While the i20 may sport an all new platform and underpinnings, its styling clearly evokes cues from the present day i30 in the Hyundai line-up plus also a few from the existing Getz. The twin-creases on the bonnet, the almost Honda-like chrome grille, the teardrop headlamps and that large air dam on the front bumper continues the modern front end look in the new i-series (so named for the cars evoking the spirit of the "i-gen" or today's youth). The character crease line just below the waistline and lower down on the flanks gives it a link to the Getz as does the C-pillar treatment. At the rear the i20 features stacked tail lamps to give it that individualistic look.

SEPTEMBER 7, 2008

No Nano? Two weeks after the controversial headline made the world news, Ravi Kant, Tata Motors' managing director, was still countering the media's questions about TML's promise that the people's car would be rolling off the production lines at the Singur plant, in the province of West Bengal

---

[7] "Indian A-Star Is Suzuki's New Alto for the World," The Economic Times of India, http://economictimes.indiatimes.com/articleshow/msid-3395977,prtpage-1.cms, accessed September 5, 2008.

[8] Large values of Indian rupees are counted in terms of thousands, lakh (100,000), crore (10,000,000) and arab (1,000,000,000).

[9] Adil Jal Darukhanawala, "Hyundai Reveals Suzuki Challenger," September 6, 2008, http://economictimes.indiatimes.com/News/News_By_Industry/Auto/Automobiles/Hyundai_reveals_Suzuki_challenger/articleshow/3451961.cms, accessed September 6, 2008.

in eastern India, later the same year. Because of the land leased to TML had been acquired by the provincial government without adequate compensation, protesters had been picketing at the gates, preventing workers from entering the factory premises.

On August 22, Ratan Tata had stated that TML would halt production if the unrest posed safety concerns. Workers stayed away on August 29, and TML suspended work on September 3, as Governor Gopalkrishna Gandhi began mediation with the provincial government. Although on September 4 Ratan Tata had reassured the workers that all possible steps were being taken to roll out Nano as scheduled, the *Hindustan Times* e-paper speculated delays of 8 to 10 months if Tata were to leave the Singur site.[10] Even if production continued, the article added, the company would only be able to produce 50,000 to 60,000 units this fiscal year against its stated target of one lakh (100,000).

Delays at Singur could both affect supply and further increase production costs. Competitors speculated that even short delays in rolling the Nanos off the production line in Singur might influence TML's market entry and subsequent market share growth. With the launches of Suzuki's A-star and Hyundai's i20 imminent, TML faced increased pressure to churn out the Nanos.

Tata Motors had successfully broken new ground in India's automotive industry (see Exhibit 2); yet competition in India's passenger car segment was tightening (see Exhibit 3). The automotive sector was a US$34-billion industry, which averaged approximately 14 per cent compound annual growth rate (CAGR) in vehicle production in the previous year. In 2006–07, India produced 11 million vehicles. Although the vehicle penetration was still low (three cars and 50 two-wheelers per 1,000 individuals), the market was accelerating quickly. In 2005–06, the industry grew 15.06 per cent (see Exhibit 4). In 2006–07, India's automotive industry produced 1.5 million passenger cars, which represented a growth rate of 21per cent CAGR over the previous four years.[11] Along with Indica, the Nano, would be the main growth focus for Tata Motors in the medium term.

Achieving Nano's ambitious milestones required several important decisions. Cost management had been a constant source of speculation. Some sources suggested that material costs had almost doubled since conception, rising from 13 per cent to 23 per cent by August 2008. Competitors had suggested that Tata might introduce the car with an artificially low introductory price, perhaps foregoing profit on the car to capture early demand. Kant was unsure whether he should engage in this public debate over costs or simply look after the business—he knew the suppliers would have to be paid. Although profitability was not the key driver behind the Nano, economic viability was important if the project was to meet its goals to innovate for the base of the pyramid.

Kant also reflected on the strengthening position of Tata Motors in global markets. According to the Society of Indian Automobile Manufacturers (SIAM), automobile export had grown 25.43 per cent from March 2006 to April 2007, compared with the same period the previous year: "Passenger vehicles exports grew by 13.05 percent, commercial vehicles exports increased by 22.58 percent, three wheelers exports by 87.17 percent and two wheelers exports grew by 20.65 percent."[12] In about three to five years, Kant felt that Tata Motors would be able to fully match the standards of international manufacturers.[13] He noted that Tata Motors' key strengths were its people and its engineering

---

[10] Jaidev Majumdar, "No Nano" Tata Threatens to Pull Out of Singur: People's Car May Get Delayed," Hindustan Times, August 22, 2008, http://epaper.hindustantimes.com/artMailDisp.aspx?article=23_08_2008_001_028&typ=1&Archtype=&pub =47, accessed on September 5, 2008.

[11] The automotive industry has a mix of large domestic private players (Tata Motors, Mahindra & Mahindra, Ashok Leyland, Bajaj Auto, Hero Honda) and major international players including Suzuki, GM, Ford, Daimler, Toyota, Honda, Hyundai, Renault, VW and Volvo. All major international players have set up manufacturing capacities in India. Source: Investment Commission of India, "Automobiles: Overview," http://www.investmentcommission.in/automobiles.htm, accessed September 6, 2008.

[12] Society of Indian Automobile Manufacturers, "Automobile Industry Performance During 2006–2007," http://www.siamindia.com/scripts/industrystatistics.aspx, accessed September 6, 2008.

[13] "Competing Globally?: It's a Work in Progress," Tata Review, May 2008, pp. 10–12, http://www.tata.com/pdf/2596-page1012_ravi_kant.pdf, accessed September 6, 2008.

orientation: not engineering in the technical sense of the word, but in our orientation with regard to processes and the systematic manner in which we view our world."[14]

> I would say Tata Motors has entered into many associations, some through acquisitions, some through joint ventures, and some through plain partnerships, like with Fiat. This is one way for us to become international class rapidly. Take, for instance, our acquisition of Tata Daewoo or Hispano Carrocera. We have saved time and got assured quality. This way we will bridge the quality gap much quicker than if we were to do it alone.[15]

Chairman Tata's leadership over the past 12 years had been tremendously important, Kant noted "This is a business that's close to his heart. It's a huge advantage that Tata Motor has, to be in a position to tap his interests and knowledge in different areas."[16]

For Ratan Tata, "companies that are not good corporate citizens—those that don't hold to standards and that allow the environment and the community to suffer—are really criminals in today's world."[17] The Nano, as all Tata Motors' milestones (see Exhibit 2) had embodied Ratan Tata's unwavering commitment to ethics:

> What I feel most proud of is that we have been able to grow without compromising any of the values or ethical standards that we consider important. And I am not harping on this hypocritically. It was a major decision to uphold these values and ethics in an environment that is deteriorating around you. If we had compromised them, we could have done much better, grown much faster, and perhaps been regarded as much more successful in the pure business sense. But we would have lost the one differentiation that this group has against others in the country. We would have been just another venal business house.[18]

The Nano complied with the Bharat III[19] and the Euro IV[20] emission standards. According to Ratan Tata, the new market for Nano would come at the expense of higher consumption and emission alternatives:

---

[14] Ravi Kant, quoted in "Competing Globally?: It's a Work in Progress," Tata Review, May 2008, p. 12, http://www.tata.com/pdf/2596-page10-12_ravi_kant.pdf, accessed September 6, 2008.

[15] Ravi Kant, quoted in "Competing Globally?: It's a Work in Progress," Tata Review, May 2008, p. 12, http://www.tata.com/pdf/2596-page10-12_ravi_kant.pdf, accessed September 6, 2008.

[16] Ravi Kant, quoted in "Competing Globally?: It's a Work in Progress," Tata Review, May 2008, p. 12, http://www.tata.com/pdf/2596-page10-12_ravi_kant.pdf, accessed September 6, 2008.

[17] Ranjit V. Pandit "What's Next for the Tata Group: An Interview with Its Chairman," The McKinsery Quarterly, April 28, 2006, http://www.mckinseyquarterly.com/Strategy/Strategy_in_Practice/Whats_next_for_Tata_Group_An_interview_with_its_chairman_1688, accessed September 6, 2008.

[18] Ranjit V. Pandit "What's Next for the Tata Group: An Interview with Its Chairman," The McKinsey Quarterly, April 28, 2006, http://www.mckinseyquarterly.com/Strategy/Strategy_in_Practice/Whats_next_for_Tata_Group_An_interview_with_its_chairman_1688, accessed September 6, 2008.

[19] According to Professor B. S. Murthy, formerly of the Indian Institute of Technology, Chennai, India, "The main requirements for BS III graduation are lower HC and NOx levels, which are now mandated separately. Probably, these are controlled by a higher and/or different catalyst formulation (to oxidise HC in the exhaust) and selected dosage of exhaust gas recirculation (preventing excessive formation of NOx). Naturally, the customers have to meet this extra cost. The low emission level in BS III norms is only a necessary, but not sufficient, condition. For complete equivalence, some more provisions need to be made. One such provision is the on-board diagnostic system (OBD) that can indicate malfunctioning of emission control and engine performance. With this and other specified add-on systems, complete graduation to Euro-III level can be attained." Source: B.S. Murthy, "Euro Versus Bharat Norms," The Hindu Business Line, February 7, 2005, http://www.thehindubusinessline.com/2005/02/07/stories/20050207002 80900.htm, accessed September 6, 2008.

[20] "Appendix I: EU Emission Standards for Petrol Vehicles," http://www.airquality.co.uk/archive/reports/cat15/0408171318SIPhase1reportAppendix1Issue3.pdf, accessed September 6, 2008.

> If you could position an all-weather car that was not a glorified scooter or a stripped down car, then I believe there would be a market potential for one million cars a year, start off a new market and cannibalize a bit from both sides. That would be the kind of volume you might see at a mature stage.[21]

Passenger safety was also essential. The Nano had already passed the full-frontal crash test and the side impact crash test. On the eve of the unveiling in Detroit, in an interview with the *Wall Street Journal*, Ratan Tata had reportedly stated: "We did not do any shortcuts. Nothing was eliminated that would interfere with safety or pollution or reliability."[22]

Nano's safety record was an important competitive advantage. Many cars in India, for example, were sold without airbags or antilock brakes, considered standard features in the West. Outfitting cars with safety features added a huge cost element. Crash-test facilities alone were a gigantic investment. The equipment required for safety and emissions control in Western markets could automatically bring the price of a cheap Chinese or Indian car up to US$6,000 to $7,000.

Despite the Nano's success, it had attracted some criticism. Although the Nano compared favorably with its global climate-friendly competition, its immediate impact on increasing India's traffic congestion soon created a global double-standard—some groups had deliberately reframed the small new car as a climate wrecker rather than a breakthrough:

> One car gets 46 miles per gallon, features fancy accessories, and sports two engines with a combined 145 horsepower. The other car reportedly gets 54 miles per gallon, runs on a diminutive 30-horsepower engine, and is positively spartan in its interior trimmings. The first is a darling of the environmentally conscious. The latter is reviled as a climate wrecker. These two vehicles are the Toyta prius and the newly unveiled Tata Nano, dubbed "the people's car."[23]

For Kant, who had already overcome so many seemingly impossible hurdles to bring a truly revolutionary idea within the grasp of Indian's masses, the social and the environmental sustainability of the Rs one-lakh car project was simply beyond questioning. The Nano had been a visionary answer to Chairman Ratan Tata's attention to the larger part of the income pyramid—TML was following his direction to "explore the large mass market that is emerging—not by following but by breaking new ground in product development and seeing how we can do something that hasn't been done before."[24] In an industry that was already putting 1.5 million cars on the road, Nano's growing market share should come at the expense of gas guzzlers and thus despite adding to the number of vehicles on the road, the impact of the Nano on emissions should be favorable. The Nano was also expected to affect the used car market, offering eco-conscious budget customers a climate-friendlier option (Exhibit 5 highlights the state and evolution of the vehicle emission regulations in India).

Sustainability had become part and parcel of Tata's brand, which ranked 57th globally in 2007 with an estimated value exceeding US$11 billion.[25] Tata Motors had played a part in this strong legacy.

---

[21] Quoted in B. A. Rao, et al., "Tata Motors' RS One-Lakh Car Project," ICFAI Business School, Chennai, India, 2007.

[22] Eric Bellman, "Tata's High-Stakes Bet on Low-Cost Car," Wall Street Journal, http://online.wsj.com/article/SB1199931024 61279857.html, accessed September 5, 2008.

[23] "Analysis: Nano Hypocrisy?" Environmental News Network, January 16, 2008, http://www.enn.com/business/article/29401, accessed September 6, 2008.

[24] Ranjit V. Pandit "What's Next for the Tata Group: An Interview with Its Chairman," The McKinsery Quarterly, April 28, 2006, http://www.mckinseyquarterly.com/Strategy/Strategy_in_Practice/Whats_next_for_Tata_Group_An_interview_with_its_chairman_1688, accessed September 6, 2008.

[25] http://www.livemint.com/2008/04/22000325/Tata-is-now-57th-most-valuable.html, last accessed October 28, 2008.

In 1998, TML had redefined the passenger car business with the launch of India's first indigenously designed, developed and produced car, the Indica, three years later. In 2005, it repeated the same success with India's first mini-truck, the Tata Ace. TML had long been at the forefront of social innovation: it had indigenously designed and manufactured India's first light commercial vehicle, the Tata 407, and India's first sports utility vehicle, the Tata Safari.

Tata Motors had a stellar, forward-looking sustainability record. Once the Nano had been successfully brought to India's eager mass market, Kant continued to look beyond the current technology frontiers. He began pondering the strategy for the MiniCat, Tata Motors' air car. Although the technology was still in the development stage, Tata Motors had signed an agreement with MDI of France for the coveted green technology. Even eco-enthusiasts[26] were eagerly awaiting the next step, although as many times before, many still doubted that the technological breakthrough was even possible, let alone within the reach of the Indian pioneer.

When asked whether he could replicate the "wow" effect of the Nano with other vehicles Kant replied:

> Why not? That's what we have done, in a way, with our small truck, the Ace, a low-price product that has become popular in the domestic market and is getting a good response outside India too.[27]

PREVIOUSLY ON TATA'S NANO

January 11, 2008

The *New York Times* noted:

> Even the usually nonconfrontational chairman of the Nobel Peace Prize-winning Intergovernmental Panel on Climate Change, Rajendra K. Pachauri, has sharply criticized the small car boom, questioning Tata Motors in particular for devoting itself to building cheap cars rather than efficient mass transportation.[28]

April 19, 2007

Forbes added:

> There is a lot riding on its small wheels. If the yet-to-be-named car is a success when it goes on sale next year, it would herald the emergence of Tata Motors on the global auto scene, mark the advent of India as a global center for small-car production and represent a victory for those who advocate making cheap goods for potential customers at the "bottom of the pyramid" in emerging markets. Most of all, it would give millions of people now relegated to lesser means of transportation the chance to drive cars. It is a hugely ambitious project—rivals have called it impossible—for any company. But it is audacious for one that hadn't even built cars a decade ago.[29]

---

[26] "Tata Car Not Ready," ECO-CAN News, http://www.eco-can.ca/eco-news/2008/8/27/breaking-news-tata-air-car-not-ready.html, accessed September 6, 2008.

[27] Ravi Kant, quoted in "Competing Globally?: It's a Work in Progress," Tata Review, May 2008, pp. 10–12, http://www.tata.com/pdf/2596-page10-12_ravi_kant.pdf, accessed September 6, 2008.

[28] Somini Sengupta, "Indians Hit the Road Amidst Elephants," New York Times, January 11, 2008, http://www.nytimes.com/2008/01/11/world/asia/11indiacar.html?_r=1&oref=slogin, accessed September 5, 2008.

[29] Robyn Meredith, "The Next People Car," Forbes, April 16, 2007, http://finance.yahoo.com/family-home/article/102865/the-next-peoples-car, accessed on September 5, 2008.

THE NANO DESIGN

Five years earlier, in March 2003, on the sidelines of the Geneva Auto Show, Tata had told a *Financial Times* correspondent that he was thinking of making "a people's car" that would cost about 2,000. Although he had emphasized the concept rather than the price tag, the promise of a car for one lakh Indian rupees (INR100,000) instantly made the headlines. "It was the media that said it," said Tata, later on, "but we decided to accept it as a challenge."[30]

In late March 2003, five young engineers from the TML plant in Pune walked into a conference room at Bombay House, the Victorian sandstone building in downtown Mumbai that served as the headquarters of the Tata group. They had been summoned at a day's notice by Ratan Tata, who had made a "promise" that had been reported in the business press worldwide.

EMISSIONS

According to Ratan Tata, because of its small size, the Nano would meet or exceed the current and future European emission standards, making it cleaner than many small cars currently on the road.[31] The initial design team envisioned Nano as a rear-engined, four-door, four-seat car. It would have a 33hp engine, providing more pep than the Model T or the VW Beetle when they drove onto the scene. The basic version would not have air-conditioning or power steering, which would be add-ons for the deluxe model, one of three variants being planned. The car would be designed with some functional characteristics in mind: replicability, modularity and repairability. The engine could be removed from underneath from its cradle conveniently, when necessary. The parts would be interchangeable. For example, the left-hand drive could be traded for a right-hand drive.

THE MARKET

TML estimated that the initial potential market for Nano would be approximately one million. Although the Nano was primarily aimed at the Indian market, TML envisioned the Nano at the top of the shopping list of the millions of Chinese, Indians, Brazilians and Russians expected to join the middle class in the coming decade. Despite outcries by environmental groups,[32] affordable, low-emissions cars were also expected to quickly gain in popularity in India and globally. A *New York Times* feature described the rush for getting on the road:

> Indians are rushing headlong to get behind the wheel, as incomes rise, car loans proliferate and the auto industry churns out low-cost cars to nudge them off their motorcycles. They bought 1.5 million cars last year, and by some estimates India is expected to pass China this year as the fastest-growing car market.[33]

---

[30] Dinesh Narayanan, "The Making of a Classic," Business World, January 22, 2008, http://www.businessworld.in/index.php/Automobiles/The-Making-Of-A-Modern-Classic.html, last accessed October 28, 2008.

[31] "With a length of 3.1 meters (about 10 feet), a width of 1.5 meters and a height of 1.6 meters, the new vehicle is 20% smaller than the cheapest car on Indian roads, the Maruti Suzuki 800." Source: Eric Bellman, "Tata's High-Stakes Bet on Low-Cost Car," Wall Street Journal, http://online.wsj.com/article/SB119993102461279857.html, accessed September 5, 2008.

[32] "Analysis: Nano Hypocrisy?" Environmental News Network, January 16, 2008, http://www.enn.com/business/article/29401, accessed September 5, 2008.

[33] Somini Sengupta, "Indians Hit the Road Amidst Elephants," New Delhi Journal, January 11, 2008, http://www.nytimes.com/2008/01/11/world/asia/11indiacar.html?_r=1&oref=slogin, accessed September 5, 2008.

MANUFACTURING

TML had built a new manufacturing plant, estimated to cost about INR17 billion (US$ .178 billion), on a new site of about 650 acres of land at Singur in the province of West Bengal, 40 kilometers from Kokata. The provincial government had acquired another 350 acres for suppliers' facilities. The co-located component manufacturers would produce specialized parts for the Nano, but were also free to supply parts and subassemblies to other automakers. The TML plant at Singur was to generate employment for 2,000 people directly and 10,000 people indirectly. It would have a capacity to produce 250,000 units per annum, expandable to 350,000 units. The first car was scheduled to roll out of Singur plant in the October–December quarter of 2008.[34]

PRODUCTION

TML would be producing about 300,000 units. The rest would be produced by independent assemblers, trained by TML and equipped with assembly lines and car kits from the company. The latter would not be allowed to use the Tata marquee. TML would also not assume any responsibility for warranty and liabilities arising from the sale of vendor-assembled cars.

> We will manufacture the car . . . we will manufacture all the mass parts for our car at one place—let's say, all the press metal parts, etc. So we may farm out the car. Not for us, but to give a livelihood to some others. So, let's say that there is the car A, which is made by us, and a car B, which is made from the parts made for car A, but which looks different and has a different badge. If you and 30 other young guys from rural areas or semi-urban areas want to manufacture this car, we would send you these parts, we would train you, we would provide you with a modular manufacturing plant that will enable you to produce the car. We will not take warranty responsibilities. We will not let you use our name. We could give 30 or 100 entrepreneurs an opportunity to start a business without having to invest in a press shop and having to design a car. Will it compete with us? To some extent, it would. We would expect our brand to take care of most of that. But it could also reach out in areas which we may never have reached otherwise. We will design a low breakeven point assembly plant which we will sell as a kit to a group of entrepreneurs who decide to set up an enterprise that could assemble cars.
>
> For now, we will manufacture the cars in the plant we will put up soon, stabilize and mature the product and then for further growth, we will encourage private entrepreneurship both in service and manufacturing. Those manufacturers could conceivably be retailers of the car also. So we will, therefore, be one level removed and if we go through that pattern, we would train those people, we will establish a system to train them and oversee the quality, so the customer does not feel any different.

---

[34] A short week after the announcement of the Singur site on May 18, 2006, local farmers began protesting, claiming that part of the land for the project had been acquired forcibly. Despite persistent protests, Ratan Tata steadfastly backed the choice and explained the developmental benefits. However, upsurges in protests in August 2008 had him consider moving out of West Bengal. In the following days, the Indian industry, including Reliance Industries chairman Mukesh Ambani, began rallying behind Tata Motors. Several states, including Haryana and Maharashtra, asked Tatas to relocate the Nano factory to their territories. On Wednesday, September 3, Tata suspended work at Singur and reportedly began evaluating alternative sites. Governor Gandhi stepped in as a mediator, and the state government agreed to work towards ending the stalemate. The following day, Ratan Tata offered reassurance that all possible steps being taken to roll out Nano as scheduled. A detailed list of stakeholder engagement events is available online at http://economictimes.indiatimes.com/News/News_By_Industry/Auto/Automobiles/The_Tata-Singur_saga_chronology/articleshow/3449464.cms, accessed September 5, 2008.

We are looking at small satellite units, with very low break-even points, where some of the cars could be assembled, sold and serviced. We would encourage local entrepreneurs to invest in these units and we would train these entrepreneurs to assemble the fully knocked down or semi-knocked down components that we would send to them and they would also sell the assembled vehicles and arrange for their servicing. This approach would replace the dealer and therefore the dealer's margin, with an assembly-cum-retail operation that would be combined with very low-cost service facilities.

The same philosophy that I am talking here can be grafted into South Africa or Namibia. Or, other countries that are looking for low-end cars. We can provide the pre-fab, the trimmings, the modular plant. We are looking at how to bring the cost of the plant down."[35]

THE TATA PROMISE: TO IMPROVE THE QUALITY OF LIFE

The Tata brand carried a powerful emotional appeal among India's growing consumer market. Domestically, the Tata name was synonymous with trust. According to the U.K.-based Brand Finance Plc, which ranked global brands annually based on their value, the Tata brand ranked 57th among the top 500 global brands, at an estimated a monetary value of US$11.8 billion (INR470.82 billion) as of December 2007. The Nano would embody Tata's promise for quality indigenous innovation—and the group's credo for putting the communities it served at the very center of its business model.

The Tata promise had deep roots in India's modern history. The group had been founded as a trading enterprise in 1868 by Jamsetji Tata, a member of the Parsi minority, one of the most enlightened and progressive communities in India. The group's founder pioneered economic growth in the country by setting up, over the decades, the country's first steel mill, power utility, luxury hotel chain, international airline and software enterprise. Jamsetji Tata's core values—integrity, understanding, excellence, unity and responsibility—had permeated all the group's companies and their leaders for four generations. The group never compromised on these values, even if it meant foregoing lucrative opportunities.

Tata made a strong link between economic and social value creation—its trusteeship structure formalized an unusual cycle of value distribution and regeneration, by channeling two-thirds of the equity of Tata Sons (the majority stakeholder for the group) into trusts. This structure helped the Tata Group to distribute between 8 and 14 per cent of the group's net profits, annually, to social causes that the trusts were focused on, including education, health services and community development.

By March 30, 2008, the Tata Group was one of India's largest business conglomerates, with revenues of US$28.8 billion, equivalent to about 3.2 per cent of the country's gross domestic product (GDP). The group consisted of 98 companies of which 27 were publicly listed. The latter had a market capitalization of US$56.52 billion[36] and a shareholder base of more than 2.9 million. Tata's interests prevailed in seven business sectors: information systems and communications; engineering; materials; services; energy; consumer products; and chemicals. The group employed 289,500 people and had operations in more than 80 countries across six continents.[37]

The Tata Group was the first business house in India and one of the global pioneers to deliberately align business excellence with its century-old social values with business excellence. As the result

---

[35] Rajeev Dubey, "Interview: Ratan Tata," Business World January 24, 2005, http://www.balendu.com/old_site/ratan_tata.htm, last accessed October 28, 2008.

[36] As on March 19, 2008.

[37] http://www.tata.com/aboutus/sub_index.aspx?sectid=8hOk5Qq3EfQ=, accessed March 19, 2008.

of strategic planning started in the early 1990s, the group launched, in 2003, a world-first corporate sustainability system: The Tata Index for Sustainable Human Development,[38] an Index that followed the Tata Business Excellence Model (TBEM), an open-ended framework that drove business excellence in Tata companies. The Tata Index reflected a collective effort, at the highest level, to direct, measure and enhance the community work undertaken by the Tata companies themselves and to share guidelines and best practices that helped the Tata companies to fulfill their social responsibilities. The Index was designed and implemented by the Tata Council for Community Initiatives (TCCI), a centrally administered agency that assisted Tata companies through specific processes:

> TCCI's charter embraces social development, environmental management, biodiversity restoration, climate change initiatives and employee volunteering.
>
> This participatory network is headed by Kishor Chaukar, a member of the Tata Group Corporate Centre, and includes chief executive officers of major Tata companies. TCCI coordinates the varied and widespread community development and environmental activities of Tata companies.
>
> TCCI is also involved in assisting Tata companies address sustainability reporting as per guidelines set by the Global Reporting Initiative. It is also the focal point for the UN Global Compact in India, which has 42 Tata companies as signatories—the highest in the world from a business group.[39]

The Index had been deployed since June 2004, with the main objective of ensuring continuous improvement in the delivery of social responsibility initiatives at the company level. The Index reiterated the conviction that sustainability mattered—to the success of their companies, to their own success as leaders and to the Tata legacy. In 2005, reporting companies averaged 452.95 points on a 1,000 point scale. Tata Motors achieved one of the highest scores, 663, which was a testimony to the centrality of sustainable strategies and business practices in its business model.[40]

TATA MOTORS LTD.

Tata Motors Ltd. (TML) was the second-largest player in the Indian passenger car market, with 16.5 per cent share, in 2007. It was also the fifth-largest medium and heavy commercial vehicle manufacturer and the second-largest medium and heavy bus manufacturer in the world.

Set up in 1945 to manufacture locomotives (trucks and buses) and other engineering products, the company had rolled its first vehicle out of its home base, the Jamshedpur plant, in 1954.[41] TML diversified into passenger car business in 1995 under the leadership of Ratan Tata, the new chairman. In 1998, it launched the country's first indigenously designed, developed and produced car, the Tata Indica, at a price tag of US$7,000.

Just when the investments on the new product portfolio were hitting home, a crisis hit. Truck and bus sales plunged in 1999. TML lost US$110 million in the fiscal year ending March 2000,

---

[38] Oana Branzei and Anant G. Nadkarni, "The Tata Way: Evolving and Executing Sustainable Business Strategies," Ivey Business Journal, March/April 2008, http://www.iveybusinessjournal.com/article.asp?intArticle_ID=750, accessed September 6, 2008.

[39] "Tata Council for Community Initiatives," http: www.tata.com/article.aspx?aartid = IV/tF-5W9eeQ=, accessed September 6, 2008.

[40] Oana Branzei and Anant G Nadkarni, " The Tata way: Evolving and Executing Sustainable Business Strategies," Ivey Business Journal, March/April 2008, http://www.iveybusinessjournal.com/article.asp?intArticle_ID=750, accessed September 6, 2008.

[41] Tata Motors, "Profile," http://www.tatamotors.com/our_world/profile.php, accessed March 19, 2008.

representing corporate India's biggest loss that year and the first red ink for TML since 1945. The crisis galvanized the company into going lean. A core group of engineers, all under the age of 35, was given the mandate for organizational transformation. By March 2003, the results of the turnaround were reflected in a robust balance sheet.

Global Presence

TML was also increasing its global profile. Since 1961, the company had been exporting its products to countries in Europe, Africa, the Middle East, Australia, South East Asia and South Asia. It also had built up assembly operations in Malaysia, Kenya, Bangladesh, Ukraine, Russia and Senegal:[42]

> Our market entry strategy has been a little more modest than a truly global one. We want to expand into geographies where, as a group, we can have a meaningful presence. Even though companies would be very satisfied in an Indian context with may be five per cent market share in a foreign country, this is, at least in our view, not a sustainable level. So in the first instance we have chosen countries where we felt we could make an impact and secondly, where we are able to participate, as we have in India, in the development of that country.[43]

One of the first steps in Tata's market entry strategy was to seek an overseas listing. In September 2004, TML became the first company from India's engineering sector to be listed on the New York Stock Exchange. The company then looked at acquisitions and joint ventures.

In 2004, it acquired Daewoo Commercial Vehicles Company, Korea's second-largest truck maker. The rechristened Tata Daewoo Commercial Vehicles Company, a 100 per cent subsidiary of TML, went on to launch several new products for both the Korean and export markets. In 2005, TML acquired a 21 per cent stake in Hispano Carrocera, a Spanish bus and coach manufacturer, with an option to buy the remaining stake. In 2006, it formed a joint venture with the Brazil-based Marcopolo, a global leader in body-building for buses and coaches, to manufacture buses and coaches for India and select international markets. TML also entered into a joint venture in 2006 with Thonburi Automotive Assembly Plant Company of Thailand to manufacture and market the company's pickup vehicles in Thailand. In 2006, TML and Fiat Auto formed an industrial joint venture at Ranjangaon (near Pune in Maharashtra, India) to produce both Fiat and Tata cars and Fiat power trains for the Indian and overseas markets. TML was already distributing and marketing Fiat-branded cars in India. In 2007, TML and Fiat Auto entered into an agreement for a Tata license to build a pickup vehicle bearing the Fiat nameplate at the Fiat plant at Córdoba, Argentina. The pickup was to be sold in South America, Central America and select European markets. TML had 18 per cent revenues from international operation in 2007, up from five per cent in 2003.

Revenue on Rebound

By 2006, the results of the post-2000 cost-cutting were becoming evident. It now took between 12 and 15 minutes to change a die on the passenger car assembly line, down from two hours in 2000. Nearly 6,000 workers had left the company with early retirement deals. The company's e-sourcing

---

[42] Tata Motors, "Profile," http://www.tatamotors.com/our_world/profile.php, accessed March 19, 2008.

[43] Ranjit V Pandit, "What Is Next for Tata Group: An Interview with its Chairman," The McKinsey Quarterly, number 4, 2005, http://www.mckinseyquarterly.com/Strategy/Strategy_in_Practice/Whats_next_for_Tata_Group_An_interview_with_its_chairman_1688, last accessed October 27, 2008.

had run 750 reverse auctions in 2006, which lowered purchasing prices by an average of seven per cent for everything from ball bearings to the milk served in the cafeteria.[44] The company had reduced its break-even from nearly two-thirds of capacity utilization to approximately one-third, which meant that even if the market shrank by close to 60 per cent, the company would still be in the black.[45] TML was also boosting its revenue by making dies for Jaguar, Ford, General Motors and Toyota, and running the made-in-India Mercedes cars through its paint shop.

By March 2007, TML had revenues of INR324.26 billion (US$7.2 billion) and employed 22,000 employees at four manufacturing facilities in Jamshedpur, Pune, Lucknow and Pantngar in India. A new plant would be opened at Singur, dedicated to manufacturing the Nano. Its dealership, sales, services and spare parts networks in India comprised more than 2,000 touch points. The company also had an auto finance operation supporting customers to purchase Tata vehicles.

The Making of a Game Changer[46]

When asked to comment on the origins of the Nano, Ratan Tata confessed:

> There has always been some sort of unconscious urge to do something for the people of India and transport has been an area of interest. As urbanisation gathers pace, personal transport has become a big issue, especially since mass transport is often not available or is of poor quality. Two-wheelers—with the father driving, the elder child standing in front and the wife behind holding a baby—is very much the norm in this country. In that form two-wheelers are a relatively unsafe mode of transporting a family. The two-wheeler image is what got me thinking that we needed to create a safer form of transport.
>
> My first doodle was to rebuild cars around the scooter, so that those using them could be safer if it fell. Could there be a four-wheel vehicle made of scooter parts? I got in touch with an industry association and suggested that we join forces and produce what, at that point, I called an Asian car: large volumes, many nations involved, maybe with different countries producing different sets of parts. . . . Nobody took the idea seriously, nobody responded.
>
> This was similar to what happened when we wanted to get going on the Indica. I had proposed a partnership with an industry body to create an Indian car, designed, developed and produced in India, something that could be conceptualised and executed as an Indian enterprise. Everybody scoffed at the concept. I remember people saying, "Why doesn't Mr. Tata produce a car that works before he talks about an Indian car." My confidence got a boost when we finally succeeded with the Indica. Willy-nilly, we decided to look at [the low-cost car] project within Tata Motors.[47]

---

[44] Robyn Meredith, "The Next People's Car," Forbes, April 16, 2007, http://finance.yahoo.com/family-home/article/102865/the-next-peoples-car, accessed September 5, 2008.

[45] Gautam Kumra, "Leading Change: An Interview with the Managing Director of Tata Motors," Voices on Transformation (2), McKinsey Quarterly. http://www.mckinseyquarterly.com/automotive/leading_change_an_interview_with_the_managing_director_of_tata_motors_1908, last accessed October 27, 2008.

[46] Anand Mahindra, Vice Chairman of Mahindra & Mahindra Ltd., speech at Nasscom Leadership Summit, February 13, 2008.

[47] Christabelle Noronha, "The Making of the Nano," January 2008, http://www.tata.com/aboutus/articles/inside.aspx?artid=Sd75BUBmzSM=, accessed September 7, 2008.

Soon after its unveiling in Detroit, Nano made *Time* magazine's "The dozen most important cars of all time starting from 1908 to the present" alongside such legends as the Ford Model T, the Volkswagen Beetle, the Chevy Belair, the Toyota Corolla, the Mini and the Honda Civic.[48]

According to Ratan Tata, the Nano targeted "families that normally ride on two-wheelers—the father driving, his kid standing in front, his wife seated behind him holding the baby—it's a safe, affordable all-weather form of transport."

But the small family car packed several technological breakthroughs. It was the first time a two-cylinder, non-opposed petrol engine would be used in a car with a single balancer shaft. Tata Motors has reportedly filed 34 patents for the design innovations embodied in the Nano. The powertrain accounted for half of them (see Exhibit 6):

> The vehicle's design, a combination of simple-to-manufacture panels and plastic mouldings, was devised by the IDEA Institute of Italy.
>
> The base version of the Nano will have a manual gearbox, but a continuously variable transmission will be offered as an option. Kinetic Engineering of Pune will supply the unit.
>
> Tata has ventures with international companies that are likely to supply parts: Tata-Yazaki makes wiring harnesses, Taco GS Yuasa makes batteries, Tata-Toyo radiators, and Tata Johnson Controls seats. Some suppliers, such as sealing firm Freudenberg, have a lot of standard solutions that required no further development cost. "We defined the requirements and delivered exactly what was wanted without over-engineering," says the company. "The sealing packages for the Nano are produced in a joint venture with NOK."
>
> Others have expertise in low-cost, high-quality manufacturing. The effect of faulty parts on margins is greater on a car like the Nano. Caparo will press and assemble some of the inner structural panels. "The body technology is conventional, but the manufacturing requires sophisticated analysis to ensure zero-fault-forward quality control at low cost," says Caparo chief executive Angad Paul.
>
> Ficosa is supplying mirrors, washer system and gear shifters. These are not standard parts, says the company's R&D director, Vicenç Aguilera: "Basing the design on cost instead of prioritising the technology required a specific development to reach Tata's quality and reliability standards."
>
> GKN produces the driveshafts, also tailored to the vehicle using every opportunity to minimise cost. "It required technological capability from Europe to support the localisation of every component in India," says the company. "The reduction of technical complexity we achieved is tremendous."
>
> Bosch developed the starter-alternator and the injection system for the engine. A system for a diesel version will come later. Wolf-Henning Scheider, president of the company's gasoline systems division, says it's a profitable business for Bosch: "For a BMW M3, the engine's the most important part of the car. For a one-lakh car, the main thing is that it has a roof, four doors and four seats. The margins are smaller as a result, but the volume per variant is higher."

---

[48] Kiron, Kasbekar, "All Right Turns," Tata Review, May 2008, http://www.tata.com/pdf/2596-page6-9_Transformation.pdf, accessed September 6, 2008.

> Engineers in Germany performed a lot of the development for Bosch's Value Motronic injectors. The engine management system was developed in China. The application work and the production engineering took place in India.
>
> The result is a system that costs less than half that of a conventional European engine. The first-generation system achieves Euro III emissions levels with on-board diagnostics (OBD). Future versions will be able to pass Euro IV without costing any more. "At the moment low-cost cars require only Euro III," says Scheider. "OBD will be the next step, which is why we have already integrated it."[49]

NANO TECHNOLOGY

The story of the Nano was a story of innovation and ingenuity, within the group and outside, a story of overcoming early skepticism and a story of persistence in "making history":[50]

> Rane Group, for instance, makes a rack and pinion steering system. It focused on reducing the weight of the materials used, replacing the steel rod of the steering with a steel tube—a major cost-reducer. Typically, the product is made of two pieces, but it was redesigned as one to save on machining and assembling costs.
>
> According to Harish Lakshman, director of the $317 million company: "The world has seen this sort of integration of two pieces into one, but applied differently—not for a new car, and not to reduce costs."
>
> GKN Driveline India, a subsidiary of global auto parts leader GKN, made the driveshaft—the component that transfers power from the engine to the wheel. The team spent a year developing 32 experimental variants to create the perfect driveshaft for the Nano. It roped in designers from the company's French and Italian operations and changed the design to make it lighter and easier to manufacture.
>
> For the Nano's rear-wheel drive system, GKN designed a smaller diameter of shaft, which made it lighter and saved on material costs. "We thought if we were successful in this, we could dictate terms to the market, and every other car manufacturer would want to work with us," says Rajendra Ojha, chief executive of GKN Driveline India.[51]

Taking the Pulse of the Project

All the suppliers have similar stories. And although none would disclose specific cost savings, most stuck to Tata's mandate to cut costs. That was, as Kant acknowledged, the biggest hurdle for the company: "then, now, and in the future,"—particularly because the prices of raw materials, such as steel, have more than doubled in the past four years, and the company has been required to follow new, tighter industry regulations.

---

[49] Simon Bickerstaffe and Tristan Honeywill, "India's Tata Low-Cost Nano Took a Lot of High-Tech," Automotive Engineer, March 2008, http://www.ae-plus.com/Key%20topics/cc-Tata-news3.htm, accessed September 26, 2008.

[50] Manjeet Kripalani, "The Story Behind the Tata Nano," BusinessWeek.com, http://www.rediff.com/money/2008/may/ 14tata.htm, accessed September 6, 2008.

[51] Manjeet Kripalani, "The Story Behind the Tata Nano," BusinessWeek.com, http://www.rediff.com/money/2008/may/ 14tata htm, accessed September 6, 2008.

Kant, who recently led negotiations to acquire luxury auto brand Jaguar Land Rover, had little time to get involved in day-to-day details of Tata's many projects. However, with the Nano, "every cost, every component price, has to be run by me," he said.

Coordinating the vendors with Tata Motors' team was a new exercise in logistics. Girish Wagh, the head of the Super Car Project Team, quickly realized it was necessary to bring everyone on board, or else, as he put it "it leads to last-minute heartache and delays."

Every morning, he would spend an hour or two on the floor of the Pune factory, insisting that everyone involved—designers, manufacturing teams, vendor development people—be there to accelerate decision-making and problem-solving. "We had to have the pulse of the project and know exactly where the hurdles were," Wagh remembered.

Over time, Wagh's team grew to comprise some 500 engineers, an impractically large group to gather on a daily basis. Instead, a core team of five engineers gathered every day at 3 p.m. to discuss the latest developments. Each engineer represented a different part of the car: engine and transmission, body, vehicle integration, safety and regulation, and industrial design.

Attention to Detail Pays Off

Fitting the parts of the car together required many head-breaking details, recalled Wagh. The engine, for instance, was designed three times. Initially, when Wagh thought they would buy an off-the-shelf engine, he had studied all the small-capacity engines available. They were unsuitable, so in early 2005 he decided to build his own.

The first was a 540 cc engine that, when fitted on the prototype, lacked the necessary power. Its capacity was increased by nine per cent, then by another nine per cent, before Wagh finally settled on a 623 cc engine. Then the foot pedal had to be realigned to create more legroom.

The body had to be changed because Ratan Tata, who stood taller than six feet, wanted it to be easy for tall people to get in and out of the car. "Imagine the plight of the body designer—he went through hundreds of iterations, then at the last minute the car length was increased by 100 millimeters!" remarked Wagh.

Cost Structure

> It was never meant to be a ₹ 1-lakh car; that happened by circumstance. I was interviewed by the [British newspaper] *Financial Times* at the Geneva Motor Show and I talked about this future product as a low-cost car. I was asked how much it would cost and I said about ₹ 1 lakh. The next day the *Financial Times* had a headline to the effect that the Tatas are to produce a ₹ 100,000 car. My immediate reaction was to issue a rebuttal, to clarify that that was not exactly what I had said. Then I thought, I did say it would be around that figure, so why don't we just take that as a target. When I came back our people were aghast, but we had our goal.[52]

Nano's cost structure had been constantly scrutinized. Guesstimate breakdowns shown in Exhibit 6 identified five major cost areas: engine and transmission (30 per cent of the sales price); body (9 per cent); electricals (9 per cent); suspension and wheels (11 per cent) and interiors

[52] Christabelle Noronha, "The Making of the Nano," January 2008, http://www.tata.com/aboutus/articles/inside aspx?artid=Sd75BUBmzSM=, accessed September 6, 2008.

(7.5 per cent).[53] Although most competitors debated whether such low costs could be accomplished, and some questioned the anticipated 5.5 per cent gross profit margins, Tata Motors' managing director had taken repeated steps to keep the cost structure in check.

Out-of-the-box thinking helped manage costs at various stages in the product's value chain, especially for input sourcing. Typically, a car manufacturer would solicit bids for components from various suppliers and award a multi-year contract to the supplier offering the lowest bid. The Nano team laid out a cost target for each component and asked suppliers to develop prototypes that exceeded those targets. The design that drove down the target the most was awarded the contract after it had been assessed on various other metrics. This non-traditional approach enabled TML to connect, upfront, with the most cost-efficient vendor for each of Nano's components. It also encouraged vendors to develop new technologies to reduce costs.

One such innovation was the "roll-forming" technology used in the making of a chassis. A highly standardized auto component, the chassis typically involved three to four pieces. Welding them together usually meant more processes, variations, time and cost. Samco Machinery, a Toronto-based supplier of roll-forming machinery to the construction industry, offered to develop a chassis made entirely from one piece of metal. A coil of narrow steel would be fed into a succession of spools to become a firm, elongated trough which could then be cut into 1.5-meter segments. Each segment would be put through a stretch bender adding angles to what was now a fully realized chassis ready to be integrated into the body of the car. According to Joseph P. Repovs, founder, chief executive officer (CEO), Samco Machinery:

> We reengineered the processes to eliminate welding, heating or banging and also wastage of metal. The new chassis is thinner, tougher and cheaper. We will be installing the roll-forming machinery at the Nano plant at Singur and this is our first major foray outside Canada.

The Nano faced little direct price competition in India or elsewhere. At ₹ one lakh, the Nano would be by far the most affordable car ever made. The Nano cost one-fourth of the price of the Mini and provided the same horsepower:

Among its global competitors (see Exhibit 1), the only car comparable to Nano in terms of pricing was the Pakistan-made Sitara. But with no doors and no roofing, Sitara looked more like a hybrid between a jeep and a golf cart than a car. Launched in 2004, Sitara had sold less than 100 units in four years. The company had not achieved scale, which was crucial to cost leadership. Bogged down in bureaucratic hurdles to capacity creation and facing competition from Chinese imports, Sitara was yet to make a dent on the Pakistani middle-class consumers.

Ravi Kant was preoccupied with Nano's affordability to the Indian consumer. In the context of the European or U.S. market, a sticker price of $2,200 was inexpensive (one-tenth of the average passenger car price). In India, however, a Nano would cost three times the country's per capita income, or two years worth of earnings for a salaried employee. The average pay for factory workers at TML was US$5,500 a year.[54]

The federal and provincial taxes added as much as 24 per cent to the price tag. The Society of Indian Automobile Manufacturers, an industry body representing 38 leading vehicle and vehicular engine manufacturers, had been lobbying the federal government for an eight percentage point reduction

---

[53] Krishna Gopalan and Kushan Mitra, "How Nano Was Built," Business Today, January 22, 2008, http://tatanano.inservices.tatamotors.com/tatamotors/index.php?option=com_content&task=view&id=215&Itemid=207, last accessed October 28, 2008.

[54] Robyn Meredith, "The Next People's Car," Forbes, April 16, 2007 http://finance.yahoo.com/family-home/article/102865/the-next-peoples-car, accessed September 5, 2008.

in post-manufacturing tax from 24 per cent to 16 per cent on small cars. Demand for the Nano (and its growing competition) was price sensitive; however, lowering the tax burden would spearhead adoption and thus recover the forgone governmental revenues within five to seven years. But most importantly, a lower tax would provide a low-cost, low-emission alternative to India's consumers and help establish India as a small car hub, churning automotive innovations for the rest of the world.

Local Competition

The proliferation of low-cost small cars in India's market was good news to the consumer, to Tata Motors and its competitors. The popularity of these cars created an added incentive for investments that could both lower the cost structure of the new technology (through alliances, co-production agreements, supplier learning) and motivate the government to lower the tax structure in an effort to boost demand and reduce emissions. India's average of three cars per 1,000 people provided the market potential for significant opportunities for second movers. Exhibit 7 highlights Tata Motors' approach towards sustainability.

Compared to the U.S. market, India's car penetration was an order of magnitude lower. For example, the total number of passenger vehicles sold in India for the year ending March 2006, was 1.3 million, equivalent to one month's sale in the U.S. market. Put differently, one billion Indians purchased approximately the same number of cars in one year as 300 million Americans purchased in one month.

The Nano and its competitors would compete head on with the scooter and motorcycle segment, seven million of which had been sold in India in 2006 (see Exhibit 3b). The unit prices of scooters and motorcycles ranged between INR30,000 and INR70,000 (US$675 to $1,600). According to McKinsey and Co. partner Ramesh Mangaleswaran, in Mumbai, about 2 million of the motorcycle owners would trade up to buy the Tata car at a price of $1,000.[55]

In 2006, an estimated 600,000 used cars (about half of the new car sales) changed hands. The size of the used car market, by volume, was estimated to be 10 per cent higher than the new car market. The number of old cars sold during the year ending March 2006 was approximately 1.5 million. About 85 per cent of the used car market consisted of small, individually owned outfits. Some of the car manufacturers had entered the market, including Maruti Suzuki (with its "True Value"), Honda ("Auto Terrace"), Mahindra & Mahindra ("First Choice"), Hyundai and Ford. The most recent entrant was a non-auto player, Reliance, which was planning to set up "auto zones" as part of expanding its retail operations. Nano was bound to be an attractive proposition to the cost-conscious (and gas-conscious) consumer.

Global Presence

Reflecting on Tata Motors' track record of economic performance (Exhibits 8 and 9), Ratan Tata reportedly said:

> If you have to be competitive in India, you have to be competitive in the world. Otherwise the Indian advantage will get eroded one day as foreign companies expand their presence in India. . . . If you have to be competitive in India, you have to be competitive in the world.[56]

---

[55] Robyn Meredith, "The Incredible Story of Tata Motors and the ₹1-lakh Car," Forbes, March 20, 2007, http://www.rediff.com/money/2007/mar/30tata.htm, accessed September 6, 2007.

[56] Kiron Kasbekar, "All Right Turns," Tata Review, May 2008, http://www.tata.com/pdf/2596-page6-9_Transformation.pdf, accessed September 6, 2007.

Nano was a winning pick. Low-cost cars were the single most important up-trend in the global automotive industry. By 2012, the market for vehicles costing less than $10,000 was likely to reach 18 million cars, or one-fifth of world auto sales, up from 12 million in 2006, according to Roland Berger Strategy Consultants.[57] The majority of low-cost cars sold in the price range of between $5,000 and $10,000, depending on size and features (see Exhibit 1).

Going global, Nano would be facing competition from three automotive segments: established carmakers diversifying abruptly into small cars; new manufacturers planning to enter the small-car market and used car dealers. Established carmakers and new manufacturers would likely compete on fuel efficiency and emission reductions; whereas used car dealers were more likely to compete on price with better features but lower miles per gallon.

Small Is In

Every major carmaker had announced its own 21st century Model T project. Toyota, Fiat, Volkswagen and Peugeot had all vowed to build cut-rate Logan-killers (a reference to the Logan, a successful bare-bones sedan manufactured by Renault). India emerged as a perfect storm for testing the new model of competition in low-cost, low-emission vehicles.

Chrysler

Chrysler was developing low-cost cars with Chinese manufacturer Chery.

Ford

The company had announced plans to invest $500 million to develop a small car in India.

General Motors

GM had announced plans to use its Korean subsidiary, GM Daewoo, to design a model selling for approximately $7,000. It was also planning to make India its export hub for small cars.

Renault Nissan

Renault already had a runaway hit with Logan, its bare-bones sedan. The automaker had started offering the roomier Logan in Europe for $7,200 in 2004—40 per cent less than rival sedans—and had since sold 450,000 of the cars in 51 countries. To make a success of the Logan, Renault manufactured in low-cost Romania. Renault had reduced the total number of parts and made assembly less complicated. It stripped out sophisticated electronics and dispensed with high-tech curved windshields. Savings of $3 per vehicle were achieved by installing identical rear-view mirrors on each side. The biggest breakthrough was the elimination of prototypes and the tooling involved in building them, both of which were expensive. As a result, Renault could move directly from digital mockup to production, an innovation that saved $40 million.

Toyota

Toyota was working on a car with a sticker price of less than $7,000 that could hit emerging markets, such as India and Brazil, by 2009. The company was banking on breakthroughs in new materials, manufacturing and low-cost factories. A successful Toyota venture in this segment could "scramble all the eggs in emerging markets," according to a competitor.[58]

---

[57] http://www.rolandberger.com/news/2006-06-30-rbsc-news-hybrid_hype.html, last accessed October 27, 2008.

[58] http://www.businessweek.com/magazine/content/07_17/b4031064.htm?chan=search, last accessed October 27, 2008.

Hyundai

Hyundai sold the cheapest new car available in the United States—the Korean-made Chevrolet Aveo—at $10,560, four times the price of Nano. Hyundai was planning to use its plant already set up in India, as a global hub for its small-car production. It was offering a popular entry-level sub-compact, the Santro, at a starting price of $6,300 in India, while still offering features such as air-conditioning and power steering standard. Moving along the high-tech production lines of its Indian plant were also cars for export to Europe, Russia, and Latin America.

Suzuki

Suzuki's product, Maruti, developed in a long-term collaboration with Maruti Udyog Ltd. (MUL) in India, was the number-one small car in India, which retailed at US$4,400 (INR200,000). MUL had pared costs to the bone with little provision for "breakthrough" reduction in costs. But it had two major advantages over a new competitor, such as TML. First, Suzuki's dies and tools had been fully depreciated. The company could thus reduce prices until it could force TML to back off, and it would still stay afloat. Second, the company had 185 True Value outlets all over the country, buying Maruti cars less than four years old (or having accumulated up to 60,000 km) and with no more than two previous owners. The cars would be reconditioned and sold to new buyers for between INR70,000 and INR80,000 (roughly US$1,775 to US$2,025)—a price lower than that of a new small car.

Global Trends

The global passenger car market was branching into a luxury segment, which continued to grow, and a frugal, low-cost stripped down segment, which provided convenience with low emissions.

Global car makers tried to straddle both segments; however, the majority found a sticker price of $3,000 or less could not even cover the input costs. Both European and North American producers focused on low- or zero-emissions premium cars, such as the Toyota Prius. These models offered high unit margins, an important attraction of a luxury car for producers. The margin on BMW, a German luxury car, was an estimated $3,300 per car, on average, compared with $400 per car on Logan, the bare-bones sedan manufactured by French auto-maker Renault.[59] Premium cars were heavier, and vehicle weight was an important consideration in fuel efficiency: the lighter the vehicle, the lower the fuel consumption.

Smaller cars typically fared better at the pump—typically, the smaller the vehicle, the better the mileage. Geely Group Co of China made a car for $3,900, which it was aiming to export to the United States by 2010. Suzuki, selling cars starting at $4,400 in India, was preparing to launch a new compact in 2008 for export to Europe. Tata's Indica, priced in 2007 at $8,500, was already selling in southern and Eastern Europe.

As growth in luxury models stalled in the United States, Europe and Japan, the major global automakers were eyeing the emerging markets for new opportunities. Tapping into these "base of pyramid" markets required redesigning models for buyers who could afford only a scooter or a motorcycle.

Nano-based Competition

Nano had fast-forwarded Tata Motors to a first-mover position in an exciting but highly competitive space, which exposed the company to both global praise and scrutiny. The attention showcased Tata

---

[59] "The Race to Build Really Cheap Cars," Business Week, April 23, 2007, http://www.businessweek.com/magazine/content/07_17/b4031064.htm?chan=search, last accessed on October 27, 2009.

group values by large deals and minute choices, all combining the social good with tomorrow's path-breaking technology.

Kant had made a long list of the strategic priorities in the short and medium term, as Tata Motors deliberately sought to outcompete its domestic and global rivals as it always did—by offering its customers the quality they had come to expect over a century of trust.

Sustaining First-Mover Advantage

Passenger cars would soon be treated as consumer durables in India; they would become commodity plays. Product differentiation would be no longer defined by low cost, giving way to the new differentiators: design and technology. The first-mover advantage would be put to test, as more and more competitors achieved manufacturing efficiency, performance, marketing network and after-sales service. The competition would no longer be based on price alone. Would Tata's leadership with trust be a sufficient differentiator? Would its world-class commitment to sustainability prevail over criticism mired in the demise of the oil on a heating planet?

Becoming a Systems Integrator

TML was at cross-roads in manufacturing. With the imminent launch of Nano, it was leapfrogging from stages 1 and 2 of Indian manufacturing, prevalent over its previous six decades, to stage 3, which would be an unfamiliar territory for the company.

Stage 1 had consisted of manufacturing trucks and buses only because the company had secured an official license to do so. The products were functional, sans frills, serving basic transportation needs. Sturdiness was all. Demand was so rampant that products had to be rationed for customers who waited in line. Everything the company produced was sold. Cost-plus was the only known formula for pricing. In this environment, manufacturers such as TML had little incentive for cost reduction although they took pride in ownership of the product. An off-shoot of this stage was for an entrepreneur to sign up with an overseas trading partner from whom to import the product for sale, at a markup, in the local market.

Stage 2 took off, post-liberalization. Companies went shopping for technologies they could adapt to local needs. They copied products, seeing them through their crude stages and gestation periods, and then refining them. The products were, in many ways, "me-toos" but, as it turned out, worked as well as, and often better than their foreign counterparts, and cost much less. Indian manufacturing had discovered its single largest competitive advantage—low labor costs—which was soon to gain importance in the global context. Indian engineers could cut costs to the bone, a skill developed by decades of selling to, what was to be known in later years as, the bottom of the pyramid segment of the Indian market. The cost-cutting led to a surge in exports of manufactured goods from India. Labor arbitrage soon became a driving force behind the export of services such as information technology (IT). Indian automotive companies, including TML, had started doing engineering work for global automakers at cut-rate prices.

With the launch of Nano, TML was moving into stage 3, where it would be involved only in product design. TML would not manufacture parts but instead would assemble components purchased from vendors. TML would be a systems integrator, making the Nano the way a hardware manufacturer, such as IBM, made its laptops, with displays from Toshiba, drives from Seagate, a chip from Intel. This approach would be a departure for TML, an automotive company that had been fully vertically integrated.[60]

---

[60] Rajeev Dubey, "Interview: Ratan Tata," Business World January 24, 2005, http://www.balendu.com/old_site/ratan_tata.htm, last accessed October 28, 2008.

Sailing in the eye of the (perfect) storm, India was quickly becoming a global center for small-car design, testing and production. According to a widely held belief, India would become a global hub for small-car production the way the United States had been for pickups. Hyundai and Suzuki were already building small cars in India, and Toyota was seriously considering setting up a hub in India.

The Nano would generate top-line growth but higher-margin variants were important for bottom-line growth. Creating luxury Nanos revived some tension between doing good and doing well, and between frugality and consumerism. Tata Motors' competitors had been criticizing the company for subsidizing the initial runs to gain strong footing and recognition in the exploding market. Frugal profit margins were not new to the group or to the company, both historically and through the last decade of restructuring. But were thin margins a matter of choice to maximize the social impact of the Nano or a powerful competitive tool to put strong values to use? How would competitors manage their product portfolios? Were low-emission models a market creation strategy? How low could or should the costs drop before the competition shifted to luxury, not so low-cost, features?

Extending Geographies

Countries with similar income levels in Africa, Southeast Asia, Eastern Europe and Latin America would open up exciting markets, not to mention neighboring China. Tata Motors had exported a small number of commercial vehicles, mainly to developing countries, but it had established bonds of trust with local distributors and customers. Its brand name would offer strong leverage for scaling up Nano's global reach.

According to Kant, however:

> The innovation wasn't in technology. It was in a mindset change. The Nano has put an end to all discussions of having variants of scooters or quadricycles as passenger vehicles on India's roads.[61]

The teamwork of young designers and the combination of talent and hunger for growth could make a world of difference to India's new generations of drivers. The job ahead for Tata was to make this decision a part of Tata Motors' history and the group's legacy in doing good.

Exhibit 1 The Nano and its competition

(a) Nano and India-based Competition

Credits: http://en.wikipedia.org/wiki/Image:Tata_Nano_Std.JPG, accessed September 5, 2008.

Credits: http://thunderror.com/maruti-a-star-the-new-alto/, accessed September 6, 2008.

(Continued)

[61] Manjeet Kripalani, "The Story Behind the Tata Nano," BusinessWeek.com, http://www.rediff.com/money/2008/may/14tata.htm, accessed September 6, 2008.

(*Continued*)

Mileage	20 km/liter	22 km/liter
Fuel tank	15 liters	28 liters
Price	INR100,000	INR194, 624
Features	Rear-wheel drive, all-aluminum, two-cylinder, 31 horsepower, 623 cc engine	Front-wheel drive, all-aluminum, three cylinder, 33 horsepower, 800 cc engine
Length	3.1 meters	3.1 meters
Width	1.5 meters	1.5 meters
Height	1.6 meters	1.6 meters

Source: "Tata Keeps His Promise," BW Online Bureau, January 10, 2008.

(b) Global Small Car Competitors

Brand	Company	Country	Features	Price (INR)
Citroen C1	Citroen	France	Petrol: 998 cc, three cylinder, 68 hp; Diesel: 1,398 cc, four cylinder, 55 hp	513,105–667,155
Sitara	Habib Motors	Pakistan	Petrol, 170 cc, single-cylinder	92,345
Smart Forfour	DaimlerChrysler	USA	Petrol & diesel, 1,124 cc–1,493 cc, three cylinder, 68–177 hp	576,305–1358,405
Oka City	Kamaz	Russia	Petrol, 749 cc, two cylinder, 35 hp	351,560
Aixam 751	Aixam Mega	France	Diesel, 479 cc, two cylinder, 12.9 hp	456,456–543,400

Source: R Sridharan, "Tata's ₹1 Lakh Car," Business Today, October 9, 2005, http://www.highbeam.com/doc/1P2-10955606.html, last accessed October 28, 2008.

Exhibit 2 Tata motors' milestones[1]

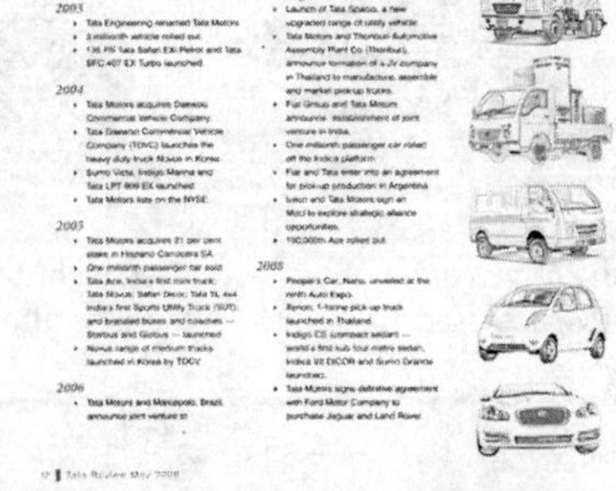

[1] *Source:* "Competing Globally?: It's a Work in Progress," Tata Review, May 2008, p. 12, used with permission; http://www.tata.com/pdf/2596-page10-12_ravi_kant.pdf, accessed September 6, 2008.

Exhibit 3

(a) The Indian Consumer

Household Income Classes	Real Annual Household Income ($)	Segment Size (Millions of Households)	Common Occupations	Assets Owned
"Global India"	>10,000	1	Businesspeople in small to mid-size enterprises; corporate and government employees; and rich farmers	1–2 bedroom house; color TV; mobile phone; refrigerator, washing machine; car
"Aspiring India"	4,000–10,000	40	Salaried employees; new services (IT and media) employees; and shopkeepers	Color TV; refrigerator; washing machine; scooter, motorcycle or small car
"Struggling India"	1,500–4,000	110	Shopkeepers; service workers (waiters, drivers and maids); and farmers	Bicycle; black & white TV; radio
"Destitute India"	<1,500	40	Subsistence farmers and farm workers	Watch

Note: (1) Data pertains to 2004.
(2) Average household size: 5.4.
Source: McKinsey Quarterly 2005 special edition "Winning the Indian Consumer".

(b) Domestic Sales of Vehicles, 2000–2007

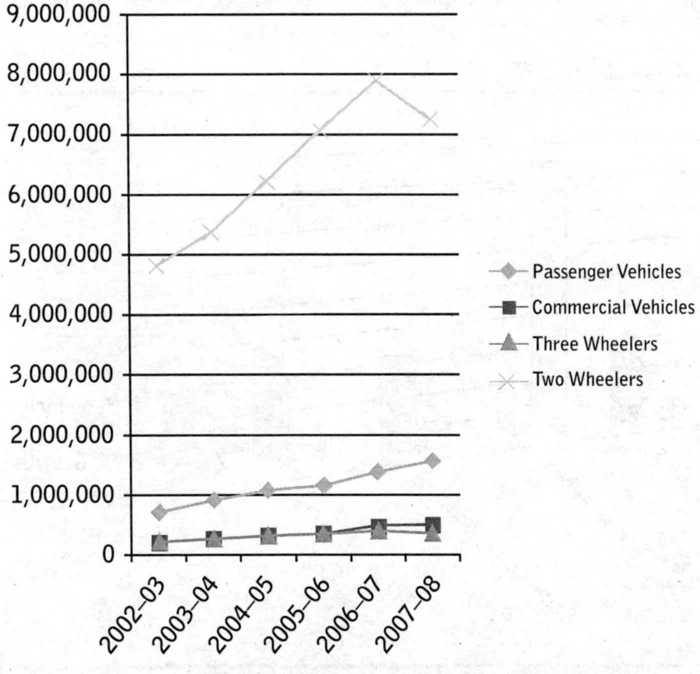

Source: Adapted from Society of Indian Automobile Manufacturers, "Domestic Sales Trend," http://www.siamindia.com/scripts/domestic-sales-trend.aspx, accessed September 5, 2008.

Exhibit 4 Vehicle production and sales in India

(a) India's Automotive Market: Major Players and Sales Volumes

		Sales Volume in India (FY 07)			
		Commercial Vehicles	**Passenger Cars**	**Two Wheelers**	**Three Wheelers**
Major Indian Private Players (FY 2007)					
Tata Motors	7,679	336,590	245.556		
Hero Honda	2,815			3,339,896	
Bajaj Auto	2,594			2,379,512	329,485
Ashok Leyland	2,067	83,104			
TVS Motors	1,090			1,513,764	
Major International Private Players (CY 06)					
Suzuki	27,049		582,228		
Hyundai	66,663		314,604		
Ford	160,126		41,451		
GM	207,349		36,894		
Toyota	204,754		50,210		
Honda	94,974		59,152	713,889	

Source: Adapted from Society of Indian Automobile Manufacturers (SIAM), and annual reports; http://www.siamindia.com/, last accessed September 5, 2008.

(b) Vehicle Production in India, 2007

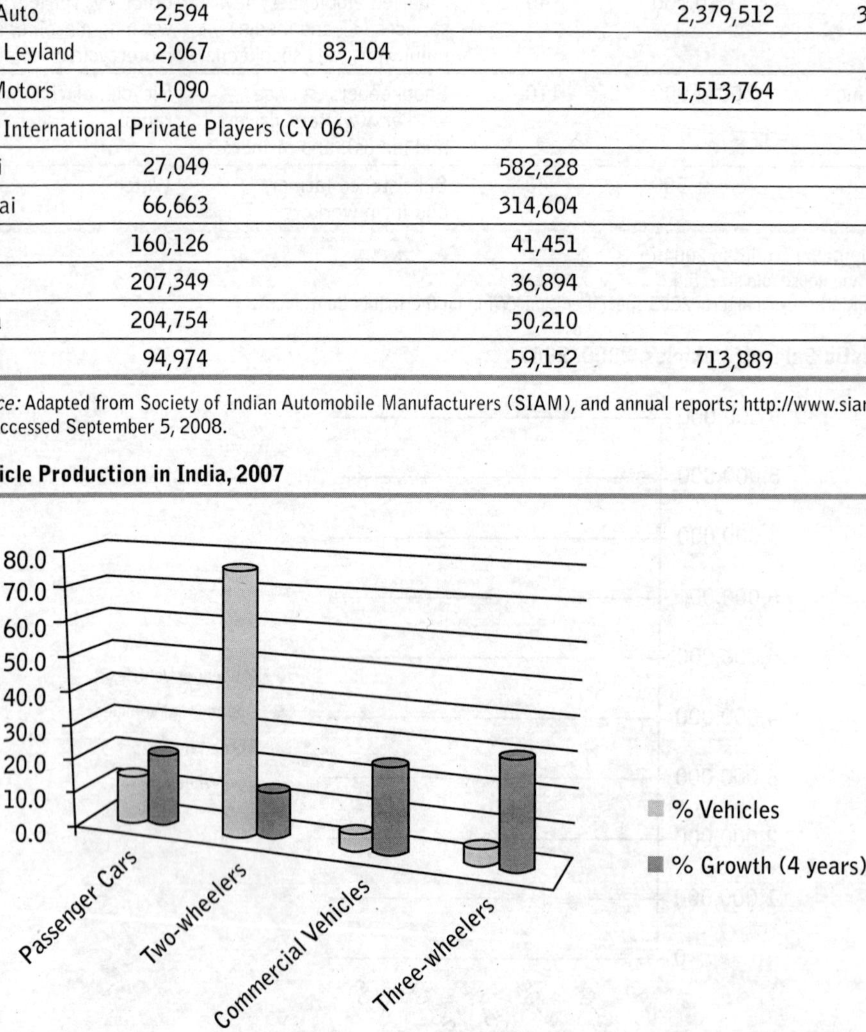

Source: Adapted from Society of Indian Automobile Manufacturers (SIAM) and annual reports. http://www.siamindia.com, last accessed September 5, 2008.

(c) The Indian Passenger Car Market, Vehicle Production Volumes, 2001–2006

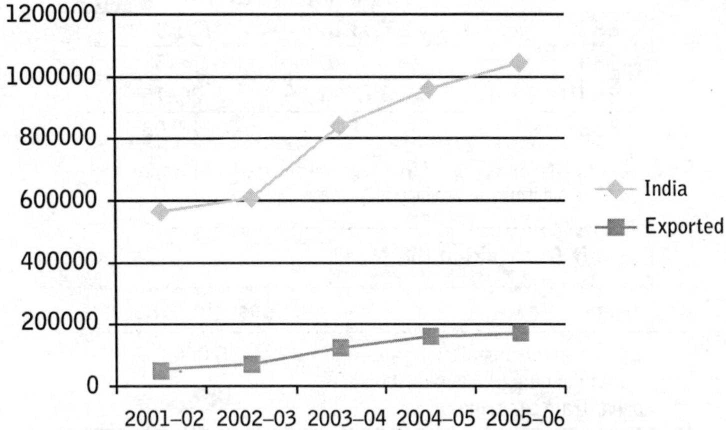

Source: Adapted from Society of Indian Automobile Manufacturers (SIAM), http://www.siamindia.com/, last accessed September 5, 2008.

Exhibit 5 Vehicle emissions regulations in India

(a) History of Emission Regulations in India[62]

1989 Idle Emission Regulation
1991 Mass Emission Regulation (CO & HC) (Hot Start; Indian Driving Cycle)
1992 Mass Emission Regulation for Diesel Vehicles
1995 Fitment of catalytic converters (CAT) for cars in four metros
1996 Tightening of emission limits (CO, HC & NOx), Evaporative Emission & Crank Case Emission
1998 Norms for CAT-fitted vehicles (50% tighter standards)
1998 From September, fitment of CAT converters in 42 major cities for petrol-driven passenger vehicles
2000 India 2000 (Euro-I equivalent) norms for all 4-wheelers; Bharat Stage-II (Euro-II equivalent) norms in the National Capital Region (NCR) for Passenger Cars and minivan or multi-purpose utility vehicles (MUVs); Extended to Mumbai and Kolkata from January 2001 and Chennai from July 200; Tightest norms in the world for two wheelers
2001 Bharat Stage II (Euro II equivalent) norms for Commercial Vehicles in Delhi and Kolkata (from October 24, 2001); Bharat Stage II norms for CVs in Mumbai and Chennai from November 1, 2001.
2005 Maruti Udyog has rolled out Euro-III compliant cars (According to a Hindu Business Line 2005 release, "Euro-III is nearly equivalent to Bharat Stage-III, which is the vehicular emission standard proposed by the Union government and to be effective from April 2005 in identified metropolitan cities having substantial vehicle population").[63]
2010 Based on the report of the Mashelkar committee on auto-fuel policy for improvement of air quality. In 2010, Bharat Stage-IV equivalent to Euro-IV is envisaged. The adoption will be initiated in metros first, and then gradually extended to vehicles plying all over India.

---

[62] Source: K.K. Gandhi, "Vehicle Emissions Standards in India," Presentation at Regional Workshop for Reducing Vehicle Emissions: Strengthening Inspection and Maintenance, November 7–0, 2001, Chongqing, PRC, http://www.adb.org/Documents/Events/2001/RETA5937/Chongqing/documents/cq_08_gandhi.pdf, accessed September 6, 2008.

[63] B.S. Murthy, "Euro versus. Bharat Norms," The Hindu Business Line, http://www.thehindubusinessline.com/2005/02/07/stories/2005020700280900.htm, accessed September 6, 2008.

(b) Bharat Stages (BS): Prescribed Emission Limits[64]

	CO (g/km)	HC+NOx (g/km)
BS I	2.72/3.16*	.97/1.30*
BS II	2.20	.50
BS III	2.30	.20/.15
BS IV	1.00	.10/.08

*Lower values are for type approval and the higher values are for conformity of production.

Exhibit 6 Making the Nano

Item	Cost (in INR)
Engine and transmission (aluminum engine block, gear box, drive-train, steering)	30,000
Body shell (steel, frame, welding)	9,000
Electricals (lights, batteries, starter motor)	9,000
Suspension and wheels	11,000
Interiors (floor mats, seats, plastics, roof trim)	7,500
Post-manufacturing tax	24,000
Sales tax	4,000
Gross profit	5,500
Sale price	100,000

Suppliers for Tata's Nano

Supplier	Product
Behr	HVAC for the luxury version
Bosch	Gasoline injection system (diesel will follow), starter, alternator, brake system
Caparo	Inner structural panels
Continental	Gasoline fuel supply system, fuel level sensor
Delphi	Instrument cluster
Denso	Windshield wiper system (single motor and arm)
FAG	Rear-wheel bearing

64 Ibid.

Ficosa	Rear-view mirrors, interior mirrors, manual and CVT shifters, washer system
Freudenberg	Engine sealing
GKN	Driveshafts
INA	Shifting elements
ITW Deltar	Outside and inside door handles
Johnson Controls	Seating
Mahle	Camshafts, spin-on oil filters, fuel filters and air cleaners
Saint-Gobain	Glazing
TRW	Brake system
Valeo	Clutch sets
Vibracoustic	Engine mounts
Visteon	Air induction system
ZF	Chassis components, including tie rods

Source: Simon Bickerstaffe and Tristan Honeywill, "India's Tata Low-Cost Nano Took a Lot of High-Tech," Automotive Engineer, March 2008, httL://www.ae-plus.com/Key%20topics/cc-Tata-news3.htm, accessed September 6, 2008.

Exhibit 7 Sustainability at Tata Motors

"The Tata Group is guided by the Principle of Trusteeship and the conviction that Free Enterprise, in order to thrive, must serve the needs of society. This is the cornerstone of our Corporate Sustainability initiatives. Tata Motors is committed, in letter and spirit, to the improvement in the quality of life of people."

Tata Motors adheres to the Global Reporting Initiative (GRI), a multi-stakeholder process to develop and disseminate globally applicable Sustainability Reporting Guidelines. It is based on the "Triple Bottom Line" of Strong Financial Performance (Profit), Strong Environmental Management (Planet) and Corporate Social Responsibility (People). Reporting began in 2002/03. A Third Party assurance audit was completed by PricewaterhouseCoopers for the 2004/05 report. The 2005/06 GRI report was based on the latest G3 guidelines; the same approach was followed for the 2006/07 report.[65]

Tata Motors received the prestigious "CII-ITC Sustainability Award 2006 for Significant Achievement on the Journey towards Sustainable Development." The award recognizes Tata Motors' corporate governance practices and economic, environmental and social performance—the Triple Bottomline concept as per guidelines of the Global Reporting Initiative (GRI):

> The assessment included, among various factors, the company's practices to engage with and initiate action on stakeholders' concerns and perceptions, proactive initiatives going beyond statutory compliances, resource use efficiency on scarce resources like water and energy, enhancement of living standards in adjacent neighbourhoods, transparency and reporting standards, processes for diversification with new products and into new markets.[66]

(*Continued*)

[65] "Company: Tata Motors Ltd.," Karmajog.org, http://www.karmayog.org/csr500companies/csr500companies_8541.htm, accessed September 6, 2008.

[66] Tata Motors, "Tata Motors Conferred with Sustainability Award–2006," media release, http://www.tata.com/company/releases/inside.aspx?artid=+XWDmdOTUuY=, accessed September 6, 2008.

(Continued)

The 2006/07 Corporate Sustainability Annual Report states:

> Tata Motors partners in the efforts of various industry forums like the CII, BCCI, SIAM and TERI. In the year 2006-07, Tata Motors has took the first steps towards assessing the "As is" status of the affirmative actions that the company has taken so far for improving the condition of the disadvantaged, particularly the Scheduled Caste and the Scheduled Tribe populations (Report Attached as Annexure II). While grappling with the issue of withstanding the threat of reservations being introduced in the private sector, the company commits itself to better the present status of the SC/ST populations by taking measures to improve their educational status, enhance employability and create entrepreneurs through mentoring and promoting leadership amongst the SC/ST community. Representatives from Tata Motors also participated in various conferences and seminars organised by BCCI, TERI and SIAM and contributed positively to the discussions regarding sustainability and industry's role in preserving the triple bottom line of people, planet and profit.[67]

Exhibit 8 Tata Motors Ltd. consolidated balance sheet

For the Year Ending March 31 (in INR Million)	2008	2007	2006
Sources of Funds			
1. Shareholders' Funds			
(a) Share Capital	3,856	3,855	3,829
(b) Reserves and Surplus	83,120	73,362	57,486
2. Minority Interest	4,683	2,500	1,739
3. Loan Funds			
(a) Secured	60,118	44,626	8,816
(b) Unsecured	55,730	28,392	24,975
4. Deferred Tax Liability	9,744	8,173	6,768
5. Total Funds Employed	**217,251**	**160,908**	**103,613**
Application of Funds			
6. Fixed assets			
(a) Gross Block	129,756	103,591	93,050
(b) Less Depreciation	60,605	54,266	48,436
(c) Net Block	69,151	49,325	44,614
(d) Capital Work-In-Progress	59,482	25,816	9,745
7. Goodwill	5,661	4,430	4,122
8. Investments	26,658	11,747	12,615

[67] Tata Motors, "CS at Non-plant Locations," Annual Report, 2006–2007, http://www.tatamotors.com/CSR-0607/page-13.php, accessed September 6, 2008.

9. Current Assets, Loans and Advances			
(a) Interest accrued in investments	12	63	65
(b) Inventories	32,946	31,670	24,810
(c) Sundry Debtors	20,605	17,022	13,545
(d) Cash and Bank Balances	38,331	11,543	13,864
(e) Loans and Advances	100,778	97,828	58,284
10. Less: Current Liabilities and Provisions			
(a) Current liabilities	113,192	72,350	64,437
(b) Provisions	23,253	16,304	13,754
11. (9-10) Net Current Assets	56,227	69,471	32,378
12. Miscellaneous Expenditure	72	119	139
13. Total Assets (Net)	**217,251**	**160,908**	**103,613**

Source: Tata Motors, Annual Report 2006–2007, page 94.

Exhibit 9 Tata Motors Ltd. consolidated income statement

For the Year Ended March (in INR Million)	2008	2007	2006
Income			
1. Sales	403,408	369,878	272,637
Less Excise duty	46,893	45,614	34,943
2. Other Income	2,675	1,531	2,435
Total Income	**359,190**	**325,795**	**240,129**
Expenses			
3. Manufacturing Expenses	312,406	283,105	207,212
Gross Profit	46,784	42,690	32,917
4. Product Development Expenses	659	850	718
5. Depreciation	7,820	6,885	6,233
6. Interest	7,443	4,058	2,4,60
Profit Before Tax	30,862	30,896	23,506
Profit After Tax	**22,347**	**21,700**	**17,281**

Source: Tata Motors, Annual Report 2006–2007, page 95.

24

Louis Vuitton in India[1]

R. Chandrasekhar wrote this case under the supervision of Professor Shih-Fen Chen solely to provide material for class discussion. The authors do not intend to illustrate either effective or ineffective handling of a managerial situation. The authors may have disguised certain names and other identifying information to protect confidentiality.

INTRODUCTION

> Luxury: from the Latin word luxus, meaning indulgence of the senses regardless of cost.[2]

In January 2008, Louis Vuitton, the fashion and leather goods business unit of LVMH Group, the Paris-headquartered luxury goods conglomerate, was at a crossroads in India. It was to open a new store, its third in the country so far, in a luxury mall scheduled to launch in a few months in the city of New Delhi. The move would be a departure from the protective environment of luxury hotels playing host to the two stores Louis Vuitton had established in the country. The new location would also mean a change in the profile of its customers in India. The company would be moving from targeting

[1] This case has been written on the basis of published sources only. Consequently, the interpretation and perspectives presented in this case are not necessarily those of LVMH Group or any of its employees.

[2] V. Vedpuriswar, "The Marketing of Luxury Brands," Catalyst Magazine, The Hindu Business Line, http://www.blonet.com/catalyst/20005/03/03/stories/2005030300170200.htm, accessed June 29, 2007.

the "super rich" who travelled, shopped abroad, and formed part of a captive pool, to what a local business magazine called those at the "next lower level," representing, in the view of Louis Vuitton's top executives, "a tipping point" for the company.[3]

Louis Vuitton had to plan its route ahead in a new landscape. The luxury mall business model, per se, was new to India.

COMPANY BACKGROUND

Louis Vuitton had its origins in Paris. In 1854 a French craftsman invented the flat-topped trunk (which stacked better during travelling than the traditional dome-shaped trunk) with a canvas cover (which, when varnished, rendered the cover waterproof).[4] The company, bearing the founder's name, flourished with the growth of travel by rail and ship. It soon opened a store in London, U.K., but for seven decades Louis Vuitton remained a single-product brand of handmade leather bags before diversifying into leather accessories. In 1987, Louis Vuitton merged with Moët Hennessy, a French wine maker of 1743 vintage, to form LVMH Group.

In its early decades, Louis Vuitton thrived in Europe because of the general attitude towards luxury in the region where aristocracies formed the ruling elite. Luxury in Europe was for the chosen few. For those chosen few, luxury was about feeling exclusive. This was to prove a contrast to the U.S. market, where luxury was about feeling special. The American luxury market had democratic roots where luxury was for all. Europe and the United States were to become the two largest consumers of luxury products but the differences were marked. European luxury brands did not have price points aimed at capturing consumers at various levels. American brands did. They had product lines that allowed luxury "nibbling."

LVMH went on an acquisition spree during the 1990s, targeting heritage brands. By 2000, the company had over 60 brands in its portfolio, each a star in its own right, in four business segments: wines and spirits; watches and jewellery; perfumes and cosmetics; and fashion and leather goods (see Exhibit 1: LVMH—Business Segments).

Louis Vuitton, the pioneering travel brand that was now the flagship brand of the company's fashion and leather goods business segment, generated over half of the group's profits. The segment included a number of other brands besides Louis Vuitton: Fendi, Donna Karan, Loewe, Marc Jacobs, Celine, Kenzo, Givenchy, Thomas Pink, Pucci, Berluti, Stefanobi, Rossimoda and eLuxury.

LVMH combined the artistic creativity of its designers with a rigorous management of resources to produce brands that were the most profitable in the world in the luxury genre. The company's operating metrics and performance standards were considered worthy of emulation by peers.

According to Antonio Belloni, Group Managing Director, LVMH:

> Because our businesses are artistic and commercial at the same time, the success of our brands lies in the quality of the collaboration between managers and designers. It is inconceivable to lead a luxury company if you don't have a true passion for creation. It is essential for the designer to absorb the culture of the brand so that he or she is in

---

[3] Priya Srinivasan, "Brussels, Madrid, New Delhi, Mumbai: Louis Vuitton's Chairman and CEO insists they are in the same league," http://archives.digitaltoday.in/businesstoday/20041219/trends4.html, Business Today, December 19, 2004, accessed December 24, 2007.

[4] *"LVMH Moët Hennessy Louis Vuitton SA," http://www.fundinguniverse.com/company-histories/, accessed December 29, 2007.*

> harmony with its universe. At the same time, the manager's role is not to interfere in the creative process, but to support it with strong teams and translate that process into products and communications that can stir emotions and excitement. Our star brands are the perfect illustration of the power of a successful symbiosis.[5]

Louis Vuitton was keen on projecting itself as a luxury brand with a distinguished heritage and not a fashion brand that changed with the times. The demand for Louis Vuitton products was strong and there was a wait list, particularly for special orders, in every market. The stores did not sell more than five units of a product at a time to a customer because the company did not want to encourage a parallel business of reselling. Its merchandise was the same in all stores. Distribution was tightly controlled. No Louis Vuitton bag was ever marked down.

The fashion and leather goods business had 14 production workshops—12 in France and one each in Spain and California—where the processes, although planned and executed with modern technology, relied on the skills of individual artisans. They were labor-intensive. The production of a single purse could entail up to 1,000 manufacturing tasks, each crucial to the desired quality. In spite of an assembly line orientation, the focus was on craftsmanship and not on mass manufacturing. Shop floor employees worked in teams of 20 to 30, each working on one product at a time. A team of 24 workers produced about 120 handbags a day.[6] The fashion and leather goods business also had an international logistics centre catering to the supply chain requirements of 382 stores in 59 countries (see Exhibit 2).

By 2007, the group had 2,048 stores worldwide. It had 71,885 employees, of whom 74 per cent were outside France, essentially in the retail networks of North and South America and Asia-Pacific. Listed on the New York Stock Exchange, LVMH had consolidated sales revenue of €16.5 billion and a net profit of €2.3 billion for the year ending December 2007 (see Exhibit 3).

ENTERING INDIA

Under pressure from Wall Street to sustain double digit growth rates, LVMH was planning to enter new markets, beyond the traditional orbit of Japan, Western Europe and the United States. It had developed a long-term strategy wherein it would not only continue to invest in brands with high potential and develop its traditional markets but also tap into the growing markets of China, India and Central Europe. The company found in the rising affluence of Asian markets, in particular, a natural growth platform. It was thus that the company started working, in 1999, towards a formal entry into India.

There was a historical reason for choosing India. In the late 19th century, more than 600 maharajahs were ruling various regional provinces in British India. They were among the wealthiest people in the country. They flooded the small factory of Louis Vuitton in Paris with requisitions for custom-made leather interiors for their Rolls-Royces and leather bags for their travel during annual vacations. It was the ongoing orders from Indian royal families, among other wealthy customers, that had helped Louis Vuitton survive the Great Depression of the 1920s. That relationship had blossomed over the decades, with the maharajahs becoming customers for later Louis Vuitton products. India was thus a familiar market for Louis Vuitton, which was a well-known brand among its ruling class.

---

[5] LVMH 2006 annual report, p. 8.

[6] Carol Matlack, "The Vuitton Money Machine: Inside the world's biggest, most profitable luxury brand," BusinessWeek online, http://www.businessweek.com/magazine/content/04_12/b3875002.htm, March 22, 2004, accessed January 15, 2008.

Yves Carcelle, Louis Vuitton's chief executive officer, was keen on leveraging the historical relationship between India and the brand when he joined the company in 1990. An alumnus of INSEAD, Paris, Carcelle had signed up with the LVMH Group as director of strategy a year earlier. He was an Indophile.[7] Bollywood movies were a particular source of fascination for him, as was Indian art.[8] He knew intuitively that India was a market for luxury products waiting to be tapped.

India was unlike the markets of the United States, Europe and the Far East in which Louis Vuitton was doing business. It was a country of 1.03 billion, the second largest mass of people occupying a single geographical territory in the world, next to China. Of these people, 72.2 per cent lived in more than 550,000 villages and the rest in about 2,000 towns and cities, and 20.1 per cent could not read or write. Indians spoke a total of 1,652 languages and dialects, evidence of the country's diversity.[9] Since becoming independent from British rule in 1947, India had followed a socialistic pattern of economic development characterized by government ownership of economic assets. Several multinational corporations (MNCs), such as Coca-Cola and IBM, had exited from India in late 1970s because, although the market was huge, the official stance at the time was anti-MNC. In 1991, the federal government started a series of liberalization measures aimed at not only diluting its role in business but promoting foreign investment in many sectors of manufacturing and services in order to make them globally competitive.

Post-liberalization, the Indian economy had grown. The percentage of those below the poverty line was coming down[10] (see Exhibit 4). The federal government had been using, since 1973, the conventional calorific method where a consumption level below 2,400 calories per day (necessary for subsistence living) was deemed below the poverty line. The money needed to buy 2,400 calories in 1973 was 51 Indian rupees (INR), equivalent to US$6.60 at the then exchange rate of INR7.74 to US$1 but equivalent to $1.16 in 2005 at the exchange rate of INR44.1 to US$1). The World Bank was using the more widely accepted criterion wherein anyone earning less than a dollar a day was considered extremely poor. Accordingly, in 2005, 266.5 million people (out of a total population of 1.08 billion) were below the poverty line (see Exhibit 5).

A country in which 87 per cent of the population lived on an income of less than $2.50 a day would not be a particularly hospitable environment even to a fashion products company. Louis Vuitton was a luxury products company, way beyond fashion. While examining its Indian option in the late 1990s, Louis Vuitton made the important observation that "the rich in India were flying to London, Dubai, Singapore, New York and Paris to shop because there was nothing available in India for them to buy."[11] It did not take long for Louis Vuitton to articulate two clear long-term goals: to open a Louis Vuitton store in every Indian city with a population of 10 million plus and to acquire a cumulative customer base of one million in India by 2010.

Four years down the line, the new venture had not yet made a direct local sale. That was because it had not yet set up a local physical presence. But the company remained upbeat about the market potential. Demand was the least of its concerns. It was busy mapping a route that could take Louis Vuitton to its stated goals without hitting road blocks.

---

[7] Sona Bahadur, "Monumental Agenda," Verve Magazine online edition, Vol. 15, Issue 7, July 2007, http://www.verveonline.com/51/fashion/yvesfull.shtml, accessed December 24, 2007.

[8] Matlack, "The Vuitton Money Machine."

[9] Census of India, Census data finder. http://www.censusindia.gov.in/Census_Data_2001/Census_data_finder/Census_Data_Finder.aspx. accessed September 07, 2008.

[10] The country's Planning Commission had used the criterion of monthly per capita consumption expenditure at INR 356.35 for rural areas and INR 538.60 for urban areas as indicative of the poverty line.

[11] Matlack, "The Vuitton Money Machine."

There were macro-management issues that needed resolution. The customs duties on imports of luxury products were high in India. Ranging between 30 per cent and 70 per cent, they had rendered domestic purchases of luxury products more expensive than offshore purchases. High tariffs were a disincentive for consumers to buying locally. The federal government did not allow foreign direct investment in a retailing venture. There was also an official ban on imports of leather products: Louis Vuitton's traditional forte.

Louis Vuitton seemed to have entered India ahead of its time, three to four years too early. "It's not a scientific way of looking at investments," a company representative said during a visit to India at the time, "but this is the business model that works in India, and it's important for us to find the right pace to do things here."[12]

The company spent the interim period preparing the ground. Louis Vuitton had to clear a number of misgivings at various levels about a luxury goods marketer entering India. One major concern was that the entry of a multinational corporation such as Louis Vuitton would place the domestic leather trade at risk. The company was convinced that, on the contrary, it would provide structure to a trade that was largely unorganized, thereby bringing stability to local business. It was also convinced that India had the potential to become not only a sourcing centre for its global requirements of leather but also a manufacturing hub.

It was not until April 2001 that the federal government lifted the ban on imports of leather goods, as part of a wider mandate to comply with the requirements of the World Trade Organization. The first hurdle had been cleared. Louis Vuitton started examining potential locations for its retail stores.

MARKET SIZE

To estimate the potential market in India for luxury products, Louis Vuitton used the periodical household income surveys conducted by the National Council of Applied Economic Research (NCAER), a premier market research agency in the country. According to NCAER, in India in 2001–02 there were 20,000 families with annual incomes of more than INR100 million. That number was expected to grow to 53,000 by 2005 and to 140,000 by 2010.

Luxury product companies strategizing their entry into India were primarily targeting high-net-worth (HNW) consumers (those with a million dollars or more in liquid financial assets). The *World Wealth Report 2005–06*, published by Merrill Lynch and Capgemini, put the number of dollar millionaires in India at 83,000 in 2005. The report also said that India recorded the world's second fastest growth in the number of HNW individuals, 19.3 per cent in 2005.[13]

Crucial to companies strategic planning were the "cocooners," so called because of the metamorphosis they were undergoing in their income levels and spending habits. Nibbling around the crust of this new age of luxury and relishing the first bite, they had the potential to develop a taste for luxury and become its loyal consumers. Cocooners were part of the burgeoning mid-segment of the Indian consumer market, numbering 97 million. According to the McKinsey Global Institute's charting of the ascendance of the Indian middle class over the longer term, their number would go up to 583 million by 2025.

---

[12] Kishore Singh, "India enthralls Louis Vuitton," www.rediff.com/money/2005/jul/09spec3.htm, July 9, 2005, accessed August 17, 2007.

[13] Joanna Punjabi, "Luxury Brands' Wish List," The Economic Times, October 12, 2007, online edition http://economictimes.indiatimes.com/ET_Cetera/Luxury_brands_wish_list/articleshow/2450540.cms, accessed January 15, 2008.

The global luxury market was valued at $169 billion in 2004.[14] Approximately 60 per cent of the business was concentrated in 35 brands. Louis Vuitton was the largest global luxury brand by revenue, at about $4 billion, followed by Gucci, Prada, Giorgio Armani, Hermès and Chanel, each at about one billion dollars annually.

The size of the luxury market in India was estimated to be about $4 billion, and expected to grow to $30 billion by 2015. The largest of its segments was luxury assets—yachts, jets, cars and homes—valued at $2.9 billion. The second largest segment was luxury services, which included such things as cruise trips and vacations, and the third, luxury products. Comprising watches, jewellery, high-end electronics, wines, spirits, perfumes, apparel and personal accessories, the luxury products market was estimated to be $444 million and growing at 20 per cent annually.

The Indian consumer market was a study of contrasts. For example, domestic car makers were developing prototypes of cars for the mass market in India where many in the countryside travelled on foot. In December 2007, Tata Motors, a leading Indian auto maker, had already launched Nano, the world's lowest priced car at $2,500. At the same time, local marketing offices of high-end luxury cars such as Rolls-Royce, Porsche, Lamborghini, Aston Martin, Ferrari, Jaguar, Maybach and BMW were exceeding their sales targets in India. When Bentley of the United Kingdom opened its sales outlet in New Delhi in 2003, the head of Indian sales said that "many people seem to think we will close down in a year."[15] The super premium luxury car cost $430,000 in India (including 114 per cent customs duty). However, demand was so encouraging by 2007 that Bentley was planning to open a second sales outlet in Mumbai in the next year.

CUSTOMERS

As a result of the *States Reorganisation Act* of 1956, the maharajahs had lost their traditional hold in post-independent India and become part of mainstream Indian society. In 1971, they lost their titles and riches with the abolition of annual financial grants, called privy purses, to which they had previously been entitled from the federal government. With these changes, many of them faded into oblivion. Others became entrepreneurs, converting their palaces into luxury hotels. But they were all influential as viral marketers. It was through them that Louis Vuitton was trying to connect with the country's new elite: start-up owners of myriad new businesses in technology, manufacturing and services; professional CEOs in their thirties and early forties; non-resident Indians returning home; small and medium retailers; big-brand franchisees; Bollywood actors (who were both customers and image makers); and "closet spenders" (like politicians and bureaucrats). It was this elite, none of whom knew Louis Vuitton as a brand, that formed the new generation of customers for Louis Vuitton in India.

BUYING BEHAVIOR

Exclusivity was an important factor influencing the buying habits of luxury consumers in India. Perched as they were at the top of the pyramid, with a sizeable gap between them and the next rung of consumers, the "super rich" sought assurance in maintaining that gap. Thus, a complex combination of gratification, social assertion and the propensity to "make statements" (or define oneself through consumption) was

---

[14] Vanita Kohli-Khandekar, Nandini Vaish and Tanmoy Neog "The Business of Luxury," Businessworld, July 24, 2006.

[15] Amy Yee, "Wealthy lap up luxury goods," The Financial Times, May 29, 2007, available online at www.ft.com.

driving the purchase decisions of this segment. Significantly, the super rich were also prone to look for the best deal, opting often for a product or brand actually aimed at a less affluent segment.

This last trait was best exemplified in India by the affluent buyers' decisions regarding cell phone services, which involved, as elsewhere in the world, buying both a subscription and a handset. The affluent were picking up the cheaper phones and subscription options simply because the service, being ubiquitous, conferred no exclusive status on them. In spite of having the financial ability to purchase super-premium brands of cell phones, they were unwilling to pay for them since the product, per se, was available to all and sundry, although at different price points. It was only when the product was equated with the "creme de la crème," establishing a clear gap between them and other consuming classes, that they were willing to pay a premium.[16]

The buying behavior of luxury consumers in developed markets such as the United States seemed somewhat similar, of late. A survey by BIGresearch LLC, a market research firm, released at the National Retail Federation Conference in New York in January 2007, showed that 32.5 per cent of women who shopped at Bergdorf Goodman, Neiman Marcus or Saks—all luxury stores—in the preceding three months also shopped at Target, a discounter, while 11.6 per cent of them went to Wal-Mart whose "Every Day Low Prices" had become a catchphrase for mass retailing.[17]

Worldwide, luxury consumers fell into three categories, based on their personal concept of luxury. The first category consisted of those who bought a luxury product for its superior functionality and quality. They were older and wealthier and willing to pay premium for products that had enduring value. They conducted extensive pre-purchase research, making decisions that were logical rather than emotional or impulsive. Messages that highlighted product quality and were information-intensive appealed to them. Consisting of connoisseurs, this category was the largest.

The second category comprised those who perceived luxury products as a reward. They saw them as status symbols with which to make the personal statement that they had "arrived." Highly driven, they were motivated by a desire to be successful. They were also eager to showcase their success to others. At the same time, they were keen on not appearing lavish or hedonistic. They wanted to make seemingly "smart" decisions that demonstrated the importance of their purchases while not leaving them open to social criticism of any kind. Marketing messages communicating "acceptable" exclusivity appealed to this group.

The third category was the smallest and consisted of younger consumers, with a higher proportion of males than the other categories. They saw luxury products as a means of self-indulgence. They enjoyed luxury products for their feel-good factor. They were emotional in their purchase decisions and were not concerned with product longevity or its enduring value.

According to a study by American Express, *Inside the Affluent Space*, the mindset of the Indian consumer was a desire to prove that "I've made it." The study had placed the Indian consumer in the second category.[18] It also showed that women, in particular, were emerging as a distinct voice inside the affluent space, signalling an important micro-trend in the marketplace.

---

[16] Adite Chatterjee, "Marketing to the Superich," Business Today, http://www.india-today.com/btoday/22041998/index.html, April 22, 1998, accessed November 10, 2008.

[17] "High income women covet luxury, but eye bargains,"17 Jan, 2008, Reuters http://economictimes.indiatimes.com/Specials/Womens_Day/High_income_women_covet_luxury_but_eye_bargains/rssarticleshow/2847217.cms, The Economic Times, January 17, 2007, accessed February 12, 2008.

[18] "Indian millionaires' club expanding fast," http://www.rediff.com/money/2006/sep/21rich.htm, September 21, 2006, accessed December 29, 2007.

2003—INDIAN LAUNCH

Typically, Louis Vuitton had its stores in boulevards ensuring a neighborhood compatible with its main brand value of exclusivity. Out of 382 stores worldwide, Louis Vuitton had 338 stores in luxury plazas housing high-end brands, with a premium aura. But Indian cities did not have high streets providing symbiotic clusters of luxury retailers. Specialty stores with nation-wide chains focusing on lifestyle products were also few. In spite of ongoing economic reforms, the Indian infrastructure was not ready to receive global luxury retailers. Location was thus a major limiting factor for a luxury marketer in India.

Louis Vuitton also had a tradition of opening stores in luxury hotels in Asia, for example, The Peninsula in Hong Kong, The Oriental in Bangkok and The Metropole in Hanoi. The company had scored a coup when it convinced P.R.S. Oberoi, the chairman and CEO of East India Hotels Ltd., a leading Indian luxury hotel chain, to turn his sprawling office at the ground floor of The Oberoi Hotel in New Delhi into the first Louis Vuitton store in the country. But space was a major constraint with these venues, since a store could not occupy more than 3,000 square feet in a luxury hotel.

The limitation of space went contrary to the ongoing luxury retailing trend, worldwide, of large formats. Louis Vuitton itself had opened a new showroom in Paris in 2005 spread over an impressive 20,000 square feet, its largest to date. The pressure of demand for space in a luxury hotel had pushed up rental costs in India to twice the global average of 10 per cent to 12 per cent of total costs. A luxury mall would offer the same ambience at half the price.

Said Yves Carcelle at the opening of Louis Vuitton's first store in India at The Oberoi Hotel in New Delhi in March 2003:

> Ten years ago, when we opened in China, 80 per cent of the citizens of Beijing still wore Mao jackets and our store was tucked away in the basement of The Palace Hotel. Now we have ten stores. We think we will develop a new generation of customers in India, people who are very aware of what is happening in the rest of the world. As with China, we find it is best to start in a hotel because in a city such as Delhi, a hotel is a gathering point for society and a hub for those who travel.[19]

The Louis Vuitton store stood the ground by itself at The Oberoi Hotel for a while before other luxury retailers like Christian Dior and Gucci joined it. The company opened its second store at the Taj Mahal Palace and Towers Hotel, a luxury hotel that was also a designated heritage building, in Mumbai in September 2004.

Louis Vuitton had been building, well before the launch of its first store in New Delhi, a database of both traditional customers and the new generation of high-net-worth individuals. It had been courting these potential customers in India with promotional brochures, invitations for special viewings of its products at select gatherings, and offers of personalized tours of the company's private museum located in Asnières, near Paris. The company did not rely on the conventional media of print and television to reach customers. Instead, it was using viral marketing, based largely on referrals and word-of-mouth, which helped log individual sales requisitions, big and small, into an order book position.

---

[19] Melanie Rickey, "Louis Vuitton, Meet India," www.fashionwindows.com/boutiques/louis_vuitton/new_delhi.asp, April 7, 2003, accessed December 24, 2007.

Most of the logs pertained to what the company called "special orders" customized to specific individual needs of design, color, embossing, packaging and other attributes. The physical store, opened first in New Delhi and then in Mumbai, was attracting the routine traffic passing through a luxury hotel in a premier city. But, it was also a processing center for "special orders" from India: for collecting sales requisitions, coordinating with the manufacturing centre in France, and arranging delivery.

Since 2000, the Indian economy had been on a growth path (see Exhibit 6). However, the country's per capita income (INR22,946 as of 2005) was well below the unit price of the products sold by Louis Vuitton at its retail store in New Delhi and Mumbai (see Exhibit 7).The size of the Indian middle class was expected to grow to 583 million, of whom 23 million—more than the current population of Australia—would be among the country's wealthiest by 2025. The number of households categorized as near rich, clear rich, sheer rich and super rich was growing progressively every year (see Exhibit 8). The largest group among India's consumers was its young people, with 51 per cent of its population below 25 years. The stock markets were creating new millionaires. Of more than 5,500 companies listed on Indian stock exchanges, about 200 had more than $1 billion in market capitalization, and 900 companies were in the $50 million to $1 billion range.

LUXURY MALL

A major stimulus for the growth of luxury brands in India had come from a decision by the federal government in February 2006 to allow 51 per cent ownership by a foreign enterprise in a local retail venture of a "single" brand. Although "multi-brand" retailers such as Wal-Mart still faced hurdles, the decision had encouraged global luxury brands—such as Versace, Gucci, Dolce & Gabbana, Armani, Chanel, Lanvin, Cartier, TAG Heuer, Girard-Perregaux, Breguet, Corum, Audemars Piguet, and Jaeger-LeCoultre—to begin to strategize their plans for the Indian market. They were all set to grow their retail presence in India.

Several real-estate entrepreneurs in India were planning to develop luxury malls. An unofficial estimate placed the number of new malls coming up, by 2010, at 300. However, not all of them had the wherewithal to readily attract luxury brands. Many were pure plays by developers with little experience in retailing, much less luxury retailing. Mall managements were not making adequate provisions for well-lit walkways, spacious parking, uncluttered traffic flows and perfumed toilets, considered basic in luxury retailing. Nor was there the sense of synergy and symbiosis that was integral to a shopping cluster.

A case in point was the experience of Ermenegildo Zegna, an Italian maker of top-of the-line suits costing about $15,000 each. The company had built up a vast clientele among travelling Indian industrialists for its *pièce de résistance*, a made-to-measure suit, over the years. Seeking to capitalize on the potential of the Indian market, Zegna had set up shop in Mumbai in October 1999 at Crossroads, the country's first shopping mall. Crossroads had been billed at the time as a poster child for premium retail in India. But, Zegna found that the mall had a store selling indigenous spices on the same level and a McDonald's restaurant elsewhere in the building. Unable to cope with low-end neighbors and poor quality footfalls, the luxury suit-maker was planning to exit from India.[20]

[20] Zegna closed its store at Crossroads in 2004 but resurfaced in 2007 with a store in a luxury hotel in Mumbai.

Worldwide, the retail ambience in which Louis Vuitton felt at home was the luxury retail cluster (LRC). Spread over several blocks, usually in a city's downtown core, an LRC enabled a luxury products company to showcase its offerings in a manner that highlighted its brand personality. The distinctive appeal of a store was reinforced by an image spillover from other stores in the neighborhood, invariably peers with which it was also competing in different categories. An LRC generated both scale economies and scope economies. The former pertained to the supply side, by which an LRC could attract traffic large enough to give scale to individual stores by the sheer number of shoppers. The latter pertained to the demand side, by which it enabled shoppers to purchase several items from different stores in a single trip. An LRC offered an opportunity for a brand to use its store design to create a unique image without interference from other stores in the same cluster. The bouquet of products and services an LRC offered drew shoppers from afar like a magnet. While at one level an LRC facilitated window shopping, it ensured, at another, that the footfalls converted into sales.

In cities that did not have LRCs, Louis Vuitton was operating in the next best alternative: luxury malls. A collection of stores bonded by shared facilities and a common infrastructure, a luxury mall limited the opportunities for store design and layout because the retail space was rented by the store owners, not owned by them. Unless the store was involved with the developer from the beginning, the luxury mall provided little control for an individual store over the choice of its neighbors. It also did not guarantee quality footfalls in the mall. The seamless arrangement of stores provided no opportunity for leisurely window shopping.

WILL IT WORK?

India's first luxury mall was to open in New Delhi in a few months. Built by DLF Ltd., the country's leading real-estate developer, Emporio, as it was to be called, would have a total retail space of 350,000 square feet. It would accommodate a total of 130 marquee brands, of which about 70 were global brands like Dior, Fendi, Armani, Dolce & Gabbana, Cartier, Versace, Hugo Boss, Escada, Tod's, Paul Smith, Piguet, Chopard, IWC and of course Louis Vuitton. DLF planned to develop luxury malls of similar size and scale in five other Indian metros — Mumbai, Kolkata, Bangalore, Chennai and Hyderabad — over the next five years. Louis Vuitton was involved with all of these. It was also involved with UB City-Collection, a luxury retail project scheduled to roll out in mid-2008 in the city of Bangalore. Spread over 10 acres, UB City was to have five medium-rise and five high-rise towers, housing brands like Dunhill, Gucci, Montblanc, Van Cleef & Arpels, and Zegna. Notwithstanding its close involvement with the developers from the beginning, the question before Louis Vuitton was basic: Will the luxury mall concept work in India?

Louis Vuitton was so far targeting customers in India who had been shopping abroad and were familiar with the company and its products. But, now, it was casting its net wider to cover those who would be discovering the brand for the first time in India. The company would have to identify, develop and nurture a new generation of luxury consumers from scratch. The process would be like hitting a moving target. Loyalty would not be a highly rated attribute among a community's nouveau riche, prone to experiment and switch from one luxury brand to the other and seeking trade-offs. Besides, demand for luxury brands in a community was not merely about consumers having the money but about their having a taste for the good life and a feel for a lifestyle. How should Louis Vuitton trigger that feeling among its new class of customers?

Exhibit 1 LVMH—business segments

	Fashion & Leather			**Wines & Spirits**			**Perfumes & Cosmetics**			**Watches & Jewellery**			**Selective Retailing**		
(in Euro Millions)	**2007**	**2006**	**2005**	**2007**	**2006**	**2005**	**2007**	**2006**	**2005**	**2007**	**2006**	**2005**	**2007**	**2006**	**2005**
Revenue	5,628	5,222	4,812	3,226	2,994	2,644	2,731	2,519	2,285	833	737	585	4,179	3,891	3,648
Profit	1,829	1,633	1,467	1,058	962	869	296	222	173	141	80	21	439	400	347
Investment	246	319	281	119	104	97	115	98	115	28	25	28	236	175	131
% Sales (Region)	20	21	22	29	31	33	8	9	–	25	25	24	39	40	40
United States	9	9	9	8	8	9	16	17	–	7	7	8	24	24	24
France	20	19	17	29	28	27	43	41	–	24	25	23	10	9	8
Rest of Europe	22	26	30	8	9	9	6	7	–	13	14	16	3	3	3
Japan	23	20	18	16	15	13	13	13	–	15	14	15	20	20	21
Rest of Asia	6	5	4	10	9	9	14	13	–	16	15	14	4	4	4
Other markets															
Product Categories	Leather bags, ready-to-wears, shoes and accessories			Champagne & wines and Cognac & spirits			Cosmetics, skin care products and fragrances			Watches, jewellery			–		
Brand and Year of Launch	LouisVuitton, 1854 Fendi, 1925 Loewe, 1846 Celine, 1945 Berluti, 1895 Kenzo, 1970 Givenchy, 1952 Stefanobi, 1991 Thomas Pink, 1984 Donna Karan, 1984 eLuxury.com, 2000			Chandon, 1959 Cloudy Bay, 1985 Cape Mentelle, 1970 Newton, 1984 Terrazas de los, 1999 Cheval des, 2003 10 Cane, 2005 Moët&Chandon, 1743 Dom Perignon, 1668 Veuve Clicquot, 1772 Krug, 1843 Mereier, 1858 Ruinart, 1729 Château d'Yquem, 1593 Hennessy, 1765 Glenmorangie, 1893			Dior, 1947 Guerlain, 1828 Givenchy, 1957 Kenzo, 1988 LBD, 1845 Benefit, 1976 Fresh, 1991 MakeUpForever, 1989 Acqua di Parma, 1916 Loewe, 1972			TAG Heuer, 1860 Zenith, 1865 Dior Watches, 1985 FRED, 1936 Chaumet, 1780 OMAS, 1780 De Beers LV, 1907			DFS, 1961 Miami Cruiseline, 1963 Sephora, 1970 sephora.com, 1999 Le Bon Marché, 1852 Samaritaine, 1870		

Source: www.lvmh.com.

Exhibit 2 Louis vuitton—global locations

#	Country	RLC/ Luxury Mall	Hotel	Dept Store	Duty-free Shop	Country Total	#	Country	RLC/ Luxury Mall	Hotel	Dept Store	Duty-free Shop	Country Total
1	Argentina	1				1	32	Mexico	8				8
2	Aruba	1				1	33	Monaco	1				1
3	Australia	8				8	34	Morocco		2			2
4	Austria	3				3	35	Netherlands	1				1
5	Belgium	3				3	36	New Zealand	4				4
6	Bermuda	1				1	37	Nor Mariana				1	1
7	Brazil	4				4	38	Norway	1				1
8	Canada	7	1	1		9	39	Panama	1				1
9	Chile	1				1	40	Philippines	1				1
10	China	6	2	2		10	41	Portugal	1				1
11	Colombia	1				1	42	Russia	3				3
12	Cyprus	1				1	43	Saudi Arabia	2				2
13	Czechoslo-vakia	1				1	44	Singapore	1	2		1	4
14	Denmark	1				1	45	South Africa	2				2
15	France	16				16	46	Spain	6				6

(*Continued*)

(*Continued*)

#	Country	RLC/ Luxury Mall	Hotel	Dept Store	Duty-free Shop	Country Total	#	Country	RLC/ Luxury Mall	Hotel	Dept Store	Duty-free Shop	Country Total
16	Germany	12				12	47	St. Barth	1				1
17	Greece	3				3	48	Sweden	1				1
18	Guam	2				2	49	Switzerland	7	1			8
19	Hong Kong	5	1			6	50	Taiwan	7		1		8
20	Hungary	1				1	51	Thailand	2	1			3
21	India		2			2	52	Turkey	3				3
22	Indonesia	2	1			3	53	Ukraine	1				1
23	Ireland	1				1	54	United Arab Emirates	3				3
24	Israel	1				1	55	UK	5		3		8
25	Italy	16				16	56	USA	112				112
26	Japan	54	1		1	56	57	Uruguay	1				1
27	Korea	4	1	11	6	22	58	Venezuela	1				1
28	Kuwait	1				1	59	Vietnam	1	1			2
29	Luxembourg.	1				1		**Total**	**338**	**17**	**18**	**9**	**382**
30	Macau	1	1			2							
31	Malaysia	2				2							

Source: www.louisvuitton.com/othercountries/stores, accessed February 12, 2008.

Exhibit 3 Lvmh financials

INCOME STATEMENT (in Millions of Euros)			
	2007	**2006**	**2005**
Net Sales	16,481	15,306	13,910
Less: Cost of Sales	5,786	5,481	5,001
Gross Profit	10,695	9,825	8,909
Less : Marketing and selling expenses	5,752	5,364	4,892
Less: General and administration expenses	1,388	1,289	1,274
Income from Operations	3,555	3,172	2,743
Less: Other operating expenses	126	120	221
Less: Interest	252	53	143
Less: Income taxes	846	839	711
Net Income	2,331	2,160	1,668
BALANCE SHEET (Year Ending December 31)			
Non-current Assets	20,266	19,620	19,537
Current Assets	10,475	9,165	8,516
Total Assets	30,741	28,785	28,053
Equity	12,528	11,594	10,484
Non-current Liabilities	10,443	10,835	10,978
Current Liabilities	7,770	6,356	6,591
Total Liabilities and Equity	30,741	28,785	28,053

Source: Annual Reports.

Exhibit 4 Percentage of population below poverty line

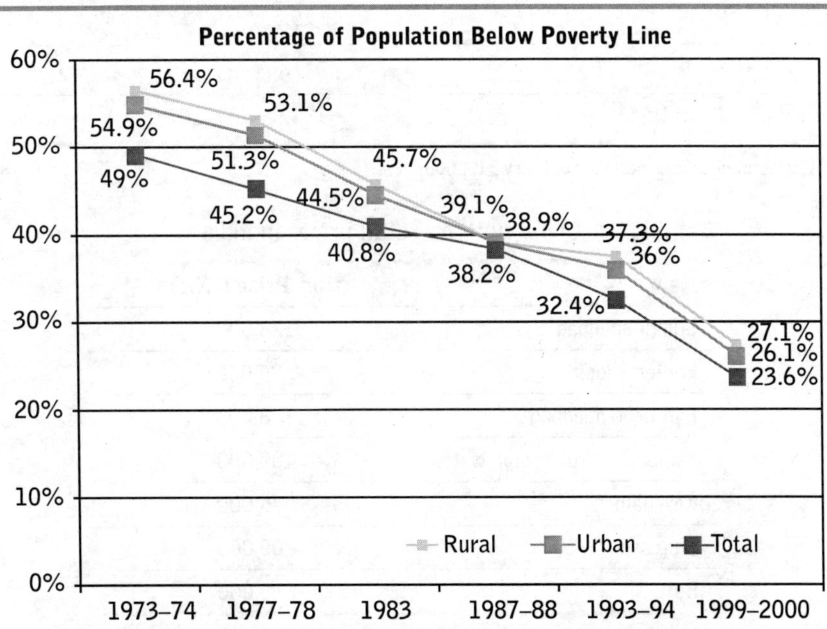

Source: Ministry of Statistics and Programme Implementation, Government of India. Central Statistical Organization (http://mospi.nic.in.in/mospi_cso_rept_pubn.htm).

Exhibit 5 The Indian timeline of poverty (as per world bank estimates)

Year	1981	1984	1987	1990	1993	1996	1999	2002	2005
Income (Population in Millions)									
$1/day	296.1	282.2	285.3	282.5	280.1	271.3	270.1	276.1	266.5
$1.25/day	420.5	416.0	428.0	435.5	444.3	441.8	447.2	460.5	455.8
$2/day	608.9	635.6	669.0	701.6	735.0	757.1	782.8	813.1	827.7
$2.5/day	650.3	686.1	725.0	766.5	808.8	841.1	875.2	911.4	938.0

Note: India's population in 2005 was 1.080 million.
Source: Shankkar Aiyar, "The Other India Story," India Today August 29, 2008, indiatoday.digitaltoday, accessed August 29, 2008.

Exhibit 6 Indian economy

	2005	2004	2003	2000
Gross domestic product (GDP) in billions INR	15,294	14,305	13,183	11,483
Per capita income (INR at 99–00 base)	22,946	20,936	18,899	17,800
Industrial production (%)	8.4	7.0	5.8	2.6
Inflation rate (%)	6.4	5.4	3.4	3.3
Imports as % of GDP	15.5	13.0	12.1	11.1
Exports as % of GDP	11.0	10.6	10.4	8.2
Forex reserves (in billions US$)	135.8	107.0	71.9	35.1

Source: www.mospi.nic.in/cso, accessed January 31, 2008.

Exhibit 7 Louis vuitton—retail prices in india

Item	Unit Price (INR)
Suhali handbag	128,000
Ladies' shoes	25,000
Eye Love handbag	128,000
Tambour Chronograph watch	189,000
Keychain	5,000
Suitcase	700,000
Belt	18,000

Sources: http://www.rediff.com/money/2003/jul/12spec3.htm, accessed June 14, 2008; http://archives.digitaltoday.in/businesstoday/20041219/trends4.html, accessed December 24, 2007.

Exhibit 8 India—income classes and number of households

Income Classes		Number of Households (000s)							
		1995–96		2001–2002		2005–2006		2009–2010 (Est)	
Category	**Annual Income Range (in US$)**	**Urban**	**Rural**	**Urban**	**Rural**	**Urban**	**Rural**	**Urban**	**Rural**
Super rich	Over 228,890	4	1	17	2	46	6	126	16
Sheer rich	114,940–228,890	9	2	34	6	87	16	219	37
Clear rich	45,980–114,940	49	14	161	41	360	94	825	212
Near rich	22,990–45,980	135	53	410	136	842	280	1,793	581
Strivers	11,500–22,990	428	223	1,204	507	2,301	911	4,629	1,544
Seekers	4,600–11,500	2,239	1,642	5,762	3,272	8,889	4,923	14,313	7,955
Aspirers	2,070–4,600	14,541	14,359	21,267	19,995	25,158	28,118	29,249	46,055
Destitutes	Less than 2,070	29,295	101,881	24,632	110,746	23,156	109,093	18,019	96,345
	Total	**46,700**	**118,175**	**53,487**	**134,705**	**60,839**	**143,441**	**69,173**	**152,745**

Source: R.K. Shukla, et al, "The Great Indian Middle Class," Report by the National Council of Applied Economic Research, www.ncaer.org/Downloads/PublicationsCatalog.pdf.

25

ROMANTIC RIDES OR FIERY THRILLS

Positioning a Motorcycle Brand in the Indian Context

Dr S. Ramesh Kumar and Dr M. Geetha

Rajesh, who had just turned 50, saw the several brands of motorcycles parked at the theater complex. They ranged from the rugged models that were about 10 years old to the dazzling ones that could set the heart pounding among the yuppies. Rajesh wondered if all these motorcycles were being used fully for their functionality (as a means of personal transport) or if there were symbolic reasons for the purchase of these motorcycles. These thoughts brought back to him the nostalgic memories of how the Yezdis and the Jawas, the brands of the yesteryears, were always considered the "in thing" during his college days. The thoughts, of course, triggered the memories of the film *Andaz* of the early seventies, which dramatized romance with its symbolic motorcycle association (through its ever popular *"Zindagi Ek Safar . . ."* song that can be heard even today in several radio stations targeting the youth). The film launched all over the country reinforced the fact that films as a medium are instrumental in dishing out products that may have a special significance on the psyche of consumers—a reality that is true even to this day.

Rajesh was brought back to the realities of his current challenges when he noticed Kiran coming over to meet him. Rajesh after his basic degree had worked in the motorcycle industry for more than two decades and had spent eight years in the sales and marketing of job profiles. His commitment and passion to work enabled him to move up to positions that involved branding and product management

---

The case was prepared for class discussion.

challenges that were normally the preserve of management graduates. His busy consultancy work with regard to marketing of durable product categories showcased his penchant for achieving success in a crowded marketplace. One of his assignments involved probably the greatest challenge he had faced in his career: working in the motorcycle industry to launch a new brand. Kiran was the product manager of a new company and he had about 6 years of experience in both FMCG (fast-moving consumer goods) and durable product categories. Kiran's educational background in management, his conceptual and analytical abilities, and his thirst to succeed by fighting against the odds were primarily the reasons for Windy Bikes Company to recruit him a few months back. The hardcore practical insight of Rajesh combined with the marketing intellect of Kiran was probably the prerequisite combination required to succeed in a market, which had several complexities and nuances reflecting the developing nature of the Indian market. They had to meet the Chief Executive Officer of Windy Bikes in about two weeks to finalize the positioning strategy for their brand.

"The motorcycle industry has been catching up over the years and with our factory capacity, there will be no problems in catering to the demand but the crucial aspect is going to be our positioning related to our brands" said Kiran. "What about finding the right brand name" asked Rajesh more out of his enthusiasm than out of a disciplined conceptual thought. "Brand name is the last of our priorities in my opinion" quipped Kiran, confident that this topic would not surface again until they had made strategic progress with the issue on hand. "What I fail to read is a specific pattern in the positioning of motorcycles. There were a few brands in the eighties and by default they had positioned themselves in different ways in terms of entering the consumers' psyche. There were just one or two bikes for style, one associated with adventure and probably one more for ruggedness. Today, the leading brands seem to have exhausted various positioning platforms" said Rajesh almost in acknowledgment of Kiran's views on the selection of the brand.

"There are already several models positioned on functional features and psychological aspects. There are also celebrity endorsements. I wonder how a brand can break this kind of clutter in the market" said Kiran. Rajesh was reminded of the ways in which companies have changed their strategies in tune with the environmental changes and competitive moves. Rajesh made an interesting observation that was applicable to the leading company Hero Honda. "Yamaha, the Japanese brand that has just around 5% in the Indian market (the brand was doing well in Japan and several other parts of Asia with a significant market share), had RX 100 brand with a strong image as a two-stroke offering before the entry of Hero Honda that was the first to enter the Indian market with a four-stroke engine. Yamaha failed to convert and sustain the image in the four-stroke category. Yamaha today is attempting to have a focused approach toward higher end offerings instead of being present in all the segments. It has launched Gladiator, a 125 cc bike, to the urban youth segment, and priced it aggressively. Hero Honda without getting complacent with its initial success in the eighties has managed its product-line, and its brands have done well over the last two decades. It has created and dropped several sub-brands without losing its focus on the respective segment." Kiran agreed and added "Feature combination and price points form an effective appeal—for instance, models with and without self-starters clearly provide a choice to the consumers, one who can afford the feature and the one who would like to have the brand but also would want to save a bit."

Rajesh continued, "TVS's Victor brand was positioned initially on multiple benefits and it was also backed up by a hot celebrity. 125 cc bikes seem to promise a huge potential." Kiran turning his attention toward the rural market mentioned "Let us not forget the rural market which is also growing and there are also bikes being created for the rural market."

The broad segments that were interested in bikes were students, government employees, private company executives, and businessmen. The segments in terms of the category of bikes were the economy segment, executive segment, and the premium segment. The executive segment had grown to about 51% of the market and this was in the price range of over ₹40,000. The economy segment that accounted for about 38% was in the range of about ₹30,000 to ₹40,000 and the premium segment was over ₹50,000 (Glamour and Karizma belong to this segment). Rajesh's observation that bikes were bought for style and prestige was confirmed by the launch of Apache by TVS. This bike was launched keeping in mind the growing personal aspirations reflected through style, looks, and riding comfort. Adding to the observation of Rajesh is also the fact that bikes, especially at the higher end, are bought just not for symbolic style. Different brands at the higher end seem to indicate that design is just not restricted to few features; it includes engine, transmission, brakes, fuel tank capacity, suspension, tires and every aspect that contributes both to the internal functioning of the bike and its external appearance. Rajesh took out a report from his briefcase and handed over the report to Kiran and told him that they should meet again after Kiran had gone through the report that he had prepared. The report had an overview of the motorcycle industry, market shares of brands and specifically what Rajesh considered was competition to map out the mind-space of the consumer—perceptual maps indicating the approach of different brands drawn on specific dimensions. Crucial to the report and also to the strategy of Windy Bikes were the results of a consumer and dealer survey that was commissioned by the company. Rajesh and Kiran had to finalize on several aspects relating to the launching of a new bike.

Exhibits 1 and 2 provide information about the motorcycle categories. Exhibits 3 to 6 refer to the attribute preferences/rankings, interest patterns, favorite pastimes/hobbies and occupations of urban motorcycle owners, respectively. Exhibits 7 to10 contain data on the factors associated with purchase, ranking of attributes, favorite pastimes/hobbies/recreation and occupations of prospective owners in urban markets. Exhibits 11 to 14 contain data on the preferences of attributes and other details concerning the demographics and psychographics of respondents of the segment belonging to owners of motorcycles in semi-urban markets. Exhibits 15 to 18 contain information about the preferences of attributes and other details concerning the demographics and psychographics of respondents of the segment belonging to prospective semi-urban consumers for the purchase of motorcycles.

Exhibit 1 Segmentation of motorcycles

	Target Income Groups	Price Range (₹'000)	Fuel Efficiency	Margins
Economy	Low	Up to 38	High	Low
Executive	Medium	38–50	High	Moderate
Premium	High	50–60	Moderate	High

Source: CRISINFAC, www.crisil.com.

Exhibit 2 Market share comparison of key players (2003-04 and 2004-05) in the motorcycle segment

	2003–04	2004–05
Bajaj	24%	28%
Hero Honda	48%	50%
TVS	16%	13%
HMSI	—	1%
Yamaha	6%	5%

Source: CRIS INFAC, www.crisil.com.

URBAN MOTORCYCLE OWNERS

The data was collected from 200 samples of a metropolitan city. The results are summarized in Exhibit 3.

Exhibit 3 Factors associated with purchase/ranking intended to purchase

(a) Responses with Purchase of Motorcycle

	1	2	3	4	5	6	7	8	9	Total
Price	45	48	39	21	15	8	7	9	8	200
Looks	46	34	23	17	13	16	33	13	5	200
Mileage	47	67	36	18	11	9	8	4	0	200
After Sales Service	5	9	19	44	36	26	18	21	22	200
Technology	17	15	26	17	33	37	37	11	7	200
Driving Pleasure	19	16	14	34	26	39	23	20	9	200
Maintenance Costs	12	9	31	23	28	28	32	20	17	200
Features	9	10	9	20	17	23	30	50	26	200
Fun	1	4	5	10	11	10	10	50	99	200
Others										

(b) Ranking of Attributes

Options	Weighted Average	Ranking
Price	6.71	II
Looks	6.04	III
Mileage	7.21	I
After Sales Service	4.58	VII
Technology	5.05	IV
Driving Pleasure	5.02	V
Maintenance Costs	4.7	VI
Features	3.68	VIII
Fun	2.3	IX

Exhibit 4 Information about interest patterns of respondents

Interests	Yes	No	Yes Percentage	No Percentage
Buy Designer/Branded Shirts/Apparel	100	100	50	50
Music	140	60	70	30
Fashion with Clothes/Watches, etc.	123	77	61.5	38.5
Reading Sports Magazines	94	106	47	53
Current Affairs/Politics	92	108	46	54
Food/Liquor	91	109	40.5	20.6
Parties with Friends	125	75	62.5	37.5
Traveling Abroad	122	78	61	39
Sports/Film-based Celebrities	85	115	42.5	57.5

Exhibit 5 Favorite pastimes/hobbies/recreation

Pastimes/ Hobbies	Sports	Films	Television	Pubs	Resorts	Friends	Books	Magazines	Internet
Number of Respondents	17	10	19	1	0	5	0	0	0
Percentage	32.69	19.23	36.53	1.92	0	9.6	0	0	0

Exhibit 6 Occupations of the respondents

Occupations	Number of Respondents	Percentage
Student	61	30.5
Executive	87	43.5
Government Employed	14	7
Professional (Doctor/Engineer/CA, etc.)	35	17.5
Others	3	1.5

PROSPECTIVE URBAN CONSUMERS FOR THE PURCHASE OF MOTORCYCLE

The data was collected from 116 samples of a metropolitan city. The results are summarized in the following.

Exhibit 7 Factors associated with purchase/ranking intended to purchase

(a) Responses with Purchase of Motorcycle

	1	2	3	4	5	6	7	8	9	Total
Price	27	25	27	12	5	15	2	1	2	116
Looks	23	10	16	17	12	11	17	6	4	116
Mileage	34	46	19	8	5	1	3	1	0	116
After Sales Service	0	1	12	11	20	24	21	14	13	116
Technology	9	16	16	12	14	13	16	16	4	116
Driving Pleasure	13	16	5	15	17	16	12	13	9	116
Maintenance Costs	4	3	6	27	23	18	13	16	6	116
Features	6	3	7	11	18	15	25	26	5	116
Fun	2	1	3	8	3	4	8	19	68	116

(b) Ranking of Attributes

Options	Weighted Average	Ranking
Price	6.89	II
Looks	5.79	III
Mileage	7.72	I
After Sales Service	3.95	VIII
Technology	5.16	IV
Driving Pleasure	5.086	V
Maintenance Costs	4.55	VI
Features	4.09	VII
Fun	2.21	IX

Exhibit 8 Information about interest patterns of respondents

Interested in	Yes	No	Yes Percentage	No Percentage
Buying Designer/Branded Shirts/Apparel	82	34	70.7	29.3
Music	105	11	90.5	9.5
Fashion with Clothes/Watches, etc.	98	18	84.5	15.5
Reading Sports Magazines	62	54	53.4	46.6
Current Affairs/Politics	80	36	69	31
Food/Liquor	52	64	45	55
Parties with Friends	81	35	69.8	30.2
Traveling Abroad	95	21	82	18
Sports/Film-based Celebrities	68	48	58.6	41.4

Exhibit 9 Favorite pastimes/hobbies/recreation

Pastimes/ Hobbies	Sports	Films	Television	Pubs	Resorts	Friends	Books	Magazines	Internet
Number of Respondents	39	18	21	3	1	23	9	2	0
Percentage	3.6	15.5	18.1	2.6	0.9	19.8	7.8	1.7	0

Exhibit 10 Occupations of the respondents

Occupations	Number of Respondents	Percentage
Student	79	68
Executive	11	9.5
Government Employed	6	5
Professional (Doctor/Engineer/CA, etc.)	20	17

SEMI-URBAN MOTORCYCLE OWNERS

The data was collected from 50 samples of a semi-urban area. The results are summarized in the following.

Exhibit 11 Factors associated with purchase/ranking intended to purchase

(a) Responses with Purchase of Motorcycle

	1	2	3	4	5	6	7	8	9	Total
Price	2	10	12	3	6	1	3	6	2	50
Looks	14	9	5	3	3	8	4	2	2	50
Mileage	21	12	5	5	2	2	0	3	0	50
After Sales Service	0	3	4	8	13	6	10	3	3	50
Technology	4	3	3	6	9	12	5	7	1	50
Driving Pleasure	3	6	9	6	6	3	12	3	2	50
Maintenance Costs	0	4	6	4	9	10	9	5	3	50
Features	3	2	3	10	2	5	8	15	7	50
Fun	1	1	3	4	0	s1	3	6	31	50
Others										

(b) Ranking of Attributes

Options	Weighted Average	Ranking
Price	5.14	III
Looks	6.32	II
Mileage	7.48	I
After Sales Service	4.56	VI
Technology	4.8	V
Driving Pleasure	5.02	IV
Maintenance Costs	4.46	VII
Features	4.3	VIII
Fun	2.36	IX

Exhibit 12 Information about interest patterns

Interests	Yes	No	Yes Percentage	No Percentage
Buying Designer/Branded Shirts/Apparel	30	20	60	40
Music	40	10	80	20
Fashion with Clothes/Watches, etc.	32	18	64	36
Reading Sports Magazines	14	36	28	72
Current Affairs/Politics	29	21	58	42
Food/Liquor	26	24	52	48
Parties with Friends	40	10	80	20
Traveling Abroad	40	10	80	20
Sports/Film-based Celebrities	29	21	58	42

Exhibit 13 Favorite pastimes/hobbies/recreation

Pastimes/ Hobbies	Sports	Films	Television	Pubs	Resorts	Friends	Books	Magazines	Net
Number of Respondents	13	15	11	2	1	5	2	0	1
Percentage	26	30	22	4	2	10	4	0	2

Exhibit 14 Occupations of the respondents

Occupations	Number of Respondents	Percentage
Student	27	54
Executive	3	6
Government Employed	0	0
Professional (Doctor/Engineer/CA, etc.)	20	40

PROSPECTIVE SEMI-URBAN CONSUMERS FOR THE PURCHASE OF MOTORCYCLE

The data was collected from 50 samples of a semi-urban area. The results are summarized in the following.

Exhibit 15 Factors associated with purchase/ranking intended to purchase

(a) Responses with Purchase of Motorcycle

	1	2	3	4	5	6	7	8	9
Price	1	25	9	3	2	8	2	2	0
Looks	10	2	7	5	3	6	6	11	2
Mileage	37	3	3	2	7	0	0	0	0
After Sales Service	0	2	7	15	9	0	10	0	9
Technology	1	14	10	3	10	7	2	5	0
Driving Pleasure	1	1	10	13	7	16	2	1	1
Maintenance Costs	2	6	5	3	12	2	14	8	0
Features	0	0	1	6	5	13	2	22	3
Fun	0	0	0	0	0	0	11	5	36

(b) Ranking of Attributes

Options	Weighted Average	Ranking
Price	6.58	II
Looks	5.17	V
Mileage	8.17	I
After Sales Service	4.59	VII
Technology	5.82	III
Driving Pleasure	5.25	IV
Maintenance Costs	4.71	VI
Features	3.33	VIII
Fun	1.52	IX

Exhibit 16 Information about interest patterns of respondents

Interests	Yes	No	Yes Percentage	No Percentage
Buying Designer/Branded Shirts/Apparel	17	35	32.7	67.3
Music	44	8	84.5	15.5
Fashion with Clothes/Watches, etc.	12	40	23.1	76.9
Reading Sports Magazines	32	20	61.5	38.5
Current Affairs/Politics	24	28	46.2	53.8
Food/Liquor	18	34	34.6	65.4
Parties with Friends	28	24	53.8	46.2
Traveling Abroad	23	29	44.2	55.8
Sports/Film-based Celebrities	22	30	42.3	57.7

Exhibit 17 Favorite pastimes/hobbies/recreation

Pastimes/ Hobbies	Sports	Films	Television	Pubs	Resorts	Friends	Books	Magazines	Internet
Number of Respondents	17	10	19	1	0	5	0	0	0
Percentage	32.69	19.23	36.53	1.92	0	9.6	0	0	0

Exhibit 18 Occupations of the respondents

Occupations	Number of Respondents	Percentage
Student	15	28.8
Executive	24	46.2
Government Employed	8	15.4
Professional (Doctor/Engineer/CA, etc.)	5	9.6

Appendix 1 (Sample calculation on how rankings were arrived at) factors associated with purchase/ranking intended to purchase

Ranking for Price

Ranks	Number of Respondents	Weights	Weighted Score
I	45	9	405
II	48	8	384
III	39	7	273
IV	21	6	126
V	15	5	75
VI	8	4	32
VII	7	3	21
VIII	9	2	18
IX	8	1	8
		Total	1,342
		Weighted Average	1,342/200 = 6.71

Note: The ranking was calculated similarly for other attributes.

Appendix 2 (Authors' weightages for various brands)

Motorcycle Brands—A Comparison of Attributes/Appeals

Motorcycles	Price (INR)	Fuel Efficiency (km)	Features	Trendy Appeal
CD Dawn	34,835	65	1	1
CD Deluxe	37,890	60	1	1
Centra	38,390	53	0	1
Boss 115	38,660	62	1	1
Yamaha Crux S	39,010	91	0	2
Victor GX	39,390	68	0	2
CT 100 DX	40,180	69	0	1
Super Splendor	43,047	65	4	4
CD 100 SS	43,520	65	–	–
Victor GLX	43,850	53	2	4
Velocity	44,730	62	1	3
Gladiator	44,990	67	5	3
Shine	45,200	65	2	1
Libero G5	46,780	65	1	2
Splendor+ Disc	48,001	65	2	2
Passion Plus Disc	49,592	65	5	3
Fiero F2 Disc	49,630	53	4	2
Fiero FX Disc	50,520	53	2	2
Discover (ES)	50,710	63	1	3
GF170 Disc	51,680	42	3	4
Unicorn (KS)	51,993	54	3	2
Achiever	52,646	52	3	4
Pulsar 150 (ES)	61,070	51	5	5
Pulsar 180 (ES)	65,450	42	5	5
Bullet 350	72,490	40	0	2
Karizma	76,303	34	6	6
Bullet Machismo	81,080	40	3	2
Electra	81,480	40	2	3
Bullet 500	98,000	35	2	2
Bajaj Platina	36,000	67	4	4

Sources:

Top Throttle Positioning. *Auto Times, The Times of India,* May 25, 2006.

Pankaj Sukhija, Riding High on Style, *The New Sunday Express,* May 28, 2006.

S. Muralidhar, Yamaha Gladiator: Into the Colosseum for 125 cc Fight, *The Hindu,* Business Line, May 28, 2006.

www.tvsmotor.in/
www.bajajauto.com/
www.herohonda.com/
www.yamaha-motor-india.com/
www.royalenfield.com/
www.honda2wheelersindia.com/
Delhi Auto Expo.,Bajaj Auto Displays, 2006, Model Lineup, *http://www.indiainfoline.com/news/news.asp?dat=73969.*
TVS Motor Records 25 pc Growth in Motorcycles Sales, *http://www.blonnet.com/2006/02/03/stories/2006020301030200.htm.*
Suzuki Motorcycle Plans Indian Launch in Oct with 125-cc Bike, h ttp://www.blonnet.com/2005/07/14/stories/2005071402530200.htm
Mobike Makers Rev Up Launches in Entry-level Segment, h ttp://www.blonnet.com/2006/06/03/stories/2006060300670500.htm
Question N Auto, www.blonnet.com/iw/2006/01/01/stories/2006010100451500.htm
Muralidhar S, Lining up the 150 cc bikes, The Hindu Businessline, May 14, 2006.
R. Cooper, Platinum Edge, The Hindu, June 14, 2006.
Glad to meet you, The Hindu, May 31, 20s06.

Note: on lifestyle positioning: Most brands of premium motorcycles have a strong lifestyle positioning. Executive segment brands and economy segment brands too have several shades of lifestyle orientation in their positioning. Other than the advertisements associated with the respective brand, these aspects were also observed in some of the Web sites of the respective brand/company. Fuel efficiency in the appendix is in kilometers, while trendy appeal and features have been assigned weightages based on authors' perception of these factors (higher number indicates a higher weightage).